The Award in International Investment Arbitration

The Award in International Investment Arbitration

Edited by

KATIA FACH GÓMEZ

Senior Lecturer in Private International Law,
University of Zaragoza, Spain

CATHARINE TITI

Tenured Research Associate Professor,
French National Centre for Scientific Research, France

OXFORD
UNIVERSITY PRESS

OXFORD
UNIVERSITY PRESS

Great Clarendon Street, Oxford, OX2 6DP,
United Kingdom

Oxford University Press is a department of the University of Oxford.
It furthers the University's objective of excellence in research, scholarship,
and education by publishing worldwide. Oxford is a registered trade mark of
Oxford University Press in the UK and in certain other countries

Published in the United States of America by Oxford University Press
198 Madison Avenue, New York, NY 10016, United States of America

British Library Cataloguing in Publication Data

Data available

Library of Congress Control Number: 2024937030

ISBN 9780192872968

DOI: 10.1093/9780191975936.001.0001

Printed and bound by
CPI Group (UK) Ltd, Croydon, CR0 4YY

FSC www.fsc.org MIX Paper | Supporting responsible forestry FSC® C013604

The manufacturer's authorised representative in the EU for product safety is
Oxford University Press España S.A. of El Parque Empresarial San Fernando de Henares, Avenida
de Castilla, 2 – 28830 Madrid (www.oup.es/en or
product.safety@oup.com). OUP España S.A. also acts as importer into Spain
of products made by the manufacturer.

Preface

The Award in International Investment Arbitration is the result of three years of work combining the experience of forty-six authors, including many internationally acclaimed experts in international investment arbitration. This book focuses on the multiple aspects of the investment award in all their complexity: from award drafting to the procedural principles that govern it; from arbitral deliberations and tribunal dynamics to post-award challenges; from the role of gender in decision-making to the impact of tribunal secretaries. Sensitive to contemporary challenges, this edited volume both addresses existing questions that have evolved over time and explores novel topics that have never been raised thus far. It is in this spirit, for example, that the book examines the usefulness of draft awards circulated to the disputing parties in order to control for errors or as a means of encouraging amicable settlement, a practice inspired by interim panel reports in the World Trade Organization, or the increasing impact of technology on award drafting.

The book is divided into six parts and it is composed of a total of 31 chapters. Part I of the book delves into the different *types and aspects of the international investment award*. In addition to assessing what an investment award is, and what it is not, and the minimum content of an enforceable award, this initial part of the book considers topics such as consent awards, compensation, and the award on costs. Part II addresses the key *procedural principles* that inform the drafting of investment awards. A careful selection is made of the principles that guide this process and the most important among them are subjected to a thorough analysis. Part III reviews *the content of investment awards*, covering topics such as fact-finding, applicable law, human rights in investment awards, counterclaims, and the impact of experts. Part IV focuses on *award drafting*, exploring rarely or never discussed topics such as tribunal dynamics and arbitral deliberations, the role of tribunal secretaries in the drafting of investment awards, and legal reasoning and persuasion. Part V studies *review and enforcement* of international investment awards. As the popularity of investment arbitration continues to grow, disputing parties make increasing use of the available review and enforcement mechanisms, which therefore become a critical element external, yet essential, to the investment award. The book's final part, Part VI, turns to *cross-cutting issues*, from empirical dimensions of investment awards to gender and investment awards, and the importance of technology for arbitral awards and proceedings.

It is our hope that *The Award in International Investment Arbitration* offers a singular reservoir of knowledge and experience. The authors of individual chapters study the complex topic of the international investment award from a variety of angles, sharing with the readers their vast practical experience and profound scholarly insights. Working closely with the extraordinary authors of this edited volume has allowed us to build a solid work, internally coherent, which we hope will benefit the reader. We are grateful to all our authors for their commitment and outstanding contributions to this volume. We are also grateful to our research institutions[1] and to Oxford University Press for allowing us to develop this ambitious book project.

Last and certainly not least, we would like to take a moment to express our sorrow at the passing of professor and arbitration expert, Armand de Mestral CM, who was one of the original contributors in this book. His loss touches us profoundly.

Katia Fach Gómez and Catharine Titi
30 June 2024

[1] For funding purposes, Katia Fach Gómez hereby declares that she is a member of the Institute IDEIR, the Aragon Research Group LegMiBIO (S12_23R), and the Spanish Research Project PID2022-137502NB-I0.

Contents

List of Contributors

Mohamed S Abdel Wahab, PhD is Professor of International Arbitration, Private International Law and English Contract Law, Cairo University; Founding Partner and Head of International Arbitration, Construction and Energy Groups, Zulficar & Partners Law Firm, Cairo, Egypt

Andrés E Alvarado-Garzón, LLM, PhD is Arbitration Lawyer, Disputes Team, Herbert Smith Freehills LLP, Frankfurt am Main, Germany

Crina Baltag, PhD, LLM, MSc, FCIArb, is Associate Professor in International Arbitration, Stockholm University, Sweden

George A Bermann, JD, BA is Professor and Director, Center for International Commercial and Investment Arbitration, Columbia Law School, Columbia University, New York, United States

Nigel Blackaby KC is Partner, Freshfields Bruckhaus Deringer, Washington DC, United States

Bianca Böhme, LLM is Research Associate, Europa-Institut, Saarland University, Saarbrücken, Germany

Gabriel Bottini is Adjunct Professor of Public International Law, University of Buenos Aires, Argentina; Partner and co-head of the International Arbitration and Litigation Group, Uría Menéndez, Madrid, Spain

Charles N Brower, BA, JD is Judge, Iran–United States Claims Tribunal; formerly Judge ad hoc, International Court of Justice, The Hague, Netherlands

Marc Bungenberg is Professor of International Economic Law, Jean Monnet Chair EU Constitutional Framework for International Dispute Settlement and Rule of Law, Director of the Europa-Institut, Saarland University, Saarbrücken, Germany

Julien Chaisse, LLM, PhD is Professor of Law, City University of Hong Kong, Hong Kong SAR

Giuditta Cordero-Moss, Dr juris, PhD is Professor, Department of Private Law, University of Oslo, Oslo, Norway

Yves Derains is Lawyer, Derains Gharavi, Paris, France

Diane A Desierto, JSD, LLM, JD is Professor of Law and Global Affairs, Faculty Director of LLM Program in IHRL, Founding Director, NDLS Global Human Rights Clinic, Notre Dame Law School and Keough School of Global Affairs, University of Notre Dame, South Bend, United States

Carlo de Stefano, PhD is Assistant Professor of International Law, Roma Tre University, Department of Law, Rome, Italy

Katia Fach Gómez, PhD, LLM (Fordham) is Senior Lecturer (Profesora titular) in Private International Law, University of Zaragoza, Spain

Susan Franck is Professor of Law, Washington College of Law, American University Washington College of Law, Washington, USA

Claudia Frutos-Peterson, PhD is Managing Partner, DC Office, Curtis, Mallet-Prevost, Colt & Mosle, LLP, Washington, DC, USA

Martin Gronemann is Research Associate, Friedrich-Alexander-Universität Erlangen-Nürnberg, Germany

Steffen Hindelang, Dr, LLM is Professor of International Investment and Trade Law, Uppsala University, Uppsala, Sweden

Kaj Hobér, BA, LLM, MCL, PhD is Professor of International Investment and Trade Law, Uppsala University, Uppsala, Sweden

Markus Krajewski is Professor, School of Law, University of Erlangen-Nürnberg, Germany

Ursula Kriebaum, Dr jur is Professor of International Law, University of Vienna, Austria

Céline Lévesque, LLL, LLB, LLM, MA is Full Professor, Faculty of Law, University of Ottawa, Canada

Ahmed Mazlom is Judicial Fellow to the Honorable Charles N Brower

Maria Julia Milesi is Counsel, Freshfields Bruckhaus Deringer US LLP, Washington DC, United States

Patricia Nacimiento, PhD is Partner, Head of German Disputes, Herbert Smith Freehills, Frankfurt, Germany

Julia Nassl is Research Assistant, Uppsala University, Uppsala, Sweden

Karsten Nowrot, Dr iur, LLM (Indiana) is Professor of Public Law, Public International Law, European Law and International Economic Law, University of Hamburg, Hamburg, Germany

Jan Ortgies, LLM, LLM (Stanford) is Head of Legal, Register of Damage for Ukraine, The Hague, Netherlands

Marija Ozolins, JD is Associate, Curtis, Mallet-Prevost, Colt & Mosle LLP, Washington, DC, USA

Rodrigo Polanco, PhD, LLM (NYU), is Senior Lecturer and Researcher, World Trade Institute, University of Bern, Switzerland; Swiss Institute of Comparative Law, Lausanne, Switzerland

Bailey Roe, JD is Associate, Arnold & Porter Kaye Scholer LLP, American University Washington College of Law, Washington, USA

Giorgio Sacerdoti is Emeritus Professor, International Law, Bocconi University, Milan, Italy

Christian Schmid, Mag iur, BA, LLM is Legal Officer, Federal Ministry of Labour and Economy of Austria, Vienna, Austria

Christoph Schreuer, Dr iur, LLM, JSD is Of Counsel, Zeiler Rechtsanwälte, Vienna, Austria

Bruno Simma is Judge, Iran–United States Claims Tribunal, The Hague, Netherlands

Emily Sipiorski, Dr iur, JD, MA is Tenured Assistant Professor, Tilburg University, Tilburg, Netherlands

SI Strong, DPhil, PhD, JD is KH Gyr Professor of Private International Law, Emory University, Atlanta, USA

Attila M Tanzi, PhD is Chair of International Law, Department of Legal Studies, University of Bologna Alma Mater Studiorum, Bologna, Italy; 3 VB Chambers, London, United Kingdom

Catharine Titi, Dr iur, FCIArb is Tenured Research Associate Professor, French National Centre for Scientific Research (CNRS), Paris, France

Marat Umerov, PhD is Counsel, Curtis, Mallet-Prevost, Colt & Mosle LLP, Washington, United States

Valentina Vadi, PhD is Adjunct Professor, Department of Political Science, University of Florence, Florence, Italy, University of Padua, Italy

Lukas Vanhonnaeker is Assistant Professor, Faculty of Law, University of Montreal, Canada

Kilian Wagner, Dr iur is Research and Teaching Assistant, University of Vienna, Austria

Friedl Weiss, LLM, PhD is Emeritus Professor, University of Vienna, Austria

PART I

KEY ASPECTS AND TYPES OF INVESTMENT AWARDS

1

What Is an Award?

Concept, Content, Drafting, Effects

Catharine Titi

I. Introduction

Awards are decisions that 'finally determine' the core issues that they have to address.[1] An award on jurisdiction finally decides whether the tribunal has jurisdiction to hear a dispute, an award on the merits decides whether substantive treaty standards have been violated, and an award on costs makes a final decision on costs. Depending on the applicable arbitration rules, awards can come in different shapes and forms: interim awards, partial awards, consent awards,[2] default awards,[3] final awards, and even awards recording the termination of proceedings.[4] However, generalizations are not always helpful. In reality, an award can only be accurately defined by taking into account the arbitration rules applicable to it. For example, an award under the 2021 Arbitration Rules of the United Nations Commission on International Trade Law (UNCITRAL) is a different animal to an award under the Convention on the Settlement of Investment Disputes between States and Nationals of Other States (ICSID Convention). The minimum content of an award, its form and substantive requirements may vary considerably between different arbitration rules.

By definition, the award is the outcome of an arbitral proceeding, therefore it must be distinguished from a judgment, which is rendered by a court. It is true that the difference between courts and tribunals is one of degree and sometimes it can be difficult to draw the line between a court and an arbitral tribunal.[5] But for the purposes of this chapter, and indeed for the purposes of this book, decisions rendered by a future

[1] Nigel Blackaby, Constantine Partasides, and Alan Redfern, *Redfern and Hunter on International Arbitration* (7th edn, Kluwer Law International/OUP 2023) para 9.08.

[2] eg Arbitration Rules of the Arbitration Rules of the Stockholm Chamber of Commerce (SCC) Arbitration Institute art 45; Arbitration Rules of the London Court of International Arbitration (2020) art 26.9. Consent awards are not considered in this chapter, but see Gabriel Bottini, 'Consent Awards' in Katia Fach Gómez and Catharine Titi (eds), *The Award in International Investment Arbitration* (OUP 2024).

[3] ICSID Convention art 45(2); ICSID Arbitration Rules r 49.

[4] SCC Arbitration Rules (2023) art 45(2).

[5] Catharine Titi, 'Investment Treaty Arbitration Caught in the Public–Private Law Divide' (2024) 45(3) Michigan Journal of International Law (forthcoming), also on SSRN <https://papers.ssrn.com/sol3/papers.cfm?abstract_id=4536824> (arguing that investment arbitration displays important commonalities with international court systems and that its presumed unique features, such as party autonomy, are not the absolute prerogative of arbitration); Jeswald W Salacuse, 'Is There a Better Way? Alternative Methods of Treaty-Based, Investor-State Dispute Resolution' (2007) 31 Fordham International Law Journal 138, 154.

Catharine Titi, *What Is an Award?* In: *The Award in International Investment Arbitration*. Edited by: Katia Fach Gómez and Catharine Titi, Oxford University Press. DOI: 10.1093/9780191975936.003.0001

investment court system such as the one provided for in investment treaties signed by the European Union are not regarded as 'awards', but as judgments, despite the fact that the European Union and its treaty partners have used the term 'award' in the hope of benefiting from international awards' compliance and enforcement mechanisms.[6]

This chapter gives an overview of what an investment award is and what it is not—in the ICSID Convention and beyond. The chapter enquires into the drafting of an investment award, considering its minimum content, notably form and substantive requirements, and its structure. Finally, the chapter considers the effects of an award, and in particular its binding character and *res iudicata* effect, and the recognition and enforcement obligations it carries.

II. Awards and Decisions

Unlike other arbitration systems, the ICSID Convention draws a distinction between a 'decision' and an 'award', whereby decisions are 'provisional' or 'interim', by contrast to an award that is de facto final. The ICSID Convention provides that '[t]he award shall deal with every question submitted to the Tribunal'.[7] This is supplemented by another provision in the ICSID Arbitration Rules, according to which the award contains 'the decision of the Tribunal on every question submitted to it'.[8] Therefore, the award must resolve all issues submitted to it. The 2006 ICSID Additional Facility Arbitration Rules contained a similar provision,[9] which has been removed from the 2022 ICSID Additional Facility Arbitration Rules. However, the distinction between awards and decisions persists under the ICSID Additional Facility Rules.[10] Since the award must include the decision of the tribunal on every question that has been submitted to it, it must incorporate all 'decisions'.[11] In particular, to the extent that these decisions are crucial to the outcome of the dispute, their findings must be incorporated in the award.[12] No provision in the ICSID Convention and the ICSID Arbitration Rules 'permit[s] or even contemplate[s] "Partial" or "Interim" awards, indeed, [...] the Rules contemplated only one, Final Award'.[13]

[6] Titi (n 5).

[7] ICSID Convention art 48(3).

[8] ICSID Arbitration Rules r 59(1)(i).

[9] eg see ICSID Additional Facility Rules (2006) art 52(1).

[10] eg see ICSID, 'Award—Additional Facility Arbitration (2022 Rules)' <https://icsid.worldbank.org/procedures/arbitration/additional-facility/award/2022>.

[11] eg *ConocoPhillips Petrozuata BV and others v Venezuela*, ICSID Case No ARB/07/30, Decision on Respondent's Request for Reconsideration (10 March 2014), Dissenting Opinion of Georges Abi-Saab [38]–[39]. See also *ConocoPhillips Petrozuata BV and others v Venezuela*, ICSID Case No ARB/07/30, Decision on the Respondent's Request for Reconsideration (9 February 2016), Dissenting Opinion by Arbitrator Andreas Bucher, [27]; *Standard Chartered Bank (Hong Kong) Limited v Tanzania (TANESCO)*, ICSID Case No ARB/10/20, Award (12 September 2016) [309]. See further Catharine Titi, '*Res iudicata* and Interlocutory Decisions under the ICSID Convention: Antinomies over the Power of Tribunals to Review' (2018) 33 (2) ICSID Review 358, 362.

[12] Anthony Sinclair, 'Article 48' in Stephan Schill and others (eds), *Schreuer's Commentary on the ICSID Convention*, vol 2 (3rd edn, CUP 2022) 1142.

[13] *Tanzania Electric Supply Company Ltd v Independent Power Tanzania Ltd*, ICSID Case No ARB/98/8, Final Award (22 June 2001) [32].

It becomes clear from the above that an ICSID award is not limited to jurisdictional and substantive issues but may also have to decide other questions, such as the apportionment of costs and any applicable interest that may be due. Contrariwise, an award does not necessarily need to include a decision on the merits. A 'decision' that declines jurisdiction is an award: it disposes of the dispute and it is final and binding. For example, according to the ICSID Arbitration Rules, if the tribunal determines 'all claims' to be 'manifestly without legal merit, it shall render an *Award* to that effect'; and, if not, it shall render 'a *decision* on the objection'.[14] If jurisdiction is declined but the jurisdictional defect is later cured, action can be recommenced, the cure constituting a *factum superveniens*, which removes the earlier award's *res iudicata* effect.[15]

In contrast with an award, a 'decision' under the ICSID Convention does not deal with every question submitted to the tribunal. So, for example, a decision upholding jurisdiction, a partial decision on the merits, a decision on costs, or a decision on the recommendation of provisional measures, are not awards but decisions under the ICSID Convention.

The distinction between awards and decisions in the ICSID system is significant because awards produce different effects than decisions. Only awards are final and binding, carry *res iudicata*, and are subject to the post-award remedies provided for in the ICSID Convention. According to Article 53 of the ICSID Convention, it is awards that are binding on the parties, that cannot be 'subject to any appeal or to any other remedy except those provided for in this Convention' and that require that parties 'shall abide by and comply with' their terms.[16] Under Article 54 of the ICSID Convention, awards only are subject to recognition and enforcement.[17] Decisions, even if they impose pecuniary obligations,[18] such as decisions on costs rendered before the award, are not covered by the effects laid out in Article 54 of the ICSID Convention. In fact, the Convention expressly states that decisions on costs need to be incorporated in the award.[19] However, once an award is rendered under the Convention, some post-award 'decisions' produce the same effects as an award: this is notably the case, for the purposes of recognition and enforcement, of a 'decision' interpreting, revising or annulling an award under Articles 50–52 of the ICSID Convention.[20] These formal remedies under the ICSID Convention become available against awards only: a request for interpretation,[21] revision,[22] and a request for annulment[23] are only possible with respect

[14] ICSID Arbitration Rules r 41(3) (emphasis added).

[15] Kaj Hobér, '*Res judicata* and *lis pendens* in International Arbitration' (2014) 366 Recueil des Cours 99, 284, 394.

[16] ICSID Convention art 53(1).

[17] ibid art 54(1).

[18] *Burlington Resources Inc v Ecuador*, ICSID Case No ARB/08/5, Decision on Reconsideration and Award (7 February 2017) [88].

[19] ICSID Convention art 61(2).

[20] ibid art 53.

[21] ibid art 50.

[22] ibid art 51; Karsten Nowrot and Emily Sipiorski, 'Review Beyond Annulment: Correction, Additional Awards, Clarification, and Revision' in Fach Gómez and Titi (n 2).

[23] ICSID Convention art 52; Steffen Hindelang and Julia Nassl, 'Annulment and Set-Aside' in Fach Gómez and Titi (n 2).

to an award. For this reason, in particular circumstances, pre-award decisions can be reconsidered by the arbitral tribunal, while the proceeding has not been terminated and the tribunal is not functus officio.[24]

In contract with ICSID awards and decisions, in non-ICSID arbitration, this distinction disappears. The 2021 UNCITRAL Arbitration Rules provide that the tribunal 'may make separate awards on different issues at different times'.[25] Each one of these awards is 'final and binding on the parties' and the parties have to carry it out 'without delay'.[26] That said, the term 'final award' is typically reserved for the award that revolves all (remaining) issues in dispute between the parties.[27] The 2020 Arbitration Rules of the London Court of International Arbitration (LCIA) also provide that the tribunal 'may make separate awards on different issues at different times, including interim payments on account of any claim, counterclaim or cross-claim (including Legal and Arbitration Costs ...). Such awards shall have the same status as any other award made by the Arbitral Tribunal'.[28] Under these rules too '[e]very award (including reasons for such award) shall be final and binding on the parties' and shall be carried out 'immediately and without any delay'.[29] The 2023 Arbitration Rules of the Stockholm Chamber of Commerce (SCC) Arbitration Institute establish that the tribunal 'may decide a separate issue or part of the dispute in a separate award'[30] and awards are 'final and binding on the parties'.[31] The parties 'undertake to carry out any award without delay'.[32] Finally, the 2021 Arbitration Rules of the International Chamber of Commerce (ICC) establish that the term 'award' includes, 'inter alia, an interim, partial, final, or additional award'.[33] The Rules make it clear that 'every' award is binding on the parties, which 'undertake to carry [it] out' 'without delay'.[34]

III. Drafting the Award: Content and Structure

In light of the different 'definitions' of the term 'award' in the ICSID system and under other arbitration rules, the minimum content of an award is markedly different in the former and latter contexts. The applicable arbitration rules are the best guide to the minimum content of an award, although common threads can be identified too. The sections that follow address in turn the minimum content of an award and its structure.

[24] See n 117.
[25] UNCITRAL Arbitration Rules (2021) art 34(1).
[26] ibid art 34(2).
[27] Blackaby, Partasides, and Redfern (n 1) para 9.19.
[28] LCIA Arbitration Rules (2020) art 26.1.
[29] ibid art 26.8.
[30] SCC Arbitration Rules (2023) art 44.
[31] ibid art 46.
[32] ibid.
[33] ICC Arbitration Rules (2021) art 2.
[34] ibid art 35(6).

A. Minimum Content

The award needs to comply with some form and substantive requirements that vary depending on the applicable arbitration rules. Typically, an award needs to be in writing,[35] and it must state the reasons upon which it is based.[36] This is simply good sense in order to ensure that the tribunal has duly reflected on the case and so as to 'record with clarity' its decisions for the parties, who are the primary addressees of the award, but also for the purposes of enforcement and for an eventual annulment or set-aside proceeding.[37] However, these rules are not absolute. So, under the 2021 UNCITRAL Arbitration Rules, the parties can agree that the award will not provide any reasoning.[38] Under the LCIA Arbitration Rules, the parties can 'agree in writing' that the award itself will not be in writing.[39] Or, under the English Arbitration Act 1966, '[t]he parties are free to agree on the form of an award', although, in the latter case too, the default rule is a reasoned award in written form.[40] To seek recognition and enforcement of an award under the New York Convention, it is necessary to provide the 'duly authenticated original award or a duly certified copy',[41] which seems to point to the need for a written instrument.[42]

The ICSID Convention, as we have already seen, expressly requires that the award deal with every question submitted to the tribunal,[43] and it must include a decision on costs.[44] If the award has been preceded by preliminary decisions, these decisions must be reflected in the award. This can happen by referring to the earlier decisions and expressly incorporating them into the award.[45] Questions are decided by a majority of votes, and the award must contain the signatures of the members of the tribunal who voted for it.[46] In other words, the award rendered by a three-member tribunal must contain the signatures of at least two of the three arbitrators. If the disputing parties agree, these signatures can be electronic.[47] The award may also contain individual or separate opinions of the tribunal members.[48]

[35] ICSID Convention art 48; UNCITRAL Arbitration Rules (2021) art 34(2), SCC Arbitration Rules (2023) art 42(1); UNCITRAL Model Law art 31(1).

[36] ICSID Convention art 48(3); SCC Arbitration Rules (2023) art 42(1); LCIA Arbitration Rules (2020) art 26.2; UNCITRAL Model Law art 31(2). On reasoning, see Bruno Simma and Jan Ortgies, 'The Reasoned Award' in Fach Gómez and Titi (n 2).

[37] Gary B Born, *International Arbitration: Law and Practice* (3rd edn, Kluwer Law International 2021) 339 (discussing the requirement for an award in writing).

[38] UNCITRAL Arbitration Rules (2021) art 34(3).

[39] LCIA Arbitration Rules (2020) art 26.2.

[40] English Arbitration Act 1966 s 52(1)–(4).

[41] New York Convention art IV(1)(a).

[42] Born (n 37) 338.

[43] ICSID Convention art 48. See text to nn 7–11.

[44] ibid art 61(2).

[45] eg *Veolia Propreté v Egypt*, ICSID Case No ARB/12/15, Award (25 May 2018) [1] ('On 13 April 2015, the Tribunal issued its Decision on Jurisdiction, *which forms part of this Award*', emphasis added).

[46] ICSID Convention art 48.

[47] ICSID Arbitration Rules r 59(2); ICSID Additional Facility Arbitration Rules r 70(2). In the latter case, electronic signatures are subject not only to the parties' agreement, but also to the law of the seat of the arbitration.

[48] ICSID Convention art 48. On this topic, see further Charles N Brower and Ahmed Mazlom, 'To Err Is Human, to Dissent Divine' in Fach Gómez and Titi (n 2); Catharine Titi, 'Investment Arbitration and the Controverted

According to the ICSID Arbitration Rules, the award must also designate the disputing parties, provide the names of the parties' representatives, expressly state that the tribunal 'was established in accordance with the Convention' and describe 'the method of its constitution'; identify the arbitrators and who they were appointed by; specify 'the date and place of the first session, case management conferences and hearings', and provide 'a brief summary of the proceeding', in other words, it must provide the procedural history of the case; contain a statement of facts 'as found by the Tribunal'; provide 'a brief summary of the submissions of the parties, including the relief sought'; and include 'a statement of the costs of the proceeding, including the fees and expenses of each member of the Tribunal, and a reasoned decision on costs'.[49] The content requirements for an award made under the ICSID Additional Facility Rules are similar,[50] with one important exception: while for an award delivered under the ICSID Convention the seat of the arbitration is immaterial,[51] this is not the case for an award made under the ICSID Additional Facility Rules. Therefore, under the ICSID Additional Facility Arbitration Rules, the award must also contain the seat of the arbitration.[52] The award is deemed to have been rendered there.[53]

Unlike awards rendered under other arbitration rules, there is no express requirement for ICSID arbitrators to date an award. The reason for this 'omission' is that, under both the ICSID Convention and the ICSID Additional Facility, the award is deemed to have been rendered on the date on which the Secretary-General of ICSID dispatches certified copies of the award to the parties.[54] Table 1.1 presents a checklist of form and substantive requirements for an ICSID Convention award. The table presents the minimum requirements but is without prejudice to additional elements that can form part of the award, such as the grant of relief and interest.[55] It is important to stress that the distinction between form and substantive requirements is schematic and used here for heuristic purposes only, since what are here termed substantive requirements can also be classified as 'form' requirements, in the sense that they relate to the form an award must take. For instance, the English Arbitration Act 1996 expressly classifies the requirement to state reasons as a 'form' requirement.[56]

Right of the Arbitrator to Issue a Separate or Dissenting Opinion' (2018) 17(1) Law and Practice of International Courts and Tribunals 197.

[49] ICSID Arbitration Rules r 59.
[50] See ICSID Additional Facility Arbitration Rules r 70(1).
[51] Broadly speaking, ICSID Convention arbitration takes place at a remove from national jurisdictions, since the Convention contains its own mechanisms for review, recognition, and enforcement of its awards. This is possible because, unlike other arbitration rules, the ICSID Convention is an international treaty with very broad membership. For a list of ICSID member states, see <https://icsid.worldbank.org/about/member-states/database-of-member-states>.
[52] ICSID Additional Facility Arbitration Rules r 70(1)(e).
[53] ibid r 71.
[54] ICSID Convention art 49(1); ICSID Additional Facility Arbitration Rules r 71.
[55] See also nn 73ff.
[56] See English Arbitration Act 1966 s 52 in conjunction with s 68(2)(h).

Table 1.1 Minimum content of an ICSID Convention award

Form requirements	Substantive requirements
Award in writing	Brief summary of the proceeding
Decided by majority of votes	Statement of facts 'as found' by the tribunal
Signatures of tribunal members who voted for the award. Signature can be electronic, so long as the parties agree	Brief summary of the parties' submissions and the relief sought
Disputing parties identified	Every question submitted to the tribunal must have been dealt with
Representatives of the parties identified	Reasons, including for the decision on costs
All arbitrators identified	Statement of the costs of the proceeding, including the fees and expenses of each arbitrator
Statement about who appointed each arbitrator	
Statement that the tribunal has been established in accordance with the ICSID Convention	
Description of the method of the tribunal's constitution	
Date and place of the first session, case management conferences, and hearings	
Date (this is the date on which the Secretary-General dispatches the award)	

In non-ICSID arbitration too, decisions are taken, in principle, by a majority of the appointed arbitrators,[57] although some arbitration rules state that questions of procedure can be decided by the presiding arbitrator.[58] Exceptionally, in the absence of a majority, provision is made for a decision on any issue to be made by the presiding arbitrator.[59] The majority rule also applies to the signing of the award. In principle, the award must bear the signatures of (at least) the majority of tribunal members, provided that it states the reason for any missing signature.[60] Exceptionally, some arbitration rules provide that the signature of the presiding arbitrator will suffice, if the award states the reason for the missing signatures.[61] These rules appear to allow the decision to be taken by the presiding arbitrator, in cases where no majority can be reached on a particular issue or even on the dispositive part of the award. That said, even if the rules allow decisions to be made by the presiding arbitrator, it is unclear that the constitution of a tribunal of three to hear a high-impact investment dispute ending up with an award supported by a single arbitrator, the president of the tribunal, will not raise legitimacy concerns.

[57] UNCITRAL Arbitration Rules (2021) art 33(1); Permanent Court of Arbitration (PCA) Arbitration Rules (2012) art 33(1); LCIA Arbitration Rules (2020) art 26.5; UNCITRAL Model Law art 29.

[58] UNCITRAL Arbitration Rules (2021) art 33(2); PCA Arbitration Rules (2012) art 33(2); SCC Arbitration Rules (2020) art 41 (2); UNCITRAL Model Law art 29.

[59] LCIA Arbitration Rules (2020) art 26.5; SCC Arbitration Rules (2023) art 41(1).

[60] UNCITRAL Arbitration Rules (2021) art 34(4); UNCITRAL Model Law art 31(1); LCIA Arbitration Rules (2020) art 26.6; SCC Arbitration Rules (2023) art 42(3); PCA Arbitration Rules (2012) art 34(4).

[61] SCC Arbitration Rules (2023) art 42(3); LCIA Arbitration Rules (2020) art 26.2.

The LCIA Arbitration Rules expressly establish that the arbitrators can, in principle, sign the award electronically and/or in counterparts that have been assembled into a single document.[62] Electronic signatures are increasingly accepted as a valid means of signing awards.[63] Given that the law of the seat matters in non-ICSID Convention arbitration, it is advisable to also take into account its requirements with respect to the form of the signatures.

Exceptionally, an additional procedural requirement is imposed by the ICC Arbitration Rules: before signature of the award, the tribunal must submit a draft of the award to the ICC International Court of Arbitration.[64] The latter may modify the form of the award and draw the tribunal's 'attention to points of substance'.[65] While any comment on substance does not limit the freedom of the tribunal as to the final outcome, the form of the award has to be approved by the Court before the tribunal renders its award.[66]

In an award rendered in non-ICSID proceedings, the arbitrators must indicate the date on which it was made and the place or seat of the arbitration.[67] Both the date and place of arbitration are crucial. The date of the award determines the moment from which various time frames start to run, such as notably for review and set-aside proceedings in local courts.[68] The place or seat of the arbitration, which does not need to correspond with the physical place where proceedings actually take place or the award is made,[69] indicates the jurisdiction whose law applies to some procedural matters and whose courts can be seized of, among others, review proceedings.[70]

Some arbitration rules expressly refer to costs, for instance, the UNCITRAL Arbitration Rules, provide that the tribunal shall determine in the award 'any amount that a party may have to pay to another party as a result of the decision on allocation of costs'.[71] The SCC Arbitration Rules make more detailed provision and specify that the tribunal 'shall include in the final award the costs of the arbitration ... and specify the individual fees and expenses of each member of the Arbitral Tribunal and the SCC'.[72]

Arbitration rules and local arbitration laws do not often expressly recognize the power of the tribunal to award interest.[73] However, tribunals routinely do so and the

[62] LCIA Arbitration Rules (2020) art 26.2.

[63] See also Ilias Bantekas, 'Form and Contents of Award' in Ilias Bantekas and others (eds), *UNCITRAL Model Law on International Commercial Arbitration: A Commentary* (CUP 2020) 814. However, it seems that electronic awards are not widespread yet, see Katia Fach Gómez, 'The Visible and Invisible Footprint of New Technologies in Investment Awards' in Fach Gómez and Titi (n 2). More generally, on the use of technology in investment arbitration, see Katia Fach Gómez, *The Technological Competence of Arbitrators* (Springer 2023).

[64] ICC Arbitration Rules (2021) art 34.

[65] ibid.

[66] ICC Arbitration Rules (2021) art 34. On draft awards, see Friedl Weiss, 'Draft Awards: Twirling Curls on a Bald Head' in Fach Gómez and Titi (n 2).

[67] UNCITRAL Arbitration Rules (2021) art 34(4); SCC Arbitration Rules (2023) art 42(2); LCIA Arbitration Rules (2020) art 26.2; UNCITRAL Model Law art 31(3); English Arbitration Act 1966 s 52(5).

[68] eg English Arbitration Act 1966 s 70(3); UNCITRAL Model Law art 33(2).

[69] eg see English Arbitration Act 1966 s 53.

[70] Gabrielle Kaufmann-Kohler and Michele Potestà, *Investor-State Dispute Settlement and National Courts* (Springer 2020) 55–77; Aniruddha Rajput, 'National Courts as Actors in Investment Arbitration' in Catharine Titi (ed), *Public Actors in International Investment Law* (Springer 2021) 48–49.

[71] UNCITRAL Arbitration Rules (2021) art 42(2); PCA Arbitration Rules (2012) art 42(2).

[72] SCC Arbitration Rules (2023) art 49(5).

[73] See also Born (n 37) 356.

award of interest is considered part of their mandate.[74] Doubts can be raised about the tribunal's power to award interest, if the applicable law makes no provision for interest and the claimant has not asked for it; awarding interest in such a case may turn out to be *ultra petita*.[75] The power of international adjudicatory bodies to award interest is recognized in the International Law Commission's (ILC) Articles on the Responsibility of States for Internationally Wrongful Acts, which provide that interest 'shall be payable when necessary in order to ensure full reparation'.[76] It is further specified that '[t]he interest rate and mode of calculation shall be set so as to achieve' full reparation.[77] Sometimes, tribunals make no distinction between pre- and post-award interest and impose interest from the moment of treaty violation until actual payment of the award.[78] According to the ILC Articles on the Responsibility of States for Internationally Wrongful Acts too, '[i]nterest runs from the date when the principal sum should have been paid until the date the obligation to pay is fulfilled'.[79] Some tribunals allow the state, eg, around ninety days to pay, after which interest accrues.[80]

The power of tribunals to award compound (as opposed to simple) interest has given rise to more debate, although compound interest seems to be progressively awarded with greater frequency.[81] The tribunal in *Continental Casualty v Argentina* held that '[t]he time value of money ... is measured in compound interest; simple interest cannot be relied upon to produce full reparation for a claimant's loss occasioned by delay in payment'.[82] In *Gemplus v Mexico*, the tribunal similarly found that 'there is now a form of "jurisprudence constante" where the presumption has shifted from the position a decade or so ago with the result it would now be more appropriate to order compound interest, unless shown to be inappropriate in favour of simple interest, rather than vice-versa'.[83] Exceptionally, some arbitration rules lay down express provisions on compound interest. The LCIA Arbitration Rules establish that:

> Unless the parties have agreed otherwise, the Arbitral Tribunal may order that simple or compound interest shall be paid by any party on any sum awarded at such rates

[74] Charles N Brower and Jeremy K Sharpe, 'Awards of Compound Interest in International Arbitration: The *Aminoil* Non-Precedent' in Gerald Aksen and others (eds), *Global Reflections on International Law, Commerce and Dispute Resolution: Liber Amicorum in Honour of Robert Briner* (ICC Publishing 2005) 155; Born (n 37) 356; Blackaby, Partasides, and Redfern (n 2) para 9.72.

[75] *Enron Corporation Ponderosa Assets, LP v Argentina*, ICSID Case No ARB/01/3, Decision on Claimants' Request for Rectification and/or Supplementary Decision of the Award (3 October 2007) [42]. See further Attila M Tanzi, 'On the Adjudicative Discretion of Investment Arbitrators: Between *ne ultra petita*, *ne infra petita*, and *jura novit curia*' in Fach Gómez and Titi (n 2).

[76] ILC Articles on the Responsibility of States for Internationally Wrongful Acts art 38(1).

[77] ibid.

[78] eg *Michael Anthony Lee-Chin v Dominican Republic*, ICSID Case No UNCT/18/3, Final Award (6 October 2023) [591]; *BG Group Plc v Argentina*, UNCITRAL, Final Award (24 December 2007) [467].

[79] ILC Articles on the Responsibility of States for Internationally Wrongful Acts art 38(2).

[80] eg *AsiaPhos Limited and Norwest Chemicals Pte Limited v China*, ICSID Case No ADM/21/1, Award (16 February 2023) [232].

[81] ILC Articles on the Responsibility of States for Internationally Wrongful Acts, Commentary, art 38, paras 8–9; Brower and Sharpe (n 74) 156–60; Blackaby, Partasides, and Redfern (n 2) paras 9.75–9.77.

[82] *Continental Casualty Company v Argentina*, ICSID Case No ARB/03/9, Award (5 September 2008) [309].

[83] *Gemplus SA, SLP SA, Gemplus Industrial SA de CV v Mexico*, ICSID Case No ARB(AF)/04/3 (16 June 2010) [16.26].

> as the Arbitral Tribunal decides to be appropriate (without being bound by rates of interest practised by any state court or other legal authority) in respect of any period which the Arbitral Tribunal decides to be appropriate ending not later than the date upon which the award is complied with.[84]

Similar provision for simple or compound interest, pre- and post-award, is made in some local arbitration laws.[85]

In some Islamic jurisdictions granting interest may be against local laws and/or against public policy, something that arbitrators must keep in mind, depending on the seat of the arbitration or where enforcement is likely to be sought.[86] However, it appears that, at least in some cases, it may be possible to grant instead compensation for 'financial damages'.[87] For example, in Iran, payment of interest is prohibited by the Constitution, but the Guardian Council has established that this prohibition does not apply to 'foreign governments, institutions, companies and persons, who, according to their own principles of faith, do not consider [interest] as being prohibited'.[88]

If the tribunal does not fully comply with form and substantive requirements, the award is defective. Depending on the kind of defect, there may be no consequences, eg if the losing party voluntarily complies with the award despite the defect. However, in some jurisdictions, failure to comply with form requirements is a ground for set-aside.[89] Under the ICSID Convention, failure to state reasons (classified here as a substantive requirement) is a standalone ground for annulment.[90] In other cases, non-compliance with obligatory requirements could end up with an impossibility to enforce, eg if the instrument is not recognized as an award. It is therefore necessary that arbitrators, who should 'make every effort' to render an enforceable award,[91] are mindful of form and substantive requirements, whose non-respect may constitute a ground for annulment and set-aside or even a ground for refusing recognition and enforcement.

B. Structure

The award will often have a title page, which will identify the document as an 'award', that the proceeding is an 'arbitration', it will state the applicable arbitration rules and investment treaty, the disputing parties, the tribunal members, the tribunal secretary, and assistant to the tribunal, if any, and the date and place of the award. The typical title

84 LCIA Arbitration Rules (2020) art 26.4.
85 eg English Arbitration Act 1966 s 49. For some examples from civil law jurisdictions, see Blackaby, Partasides, and Redfern (n 2) para 9.76.
86 Blackaby, Partasides, and Redfern (n 2) para 9.71, n 99.
87 ibid.
88 ILC Commentary (n 81), art 38, para 10, n 620, citing JY Gotanda, *Supplemental Damages in Private International Law* (Kluwer 1998) 38–40.
89 eg English Arbitration Act 1966 s 68(2)(h). For the use of the term 'form' requirement, see n 56.
90 ICSID Convention art 52(1).
91 Blackaby, Partasides, and Redfern (n 2) para 9.15; ICC Arbitration Rules (2021) art 42.

INTERNATIONAL CENTRE FOR SETTLEMENT OF INVESTMENT DISPUTES

In the arbitration proceeding between

[NAME OF CLAIMANT]

Claimant

and

[NAME OF RESPONDENT]

Respondent

ICSID Case No. ARB/[XX]

AWARD

Members of the Tribunal

[XXXX]

Secretary of the Tribunal

[XXXX]

Assistant to the Tribunal

[XXXX]

Date of dispatch to the Parties: [XXXX]

Figure 1.1 Cover page template of an ICSID award

page of an award rendered under the ICSID Convention includes the information provided in Figure 1.1.

An ICSID-administered non-ICSID Convention arbitration will also identify the place of arbitration. Often a second page will identify the representatives of the parties, although these can also be listed in the body of the award. The following paragraphs outline a possible structure of an investment award.

The main body of the award tends to start with a very short *introduction* to or summary of the dispute, briefly identifying the applicable law and arbitration rules and the facts that give rise to the dispute. This part, or a following separate part, also identifies the disputing parties and their representatives. The award continues by providing the *procedural history* of the dispute: from the notice of arbitration to the constitution of the tribunal, indicating which arbitrator was appointed by whom, from the preliminary hearing to the post-hearing phase, the issuance of eventual procedural orders, etc. The ensuing part will be focused on the *factual background* of the dispute, including disputed facts; the parties' *claims* and the *relief sought*; then the tribunal will apply the applicable law to the facts.

In particular, the *parties' arguments* will be presented in detail in relation to the claims and defences. It is practical for the arbitrator or arbitrators to copy and paste the parties' arguments, in order to avoid omissions or mistakes. In this part, separately or in conjunction with the parties' claims and arguments, the award will identify the issues or questions that are to be decided by the tribunal. The tribunal must stay within these issues to avoid including topics that are *ultra petita*.[92] The particular structure of the award with respect to the parties' arguments will of course depend on the type of award it is. For example, in a unitary (ie non bifurcated) proceeding, the award will first address *jurisdiction* and *admissibility*, then *liability*, that is, the merits, followed each time by the *tribunal's conclusions*. A non-ICSID jurisdictional award will address only jurisdiction and admissibility. In a bifurcated ICSID proceeding the award may simply incorporate the decision on jurisdiction, instead of addressing again the parties' positions with respect to jurisdiction.[93] The tribunal's examination of jurisdiction and admissibility will rely on, among others, the instrument of consent, usually the arbitration clause in an investment treaty. The tribunal's examination of the merits and liability, will discuss the law applicable to the substance of the dispute.[94]

If the tribunal finds that there has been a violation of the treaty, it must make a determination on *damages* and *quantum*, including, as the case may be, pre- and/or post-award *interest*.[95] In respect of damages and quantum too, the award will typically present the parties' and eventual experts' submissions on the matter and will then add the tribunal's conclusions.

Customarily, tribunals grant monetary relief to investors whose treaty rights have been violated, and only exceptionally do they grant non-pecuniary remedies.[96] The preponderance of monetary awards derives in part from the fact that many arbitration rules make reference to monetary awards but are silent about other types of relief. In addition, questions can be raised about specific performance in investment disputes, when the contested state measures are national legislation. When it comes to enforcement under the ICSID Convention, states' enforcement duty is limited to 'the pecuniary obligations' imposed by the award.[97]

Irrespective of whether a tribunal awards damages, the award must make a determination on the apportionment of *costs*.[98] Finally comes the dispositive or operative part of the award, which typically states that 'for the reasons stated above' the tribunal

92 Tanzi (n 75).

93 See text to n 45.

94 See George A Bermann, 'The Applicable Law in Investor-State Dispute Settlement' in Fach Gómez and Titi (n 2).

95 See text to n 73. See also Kaj Hobér, 'Compensation' in Fach Gómez and Titi (n 2).

96 Gisèle Stephens-Chu, 'Is it Always All about the Money? The Appropriateness of Non-Pecuniary Remedies in Investment Treaty Arbitration' (2014) 30(4) Arbitration International 661.

97 ICSID Convention art 54(1); Marc Bungenberg, Andrés E Alvarado-Garzón, and Bianca Böhme, 'Recognition and Enforcement of ICSID Convention Awards' in Fach Gómez and Titi (n 2).

98 eg see ICSID Convention art 61; UNCITRAL Arbitration Rules (2021) art 42(1). See also text to nn 44, 49, 71–72; Susan Franck and Bailey Roe, 'The Cost Award' in Fach Gómez and Titi (n 2); Irmgard Marboe, 'Article 61' in Schill and others (n 12) 1661; Gabriel Bottini and others, 'Excessive Costs and Recoverability of Cost Awards in Investment Arbitration' (2020) 21 (2–3) Journal of World Investment & Trade 251. While tribunals have broad discretion in apportioning costs, the applicable arbitration rules and/or investment treaty will sometimes provide some guidance. For example, the tribunal's decision on cost may be influenced by the determination of whether there has been a violation of the treaty, especially in cases when the tribunal is mandated by the applicable rules to follow the loser pays principle. Often the broad freedom tribunals have in apportioning costs will be streamlined by the requirement to take into account the circumstances of the particular case and achieve an apportionment of costs that is 'reasonable', see Catharine Titi, *The Function of Equity in International Law* (OUP 2021) 194.

decides X, Y, Z, and then uses directive language (eg the respondent shall pay X amount in respect of damages, or the claimant shall pay X in respect of costs). The dispositive part of the award must give clear directions to the parties, it must solve the dispute and leave no doubt about what the parties have to do, if anything. After that, the date of signature is added (both for ICSID and non-ICSID awards) and (for non-ICSID awards) the place of arbitration.

IV. The Effects of an Award: Binding Character, *res iudicata*, Recognition, and Enforcement

Pursuant to Article 53 of the ICSID Convention, an award is binding on the parties and it is not subject to appeal or any other remedy except as provided for in the Convention.[99] This article establishes what could be termed the award's internal binding effect, focused on how the award affects the parties to the proceeding.[100] As we have seen, other arbitration rules make similar provision with regard to the finality and binding effect of awards (although, unlike the ICSID Convention, they do not establish a self-contained review system).[101]

Article 53 of the ICSID Convention is complemented by the following provision, Article 54, which instructs ICSID member states to recognize an award as binding and enforce the pecuniary obligations imposed by it.[102] This obligation broadens the addressees of the award's binding nature and sets out its external binding effect.[103] Given that states' obligation to recognize the award as binding and enforce the pecuniary obligations imposed by it is owed to other member states by virtue of an international treaty (the ICSID Convention), its violation could engage the international responsibility of the state.[104] In non-ICSID arbitration, states' obligation to recognize as binding and enforce an international award arises from the New York Convention, a treaty external to the arbitration rules themselves.[105] Unlike the ICSID Convention, which requires member states to treat an award, for the purposes of recognition and enforcement, 'as if it were a final judgment of a court in that State',[106] recognition and enforcement of awards under the New York Convention is not automatic. The winning party has to present the award to the enforcement court in a New York Convention member state for the court to recognize the award following a narrow review of its enforceability.[107] According to the UNCITRAL Model Law, '[a]n arbitral award, irrespective of the

99 ICSID Convention art 53(1).
100 Titi (n 11) 360.
101 See text to nn 26–34.
102 ICSID Convention art 54(1). On enforcement of ICSID awards, see Bungenberg, Alvarado-Garzón, and Böhme (n 97).
103 Titi (n 11) 360.
104 August Reinisch, 'Article 53' in Schill and others (n 12) 1448, 1462.
105 See Giuditta Cordero-Moss, 'Recognition and Enforcement of non-ICSID Convention Awards' in Fach Gómez and Titi (n 2).
106 ICSID Convention art 54(1).
107 Cordero-Moss (n 105).

country in which it was made, shall be recognized as binding and, upon application in writing to the competent court, shall be enforced'.[108] Exceptionally, recognition and enforcement of non-ICSID Convention awards can be refused on some grounds provided for in local laws and the New York Convention.[109]

An award's finality or binding character is inextricably linked to the *res iudicata* effect it carries. *Res iudicata* means that the claims the award has dealt with and decided cannot be the subject of another judicial or arbitral proceeding.[110] In *Ampal v Egypt*, the tribunal considered an earlier award rendered in a contract-based arbitration bearing on the same claims and parties.[111] Since that award had decided the questions as between the parties and was binding upon them (internal binding effect), the tribunal concluded that the findings of this earlier award had a *res iudicata* effect between the parties to the proceeding before it.[112] Other tribunals have focused on the award's external binding effect to determine *res iudicata*.[113] In *Standard Chartered Bank v Tanzania*, the tribunal held that while ICSID *decisions* are binding within the proceedings, this does not make them *res iudicata*.[114] For this tribunal, an important aspect of *res iudicata* is that 'the judgment in question produces effects on the parties outside the proceedings in which it is granted'.[115] In reality, an award can have *res iudicata* effect, even when it is not possible to enforce it—so, the *res iudicata* effect of an award granting non-pecuniary remedies is not affected by the fact that only pecuniary obligations are enforceable under the ICSID Convention.[116] As for ICSID decisions, not only do they not carry *res iudicata*, but, *pace* the *Standard Chartered Bank* tribunal, neither are they binding; they are certainly not binding beyond the duration of the proceeding and, even within the proceeding, they can be revisited by a tribunal.[117]

[108] UNCITRAL Model Law (2006) art 35(1).

[109] New York Convention art V; UNCITRAL Model Law (2006) art 36.

[110] August Reinisch, 'Article 54' in Schill and others (n 12) 1485.

[111] *Ampal-American Israel Corporation and others v Egypt*, ICSID Case No ARB/12/11, Decision on Liability and Heads of Loss, 21 February 2017 [248]–[270].

[112] ibid [259], [270].

[113] See also Reinisch (n 110) 1485 and Reinisch (n 104) 1147, arguing that the obligation to recognize an award as binding renders it *res iudicata*.

[114] *Standard Chartered Bank (Hong Kong) Limited v Tanzania (TANESCO)*, ICSID Case No ARB/10/20, Award (12 September 2016) [313].

[115] ibid.

[116] ICSID Convention art 54(1). See Christoph Schreuer, 'Non-Pecuniary Remedies in ICSID Arbitration' (2004) 20 (4) Arbitration International 325, 326, citing Aron Broches.

[117] Titi (n 11). In reality, many pre-award decisions do not impose obligations on the parties. A decision upholding jurisdiction does not usually require any party to do anything. Therefore, it makes little sense to talk about its binding effects. Exceptionally, decisions can impose obligations, this is especially the case of decisions on provisional measures. Unlike other arbitration rules, decisions on provisional measures under the ICSID Convention are not expressly binding. The Convention and the Arbitration Rules state that the tribunal can 'recommend' (rather than 'order') provisional measures (see ICSID Convention art 47; ICSID Arbitration Rules r 47) and the same conclusion can be reached in light of the Convention's drafting history, see Chester Brown, 'Article 47' in Schill and others (n 12) 1060; David D Caron, 'Interim Measures of Protection: Theory and Practice in Light of the Iran–United States Claims Tribunal' (1986) 46 Zeitschrift Für Ausländisches Öffentliches Recht Und Völkerrecht 465, 478, 511; Hobér (n 15) 284; Cameron Miles, *Provisional Measures before International Courts and Tribunals* (CUP 2017) 285–87; cf Anthony C Sinclair and Odysseas G Repousis, 'An Overview of Provisional Measures in ICSID Proceedings' (2017) 32 (2) ICSID Review 431, 433. For a different interpretation, see Charles N Brower and Ronald EM Goodman, 'Provisional Measures and the Protection of ICSID Jurisdictional Exclusivity Against

The ICSID Convention attributes *res iudicata* and binding effect to awards only.[118]

V. Conclusion

This chapter has given an overview of what an investment award is and what it is not. It has discussed the differences between awards and pre-award decisions in the ICSID Convention and explained what these differences mean for our understanding of awards in the ICSID system and beyond. Next, the chapter enquired into the drafting of investment awards. First, it focused on minimum content requirements, notably form and substantive requirements, from run-of-the-mill obligations, such as the need to identify the parties' representatives in the award to the substantive requirement to state reasons when awarding costs. Second, it explored the typical structure of an investment award. This part of the chapter thus provided a basic checklist and a roadmap for drafting. In addition, it paid close attention to a particular question, that of the power of tribunals to award interest as part of their mandate. Finally, the chapter considered the effects of an award, and in particular its binding character and *res iudicata* effect, and the recognition and enforcement obligations it carries. The chapter commented on the duty of arbitrators to render an enforceable award, which in turn requires that, when drafting, it is important to be mindful of the grounds for annulment and set-aside as well as the grounds for refusing recognition and enforcement.

Municipal Proceedings' (1991) 6 (2) ICSID Review 431, 440. For provisional measures outside the ICSID Convention, see eg UNCITRAL Arbitration Rules (1976) art 26 (providing that 'interim measures may be established in the form of an interim award') in conjunction with art 32(2) (establishing the binding nature of 'awards'). Even so, ICSID tribunals have consistently treated recommendations of provisional measures as binding on the parties (internal binding effect), eg *Emilio Agustín Maffezini v Spain*, ICSID Case No ARB/97/7, Procedural Order No 2 (28 October 1999) [9]; *Víctor Pey Casado and President Allende Foundation v Chile*, ICSID Case No ARB/98/2, Decision on Provisional Measures (25 September 2001) [17]ff; *Tokios Tokelés v Ukraine*, ICSID Case No ARB/02/18, Procedural Order No 3 (18 January 2005) [6] n 12; *Perenco Ecuador Limited v Ecuador*, ICSID Case No ARB/08/6, Decision on Provisional Measures (8 May 2009) [74]; *Quiborax SA and Non Metallic Minerals SA v Bolivia*, ICSID Case No ARB/06/2, Award (16 September 2015) [579] n 738; *Valle Verde Sociedad Financiera SL v Venezuela*, ICSID Case No ARB/12/18, Decision on Provisional Measures (25 January 2016) [75] n 30. However, ICSID member states are under no obligation to recognise as binding and enforce decisions granting provisional measures, see Brown, 'Article 47' in Schill and others (n 12) 1060). In any case, decisions granting provisional measures under the ICSID Convention are not *res iudicata* and provisional measures can be modified or revoked by the tribunal 'at any time', according to ICSID Arbitration Rules r 47(6). Besides, provisional measures are without prejudice to whether the tribunal actually has jurisdiction to hear the dispute. If the tribunal ultimately declines jurisdiction, the provisional measures automatically lapse, eg *Bayindir Insaat Turizm Ticaret Ve Sanayi AS v Pakistan*, ICSID Case No ARB/03/29, Decision on Jurisdiction (14 November 2005) [47]; *SGS Société Générale de Surveillance SA v Pakistan*, ARB/01/13, Procedural Order No 2 (16 October 2002); *Víctor Pey Casado and President Allende Foundation v Chile*, ICSID Case No ARB/98/2, Decision on Provisional Measures (25 September 2001) [14]; *Millicom International Operations BV and Sentel GSM SA v Senegal*, ICSID Case No ARB/08/20, Decision on the Application for Provisional Measures (24 August 2009) [38].

[118] In *Burlington v Ecuador*, the tribunal described the *res iudicata* effect of awards, as opposed to decisions, with the reasoning that 'the requirement for incorporation of earlier decisions into the award, the absence of remedies against these decisions, and the fact that the Contracting States' obligation to recognize and enforce only attaches to the award, not to earlier decisions, show that *res judicata* attaches to the "award" in the ICSID meaning and not to earlier decisions', *Burlington Resources Inc v Ecuador*, ICSID Case No ARB/08/5, Decision on Reconsideration and Award (7 February 2017) [89].

2

The Award on Jurisdiction and Merits

*Giorgio Sacerdoti and Carlo de Stefano**

I. Introduction

The 'award' rendered by an international investment tribunal, be it on the merits or the jurisdictional aspects of a dispute, truly is a classic international decision (*décision internationale*).[1] In particular, the operative part of the award or decision is mandatorily anticipated by the substantial motivation ('reasoning') of the tribunal in fact and in law, which includes the illustration of the arguments advanced by the parties, the articulated *exposé* of the logical reasoning undertaken by the adjudicators, and references to the authorities and precedents that corroborate the conclusions of the arbitrators.[2] In this respect, international investment arbitration adheres to the common law (and German) 'persuasive model' rather than to the practice of civil law jurisdictions ('*juridictions latines*').[3] This is confirmed by the right of individual arbitrators to issue and append to the award a separate or dissenting opinion.[4] These are but few explanations about the length of international investment awards, especially when they address the merits of the dispute. The deliberations of the tribunal are secret and, when the adjudicative organ has a plural composition, they are adopted on the basis of the principle of collegiality of the formation of the judgment, including through the collective exchange of views between the members of the tribunal.[5] The award or decision

* This chapter constitutes the result of a collaborative work. However, sections III–IV are attributed to Giorgio Sacerdoti and sections I–II and V–VII to Carlo de Stefano.

[1] Gaetano Morelli, *La sentenza internazionale* (CEDAM 1931); John Collier and Vaughan Lowe, *The Settlement of Disputes in International Law: Institutions and Procedures* (OUP 1999) 253–57.

[2] Hélène Ruiz Fabri and Jean-Marc Sorel (eds), *La motivation des décisions des juridictions internationales* (Pedone 2008) 285.

[3] Carlo Santulli, *Droit du contentieux international* (2nd edn, LGDJ 2015) 488.

[4] ICSID Convention art 48(4); ICSID Arbitration Rules r 59(3); ICSID Additional Facility Arbitration Rules r 70(3). See Albert Jan van den Berg, 'Dissenting Opinions by Party-Appointed Arbitrators in Investment Arbitration' in Mahnoush H Arsanjani and others (eds), *Looking to the Future: Essays on International Law in Honor of W Michael Reisman* (Martinus Nijhoff 2011) 821.

[5] In full consistency with the principle of collegiality in the deliberations of the arbitrators, the arbitral tribunal may avail itself of an administrative secretary, who is usually proposed by the president. In ICSID arbitration, the tribunal's secretary is by default a legal counsel of the Centre's Secretariat and, in addition, the arbitral tribunal or the president alone may nominate an assistant to the tribunal. On the (legitimate) role of tribunal's secretaries in ICC arbitration, the Belgian Court of Cassation recently confirmed a decision of the Tribunal of First Instance of Brussels, which held that the delegation of tasks by arbitrators to administrative secretaries does not violate the arbitration agreement as long as the tribunal reviews and corrects the draft(s) according to its own views. cf Belgian Court of Cassation, *Emek Inşaat Şti Ltd & WTE Wassertechnik Gmbh v European Commission*, C.21.0548.F/1, Judgment (24 April 2023). See Claudia Frutos-Peterson and Marat Umerov, 'The Role of Tribunal Secretaries in the Drafting of Investment Awards' in Katia Fach Gómez and Catharine Titi (eds), *The Award in International Investment Arbitration* (OUP 2024).

Giorgio Sacerdoti and Carlo de Stefano, *The Award on Jurisdiction and Merits* In: *The Award in International Investment Arbitration*. Edited by: Katia Fach Gómez and Catharine Titi, Oxford University Press. © Katia Fach Gómez and Aikaterini Titi 2024.
DOI: 10.1093/9780191975936.003.0002

is adopted by majority, if unanimity is not reached.[6] A typical feature of international (but also domestic) commercial arbitration, as also found in the arbitration rules of institutions administering investment arbitrations, is the non-publicity of decisions or awards. These are in principle not public, except if the parties agree otherwise.[7] After the means of recourse have been exhausted, or if they are unavailable, an international investment award is final and produces the effect of *res judicata* (*chose jugée*) as between the parties,[8] based on the triple identity test regarding the parties, the underlying cause of action and object (or subject matter) of the dispute.[9] Nevertheless, international investment awards (and decisions) may be subject to reconsideration both in the system established by the International Centre for Settlement of Investment Disputes (ICSID or the Centre) and in non-ICSID arbitrations, as explained below.

In ICSID arbitrations, the decision that affirms the jurisdiction of the Centre is referred to as 'decision on jurisdiction'. As mentioned below, it may not be subject to review immediately, but the jurisdictional findings of the tribunal may form the object of an application for annulment[10] at a later stage in conjunction with the (final) award. Instead, the decision of an ICSID tribunal that does not uphold its jurisdiction and hence terminates an arbitral proceeding in its entirety is denominated as 'award'.[11] In non-ICSID arbitrations, such as those administered by the Permanent Court of Arbitration (PCA), the International Court of Arbitration of the International Chamber of Commerce (ICC), or the Arbitration Institute of the Stockholm Chamber of Commerce (SCC), the decision on jurisdiction is defined as 'partial award', 'interim award', or, if it denies the tribunal's competence, as 'final award'. The decision on jurisdiction is frequently coupled with the tribunal's determination on the admissibility of the arbitral claim.[12] The arbitral tribunal's decision on the merits of the investment dispute is instead normally named an 'award' ('*sentence arbitrale*', '*laudo*', '*lodo*', '*Urteil*'). The award on the merits usually contains the arbitrators' findings on the substantive liability of the state. If the state is found liable for a breach to the prejudice of the investor, the final award will include the evaluation, determination, and quantification of the damages suffered by the latter as well as the sentencing of the state to pay damages to the investor. More rarely, the decision on the quantum of damages may be issued separately at a later stage.[13] In this case, under the ICSID rules the arbitral tribunal issues

[6] Stephen M Schwebel, 'The Majority Vote of an International Arbitral Tribunal' in Christian Dominicé, Robert Patry, and Claude Reymond (eds), *Études de droit international en l'honneur de Pierre Lalive* (Helbing and Lichtenhahn 1993) 671.

[7] ICSID Convention art 48(5); UNCITRAL Arbitration Rules art 34(5). See, however, UNCITRAL Rules on Transparency in Treaty-based Investor-State Arbitration (effective 1 April 2014) art 3.

[8] Aaron Broches, 'Awards Rendered Pursuant to the ICSID Convention: Binding Force, Finality, Recognition, Enforcement, Execution' (1987) 2(2) ICSID Review 287. The authority of *res judicata* is limited to the actual *decisum* of the award, including with respect to the effect of *ne bis in idem*. See Catharine Titi, 'What Is an Award? Concept, Content, Drafting, Effects' in Fach Gómez and Titi (n 5).

[9] Kaj Hobér, '*Res Judicata* and *Lis Pendens* in International Arbitration' (2014) 366 Recueil des Cours 376–401.

[10] ICSID Convention art 52.

[11] eg *Itisaluna Iraq LLC, Munir Sukhtian International Investment LLC, VTEL Holdings Ltd, VTEL Middle East and Africa Limited v Iraq*, ICSID Case No ARB/17/10, Award (3 April 2020).

[12] For a recent example, see *Mathias Kruck and others v Spain*, ICSID Case No ARB/15/23, Decision on Jurisdiction and Admissibility (19 April 2021).

[13] eg *Sevilla Beheer BV and others v Spain*, ICSID Case No ARB/16/27, Award (22 May 2023).

a 'decision' on liability,[14] while the determination of the quantum will ultimately take the form of a (final) 'award'.[15] In the rare instances when an investment tribunal finds a counterclaim admissible, the tribunal will rule on the merits of the counterclaim and any amount of damages it establishes as due by the investor to the state in the same final award.[16] The final award also invariably determines, as provided in the relevant arbitration rules (including institutional rules), the amount of costs of the proceedings and its apportionment among the parties.[17]

Investment arbitration awards benefit from favourable enforcement regimes whose application depends on the rules under which the main proceedings were administered.[18] The circulation of ICSID awards is governed by the Convention on the Settlement of Investment Disputes between States and Nationals of Other States of 18 March 1965 (ICSID or Washington Convention), in particular by Articles 53–55.[19] Non-ICSID investment awards may circulate in countries other than those in which, or pursuant to whose law, they were rendered (where they are as a rule considered as domestic awards, subject to the local law requirements as to proceedings, issuance, and challenges) pursuant to the Convention on the Recognition and Enforcement of Foreign Arbitral Awards of 10 June 1958 (New York Convention), notably under its Article V.[20] In this case, there is no particularity of investor-state arbitration in so far as the ensuing awards are governed by the same rules as international commercial awards with respect to their recognition and enforcement in the jurisdictions where such recognition and enforcement are sought.[21]

II. Bifurcation of Proceedings

Before addressing discretely the features of the decision on jurisdiction and the award on the merits with regard to investment disputes, it is appropriate to mention that arbitral proceedings may be bifurcated.[22] In particular, 'in investment treaty arbitrations, bifurcation remains relatively straightforward and largely arises where there is an objection to jurisdiction'.[23] In this scenario, arbitration proceedings would be divided into

[14] eg *Mathias Kruck and others v Spain*, ICSID Case No ARB/15/23, Decision on Jurisdiction, Liability and Principles of Quantum (14 September 2022).

[15] *Mathias Kruck and others v Spain*, ICSID Case No ARB/15/23, Award (6 October 2023).

[16] See Carlo de Stefano, 'Equality and Asymmetry in Treaty-Based Investment Arbitration: Counterclaims by Host States' in Daniele Amoroso and others (eds), *More Equal than Others? Perspectives on the Principle of Equality from International and EU Law* (TMC Asser Press 2022) 303.

[17] See Susan Franck and Bailey Roe, 'The Cost Award' in Fach Gómez and Titi (n 5).

[18] Giorgio Sacerdoti, 'Investment Arbitration Under ICSID and UNCITRAL Rules: Prerequisites, Applicable Law, Review of Awards' (2004) 19(1) ICSID Review 1.

[19] See section VI of this chapter.

[20] ibid.

[21] See Carlo de Stefano, 'The Circulation of International Investment Awards under the New York Convention' in Ana Mercedes López Rodríguez and Katia Fach Gómez (eds), *60 Years of the New York Convention on the Recognition and Enforcement of Foreign Arbitral Awards: Key Issues and Future Challenges* (Kluwer Law International 2019) 441–55.

[22] John Yukio Gotanda, 'An Efficient Method for Determining Jurisdiction in International Arbitrations' (2001) 40 Columbia Journal of Transnational Law 11.

[23] Lucy Greenwood, 'Revisiting Bifurcation and Efficiency in International Arbitration Proceedings' (2019) 36(4) Journal of International Arbitration 421, 422; Lucy Greenwood, 'Does Bifurcation Really Promote

two main segments: a first phase will be devoted to issues related to the jurisdiction of the tribunal (and often also to the admissibility of the claim); a second phase will be devoted to the substance of the dispute, namely its merits, including the assessment of damages. Obviously, the merits phase of the bifurcated arbitration proceedings will be held only when an affirmative decision on jurisdiction has been adopted by the tribunal in the first phase. It is also possible for the arbitrators to decide in favour of the trifurcation of proceedings. In this scenario, an additional third phase would be dedicated specifically to the determination of the quantum of damages.[24] Accordingly, the second phase of the investment arbitration will end with an award or decision on liability or 'principles of liability', sometimes including 'principles', 'directions', or 'guidelines' on quantum,[25] and the subsequent procedural phase will revolve around the actual quantification of damages. In recent arbitrations based on intra-EU bilateral investment treaties (BITs) or in arbitrations under the Energy Charter Treaty (ECT) involving member states and investors of another member state, tribunals have decided to bifurcate the proceedings in order to temporally prioritize their jurisdictional decision on the so-called intra-EU objection or *Achmea* issue.[26]

Alongside procedural fairness, the main rationale for bifurcation of proceedings is efficiency, which may be predicated to be effectively served in case the first phase of the investment arbitration is likely to result in a final award disposing of the proceedings (eg a decision declining the jurisdiction of the tribunal). Article 41(2) of the ICSID Convention and the new Rule 42 of the ICSID Arbitration Rules applies to the bifurcation of the proceedings. In particular, a party's application for bifurcation consists in the 'request that a question be addressed in a separate phase of the proceeding ("request for bifurcation")'.[27] Typically, the object of the request may be a 'preliminary objection' relating to the lack of jurisdiction of the Centre or competence of the tribunal.[28] For such issues, the arbitral tribunal may decide also 'on its own initiative'.[29] Under the current UNCITRAL Arbitration Rules, Article 23(3) establishes that the arbitral tribunal may rule on a jurisdictional plea 'either as a preliminary question or in an award on the merits'.[30] This rule supersedes the provision contained in Article 21(4) of the 1976 version of the UNCITRAL Rules, which reflected a rebuttable presumption of bifurcation with respect to jurisdictional objections: 'In general, the arbitral tribunal should rule on a plea concerning its jurisdiction as a preliminary question. However, the arbitral tribunal may proceed with the arbitration and rule on such a plea in their

Efficiency?' (2011) 28(2) Journal of International Arbitration 105; Massimo Benedettelli, 'To Bifurcate or Not to Bifurcate? That Is the (Ambiguous) Question' (2013) 29(3) Arbitration International 493.

[24] eg *Total SA v Argentina*, ICSID Case No ARB/04/01, Award (27 November 2013).

[25] eg *RREEF Infrastructure (GP) Limited and RREEF Pan-European Infrastructure Two Lux Sàrl v Spain*, ICSID Case No ARB/13/30, Decision on Responsibility and on the Principles of Quantum (30 November 2018).

[26] See eg *Eskosol SpA in liquidazione v Italy*, ICSID Case No ARB/15/50, Decision on Termination Request and Intra-EU Objection (7 May 2019).

[27] ICSID Arbitration Rules r 42.

[28] ibid r 43.

[29] ibid.

[30] UNCITRAL Arbitration Rules art 23(3).

final award.'[31] In any event, also under the 1976 UNCITRAL Arbitration Rules an arbitral tribunal could make use of a certain margin of discretion ('the arbitral tribunal may proceed with the arbitration') in granting a request for bifurcation based on jurisdictional grounds.[32] At present, it is generally accepted that 'there is no presumption in favour of bifurcation in ICSID proceedings.'[33]

The requesting party bears the burden of proving that its application for bifurcation is well founded[34] and, as the *Mesa Power* tribunal pointed out, 'the burden of full-fledged proceedings' should not be imposed 'on a party that disputes being subject to arbitration',[35] which usually is the respondent state. Accordingly, an arbitral tribunal does entertain discretion to preliminarily decide the determination of discrete issues (including questions of merits), if it believes that doing so would serve the interests of fair and efficient resolution of the case. Under the UNCITRAL Rules, this conclusion is supported by Article 17(1), which states that 'the arbitral tribunal may conduct the arbitration in such manner as it considers appropriate, provided that the parties are treated with equality and that at an appropriate stage of the proceedings each party is given a reasonable opportunity of presenting its case.'[36] This general authority includes the power to sequence the presentation and determination of issues in whatever manner appears sensible in the particular circumstances in order to serve justice in the most appropriate way and in the best interests of a pending case. Finally, and very importantly, as remarked by the *Tulip* tribunal, an arbitral tribunal, when confronted with an application for bifurcation, should only discharge the task of deciding whether to grant or not the application.[37] This entails that the arbitrators should not decide or even prejudge at that juncture the issues that are sought to be bifurcated.

As mentioned above, the main rationale for the bifurcation of arbitral proceedings is efficiency, namely the avoidance of dissipation of resources, especially time and costs. While the UNCITRAL Rules do not set forth any particular standard applicable to the decision on bifurcation, nor even a list of specific factors to be taken into consideration or weighed, the new ICSID Arbitration Rules of 2022 codify the traditional three-tiered

[31] UNCITRAL Arbitration Rules (1976) art 21(4). See *Glamis Gold Ltd v United States of America*, UNCITRAL, Procedural Order No 2 (Revised) (31 May 2005) [9]: 'Article 21(4) establishes a presumption in favor of the tribunal preliminarily considering objections to jurisdiction.'

[32] *Glamis Gold Ltd v United States of America* (n 31) [9]: 'Simultaneously, however, Article 21(4) does not require that pleas as to jurisdiction must be ruled on as preliminary questions. The choice not to do so is left to the tribunal's discretion.' See also *Canfor Corporation v United States of America*, UNCITRAL, Decision on the Place of Arbitration, Filing of a Statement of Defense and Bifurcation of the Proceedings (23 January 2004) [46].

[33] *Canepa Green Energy Opportunities I, Sárl and Canepa Green Energy Opportunities II, Sárl v Spain*, ICSID Case No ARB/19/4, Procedural Order No 3—Decision on Bifurcation (28 August 2020) [66].

[34] ibid (holding that the requesting party 'bears the burden of demonstrating that the facts currently in the record merit a conclusion by the Tribunal that bifurcation is merited').

[35] *Mesa Power Group, LLC v Canada*, PCA Case No 2012-17, Procedural Order No 2 (18 January 2013) [16].

[36] UNCITRAL Arbitration Rules art 17(1); UNCITRAL Arbitration Rules (1976) art 15(1).

[37] *Tulip Real Estate Investment and Development Netherlands BV v Turkey*, ICSID Case No ARB/11/28, Decision on the Respondent's Request for Bifurcation (2 November 2012) [36]. Accord, *Canepa Green Energy Opportunities I, Sárl and Canepa Green Energy Opportunities II, Sárl v Spain*, ICSID Case No ARB/19/4, Procedural Order No 3—Decision on Bifurcation (28 August 2020) [64]; *Carlos Sastre and others v Mexico*, ICSID Case No UNCT/20/2, Procedural Order No 2 (13 August 2020) [24]; *Red Eagle Exploration Limited v Colombia*, ICSID Case No ARB/18/12, Decision on Bifurcation (3 August 2020) [36]; *Hela Schwarz GmbH v China*, ICSID Case No ARB/17/19, Procedural Order No 3 (17 December 2018) [72].

test that should be applied by the arbitral tribunal. While the *timeliness* of the application for bifurcation of proceedings remains a relevant criterion (as early as possible and 'no later than in the statement of defence'),[38] ICSID Arbitration Rules 42(4) and 44(2) establish that:

> [i]n determining whether to bifurcate, the Tribunal shall consider all relevant circumstances, including whether:
> (a) bifurcation would materially reduce the time and cost of the proceeding;
> (b) determination of the questions to be bifurcated would dispose of all or a substantial portion of the dispute; and
> (c) the questions to be addressed in separate phases of the proceeding are so intertwined as to make bifurcation impractical.

This list of factors is not exhaustive and the criteria that are encapsulated therein are, as a tendency, cumulative.[39] In both UNCITRAL and ICSID proceedings, investment tribunals have identified a number of standards that may be relevant to assessing the appropriateness of bifurcation in any particular case. These include inter alia whether the objection is substantial and/or not frivolous,[40] whether the objection has the potential to dispose of the entire case, or at least to result in a material reduction of scope in the subsequent phase of proceedings,[41] and whether the jurisdictional (or admissibility or merits) question at issue is sufficiently discrete from and not intertwined with the factual and legal issues that would need to be heard in later phases, so that it may be resolved without the parties being put to the burden and expense of potentially duplicative presentations.[42] More generally, in addressing the overarching question of procedural economy and efficiency, tribunals consider 'whether the costs and time

[38] UNCITRAL Arbitration Rules art 23(2).

[39] *Carlos Sastre and others v Mexico*, ICSID Case No UNCT/20/2, Procedural Order No 2 (13 August 2020) [43]: 'The Tribunal agrees that these criteria should be taken into consideration when deciding bifurcation. The three factors identified are not "stand-alone" criteria. All three elements of the test must be cumulatively satisfied to decide a preliminary objection to jurisdiction in a separate phase.' See also *Orazul International España Holdings SL v Argentina*, ICSID Case No ARB/19/25, Decision on the Respondent's Request for Bifurcation (7 January 2021) [31]; *A11Y Ltd v Czech Republic*, ICSID Case No UNCT/15/1, Procedural Order No 2—Decision on Bifurcation (5 October 2015) [58].

[40] In this respect, the applicable threshold is higher than mere non-frivolousness of the objection that is sought to be bifurcated. According to *Glencore Finance (Bermuda) Limited v Bolivia*, PCA Case No 2016-39, Procedural Order No 2: Decision on Bifurcation (31 January 2018) [42]: 'although the Tribunal recognizes that the objection is not frivolous, and the contextual arguments posed by the Respondent in this regard are capable of being argued and worth exploring in depth, it is not convinced that this objection is sufficiently serious and substantial as to justify bifurcation'; *Eco Oro Minerals Corp v Colombia*, ICSID Case No ARB/16/41, Procedural Order No 2 (28 June 2018) [51]: 'The Tribunal further determines that, with respect to the first limb of the three-part test, for an objection to be held to be "serious and substantial" a higher threshold must be applied than merely requiring that the objection is not frivolous or vexatious'; *Red Eagle Exploration Limited v Colombia*, ICSID Case No ARB/18/12, Decision on Bifurcation (3 August 2020) [42].

[41] *Glamis Gold Ltd v United States of America* (n 31) [12(c)]; *Josias Van Zyl and others v Lesotho*, PCA Case No 2016-21, Procedural Order No 1 (3 November 2016) [49]; *Emmis International Holding, BV, Emmis Radio Operating, BV, MEM Magyar Electronic Media Kereskedelmi és Szolgáltató Kft v Hungary*, ICSID Case No ARB/12/2, Decision on Respondent's Application for Bifurcation (13 June 2013) [49].

[42] See *Glamis Gold Ltd v United States of America* (n 31) [12(c)]; *Tulip Real Estate Investment and Development Netherlands BV v Turkey* (n 37) [36]–[38]; *Philip Morris Asia Limited v Australia*, UNCITRAL, PCA Case No 2012-12, Procedural Order No 8 (14 April 2014) [108]; *Marco Gavazzi and Stefano Gavazzi v Romania*, ICSID

required of a preliminary proceedings, even if the objecting party is successful, will be justified in terms of the reduction in costs at the subsequent phase of proceedings'.[43]

However, concerning the various standards that are applicable for the purposes of adopting a decision on bifurcated issues, as one tribunal noted, '[t]here is no consensus on whether they are to be considered holistically or sequentially (much less in what sequence); whether any particular factor is mandatory; or whether certain factors should be weighted more heavily than others for purposes of reaching an eventual result'.[44] Given the absence of standards in the UNCITRAL Rules and the non-exhaustiveness of the test(s) provided in the ICSID Arbitration Rules, no one-size-fits-all analytical structure should be imposed on a tribunal's reasoning process, leaving each tribunal sufficiently free to consider all factors that it considers relevant 'in the particular circumstances of its case'.[45]

The potential to narrow issues in dispute (and thereby rationalize the order of phases of a pending case) is an important element in deciding whether to prioritize a decision on a specific issue before the natural progression of others. However, deciding such an issue may be often possible only after the parties have submitted their full initial statement of claim or defence.[46]

III. Decisions and Awards on Jurisdiction

As mentioned above, the arbitral tribunal may rule on jurisdictional objections either as a preliminary question (ie as a bifurcated issue) or in the award on the merits.[47] In case of bifurcation of proceedings, the award that determines jurisdictional issues (eg the question of the state's lack of consent to arbitrate)[48] is denominated as a 'decision

Case No ARB/12/25, Procedural Order No 2 (13 September 2013) [12]; *MetLife, Inc, MetLife Servicios SA and MetLife Seguros de Retiro SA v Argentina*, ICSID Case No ARB/17/17, Procedural Order No 2 (21 December 2018) [23]; *Hela Schwarz GmbH v China*, ICSID Case No ARB/17/19, Procedural Order No 3 (17 December 2018) [77]–[78]; *Canepa Green Energy Opportunities I, Sárl and Canepa Green Energy Opportunities II, Sárl v Spain*, ICSID Case No ARB/19/4, Procedural Order No 3—Decision on Bifurcation (28 August 2020) [87]:

> the Tribunal majority regards the steps needed to address the objection as most efficiently undertaken in the context of a full briefing by the Parties on the merits, rather than an analysis conducted only in a jurisdictional proceeding. As such, the Tribunal majority does not see this objection to the Tribunal's jurisdiction as most efficiently addressed in a bifurcated proceeding.

43 *Glamis Gold Ltd v United States of America* (n 31) [12(c)]; *Apotex Holdings Inc, Apotex Inc v United States*, ICSID Case No ARB(AF)/12/1, Procedural Order Deciding Bifurcation and Non-Bifurcation (25 January 2013) [10] (considering the exercise one of 'weighing for both sides the benefits of procedural fairness and efficiency against the risks of delay, wasted expense and prejudice').

44 *Gran Colombia Gold Corp v Colombia*, ICSID Case No ARB/18/23, Procedural Order No 3—Decision on the Respondent's Request for Bifurcation (17 January 2020) [26].

45 ibid. See also *Apotex Holdings Inc, Apotex Inc v United States* (n 43) [10] (acknowledging that '[t]here is no bright dividing-line' in the application of bifurcation factors, and the tribunal must decide the application 'in the particular circumstances of this case. It serves no purpose for this Tribunal to follow blindly what other tribunals have or have not done in other circumstances, particularly with hindsight').

46 Jansen Calamita and Elsa Sardihna, 'The Bifurcation of Jurisdictional and Admissibility Objections in Investor-State Arbitration' (2017) 16(1) Law and Practice of International Courts and Tribunals 44, 50–51.

47 See section II of this chapter.

48 Andrea M Steingruber, *Consent in International Arbitration* (OUP 2012) 253ff.

on jurisdiction' (or 'decision') in the ICSID system in case of affirmation of the jurisdiction, 'separate award' pursuant to the UNCITRAL Arbitration Rules, the PCA Arbitration Rules and the SCC Arbitration Rules, 'interim award' or 'partial award' (on jurisdiction) in ICC arbitration. The jurisdictional award does not merely consist in a procedural decision, like a procedural order (PO). It is an arbitral decision that is capable of disposing of the entire proceedings in case of a denial of jurisdiction or crystallizing irrevocably the competence of the tribunal to adjudicate the dispute, irrespective of the final outcome of the case on the merits. The decision or award on jurisdiction may additionally contain the determination of preliminary questions that are not jurisdictional in nature but rather pertain to the admissibility of the claim, for example the interpretation and application of a denial of benefits clause.[49] Notably, the arbitral tribunal is the judge of its own competence based on the widely accepted principle of *Kompetenz-Kompetenz*.[50] The formal and substantive requirements established by the international conventions and arbitration rules for the rendering of an 'award',[51] analysed below,[52] are also applicable to jurisdictional awards. For instance, an award dealing with jurisdiction only and terminating the proceedings will also decide on the costs of the arbitration.

In both ICSID and non-ICSID arbitrations, the decision on jurisdiction is based on an analysis of the parties' submissions relating to the competence of the tribunal. Usually, the respondent state objects to the jurisdiction, while the claimant investor argues that the tribunal is vested of jurisdiction in relation to its claims. However, in case of a state's counterclaim, the scenario is reversed: the respondent submits that its counterclaim falls within the tribunal's treaty-based jurisdiction, while the claimant alleges that the parties' consent has not been conferred to such an extent and/or a direct connectedness with the main claim is not established.

In order for an arbitral tribunal to affirm its jurisdiction, it must consider whether it has jurisdiction *ratione personae*, *ratione materiae*, *ratione temporis*, and/or *ratione voluntatis* depending on which of them is being contested. These jurisdictional conditions are usually codified by international investment agreements (IIAs) through express provisions. This means that a tribunal must primarily conclude that the jurisdictional requirements set forth in the applicable treaty are satisfied in the case at issue. With regard to ICSID arbitration, Article 25 of the Washington Convention governs the jurisdiction of the Centre by establishing its 'outer limits'.[53] This entails that an

[49] Carlo de Stefano, 'Denial of Benefits Clauses in International Investment Agreements: Burden of Proof and Notice to Claimant' (2016) 30(1) Diritto del Commercio Internazionale 143.

[50] *Ex multis*, Horacio A Grigera Naón, '"Misères et splendeurs" of the Kompetenz-Kompetenz Principle in International Arbitration (A Transatlantic Comparison)' in *Mélanges en l'honneur du Professeur Pierre Mayer. Liber amicorum* (LGDJ 2015) 273.

[51] eg ICSID Convention art 48.

[52] See section VI of this chapter.

[53] Aaron Broches, 'The Convention on the Settlement of Investment Disputes between States and Nationals of Other States' (1972-II) 137 Recueil des Cours 361. The ICSID Convention posits a notion of 'outer limits' that represents an expression of a principle that is applicable in general in international investment arbitration, even if under the aegis of different institutions and where other arbitration rules are at issue. With regard to the application of the doctrine of jurisdictional 'outer limits' in ISDS also outside ICSID arbitration in relation to the objective notion of 'investment', see *Romak SA (Switzerland) v Uzbekistan*, UNCITRAL, PCA Case No AA280, Award (26 November 2009) [207]; *Alps Finance and Trade AG (AFT) v Slovakia*, UNCITRAL, Award (5 March 2011) [243];

ICSID tribunal must establish that it is vested with jurisdiction both with respect to the objective notion encapsulated in Article 25 of the Convention *and* pursuant to the subjective definitions codified in the applicable treaty (so-called double-barrelled test).[54]

Concerning jurisdiction *ratione personae*, the investor must demonstrate that it is a national of a state party to the applicable treaty (and, in ICSID arbitration, of a contracting state to the ICSID Convention) other than the respondent state. Notably, in the ICSID system, there is a categoric prohibition of claims by dual nationals under Article 25(2)(a) of the Washington Convention, irrespective of the application of the rule of effectiveness and predominancy of the nationality that is invoked by the claimant, which remains relevant in non-ICSID investment arbitration.[55] With regard to jurisdiction *ratione materiae*, the claimant's investment must fulfil the definition of 'investment' contained in the applicable treaty, for example in the relevant BIT (such a definition is frequently 'asset-based' or, less frequently, 'enterprise-based'). In addition, the investor's economic activity must fulfil the objective notion of 'investment' encapsulated in Article 25 of the ICSID Convention, as interpreted and developed by the arbitral case law (the '*Salini* test' or criteria). In particular, such an objective notion demands a certain duration of performance of the investment, the assumption of a certain risk, the contribution of economic resources (money, assets, and/or personnel), and a positive impact to the development of the host state.[56] While the first three components (duration, risk, and contribution of economic resources) are well established in the case law of international tribunals, the fourth, that is the contribution to the economic development of the host state, is controversial and is not always considered as an independent test in arbitral practice.[57] Regarding jurisdiction

Christian Doutremepuich and Antoine Doutremepuich v Mauritius, PCA Case No 2018-37, Award on Jurisdiction (23 August 2019) [118]. Contra, *Mytilineos Holdings SA v The State Union of Serbia and Montenegro, and Serbia*, UNCITRAL, Partial Award on Jurisdiction (8 September 2006) [117]–[118] (holding that the only requirements that have to be fulfilled in order to confer *ratione materiae* jurisdiction on a non-ICSID tribunal are those under the BIT).

[54] eg *Malaysian Historical Salvors Sdn, Bhd v Malaysia*, ICSID Case No ARB/05/10, Award on Jurisdiction (28 May 2007) [55]: 'Under the double barrelled test, a finding that the Contract satisfied the definition of "investment" under the BIT would not be sufficient for this Tribunal to assume jurisdiction, if the Contract failed to satisfy the criterion of an "investment" within the meaning of Article 25'.

[55] The doctrine of dual nationals' active or dominant nationality corresponds to customary international law. See Iran–United States Claims Tribunal, Full Tribunal, *Case No A/18*, Decision on the Question of Jurisdiction over Claims of Persons with Dual Nationality (6 April 1984), 5 IUSCTR 251, 263, 265 (1984-I); Iran–United States Claims Tribunal, Chamber Two, *Nasser Esphahanian v Bank Tejarat*, Award No 31-157-2 (29 March 1983), 2 IUSCTR 157, 160–61, 168 (1983-I); Iran–United States Claims Tribunal, Chamber One, *Rana Nikpour v Iran and Foundation for the Oppressed*, Interlocutory Award No ITL 81-336-1 (18 February 1993), 29 IUSCTR 67, 75 (1993). For the earlier practice of mixed arbitral tribunals, see *Canevaro Case (Italy v Peru)*, Award (1912) 11 RIAA 397, in George Grafton Wilson (ed), *The Hague Arbitration Cases* (Ginn 1915) 238; *Mergé Case (United States of America v Italy)*, Decision No 55 (1955) 14 RIAA 236, 247.

[56] *Salini Costruttori SpA and Italstrade SpA v Morocco*, ICSID Case No ARB/00/4, Decision on Jurisdiction (23 July 2001) [52]. See Emmanuel Gaillard and Yas Banifatemi, 'The Long March Towards a Jurisprudence Constante on the Notion of Investment' in Meg Kinnear and others (eds), *Building International Investment Law: The First 50 Years of ICSID* (Kluwer Law International 2015) 97.

[57] *LESI SpA and ASTALDI SpA v Algeria*, ICSID Case No ARB/05/3, Decision (12 July 2006) [72(iv)]; *Victor Pey Casado and President Allende Foundation v Chile*, ICSID Case No ARB/98/2, Award (8 May 2008) [232]; *Alpha Projektholding GMBH v Ukraine*, ICSID Case No ARB/07/16, Award (8 November 2010) [312]. See Farouk Yala, 'La notion d'investissement dans la jurisprudence du CIRDI : Actualité d'un critère de compétence controversé (Les affaires Salini, SGS et Mihaly)' in Charles Leben (ed), *Le contentieux arbitral transnational relatif à l'investissement. Nouveaux développements* (LGDJ-Anthemis 2004) 281–306.

ratione temporis, a dispute concerning an eligible investor or investment must, as a rule, have arisen after the date of entry into force of the IIA.[58] Pre-existing investments are usually also protected by IIAs.[59] Finally, an international investment tribunal must ascertain its jurisdiction *ratione voluntatis*, which means it has to establish that the respondent state effectively consented to arbitrate the foreign investment dispute or claims brought by a foreign investor. An interesting arbitral practice concerning this jurisdictional condition pertains to the possibility for investors to import via the most-favoured-nation (MFN) clause of the applicable treaty the state's consent to ICSID arbitration contained in the comparator treaty. This question concerning jurisdiction *ratione voluntatis* has been answered preponderantly in the negative by international tribunals.[60]

In general, the burden of proof relating to facts, on which the establishment of jurisdictional requirements depends, must be fully discharged by the party alleging those facts in an international investment arbitration (ie the claimant with regard to the various conditions establishing the tribunal's jurisdiction and, correspondingly, the respondent with respect to a possible counterclaim).[61] This entails that the *Oil Platform* test is not applicable in this respect. The test, as formulated by Judge Higgins in her Separate Opinion with regard to the preliminary objection in the *Oil Platform* case, posits that the decision whether an international court is vested of jurisdiction should be definitive in the jurisdictional phase and should be based also on the *pro tempore* finding that the facts, as alleged by the claimant, if established, could result in a breach of the applicable international obligations.[62] Evidently, the *pro tem* or prima facie evidentiary standard applies to facts pertaining to the merits of a given dispute, which however are relevant for the purposes of preliminary ascertainment of the tribunal's jurisdiction, including in international investment arbitration. Consequently, a fact embodying a condition to the tribunal's jurisdiction must be fully proved at a preliminary stage (eg in the procedural phase preceding the issuance of a decision or award on a bifurcated jurisdictional issue) by the party that alleges it. The same standard of proof applies to facts basing an objection to the admissibility of the claimant's claim, for example the operation of a denial of benefits provision, a burden which should be discharged by the respondent state.[63] The distinction between facts establishing a breach of the applicable treaty as an objective element of international responsibility and facts

[58] Zachary Douglas, *The International Law of Investment Claims* (CUP 2009) 333: 'The most common stipulation is that the jurisdiction of the investment treaty tribunal is limited to investment disputes arising after the treaty has entered into force'. See, *ex multis*, *Valeria Italia Srl in liquidation v Albania*, PCA Case No 2018-49, Award on Jurisdiction (17 August 2021) [181]–[204].

[59] Eric de Brabandere and Saskia Lemeire, 'The Jurisdiction *Ratione Temporis* of International Investment Tribunals—Some Observations on the Decision of the Tribunal in *Ping An v Belgium*' [2016] Belgian Review of Arbitration 139–49.

[60] eg *Itisaluna Iraq LLC, Munir Sukhtian International Investment LLC, VTEL Holdings Ltd, VTEL Middle East and Africa Limited v Iraq*, ICSID Case No ARB/17/10, Award (3 April 2020).

[61] See Christoph Schreuer, 'Burden and Standard of Proof on Jurisdiction' in Fach Gómez and Titi (n 5).

[62] *Oil Platform (Iran v United States of America)*, Preliminary Objection, Judgment, Separate Opinion of Judge Higgins, [1996] ICJ Rep 803 [31]–[32], [34]. Investment tribunals have comprehensively applied the evidentiary standard proposed by Judge Higgins. See, inter alia, *Gustav FW Hamester GmbH & Co KG v Ghana*, ICSID Case No ARB/07/24, Award (18 June 2010) [143].

[63] Douglas (n 58) 469.

representing requirements for the tribunal's jurisdiction (or the admissibility of the claim) is of threshold importance and reasonably supports a different standard of the burden of proof at the initial stage of the arbitration.[64]

IV. The Non-Finality of ICSID Decisions on Jurisdiction: Issues of Reconsideration

A definitive decision affirming the competence of the tribunal in ICSID arbitration without deciding the merits nor concluding the case does not constitute *res judicata* since it is not a final award that decides all issues in dispute between the parties. As a consequence, it is not governed by Articles 48–54 of the Washington Convention, in particular by Article 53, which provides for the finality of ICSID awards.[65] Not being an award, such a decision may not be challenged immediately, but only at a later procedural stage in conjunction with an application for annulment of the final award pursuant to Article 52 of the ICSID Convention, which lists five exhaustive and restrictive grounds for annulment.[66] The conclusions on jurisdiction of an ICSID tribunal issued through a preliminary decision are to be later incorporated, usually as an annex, in the final award rendered upon the closure of the arbitral proceedings entailing the entire discharge of the arbitrator's adjudicative function.[67]

This distinction between decisions on jurisdiction and awards represents a specificity of investment arbitrations under the ICSID Convention. Since such decisions are not final and are not subject to the regime of awards, a discussion has developed as to whether such decisions may be reconsidered with a view to amending or revising them during the further proceedings, reopening the issue of jurisdiction, and under which conditions.[68] On the one hand, decisions on jurisdiction are formally like any other procedural decisions that may be and are often modified or updated according to the demands entailed by the development of the case. Indeed, an ICSID decision on jurisdiction may be subsumed within the variety of 'decisions' of the tribunal that may be issued throughout the arbitral proceeding pursuant to Rule 27 of the ICSID Arbitration Rules, which does not establish a distinction between decisions of a procedural nature

[64] *Phoenix Action, Ltd v Czech Republic*, ICSID Case No ARB/06/5, Award (15 April 2009) [64].

[65] See ICSID Convention art 48(3), which establishes that '[t]he award shall deal with every question submitted to the Tribunal, and shall state the reasons upon which it is based'. The non-finality is widely affirmed in ICSID case law, although in rare instances tribunals have held decisions on jurisdiction to be *res judicata* as a basis to reject requests of reconsideration, see to this effect *ConocoPhillips Petrozuata BV, ConocoPhillips Hamaca BV and ConocoPhillips Gulf of Paria BV v Venezuela*, ICSID Case No ARB/07/30, Decision on Respondent's Request for Reconsideration, with an extensive Dissenting Opinion of Georges Abi-Saab (10 March 2014) [38]–[39]. This holding was expressly rejected by the tribunal *Standard Chartered Bank (Hong Kong) Limited v Tanzania Electric Supply Company Limited*, ICSID Case No ARB/10/20, Award (12 September 2016) [322], whose position has been generally followed on the issue by subsequent ICSID tribunals, see below n 81.

[66] ICSID Convention art 52(1).

[67] ibid art 48(3). See *ConocoPhillips v Venezuela*, Dissenting Opinion of Georges Abi-Saab (n 65) [38]–[39] (observing that 'incorporation of such interlocutory decisions in the final Award is not only a matter of practice… It is a matter of legal necessity and obligation, given the specificity of the procedural system of ICSID').

[68] For a general discussion of this issue, see Catharine Titi, '*Res Iudicata* and Interlocutory Decisions under the ICSID Convention: Antinomies over the Power of Tribunals to Review' (2018) 33(2) ICSID Review 358.

and those of substance.[69] On the other hand, decisions on jurisdiction resolve a fundamental issue relating to the competence of the tribunal to carry on the procedure and must enjoy a high level of stability since they are the basis of the subsequent proceedings in the merits.

As to the standard of their reconsideration, reference has been made by analogy, or a fortiori, to Article 51(1) of the ICSID Convention:

> Either party may request revision of the award by an application in writing addressed to the Secretary-General on the ground of discovery of some fact of such a nature as decisively to affect the award, provided that when the award was rendered that fact was unknown to the Tribunal and to the applicant and that the applicant's ignorance of that fact was not due to negligence.

In support of the power of a tribunal to examine a request of reconsideration of a previous decision affirming the tribunal's jurisdiction it has been held that '[t]ribunals make decisions on procedural matters, on provisional measures, all of which are subject to being reviewed, reconsidered and revised, notwithstanding the absence of anything in the Convention authorizing this. Thus, the mere fact that something is characterized as a decision of a tribunal cannot automatically make it *res judicata*.'[70] The same tribunal has further held that 'the fact that a decision is binding on the parties does not mean the same thing as saying that it is *res judicata*' and stated that:

> [d]ecisions of tribunals are of course binding within the scope of the proceedings, but this does not make them res judicata. That is so with procedural orders and provisional measures as pointed out earlier. An essential feature of *res judicata* is that the judgment in question produces effects on the parties outside the proceedings in which it is granted. But decisions of tribunals only have effect within the proceedings until they have been incorporated into the final award.[71]

Even if not expressly mentioned by the ICSID Convention and ICSID Arbitration Rules, an ICSID decision on jurisdiction may be thus subject to reconsideration based on the inherent powers of arbitral tribunals in order to address relevant changes in circumstances such as supervening and decisively important facts. Support for this

[69] ICSID Arbitration Rules r 27:

(1) The Tribunal shall make the orders and decisions required for the conduct of the proceeding.
(2) Orders and decisions may be made by any appropriate means of communication, shall indicate the reasons upon which they are made, and may be signed by the President on behalf of the Tribunal.
(3) The Tribunal shall consult with the parties prior to making an order or decision it is authorized by these Rules to make on its own initiative.

[70] *Standard Chartered Bank (Hong Kong) Limited v Tanzania Electric Supply Company Limited* (n 65) [311].

[71] ibid [312]–[313], followed by *Burlington Resources Inc v Ecuador*, ICSID Case No ARB/08/05, Decision on Reconsideration and Award (7 February 2017) [108] and the cases concerning the ECT mentioned in n 76. See also *Waste Management, Inc v Mexico*, ARB(AF)/00/3, Award (30 April 2004) [17]; *Compañiá de Aguas del Aconquija SA and Vivendi Universal SA v Argentina*, ICSID Case No ARB/97/3 (formerly *Compañía de Aguas del Aconquija, SA and Compagnie Générale des Eaux v Argentina*), Decision on Jurisdiction (14 November 2005) [78].

conclusion can also be found in Article 41(1) of the ICSID Convention which grants general power to ICSID tribunals to determine their own competence.[72] Moreover, Article 44 of the ICSID Convention expressly provides that '[i]f any question of procedure arises which is not covered by this Section or the Arbitration Rules or any rules agreed by the parties, the Tribunal shall decide the question'.[73]

The subsequent issue is the identification of the conditions that are required to grant reconsideration. Following the criteria applied in the *Standard Chartered Bank* case, tribunals have considered that in exercising their power to reconsider a decision, they 'should be guided by, although not bound by, the limitations on reopening that apply to awards'.[74] By adhering to this guideline, tribunals refrain from reopening a decision for any reason invoked by a party at their discretion. They follow instead certain streamlined conditions mentioned in the ICSID Convention in respect of awards, thus restricting the scope of review to those cases where there are sufficiently compelling reasons to reconsider what has already been decided. In particular, the tribunals tend to apply by analogy, or as a guideline, the conditions of Article 51 of the ICSID Convention, which directly regulates the revision of final awards, to the reconsideration of jurisdictional (or other) decisions. Thus, the circumstances listed in Article 51 of the Washington Convention—namely, first, a 'fact of such a nature that as decisively to affect' the decision; second, that was 'unknown to the Tribunal and to the applicant'; and, third, 'the applicant's ignorance of the fact was not due to negligence'—are considered as the basic orienting criteria for tribunals to resolve whether to accord a request for reconsideration.[75]

Case law on reconsideration of decisions on jurisdiction has 'exploded' in respect of disputes concerning the compatibility with the ECT of measures adopted by a number of EU member states (especially Spain) that reduced or withdrew incentives initially granted to undertakings investing in the establishment of renewable energy plants. ICSID tribunals have uniformly affirmed their jurisdiction against respondents' objections that 'intra-EU' disputes (ie disputes between investors of a member state against another member state) are not arbitrable in light of EU law.[76] Subsequently, the Court

[72] ICSID Convention art 41. It has been observed that the power of an ICSID tribunal to reconsider an affirmative decision on jurisdiction descends from the ICSID Arbitration Rules r 41(2). See Ursula Kriebaum, 'Article 41' in Stephan Schill and others (eds), *Schreuer's Commentary on the ICSID Convention* (3rd edn, CUP 2022) 762.

[73] ICSID Convention art 44.

[74] *Standard Chartered Bank (Hong Kong) Limited v Tanzania Electric Supply Company Limited* (n 65) [322].

[75] See *Portigon AG v Spain*, ICSID Case No ARB/17/15, Decision on Request for Reconsideration (20 October 2022) [62]ff.

[76] See *Greentech Energy Systems A/S and others v Italy*, SCC Case No 2015/095, Final Award (23 December 2018) [335]–[355]; *Foresight Luxembourg Solar 1 SÁRL and others v Spain*, SCC Case No 2015/150, Final Award (14 November 2018) [221]; *UP (formerly Le Chèque Déjeuner) and CD Holding Internationale v Hungary*, ICSID Case No ARB/13/35, Award (9 October 2018) [252]–[267]; *Vattenfall AB and others v Germany*, ICSID Case No ARB/12/12, Decision on the *Achmea* Issue, 31 August 2018 [232]; *Infrastructure Services Luxembourg Sàrl and Energia Termosolar BV (formerly Antin Infrastructure Services Luxembourg Sàrl and Antin Energia Termosolar BV) v Spain*, ICSID Case No ARB/13/31, Award (15 June 2018) [204]–[230]; *Masdar Solar & Wind Cooperatief UA v Spain*, ICSID Case No ARB/14/1, Award (16 May 2018) [296]–[342], [431]–[466]; *Marfin Investment Group v Cyprus*, ICSID Case No ARB/13/27, Award (26 July 2018) [595]; *WNC Factoring Limited v Czech Republic*, PCA Case No 2014-34, Award (22 February 2017) [301]; *9REN Holding Sarl v Spain*, ICSID Case No ARB/15/

of Justice of the EU (CJEU), in its *Achmea* decision of 6 March 2018,[77] stated that investment arbitration on the basis of 'intra-EU' BITs was indeed incompatible with EU law, and with the later *Komstroy* decision of 2 September 2021 extended this holding to 'intra-EU' arbitration under the ECT. As a consequence, according to the CJEU, the consent of respondent member states to ICSID arbitration was invalid due to its incompatibility with EU law.[78] Thereafter, respondents EU member states (notably Spain and Italy) have petitioned (sometimes more than once) ICSID tribunals hearing those cases to reconsider the matter of jurisdiction. Most tribunals have declared the petition admissible by reference to Article 51 ICSID Convention, considering that these CJEU judgments could be considered as supervenient new facts of such a nature that might decisively affect their determination.[79]

In so deciding, tribunals have considered that the *Komstroy* judgment, although not a fact in the strict sense, can be considered an occurrence that may potentially have a significant impact on the outcome of a decision.[80] However, all ICSID tribunals that have declared reconsideration of their previous decision admissible in view of the subsequent *Komstroy* decision have rejected on its substance the request for reconsideration, confirming their previous decision on the existence of their jurisdiction, holding that the CJEU decision(s) were not relevant and, moreover, not decisive from the viewpoint of the ICSID system.[81]

15, Award (31 May 2019) [168]–[173]; *Cube Infrastructure Fund SICAV and others v Spain*, ICSID Case No ARB/15/20, Decision on Jurisdiction, Liability and Partial Decision on Quantum (19 February 2019) [118]–[160]; *Landesbank Baden-Württemberg and others v Spain*, ICSID Case No ARB/15/45, Decision on the Intra-EU Jurisdictional Objection (25 February 2019) [88]–[194]; *NextEra Energy Global Holdings BV and NextEra Energy Spain Holdings BV v Spain*, ICSID Case No ARB/14/11, Decision on Jurisdiction, Liability and Quantum Principles (12 March 2019) [332]–[357]; *Eskosol SpA in liquidazione v Italy*, ICSID Case No ARB/15/50, Decision on Termination Request and Intra-EU Objection (7 May 2019) [76]–[235]; *SolEs Badajoz GmbH v Spain*, ICSID Case No ARB/15/38, Award (31 July 2019) [223]–[237]; *InfraRed Environmental Infrastructure GP Limited and others v Spain*, ICSID Case No ARB/14/12, Award (2 August 2019) [256]–[274]; *OperaFund Eco-Invest SICAV PLC and Schwab Holding AG v Spain*, ICSID Case No ARB/15/36, Award (6 September 2019), unpublished; *Silver Ridge Power BV v Italy*, ICSID Case No ARB/15/37, Award (26 February 2021) [191]–[238].

77 Case C-284/16 *Slowakische Republik (Slovak Republic) v Achmea BV*, Judgment of the Court (Grand Chamber), ECLI:EU:C:2018:158 (6 March 2018).

78 Case C-741/19 *République de Moldavie v Komstroy LLC*, Judgment of the Court (Grand Chamber), ECLI:EU:C:2021:655 (2 September 2021).

79 See the cases listed in n 81.

80 See eg *Portigon AG v Spain* (n 75) [69].

81 See *Landesbank Baden-Württemberg and others v Spain*, ICSID Case No ARB/15/45, Decision on the Respondent's Application for Reconsideration of the 'Intra-EU' Jurisdictional Decisions (22 February 2023) [34]–[51]; *Rockhopper Italia SpA, Rockhopper Mediterranean Ltd, and Rockhopper Exploration Plc v Italy*, ICSID Case No ARB/17/14, Decision on Italy's Request for Reconsideration of 29 September 2021 (20 December 2021) [20]–[51]; *Cavalum SGPS, SA v Spain*, ICSID Case No ARB/15/34, Reconsideration Decision (10 January 2022) [36]–[98]; *Infracapital F1 Sàrl and Infracapital Solar BV v Spain*, ICSID Case No ARB/16/18, Decision on Respondent Request for Reconsideration regarding the Intra-EU Objection and the Merits (1 February 2022) [77]–[116] and Second Decision on Reconsideration (19 August 2022) [28]–[48]; *Sevilla Beheer BV and others v Spain*, ICSID Case No ARB/16/27, Decision on Respondent's Second Request for Reconsideration (30 January 2023) [19]–[33]; *Portigon AG v Spain* (n 75). For a criticism of this case law, see Giorgio Sacerdoti, 'After *Komstroy*. Have the EU Member States Withdrawn by the Lisbon Treaty, as an Inter-Se Agreement under Article 41 VCLT, their Consent to ICSID Jurisdiction on ECT Intra-EU Investment Disputes?' in Massimo Benedettelli and others (eds), *Arbitration as Balanced Administration of Justice. Essays in Honour of Piero Bernardini* (Brill 2024) 371.

V. The Finality of Awards on Jurisdiction in Non-ICSID Arbitrations

The situation is quite different under non-ICSID regimes. In non-ICSID investment arbitrations, a tribunal's partial or interim award on jurisdiction (in commercial and investment arbitration alike) constitutes *res judicata* pursuant to the applicable *lex (loci) arbitri*, which is usually a national law. Looking first at domestic regulation on the matter, Article 186(3) of the Swiss Federal Private International Law Act (PILA) of 18 December 1987, for instance, provides that a decision of the arbitral tribunal on its jurisdiction takes the form of an 'interlocutory decision' (*décision incidente*) which is issued as an award.[82] Such awards on jurisdiction 'have *res judicata* effect, even though they do not put an end to the arbitration.'[83] Such an award can and must be challenged immediately and separately from the (future) final award, leading possibly to the suspension of the proceedings on the merits until the resolution of the matter by the competent state court.

A perusal of international arbitration rules confirms that deciding jurisdictional issues by (interim) awards that are as such final and subject to immediate challenge before national courts is the dominant choice. Thus, the UNCITRAL Arbitration Rules provide in Article 34 that '[t]he arbitral tribunal may make separate awards on different issues at different times'[84] and '*[a]ll* awards shall be made in writing and shall be final and binding on the parties.'[85] The PCA Arbitration Rules follow this approach verbatim in Article 34.[86] Under the SCC Arbitration Rules, 'separate awards' pursuant to Article 44 encompass jurisdictional awards and are equated to SCC awards in general in terms of finality.[87] The same conclusion may be stated with regard to the Hong Kong International Arbitration Centre (HKIAC) Administered Arbitration Rules, which refer to 'separate awards regarding different issues at different times and in respect of all parties involved in the arbitration in the form of interim, interlocutory, partial or final awards', including awards on jurisdiction.[88] Similarly, the Investment Arbitration Rules of the Singapore International Arbitration Centre (SIAC Investment Rules) establish that 'the Tribunal may make separate awards on different issues at different times'[89] and *any* of such awards 'shall be final and binding on the parties from the date it is made.'[90]

It appears therefore that international investment awards on jurisdiction rendered outside the ICSID system are characterized by the status of 'interim finality'. Accordingly, an interim award ruling on jurisdictional issues that has not been successfully challenged in the country of the seat of the arbitration is inter alia capable

[82] PILA art 186(3) (French official text): 'En général, le tribunal arbitral statue sur sa compétence par une décision incidente'.
[83] Gabrielle Kaufmann-Kohler and Antonio Rigozzi, *International Arbitration: Law and Practice in Switzerland* (OUP 2015) [7.105].
[84] UNCITRAL Arbitration Rules art 34(1).
[85] ibid art 34(2) (emphasis added).
[86] PCA Arbitration Rules art 34(1)–(2).
[87] SCC Arbitration Rules art 46.
[88] HKIAC Administered Arbitration Rules arts 35(1)–(2).
[89] SIAC Investment Rules r 30.5.
[90] ibid r 30.11.

of barring parallel proceedings before national courts in other jurisdictions, if recognized pursuant to the New York Convention. As acknowledged by the 'Final Report on Interim and Partial Awards' of the ICC Commission on International Arbitration of 1990, 'decisions on jurisdiction issues are frequently reviewable by the national courts at the place of arbitration' and, accordingly, 'parties may wish to have a decision on jurisdiction in the form of an interim award so that the appellate procedure will not have to wait until the end of the arbitration'.[91] In any case, especially with respect to Model Law countries, the denomination of the decision as an 'award' or the lack thereof would not be decisive for the purposes of judicial review.[92]

Irrespective of being subject to a nullity challenge, awards on jurisdiction may be subject to reconsideration by the same arbitral tribunal that has issued them in case this is provided in the applicable arbitration rules or the *lex arbitri*. For instance, the ICC Secretariat's Note on Correction and Interpretation of Arbitral Awards actually clarifies that '[w]here the relevant national law or court practice provide specific circumstances in which an arbitral tribunal may render certain decisions other than corrections or interpretation regarding an award which had been approved and notified, such situations shall be treated in the spirit of this Note'.[93] This entails that the applicable *lex arbitri* may provide legitimate and sufficient grounds for a motion for reconsideration or revision with respect to a tribunal's partial award on jurisdiction. It is well understood that only extraordinary new or newly discovered facts (such as, for instance, fraud) justify making an exception to the *res judicata* effect of 'awards', which can be corroborated also by general principles of law, such as arbitral due process, fairness and equity, and common sense in connection with a supervening change of circumstances.[94] At the same time, there is a marked tendency in the literature to suggest that, even in the absence of express authority in either municipal arbitration laws or institutional rules, arbitral tribunals enjoy inherent powers to revise or revoke an award in exceptional circumstances.[95]

VI. The (Final) Award on the Merits

The award that puts an end to the arbitral proceedings is the final award through which an investment arbitration tribunal ultimately discharges its adjudicative function. This

[91] ICC Commission on International Arbitration, 'Final Report on Interim and Partial Awards' para 17, (1990) 1 (2) ICC International Court of Arbitration Bulletin 1, 26.

[92] ibid. The denomination of the decision as 'award' is immaterial in so far as the requirements concerning the reasoning pursuant to the UNCITRAL Model Law art 31(2) are satisfied.

[93] ICC Secretariat, 'Note on Correction and Interpretation of Arbitral Awards' (31 March 2014) 3.

[94] Award in ICC Case No 6079, summarized in Dominique Hascher, 'L'autorité de la chose jugée des sentences arbitrales' in *Droit international privé: Travaux du Comité français de droit international privé (2000–2002)* (Pédone 2004) 17, 27:

> A défaut d'indication contraire dans l'acte de mission, précisent-ils, le tribunal arbitral, qui peut se prononcer par voie de sentence partielle, peut aussi décider de modifier sa décision précédente dès lors que le bon sens, l'équité ou la loyauté procédurale ('common sense, arbitral due process or fairness') l'imposent si les circonstances ont évolué.

[95] Gary B Born, *International Commercial Arbitration* (3rd edn, Kluwer Law International 2021) §24.07.

award normally contains the determinations of the arbitral tribunal on jurisdiction, merits (liability) and quantum of damages, or, in case of bifurcation of proceedings, on liability and quantum, or, in case of trifurcation of proceedings, on quantum only, as well as on costs. The classic content of the award on the merits in investment arbitration proceedings consists in the interpretation and application of the substantive provisions of the applicable law(s) to the dispute in question. The applicable law may be embodied not only in an IIA (a BIT, in the majority of cases) but also in a contract entered into directly by the state with the investor or in a national investment statute. Notably, the award on the merits contains the tribunal's ascertainment about the substantive responsibility of the respondent state with respect to its treatment of the claimant(s) (foreign) investor(s).[96] Thus, in the award on the merits the arbitral tribunal establishes whether or not the host state has breached primary norms of international law based on custom and/or treaty that granted protection to eligible foreign investors. The most common substantive standards of treatment provided under IIAs, especially BITs, are contingent (relative) and non-contingent (absolute).[97] Relative standards are the MFN treatment and the national treatment. Absolute standards are, for instance, the fair and equitable treatment (FET), the full protection and security (FPS), the prohibition of unlawful expropriation (direct and indirect), as well as the obligation of observance of contractual obligations entered into by the state, or also a state-owned enterprise (SOE), with the investor ('umbrella clause'). Consequently, the award on the merits may adjudicate both treaty and contract claims.[98]

The ICSID Convention regulates the 'award' in Article 48: the award shall be adopted by majority,[99] be in written form, and duly signed.[100] In addition, the award 'shall deal with every question submitted to the Tribunal',[101] namely it should be neither *infra petita* nor *ultra petita*.[102] To such an extent, it incorporates all the previous decisions (eg a decision on jurisdiction and/or, if applicable, a decision on liability, that have been rendered in the course of the proceedings). ICSID awards are thoroughly motivated,[103] which in part may explain their traditional length, and, in case of defects concerning the arbitrators' reasoning, may be even subject to an application for annulment for failure to state the reasons on which they are based.[104] ICSID awards are not public and 'the Centre shall not publish [them] without the consent of the parties'.[105]

[96] It has been already mentioned that the award on the merits may rule on the counterclaims submitted by the respondent state. See section I of this chapter.
[97] See, *ex multis*, the Issue Series on Investment Agreements published by UNCTAD <https://unctad.org/publications-search?f%5B0%5D=product%3A615>.
[98] James Crawford, 'Treaty and Contract in Investment Arbitration' (2008) 24(3) Arbitration International 351.
[99] ICSID Convention art 48(1).
[100] ibid art 48(2).
[101] ibid art 48(3).
[102] Attila M Tanzi, 'On the Adjudicative Discretion of Investment Arbitrators: Between *ne ultra petita*, *ne infra petita*, and *jura novit curia*' in Fach Gómez and Titi (n 5).
[103] ICSID Convention art 48(3).
[104] ibid art 52(1)(e).
[105] ibid art 48(5). In this respect, see ICSID Arbitration Rules (2022) r 62 (Publication of Awards and Decisions on Annulment): '(1) With consent of the parties, the Centre shall publish every Award, supplementary decision on an Award, rectification, interpretation, and revision of an Award, and decision on annulment', and '(4) Absent consent of the parties pursuant to paragraphs (1)–(3), the Centre shall publish excerpts of the documents referred

Moreover, pursuant to Article 48(4) of the Convention, any arbitrator may attach an individual opinion, either separate, concurring, or dissenting, to the award of the majority of the tribunal.[106] In addition, Article 48 of the Washington Convention is complemented by Rule 59 of the ICSID Arbitration Rules, which expressly provides additional requirements of a formal and substantive nature, such as data on the dispute, parties, arbitrators; a brief summary of the proceeding; a statement of the relevant facts as found by the tribunal; the submissions of the parties, including the relief sought; the decision of the tribunal on every question submitted to it, and the reasons on which the award is based; and a reasoned decision on costs.[107]

Institutional arbitration rules that are more frequently applied in non-ICSID investment arbitrations also establish mandatory requirements relating to the contents and the rendering of the award.[108] Such requirements are also integrated by the conditions prescribed under the *lex arbitri*, usually the municipal law of the country of seat of the arbitration.

Having regard to post-award remedies (other than annulment challenges), ICSID awards may be subject to interpretation[109] and revision.[110] As far as practicable, the relevant decision shall be rendered by the original ICSID tribunal. Non-ICSID awards may be subject to correction (for clerical, computational, or typographical errors, or any errors of similar nature contained in an award) and interpretation, which shall be decided, if possible, by the original tribunal.[111]

Also with respect to the effects of international investment awards and their enforceability, a fundamental distinction should be outlined between ICSID and non-ICSID arbitration. The effects of ICSID awards are governed by Articles 53–55 of the ICSID Convention, which lay down a unique system of quasi-automatic universal recognition justified by their nature as international awards.[112] The effects of non-ICSID

to in paragraph (1)'. It is followed by a detailed procedure spelled out in the subsequent paragraphs which protects confidentiality by allowing parties to obtain redaction (ie non-publication) of any party of the award (which include decisions on jurisdiction annexed to it) which they do not want to disclose. ICSID Arbitration Rules r 63 lays down similar provisions and procedures in respect of orders and decisions. When proposing updating the 2006 Arbitration Rules, the ICSID Secretariat had proposed to make publication of the awards a default rule, but most member states objected, expressing their preference that the existing regime be maintained (as it has been).

[106] ICSID Convention art 48(5).

[107] ICSID Arbitration Rules r 59(1).

[108] eg ICC Arbitration Rules art 32; UNCITRAL Arbitration Rules arts 33–34; PCA Arbitration Rules arts 33–34; SCC Arbitration Rules arts 41–42; SIAC Investment Rules r 30; LCIA Arbitration Rules art 26.

[109] ICSID Convention art 50.

[110] ibid art 51. See also Karsten Nowrot and Emily Sipiorski, 'Review Beyond Annulment: Correction, Additional Awards, Clarification, and Revision' in Fach Gómez and Titi (n 5).

[111] eg ICC Arbitration Rules art 36; LCIA Arbitration Rules r 27; UNCITRAL Arbitration Rules arts 37 and 38.

[112] See Aaron Broches, 'Awards Rendered Pursuant to the ICSID Convention: Binding Force, Finality, Recognition, Enforcement, Execution' (1987) 2(2) ICSID Review 287; Georges R Delaume, 'Enforcement of State Contract Awards: Jurisdictional Pitfalls and Remedies' (1993) 8 ICSID Review 29; Santiago Tawil, 'Binding Force and Enforcement of ICSID Awards: Untying Articles 53 and 54 of the ICSID Convention' in Albert Jan van den Berg (ed), *50 Years of the New York Convention* (Kluwer Law International 2009) 327; Stanimir A Alexandrov, 'Enforcement of ICSID Awards: Articles 53 and 54 of the ICSID Convention' in Cristina Binder and others (eds), *International Investment Law for the 21st Century: Essays in Honour of Christoph Schreuer* (OUP 2009) 322; Marc Bungenberg, Andrés E Alvarado-Garzón, and Bianca Böhme, 'Recognition and Enforcement of ICSID Convention Awards' in Fach Gómez and Titi (n 5). For the application of arts 53–55 of the ICSID Convention in Italy, see Carlo de Stefano, 'Il primo lodo ICSID riconosciuto in Italia' (2019) 29(3) Rivista dell'Arbitrato 539.

investment awards as between the parties are prescribed by the applicable institutional arbitration rules and national laws as *lex arbitri*. The international arbitration rules that are more frequently applied in transnational practice (and mostly do not distinguish between commercial and investment awards) provide that the award shall be final and binding on the parties and shall be carried out without delay.[113] The recognition and enforcement of the award is governed by the New York Convention, whose Article III establishes that '[e]ach Contracting State shall recognize arbitral awards as binding and enforce them in accordance with the rules of procedure of the territory where the award is relied upon',[114] and may be denied only upon application of the seven restrictive exceptions enumerated in Article V.[115] In general, it may be observed that states usually comply spontaneously with international awards, even notwithstanding sovereign immunity issues.[116]

VII. Concluding Remarks

This chapter has attempted to illustrate, succinctly but comprehensively, the basic features of awards/decisions on jurisdiction and awards on the merits in international investment disputes, highlighting the fundamental distinction between ICSID and non-ICSID proceedings. Recent cases, such as those mentioned on intra-EU disputes, reveal an unprecedented practice concerning the bifurcation of proceedings and clarify the scope and extent of the reconsideration of awards and decisions in ICSID arbitration. Consolidated practice has established that ICSID decisions on jurisdiction do not constitute *res judicata* and do not benefit from the effect of finality that is peculiarly applicable to (final) awards pursuant to Article 53 of the Washington Convention. This contribution confirms a persisting dichotomy ('to ICSID or not to ICSID?') between ICSID and non-ICSID proceedings and the ensuing awards (including decisions on jurisdictional issues). Therefore, the applicable procedural regime depends on the choice(s) made by states as parties to international investment treaties and, even more, by claimant investors when presenting the introductory act of the arbitration proceedings. The legal consequences remain relevant also in terms of the challenge of awards and their recognition and enforcement.

113 ICC Arbitration Rules art 35(6); UNCITRAL Arbitration Rules art 34(2); PCA Arbitration Rules art 34(2); SCC Arbitration Rules art 46; SIAC Investment Rules r 30.11; LCIA Arbitration Rules art 26.8.

114 New York Convention art III. See Andreas Börner, 'Article III' in Herbert Kronke and others (eds), *Recognition and Enforcement of Foreign Arbitral Awards—A Global Commentary on the New York Convention* (Kluwer Law International 2010) 115; Giuditta Cordero-Moss, 'Recognition and Enforcement of Non-ICSID Convention Awards' in Fach Gómez and Titi (n 5).

115 New York Convention art V(1)(a)–(e)–(2)(a)–(b). See commentaries in Kronke and others (n 114) 205ff.

116 Antonio Remiro Brotóns, 'La reconnaissance et l'exécution des sentences arbitrales étrangères' (1984-I) Recueil des Cours 260: 'l'on peut se sentir soulagé par le fait que, en règle générale, les États respectent aussi, spontanément, les sentences qui les touchent'.

3

Compensation

Kaj Hobér[*]

I. Introduction

The determination of compensation is one of the most important parts of an investment arbitration award. Once a claimant has surpassed the hurdles of jurisdiction and merits, the decision on compensation will determine the monetary relief to be awarded, which is generally the crux of the relief being sought. Put in general terms, compensation should typically correspond to the economic value of the property rights in question. However, this is most often not a simple exercise, as the value of an asset or enterprise depends on many factors, the importance of which may vary depending on the nature and function of the asset or enterprise.

This chapter will provide an overview of compensation in investment arbitrations, including the basis for the right to compensation, the standards of compensation, and the most common methods for calculation of compensation. As will be seen from the discussion, there is no set formula for such calculations, and tribunals are required to analyse each case to determine what is the most appropriate method to be applied based on the facts before them. Nonetheless, precedents and trends have developed over time which provide parties and arbitrators with guidance as to how to approach this complex subject. The determination of compensation in investment arbitration has become more sophisticated over time, as counsel and arbitrators become more familiar with the economic models used, and decisions on compensation have become more refined and well reasoned. Reference will be made to both landmark and recent arbitration cases to illustrate the approaches taken by international tribunals in practice.

Case management techniques will also be discussed, which aim to assist the parties and the tribunal during the course of the proceedings. The intention of these techniques is to narrow the submissions and evidence on compensation, in particular expert evidence, in order to focus on the true areas of disagreements between the parties and the basis for such differences. The chapter will finish by discussing the drafting of decisions on compensation in the arbitral award, with the aim of providing practical suggestions to arbitrators when dealing with this subject, as well as insight for counsels on how effectively to tailor their submissions.

* With thanks to Tim Robbins (independent arbitrator at Robbins Arbitration) for his assistance with the preparation of this chapter.

Kaj Hobér, *Compensation* In: *The Award in International Investment Arbitration*. Edited by: Katia Fach Gómez and Catharine Titi, Oxford University Press. © Katia Fach Gómez and Aikaterini Titi 2024. DOI: 10.1093/9780191975936.003.0003

II. Right to Compensation

The obligation to pay compensation may arise in different ways in international investment law. In general, it will be based on the underlying treaty from which the claims arise. With respect to expropriation, while it is generally accepted under international law that states are permitted to expropriate both the property and rights of foreigners, it is equally accepted that such expropriation can only take place under certain circumstances. It is the prevailing view that under customary international law, a state must adhere to certain standards for an expropriation to be lawful. These requirements are generally summarized in four points: (1) the measure in question must serve a public purpose; (2) the measure must not be arbitrary or discriminatory; (3) the expropriation procedure must observe due process; and (4) the expropriatory measure must be accompanied by compensation. There is therefore a freestanding right to compensation under international law, although debates on the standard to be applied still exist. While not all financial injuries experienced by investors entitle them to compensation, those damages which result from a violation of a state's obligations under international law give rise to a right to compensation.[1]

As a practical matter, the right to compensation is most often found in the provisions of the relevant treaty pursuant to which the claims are being brought. The most serious threat to a foreign investment is generally expropriation, and as such the provisions of an investment treaty protecting against expropriation are viewed as the cornerstone of such treaties. Given the proliferation of bilateral and multilateral treaties over the past several decades, the vast majority of claims for compensation will therefore arise under the terms of an applicable treaty. This is of course driven primarily by the motivation of investors to have recourse to the dispute resolution provisions within treaties so that their claims are heard by an international tribunal, as opposed by the national courts of the expropriating state.

It should be noted that there is an ongoing debate regarding the role that compensation plays in determining the lawfulness of an expropriation. While the determination of whether an expropriation is lawful or unlawful will not be addressed in this chapter, this distinction is relevant with regard to the standard of compensation to be applied.

Following from this, there has been some debate regarding if and how the lawfulness of the expropriation affects the amount of compensation. The prevailing view which has developed amongst international tribunals is that, in the case of lawful expropriations, the standard of compensation in the relevant treaty shall be applied. By contrast, unlawful expropriations will be governed by customary international law and the general rules of state responsibility should apply, and as such compensation for these

[1] For a more in-depth discussion of the right to compensation, see the following: Kaj Hobér, *The Energy Charter Treaty* (OUP 2017) 260–67; Irmgard Marboe, 'Chapter 25: Compensation and Damages in Investment Treaty Arbitration' in Katia Yannaca-Small (ed), *Arbitration under International Investment Agreements: A Guide to the Key Issues* (2nd edn, OUP 2018) para 25.04.

cases may be different compared to a situation in which the expropriation was deemed to be lawful.[2]

III. Standard of Compensation

The standard of compensation will depend on the terms of the applicable treaty under which the investor is seeking relief. and, in cases of expropriation, whether the expropriation was lawful or unlawful. For expropriation, many modern investment treaties incorporate a standard, or variation thereon, which has become known as the Hull formula, according to which expropriation is lawful only if accompanied by compensation that is 'prompt, adequate and effective'. The reference to 'prompt' is generally understood to mean that payment is made without undue delay, within a reasonable period of time, or potentially as soon as possible. 'Adequate' compensation is generally understood to be a reference to the fair market value of the expropriated investment, although some BITs may describe the standard in greater detail. The requirement for 'effective' generally means that the compensation must be in a freely convertible currency, or at least in a way that the compensation is transferable. The language for the relevant treaty will have to be examined to determine whether this or another standard for compensation should be applied.[3]

In practical terms however, the vast majority of investment arbitrations deal with cases of unlawful expropriation, and therefore the general rules of state responsibility will apply. The seminal judgment in the *Chorzów Factory* case rendered by the Permanent Court of International Justice in 1928 discussed compensation for expropriation at length, and the principles therein are still valid today. In that case, the Court held that an unlawful act shall be treated under the general principles of state responsibility, and that the reparation 'must, as far as possible, wipe out all the consequences of the illegal act and re-establish the situation which would, in all probability, have existed if that act had not been committed'.[4]

This approach has been adopted with increasing frequency by international investment tribunals. In *ADC v Hungary*, for example, the tribunal stated that for unlawful expropriations, the standard of compensation contained in the applicable treaty was not decisive, but instead that customary international law should be applied.[5] The ultimate objective of compensation in cases of unlawful expropriation is to wipe out all

[2] See Irmgard Marboe, *Calculation of Compensation and Damages in International Investment Law* (2nd edn, OUP 2017) paras 3.81–3.96; David Khachvani, 'Compensation for Unlawful Expropriation: Targeting the Illegality' (2017) 32(2) ICSID Review 385, 392–94; see also the discussion in *ADC Affiliate Limited and ADC and ADMC Management Limited v Hungary*, ICSID Case No ARB/03/16 (2 October 2006) [479]–[495].

[3] For a more detailed discussion of standards of compensation, see *Marboe* (n 2) ch 3; Sergey Ripinsky and Kevin Williams, *Damages in International Investments Law* (British Institute of International and Comparative Law 2008) 17–48; Campbell McLachlan, Laurence Shore, and Matthew Weiniger, *International Investment Arbitration* (OUP 2017) paras 9.01–9.15.

[4] *Case Concerning the Factory at Chorzów (Germany v Poland)*, PCIJ Rep Ser A No 9 (26 July 1927), ICGJ 247, 47–48.

[5] See *ADC v Hungary* (n 2).

consequences of the unlawful act. This is the same standard for compensation which is generally adopted in all cases of breach of international obligations. This principle is enshrined in Article 31 of the International Law Commission's Articles on State Responsibility (ILC Articles), which provides as follows:

1. The responsible State is under an obligation to make full reparation for the injury caused by the internationally wrongful act.
2. Injury includes any damage, whether material or moral, caused by the internationally wrongful act.

While the ILC Articles do not automatically apply in investor-state arbitrations, they are frequently referred to by both parties and tribunals in such disputes, including with respect to issues of quantum. Article 35 of the ILC Articles explains that restitution is the primary remedy for internationally wrongful acts. In case of expropriations, it is unusual that restitution will be a realistic remedy. In practice, therefore, the focus is almost always on monetary compensation. This is addressed in Article 36 of the ILC Articles which reads:

1. The State responsible for an internationally wrongful act is under an obligation to compensate for the damage caused thereby, insofar as such damage is not made good by restitution.
2. The compensation shall cover any financially assessable damage including loss of profits insofar as it is established.

Put in general terms, compensation for expropriated property should typically correspond to the economic value of the property in question. The value of an asset depends on many factors, the importance of which may vary depending on the nature and function of the asset. However, it should be observed that the fact that a *standard* of compensation is applicable (eg fair market value), does not mean that a *valuation method* has been selected. This subject will be addressed in the following section.

IV. Determining Compensation

A. Valuation Methods

There are a variety of approaches to valuation that can be adopted, which can broadly be grouped into categories of market-, income-, or asset-based valuations. Consideration should be given to all three approaches, if advanced by the parties and their experts. The approach to be adopted will depend on various factors, including the standard of compensation, the nature of the assets, and the submissions of the parties' experts on valuation. In its determination, the tribunal must consider whether the objective is to put the injured party back in the position as if the investment had never been made, or into a position in which the injurious conduct had never occurred.[6]

1. Market Approach

The market value approach has been described as a method which compares the business to similar businesses, business ownership interests, and securities that have been exchanged in the market, and any relevant transactions of shares in the same business. Market-based methods look to the past, rather than the future, for the basis of valuation. The tribunal in *CMS v Argentina* defined market value as:

> the price, expressed in terms of cash equivalents, at which the property would change hands between a hypothetical willing and able buyer and a hypothetical willing and able seller, acting at arms' length in an open and unrestricted market, when neither is under compulsion to buy or sell and when both have reasonable knowledge of the relevant facts.[7]

While this was not an expropriation case, the tribunal nonetheless decided it was appropriate to use the expropriation standard of compensation.

The most common sources of information and evidence to support a market-based valuation are public stock markets where interests in similar companies are traded, the acquisition markets in which entire businesses are sold, and prior transactions in the ownership of the business are valued. However, it is essential to consider whether the comparisons used are suitable, looking to the nature and size of the other businesses, whether there is sufficient verifiable data, and whether comparable transactions were conducted at arm's length.[8]

In cases in which shares are being valued in a company which is itself publicly traded, the value of the interest can be calculated by multiplying the price of a single share by the number of shares issued. However, it should be noted that the company's total stock price may not necessarily reflect the value of a company, as discounts and premiums have to be taken into consideration depending on the percentage of control and the marketability of the shares, or lack thereof. Stock market prices may also be quite volatile, and thus it may be preferrable to observe stock prices over a longer period of time. It is not uncommon to use stock prices in combination with other methods, as a way of controlling results achieved by other valuation methods.[9]

Prior transactions can be a useful indicator of value under the market approach, and are often favoured in international practice as reliable evidence of the value of an asset. More recent transactions conducted at arm's length would generally be considered the

[6] For a more detailed discussion of valuation methods, see Mark Kantor, *Valuation for Arbitration* (Kluwer Law International 2008) ch 2; Marboe (n 2) chs 4 and 5, paras 4.01–5.369; Ripinsky and Williams (n 3) 182–236; McLachlan, Shore, and Weiniger (n 3) paras 9.17–9.94.

[7] *CMS Gas Transmission Company v Argentina*, ICSID Case No ARB/01/8, Award (12 May 2005) [402].

[8] For a detailed discussion of comparability in the market approach, see Kantor (n 6) ch 3, 119–30.

[9] For a detailed discussion of discounts, see ibid ch 8, 253–64.

best evidence of fair market value, in particular in the case of unlisted companies. In most cases, tribunals will prefer data from actual transactions over projections created by experts, in particular where those projections were prepared during the course of the dispute. In *Enron v Argentina*, the tribunal relied on market transactions involving the asset being valued, stating that these were an 'accurate reflection of the current market value of the company'. While the tribunal accepted that the income-based approach forwarded by the claimants was valid, it found the case-specific transactions involving prior sales of the claimants' shares better to reflect the value of such participation.[10]

It is essential that when assessing value on the basis of prior transactions that one must avoid confusing price with value, as it may be necessary to take into account other factors for adjustments. For example, when previous transactions were entered into by a specific buyer with specific intentions, the price paid may not reflect the actual value. The ICSID tribunal in *Azurix v Argentina* found that the price of USD438.55 million paid by the claimant for a water concession was unreasonably high, and decided that a reasonable person would have paid far less, awarding damages of USD60 million plus verified additional capital investments, which was significantly less than the transaction price.[11]

It is also possible to use prices offered for prior transactions that were not completed, although these prices may have less evidentiary weight and will often require adjustments, potentially due to the fact that the price offered may have been a factor as to why the transaction did not materialize, or where adjustments are required due to the physical quality and maintenance of the assets or other factors. The Iran–US Claims Tribunal in *James A Saghi v Iran*[12] adjusted its valuation to take account of the negative effects of the Iranian revolution and inflation, and, in *United Painting v Iran*,[13] it adjusted prior offers for the asset due to likely depreciation since those offers were made. The tribunal in *Khan Resources v Mongolia*[14] relied on three prior offers for the purchase of the mine in question, but made adjustments on the basis that those offers suffered from clear 'value-affecting factors'.

The market-based approach can also be used by relying on calculations of a 'unit of comparison'. In real estate, the unit is the price per square metre (or foot), while in business valuations these units are generally in the form of some measurement of asset value or income-producing capacity. Tribunals have become familiar with the use of multiples for valuation purposes, as the concept is relatively straightforward and the tribunal will be able to assess the basis for the assumptions used by the parties and exercise its judgment.

However, while multiples are relatively simple to use, expertise is still required properly to assess compatibility with the assets at hand in order to avoid misapplication.

[10] *Enron Corporation and Ponderosa Assets, LP v Argentina*, ICSID Case No ARB/01/3, Award (22 May 2007) [387]–[388].

[11] *Azurix v Argentina*, ICSID Case No ARB/CAF/01/12, Award (14 July 2006) [426].

[12] *James A Saghi v Iran* (1993) 29 Iran–USCTR 20.

[13] *United Painting Company Inc v Iran* (1987) 23 Iran–USCTR 223.

[14] *Khan Resources v Mongolia*, PCA Case No 2011-09, Award (2 March 2015) [418]

The tribunal in *Yukos v Russia* used the comparable companies' approach, based on data available from a range of other Russian and international oil companies.[15] While the claimants had proposed using various operating and financial metrics from a pool of sufficiently similar companies to extrapolate the enterprise value of Yukos, the tribunal considered the data from trading prices on the Moscow Stock Exchange to be a more reliable comparison. Using the best estimate of value of Yukos as at the expropriation date, the tribunal multiplied that value by a factor derived from developments in the RTS Oil and Gas Index from the date of expropriation up to 30 June 2014. The tribunal preferred this method over the discounted cash flow (DCF) approach (discussed in the next section), as the market approach allowed them to verify data on value which was publicly available and used in business practice.

2. Income Approach

The most common method of valuation under the income approach is the DCF method. This method focuses on the future income of the asset being valued, applying a discount to that income to adjust for present day value, and reflects the view that the value of an asset is best represented by the potential to yield financial benefits to its owner. This approach is often favoured when no actual market for the assets exists, but where reliable data for the company itself is available. In *PV Investors v Spain*, the tribunal preferred using the DCF method as the claimants' plants had been operational for over a decade, providing a reliable source of past financial performance, and because there was no major uncertainty regarding the plants' future cash flows.[16]

The first step in the DCF method is to determine how one is to identify and measure the income stream which will form the basis of the valuation. Reference is generally made to cash flow, rather than net earnings or future profit, as using cash flow is viewed as a better indicator of value. One must then forecast the future cash flow, which requires the collection of substantial financial information so as to analyse the past and present cash flow of the asset being valued. Past performance is particularly important, although not determinative. One must take into account economic and political factors which may have influenced cash flow in the past, as well as uncertainties relating to the pricing of goods or products produced.

Another essential consideration is to determine the relevant 'valuation drivers' in relation to the asset being valued. This may include the price of commodities, the size of the market share that the company occupies, as well as the importance of the country as a market to the company being valued. In *Phillips Petroleum v Iran*, the value of petroleum concessions was being assessed, about which the tribunal had the following to say:

> While experience shows that forecasting future crude oil prices is difficult and open to a high risk of being proved wrong by the subsequent realities of the actual market, the

[15] *Yukos v Russia*, PCA Case No 2005-04/AA227, Award (18 July 2014) [1788]–[1789].

[16] *PV Investors v Spain*, PCA Case No 2012-14, Award (28 February 2020) [691].

> Tribunal's objective here is to determine the range of expectations that seemed reasonable in September 1979, not the accuracy of those expectations in fact.[17]

Both positive and negative factors need to be taken into account, and forecasts must be tested for both plausibility and reasonableness. Business plans may also be relevant to consider, if they were prepared and approved independently of and prior to the dispute. Long-term contracts, where applicable, can be highly relevant. Tribunals will assess the particular formulation of these contracts, and whether the terms of the contracts may change over time. Where long-term contract extensions require the consent of both parties, tribunals will generally not include such extensions in their valuation considerations.[18]

The third step in the DCF method is to calculate the 'present day' value of the expected total amount of the income. For this, a discount factor is applied to take into account the fact that the longer a creditor has to wait for money, the lower its present-day value would be. There are various approaches to determine the discount rate, two of which are to use the weighted average cost of capital (WACC), or the closely related capital asset pricing model (CAPM). The tribunal's determination of the appropriate discounting will be based on the submissions of the parties, which evaluations have become increasingly more detailed in recent years.

Country risk premiums are often also taken into account when calculating discount rates, as such risks are considered to be 'obvious to the least sophisticated businessman'. As stated by the tribunal in *Tidewater v Venezuela*:

> the country risk premium quantifies the general risks, including political risks, of doing business in a particular country, as they applied on that date and as they might then reasonably have been expected to affect the prospects, and thus the value to be ascribed to the likely cash flow of the business going forward.[19]

For cases of unlawful expropriation, as discussed in section III, the standard is full compensation for the loss, in that the compensation should, as far as possible, restore the situation that would have existed had the unlawful act not occurred. It follows that this involves the comparison of two scenarios, that is, the future income after the breach and the future income without the breach.

It should be noted that in cases where there is consideration of whether the asset lacks potential as a going concern, tribunals have often declined to apply the income-based valuation methods and have taken instead other approaches. In *Impregilo v Argentina*, the tribunal declined to apply an income-based valuation based on its doubts of the profitability of the concession, and instead based its valuation on the actual investments

[17] *Phillips Petroleum Co Iran v Iran* (1989) 21 Iran–USCTR 79 [163].

[18] See for example *Bridas SAPIC v Turkmenistan*, ICC Case No 9058/FMS/KGA, Partial Award (25 June 1999) [1270], [1272].

[19] *Tidewater v Venezuela*, ICSID Case No ARB/10/5, Award (13 March 2015) [186].

made by the claimant.[20] In *Hassan Awdi v Romania*, the DCF approach proposed by the claimants was also rejected based primarily on the companies' history of losses; instead the tribunal determined compensation on a 'sunk costs' basis.[21]

3. Asset Approach

There are a number of asset-based approaches for valuation, although as a general rule these are not often relied on aside from in specific situations. While these approaches may be simpler than income or market-based approaches, using a more straightforward valuation process, they are often not considered to provide accurate reflections on the value of assets for a variety of reasons. Most notably, these approaches do not take into account future value and potential for profit. The primary advantages of this approach are that it is generally much more straightforward and less speculative, and evidence is usually available with no need to undertake complex forecasting nor a discounting process.

'Book value' of an asset falls within this category, which is based on a company's balance sheet in which assets appear at their original cost less applicable depreciation. However, in addition to the reasons already mentioned, this method is generally considered as inappropriate due to differences in bookkeeping between countries.

One can also use the 'replacement value', which uses the current costs of an asset with similar characteristics in the market, rather than historical prices paid for the asset. However, this approach does not take into account any future prospects, such as lost income, and while it is the most commonly used of the asset-based approaches, it should only be used in specific cases.

Yet another approach is the 'liquidation value', which proceeds on an asset-by-asset sale as opposed to a sale of the entire business. This approach is generally used when the business or assets being valued are deemed not to have any prospects of generating profit in the future, and would be considered as the lower end of the value of any asset.

4. Utilizing Multiple Valuation Methods

The use of multiple valuation methods can be an important and effective tool for tribunals to seek consistency of valuations across different methodologies. In the event that different approaches lead to substantial differences in valuation, this may be an indication that there are underlying problems with one or more of the valuations. Conversely, in the event that different approaches produce broadly consistent results, tribunals can take greater comfort in adopting the methodologies and conclusions reached.

In *CME Czech Republic BV v Czech Republic*, the tribunal calculated compensation by reference to a prior transaction which the claimant had entered into with a third-party purchaser, as well as considering the DCF calculations of the parties. In the end, the tribunal did not rely on the DCF calculations but used them as confirmation of its

[20] *Impregilo v Argentina*, ICSID Case No ARB/07/17, Award (21 June 2011) [381].
[21] *Hassan Awdi v Romania*, ICSID Case No ARB/10/13, Award (2 March 2015) [514].

findings based on the third-party transaction.[22] The tribunal in *Enron v Argentina* used a similar approach, and made reference to stock exchange value and share sales at the relevant times to assess the reasonableness of the DCF calculations put forward by the experts.[23]

It is further possible to use multiple valuation methodologies within the same valuation. In *Enron v Argentina*, the tribunal applied a DCF valuation for the calculation of compensation prior to Argentina implementing emergency measures, and thereafter it used transaction data for a market-based valuation which reflected the impact of the measures imposed by the government.[24]

B. Valuation Date

Determination of the valuation date is an essential, and often crucial, aspect of any valuation exercise.[25] As the value of an asset will invariably change over time, the tribunal's selection of a valuation date can have significant consequences for the calculation of compensation. A poignant example of this importance can be seen in a series of cases involving Argentina, in which tribunals were considering substantially identical economic, political, and regulatory events. Despite this, each of the tribunals determined different valuation dates, ranging over a period of approximately eighteen months. The choices of these dates may have affected valuations by tens, if not hundreds, of millions of dollars.[26]

Generally, according to the international standard of compensation for lawful expropriations, the date immediately preceding the date of the expropriation is the valuation date. In the case of unlawful expropriations, the tribunal should undertake an exercise to assess the value at two dates: first, the date of the expropriation, and second at the date of the award. This allows the tribunal to assess the value of the enterprise at the date of its award in the event that the expropriation had not taken place, in order to come as close as possible to providing full compensation. A claimant, in cases of unlawful expropriation, would then have the choice of selecting between the expropriation date and the date of the award. The *ADC v Hungary* tribunal was the first to decide that, in the case of an unlawful expropriation, the higher value at the time of the award should be chosen as it represented the best alternative for restitution as required under the law of state responsibility, reasoning which numerous tribunals have since followed.[27] In *Yukos v Russia*, the tribunal held that in the case of unlawful expropriations, the claimant should be entitled to select either the date of the expropriation or

[22] *CME Czech Republic v Czech Republic*, UNCITRAL, Final Award (14 March 2003) [514] and [560].
[23] *Enron v Argentina* (n 10) [424]–[439].
[24] ibid [389], [424]–[428].
[25] For a more detailed discussion of valuation dates, see Marboe (n 2) paras 3.266–3.342; Kantor (n 6) 60–66; Hobér (n 1) 280–82.
[26] See *CMS v Argentina* (n 8); *LG&E Energy Corp and others v Argentina*, ICSID Case No ARB/02/1; *Enron v Argentina* (n 10).
[27] *ADC v Hungary* (n 5) [497].

the date of the award. The tribunal expanded on the consequences that flow from the application of this principle as twofold: first, that investors must enjoy the benefits of unanticipated events that increase the value of an expropriated asset up to the date of the decisions; and, second, that investors do not bear the risk of unanticipated events decreasing the value of an expropriated asset over the time period.[28]

A challenging aspect of determining the valuation date is in the case of indirect expropriation, in particular where the expropriation did not occur in one instance, but through a combination of acts and omissions over a long period of time. This is also referred to as creeping or consequential expropriation. The tribunal is often required to apply some level of discretion, but international practice shows that the valuation date in such cases is often determined to be the date when the deprivation of property rights has become irreversible, which would normally be at a relatively late stage. This was the approach taken in *International Technical Products v Iran*, where the tribunal found that where:

> the alleged expropriation is carried out by way of a series of interferences in the enjoyment of the property, the breach forming the cause of action is deemed to take place on the day when the interference has ripened into more or less irreversible deprivation of the property rather than on the beginning dates of the events.[29]

In some cases of indirect or creeping expropriation, tribunals have felt the need to distinguish between the expropriation date and the valuation date. In *Amoco International Finance v Iran*, the tribunal determined that the valuation date should be fixed earlier than the formal date of expropriation, viz, on the date at which they determined that Iran had ceased adhering to the joint decision-making process for the joint venture, which eventually led to the demise of the company.[30]

C. Interest

Claims for interest are a common element of claims for compensation. In order fully to compensate an injured party, in addition to awarding compensation it will be necessary to compensate for the delay with which the payment to that party is made 'to ensure that the present value of the judgment equals the present value of the harm and the start date for the prejudgment interest should be the date of breach or loss'.[31] It is widely accepted that international tribunals have jurisdiction to award interest on compensation.[32]

[28] *Yukos v Russia* (n 15) [1763]–[1769].
[29] *International Technical Products v Iran* (1985) 9 Iran–USCTR 206 [240]–[241].
[30] *Amoco International Finance v Iran* (1987) 15 Iran–USCTR [189], [182].
[31] *RREEF Infrastructure (GP) Limited and RREEF Pan-European Infrastructure Two Lux SARL v Spain*, ICSID Case No ARB/13/30, Final Award (11 December 2019) [65].
[32] For a more detailed discussion of interest, see Marboe (n 2) paras 6.01–6.309; Ripinsky and Williams (n 3) ch 9, 361–404; McLachlan, Shore, and Weiniger (n 3) paras 9.171–9.189.

There are three main issues to address when dealing with interest: the rate of interest, the period(s) during which interest should be paid, and whether interest should be calculated on a simple or compound basis. A distinction should also be drawn between pre-award and post-award interest. The latter is best characterized as default for non-payment of an identified debt, while pre-award interest is viewed as forming part of the compensation awarded.

There are a number of approaches which can be used to determine interest. Unless the relevant investment protection treaty provides for a specific rate of interest or the parties have agreed on a rate, the decision ultimately will be based on the facts and circumstances of the individual case and subject to the discretion of the tribunal. The tribunal could focus on the borrowing rate with reference to the prime interest rate, the actual borrowing rate of the investor if that can be established, interbank interest rates, or some form of average borrowing rate. Alternatively, the tribunal could refer to the interest that the investor would have earned if it had been paid in time, such that it had the funds available to make alternative investments. In *RREEF Infrastructure v Spain*, the tribunal agreed with the claimants in that the calculation of interest should be done at Spain's borrowing rate based on the yield on Spanish ten-year bonds, which it determined to be 'appropriate to afford full reparation in the framework of a private investment realized on a market basis'.[33]

Tribunals seem to be increasingly unwilling to distinguish between pre- and post-award interest. In *Micula v Romania*, the tribunal did 'not see why the cost of the deprivation of money (which interest compensates) should be different before and after the Award... Both are awarded to compensate a party for the deprivation of the use of its funds'.[34] Similar approaches were taken by the tribunals in *PV Investors v Spain* and *RREEF Infrastructure v Spain*.[35]

The difference between awarding simple and compound interest can be substantial, in particular due to the length of interval used for compound interest. While most international financing and investment activities incorporate compound interest into their terms, traditionally most international tribunals were reluctant to award compound interest. However, recent investment treaty arbitrations have shown a growing trend towards awarding compound interest, as this is often viewed as better reflecting actual economic and financial realities.[36]

D. Calculation of Amounts

Valuation exercises can easily become lengthy and complex phases of the arbitration, which can vary greatly depending on the timing and degree of case management. When valuation becomes relevant, tribunals should take a hands-on approach to

33 *RREEF Infrastructure* (Final Award) (n 31) [68].
34 *Micula v Romania*, ICSID Case No ARB 05/20, Award (11 December 2013) [1269].
35 See *PV Investors* (n 16) [853]; *RREEF Infrastructure* (Final Award) (n 31) [65].
36 *RREEF Infrastructure* (Final Award) (n 31) [68].

setting parameters for the preparations of expert reports, with the aim of minimizing unnecessary submissions and focusing the parties' efforts on explaining material differences between their positions and approaches.

At the appropriate stage of the proceedings, following consultation with the parties, the tribunal should issue appropriate directions with regard to expert evidence, whether in the form of procedural directions or otherwise. For most cases, instructions to the experts should require their reports to include the following elements: (1) an explanation of the facts they use as the basis for their findings; (2) an explanation of the methodology (or methodologies) being used; (3) a clear statement of the assumptions which are being used for the calculations; and (4) a clear indication of the instructions which they received from the party for which the report was prepared.[37]

The method(s) of valuation may be a central point of disagreement between the parties, which can lead to vastly different valuations and complicate the tribunal's determination of compensation. To the extent possible, the experts should be invited to reach agreement on the method of valuation and, in the absence of such an agreement, the experts should clearly state their reasons for disagreement. In the event that the experts adopt different methodologies for valuation and/or valuation date, they should also be invited to reach agreement on the validity of the methodology used by the opposing expert, even though they do not agree on its applicability in the case at hand.

While often not realistic, in appropriate cases the parties should be encouraged to have their experts prepare a joint report setting out areas of agreement and explaining points of disagreement.[38] The more the parties are able to narrow the issues for the tribunal, the more efficient the proceedings will be and the greater the chance for the tribunal accurately to understand and assess the parties' respective positions on valuation. While parties are sometimes of the view that joint expert reports would not serve the interests of their case, in situations where the methodologies adopted in expert reports are substantially divergent, the parties run the risk of having their approach disregarded if the tribunal adopts the approach of the opposing side, which may be the only option open to the tribunal if there is no joint report.

Case management conferences are essential tools in this respect. The widespread adoption of virtual conferencing has reduced concerns of time and costs associated with in-person meetings. As such, in addition to the initial case management conference, further conferences can and should be held at any point of the proceedings where it appears that the parties are at an impasse and could benefit from the guidance of the tribunal.

[37] There are a number of sources of soft law which can be used for reference, or adopted in full as guidance in the proceedings. These include the International Bar Association (IBA) Rules on the Taking of Evidence in International Arbitration, although for expert evidence it may be preferrable to refer to the Chartered Institute of Arbitration (CIArb) Protocol for the Use of Party-Appointed Expert Witnesses in International Arbitration. The CIArb Protocol not only includes guidance as to the standard requirements of form and content for expert witnesses, but also sets out a detailed procedure for expert consultation, with the aim of encouraging collaboration between the experts.

[38] See as an example CIArb Protocol art 6.1(b).

In the event of disagreements on key metrics, it may be useful to bifurcate the valuation process. In this approach, following submissions by the parties, the tribunal would provide an indication and/or finding as to its determination on certain issues such as valuation date and valuation method. Doing so will provide guidance to the parties and put the experts on the same page, potentially reducing the complexity of the valuation process.

In *RREEF Infrastructure*, the tribunal made a preliminary finding on certain matters relating to damages, including that the respondent was in breach of its obligations to ensure a reasonable rate of return on the claimants' investments, in so far as it failed to ensure a reasonable rate of return above a particular rate. The tribunal then directed that the parties attempt to reach an agreement on the amount of compensation to be paid by the respondent, in accordance with the tribunal's preliminary findings.[39]

In an interim award, the tribunal in *Cavalum v Spain* issued clear directions for the assessment of damages, including the valuation date and the operating life of the relevant assets, as well as parameters for determination of the reasonable rate of return and for the calculation of the WACC.[40] The tribunal in *Sevilla Beheer v Spain* issued directions that the parties were to provide a joint calculation of the investor's rate of return, setting parameters for such calculation including the initial investment costs and that the calculation was to be on an 'operation' rather than an 'exit' rate of return, and directed the parties to attempt to reach agreement on any other outstanding issues that could arise during the course of the joint calculation.[41]

The tribunal and parties should also discuss the format and structure of the testimony of the experts at the hearing. While counsel will sometimes request the opportunity for experts to provide an explanation of their reports, either on direct examination or by means of a presentation, the tribunal should consider whether this will be a helpful exercise. If the tribunal has reviewed and understood the reports, then further explanations by the experts may prove to be of little use. With regard to cross examination of experts, the time required should be discussed in advance, and where agreement is not reached the tribunal should issue directions after considering the parties' respective positions. Appropriate time limits will allow counsel to structure their questioning so as to cover all necessary points, while ideally focusing on the main issues relevant to valuation for the tribunal's consideration.

There are other standard ways of focusing the parties' submissions, whether by limiting the number of experts, limiting the number of exchanges, and limiting the length of reports. In the absence of party agreement on these items, the tribunal should consider whether introducing such measures may be in the interests of both the efficiency of the proceedings, as well as of benefit to the tribunal's analysis. Such limits do not

[39] *RREEF Infrastructure (GP) Limited and RREEF Pan-European Infrastructure Two Lux SARL v Spain*, ICSID Case No ARB/13/30, Decision on Responsibility and Principles of Quantum (30 November 2018) [600].

[40] *Cavalum v Spain*, ICSID Case No ARB/15/34, Decision on Jurisdiction, Liability and Directions on Quantum (31 August 2020) [698].

[41] *Sevilla Beheer and others v Spain*, ICSID Case No ARB/16/27, Decision on Jurisdiction, Liability and Principles of Quantum (11 February 2022) [1019]–[1020].

necessarily affect a party's ability to present its case in full, but instead can act to focus the parties' attention on the most relevant aspects of their respective cases with respect to the material issues before the tribunal.

As a general principle, when calculating amounts, tribunals should typically consider the overall economic circumstances in a host country, including financial crises, when undertaking valuations. Any comparison of the hypothetical financial situations of the claimant in an unlawful expropriation should take into consideration economic factors which would have applied regardless of the expropriation. Several methods of valuation include appropriate methods of reflecting such risk.

E. Contributory Negligence

In the event the injured party has acted negligently in such a way as to have contributed to the damages suffered, the obligation of the state to pay damages can be reduced or offset. This principle is reflected in Article 39 of the ILC Articles on State Responsibility. Under the ILC Articles, contributory negligence is to be considered an aspect of quantification; however, in practice, it may also go to causation and preclude liability. Where a tribunal intends to apply this doctrine, it should take care not to do so in a generalized manner but should ground the reduction of compensation on the facts and circumstances of the individual case.[42]

Not just any contributory act will suffice, and this doctrine appears to be applied rather restrictively in practice. The tribunal in *Yukos v Russia* stated that the contribution must be 'material and significant' and that the tribunal 'has a wide margin of discretion in apportioning fault'.[43] In that case, the tribunal found fault with the claimants relating to what the tribunal considered to be abuse of the low-tax regions through their trading entities, while dismissing the claimant's actions in relation to depreciation of the auction price and actions in connection with the bankruptcy proceedings as insufficient to rise to the level of contributory fault. Weighing the various arguments of the parties on this issue, the tribunal exercised its 'wide discretion' and attributed 25 per cent of the loss suffered to the claimants and 75 per cent to Russia, holding that this was 'fair and reasonable in the circumstances of the present case', without providing extensive reasoning as to the conclusion on allocation.[44]

F. Mitigation of Damages

It is a generally accepted principle of law that parties have a duty to mitigate damages, and that therefore they have a responsibility to take reasonable steps to reduce their

[42] For a more detailed discussion of contributory negligence, see Marboe (n 2) paras 3.242–3.254; Kantor (n 6) 105–12; Ripinsky and Williams (n 3) 314–19.
[43] *Yukos v Russia* (n 15) [1599]–[1600].
[44] ibid [1610]–[1637].

losses. In the event the injured party fails to do so, the recoverable damages may be reduced accordingly. An issue which may arise in this context is whether the investor has a duty to take all reasonable measures to mitigate its losses, or to demonstrate that the mitigation measures it had in fact taken were reasonable in the circumstances.[45]

In the case of *MTD v Chile*, the tribunal found that, while Chile had breached its obligations, the claimants had also failed to protect themselves from business risks inherent in their investments in Chile. The tribunal found that responsibility for the claimants' loss was equally divided, and therefore concluded that Chile should pay 50 per cent of the assessed damages. On application for annulment, the annulment committee declined to annul the award, including for reasons that the tribunal had allegedly failed to set out an express basis for its 50:50 split of responsibility. The committee explained that, since estimating the impact of contributory fault was a difficult task, the arbitrators were entitled to a 'range of estimation for their damages awards in such cases, especially with respect to investment treaty claims'.[46]

G. Causality

Compensation should only be payable for the consequences of injuries which were caused by the respondent state's conduct. The injured party bears the burden of proving that the damages which are being claimed flowed from the wrongful act and the injury.[47] The tribunal in *SD Myers v Canada* required a 'sufficiently causal link', elaborating that this meant that the harm must 'not be too remote' and that the breach was the 'proximate cause of the harm', while rejecting the use of the term 'foreseeability' as often used in cases for breach of contract.[48]

For matters which involve indirect expropriation through changes to regulatory regimes or similar circumstances, tribunals usually refuse to take a binary approach in either finding that a breach led to full reparation or that no breach had occurred and therefore no damages are payable. In *RREEF Infrastructure v Spain*, the tribunal held that the 'breach does not amount to the total loss or deprivation of an asset', and therefore that 'it is only to the extent that the modifications [to the regulatory regime] would have exceeded the limits of what is reasonable that compensation would be due and should be calculated'.[49] The tribunal therefore determined that the only legitimate expectation of which the claimants could avail themselves was that of a 'reasonable return'.[50] The tribunal in *FREIF Eurowind Holdings v Spain*, using the same approach, determined that Spain had not frustrated the expectation of a reasonable return as the

[45] For a more detailed discussion of mitigation, see Marboe (n 2) paras 3.255–3.265; Kantor (n 6) 113–15; Ripinsky and Williams (n 3) 319–25.
[46] *MTD Chile, SA v Chile*, ICSID Case No ARB/01/7, Decision on Annulment (21 March 2007) [39].
[47] For a more detailed discussion of causation, see Kantor (n 6) 105–12; Ripinsky and Williams (n 3) 135–148.
[48] *SD Myers v Canada*, Second Partial Award (21 October 2002), UNCITRAL [140], [159]–[160].
[49] *RREEF Infrastructure* (Decision on Responsibility and Principles of Quantum) (n 40) [518], quoting *Joseph Charles Lemire v Ukraine*, ICSID Case No ARB/06/18, Award (28 March 2011).
[50] ibid [515]–[521].

actual return for the assets in that matter exceeded the reasonable rate determined by the tribunal.[51]

Issues of attribution may also become relevant with respect to causation, as the tribunal will need to find not only that the impugned actions resulted in the injury for which compensation is being sought, but also that the actions were taken by an entity which can be attributed to the respondent state. In *Yukos v Russia*, while the tribunal found that Russia was responsible for the actions of its 'organs, executive, judicial and administrative, in the actions that they took against and in relation to Yukos and its stockholders', it declined to attribute the actions of the bankruptcy administrator to Russia.[52]

H. Moral Damages

Historically, moral damages were not a prominent feature of investment arbitrations, which typically addressed purely economic and material damages. More recently however investors have been increasingly seeking compensation for non-material damages.[53] The principle of moral damages is recognized by most national laws, and is reflected expressly in Article 31 of the ILC Articles, which includes compensation for injuries 'whether material or moral'. Such damages can generally be categorized into three types: (1) damage to personality rights of individuals (including individual pain and suffering); (2) damage to reputation; and (3) legal damage (ie harm that results ipso facto from the violation of an international obligation).

While tribunals have been willing to recognize the rights to moral damages, per se, they have generally not been willing to award such damages due to the high threshold that has been established in jurisprudence. The first such case is thought to be *Benvenuti & Bonfant v Congo*, decided in 1980, in which the tribunal was authorized by the parties to decide *ex aequo et bono*.[54] In *Desert Line v Yemen*, one of the few recent cases in which moral damages have been awarded, the claimant was seeking approximately USD40 million for 'moral damages including loss of reputation'. The tribunal reduced the amount awarded to USD1 million, noting that this sum was more symbolic given the scale of the project at the heart of the dispute.[55]

V. Conclusion: Drafting the Compensation Part of the Award

A tribunal should approach drafting the compensation portion of the award methodically, much in a similar way that an expert would prepare his or her report. The issues

[51] *FREIF Eurowind Holdings v Spain*, SCC Case No 2017/060, Final Award (21 March 2017) [557]–[560].
[52] *Yukos v Russia* (n 15) [1480].
[53] For a more detailed discussion of moral damages, see Marboe (n 2) paras 5.342–5.369; Ripinsky and Williams (n 3) 307–12; McLachlan, Shore, and Weiniger (n 3) paras 9.147–9.155.
[54] *SARL Benvenuti & Bonfant v Congo*, ICSID Case No ARB/77/2, Award (15 August 1980). For further discussion of this case, see Catharine Titi, *The Function of Equity in International Law* (OUP 2021) 147–51.
[55] *Desert Line Projects LLC v Yemen*, ICSID Case No ARB/05/17, Award (6 February 2008) [289]–[291].

for determination should be identified, which may include decisions on the standard of compensation, valuation date, and the method of valuation. The tribunal's decisions must of course be founded in the parties' submissions, be well reasoned, and provide a clear, coherent, and logical explanation for the conclusions reached. The absence of sufficient reasoning to support the tribunal's conclusions on these issues may constitute a ground for set-aside of the award.

When preparing submissions, not only on compensation but indeed on all issues, it serves parties well to keep the tribunal's decision-making process and the drafting of the award in mind. A party who has clearly set out the issues, the relevant principles, and a well-reasoned application of those principles to the facts, in a way which is both easy for the tribunal to understand and reasonable to accept, will improve the chances of its position being adopted by the tribunal.

When approaching the valuation assessment in the award, a tribunal should have a clear understanding of the areas of agreement and disagreement as between the parties and their experts. Awards should generally contain reasonably comprehensive summaries of the parties' positions on compensation and valuation, setting out the areas of agreement and disagreement, prior to the tribunal's reasoning and decisions. In *RREEF Infrastructure v Spain*, for example, the tribunal started its assessment of damages by clearly setting out the points on which the experts had agreed.[56]

When selecting between competing methods of valuation, the tribunal should explain in a clear and understandable way why it prefers one method over another for determining value. When deciding between competing methodologies in calculating the WACC, the tribunal in *RREEF Infrastructure v Spain* set out a list of reasons supporting its decision to prefer one expert's position over the other.[57]

As a rule, it is not recommended that a tribunal simply decides between two opposing views and adopts the chosen report in its entirety, along with the accompanying figures for compensation. The tribunal needs to be discerning in its adoption of the contents of an expert report and should directly address aspects of the expert report which were criticized or questioned by the opposing side. In *PV Investors v Spain*, the tribunal decided to utilize the claimant's expert's methodology for valuation. It then addressed both the reasons supporting its decisions as well as the criticisms argued by the respondent.[58] While it may not be practical or necessary to address every question raised in relation to an expert report, the tribunal should ensure that all material elements of the valuation methodology which it applies have either been agreed between the experts or are supported by comprehensive reasoning in the award.

It can be said that valuation is an art, not a science. Indeed, there is often a substantial amount of discretion involved on the part of a tribunal when determining the value of assets. However, that discretion should only be applied when necessary. Where sufficient data and analysis are presented so that clear conclusions can be drawn, the

[56] *RREEF Infrastructure* (Final Award) (n 31) [19]–[20].
[57] ibid 27.
[58] *PV Investors* (n 16) [688]–[697].

tribunal must limit the exercise of its discretion accordingly. The ultimate goal is for the determination of compensation to be as well grounded on facts as possible, and not a weighing exercise between two opposing opinions. The tribunal in *Yukos v Russia* reviewed the parties' positions in detail on the valuation of the claimant's lost dividends. After extensively setting out its observations on the subject and stating which particular circumstances it was taking into account, the tribunal expressly exercised its discretion in determining the dividend payments which Yukos would have paid to its shareholders.[59]

59 *Yukos v Russia* (n 15) [1791]–[1811].

4

The Cost Award

Susan Franck and Bailey Roe[*]

I. Introduction

As humans are human, when divergent incentives, experiences, and expectations intersect in an international investment, conflict is inevitable.[1] With variations in commercial realities, power differentials, cultural experiences, expectations of legal norms, or challenges from political contexts, some conflicts will mature into full-blown disputes.[2] When those disputes crystallize into formal arbitrations, a myriad of derivative fiscal costs become inevitable. The core challenge is not whether costs will occur but *when and how* they will be incurred, assessed, and distributed. Stakeholders can 'pay now, or pay later' but will pay for the privilege of dispute settlement.[3]

Cost awards are fundamental to the efficacy of international dispute settlement. Beyond fiscal expense, choices about costs reflect societal norms about what is valued. Costs—and cost allocation—impact whether parties can and will pursue their claims or defences as well as considerations about fiscal exposure to potential costs (and cost-shifting), incentives for party settlement, strategies for refining dispute resolution, and the ultimate utility of adjudication.

While others in this collective volume explore awards through the prism of jurisdiction, merits, or damages, this chapter focuses on investment treaty arbitration (ITA) cost awards, including fiscal costs, standards for assessment, and tribunal cost allocation.[4] First, this chapter explores the impact of international arbitration costs. Second, it provides an overview of the definition and doctrine of costs. Third, it explores ITA costs reform, focusing on recent efforts at the International Centre for Settlement of Investment Disputes (ICSID). Fourth, it provides observations about the challenges and opportunities for the future. Finally, the chapter concludes that the applicable laws

* The authors are grateful for the research support and editorial assistance of Vicky Cheng.

1 See generally Jay Payleitner, *Don't Take the Bait to Escalate: Conflict Is Inevitable, Being a Jerk Is Optional* (Simon and Schuster 2022).

2 Mariana Hernandez Crespo, 'A New Chapter in Natural Resource-Seeking Investment: Using Shared Decisions System Design ("SDSD") to Strengthen Investor-State and Community Relationships' (2017) 18 Cardozo Journal of Conflict Resolution 551, 571–72; Roberto Echandi, 'Complementing Investor-State Dispute Resolution: A Conceptual Framework for Investor-State Conflict Management' in Pierre Sauvé and Roberto Echandi (eds), *Prospects in International Investment Law and Policy* (CUP 2013) 288–89.

3 See eg Susan Franck, 'Integrating Investment Treaty Conflict and Dispute Systems Design' (2007) 92 Minnesota Law Review 161.

4 While indirectly impacting ITA costs, this chapter does not discuss security for costs or third-party funding due to space constraints. See also nn 8–9 (discussing the definition of a 'cost award' for the purposes of this chapter and noting doctrinal distinctions).

Susan Franck and Bailey Roe, *The Cost Award* In: *The Award in International Investment Arbitration*. Edited by: Katia Fach Gómez and Catharine Titi, Oxford University Press. © Katia Fach Gómez and Aikaterini Titi 2024. DOI: 10.1093/9780191975936.003.0004

must structure arbitral discretion to permit ex ante management of parties' (and their counsel's) expectations, give arbitrators better guidance, encourage clear articulation of the law and justification of cost awards, and reflect rule of law values required for the peaceful, non-abusive resolution of international disputes.

II. The Importance and Impact of Cost Awards

The volume of ITA cases has increased since the first investment treaty was signed and the first award rendered.[5] Shifts in globalization,[6] a massive network of treaties, and humanity's propensity to generate conflict[7] create foreseeable risks of ITA. As this risk has materialized for investors and states, arbitration costs and cost management concerns have become more pervasive. Yet even with more publicly available awards and precision in treaties, cost awards remain the wild west and represent the last bastion of unfettered discretion in ITA.

While decisions about jurisdiction, merits, and damages may create consternation,[8] cost awards present unique challenges.[9] Such awards on costs often require parties to pay millions of dollars in legal fees to cover the opposing party's and/or tribunal's legal and/or administrative expenses, among other costs. To complicate matters, uncertainty about who should bear these costs (and on what basis) creates further confusion and frustration.[10]

The costs of arbitration generally, and ITA specifically, are often referred to as 'the sting in the tail'[11] or the 'worst feature' of international arbitration.[12] Various analyses

[5] See generally Susan Franck, *Arbitration Costs: Myths and Realities in Investment Treaty Arbitration* (OUP 2019) 113–20; International Centre for Settlement of Investment Disputes (ICSID), 'The ICSID Caseload–Statistics: 2021–2 Edition' (28 July 2021) <https://icsid.worldbank.org/resources/publications/icsid-caseload-statistics>; United Nations Conference on Trade and Development (UNCTAD), 'Investor-State Dispute Settlement Cases Pass the 1,000 Mark: Cases and Outcomes in 2019', IIA Issues Note (July 2020) <https://unctad.org/system/files/official-document/diaepcbinf2020d6.pdf>. See also Yas Banifatemi, 'The Law Applicable to Investment Treaty Arbitration' in Katia Yannaca-Small (ed), *Arbitration under International Investment Agreements* (OUP 2010) 191, 193–94.

[6] See generally UNCTAD, *World Investment Report 2019: Special Economic Zones* (United Nations 2019); UNCTAD, *World Investment Report 2021: Investing in Sustainable Recovery* (United Nations 2021).

[7] Franck (n 5) 6–22.

[8] As other chapters in this book acknowledge, the definition of what constitutes an ITA 'award' is a thorny doctrinal issue, given variations in cases governed by the ICSID Convention (which only permits one final 'award') and other regimes often governed by the New York Convention (which may permit multiple awards, including partial or interim awards, in addition to the final award). For the purposes of this chapter, an 'award' is any dispositive substantive decision on a matter in dispute. See also Catharine Titi, 'What Is an Award? Concept, Content, Drafting, Effects' in Katia Fach Gómez and Catharine Titi (eds), *The Award in Investment Arbitration* (OUP 2024).

[9] A 'cost award' for the purposes of this chapter is a substantive decision by a tribunal on a matter related to the fiscal costs of an international arbitration. Cost awards, namely decisions that identify a matter related to costs, can typically be made at any time during the life of a dispute. For example, it may be a decision made early in the case that identifies in advance how tribunals will assess costs. It may also be a cost assessment rendered in connection with other substantive decisions, whether interim or final as regards the allowable costs, the proportion paid by which parties, and the grounds upon which costs will (or will not be) shifted.

[10] Ilija M Penuliski, 'A Dispute Systems Design Diagnosis of ICSID' in Michael Waibel and others (eds), *The Backlash against Investment Arbitration* (Harvard Law School 2010) 507–08.

[11] Klaus Reichert and James Hope, 'Costs—The Sting in the Tail' (2006) 1 Global Arbitration Review 30.

[12] Queen Mary and White & Case, *2015 International Arbitration Survey: Improvements and Innovations in International Arbitration* (2015) <www.arbitration.qmul.ac.uk/research/2015/> (hereinafter 2015 *Arbitration Survey*) 2, 5.

suggest that the average total cost of an ITA dispute is roughly USD12 million[13]—with the parties' combined legal fees and expenses costing around USD11 million (around 91 per cent of average total ITA costs) and tribunal and administrative support costs around USD1 million (9 per cent of the total ITA costs).[14] Costs are fiscally critical as, in many instances, they make up roughly 20–30 per cent of the amounts awarded.[15] Given this serious fiscal exposure, many stakeholders have focused on costs and cost awards to promote structural reform.[16]

Cost assessments—whether they occur at an early stage of the proceedings or in the final award—are central to parties' appreciation of their risk and estimations of financial exposure in an ITA proceeding, which inform core choices about dispute management.[17] Without explicit treaty provisions or ex ante agreement on cost allocation, tribunals' cost awards (and cost-shifting) are more difficult to predict than other matters. Uncertainty in costs—over who will pay, how much will be spent, and why—undermines stakeholders' expectations about, satisfaction with, and commitment to international arbitration.[18] This lack of clarity also hamstrings the parties' ability to weigh the value of arbitration and promotes troubling incentives for parties deciding on procedural tactics.[19]

Cost awards further implicate other aspects of ITA's integrity, including its effects on economically disadvantaged stakeholders, like smaller investors and developing

[13] One study using time-bound data identified, upon adjustment for inflation to 2018 levels, the average cost of investors' counsel was roughly USD5.7 million and respondents' counsel was USD4.7 million. For cases containing complete costs data for both parties' legal teams, the average inflation-adjusted total cost of counsel was roughly USD10.7 million. Likewise, the total cost of tribunal, institutional, and administrative expenses were just under USD1 million in inflation-adjusted terms. See Franck (n 5) 202–11. In 2018, Commission and Molo identified: the average cost of investor counsel was around USD6 million, the cost of respondent counsel was around USD4.6–5.2 million, and tribunal and administrative costs were roughly USD1 million. Jeffrey Commission and Rahim Moloo, *Procedural Issues in International Investment Arbitration* (OUP 2018) 186–91; Jeffery Commission, '2018 ICSID Awards: Year in Review', Burford Capital (14 January 2020) <www.burfordcapital.com/insights/insights-container/2018-icsid-awards-year-in-review/>. In 2017, Hodgson and Campbell identified the average cost of investor counsel was around USD6 million, state counsel was around USD4.9 million, and tribunal expenses were less than USD1 million. Matthew Hodgson and Alastair Campbell, 'Damages and Costs in Investment Treaty Arbitration Revisited' *Global Arbitration Review* (14 December 2017) <https://globalarbitrationreview.com/article/damages-and-costs-in-investment-treaty-arbitration-revisited>; Matthew Hodgson and others, '2021 Empirical Study: Costs, Damages and Duration in Investor-State Arbitration', British Institute of International and Comparative Law (June 2021) <www.biicl.org/documents/136_isds-costs-damages-duration.pdf>.

[14] Franck (n 5) 202–08, fig 6.1.

[15] ibid 208–11, 299–302.

[16] See generally ibid (compiling sources); Diana Rosert, 'The Stakes Are High: A Review of the Financial Costs of Investment Treaty Arbitration', International Institute of Sustainable Development (July 2014) <www.iisd.org/system/files/publications/stakes-are-high-review-financial-costs-investment-treaty-arbitration.pdf> 14.

[17] See generally Franck (n 5); Stephan Schill, 'Arbitration Risk and Effective Compliance: Cost-Shifting in Investment Treaty Arbitration' (2006) 7 Journal of World Investment and Trade 653, 656, 658 n 28.

[18] Franck (n 5); Ank A Santens, 'Costs in International Arbitration: A Plea for a Debate on Early Guidance by the Arbitral Tribunal on the Principles It Will Apply When Deciding on Costs' (*Kluwer Arbitration Blog*, 10 June 2009) <http://arbitrationblog.kluwerarbitration.com/2009/06/10/costs-in-international-arbitration-a-plea-for-a-debate-on-early-guidance-by-the-arbitral-tribunal-on-the-principles-it-will-apply-when-deciding-on-costs/>; John Y Gotanda, 'Consistently Inconsistent: The Need for Predictability in Awarding Costs and Fees in Investment Treaty Arbitration' (2013) 28 ICSID Review 420, 421.

[19] Cost considerations are a driving factor at every stage of arbitration, especially when parties assess the utility of arbitration against other forms of dispute resolution. See, eg, Michael Erdle, 'Costs in International Arbitration: What's "Reasonable?"', *Slaw* (9 June 2021) <www.slaw.ca/2021/06/09/costs-in-international-arbitration-whats-reasonable/>; Susan Franck, 'The Fundamentals of Arbitration', *Oxford Research Encyclopedia* (19 November 2020) <https://doi.org/10.1093/acrefore/9780190625979.013.369>.

states. From an investor's perspective, smaller commercial ventures with limited resources and lower value claims may be unable to access justice, even with cognizable claims.[20] From a state's perspective, cost issues can create perverse incentives. On the one hand, potentially problematic state conduct could go unscrutinized—and more generally, states could become incentivized to be less mindful of investor rights—if potential claimants decline for economic reasons to file ITA claims.[21] On the other hand, countries with limited public resources could face a *Sophie's Choice* of denying their citizens basic resources, raising taxes to pay for arbitration costs, or failing to comply with their international legal obligations.[22]

ITA, both in procedure and substance, should demonstrate legal rigor, rather than irrationality, inconsistency, or abuse of discretion.[23] Precision and predictability aid better expectations management, encourage realistic views about possible outcomes, and minimize unfair surprises.[24] As different arbitration costs involve risks of fiscal exposure that have quite distinct magnitudes, cost reforms should address concerns in a nuanced manner, reflect norms about access to justice and equality of arms, and support procedural (and often substantive) legitimacy.[25]

III. The Definitions and Doctrine of Cost Awards

Given the heterogeneity of legal cultures and applicable law, 'costs' can mean different things to different stakeholders.[26] Rather than engaging in crosstalk, this section first identifies definitions of costs that have been adopted in the cost awards of ITA tribunals. It then presents an outline of the law applicable to cost assessments, provides an

[20] Katia Fach Gómez and Catharine Titi, 'Facilitating Access to Investor-State Dispute Settlement for Small and Medium-Sized Enterprises: Tracing the Path Forward' (2023) 34 (7) European Business Law Review 1039; Tom Fecak, *International Investment Agreements and EU Law* (Kluwer Law International 2016) 115; Kristen E Boon, 'Investment Treaty Arbitration: Making a Place for Small Claims' (2018) 19 Journal of World Investment & Trade 667, 668; Alexander Gebert, 'Legal Protection for Small and Medium-Sized Enterprises through Investor-State Dispute Settlement: Status Quo, Impediments, and Potential Solutions' in Thilo Rensmann (ed), *Small and Medium-Sized Enterprises in International Economic Law* (OUP 2017) 292.

[21] Franck (n 5) 232; David Smith, 'Shifting Sands: Cost-and-Fee Allocations in International Investment Arbitration' (2011) 41 Virginia Journal of International Law 749, 775.

[22] Hena Schommer, 'Environmental Standards in US Free Trade Agreements: Lessons from Chapter 11' (2007) 8 Sustainable Development Law and Policy 36, 36; Joshua B Simmons, 'Validation in Investor-State Arbitration: Towards a More Exact Science' (2012) 30 Berkeley Journal of International Law 196, 196; Nicholas Bouchardie and others, 'Focus on Costs in International Arbitration, *Lexology* (30 October 2009) <www.lexology.com/library/detail.aspx?g=5663aa4f-ea22-4ba1-9967-77500a8fbedf> ('costs often undermine the efficiency of investment arbitration proceedings').

[23] See generally Daniel Kahneman, Olivier Sibony, and Cass R Sunstein, *Noise: A Flaw in Human Judgment* (Little, Brown Spark, Hachette Book Group 2021) (discussing the impact of bias (ie skew) and 'noise' (ie an overly broad scope of variability) on various legal decisions).

[24] Susan Franck, 'Considering Recalibration of International Investment Agreements: Empirical Insights' in Jose E Alvarez and others (eds), *The Evolving International Investment Regime: Expectations, Realities, Options* (OUP 2011) 75.

[25] Franck (n 5) 182; Ronald J Allen, 'How to Think about Errors, Costs, and Their Allocations' (2012) 64 Florida Law Review 885.

[26] There has been a tremendous focus on how 'costs' (and cost awards) affect the legitimacy of ITA. See UNCTAD, 'Recent Developments in the IIA Regime: Accelerating IIA Reform', IIA Issues Note (August 2021) <https://unctad.org/system/files/official-document/diaepcbinf2021d6_en.pdf> (citing ongoing concerns surrounding cost reduction and the promotion of transparency); see also 2015 *Arbitration Survey* (n 12) 2, 5; Santens (n 18).

evaluation of the ratio of cost awards, and proffers a conceptual framework to understand cost awards and their implications.

A. Defining ITA Costs

A cost award is a tribunal's dispositive decision resolving the treatment of core ITA costs. Such awards include written determinations identifying the *quantity* of party and/or tribunal costs, the applicable *law and standards* for cost assessment, and the *allocation, shifting, or splitting* of ITA costs. This section focuses on both unquantifiable and quantifiable transactional costs that create tangible fiscal and reputational exposure for the parties, as an explanation of 'true costs' likely includes both fiscal and non-fiscal elements.[27]

Certain ITA costs are unquantifiable. For example, international investment disputes derive from treaties and generate unique social and political considerations and expenses. Such costs may include public funds spent on ITA and social and regulatory costs deriving from uncertainty. Likewise, political costs can arise from defending claims in the public eye and from sacrificing sovereignty or raising domestic taxes to cover ITA costs (including impact upon civil society and national harmony). Other elements could include the opportunity cost of committing resources to ITA that would otherwise be allocated elsewhere and reputational costs (including those that impact the credit rating of sovereign debt or influence foreign investment decisions within a country). While difficult to quantify, these costs are non-trivial and have downstream consequences.

In contrast, other ITA costs are traceable and tangible. These transactional costs—namely, costs relating to lawyers, experts, arbitrators, institutions, and derivative expenses—are easier to quantify, measure, and analyse given their fiscal nature.[28] Two critical categories of costs include parties' legal costs (PLC) and tribunal and institutional administrative expenses (TCE). If 'the worst thing a client can ever be is surprised',[29] precision in cost assessments aids expectation management, encourages realistic views on potential outcomes, and minimizes unfair surprise.

PLC involves the cost of retaining lawyers to pursue adjudication, including costs of each party's legal counsel, counsel's administrative fees (data storage, document processing, expert witnesses, translations, travel, etc), and other expenses of party advocacy.[30] PLC costs are unavoidable.

[27] Finding a reliable, clear, and scientifically sound ex ante way to measure non-fiscal costs is challenging and the remainder of this chapter focuses on reforms addressing quantifiable, fiscal costs.

[28] Susan Franck, 'Rationalizing Costs in Investment Treaty Arbitration' (2011) 88 Washington University Law Review 769, 782–83; Franck (n 5) ch 4. It is nevertheless possible that some direct costs, particularly from counsel, remain unquantified, as firms may choose to underbill (by either writing off accrued time or redirecting costs to non-client accounts, like business development) or overbilling, which in some jurisdictions is a violation of counsel's ethical obligations.

[29] See Franck (n 24) (referring to observations by Sherry Williams).

[30] John Gotanda, 'Awarding Costs and Attorneys' Fees in International Commercial Arbitration' (1999) 21 Michigan Journal of International Law 1, 9–10; Franck (n 5), Companion Website, Codebook <https://global.oup.com/booksites/content/9780190054434/> (*OUP Codebook*) (defining PLC as 'costs incurred by either a Claimant

TCE represents the broad set of ITA administrative costs.[31] It includes administrative charges (whether by an arbitral institution or organization hosting or administering the arbitration), arbitrators' fees and expenses, costs for tribunal-appointed experts, fees of the tribunal secretaries (if any), and other arbitrator-related expenses (ie hotels and flights).[32] These costs are of a smaller order of magnitude than other costs,[33] triggering different normative concerns. With no state entity or transnational body picking up the tab, TCE costs are also inevitable.

B. The Applicable Law of Costs

Unlike public international law disputes where states generally pay their own way, ITA exhibits more variability.[34] The core ITA costs (PLC and TCE) have distinct doctrinal rules[35] and are of materially different financial magnitude.[36] This section offers a brief overview of the primary sources of applicable law in ITA that should (and must) influence tribunals' analysis and cost awards: investment treaty language, party agreement, and institutional or ad hoc (ie UNCITRAL) arbitral rules.[37]

Treaties are the first source of law governing cost awards—eg, by stating how the tribunal must apportion costs or listing elements tribunals must consider.[38] Unfortunately, few investment treaties offer guidance on cost assessments[39] and many fail to address costs altogether.[40]

in bringing a claim or a Respondent in defending a claim. PLC might include, for example, (1) attorney fees, (2) expert and consultant fees, (3) travel expenses, and (4) administrative expenses').

[31] See nn 14 and 21.

[32] Micha Bühler, 'Awarding Costs in International Commercial Arbitration: An Overview' (2004) 22 ASA Bulletin 249, 249; see also *OUP Codebook* (n 30) (defining TCE as 'costs incurred by the tribunal and the arbitral institution (if any) in adjudicating the claims and arguments made by the parties. TCE might include, for example, (1) tribunal's fees, (2) the tribunal's travel expenses, (3) the costs of experts consulted by the tribunal, (4) the costs of hearing rooms and transcripts, and (5) the administrative expenses of the institution').

[33] See nn 14 and 21.

[34] See eg Statute of the International Court of Justice (ICJ Statute) art 64 ('Unless otherwise decided by the Court, each party shall bear its own costs'); Chester Brown, *A Common Law of International Adjudication* (OUP 2007) 193–95, 216–20; Marc L Busch and others, 'Does Legal Capacity Matter? A Survey of WTO Members' (2009) 8 World Trade Review 559, 570–71; Christine Sim, 'Security for Costs in Investor–State Arbitration' (2017) 33 Arbitration International 427, 431–32 (outlining the 'classic view' of public international law dispute resolution is that parties bear equal costs).

[35] Arbitration Rules of the Commission on International Trade Law (UNCITRAL) (1976) art 40(1)–(2) (providing that procedural costs are 'borne by the unsuccessful party', but for legal costs, the tribunal is 'free to determine which party shall bear such costs or may apportion such costs between the parties if it determines that apportionment is reasonable'); UNCITRAL Arbitration (2010) arts 40, 42.

[36] PLC is comparatively larger than TCE. See nn 14–16; Franck (n 5) 202–11.

[37] Franck (n 5) 193–99.

[38] Some investment treaties, particularly involving Eastern European countries, used the 'pay your own way' approach, akin to cost allocation in public international law. See eg Netherlands–Poland bilateral investment treaty (BIT) (1992) art 12(9) ('Each Party shall bear the cost of the arbitrator appointed by itself and its representation. The cost of the chairman as well as the other costs will be borne in equal parts by the Parties'); Czech Republic–Albania BIT (1994) art 9(5); Bulgaria–Hungary BIT (1994) art 8(6); cf ICJ Statute art 64 (outlining how parties before the ICJ each bear their own respective costs).

[39] Schill (n 17) 658 n 28 (noting that investment treaties 'only occasionally ... expressly address the allocation of costs in investor-state disputes').

[40] See generally United Nations Convention on the Recognition and Enforcement of Foreign Arbitral Awards, June 10, 1958, 21 UST 2518, 330 UNTS 3 (establishing grounds to enforce arbitration awards (or contest

In contrast, the negotiators of the ICSID Convention debated costs throughout their drafting in the 1960s, exploring how to allocate costs most effectively.[41] An early draft required that all parties would pay their own way for both PLC and TCE, subject only to cost-shifting for bad-faith or frivolous dispute settlement.[42] There was, however, a material debate on the standards for allocating costs. The Austrian delegate, Ms Villgrattner, pushed to impose the opposite default, using a 'loser pays' rule often associated with civil law systems.[43] A Brazilian delegate suggested an amendment to 'loser pays' rules, but only for TCE.[44] Both proposals were rejected. After Ms Villgrattner amended her proposal to provide for broad tribunal flexibility, this standard was accepted.[45] By failing to take a stand on costs or otherwise offer guidance, the ICSID Convention left a void ripe for arbitrator discretion.[46]

The second source of applicable law is party agreement, which derives from a fundamental principle of international arbitration: consent. If parties in a live dispute reach an express agreement ex post about how to resolve costs, that agreement controls. Unfortunately, there is little evidence that agreements of this nature exist.

The third source of legal guidance for tribunals making cost awards comes from the implied agreement of the parties, namely the applicable arbitration rules. Investment

enforcement) without substantive cost guidance). See also C Mark Baker and Denton Nichols, *International Arbitration Report: Issue 16* (June 2021) 21.

[41] See Susan Franck, 'Reforming World Bank Dispute Resolution: ICSID in Context' (2023) 44 Michigan Journal of International Law 349 (discussing ICSID Convention history and the importance of its travaux); Sergio Puig, 'Emergence & Dynamism in International Organizations: ICSID, Investor-State Arbitration & International Investment Law' (2013) 44 Georgetown Journal of International Law 531.

[42] Multiple conversations on costs surrounded administrative support to finance ICSID infrastructure (rather than costs of a specific case). ICSID, *Convention on the Settlement of Investment Disputes between States and Nationals of Other States: Documents Concerning the Origin and the Formation of that Convention*, vol II (World Bank 1968) pt 1, documents, 175–76, 254–55. An earlier version of the ICSID Convention provided specific rules on cost-shifting. Namely, '[e]xcept as otherwise agreed by the parties, each party . . . shall bear its own expenses, and any fees and expenses of the Center . . . and arbitrators shall be divided between and borne equally by the parties; provided, however, that if . . . [an] Arbitral Tribunal determines that a party has instituted the proceedings frivolously or in bad faith, it may assess any part or all of such fees and expenses against that party.' ibid 166–67, 225; see also 43–44, 177.

[43] Ms Villgrattner initially suggested an amendment where 'the losing party should always bear the entire coste [*sic*] and expenses' with some flexibility for partial party success, ibid 873. Ms Villgrattner was the Austrian delegate and one of only three women involved in negotiating the ICSID Convention. Franck (n 41) 370 n 106.

[44] The Brazilian delegation made what Broches deemed an 'intermediate' proposal. First, it suggested making a distinction between PLC and TCE, which was supported by Japan. Brazil then also recommended that parties pay their own PLC irrespective of the outcome (ibid).

[45] Ms Villgrattner revised her amendment to focus on permitting the tribunal 'to make the decision with respect to costs as it [s]aw fit except where the parties had otherwise [a]greed' (ibid). Broches then confirmed 'the amended Austrian proposal appeared to enjoy the largest acceptance and that the Article would therefore be amended accordingly' (ibid). Ms Villgrattner subsequently confirmed that costs 'would fall under the provisions of Article 57 dealing with enforcement' (ibid).

[46] The ICSID Convention, Chapter V (arts 59–61), technically discusses costs. The relevant provisions only require tribunals to assess costs and that assessment becomes part of the award. There is no guidance about how, when, or why such power should be exercised. See ICSID Convention art 61(2) ('In the case of arbitration proceedings the Tribunal shall, except as the parties otherwise agree, assess the expenses incurred by the parties in connection with the proceedings, and shall decide how and by whom those expenses, the fees and expenses of the members of the Tribunal and the charges for the use of the facilities of the Centre shall be paid. Such decision shall form part of the award'); see also Christoph Schreuer and others, *The ICSID Convention: A Commentary* (2nd edn, CUP 2009) 1222–26, 1229, 1236 (describing ICSID cost-shifting practices as 'neither clear nor uniform' and discussing doctrine) ibid 112 (discussing the Convention's legislative history on costs); Lester Nurick, 'Costs in International Arbitration' (1992) 7 ICSID Review 57, 59–60 (same).

treaties often offer investors choices about where to initiate ITA, including at ICSID, other arbitral institutions, or through an ad hoc proceedings using the UNCITRAL Rules.[47] Once investors select an option from the applicable treaty, the venue's rules become implied terms of the parties' agreement. As such, the provisions on costs in the applicable institutional rules (eg ICSID, UNCITRAL, SCC, ICC, LCIA, ICDR)[48] provide invaluable structure for cost awards. The vacuum of guidance on costs and cost assessments has left these rules as the primary source of legal authority for tribunals and parties.[49]

C. The Ratio of Cost Awards

A clear definition of costs and legal standards to direct cost assessments is a constructive starting place for understanding the financial risks related to costs. The more profound challenge, however, is understanding *why* tribunals make their decisions about costs—even if their justifications are somewhat superficial.

There is a perplexing puzzle regarding the justification of cost awards in ITA. A content analysis of 272 ITA awards revealed that tribunals consistently failed to bolster their decisions with legal authority and have offered minimal legal reasoning to support their conclusions.[50] This pattern held regardless of whether the costs were PLC or TCE.

For PLC, 88 final awards (and twelve non-final awards) relied on legal authority, leaving 172 awards—or 63 per cent of the analysed awards—without *any* legal authority to justify the conclusion.[51] Tribunals were better at explaining themselves than providing legal authority, with roughly two-thirds of awards (135 final awards and 55 non-final awards) providing some rationale for PLC determinations. However, approximately 30 per cent of awards did not explain their PLC decisions.[52] See Table 4.1.

[47] Some treaties only offer investors one option, like arbitration at ICSID or an ad hoc venue. Other treaties offer investors multiple venues to commence arbitration. While historically these focused on the ICSID, ICC, SCC, or ad hoc proceedings, this has begun expanding to other venues. See, eg, Todd Allee and Clint Peinhardt, 'Delegating Differences: Bilateral Investment Treaties and Bargaining over Dispute Resolution Provisions' (2010) 54 International Studies Quarterly 1; Joachim Pohl, Kekeletso Mashigo, and Alexis Nohen, 'Dispute Settlement Provisions in International Investment Agreements: A Large Sample Survey', OECD Working Papers on International Investment 2012/02 (2012) <http://dx.doi.org/10.1787/5k8xb71nf628-en> (last visited 20 June 2022); Jason W Yackee, 'Do Bilateral Investment Treaties Promote Foreign Investment: Hints from Alternative Evidence' (2010) 51 Virginia Journal of International Law 397.

[48] See Franck (n 5) 194–97 (describing how institutional rules provide the doctrine for cost allocation); see also nn 92–107.

[49] In ICSID Convention cases, the applicable investment treaty and Convention contain the applicable law. The New York Convention and the ICSID Additional Facility Rules incorporate domestic arbitration laws of the place of arbitration (and places of enforcement) (see n 8). In theory, the law from the place of arbitration could provide guidance for cost awards. A lack of national legislation on cost-shifting undermines the value of the theory, as there is still minimal (if any) direction from national law.

[50] Franck (n 5) 233–37.

[51] ibid 234–35. Although statistical tests suggested more recent cases were more likely to use authority to justify cost decisions, this improvement was arguably a function of the poor quality of the oldest cost awards, which tended to cite to nothing (ibid 248–50).

[52] ibid 234–35.

Table 4.1 Frequency of tribunal use of legal authority and rationale to explain both PLC and TCE decisions in awards ($n = 272$)

	PLC[1]	TCE[2]
Legal authority provided	37% (n = 100 awards)	39% (n = 105 awards)
Provided reasoning to justify decision	70% (n = 190 awards)	71% (n = 194 awards)

[1] See Susan Franck, *Arbitration Costs: Myths and Realities in Investment Treaty Arbitration* (OUP 2019) 234–35, fig 7.1 and table 7.1 (providing information on legal authority and rationale for PLC decisions); see also ibid 238, table 7.3 (discussing types of authorities used to make PLC decisions).

[2] See ibid 236, table 7.2 (providing information on legal authority and rationale for TCE decisions).

The pattern of explanation gaps—both for authority and rationale—was similar for TCE decisions. When justifying their own costs and expenses, and despite materials being readily available, 61 per cent of awards provided no legal authority.[53] Tribunals were better at delivering some facial reasoning for their choices by some explanation justifying their TCE decisions. This time, only 29 per cent of awards failed to explain the tribunal's allocation of its own expenses.[54]

Although an important proportion of cost awards failed to include adequate reasoning, one positive aspect was that roughly two-thirds of awards tried to explain the logic underpinning the PLC and TCE decisions. However, the justifications tribunals used varied considerably. They included factors such as parties' relative success on various issues, procedural misconduct, the complexity and novelty of the legal issues in dispute, the gravity of any breaches by the municipal laws of the state, the proportionality of incurred costs, and institutional concerns about equity.[55] In contrast, it was rare to see tribunals reference concepts like party equality of arms, public interest considerations, or party settlement efforts.[56]

D. Cost Awards: A Conceptual Frame

The quantitative gaps in explanation of cost assessments are fundamental. Unlike dispositive decisions on jurisdiction, merits, or damage—cost awards are not a 'one and done' matter. Instead, costs arise throughout a proceeding and cost decisions can be made at multiple junctures.[57]

[53] ibid 236.
[54] ibid.
[55] ibid 239–43, 246–47.
[56] ibid.
[57] Costs and cost management could be addressed in the initial procedural order. See generally Franck (n 19); Franck (n 5). Given limited availability of procedural orders, little is known about how often this technique is used. See generally Sebastian Puerta and Tim R Samples, 'Investment Law's Transparency Gap' (2022) 55 Cornell International Law Journal 9.

Tackling costs sooner rather than later is sensible, as Benjamin Franklin's 'Advice to a Young Tradesman'—that 'time is money'[58] —is justified empirically. In ITA, data demonstrates that as case length increases, so does cost; as case length decreases, so too do case costs.[59] This point is fundamental as case length was the *only* reliable variable associated with cost increases or decreases.

Unfortunately, data reflects that while over 95 per cent of final awards included cost determinations, only 8 per cent of non-final awards on other dispositive matters contained a dispositive decision on costs.[60] Given the material fiscal consequences, one can imagine stakeholders' latent (and justified) irritation after learning about the factors affecting a tribunal's costs determination at a late stage, when it is no longer possible to adapt party behaviour.

The 'noise' (ie broad scope of variability)[61] in the treatment of costs is regrettable, particularly when disconnected from legal standards, and impacts the efficiency, predictability, value, and coherence of a single aspect of ITA that involved (using 2018-inflation adjusted data) roughly USD11 million for every case. It is also likely why one commentator quipped that, '[i]f Tolstoy had been an international arbitration lawyer, he might have said that "efficient proceedings are all alike; every inefficient proceeding is inefficient in its own way"'.[62]

Without a tribunal that offers advance guidance on the applicable law and standards of costs, cost awards will continue to be inefficient, unpredictable, and confusing.

IV. Reform of Cost Awards

Costs are central to the debate about ITA's future.[63] This section explores options within ITA's existing framework for implementing targeted reforms. It first focuses on opportunities to reform international investment treaties directly. Then, it focuses on ICSID's recent reforms and offers some comparisons to the rules and practices of other institutions. Finally, it considers how national law could serve as a resource to nudge stakeholders addressing costs in ITA awards.

[58] Benjamin Franklin, 'Advice to a Young Tradesman' (1748), reprinted in *The Oxford Dictionary of Quotations* (3rd edn, OUP 1979) 218.

[59] All analyses revealed a strong, reliable, and positive relationship between case length and different ITA costs. As case length increased, so did ITA costs; and as case length decreased, so too did costs. See generally Franck (n 5) 136–40.

[60] ibid 200–02.

[61] See Kahneman, Sibony, and Sunstein (n 23).

[62] Anthony Sinclair and Sarah Macrory, 'ICSID Arbitration: How Long Does It Take?' (2009) 4 Global Arbitration Review 4.

[63] Whether debates involve relative costs of arbitration as opposed to other forms of dispute settlement, consideration of forming a permanent court to help contain 'costs' in the more general sense, or active debates about reforming ICSID and other institutional rules, costs remain contentious. See Malcolm Langford and others, 'Special Issue: UNCITRAL and Investment Arbitration Reform: Matching Concerns and Solutions—An Introduction' (2020) 21 Journal of World Investment & Trade 167, 173 (explaining that procedural reforms will have 'substantive implications' such that a space is created to more easily discuss and enact changes to the substantive provisions of investment treaties). See also Gabriel Bottini and others, 'Excessive Costs and Recoverability of Costs Awards in Investment Arbitration' (2020) 21 Journal of World Investment & Trade 251.

A. Reforming Investment Treaties

While factors impacting treaty negotiations are numerous and complex, investment treaties provide unique opportunities for cost-related reform. Many bilateral and multilateral investment treaties include 'sunset' clauses for potential treaty termination.[64] These clauses create a natural inflection point for considering new treaty innovations.[65]

At present, treaties vary in how they manage issues of costs, including cost allocation and cost-shifting. The first approach taken is to omit any language related to costs.[66] This approach seems simple, as it eliminates conflict that may arise in negotiating cost matters when disputes are only a theoretical possibility and have not yet crystallized. However, there are negative externalities in failing to address costs at this stage as parties later find themselves without clear guidance when they plan for dispute management, allocate internal budgets, and argue about costs in an arbitral proceeding; and arbitrators similarly lack guidance to decide cost matters.

The second approach to costs involves specifying in the treaty how costs will be allocated, usually by stipulating that each party will bear its own costs, with the shared costs split equally between the parties.[67] Under this method, arbitrators have little trouble allocating costs during or after an arbitration, but there is little to no room for case-by-case flexibility.

Over time, the need for reform has persisted as treaties have failed to provide sufficient guidance to transparently resolve cost issues while still allowing for flexibility in cases where concerns about fairness would be triggered. Given the challenges inherent in reforming treaties, the remainder of this section contemplates alternatives for clear guidance, namely reform of institutional rules and national arbitration laws.

B. Institutional Rules and Reform

Unlike investment treaties, institutional rules present a streamlined source of applicable law ripe for reform. As ICSID is central to ITA, this section focuses primarily on ICSID's history and recent rule amendments while comparing the approaches of other institutions.

[64] See Jarrod Hepburn, 'Domestic Investment Statutes in International Law' (2018) 112 American Journal of International Law 658, 685 ('In general, investment treaties permit unilateral termination with prior notice, subject to a "sunset" period of continued effect for a specified number of years, often ten'); Frederic G Sourgens, 'Keep the Faith: Investment Protection Following the Denunciation of International Investment Agreements' (2013) 11 Santa Clara Journal of International Law 335, 376.

[65] Investment treaty negotiations involve multiple stakeholders and divergent interests. With much at stake and complicated political dynamics, costs receive short shrift at the negotiating table. Nevertheless, when renegotiating treaties, states should seize the opportunity to provide cost reform, as a basic form of risk management.

[66] Schill (n 17).

[67] See n 38 and accompanying text.

1. ICSID: History of Cost Rules

ICSID's first set of Rules was enacted in 1968, with the original *Brown Book* (named for its brown cover) providing insights about interpretation and application.[68] Although the cost rule (then Rule 27) contained some general direction, the *Brown Book*'s notes provided minimal clarity on cost assessments.[69]

ICSID later added the Additional Facility and Fact Finding in 1978 to provide stakeholders additional services and minor rule revisions. Later, in the 1985 'Official Documents', the substance of the cost rules moved to Rule 28, but the content remained the same. Namely, the rules failed to provide guidance about allocation of costs in the absence of party agreement.[70] Other ICSID reforms, including the 2006 revisions to the Arbitration Rules, made more material advancements but did not revise the cost provisions.[71]

Put differently, for over fifty years, the ICSID arbitration rules provided no clear guidance on costs, merely stating: '[T]he Tribunal may, unless otherwise agreed by the parties, decide: (a) at any stage of the proceeding, the portion which each party shall pay . . . (b) with respect to any part of the proceeding, that the related costs . . . shall be borne entirely or in a particular share by one of the parties'.[72] The broad generality meant tribunals would have virtually unfettered discretion.[73]

2. ICSID Costs Reform

The most recent reform to the ICSID Arbitration Rules started in October 2016. After nearly six years—with multiple working papers that were drafted, reviewed, debated, and edited following extensive public consultation—new rules came into effect on 1 July 2022.[74] This time: costs-related reform was central to ICSID's revision process.

One general category of revisions involved streamlining procedures for systemic efficiency. The focus on 'saving costs along the way' materialized in several rules seeking to decrease case length and minimize costs. These measures included mandating one case management conference, streamlining timetables (including the table applicable

[68] ICSID, 'ICSID Regulations and Rules', Doc ICSID/4/Rev.1 (1975) <https://icsid.worldbank.org/sites/default/files/ICSID%20Regulations%20and%20Rules%201968%20-%20ENG.pdf> (hereinafter *Brown Book*).

[69] ibid 96–97. The *Brown Book* cross-references other provisions addressing costs, discussing costs of witness and site visitations. The most relevant guidance notes that tribunals, 'may decide to charge one party (always without prejudice to the ultimate disposition, pursuant to Article 61(2) of the Convention, of the cost of the proceeding) with all or a major share of the cost of a particular part of the proceeding' ibid 97. It failed to discuss providing reasons for cost decisions.

[70] ICSID Arbitration Rules (1985) rr 28 and 47(1)(j).

[71] The text of arts 28 and 47(1)(j) was identical.

[72] *Brown Book* (n 68) r 27; ICSID Arbitration Rules r 28. ICSID's Additional Facility Rules were similarly vague. See ICSID Additional Facility Rules art 59 ('Unless the parties otherwise agree, the Tribunal shall decide how and by whom the fees and expenses of the members of the Tribunal, the expenses and charges of the Secretariat and the expenses incurred by the parties in connection with the proceeding shall be borne').

[73] See ICSID, 'Cost Submissions—ICSID Convention' <https://icsid.worldbank.org/services/arbitration/convention/process/cost-submissions> (using pre-2022 ICSID Rules to note a tribunal has 'broad discretion to allocate costs between the parties in the final award. It may allocate costs with regard to the proceeding as a whole or with regard to a particular part of the proceeding. Its decision in the award becomes binding and enforceable').

[74] ICSID, 'ICSID Rules and Regulations Amendment' <https://icsid.worldbank.org/resources/rules-amendments>.

to arbitrator appointment), promoting consolidation, aiding bifurcation, and providing award deadlines.[75] To offer a conduit for channelling disputes towards appropriate (and cost-effective) dispute resolution, ICSID also established new mediation and expedited arbitration rules.[76]

Those general changes notwithstanding, the most material change on costs involved revising two core provisions: one concerning standards and obligations for cost allocation (Rule 52) and another on award content (Rule 59). While some elements may reflect aspects of existing ICSID practice, the textual guidance alters how tribunals will address cost matters. Rather than surrendering to the legal vacuum, the new rules structure arbitral discretion to enhance precision and clarity.

First, ICSID's arbitration rules—for the first time in its history—provide factors to constrain and guide tribunal discretion on costs. Expressly permitting tribunals to make cost assessments 'at any time',[77] the new rules offer a standard for the four variables tribunals *must* consider, namely:

> In allocating the costs of the proceeding, the tribunal shall consider all relevant circumstances, including:
> (a) the outcome of the proceeding or any part of it;
> (b) the conduct of the parties during the proceeding, including the extent to which they acted in an expeditious and cost-effective manner and complied with these Rules and the orders and decisions of the tribunal;
> (c) the complexity of the issues; and
> (d) the reasonableness of the costs claimed.[78]

By including specific factors alongside the invitation to the tribunal to consider 'all relevant circumstances', ICSID balanced the need for flexibility with the goals of clarity and transparency.[79] As a result, this framework enables parties and tribunal members to appreciate costs more fully and accurately, provide early cost guidance, and incentivize desirable behaviour.[80]

In contrast to the old rules, the 2022 rules create an affirmative obligation that 'all decisions on costs are reasoned'.[81] This rationale requirement represents a core advance given the empirical data that demonstrates the previous widespread failure to cite authority or explain multi-million-dollar cost decisions.

[75] ICSID Arbitration Rules (2022) rr 10–12, 15–21, 31, 42–46, 58.
[76] ICSID, 'ICSID Releases 2022 Versions of Its Rules and Regulations' (22 June 2022) <https://icsid.worldbank.org/news-and-events/communiques/icsid-releases-2022-versions-its-rules-and-regulations>.
[77] ICSID Arbitration Rules (2022) r 52(3).
[78] ibid r 52(1). Cost allocations are slightly different for some preliminary objections. When tribunals render an award determining a claim is 'manifestly without legal merit', the default is that tribunals 'shall award the prevailing party its reasonable costs, unless the Tribunal determines that there are special circumstances justifying a different allocation of costs' ibid r 52(2).
[79] ICSID replicated the cost rules for Additional Facility arbitration. ICSID Additional Facility Arbitration Rules (2022) r 62(1), (3).
[80] See Smith (n 21) 776; Franck (n 5).
[81] ICSID Arbitration Rules (2022) r 52(4); ICSID Additional Facility Arbitration Rules (2022) r 62(4).

The second core rule change involves the required elements of an ICSID award. Rule 59 lists the features an award must possess and mirrors Rule 52's obligation to provide reasoned cost decisions. While the requirement that a final award must include a cost determination is not new, Rule 59 now requires 'a statement of the costs of the proceeding, including the fees and expenses of each member of the Tribunal'.[82] These changes neatly achieve two goals—parties gain greater insight into the contributions of each arbitrator and tribunals must provide 'reasoned' cost decisions, presumably using legal authority and reasoning.

Because Rule 50 defines the 'cost of the proceedings' to include both PLC and TCE,[83] the new rule *requires* tribunals to provide fiscal information on counsel's expenses. This requirement is subtle but transformative, as many arbitral tribunals have skipped providing detailed fiscal information on PLC or the tribunal member's own respective costs.[84] Moreover, transparently offering financial information in an award enables accurate empirical research and aids stakeholders in making realistic risk assessments.

ICSID awards historically provided some information on fiscal tribunal costs or a numerical proportion for costs. The amount was often a lump sum. By combining fees from three people into one expense, it was impossible to identify which arbitrator was responsible for which portion of the overall cost. As anonymity and lack of scrutiny can incentivize error and imprecision, focusing on individual conduct is vital. For costs, transparency has a unique power to foster rigor, honesty, and billing accuracy. As arbitrators have their fees readily available and can easily provide a brief sentence, the benefit[85] outweighs the light burden of providing real fiscal data.

For tribunals subjected to academic or public scrutiny, it becomes possible to make a detailed assessment of the efforts of the tribunal as a whole as well as enhancing the capacity to scrutinize conduct of individual arbitrators. A simple comparison can demonstrate the value of offering this clarity. Consider *Ping Ahn* and *Ansung Housing*.[86] In 2015, the *Ping Ahn* tribunal concluded, that '[p]arties shall bear equally the fees and expenses of the members of the tribunal and the charges of the Centre' without providing any information on tribunal fees (either as a composite or on an individual basis).[87] *Ansung Housing*, by contrast, contained detailed financial information about TCE, with the Chair (Albert Jan van den Berg) charging roughly USD34,000, both party-appointed arbitrators (Lucy Reed and Michael Pryles) charging less than USD30,000 each, and ICSID's administrative fees totalling USD32,000.[88] The details permit a constructive comparison of the relative charges of

[82] ICSID Arbitration Rules (2022) r 59(1)(j); ICSID Additional Facility Arbitration Rules (2022) r 70(1)(j).

[83] ICSID Arbitration Rules (2022) r 50; ICSID Additional Facility Arbitration Rules (2022) r 60.

[84] See Franck (n 5) 136–40 (identifying challenges from cost awards missing fiscal data).

[85] Hiding arbitrators' charges does not promote integrity or public confidence. Instead, it risks arbitrators making outsized hourly charges or a lack of effort in exercising their arbitral mandate.

[86] Both cases involved early dismissal (r 41(5) or jurisdictional bases), included a Chinese party, and generated awards of fifty to sixty pages.

[87] *Ping An Life Ins Co of China, Ltd v Belgium*, ICSID Case No ARB/12/29, Award (30 April 2015) [240].

[88] *Ansung Housing Co, Ltd v China*, ICSID Case No ARB/14/25, Award (9 March 2017) [166]–[169].

all arbitrators.[89] Ultimately, providing specific information is more valuable than an information void.

Despite the utility of their reform, ICSID missed other opportunities to change cost dynamics constructively. For example, ICSID could have codified additional factors to incentivize constructive party behaviour. Likewise, ICSID could have differentiated how to shift different costs. As PLC and TCE have distinct doctrinal bases and orders of magnitude, providing a textual nudge to separate these costs reminds tribunals to treat different costs differently to maximize desired behaviour and manage party expectations. In situations where tribunals wish to send a light-touch signal, the ICSID Rules could have used different standards for shifting TCE given its small magnitude. Likewise, the Rules could have offered specific standards for the larger PLC element to create strong incentives. Nevertheless, ICSID's new requirement of specificity is preferable to the prior vacuum and reflects a fundamental and positive evolution.

3. Other Institutional Reforms on Costs

ICSID's attention to costs is not unique as other arbitral institutions have also focused in this area. Yet, there is variation in how such institutions amended rules to guide both costs and cost-shifting.

The International Chamber of Commerce (ICC) 2021 Arbitration Rules focused on cost containment[90] by tackling joinder, consolidation, third-party funding, and remote hearings. Lacking a material change in cost rules,[91] ICC Article 38 still permits tribunals to make cost decisions at any time, allows cost-shifting, and explains that tribunals 'may take into account such circumstances as [they] consider[] relevant, including the extent to which each party has conducted the arbitration in an expeditious and cost-effective manner'.[92] The ICC's primary substantive nudges were the soft focus on expeditiousness and cost-effectiveness,[93] with perhaps only the Singapore International Arbitration Centre (SIAC) offering less guidance for tribunal cost decisions.[94]

[89] One recent 175+ page award dismissing the case benefited from ICSID's recent transparency efforts embodied in the new rule. The chair (Lord Nicholas Phillips), who typically conducts tribunal management, charged USD227,198. One party-appointed arbitrator (Christopher Thomas) charged much less, USD158,722, which mirrored ICSID's administrative fees. The other party appointee (Horacio Grigera-Naón) charged USD205,875—representing 91 per cent of the chair's fees. There was no dissenting opinion. *Bridgestone Licensing Servs, Inc v Panama*, ICSID Case No ARB/16/35, Award (14 August 2020).

[90] See ICC, 'ICC Unveils Revised Rules of Arbitration', ICCwbo.org (10 August 2020) (suggesting the new rules will provide 'greater efficiency, flexibility[,] and transparency').

[91] See ICC, 'ICC Arbitration Rules 2017 and 2021 Compared Version', ICCwbo.org, art 38 <https://iccwbo.org/content/uploads/sites/3/2020/12/icc-2021-2017-arbitration-rules-compared-version.pdf>.

[92] ICC Arbitration Rules (2021) art 38(3)–(5).

[93] Article 38 permits a theoretical decrease of PLC, as only 'the *reasonable* legal and other costs' are part of a costs determination, presumably excluding unreasonable costs. ibid art 38(1) (emphasis added). There is no explanation of what is 'reasonable'. At the ICC, TCE is a function of amount in dispute; but the rules permit the ICC Court to impose 'a figure higher or lower' than normal fees when 'deemed necessary due to the exceptional circumstances of the case' ibid art 38(2).

[94] SIAC Arbitration Rules (2016) arts 34–37; but see ibid art 39.4 (granting tribunals power to award costs 'if a party breaches the provisions' of confidentiality rules). Compare SIAC Investment Rules (2017) arts 33–35 (failing to articulate grounds for cost assessments other than third-party funding and not explaining how funding impacts assessments); see also n 103 (noting HKIAC's focus on third-party funding).

At the other end of the spectrum, the London Court of International Arbitration (LCIA) provides detailed cost guidelines. The LCIA's 2020 revisions focused on virtual hearings, electronic communication, and e-awards rather than changing the cost provisions.[95]

The default cost rules of the LCIA remain the most detailed of the major international arbitration institutions. Beyond maintaining traditional tribunal discretion to reduce the scope of shiftable PLC,[96] LCIA tribunals must make decisions on PLC and TCE by employing 'the general principle that costs should reflect the parties' relative success and failure in the award or arbitration or under different issues', allowing for an exception only when 'it appears to the Arbitral Tribunal that in the circumstances the application of such a general principle would be inappropriate'.[97] Requiring written reasons for all cost assessments,[98] the LCIA Rules have tribunals consider 'the conduct of the parties and that of their authorized representatives in the arbitration, including any cooperation in facilitating the proceedings as to time and cost and any non-cooperation resulting in undue delay and unnecessary expense'.[99]

Other prominent institutions—like the Stockholm Chamber of Commerce (SCC)[100] and Hong Kong International Arbitration Centre (HKIAC)[101]—have approaches to costs somewhere between the practices of the ICC and LCIA. Like other institutions, their rules focus on fee reasonableness.[102] Still, they include unique aspects, like the HKIAC's reference to third-party funding[103] and the SCC's incentive for tribunals to contain their costs.[104]

Ultimately, none of the institutional rules (or the UNCITRAL Arbitration Rules)[105] provide clarity on how tribunals can exercise their adjudicative authority to assess costs or offer context as to what can be appropriate or reasonable. The institutions delineating specific factors are the most helpful in managing expectations and guiding tribunals, but the challenge remains as to how to provide predictability of application.

[95] Evgeniya Rubinina, 'The LCIA Publishes its 2020 Rules: A Light-Touch Update to Meet Modern Needs' (*Kluwer Arbitration Blog*, 13 August 2020) <http://arbitrationblog.kluwerarbitration.com/2020/08/13/the-lcia-publishes-its-2020-rules-a-light-touch-update-to-meet-modern-needs/>.

[96] Akin to ICC 'reasonableness', the LCIA focuses on an 'appropriate' PLC and requiring the tribunal 'decide the amount of such [parties'] Legal Costs on such reasonable basis as it thinks appropriate'. LCIA Arbitration Rules (2020) art 28.3; see also n 93 (discussing ICC rules for reasonable PLC).

[97] LCIA Arbitration Rules art 28.4.

[98] ibid ('Any decision on costs by the Arbitral Tribunal shall be made with reasons in the order or award containing such decision (unless it is a Consent Award)').

[99] ibid.

[100] SCC Arbitration Rules (2017) arts 49–51. The core standards motivating SCC cost-shifting involves a focus on 'the outcome of the case, each party's contribution to the efficiency and expeditiousness of the arbitration and any other relevant circumstances' (see ibid arts 49(6) TCE; 50 (PLC)).

[101] HKIAC Administered Arbitration Rules (2018) arts 34–35. The core of HKIAC's cost-shifting standard involves permitting tribunals to 'apportion all or part of the costs of the arbitration' based upon a determination of what 'is reasonable, taking into account the circumstances of the case' ibid 34.3.

[102] SCC Arbitration Rules r 50; HKIAC Arbitration Rules arts 34.1(b)–(d) and 34.2.

[103] HKIAC Arbitration Rules art 34.4.

[104] See SCC Arbitration Rules r 49.3 (determining TCE is set by whether the tribunal 'has acted in an efficient and expeditious manner, the complexity of the dispute and any other relevant circumstances').

[105] UNCITRAL Arbitration Rules' (2013) arts 40–42; see generally n 35; Catharine Titi, *The Function of Equity in International Law* (OUP 2021).

C. Potential Reform: National Law

Beyond treaty and rule reform, national arbitration laws provide an opportunity for transparency and clarity in cost awards. Unfortunately, such reform may prove challenging, as ICSID Convention cases are self-contained and restrict the applicable law to the underlying investment treaty and ICSID Convention, and national law may not apply to cost decisions in those cases.

However, not all ITA disputes operate under the ICSID Convention. For instance, ICSID Additional Facility cases and other arbitrations (whether ad hoc or institutional) may be governed by the New York Convention, where the national law from the place of arbitration plays a potential role. Beyond a psychological nudge, providing clarity on cost-shifting obligations through national law empowers states to create clear ex ante 'guide rails' for party expectations and tribunal discretion. For jurisdictions with enhanced predictability, providing national legislation that identifies clear cost-shifting rules would aid those making risk assessments about arbitration costs and the utility of dispute settlement.

V. The Implications and Challenges

Irrespective of the applicable doctrine, the question remains how arbitrators' residual discretion impacts cost awards. Even with clear ex ante legal standards, tribunals' cost awards may derive from practical politics, with arbitrators using costs as a negotiation or horse-trading tool. Alternatively, decisions may not derive from anything nefarious. Instead, in many instances cost awards simply reflect cognitive depletion by the arbitrators after wrestling for a long time with many complicated issues involving jurisdiction, merits, and quantum.

The lack of clear guidelines for cost-shifting makes concerns about cognitive depletion more pressing. Studies indicate that where arbitrators have relevant standards and applicable law to use in making determinations of this type, they will rely on such standards and produce predictable and reliable results.[106] When arbitrators' work is not governed by clear applicable law, a vacuum persists that creates a void of unfettered discretion. While it may be desirable for arbitrators to be immune to cognitive illusions, biases, and depletion—they are not. Pretending arbitrators are infallible or not subject to normal human error risks ITA's integrity and places parties and tribunals in a position to fail.

Irrespective of the applicable law, cost assessments in ITA will continue to be somewhat unpredictable and quixotic for the foreseeable future—even with ICSID's material advancements. For this reason, stakeholders should focus on the tools that they presently have in their cost management arsenals.

[106] Susan Franck and others, 'Inside the Arbitrator's Mind' (2017) 66 Emory Law Journal 1115.

Clarity and consistency in cost awards derive from applicable law, and risk will result whenever there is either a legal vacuum or uncertainty. Stakeholders should mitigate this risk whenever they can. For example, where there is a direct contractual relationship or investment contract, parties should address costs in the relevant dispute resolution clause rather than gaming costs after the fact. Likewise, states can use their 'power of the pen' to negotiate and draft cost allocation rules in international treaties or national legislation. Meanwhile, arbitration rules should continue to provide enhanced guidance and clarity as to what tribunals must do; and it should not be optional for tribunals to hide from the financial and reputational implications of the parties' conduct or their own.

While ITA does not create de jure precedent, stakeholders are interested in some predictability on costs. Without it, investors and states could flip a coin to resolve the distribution of millions of dollars in PLC and TCE. In their ruling on costs, arbitrators should provide legal authority and rationales to explain their decision-making rather than simply a general gestalt. These explanations would enable parties to understand cost decisions and allow future arbitrators to consider the insights of those who have dealt with similar considerations.

As a final reminder, tribunals and institutions are not the only entities tasked with containing costs and increasing certainty about the ultimate allocation of costs. Parties and counsel also play a fundamental role. Even with clear cost rules, parties and their lawyers often 'leave no stone unturned', which inevitably increases (rather than decreases) costs. Under these circumstances, counsel should *counsel*, helping clients make hard decisions in a world of limited resources and constrained choices. Low-cost advocacy is not possible when many people must conduct significant work to prosecute or defend claims working across multiple jurisdictions and languages. Likewise, where institutions or tribunals suggest addressing costs earlier and providing parties with guidance, lawyers should not game the system or wait until the end on the assumption they will be victorious.

Optimism, egocentrism, and bias blind spots are fundamental cognition errors that inevitably affect counsel and clients' perception of what is possible.[107] The better course is for tribunals to explore cost rules early in the case, create clear rules of engagement in a procedural order as early as possible, and then for parties and counsel to stick to those ground rules. Given what is at stake in a contentious area of international law, transparency, clarity, and the expectation management of ITA costs are fundamental to promoting proper debates, quality decision-making, and the integrity of international dispute settlement.

VI. Conclusion

One of the only certainties about costs and cost allocation in awards is their uncertainty and it is the job of the ITA community to identify opportunities for reform. Only then

[107] Franck (n 5) 33–55.

will it be possible to persuade arbitral institutions (like ICSID) to enhance their rule-making on costs, and enable tribunals, counsel, and parties likewise to be constructive on that issue.

Ultimately, the law can and must provide a framework to structure tribunal discretion and aid ex ante expectation management. Giving tribunals better guidance by encouraging clear articulations of the applicable law, incentivizing or even requiring tribunals to provide adequate analysis justifying cost awards, and ensuring that cost information is provided transparently will enable ITA to reflect rule of law values necessary to support the peaceful, non-abusive resolution of international disputes.

5
Consent Awards

Gabriel Bottini

I. Introduction

The basic purpose of international dispute settlement procedures is to resolve disputes that the parties could not settle between themselves before these procedures were triggered. Involving a neutral third party is intended to ensure that the parties' respective positions are considered and ultimately that the dispute is resolved in an impartial and independent manner, by someone who is not a party to the dispute. The parties are, by definition, neither impartial nor independent vis-à-vis the dispute and each party will pursue its own interests, sometimes at the expense of those of the other party. At the same time, however, the parties are more familiar with the details of the dispute and their overall relationship than anybody else. Further, particularly in the context of investment disputes, the parties will together be ideally placed to determine the terms of a mutually satisfactory resolution (to the maximum extent possible in the circumstances). A resolution agreed by the parties may or may not allow for the investment in question to continue, but will at least represent an instance of joint action by the parties that may facilitate subsequent cooperation and even new investment projects in the host country.[1]

As a general matter, the basis of an arbitral award is different from that of a settlement. The aim of an award is to resolve the dispute based on the tribunal's final determination of the parties' rights and liabilities. The tribunal's decision will be informed by and to a certain extent reflect the parties' respective positions, but it will not be a product of the parties' joint wishes. While the parties' submissions delimit the tribunal's jurisdiction, in the end it is the neutral application of the law that determines the outcome. In this way, arbitral awards can contribute to upholding the rule of law, particularly in the field of international investment.[2] However, the purpose of a tribunal-imposed resolution of the investment dispute is not to find the outcome that best suits both parties. Typical merits decisions in investment arbitration include, on the one hand, a partial or total acceptance of the investor's claim that will see the host state's measure deemed a breach of international law for which it may have to pay damages. Or, on the other hand, the claim is rejected, in which case the investor will not be awarded compensation for the alleged damage to the investment, at least not by an international tribunal. In either

[1] Stephan Schill (ed), *Schreuer's ICSID Convention: A Commentary* (3rd edn, CUP 2022) 1142.
[2] Georges R Delaume, 'Convention on the Settlement of Investment Disputes between States and Nationals of Other States' (1966) 1 International Lawyer 64, 66.

Gabriel Bottini, *Consent Awards* In: *The Award in International Investment Arbitration*. Edited by: Katia Fach Gómez and Catharine Titi, Oxford University Press. © Katia Fach Gómez and Aikaterini Titi 2024. DOI: 10.1093/9780191975936.003.0005

case, there may be serious consequences for the losing party that hinder the successful continuation of the investment project (if it is still ongoing),[3] not least due to the mistrust that the dispute may have created between the parties—something that the award is not designed to mend.

However, arbitral rules often provide for the possibility that the tribunal issue an award containing a settlement agreed by the parties as opposed to a third-party resolution of the dispute. While not the typical function of arbitral tribunals, a consent or settlement award[4] may be of interest to the parties, particularly in terms of facilitating the settlement's enforcement.[5] This is because if the parties do not voluntarily comply with the settlement or they disagree on its implementation, any of them may seek its enforcement under the applicable arbitral rules.[6] Yet this particular exercise of the arbitral function poses questions, not least as to the limits of the parties' freedom to determine the contents of a settlement award, and the arbitral tribunal's powers vis-à-vis the parties' joint wish to have their settlement embodied in an award. These questions relate to potential grounds for annulling settlement awards in investment arbitration that arise from limits imposed by the applicable law and the extent to which these grounds overlap with those applicable to 'ordinary' awards.

Section II of this chapter discusses the contents and interpretation of the provisions on consent awards in the most widely used arbitral rules in investment arbitration. Section III analyses the law applicable to consent awards and the authority of arbitral tribunals to issue them. Section III then explores the limits on the content of consent awards and the applicable annulment and enforcement frameworks, with a conclusion in section IV.

II. The Rules

The main arbitral rules used in investment arbitration grant arbitral tribunals the power to issue an award embodying a settlement reached by the parties. This is true of the 2022 ICSID Arbitration Rules and the 2021 Arbitration Rules of the United Nations Commission on International Trade Law (UNCITRAL), which are analysed below, as well as of the 2021 Rules of Arbitration of the International Chamber of Commerce, the 2020 Arbitration Rules of the London Court of International Arbitration, and the 2023 Arbitration Rules of the Arbitration Institute of the Stockholm Chamber of

[3] See Jan K Schäfer, 'Alternatives to Investment Arbitration' in Marc Bungenberg and others (eds), *International Investment Law: A Handbook* (C.H. Beck/Hart 2015) 1186, 1192 (arguing that '[w]hile a successful claim for damages might help deter a host State from engaging in a similar violation in the future, it might not further the goals of the investor claimant who simply wants to continue enjoying the investment').

[4] The terms consent award and settlement award are used interchangeably here.

[5] See Yaraslau Kryvoi and Dmitry Davydenko, 'Consent Awards in International Arbitration: From Settlement to Enforcement' (2015) 40 Brooklyn Journal of International Law 827, 835.

[6] On international arbitration generally, see Nigel Blackaby and others, *Redfern and Hunter on International Arbitration* (6th edn, OUP 2015) 513; on ICSID arbitration, see Aron Broches, 'The Convention on the Settlement of Investment Disputes between States and Nationals of Other States' (1972) 136 Recueil des Cours de l'Académie de Droit International 331, 338.

Commerce (SCC), among others.[7] There are a few non-fundamental yet not wholly irrelevant differences among the rules, which may have an impact on procedural matters relating to settlement awards. The most consequential difference relates to the frameworks applicable to the annulment, recognition, and enforcement of awards. In principle, these frameworks apply to settlement awards, although the extent to which this may differ in some respects vis-à-vis their application to ordinary awards is less straightforward.

A. 2022 ICSID Arbitration Rules

1. The Relevant Provision

The ICSID Convention contains detailed provisions on awards' content, post-award remedies, and recognition and enforcement of awards,[8] which are all key features of ICSID arbitration. However, the Convention itself does not provide for settlement awards. These awards are regulated in what is now Rule 55(2)(b) of the ICSID Arbitration Rules. ICSID Arbitration Rule 55, which deals with settlement and discontinuance by agreement of the parties, reads as follows:

> (1) If the parties notify the Tribunal that they have agreed to discontinue the proceeding, the Tribunal shall issue an order taking note of the discontinuance.
> (2) If the parties agree on a settlement of the dispute before the Award is rendered, the Tribunal:
> (a) shall issue an order taking note of the discontinuance of the proceeding, if the parties so request; or
> (b) may record the settlement in the form of an Award, if the parties file the complete and signed text of their settlement and request that the Tribunal embody such settlement in an Award
> (3) The Secretary-General shall issue the order referred to in paragraphs (1) and (2) (a) if the Tribunal has not yet been constituted or if there is a vacancy on the Tribunal.[9]

Compared to Rule 43(2), which regulated settlement or consent awards in the 2006 ICSID Arbitration Rules, Rule 55(2)(b) contains only 'stylistic' changes.[10] The same provision is contained in Rule 65(2)(b) of the ICSID Additional Facility Arbitration Rules.[11] Conciliation commissions may embody a settlement agreement by the parties

[7] See also 2021 Rules of Arbitration of the International Chamber of Commerce art 33; 2020 LCIA Arbitration Rules art 26.9; 2023 SCC Arbitration Rules art 45.

[8] See ICSID Convention, ch IV, ss 4–6.

[9] ICSID Arbitration Rules (2022) r 55.

[10] Proposals for Amendment of the ICSID Rules—Working Paper, ICSID Secretariat, 2 August 2018 ('Working Paper #1') para 559.

[11] ICSID Additional Facility Arbitration Rules (2022) r 65(2)(b).

in their reports terminating the conciliation, although these reports are of course not awards.[12]

The issue of settlement awards does not seem to have been raised during the ICSID Convention negotiations. Distinguishing between provisions dealing with conciliation proceedings and provisions dealing with arbitration proceedings, the Report of the Executive Directors on the ICSID Convention stated that 'the differences between the two sets of provisions reflect the basic distinction between the process of conciliation which seeks to bring the parties to agreement and that of arbitration which aims at a binding determination of the dispute by the Tribunal'.[13] The ICSID Convention's *travaux préparatoires* contain extensive discussions about the effects of awards, not least with a view to their recognition, enforcement, and execution,[14] but they make no reference to the possibility of awards embodying an agreement by the parties that puts an end to the dispute.

The provision on settlement awards was included in Rule 43(2) of the first version of the ICSID Arbitration Rules, which were adopted by ICSID's Administrative Council in 1967 and came into effect on 1 January 1968.[15] The text of the two paragraphs of Rule 43, which according to the non-binding explanatory notes prepared by ICSID's Secretariat ('Explanatory Notes') dealt 'with the contingency of the parties agreeing to settle their dispute or to discontinue the proceeding on some other basis',[16] remained unchanged by the 2006 amendments[17] and until the 2022 non-substantive amendment.

2. Interpretation

Like its predecessor (Rule 43 in the 2006 Rules), ICSID Arbitration Rule 55 deals with settlement and discontinuance by agreement of the parties. Rule 56 governs discontinuance at the request of a party and Rule 57 discontinuance for failure of the parties to act. Unlike the former Rule 43, Rule 55 distinguishes between the case where the parties agree to discontinue the proceeding (paragraph (1)) and the case where they agree on a settlement and then ask the tribunal to discontinue the proceeding (paragraph (2)(a)).[18] In both situations the tribunal, or the Secretary-General if the tribunal has not yet been

[12] See ICSID Conciliation Rules (2022) r 35(2); ICSID Additional Facility Conciliation Rules (2022) r 43(2). See also ICSID Mediation Rules (2022) r 22(1)(a).

[13] Report of the Executive Directors on the Convention on the Settlement of Investment Disputes between States and Nationals of Other States, 10 September 1964, para 37.

[14] See generally *History of the ICSID Convention: Documents Concerning the Origin and the Formulation of the Convention on the Settlement of Investment Disputes between States and Nationals of Other States*, vols II-1 and II-2 (1968) <https://icsid.worldbank.org/resources/publications/the-history-of-the-icsid-convention>.

[15] See ICSID Regulations and Rules, ICSID/4/Rev. 1, 3 <https://icsid.worldbank.org/sites/default/files/ICSID%20Regulations%20and%20Rules%201968%20-%20ENG.pdf>.

[16] ICSID, Explanatory Notes prepared by the Secretariat of the Centre (1968) 109. Szasz noted that the explanatory notes 'had originally been prepared for the benefit of the Administrative Council in considering the definitive texts of the Rules', but 'were not adopted by the Council and have no legal force'. Paul C Szasz, 'A Practical Guide to the Convention on Settlement of Investment Disputes' (1968) 1 Cornell International Law Journal 1, 8.

[17] See ICSID Arbitration Rules 2006 r 43 <https://icsid.worldbank.org/sites/default/files/ICSID%20Convention%20English.pdf>.

[18] The need for this distinction is not readily apparent.

constituted or if there is a vacancy on the tribunal as per paragraph (3), shall issue an order taking note of the discontinuance if the parties so request.

Rule 55(2)(b) is the provision that specifically deals with settlement awards. The power of ICSID tribunals to issue an award embodying a settlement is premised on them receiving a joint request from the parties to that effect and on the parties filing 'the complete and signed text of their settlement'.[19] On the one hand, it is clear from the use of the word 'may' at the beginning of the provision that the tribunal is not obliged to issue an award under Rule 55(2)(b), even if the parties so request.[20] On the other hand, it is also clear that ICSID tribunals do not have the power to issue an award under Rule 55(2)(b) if the parties do not jointly request it.[21]

There are no specific formal requirements to be met by this type of request,[22] other than the need for the parties to present the settlement itself in full. If the parties were not willing to present the 'complete and signed text of their settlement', an express requirement of Rule 55(2) would not be fulfilled, and this should prevent the tribunal from issuing a settlement award. To the extent that the tribunal does not have full knowledge of the contents of the settlement, it cannot properly exercise its discretion not to issue a settlement award, for example when 'it considers it improper for the Tribunal to become a party to a particular settlement'[23] or that the settlement is otherwise not permissible under the applicable law.[24]

As with any other ICSID award, settlement awards may only be issued by an arbitral tribunal.[25] Neither the ICSID Convention nor the ICSID arbitration rules grant the Secretary-General the power to issue settlement awards (or any other award for that matter).[26] As already noted, ICSID Arbitration Rule 55(3) grants the Secretary-General the power to issue an order taking note of the discontinuance. Even if they put an end to the proceeding, however, discontinuance orders do not have the status of awards. Thus, the provisions governing awards in the ICSID Convention and the ICSID Arbitration Rules are not applicable to these orders.[27]

By the same token, in principle all the provisions of the ICSID Convention and the ICSID Arbitration Rules that regulate awards also apply to settlement awards.[28] Rule 55

[19] ICSID Arbitration Rules (2022) r 55(2)(b).

[20] See Explanatory Notes (n 16) 109; Schill (n 1) 1138; Alexandra Munoz and Tess Pickard, 'Rule 43—Settlement and Discontinuance' in Julien Fouret, Rémy Gerbay, and Gloria M Alvarez (eds), *The ICSID Convention, Regulations and Rules: A Practical Commentary* (Edward Elgar Publishing 2019) 1210.

[21] This is so even if the parties have otherwise reached a settlement on the merits of the dispute, in whole or in part. See *Fedax NV v Venezuela*, ICSID Case No ARB/96/3, Award (9 March 1998) [28].

[22] However see Munoz and Pickard (n 20) 1210 (suggesting that the request must be in writing).

[23] ICSID (n 16) 109. The tribunal that issues a settlement award does not strictly speaking become a party to the settlement. However, the tribunal's intervention transforms the legal nature and effects of the settlement by turning it into an ICSID award.

[24] See section III.

[25] ICSID (n 16) 109.

[26] See ibid; Munoz and Pickard (n 20) 1210

[27] Schill (n 1) 1138.

[28] However see ICSID (n 16) 109 ('Articles 50 to 52 of the Convention (interpretation, revision and annulment) cannot have full application with regard to [a settlement] award'); Schill (n 1) 1138 ('only some of the Convention's provisions on awards will apply to [a settlement] award'); Munoz and Pickard (n 20) 1213 ('Certain provisions of the ICSID Convention will however be less relevant to an award rendered pursuant to Rule 43(2)').

does not introduce any restriction in this regard and clearly establishes that an award embodying a settlement by the parties is an award.[29] Aside from the need for settlement awards to contain a decision on the assessment and distribution of costs per Article 61(2) of the ICSID Convention,[30] it has been argued that 'otherwise the obligation to deal with every question and to state reasons will not apply to such an award'[31] and that this obligation is 'easily met' since 'the tribunal only needs to recite the fact that the parties have agreed the issues that were in dispute and that they have been settled'.[32] However, the requirement that the award contain reasons is an important feature of ICSID arbitration[33] and there is no reason why this requirement should not apply to settlement awards.[34] Of course, under Article 48(3) of the ICSID Convention a tribunal's duty to give reasons is closely related to the duty to deal with every question submitted to it. The fact that the parties have reached a settlement and asked the tribunal to record it in an award will have an impact on the questions that are submitted to the tribunal following the settlement.[35] Embodying the settlement in an award may be the only remaining question before the tribunal.[36] However, the settlement may be partial in that some questions may be left for the tribunal to resolve and thus the award will only partially be issued under Rule 55(2)(b).[37]

B. 2021 UNCITRAL Arbitration Rules

1. The Relevant Provision

The 2021 UNCITRAL Arbitration Rules contain only one article dealing specifically with '[s]ettlement or other grounds for termination', which is Article 36:

[29] That said, given the specific purpose of settlement awards to record a settlement by the parties rather than the tribunal's determination of the dispute, the relevant provisions of the ICSID Convention and the ICSID Arbitration Rules should be applied taking that specific purpose into account.

[30] Article 61(2) provides that the tribunal shall assess the parties' expenses and decide on the apportionment of the fees and expenses incurred in the proceedings 'except as the parties otherwise agree'. In this respect, a settlement agreed by the parties will often contain provisions on costs incurred in the arbitration. See eg *Joseph Charles Lemire v Ukraine*, ICSID Case No ARB(AF)/98/1, Award (18 September 2000) [14]; *EVN AG v The Former Yugoslav Republic of Macedonia*, ICSID Case No ARB/09/10, Award (2 September 2011) [16]; *Amir Masood Taheri v United Arab Emirates*, ICSID Case No ARB/21/19, Award under ICSID Arbitration Rule 43(2) (28 November 2022) [27].

[31] Schill (n 1) 1138.

[32] Munoz and Pickard (n 20) 1213.

[33] Aron Broches, 'Observations on the Finality of ICSID Awards' (1991) 6 (2) ICSID Review 321, 331.

[34] See, however, Article 26.9 of the 2020 LCIA Arbitration Rules ('A Consent Award need not contain reasons or a determination in relation to the Arbitration Costs or Legal Costs'); 2021 UNCITRAL Arbitration Rules art 34.1.

[35] There can be no doubt that, inter alia, the other provisions of Article 48 of the ICSID Convention dealing with the requirements applicable to awards as to majority of votes, formalities, individual opinions, and consent to publication are applicable to settlement awards. For example, individual opinions have been appended to settlement awards. See *Abaclat and others v Argentina*, ICSID Case No ARB/07/5, Declaration appended to the Award by Arbitrator Santiago Torres Bernárdez (29 December 2016).

[36] Under the ICC Rules, it has been observed that 'the simple statement that an Award is based on a settlement would appear to be an adequate reason for [a consent award]'. Yves Derains and Eric A Schwartz, *A Guide to the ICC Rules of Arbitration* (2nd edn, Kluwer Law International 2005) 312.

[37] See *Tanzania Electric Supply Company Limited v Independent Power Tanzania Limited*, ICSID Case No ARB/98/8, Award (12 July 2001) [58]–[65].

1. If, before the award is made, the parties agree on a settlement of the dispute, the arbitral tribunal shall either issue an order for the termination of the arbitral proceedings or, if requested by the parties and accepted by the arbitral tribunal, record the settlement in the form of an arbitral award on agreed terms. The arbitral tribunal is not obliged to give reasons for such an award.
2. If, before the award is made, the continuation of the arbitral proceedings becomes unnecessary or impossible for any reason not mentioned in paragraph 1, the arbitral tribunal shall inform the parties of its intention to issue an order for the termination of the proceedings. The arbitral tribunal shall have the power to issue such an order unless there are remaining matters that may need to be decided and the arbitral tribunal considers it appropriate to do so.
3. Copies of the order for termination of the arbitral proceedings or of the arbitral award on agreed terms, signed by the arbitrators, shall be communicated by the arbitral tribunal to the parties. Where an arbitral award on agreed terms is made, the provisions of article 34, paragraphs 2, 4 and 5, shall apply.

Paragraph 1 of Article 36 contains only a stylistic change vis-à-vis the same provision contained in the 1976 UNCITRAL Arbitration Rules (Article 34). Paragraph 2, which deals with arbitral tribunal orders terminating the proceedings, differs from its predecessor, which stated: 'The arbitral tribunal shall have the power to issue such an order unless a party raises justifiable grounds for objection.' This provision of the 1976 Arbitration Rules appears more general as to the potential grounds to object to a termination order by the arbitral tribunal. Finally, the second sentence of paragraph 3 also contains a change in respect of the equivalent provision of the 1976 Arbitration Rules, in that the latter stated: 'Where an arbitral award on agreed terms is made, the provisions of article 32, paragraphs 2 and 4 to 7, shall apply.' The provision in Article 32, paragraph 7, of the 1976 Arbitration Rules was not included in the 2021 Arbitration Rules.[38] Paragraph 6 of what is Article 34 in the 2021 Arbitration Rules states: 'Copies of the award signed by the arbitrators shall be communicated to the parties by the arbitral tribunal.' This provision does not apply to settlement awards under the 2021 Arbitration Rules given the change introduced to paragraph 3 of Article 36.[39]

2. Interpretation

Similar to Rule 55(2)(b) of the ICSID Arbitration Rules, Article 36(1) of the 2021 UNCITRAL Arbitration Rules distinguishes between an arbitral tribunal order terminating the proceedings that is issued following an agreement by the parties to settle the dispute, and a settlement award.[40] An order for the termination of the proceedings

[38] 1976 UNCITRAL Arbitration Rules art 32.7: 'If the arbitration law of the country where the award is made requires that the award be filed or registered by the arbitral tribunal, the tribunal shall comply with this requirement within the period of time required by law.'

[39] While Article 34.6 of the 2021 UNCITRAL Arbitration Rules deals essentially with a logistical issue, the need to introduce a distinction between settlement awards and other awards in this respect is not completely clear.

[40] David D Caron and Lee M Caplan, *The UNCITRAL Arbitration Rules: A Commentary* (2nd edn, OUP 2013) 782.

is not an award[41] and thus the provisions of the 2021 UNCITRAL Arbitration Rules that govern awards are not applicable to such an order. Here a settlement award may only be issued if 'requested by the parties and accepted by the arbitral tribunal'. Article 36(1) does not establish that the request must be in a particular form other than it has to come from all the parties,[42] which does not mean that it has to be simultaneous, provided that it is clear that the parties wish their settlement to be recorded in an award.[43]

Article 36(1) provides that '[t]he arbitral tribunal is not obliged to give reasons for [a settlement award]'. Article 55(2) of the ICSID Arbitration Rules does not contain a similar provision although, as noted above, the extent to which an ICSID tribunal must provide reasons in a settlement award is subject to some debate.[44] This difference between the UNCITRAL and ICSID Arbitration Rules may be related to the duty of arbitral tribunals to give reasons in their awards generally, which also differs under the two sets of Arbitration Rules. Under Article 34(3) of the 2021 UNCITRAL Arbitration Rules, '[t]he arbitral tribunal shall state the reasons upon which the award is based, unless the parties have agreed that no reasons are to be given'. This article represents the compromise reached between the stance of civil law countries, which proposed that reasons be required, and that of the United Kingdom and the United States, which proposed that there be no requirement to state reasons.[45] A similar proposal was rejected in the context of the ICSID Convention negotiations, which according to Aron Broches 'underscore[d] the importance attached by the drafters to the statement of reasons'.[46]

III. Jurisdiction, Annulment, and Enforcement

As noted in the previous section, both the 2021 UNCITRAL Arbitration Rules and the 2022 ICSID Arbitration Rules, as well as other relevant arbitration rules,[47] characterise consent awards as awards. Aside from the requirement to give reasons in the award, which is optional under the 2021 UNCITRAL Arbitration Rules for consent awards, the latter are governed by the same provisions as awards generally. No other exclusions are provided for.[48] Importantly, consent awards are final and binding upon the parties in the terms of Article 53 of the ICSID Convention and Article 34(2) of the

[41] ibid.

[42] But see ibid 783 ('Although not required by the Rules, it is preferable that the request be in writing and signed by both parties') (footnote omitted).

[43] See Howard M Holtzmann and Joseph E Neuhaus, *A Guide to the UNCITRAL Model Law on Commercial Arbitration: Legislative History and Commentary* (Kluwer 1989) 822–23 (noting within the framework of the UNCITRAL Model Law on Commercial Arbitration that the request for a settlement award may come from one of the parties provided that both parties' consent is clear). See also the 2020 LCIA Arbitration Rules art 26.9 (providing that a consent award 'shall contain an express statement on its face that it is an award made at the parties' joint request and with their consent').

[44] See further Bruno Simma and Jan Ortgies, 'The Reasoned Award' in Katia Fach Gómez and Catharine Titi (eds), *The Award in Investment Arbitration* (OUP 2024).

[45] Caron and Caplan (n 40) 750–52.

[46] Broches (n 33) 331.

[47] See 2021 Rules of Arbitration of the International Chamber of Commerce art 33; 2020 LCIA Arbitration Rules art 26.9; 2023 SCC Arbitration Rules art 45.

[48] With respect to the ICC Rules, see Derains and Schwartz (n 36) 312.

2021 UNCITRAL Arbitration Rules. Except for specific remedies that may be available for ordinary awards too, such as requests for interpretation, rectification, supplementary decisions or revision of awards,[49] upon rendering the consent award the arbitral tribunal becomes *functus officio*.[50] As discussed in section III.B, requests for the annulment of consent awards are decided by *ad hoc* committees in the case of ICSID awards and by the courts of the seat of the arbitration in the case of UNCITRAL awards, while in both cases ultimately 'compliance with, and enforcement of, the award become matters for the parties and national courts'.[51]

While under both Rule 55(2)(b) of the 2022 ICSID Arbitration Rules and Article 36(1) of the 2021 UNCITRAL Arbitration Rules it is clear that arbitral tribunals have discretion as to whether to render a consent award upon a request from the parties,[52] none of these provisions establish any criteria relevant to the arbitral tribunal's exercise of that discretion. However, limits to that discretion may be derived from other provisions of the arbitration rules or from the law applicable to the award itself. These limits may relate to jurisdictional aspects or to the substance of the consent award, which itself comes from the parties' settlement agreement. Real or perceived infringements of these limits may in turn give way to requests for annulment or otherwise affect the recognition and enforcement of consent awards.

A. Applicable Law And Jurisdictional Aspects of Consent Awards

By definition, consent awards embody a settlement by the parties that puts an end to the dispute before the arbitral tribunal.[53] However, the consent award and the settlement agreement are related yet different instruments.[54] On the one hand, a settlement agreement is generally a contract whereby the parties agree to settle their dispute,[55] which is usually subject to one or more national laws.[56] On the other hand, in investment treaty arbitration the consent award is not a contract but an award issued by an international arbitral tribunal. The jurisdiction of arbitral tribunals in deciding investment treaty claims is based on an international treaty, ie the applicable international

[49] ICSID Convention arts 50 and 51; 2022 ICSID Arbitration Rules r 61; 2021 UNCITRAL Arbitration Rules arts 37–39.

[50] On awards generally, see Gary Born, *International Arbitration: Cases and Materials* (2nd edn, Wolters Kluwer 2015) 1059.

[51] ibid (footnote omitted).

[52] However see Blackaby and others (n 6) 515 ('At one time, various sets of rules (including the ICC Rules prior to 1998) seemed to leave the tribunal with no discretion, but modern rules and legislation permit the arbitral tribunal to refuse to make a consent award') (footnote omitted).

[53] Jean-François Poudret and Sébastien Besson, *Comparative Law of International Commercial Arbitration* (2nd edn, Sweet & Maxwell 2007) 648.

[54] See *Abaclat and others v Argentina*, ICSID Case No ARB/07/5, Declaration appended to the Award by Arbitrator Santiago Torres Bernárdez (29 December 2016) [9].

[55] See Kryvoi and Davydenko (n 5) 832. Aside from the parties to the dispute, the settlement agreement may also include other parties. See *Isolux Corsán Concesiones SA v Peru*, ICSID Case No ARB/12/5, Award (25 March 2014) [13].

[56] But see *St Marys VCNA, LLC v Canada*, PCA Case No 2012-19, Consent Award (29 March 2013) 9 (settlement agreement governed by 'the laws of the Province of Ontario and such rules of international law as may be applicable').

investment agreement (IIA), and it is thus an international law jurisdiction.[57] In the case of ICSID tribunals, their jurisdiction is also governed by another treaty, the ICSID Convention, from which they also derive their powers.[58] Thus, consent awards issued by tribunals constituted under IIAs are subject to international law and the arbitration rules to which the applicable investment treaty refers,[59] specifically the provisions governing awards in general and consent awards in particular. However, in investment arbitration even treaty claims often require consideration of the host state's national law alongside international law.[60] Here national law will also be part of the law applicable to the consent award, not least for the purposes of recognition and enforcement.[61]

As regards jurisdiction and the arbitral tribunal's authority in principle to issue a consent award, no procedural issue arises in the arbitration if the arbitral tribunal has affirmed its jurisdiction over the dispute before rendering the consent award.[62] The situation is different, however, if jurisdiction has not been determined at the time the parties request the arbitral tribunal to issue a consent award. In this case, the question is whether the arbitral tribunal must be satisfied that it has jurisdiction in order to issue the consent award requested by the parties. Published consent awards show that investment tribunals generally do not consider whether they have jurisdiction in issuing the consent award.[63] Yet under the ICSID Convention it has been argued that the tribunal must first 'find that it has the authority to resolve the dispute', since through a consent award the tribunal 'does not decide on the merits, [but] it does dispose of the dispute'.[64] The ICSID Secretariat's Explanatory Notes state that the arbitral tribunal may at its discretion refuse to comply with a request from the parties to issue a consent award, inter alia because 'it may instead decide that it lacks jurisdiction'.[65]

[57] See Chittharanjan F Amerasinghe, *Jurisdiction of International Tribunals* (Kluwer Law International 2003) 11–12.

[58] See Aron Broches, 'Convention on the Settlement of Investment Disputes: Some Observations on Jurisdiction' (1966) 5 Columbia Journal of Transnational Law 263, 278.

[59] In principle, the analysis of the law applicable to consent awards per se would not vary significantly in the case of an ICSID tribunal hearing a contract-based claim, given the application of the ICSID Convention. However, it would differ in the case of a non-ICSID tribunal hearing such a claim due to the arbitral tribunal's jurisdiction not deriving from an instrument of international law but rather from the contract in question. See ibid. The extent to which the latter type of arbitration could still be deemed an investment arbitration would depend on the specific circumstances of the case.

[60] See eg *Venezuela Holdings, BV and others v Venezuela*, ICSID Case No ARB/07/27, Decision on Annulment (9 March 2017) [181]. See also Martin Jarret, 'The International Validity of Domestic Law in Investment-Treaty Arbitration' (2023) 39 Arbitration International 1, 2.

[61] See section III.B.

[62] See *Mobil Investments Canada Inc v Canada (II)*, ICSID Case No ARB/15/6, Award (4 February 2020) [8]. However, the arbitral tribunal's jurisdiction may be debated in the annulment or enforcement phase of consent awards. The tribunal may have decided part of the merits of the dispute before issuing the consent award. See eg *Antoine Goetz et consorts v Burundi*, ICSID Case No ARB/95/3, Award (10 February 1999) [134]–[137].

[63] See eg *Miminco LLC and others v Congo*, ICSID Case No ARB/03/14, Award (19 November 2007); *Vattenfall AB, Vattenfall Europe AG, Vattenfall Europe Generation AG v Germany (I)*, ICSID Case No ARB/09/6, Award Embodying the Parties' Settlement Agreement (11 March 2011); *Trans-Global Petroleum, Inc v Jordan*, ICSID Case No ARB/07/25, Consent Award (8 April 2009); *Enel Fortuna SA v Panama*, ICSID Case No ARB/19/5, Award (18 August 2021). But see *TCW Group, Inc and Dominican Energy Holdings, LP v The Dominican Republic*, PCA Case No 2008-06, Consent Award (16 July 2009) [1]; *AbitibiBowater Inc v Canada*, ICSID Case No UNCT/10/1, Consent Award (15 December 2010) [9], [13], [18] (considering the effect 'on the Tribunal's continued jurisdiction' once the settlement agreement had taken effect).

[64] Munoz and Pickard (n 20) 1211; Kryvoi and Davydenko (n 5) 838.

[65] ICSID (n 16) 109; Schill (n 1) 1138.

However, upon issuing a consent award under ICSID Arbitration Rule 55(2)(b) the tribunal does not decide the dispute but rather records the parties' settlement in the form of an award. As already noted, the consent award itself will have the same status as an ordinary award. But, in principle, when issuing a consent award the arbitral tribunal does not consider or speak to the merits of the claims.[66] Thus, the arbitral tribunal does not exercise jurisdiction over the claims or the dispute, which has been settled by the parties, but a special jurisdiction over the settlement agreement. In the case of ICSID tribunals, this special jurisdiction derives, first, (albeit indirectly) from the ICSID Convention, which governs their constitution and in Article 44 refers inter alia to the arbitration rules in effect on the date when the parties consented to arbitration and to any rules agreed by the parties; second, from ICSID Arbitration Rule 55(2)(b), which specifically provides for consent awards; and third, from the parties' consent as expressed in their joint request for a consent award.

Within the ICSID framework, '[c]onsent of the parties is the cornerstone of the jurisdiction of the Centre'.[67] Indeed, after a request for arbitration has been registered, and provided that the applicable procedure has been followed, the ICSID Convention establishes a treaty framework under which ICSID tribunals are 'validly constituted even though the consent of the parties was defective'.[68] Hence, an ICSID tribunal arguably has authority to issue a consent award based on the ICSID Convention, the ICSID Arbitration Rules and the parties' joint request (at least in Aron Broches' view as to when consent to ICSID jurisdiction may be given)[69] even if consent to the ICSID's jurisdiction was not given before the tribunal was constituted.

It may be argued, therefore, that an ICSID tribunal hearing a treaty claim does not have to satisfy itself that the claim falls within the provisions of the applicable treaties for jurisdictional purposes[70] in order to issue a consent award. But while consent is a fundamental tenet of ICSID's jurisdiction, in ICSID arbitration 'consent is not enough'.[71] Under the ICSID Convention, 'jurisdiction' means 'the limits within which the provisions of the Convention will apply and the facilities of the Centre will be available for conciliation and arbitration proceedings'.[72] These limits apply to any exercise of jurisdiction under the ICSID Convention. Hence, for an ICSID tribunal to render a consent award, the dispute that has been settled must fulfil the *ratione personae* and *ratione materiae* requirements established in Article 25 of the ICSID Convention,[73]

[66] In *IBM v Ecuador* the tribunal noted in the consent award that it was expressing no views on the terms of the settlement agreement. See *IBM World Trade Corp v Ecuador*, ICSID Case No ARB/02/10, Award (22 July 2004) [9].

[67] Report of the Executive Directors on the ICSID Convention (n 13) para 23.

[68] Broches (n 6) 368. Of course, any defects affecting the consent of the parties, let alone the absence of consent, may give rise to preliminary objections that the tribunal would have to consider. See ICSID Convention art 41(2).

[69] Broches (n 58) 277–78.

[70] For the jurisdictional test under international law see *Oil Platforms (Iran v USA)*, Preliminary Objection, Judgment, [1996] ICJ Rep 803 [16].

[71] Broches (n 6) 352.

[72] Report of the Executive Directors on the ICSID Convention (n 13) para 22.

[73] This is why an ICSID arbitration cannot be commenced for the sole purpose of constituting a tribunal that would issue a consent award, since in that case ICSID would have no jurisdiction due to the absence of a dispute. See Schill (n 1) 1138; Munoz and Pickard (n 20) 1210. See also *Azpetrol International Holdings BV, Azpetrol*

ie the 'outer limits' of ICSID's jurisdiction.[74] Conversely, in the context of investment treaty arbitration and provided that the parties have consented, an ICSID tribunal may not have to consider whether all the jurisdictional requirements of the applicable investment treaty are present to issue a consent award.[75]

Under the UNCITRAL Rules, it has been argued that arbitral tribunals' discretion to record a settlement in an award is 'circumscribed by the duty to record only those settlements that fall within the arbitral tribunal's jurisdiction, as established by the arbitration agreement'.[76] Yet if the settlement 'involves new subject matter outside the scope of the original agreement, the arbitral tribunal may interpret the settlement agreement as an implied amendment of the arbitration agreement'.[77] In investment treaty arbitration, although the arbitration agreement is entered into between the claimant investor and the host state,[78] it is based on the applicable IIA, which only the state parties can amend. Furthermore, unlike arbitration under the ICSID Convention, in treaty arbitration under the UNCITRAL Rules there is no treaty conferring jurisdiction on the arbitral tribunal other than the applicable IIA. Thus, to issue a consent award in relation to a treaty dispute, an UNCITRAL tribunal must have jurisdiction under the applicable IIA.[79]

B. Limits on the Contents of Consent Awards: Annulment and Enforcement

Under Rule 55(2)(b) of the 2022 ICSID Arbitration Rules and Article 36(1) of the 2021 UNCITRAL Arbitration Rules, arbitral tribunals have the power but are not required to render a consent award at the request of the parties.[80] During the negotiations of

Group BV, and Azpetrol Oil Services Group BV v Azerbaijan, ICSID Case No ARB/06/15, Award (8 September 2009) [105].

[74] See Broches (n 6) 351.

[75] However, see Munoz and Pickard (n 20) 1212–13 (arguing that parties should only request an ICSID tribunal to issue a consent award 'if they are sure that it has the authority to resolve the dispute pursuant to Article 25 of the ICSID Convention and pursuant to the instrument under which the arbitration is commenced').

[76] Caron and Caplan (n 40) 784.

[77] ibid.

[78] See Zachary Douglas, 'The Hybrid Foundation of Investment Treaty Arbitration' (2003) 74 British Yearbook of International Law 151, 184. See also Zachary Douglas, *The International Law of Investment Claims* (CUP 2009) 35.

[79] A different question is what standard of review the UNCITRAL tribunal should apply to determine whether it has jurisdiction given that both parties are requesting it to issue a consent award. The Iran–US Tribunal left this question open. See *Iran* and *United States*, Case A/1 (1983 Tribunal Rules) 152–53. Subject to any restrictions stemming from the law of the state of the seat of the arbitration, there would seem to be no fundamental obstacle for a UNCITRAL tribunal to apply a prima facie test for this purpose, similar to the one applied by international tribunals to decide on provisional measures applications. On the jurisdictional test applicable to provisional measures requests, see Ibrahim FI Shihata and Antonio R Parra, 'The Experience of the International Centre for Settlement of Investment Disputes' (1999) 14 ICSID Review 299, 326.

[80] Whether arbitral tribunals may issue consent awards in the absence of provisions granting them the power to do so is not a straightforward matter, not least because of the special nature of this exercise of jurisdiction and the fact that it is not necessary to put an end to the proceedings. But see Kryvoi and Davydenko (n 5) 836 (arguing that arbitrators have an inherent power to issue consent awards); Julian DM Lew, Loukas A Mistelis, and Stefan M Kröll, *Comparative International Commercial Arbitration* (Wolters Kluwer 2003) 636 ('Arguably tribunals always have [the discretion to issue consent awards] even if not expressly provided for in the rules').

the 1976 UNCITRAL Arbitration Rules, a proposal to deny arbitrators the power to refuse to issue consent awards was rejected on the basis that the arbitrators' discretion in this regard 'was useful and should be retained, as the settlement agreed on by the parties might be unlawful or contrary to public policy'.[81] The ICSID Secretariat's Explanatory Notes refer to the tribunal deciding that it lacks jurisdiction or otherwise considering it improper to be associated with the settlement agreement as reasons to exercise its discretion not to render a consent award.[82] Whatever the motive for the refusal, under both sets of rules tribunals appear to have full discretion to refuse to issue a consent award, in which case they are not required to give reasons for the refusal. Thus, under both the ICSID and UNCITRAL Arbitration Rules there would seem to be little or no room to question this refusal.[83] Aside from the fact that the relevant provisions impose no limit on the tribunals' discretion, a potential abuse of this discretion (for example, a refusal for improper motives) would deprive the parties of the benefit of a consent award, but would otherwise not prevent them from putting an end to the arbitration through a procedural order[84] or indeed to the dispute through the settlement agreement.

Yet when the arbitral tribunal does issue a consent award, it must comply with the law applicable to the award. And given that consent awards incorporate and to a certain extent give 'a measure of approval'[85] to the settlement agreement, restrictions affecting the latter's validity also impinge on the consent award's validity.[86] In terms of international law, clear limits are placed on the object of settlement agreements (and thus settlement awards) through peremptory norms or jus cogens,[87] against which no agreement is allowed.[88] In the field of international investment law, the principle of self-determination may be relevant in certain cases, although the importance of fundamental provisions on human rights cannot be disregarded here as well.[89] The validity of consent awards that breach applicable provisions of national law may also be questioned, especially mandatory provisions of the law of the seat of the arbitration in the case of non-ICSID arbitrations.[90] In turn, violations of legal restrictions to the consent award's object may lead to its annulment or oppositions to its recognition and enforcement.

[81] See UNCITRAL Yearbook, vol VI: 1975, UN Doc A/CN.9/SER.A/1975, 42. See also UNCITRAL Yearbook, vol VII: 1976, UN Doc A/CN.9/SER.A/1976, 189. See also Derains and Schwartz (n 36) 311.

[82] ICSID (n 16) 109. See also Munoz and Pickard (n 20) 1212 (noting that in deciding whether to render a consent award arbitral tribunals should 'bear in mind the risk that [consent awards] may be used for improper purposes, such as money laundering').

[83] See however Caron and Caplan (n 40) 785 (discussing under which circumstances a refusal to record a settlement agreement in an award may be appropriate).

[84] In the event of a settlement, arbitral tribunals are required to issue an order terminating the arbitral proceedings. See 2022 ICSID Arbitration Rules r 55(2)(a); 2021 UNCITRAL Arbitration Rules arts 36(1).

[85] Blackaby and others (n 6) 513.

[86] See however Sundra Rajoo, *Law, Practice and Procedure of Arbitration* (2nd edn, LexisNexis 2017) 573 ('However the invalidity of the settlement agreement does not automatically invalidate an award').

[87] See Kryvoi and Davydenko (n 5) 859.

[88] On the concept of peremptory norms, see eg Malcolm Shaw, *International Law* (9th edn, CUP 2021) 105–9; Mathias Forteau, Alina Miron, and Alain Pellet, *Droit International Public* (9th edn, LGDJ 2022) 259–70.

[89] See James Crawford, *Brownlie's Principles of Public International Law* (9th edn, OUP 2019) 581–82.

[90] See Blackaby and others (n 6) 513–14.

As no exclusions are provided for ICSID awards, all the provisions of the ICSID Convention and the ICSID Arbitration Rules on post-award remedies also apply to consent awards. It has been argued, however, that in the case of consent awards the application of these remedies is 'severely restricted', that the annulment grounds in Article 52(1) 'would hardly apply', and that '[f]ailure to state reasons clearly would not apply'.[91] Yet a restrictive application of the provisions on post-award remedies is not provided for in the applicable rules. Generally, these provisions are less likely to be applied in the case of consent awards given their specific object and more limited content. However, even interpretation of a consent award under Article 50 of the ICSID Convention may be called for given that the content of consent awards is not strictly limited to the settlement agreement. And as already noted, under the ICSID rules the requirement that the award contain reasons applies to consent awards and thus the corresponding annulment ground in Article 52(1)(e) may also be applicable to a consent award. Further, there is no doubt that the ICSID Convention's provisions on recognition and enforcement of awards apply to consent awards.[92] Thus, under Article 54(1) of the ICSID Convention, consent awards are binding and their pecuniary obligations are to be enforced in any of the Convention's contracting states as final judgments of local courts.

As regards consent awards issued under the UNCITRAL Rules, their status for the purposes of annulment proceedings, recognition, and enforcement depends, in the case of investment treaty arbitration, on any specific provisions in the applicable IIA and on the law of the seat of the arbitration. To the extent that they have the same status and effect as ordinary awards under the law of the seat, as provided for example in Article 30(2) of the UNCITRAL Model Law on International Commercial Arbitration,[93] the annulment grounds applicable to ordinary awards will apply to consent awards before the courts of that state. Furthermore, aside from the local laws applicable to foreign arbitral awards, it is generally accepted that the 1958 New York Convention on the Recognition and Enforcement of Foreign Arbitral Awards (New York Convention) is applicable to the recognition and enforcement of consent awards in countries other than that of the seat.[94] In cases where the settlement agreement embodied in the consent award seeks to somehow legitimize illegal activities such as money laundering, tax evasion or bribery, this may give rise to defences against recognition and enforcement,

[91] Schill (n 1) 1139. See also Munoz and Pickard (n 20) 1213 (arguing that application of post-award remedies 'will be restricted' and some annulment grounds 'would not apply at all' such as failure to state reasons); Kryvoi and Davydenko (n 5) 855 (annulment ground for failure to state reasons 'should not apply because the ICSID Arbitration Rules specifically allow consent awards').

[92] Schill (n 1) 1139–40; Munoz and Pickard (n 20) 1212.

[93] See UNCITRAL Model Law on International Commercial Arbitration (1985), with amendments as adopted in 2006,

[94] See Albert Jan van den Berg, *The New York Arbitration Convention of 1958: Towards A Uniform Judicial Interpretation* (Kluwer Law International 1981) 49–50; Gino Lörcher, 'Enforceability of Agreed Awards in Foreign Jurisdictions' (2001) 17 Arbitration International 275; Richard H Kreindler, 'Settlement Agreements and Arbitration in the Context of the ICC Rules' (1998) 9 (2) ICC Bulletin 22; Lew, Mistelis, and Kröll (n 80) 636; Caron and Caplan (n 40) 783. But see Irina M Coman, 'The Role of "Consent Awards" in International Arbitration' (2021) 15 Romanian Arbitration Journal 113, 115 (stating that 'there is still a slight uncertainty when it comes to enforceability under the NYC').

for example as being contrary to the public policy of the country where recognition and enforcement is sought in the terms of Article V(2)(b) of the New York Convention.[95]

IV. Conclusion

The ideal outcome of dispute settlement procedures is the amicable settlement of the dispute and nobody is better placed to determine the terms of a settlement that is satisfactory to the parties than the parties themselves. In the field of international investment, an agreed settlement may allow for the investment in question to continue or may foster new investments involving the investor and the host state parties to the dispute. Provisions on consent awards in arbitral rules facilitate settlement agreements by providing the parties with the option to accord these agreements the status of an award, with the corresponding enforcement safeguards in case any of the parties fails to implement the agreement.

According to the database of the United Nations Conference on Trade and Development (UNCTAD), as of 31 December 2022 out of 1257 known treaty-based investment arbitration cases, which include arbitrations conducted under different arbitration rules, 171 had been settled and 121 discontinued.[96] The share of settled or otherwise discontinued ICSID arbitrations (36 per cent) is somewhat higher but not substantially different.[97] Within the settled or otherwise discontinued ICSID arbitrations, in only 11 per cent of the cases a settlement agreement was embodied in an award at the parties' request.[98] Given that according to the UNCITRAL figures the number of settled cases is higher than that of discontinued cases (and that discontinued cases may also involve a settlement by the parties), there would seem to be room for a greater recourse to consent awards. As was the case decades ago with investment arbitration generally, the lack of familiarity with the relevant provisions among international arbitration users may be one of the factors preventing a sustained increase in the number of consent awards. In this respect, the fact that a good number of consent awards are not published[99] does not help. While there may be good reasons for all or part of the

[95] See generally Flore Poloni and Nicolas Brooke, 'Arbitral Tribunals Beware: Better Keep an Eye on Potential Corruption Involving Consent Awards' (*Kluwer Arbitration Blog*, 19 January 2021) <http://arbitrationblog.kluwerarbitration.com/2021/01/29/arbitral-tribunals-beware-better-keep-an-eye-on-potential-corruption-involvingconsent-awards/>.

[96] See UNCTAD, 'Investment Dispute Settlement Navigator' (Investment Policy Hub) <https://investmentpolicy.unctad.org/investment-dispute-settlement?status=6> (information correct as of 16 September 2023).

[97] See ICSID, 'ICSID Caseload—Statistics. Issue 2023—2' (ICSID Caseload—Statistics) 12.

[98] ibid 14.

[99] See *Samsung Engineering Co, Ltd v Oman*, ICSID Case No ARB/15/30, Final Award Embodying Parties' Settlement (17 January 2018); *SGS Société Générale de Surveillance SA v Philippines*, ICSID Case No ARB/02/6, Award embodying the parties' settlement agreement (11 April 2008); *Türkiye Petrolleri Anonim Ortaklığı v Kazakhstan*, ICSID Case No ARB/11/2, Award embodying the parties' settlement agreement (18 August 2014); *Société d'Energie et d'Eau du Gabon and Veolia Africa v Gabon*, ICSID Case No ARB/18/36, Award embodying the parties' settlement agreement (29 March 2019); *Enel Green Power SpA v El Salvador*, ICSID Case No ARB/13/18, Award embodying the parties' settlement agreement (14 September 2015); *Compagnie Française pour le Développement des Fibres Textiles v Côte d'Ivoire*, ICSID Case No ARB/97/8, Award embodying the parties' settlement agreement (4 April 2000); *Guadalupe Gas Products Corporation v Nigeria*, ICSID Case No ARB/78/1, Award embodying the parties' settlement agreement (22 July 1980); *Barmek Holding AS v Azerbaijan*, ICSID Case No ARB/06/16, Award embodying the parties' settlement agreement (28 September 2009); *WRB Enterprises and*

settlement agreement to remain confidential, arbitral institutions are well placed to encourage parties to consent to the publication of consent awards (with any redactions that may be necessary). As more consent awards become public, their benefits and the requirements applicable to them will be better understood.

Grenada Private Power Limited v Grenada, ICSID Case No ARB/97/5, Award embodying the parties' settlement agreement (21 December 1998); *Petronor E&P Gambia Limited and APCL Gambia BV v Gambia*, ICSID Case No ARB/17/38, Award embodying the parties' settlement agreement (27 October 2020); *Millicom International Operations BV and Sentel GSM SA v Senegal*, ICSID Case No ARB/08/20, Award (27 November 2012); *Cemex Asia Holdings Ltd v Indonesia*, ICSID Case No ARB/04/3, Award embodying the parties' settlement agreement, pursuant to Arbitration r 43(2) (23 February 2007); *MTN (Dubai) Limited and MTN Yemen for Mobile Telephones v Yemen*, ICSID Case No ARB/09/7, Award (25 June 2010); *Consolidated Exploration Holdings Lt and others v Kyrgyz Republic*, ICSID Case No ARB(AF)/13/1, Award (1 September 2015).

6

Draft Awards

Twirling Curls on a Bald Head

*Friedl Weiss**

I. Introduction

Generally, a decision in international investment arbitration refers to the position of an arbitral tribunal in relation to any kind of question relating to the conduct or the resolution of the dispute. Arbitration rules in investment arbitration allow tribunals to decide on a subject through either an award, a decision, or an order. There is no clear definition of the notion of award. ICSID arbitration, however, distinguishes between decisions and awards. Only awards may be subject to a post-award remedy.[1]

The draft award is a preliminary, non-binding decision in the decision-making process that is issued by an arbitral tribunal. It is commonly issued after a tribunal's consideration of evidence and the parties' arguments on such issues as jurisdiction, liability and damages and may include a proposed resolution of the issue. An arbitral tribunal's draft final award is an unfinished award. As such, prior to its issuance, it obviously lacks any legal force or effect whatsoever, even if impeccably drafted, closely similar or nearly identical to the final version. While different arbitration rules may feature draft awards under inconsistently used terminology, draft awards are not interlocutory, separate, single, provisional (interim/conservatory),[2] additional,[3] early determination awards,[4]

* I would like to express my deepest gratitude to Christoph Schreuer for his valuable and critically constructive feedback, saving me from making the most egregious mistakes in a draft of this chapter. Those that remain are entirely my own responsibility.

[1] Andrew Willcocks and Karla Lucero Andrade, 'Decision in Investment Arbitration' *Jus Mundi* (7 April 2023). See further Catharine Titi, 'What Is an Award? Concept, Content, Drafting, Effects' in Katia Fach Gómez and Catharine Titi (eds), *The Award in International Investment Arbitration* (OUP 2024).

[2] The aim of these temporary remedies which are granted under special circumstances is to preserve parties' rights—both substantive and procedural—pending the decision on the merits. International tribunals usually possess an express power contained in their constitutive instrument to grant provisional measures, see eg ICSID Convention art 47 and Arbitration Rule 39; UNCITRAL Arbitration Rules (2021) art 26; Chester Brown, *A Common Law of International Adjudication* (OUP 2007) 123.

[3] See eg 2021 ICC Arbitration Rules art 36(3) providing that within thirty days of receipt of the award, a party may request the arbitral tribunal to issue an additional award to rule upon claims raised during the proceedings but left unaddressed in the award; the new rules are accompanied by a revised Note to Parties and Arbitral Tribunals on the Conduct of the Arbitration under the ICC Rules of Arbitration (dated 1 January 2021) (hereinafter 'Note to Parties'). This revision of the 2017 Rules aligns ICC Arbitration Rules with those other rules which already deal with this issue: see eg 2013 Hong Kong International Arbitration Centre (HKIAC) Arbitration Rules art 40, 2014 London Court of International Arbitration (LCIA) Arbitration Rules art 27, 2016 Singapore International Arbitration Centre (SIAC) Arbitration Rules art 33, and 2017 Stockholm Chamber of Commerce (SCC) Arbitration Rules art 48.

[4] See eg Rules of Procedure of the Iran–United States Claims Tribunal (IUSCT) art 32 on form and effect of award; Arbitration Rules of the London Chamber of Arbitration and Mediation (LCAM) art 39.1 allows the

Friedl Weiss, *Draft Awards* In: *The Award in International Investment Arbitration*. Edited by: Katia Fach Gómez and Catharine Titi, Oxford University Press. © Katia Fach Gómez and Aikaterini Titi 2024. DOI: 10.1093/9780191975936.003.0006

or conservatory measures.[5] Put simply, draft awards are 'work-in-progress'—or preliminary versions of a tribunal's ruling on a given matter.[6] The purpose of a draft award is to provide an indication of the tribunal's findings and reasoning on certain issues as well as an opportunity to comment, object to, and review the draft award before the final award is rendered.

It is, of course, acknowledged that perhaps the most attractive feature of arbitration as a 'one shot', tailor-made dispute resolution mechanism is the finality, that is the irreversibility and non-reviewability of awards[7] and the absence of appeals.

In ongoing discussions about procedural reforms of international dispute settlement mechanisms it has often been pointed out that domestic jurisdictions never presume adjudicative infallibility. In fact, they practically always provide some kind of review or remedy for such possible contingencies beyond the mere correction of clerical errors and possibly opaquely formulated awards. Still, draft awards do not appear to be reviewable by domestic courts under any legal system, if only because they are not binding on the parties concerned so that the dissatisfied party lacks legal standing to seek their review.[8] Although, under the autonomous ICSID arbitration system, final awards are not as such sacrosanct, as it were, the role of domestic courts is limited to their recognition and enforcement.[9] True, arbitral institutions too may allow the internal scrutiny of draft awards, commonly carried out by the members of the arbitral tribunal themselves, but to a far lesser extent.[10] Some commentators, therefore, have advocated 'encouraging arbitrators, at least in some circumstances, to distribute draft

arbitral tribunal to 'decide a separate issue or part of the dispute in a separate award or awards, made at different times'; the LCAM Rules also permit the correction and interpretation of an award (art 42), as well as the making of an additional award (art 43); Arbitration Rules of the SCC 2023 art 44 provides rules for separate awards on separate issues or part of the dispute, other of its provisions for corrections and interpretation and additional awards; 2018 HKIAC Administered Arbitration Rules arts 35, 40 (correction or interpretation), 43.

[5] 2021 Arbitration Rules of the International Chamber of Commerce (ICC) art 28 on conservatory and interim measures; Rules of Investment Arbitration and Mediation of the Vienna International Arbitral Centre (VIAC) art 33.

[6] Julio-César Betancourt, 'Is an Arbitral Tribunal's Draft Award Susceptible to Judicial Review?' (*Kluwer Arbitration Blog*, 18 June 2020).

[7] Stephan Schill and others, *Schreuer's Commentary on the ICSID Convention*, vol 2 (3rd edn, CUP 2022) 1447–57 ('Article 53'); 1478–85 ('Article 54').

[8] Luis Capiel and Alicia Larrazabal, 'Is Arbitration in Venezuela in Danger?' (*Kluwer Arbitration Blog*, 27 May 2020), commenting on the Venezuelan Supreme Court's decision to stay institutional arbitration proceedings. See also comment thereon by Betancourt (n 6).

[9] Discussing three types of post-award recourse—set-aside by the courts of the seat of the arbitration, opposition to enforcement action in courts of third states, and award annulment in ICSID cases, see Freya Baetens, 'Keeping the status quo or Embarking on a New Course? Setting Aside, Refusal of Enforcement, Annulment and Appeal' in Andreas Kulick (ed), *Reassertion of Control over the Investment Treaty Regime* (CUP 2016) 103–27. Barbara Helene Steindl showed that the grounds for annulment in Article 52 of the ICSID Convention are drafted in a more restrictive language than the grounds for set-aside under Article 34 of the UNCITRAL Model Law, but also that 'apart from some state courts sitting on set-aside in the host state, state courts also seem to apply the grounds for annulment more restrictively than ICSID ad hoc Committees generally do', Barbara Helene Steindl, 'ICSID Annulment vs Set Aside by State Courts—Compared to ICSID ad hoc Annulment Committees, Is It the State Courts that Are Now More Hesitant to Set Aside Awards?' (2015) 4 Yearbook on International Arbitration 181, 202. See also Gabriel Bottini, 'Present and Future of ICSID Annulment: The Path to an Appellate Body?' (2013) 31 (3) ICSID Review 712. See also Albert Jan van den Berg, 'Should the Setting Aside of the Arbitral Award Be abolished?' (2024) 29 (2) ICSID Review 263.

[10] See eg ICC Arbitration Rules (2021) art 34 and SIAC Rules (2016) Rule 32.3, referenced in Betancourt (n 6).

awards before they are issued as final',[11] or that 'institutions should at least consider adding rules that regulate these specific issues [revision proceedings] in case the *lex arbitri* allows for the revision of awards by the original tribunal'.[12]

However, the recently amended International Centre for Settlement of Investment Disputes (ICSID) and United Nations Commission on International Trade Law (UNCITRAL) rules focus on institutional and structural investor-state dispute settlement (ISDS) reforms. Likewise, recent trade and investment treaties, whether concluded or under negotiation, contain clauses on improved institutional and procedural mechanisms including the establishment of a multilateral investment tribunal and a multilateral appellate mechanism.[13] But rules on draft awards as such were not included. Likewise, the Multi-Party Interim Appeal Arbitration (MPIA), a contingency arrangement of some members of the Word Trade Organization (WTO) pending any future reactivation of the WTO's currently defunct Appellate Body, sought to 'preserve the essential principles and features of the WTO dispute settlement system', not to reform it.[14]

Reason enough, it would seem, to have a closer look at samples of selected arbitration and dispute settlement practice on draft awards, using probative practice examples from the WTO's proximate procedures for the review of WTO interim panel reports for comparative calibration.[15]

II. Draft Awards: Texts and Practice

A. Texts on Draft Awards

Provisions on draft awards in the sense of unfinished awards, may feature in rules for international dispute settlement, albeit under idiosyncratically crafted names and

[11] Lawrence W Newman and David Zaslowsky, 'The Case for Distributing Draft Awards' (2021) New York Law Journal 93. The new 'Note to Parties' under the 2021 ICC Rules of Arbitration confirms that 'the arbitral tribunal may encourage the parties to consider settling all or part of their disputes. either by negotiation or through any form of amicable dispute resolution method, such as mediation under the ICC Mediation Rules'.

[12] Sven Lange and Felipe Volio Soley, 'Justice versus Finality: Is It Time to Revisit the Rules on the Revision of Arbitral Awards?' (*Kluwer Arbitration Blog*, 11 November 2022).

[13] A number of trade and investment agreements concluded by the EU provide for an investment court system: Canada–EU Comprehensive Economic and Trade Agreement (CETA) (art 8.29), EU–Vietnam Investment Protection Agreement (art 3.41), EU–Singapore Investment Protection Agreement (art 3.12), EU–Mexico Agreement in Principle (Section C of the chapter on Investment); cf Report of the EU Commission of 11 August 2022 on the 7th Round of negotiations between the EU and Mexico for modernizing the trade part of the EU—Mexico Global Agreement (12–22 December 2017); Submission of the European Union and its Member States to UNCITRAL Working Group III, 'Establishing a Standing Mechanism for the Settlement of International Investment Disputes', 18 January 2019; Gabrielle Kaufmann-Kohler and Michele Potesta, *Investor-State Dispute Settlement and National Courts: Current Framework and Reform Options* (Springer 2020); Friedl Weiss, 'The WTO—A Suitable Case for Treatment? Is It "Reformable"' in Antonio Segura Serrano (ed), *The Reform of International Economic Governance* (Routledge 2016) 119–41.

[14] Gabrielle Marceau and Jenya Grigorova 'On the Multiparty Interim Appeal Arbitration Arrangement. Overview and Explanation' January 2022 (unpublished).

[15] Understanding on Rules and Procedures Governing the Settlement of Disputes (DSU); Friedl Weiss, 'Trade and Investment' in Peter Muchlinski, Federico Ortino, and Christoph Schreuer (eds), *The Oxford Handbook of International Investment Law* (OUP 2008) 182–223.

functions. These include draft awards *eo nomine*,[16] decisions including interim decisions, rulings, findings, even interim panel reports,[17] and arbitration panels, to name but the most common. For instance, in the practice of the International Chamber of Commerce (ICC), all draft awards are subject to further scrutiny by the ICC Court which 'may lay down modifications as to the form of the award and, without affecting the arbitral tribunal's liberty of decision, may also draw its attention to points of substance'.[18] Approval will be notified by the Secretariat of the Court to the arbitral tribunal which then signs the award rendering it final and enforceable, thereby concluding this quality-control mechanism.[19]

1. Precis of Important Arbitration Rules

ISDS is intended to protect foreign investors, by providing reliable dispute settlement mechanisms giving investors compensation for the damage caused in case the host state acts in a way which would be inconsistent with its legal obligations.[20] In recent years investment arbitration for the settlement of cross-border disputes between foreign investors and host states (ISDS), has had to face up to a seriously bad press, to put it metaphorically. Nearly every aspect of ISDS is the subject of animated prolonged and ongoing debates.

But in 1984, 2006, and 2022 the ICSID member states—*cognita ab experientia*—succeeded in amending the ICSID Arbitration Rules together with the other Regulations and Rules.[21] Yet, as mentioned, draft awards, *eo nomine*, do not feature in any of them.[22] Likewise, no reference to draft awards is to be found in the reworked 2021 UNCITRAL

[16] 2021 ICC Arbitration Rules art 27 on the closing of the proceedings and the date for submission of draft awards.

[17] CETA art 29(9).

[18] 2021 ICC Arbitration Rules art 34. The court's decision formulating its position is communicated by the Secretariat to the arbitral tribunal, but not the parties, who are not informed of the court's deliberations.

[19] Felix Dasser and Emmanuel O Igbokwe, 'The Award and the Courts, Efficient Drafting of the Arbitral Award: Traditional Ways Revisited—Lesson Learned from the Past?' in Christian Klausegger and others (eds), *Austrian Yearbook of International Arbitration* (Manz'sche Verlags- und Universitätsbuchhandlung 2019) 279–315. For the separate and controversial discussion of the proper scope of the role of arbitral secretaries in this regard—drafting only procedural and factual sections of awards or also substantive parts, see Michael Polkinghorne and Charles B Rosenberg, 'The Role of the Tribunal Secretary in International Arbitration: A Call for a Uniform Standard' (2014) 8 Dispute Resolution International 107–26. See further Claudia Frutos-Peterson, Marat Umerov, and Marija Ozolins, 'The Role of Tribunal Secretaries in the Drafting of Investment Awards' in Fach Gómez and Titi (n 1).

[20] Organisation for Economic Co-operation and Development (OECD), 'Appointing Authorities and the Selection of Arbitrators in Investor-State Dispute Settlement: An Overview Compilation of Initial Comments Received', March 2018, 23 <www.oecd.org/investment/investment-policy/ISDS-Appointing-Authorities-Arbitration-March-2018.pdf>

[21] ICSID, 'ICSID Rules and Regulations Amendment' <https://icsid.worldbank.org/resources/rules-amendments>

[22] ICSID Convention art 51 allows a written request for the revision of an award on the ground of discovery of a fact decisively affecting the award but unknown to the tribunal and the applicant prior to the issuance of the award; cf also Arbitration Rules rr 58–69, especially rule 61 according to which a party may request a supplementary decision specifying any question which the tribunal omitted to decide in the Award (para 2(c)(i)), any clerical, arithmetical or similar error in the award to be corrected (para 2(c)(ii)); ICSID Additional Facility Arbitration Rules rr 72 and 87 allow a tribunal on its own initiative to 'rectify any clerical, arithmetic or similar error in the Award', and a party to 'request a supplementary decision, rectification or interpretation of an Award' permit requests for a supplementary decision on rectification of an award, and applications for interpretation of an Award which shall become part of the award.

Arbitration Rules,[23] nor in the Rules of Procedure of the Iran–United States Claims Tribunal which incorporate them.[24] However, the 2021 ICC Arbitration Rules which define and regulate the management of cases received by the International Court of Arbitration contain several provisions which explicitly deal with draft awards.[25]

Distinct from provisions on draft awards are those which concern review of final awards.[26] Manifestly, arbitration rules continue to evolve and to be revised as practice requires, without reflecting an approach acceptable across jurisdictions. Nonetheless, in the almost complete absence of explicitly pertinent procedural rules on draft awards, arbitral practice may in some cases be inspired by or taking note or account of proximate rules operating under other dispute settlement mechanisms.[27]

2. WTO's Understanding on Rules and Procedures Governing the Settlement of Disputes

'Draft Reports' in the dispute settlement system of the WTO exhibit characteristic features which—to some extent—appear functionally similar, possibly equivalent to comparable draft arbitration awards based on some of the mentioned arbitration rules. However, by contrast to the mentioned relative dearth of explicit ISDS rules and practice on draft awards, the contracting parties of the General Agreement on Tariffs and Trade (GATT)[28] and—since 1995—the members of the WTO have designed and developed such rules and practice.[29] Indeed, the so-called Interim Review Stage based

[23] See also <https://uncitral.un.org/en/texts/arbitration/contractualtexts/arbitration>

[24] However, Article 36 of the Rules of the IUSCT (last revised in 1983) allows either arbitrating party to request the arbitral tribunal 'to correct in the award any errors in computation, any clerical or typographical errors, or any errors of similar nature'; see thereon Decision on Correction to Award and Decision on Request for Correction and Additional Award No DEC 137-A15 (II:A)/A26 (IV)/B-43-FT in Cases of the Full Tribunal Nos A15 (II:A), A 26 (IV), and B 43.

[25] ICC Arbitration Rules art 27 on the closing of the proceedings and the date for submission of *draft* awards; ICC Arbitration Rules appendix I (Statutes of the International Court of Arbitration) art 5 on special committees; art 6 on single-member committees; and ICC Arbitration Rules appendix II (Internal Rules of the International Court of Arbitration) art 7 on scrutiny of arbitral awards.

[26] On post-award procedures and remedies of supplementation, rectification, interpretation, revision and annulment see ICSID Convention arts 49–53; see also 2021 UNCITRAL Arbitration Rules arts 37 (interpretation), 38 (correction), 39 (additional award); LCAM arts 42 and 43 allow the arbitral tribunal both to correct any clerical, typographical or computational errors in an award and the making of an additional award; 2023 SCC Arbitration Rules arts 44 and 47 allow separate awards on separate issues or part of the dispute, as well as corrections and interpretation and additional awards. See also Karsten Nowrot and Emily Sipiorski, 'Review beyond Annulment: Correction, Additional Awards, Clarification, and Revision' in Fach Gómez and Titi (n 1).

[27] In 1946 a Preparatory Committee of the UN Conference on Trade and Development discussed, but ultimately declined to retain the possibility of recourse to the ICJ for the settlement of their trade disputes, Memorandum E/PC/T/C.V/35 of 21 November 1946, 2; ICSID Convention art 51 is modelled on the Statute of the International Court of Justice art 61, Schill and others (n 7) 1201. See also n 313 in AB Report *US—Stainless Steel (Mexico)*, WT/DS344/AB/R, 30 April 2008 [161], wherein the AB discusses the International Criminal Tribunal for the Former Yugoslavia (ICTY)—Case No IT-95-14/1-A, *Prosecutor v Aleksovski*, Judgment (24 March 2000) [113] and *Saipem SpA v Bangladesh*, ICSID Case No ARB/05/07, Decision on Jurisdiction and Recommendation on Provisional Measures (21 March 2007) [67], to draw significance from how other international fora regard dispute decision consistency.

[28] A first attempt to codify, improve, and refine the basic GATT mechanism for the management of disputes based on Articles XXII and XXIII was made in the form of the 1979 Tokyo Round Understanding on Notification, Consultation, Dispute Settlement and Surveillance, L/4897, BISD 26S/210.

[29] World Trade Organization Secretariat, *A Handbook on the WTO Dispute Settlement System* (2nd edn, CUP 2017). For an appraisal of the preceding GATT practice, see William J Davey, 'Dispute Settlement in GATT' (1987) 11 (1) Fordham International Law Journal 51.

on Article 15 of the WTO's Understanding on Rules and Procedures Governing the Settlement of Disputes (DSU) [30] consists of a set of specific procedural steps dedicated to the review of 'interim reports', that is almost final panel reports, essentially draft panel reports.[31] Paragraph 1 of Article 15 states that 'the panel shall issue the descriptive (factual and argument) sections of its draft report to the parties to the dispute. Within a period of time set by the panel, the parties shall submit their comments in writing.' This gives parties an opportunity to comment on the panel's interim report, prior to its finalization, mostly in order to rectify any errors of relevant fact and parties' arguments.

Paragraph 2 of Article 15 stipulates that after the expiration of the set period of time for receipt of comments from the parties, the panel 'shall issue an interim report to the parties, including both the descriptive sections and the panel's findings and conclusions'.[32] Also, again within a period of time set by the panel:

> a party may submit a written request for the panel to review precise aspects of the interim report prior to circulation of the final report to the Members. At the request of a party, the panel shall hold a further meeting with the parties on the issues identified in the written comments.

Thus, Article 15 of the DSU provides for an 'interim review stage' consisting of three components:

(i) the issuance of the descriptive part of a panel report (facts and arguments only) with the parties given an opportunity to submit written comments prior to the report's finalization;
(ii) the subsequent issuance of an 'interim report', including both the descriptive part and the panel's findings and conclusions, with the parties afforded an opportunity to provide comments in writing and/or at a meeting with the panel prior to the report's finalization; and
(iii) the inclusion of a discussion of the arguments made at the interim review stage in the final report.[33]

During the Uruguay Round of multilateral trade negotiations (September 1986–April 1994), advocates of this innovative, more comprehensive, and robust review

[30] Understanding on Rules and Procedures Governing the Settlement of Disputes (DSU), Annex 2 to the WTO Agreement.

[31] For an excellent overview including of its historical antecedents, see Andrea Mastromatteo and Sagnik Sinha, 'Interim Review: Dispute Settlement of the World Trade Organization (WTO)' in *Max Planck Encyclopedia of International Procedural Law* (OUP 2018) para 14.

[32] The 1979 Understanding did not provide for parties' written comments and suggestions regarding the substantive part of a panel report relating to the scope and merits of the legal reasoning since the findings, conclusions, and recommendations were only disclosed to the parties in the final report. Errors of law, therefore, could only be raised in the GATT Council, a political body. Due to the positive consensus rule then applicable to the adoption of panel reports in the Council, a party that had done so could block its adoption.

[33] See Mastromatteo and Sinha (n 31) 5.

process had argued that it might more readily persuade recognizably losing parties to accept a panel's conclusions and to refrain from appealing final panel reports. Still, the limited function of the interim review stage was confirmed by the very existence of a novel appeal procedure in which parties may raise 'issues of law covered in the panel report and legal interpretations developed by the panel'.[34]

Finally, Paragraph 3 of Article 15 of the DSU postulates that 'the final panel report shall include a discussion of the arguments made at the interim review stage. The interim review stage shall be conducted within the time-period set out in paragraph 8 of Article 12.'[35]

B. Practice: What Is and What Isn't Reviewable

1. Review of Interim Panel Reports

As the DSU's Interim Review Stage was one of the procedural innovations introduced during the Uruguay Round, WTO panels have extensively scrutinized Article 15 of the DSU, thereby providing interpretative clarifications of its key concepts.[36]

i. Requests to review 'precise aspects' of the interim report

In *Japan—Alcoholic Beverages* II, the panel noted that, drawing 'guidance from Article 15.2 DSU... with the broadest possible interpretation', the purpose of the interim review stage was to consider 'specific and particular aspects' of the interim report which it considered 'sufficiently specific and detailed', but 'not to provide the parties with an opportunity to introduce new legal issues and evidence, or to enter into a debate with the panel'.[37] Likewise, another panel declined a request for a 'whole of report review' as not being related to 'precise aspects' of the interim report.[38]

ii. No new evidence, no new arguments, no arguments on new grounds

The explicit confirmation of this finding by the WTO's Appellate Body (AB)[39] 'that the interim review stage is not the appropriate time to introduce new and unanswered

[34] DSU art 17.6.

[35] ibid art 12.8 aims at more efficient panel procedures, requiring that their total duration until the date the final report is issued to the parties to the dispute 'shall, as a general rule, not exceed six months'.

[36] This section analyses summarized excerpts from the WTO Analytical Index DSU—Art 15 (DS Reports), current as of August 2023.

[37] Panel Report, *Japan—Alcoholic Beverages II*, WT/DS8, 10, 11/R, 11 July 1996 [5.2]. The AB confirmed that the interim review stage is not an appropriate time to introduce new evidence, AB Report, *EC—Sardines*, WT/DS231/AB/R, 26 September 2002 [301].

[38] Panel Report, *Australia—Salmon*, WT/DS18/R, 12 June 1998 [7.3]. Statement also recalled in Panel Report *US/Canada—Canada—Continued Suspension*, WT/DS321/R, 31 March 2008 [6.16]-[6.17], and *US—Continued Suspension*, WT/DS320/R, 31 March 2008 [6.18].

[39] See DSU art 17. The AB became defunct in December 2019. On 27 March 2020, some WTO Members agreed to a Multi-Party Interim Appeal Arbitration Arrangement (MPIA) based on DSU art 25 as a 'contingency measure ... in order to preserve the essential principles and features of the WTO dispute settlement system'. See MPIA preamble <https://trade.ec.europa.eu/doclib/docs/2020/march/tradoc_158685.pdf>

evidence'[40] was quoted and consistently followed by several panels.[41] Some of them have taken the view that 'to include such newly-submitted evidence ... would ... be unfair and would deprive the [United States] of the due process to which it is entitled in dispute settlement in the WTO'.[42] Several panels ruled out rearguing a case on new grounds,[43] some pointing to the limited function of the interim review stage which is 'confirmed by the existence of an appeal procedure, where parties may address issues of law covered in the panel report and challenge legal interpretations developed by the panel (Article 17.6 of the DSU)'.[44]

Similarly, one panel affirmed its understanding that 'the purpose of the interim review stage is not to allow a party to raise new arguments or develop arguments which were at most merely alluded to during the course of the proceeding',[45] but nonetheless considered it 'useful to address certain points made' by a party in its request for review.[46]

iii. Facts of the descriptive part of the interim report

As to the issuance of the descriptive (factual and arguments) part of the report, panels have invariably dealt with challenged factual matters in the 'findings' section of the report, 'to the extent ... necessary ... to resolve ... disputed factual issues',[47] rather than in the section on Factual Aspects of the descriptive part.

Commenting on the interim report containing the panel's findings, one party provided additional comments on the descriptive part (request for review of the language), though outside the two-week period previously allocated by the panel for such comments. Nonetheless, the panel decided to accept them 'in order to ensure the accuracy of the description of the facts in this Report'.[48]

iv. Requests to change conclusions, findings

One panel was persuaded by a party's request for interim review to reconsider certain evidence. It accepted that its original conclusion 'was incorrect as a matter of fact'

[40] AB Report, *EC—Sardines*, WT/DS231/AB/R, 26 September 2002 [301]; Panel Report, *US—Tuna II (Mexico)*, WT/DS381/R, 15 September 2011 [6.3].

[41] Panel Report, *EC—Approval and Marketing of Biotech Products*, WT/DS291/R, 29 September 2006 [6.134]; Panel Report, *EC—Bananas III (Article 21.5—United States)* [6.18]; Panel Report, *Russia—Pigs*, WT/DS475/R, 19 August 2016 [6.16]; Panel Report, *EC—Sardines*, WT/DS231/R, 29 May 2002 [6.16]; Panel Report, *EC—Selected Customs Matters*, WT/DS315/R, 16 June 2006 [6.6]; Panel Report, *EC—Seal Products*, WT/DS401/R, 25 November 2013 [6.55].

[42] Panel Report, *EC and Certain Member States—Large Civil Aircraft*, WT/DS316/R, 30 June 2010 [6.311].

[43] eg Panel Report, *Japan—Apples (Article 21.5—US)*, WT/DS245/RW, 23 June 2005 [7.23]; Panel Report, *Indonesia—Chicken (Article 21.5—Brazil)*, WT/DS484/RW, 10 November 2020 [6.43, 6.59, and 6.65].

[44] Panel Report, *US—1916 Act (EC)*, WT/DS136/R, 31 March 2000, n 279; however, a dissenting member of the Appellate Division in *Australia—Tobacco Plain Packaging* found the alleged limited nature of the interim review process not expressed in the text of DSU art 15.2, AB Reports, WT/DS435/AB/R, WT/DS441/AB/R, 9 June 2020 [6.542].

[45] eg Panel Report, *Canada—Renewable Energy/Canada—Feed-in Tariff Program*, WT/DS/426/R, 19 December 2012 [6.113]; Panel Report, *EC and Certain Member States—Large Civil Aircraft*, WT/DS316, 30 June 2010 [6.311]; Panel Report, *US—COOL (Article 21.5—Canada and Mexico)*, WT/DS385/RW, 20 October 2014 [6.70]–[6.76]; AB Report, *US—COOL (Article 21.5—Canada and Mexico)*, WT/DS385/AB/RW, 18 May 2015 [5.379].

[46] Panel Report, *US—Zeroing (EC) (Article 21.5—EC)*, WT/DS294/RW, 17 December 2008 [7.26].

[47] Panel Report, *US—Clove Cigarettes*, WT/DS406/R, 2 September 2011 [2.3].

[48] ibid [6.3]; also Panel Report, *EC—Salmon (Norway)*, WT/DS337/R, 16 November 2007 [6.9]–[6.10].

and changed its conclusion.[49] Another panel considered a request for review of 'precise aspects' of its interim report to legitimately include requests for 'reconsideration' of specific factual or legal findings, but not—as previously emphasized by the AB[50]—for the introduction of new and unanswered evidence. That panel did not, therefore, 'find it necessary to exclude *a prio*ri from consideration any request for review from either party on the sole basis that it would seek reconsideration by the panel of some of its determinations'.[51]

In light of a party's explanation of the record of evidence, one panel reconsidered its findings of violation, changed them to a finding of no violation of a subsidy programme and revised the respective parts of the interim report.[52] Another panel felt obliged to revise its findings with respect to certain additional arguments presented at the interim review stage, but not addressed in the interim report, even though it was of the view that these arguments could have been raised in a more coherent manner.[53]

v. Jurisdictional issues

Faced with new arguments, one panel acknowledged that Article 15 of the DSU does not appear to prohibit raising them at the interim review stage. That panel, however, also noted that Appendix 3 to the DSU provides 'well defined steps in the proceedings during which the parties may raise arguments in support of their positions'. It further pointed out that:

> the fact that the interim review takes place at the very end of those proceedings, once all submissions have been made, hearings have taken place and a draft report has been issued to the parties, is evidence that this stage of the proceedings is not meant to address issues which could have been better addressed in the written and oral proceedings conducted by the Panel.

Moreover, dispute settlement in good faith (DSU art 3.10) implies that arguments should not be withheld until the interim review stage when they could legitimately have been 'raised at a much earlier stage of the proceedings, in light of the claims developed in the first submissions'. Nonetheless, that panel also found that since 'since Article 15.3 of the DSU provides that the final report shall include a discussion of the arguments made at the interim review stage', it could also consider some issues of jurisdiction raised for the first time at that stage.[54] The AB agreed, both 'that the interim review was not an appropriate stage in the panel's proceedings to raise objections to the

[49] Panel Report, *EC and Certain Member States—Large Civil Aircraft*, WT/DS316/R, 30 June 2010 [6.230]–[6.231].
[50] See AB Report, *EC—Sardines*, WT/DS231/AB/R, 26 September 2002 [301].
[51] Panel Report, *US—Tuna II (Mexico)*, WT/DS381/R, 15 September 2011 [6.3].
[52] Panel Report, *India—Export Related Measures*, WT/DS541/R, 31 October 2019, annex A-2 [5.12]–[5.20].
[53] Panel Report, *Korea—Imports of Certain Paper*, WT/DS312/R, 28 October 2005 [6.5].
[54] Panel Report, *US—1916 Act (EC)*, WT/DS136/R, 31 March 2000 [5.18]–[5.19].

panel's jurisdiction for the first time', and that these 'should be raised as early as possible', but also that, as in this case, 'some issues of jurisdiction may be of such a nature that they have to be addressed by the panel at any time'.[55]

vi. Correction or clarification of errors of fact

When neither party had claimed that the panel had made any substantive error in its assessment of the facts, but one had requested review 'without prejudice' to its position on all the aspects of the panel's report, the panel considered that 'if it had misunderstood or misrepresented some of the factual aspects of the case in its findings, the parties would need the interim review stage in order to make the necessary corrections or clarifications because, unlike errors of law, errors of fact cannot usually be modified on appeal'. It added, that 'the parties should take advantage of this last opportunity to rectify the factual assessments of the Panel otherwise the Panel could unnecessarily be at risk of being accused of not having made an objective evaluation of the facts'.[56]

A panel expressed surprise that a party's request for interim review provided only 'some examples' of the 'numerous and serious errors in the reasoning of the Panel on the scientific issues underpinning the dispute' but failed to provide a 'detailed and complete list of all omissions and errors' and 'reserve[d] the right to make all its comments at the appeal stage', rather than before the panel, at the procedural stage 'expressly designed for the purpose of considering any and all comments on the interim report'. Providing only 'some examples', that panel found, 'suggests that it has already decided to appeal the panel report unless the panel makes changes which [the party] will not specify'.[57]

vii. Status of un-appealed parts of panel findings

Un-appealed parts of a final panel report are not to be regarded as some kind of variant specimen of a draft report. However, they become legally binding only upon adoption by the Dispute Settlement Body (DSB), since both final panel reports and AB Reports must be treated by the parties to a particular dispute as a final resolution to that dispute.[58] Although unadopted panel and AB Reports have no formal legal value in the WTO system, the reasoning contained in them may nonetheless provide persuasive guidance to a subsequent panel or the AB involving the same legal questions.[59] In this regard, as pointed out by Gabrielle Marceau and Jenya Grigorova, no changes were

[55] ibid [54].

[56] Panel Report, *EC—Asbestos*, WT/DS135/R, 18 September 2000 [7.2]; DSU art 11.

[57] Panel Reports, *Canada—Continued Suspension*, WT/DS321/R, 31 March 2008 [6.14], and *US—Continued Suspension*, WT/DS320, 31 March 2008 [6.15].

[58] DSU arts 16(4), 17(14); in *EC—Bed Linen (Article 21.5—India)*, the AB confirmed that 'in our view, an unappealed finding included in a panel report that is adopted by the DSB must be treated as a final resolution to a dispute between the parties in respect of the particular claim and the specific component of a measure that is the subject of that claim', WT/DS141/AB/RW, 8 April 2003 [93].

[59] AB Report, *Japan—Alcoholic Beverages II*, WT/DS8/R, 11 July 1996, DSR 1996: I, 97, 108.

introduced by the MPIA.[60] Only final panel reports may be appealed before the MPIA arbitrator, a process initiated by a party's request that the panel suspends its proceedings after the panel has issued its final report. Such a request, as explained by Gabrielle Marceau, will be automatically deemed 'to constitute a joint request by the parties for suspension of the panel proceedings for 12 months' so as to provide for the possibility of both complainant and respondent to appeal.[61]

2. Concluding remarks on reviewed Interim Panel Reports

The above summary survey shows that the practice of WTO panels in reviewing precise aspects of their legal findings and interpretations has been varied. While some panels have accepted that under Article 15.2 of the DSU a party could request review of the panel's legal findings and interpretations,[62] or even reversed findings on a claim made in the interim report as being outside its terms of reference,[63] others considered it inappropriate to re-argue a case on new grounds at the interim review stage,[64] or modify their analysis based on arguments first raised during the interim review when they could have been raised earlier in the proceedings.[65] Some clearly viewed matters of legal interpretation that had already been discussed in the course of a proceeding as 'not properly within the permissible scope of the interim review process' and 'best left for appeal rather than the interim review'.[66]

According to Article 15.3 of the DSU, 'the findings of the final report shall include a discussion of the arguments made at the interim review stage'. These are typically set out in the interim review section of the final panel report preceding its findings. They normally include a description of requests for review made by the parties, how the panel has dealt with them, and explaining which, if any of the specific aspects of the interim report the panel had agreed to change.[67]

In light of the above surveyed select practice of WTO interim review panel reports, the conclusion seems apposite that (almost) 'everything goes'. Indeed, by interpreting the phrase 'precise aspects of the interim report' broadly, some panels have shown a willingness to review even their legal findings.

Overall, and despite a number of recognized textual and operational flaws,[68] the introduction of the new and innovative DSU, including an interim review stage, has

[60] The MPIA Arrangement consists of three separate documents: a communication restating fundamental aspects as well as key features of the MPIA; annex 1 containing a template AAA (Agreed Procedures for Arbitration under DSU art 25) including a series of steps to make them operational in particular disputes, should a party wish to appeal the panel report; annex 2 contains rules governing the composition of the pool of arbitrators (para 4 of Communication JOB/DSB/1/add.12).

[61] Under DSU art 12.12, only the complainant can request the panel to suspend its work, see Marceau and Grigorova (n 14) 4.

[62] Panel Report, *US—Tuna II (Mexico)*, WT/DS381/R, 16 May 2012 [6.35].

[63] Panel Report, *US—Carbon Steel*, WT/DS213/R, 3 July 2002 [7.24] and [8.135]–[137].

[64] Panel Report, *Japan—Apples (Article 21.5—US)*, WT/DS245/RW, 23 June 2005 [7.23]–[7.24].

[65] Panel Reports, *China—Auto Parts*, WT/DS342/R, 18 July 2008 [6.31]–[6.32].

[66] Panel Report, *Indonesia—Iron or Steel Products*, WT/DS496/R, 18 August 2017, annex A-3 [2.3]–[2.4].

[67] See Mastromatteo and Sinha (n 31) 33.

[68] Possible drafting or operational imperfections were anticipated by the drafters in the Ministerial Decision on the Application and Review of the Understanding on Rules and Procedures Governing the Settlement of 14

worked reasonably well. It contributed to the quality of WTO panel reports, thereby enhancing their legitimacy. At the very least, it was observed, it is 'saving parties from the added burden of appealing erroneous findings that could be easily corrected before issuance of the final report'.[69] Moreover, since interim panel reports include the panel's findings and conclusions, parties can accurately assess whether and to what extent, if at all, their legal arguments deployed in the panel proceedings have prevailed or failed to convince the panel. Accordingly, a predictably losing party might be prompted to make an eleventh-hour attempt to seek settlement before circulation of the final panel report to the members of the WTO. After all, one should recall that 'a solution mutually acceptable to the parties to a dispute and consistent with the covered agreements is clearly to be preferred'.[70] 'Settlement' at any time is the 'top price' to be gained under the DSU. So-called retaliation is only the 'last resort' which cannot be used unilaterally but requires authorization by the DSB.[71]

Yet, statistics evidence an increasing number of appeals. This might be seen as an indication that due, perhaps, to a variety of domestic policy or strategic reasons, WTO members often seem prepared both to eschew a negotiated settlement in mandatory consultations at the start of the proceedings,[72] and even—having become aware of recognizably adverse panel findings in the interim panel report—to forego potential benefits of a confidentially reached 'last minute' mutually agreed settlement at the interim review stage.[73]

III. A Comparison between the WTO Practice on Draft Decisions and Some Review Mechanisms in ICSID Arbitration

As noted, most institutional arbitration rules lack express rules on draft awards, let alone on their revision. The ICSID Convention, however, contains some limited post-award remedies in respect of an award (art 48), as opposed to decisions issued by the arbitral tribunal during the proceedings.[74]

April 1994 which invited the Ministerial Conference to complete a full review of dispute settlement rules and procedures within four years and to take a decision thereafter on whether to continue, modify or terminate such dispute settlement rules and procedures. The review started in 1997 but never achieved agreed outcomes. The Doha Ministerial Declaration mandated further 'negotiations on improvements and clarifications' of the DSU (WTO/MIN(01)DEC/1, 9–14 November 2001 [30]), but Members were unable to conclude negotiations by the stipulated and extended deadline of May and 1 August 2004. Currently DSU review is being carried out within a framework of twelve 'thematic' issues covering a broad range of proposals made by members.

69 Mastromatteo and Sinha (n 31) 35.

70 DSU art 3.7; 'settlement' is also echoed, though less emphatically, in one of the case management techniques recommended by the 2021 ICC Arbitration Rules which consists of 'encouraging the parties to consider settlement of all or part of the dispute', appendix IV, art 1 (h).

71 So-called retaliation involves 'the possibility of suspending the application of concessions or other obligations under the covered agreements on a discriminatory basis vis- à-vis the other Member' ibid art 3.7 last sentence.

72 ibid art 4.

73 ibid art 3.7. WTO Members attribute the relatively infrequent success of consultations—approximately in only 25 percent of cases—to a lack of good faith in negotiating a mutually satisfactory settlement and have, consequently proposed shortening the 60-day time limit allocated to them (ibid art 4.7).

74 These are: supplementation and rectification (art 49(2); interpretation (art 50); revision (art 51); annulment (art 52). A party believing that the tribunal omitted to decide a question in the award may request a supplementary

Unsurprisingly, practice regarding these post-award remedies based on ICSID provisions differs, of course, fundamentally—ie conceptually, systemically, in scope, detail and interpretation—from DSU rules and practice on (draft) interim panel reports. Any direct comparison with WTO's interim review panel reports would therefore seem pointless. Nonetheless, some similarities with ICSID arbitration rules and practice on interpretation and involving substantive alteration of the original award are discernible. Highlighting some of these below might yield useful insights.

A. Article 50 ICSID Convention: Request for Post-Award Interpretation

Parties in dispute about the meaning or scope of points settled in an award's operative section may request their clarification. They rarely do. Such a request for 'authoritative interpretation'[75] must be related to clarification of what has been decided with binding force, without new facts and arguments being added. Otherwise, it would be considered 'outside the scope of the original award'.[76] A request under the Additional Facility Rules for a tribunal to reconsider or alter its decision is not one for interpretation.[77] To be admissible, the application for interpretation must identify 'precise points in dispute',[78] as it has to be balanced against the principle of the binding finality of ICSID awards.[79] A general request will not suffice.

A decision on interpretation is not an award itself, but will become part of a binding award for purposes of recognition and enforcement.[80] Requests for interpretation are not subject to a time limit, nor to a duty of notification of the other party, but the Secretary General is bound to safeguard 'due process' ie rights of the other party.[81]

Article 50 of the ICSID Convention, concerning post-award interpretation of points settled in an award, is scarcely comparable to matters covered in an Interim Panel Report, subject to review at the Interim Panel Stage (DSU art 15). The former is focused

decision or rectification (ICSID Convention art 49(2), Arbitration Rule r 49); in case of a dispute between the parties as to the scope or meaning of the tribunal's award, either party may request interpretation of the award (ICSID Convention art 50, Arbitration Rules rr 50, 51, 53, 54); if a party discovers a new fact which could decisively affect the award which was unknown to the tribunal when it rendered the award and to the party can apply for the revision of the award within ninety days, provided its ignorance of the fact is not due to negligence (ICSID Convention art 51, Arbitration Rules rr 50, 51, 53, 54); a party may also apply for the exceptional recourse of a full or partial annulment of an award on specific grounds as a safeguard against the violation of fundamental legal principles relating to the process (ICSID Convention art 52, Arbitration Rules rr 50, 52–55), excerpt summary from <https://icsid.worldbank.org/node/12236>. On this topic, see also Nowrot and Sipiorski (n 26).

[75] *ATA Construction v Jordan*, ICSID Case No ARB/08/2, Decision on Interpretation and Provisional Measures (7 March 2011) [39].

[76] *Wena Hotels v Egypt*, ICSID Case No ARB/98/4, Decision on Interpretation (31 October 2005) [127], [129].

[77] *Minotte and Lewis v Poland (AF)*, ICSID Case No ARB (AF)/10/1, Decision on the Request for Interpretation of the Award (22 October 2014) [12].

[78] Arbitration Rule 50 (1)(c)(i), *Wena Hotels v Egypt*, ICSID Case No ARB/98/4, Decision on Interpretation (31 October 2005) [76].

[79] *Wena Hotels v Egypt*, ICSID Case No ARB/98/4, Decision on Interpretation (31 October 2005) [103].

[80] Schill and others (n 7) 1194, paras 36–37.

[81] ibid para 33; note that an application for interpretation under ICSID Arbitration Rule 50(1)(c)(i) shall state 'precise points in dispute', whereas an application under Rule 69 (3) of the amended Arbitration Rules 2022 must merely specify 'the points in dispute'.

on the clarification of 'precise points' of binding force, while precluding the raising of new facts and arguments. Arguably, such authoritative clarification ultimately benefits recognition and enforcement of awards.

On the other hand, the practice of reviewing 'precise aspects' of an interim panel report (DSU art 15.2) interpreted broadly, though at times in varied, or even contradictory, ways, reflects an obverse approach. Challenged factual matters may generally be reviewed, but not new or additional evidence or arguments. Issues and errors of law and legal interpretations developed by the panel can subsequently be raised on appeal.[82] Facts, of course, cannot.

B. Article 51 of the ICSID Convention: Request for Revision of the Award

Practice under Article 51, such as it is, appears more pertinently comparable with the WTO's 'draft reports' in form of the interim panel report than that under Article 50. A party's request for a revision of an award involving its substantive alteration may be triggered by the discovery of decisive facts which could have been, but were not, considered in the arbitration proceedings because they were unknown at the time the award was made. That time, for the parties, will be the date of completion of the presentations of their case, and for the tribunal the date after which it cannot change the original award.[83] An application for revision must be made within ninety days of the discovery of the relevant facts and comply with certain requirements.[84] It must also specify the newly discovered facts, provide evidence that these were unknown both to the applicant and the tribunal, and the absence of negligence on the part of the applicant.

But what are decisive new facts? The answer is, for instance, a new document, but not a clerical error; the non-existence of facts, but not elements of domestic law for which evidentiary proof is required in cases where the presumption of *jura novit curia* is not applicable. An application for revision will be inadmissible if a party could have raised a decisive fact before the award's signature, but failed to do so. By contrast, as was briefly exemplified above,[85] WTO panels tend to adhere to a more flexible practice in handling facts.

Hitherto, Article 51 has yielded scant practical applications, which evidently shows that only very limited use has been made of that provision.[86] Essentially, an Article 51 review of an award is aimed at its alteration due to the discovery of decisive new facts, not merely—unlike in WTO's interim review—at the correction of substantive errors in a panel's assessment or inaccurate representation of previously known facts. To that extent it differs significantly from the WTO's interim review of 'sufficiently specific and

[82] DSU art 17.6.
[83] Schill and others (n 7) 1210, para 28.
[84] ibid 1203, para 7.
[85] See text to nn 48–52, 57–58.
[86] Schill and others (n 7) 1203–04, para 8.

detailed' aspects of (draft) interim panel reports, which precludes as inappropriate 'to introduce new legal issues and evidence, or to enter into a debate with the panel'.[87]

IV. Concluding Remarks

Draft awards, actually, are not awards but preliminary, non-binding decisions or rulings by an arbitral tribunal on certain matters—such as liability—before the final award is rendered. In an ICSID case, recourse cannot be taken against them, only against the award after it is rendered. Nonetheless, they can be an important tool for managing the arbitration process and promoting efficient resolution of investment disputes.

Besides permitting the identification and corrections of any errors, omissions, or ambiguities in the tribunal's reasoning or analysis—repair is better than despair—draft awards can also provide additional evidence or arguments that could influence the final decision. This can be particularly useful in complex cases where the tribunal may need to consider a number of different issues before reaching a final decision. By issuing a draft award a tribunal can help streamline the arbitration process and provide the parties with greater clarity on the issues in dispute and, possibly, guidance on the tribunal's views on the merits of the case. In light of these, the WTO's interim panel reports, a particular 'species' of draft awards in WTO dispute settlement, may provide a last-ditch incentive to the litigant state parties to negotiate a mutually acceptable settlement. Should explicit rules comparable to those on interim panel reports be usefully formulated for investment arbitration procedures? Would various practice constituencies welcome possible lateral cross-system inspiration for the drafting of future common, conceivably even harmonized procedural rules? Recognize probably attendant shared benefits of certainty and predictability, or rather prefer retaining systemic integrity of familiar procedural 'home turf'? One might also recall the concern, articulated in the Report of the Study Group of the International Law Commission, about the fragmentation of international law.[88]

At any rate, as some have already suggested, more general discussion of the acknowledged similarities and differences between WTO dispute settlement and investment arbitration would not come amiss.[89] Even though the issue of draft reports and (draft) interim panel reports may not top the list of topics in such discussions, there would be enough common ground to cover. A mutually fruitful systemic reappraisal might help

[87] See n 37.

[88] Martti Koskenniemi, 'Fragmentation of International Law: Difficulties Arising from the Diversification and Expansion of International Law' (2006) ILC Report. A/CN.4/L.682 and Add.1 <https://digitallibrary.un.org/record/574810?ln=es>. See also the Ministerial Declaration of 15 December 1993 on the Contribution of the World Trade Organization to Achieving Greater Coherence in Global Economic Policymaking <www.wto.org/english/docs_e/legal_e/32-dcohr.pdf>

[89] Bjorklund, for instance, advocates such a discussion, but also points out that 'panel decisions attract a lot of criticism because they are technocratic, illogical, hard to read, and frequently overturned on appeal', and asks whether they are necessarily the best model, OECD, 'Appointing Authorities and the Selection of Arbitrators in Investor-State Dispute Settlement: An Overview Compilation of Initial Comments Received', OECD Working Paper, March 2018, 25 <www.oecd.org/investment/investment-policy/ISDS-Appointing-Authorities-Arbitration-March-2018.pdf>

institutions concerned escape from their self-made bubbles of obtusely self-contained procedural regimes. It might possibly even contribute to further improvements of their efficiency and consistency.

After all, as was pointed out by Meg Kinnear, the substantive obligations of states under negotiated treaties or contracts which are adjudicated in the ICSID system of dispute settlement 'are very much defined and controlled by states'.[90] Such control is also a distinct characteristic of the WTO system of dispute settlement, including an explicit preference for a negotiated 'solution mutually acceptable to the parties' (DSU art 3(7)). Furthermore, at the beginning of 2023 at least 110 Members of the WTO stand poised to reach a new agreement on investment facilitation for development (IFD) covering goods trade and liberalization of services trade so as to incorporate IFD into the WTO rulebook.[91]

[90] Meg Kinnear reflecting on the enduring qualities of the ICSID dispute resolution system, as well as how ICSID continues to evolve, in John EC Brierly Memorial Lecture, 'Continuity and Change in the ICSID System: Challenges and Opportunities in the Search for Consensus' (2019) <www.mcgill.ca/pjrl/activities/brierley-lectures>

[91] Anabel González, 'A New WTO Deal to Facilitate Investment Could Be Ready in 2023: It Could Not Be More Timely' (*Thoughts from Geneva*, 2023) <www.wto.org/english/blogs_e/ddg_anabel_gonzalez_e/blog_ag_18jan23_e.htm>

PART II

PROCEDURAL PRINCIPLES

7

The Legal Nature of the Treaty-Based Consent to Investment Arbitration

Martin Gronemann and Markus Krajewski

I. Introduction

As a condition for any arbitral proceeding and award, investor-state arbitration also requires the consent of the parties. The host state can give its consent ad hoc, in an investor-state contract, through national legislation or via the investor-state dispute settlement clause of an international investment agreement (IIA). The method by which investors use state consent embedded in an IIA is today known as 'arbitration without privity'[1] or 'treaty-based arbitration',[2] and when it first served as the basis for the jurisdiction of an arbitral tribunal in 1990, it was considered new and revolutionary. Today it is a common practice, and it constitutes an important factor for the increase of investor-state arbitration proceedings since the 1990s.[3]

However, deriving host state consent from an IIA has been and remains controversial. While one commentator praises it as a 'new world of arbitration',[4] others condemn it as the magic of 'legal wizards'[5] or the 'original sin'[6] of international investment law. It is therefore not surprising that many aspects of state consent in international investment law are unclear.[7] This also includes the topic that this chapter examines: what is the legal nature of the treaty-based state consent? The term 'legal nature' refers to the legal concept as well as inherent characteristics that define state consent, and, accordingly, how it is legally handled. The answer to this question is not merely of academic significance. The legal nature of state consent has important practical implications, such as the question of the irrevocability of state consent. Whether and when state

[1] See eg Jan Paulsson, 'Arbitration without Privity' (1995) 10 ICSID Review 232; Christoph H Schreuer, 'Article 25' in Stephan Schill and others (eds), *Schreuer's Commentary on the ICSID Convention* (CUP 2022) para 762.

[2] See eg Christoph H Schreuer, 'Landmark Investment Cases on State Consent' in Hélène Ruiz Fabri and Edoardo Stoppioni (eds), *International Investment Law: An Analysis of the Mayor Decisions* (Hart 2022) 259.

[3] Gus Van Harten, 'Private Authority and Transnational Governance: The Contours of the International System of Investor Protection' (2005) 12 Review of International Political Economy 600, 609; Gus Van Harten, *The Trouble with Foreign Investor Protection* (OUP 2020) 22f; Muthucumaraswamy Sornarajah, *Resistance and Change in the International Law on Foreign Investment* (CUP 2015) 2; ICSID, 'The ICSID Caseload—Statistics', Issue 2020-1, 7, 11.

[4] Paulsson (n 1) 232.

[5] Van Harten (n 3) 2.

[6] Sornarajah (n 3) 139.

[7] Bernhard Wychera and Winslow Mimnagh, 'The Nature of State Consent' in Christian Klausegger and others (eds), *Austrian Yearbook on International Arbitration 2019* (Manz'sche Verlags- und Unversitätsbuchhandlung 2019) 395.

Martin Gronemann and Markus Krajewski, *The Legal Nature of the Treaty-Based Consent to Investment Arbitration* In: *The Award in International Investment Arbitration*. Edited by: Katia Fach Gómez and Catharine Titi, Oxford University Press.
 DOI: 10.1093/9780191975936.003.0007

consent becomes irrevocable is decisive for states' scope of action after IIAs enter into force. Depending on the legal nature of consent, different rules of interpretation may be used by arbitral tribunals. These questions have been relevant in the context of the denunciation of the Convention on the Settlement of Investment Disputes between States and Nationals of other States (ICSID Convention)[8] by Bolivia,[9] Venezuela,[10] and Ecuador[11] between 2007 and 2012.[12] In these cases, the legal nature of the state consent to arbitration is particularly decisive for the jurisdiction of the arbitral tribunals because it influences whether or for how long investors can still rely on the host state's consent in order to establish the tribunals' jurisdiction after the host state has denounced the ICSID Convention.[13] Accordingly, if the consent of a host state had already been invalid, the later subsequent award would have been exposed to the risk of annulment.

This chapter will begin its analysis of the legal nature of the state consent with an assessment of existing approaches with respect to it (II). These consider consent from a private law perspective (II.A), employ public international law (II.B), or ascribe a dual nature to the consent (II.C). In contrast to the existing opinions, this contribution proposes a different approach, which divides the search for the legal nature of consent into two steps. The first step identifies the conflict of laws rule determining the law applicable to the consent, which is challenging due to the particularities of investor-state arbitration (III.A). In this regard, the authors argue that party autonomy and the principle of the 'closest connection' constitute a specific conflict of laws rule to the state consent (III.B). In a second step, this conflict of laws rule directs to the legal system with the closest connection to the state consent. In the respective applicable legal system, its legal nature should be identified (III.C). The chapter then concludes by summarizing its main findings (IV).

II. Revisiting Current Perspectives and Complexities

Private law approaches attempt to classify the legal nature of consent and the formation of 'perfected consent'[14] through various models borrowed from private law systems.

[8] Convention on the Settlement of Investment Disputes between States and Nationals of other States (concluded 18 March 1965, entered into force 14 October 1966) 575 UNTS 159.

[9] ICSID, News Release, 'Denunciation of ICSID Convention', 16 May 2007 <https://icsid.worldbank.org/news-and-events/news-releases/denunciation-icsid-convention>

[10] ICSID, News Release, 'Venezuela Submits a Notice under Article 71 of the ICSID Convention', 26 January 2012 <https://icsid.worldbank.org/news-and-events/news-releases/venezuela-submits-notice-under-article-71-icsid-convention>

[11] ICSID, News Release, 'Denunciation of the ICSID Convention by Ecuador', 9 July 2009 <https://icsid.worldbank.org/news-and-events/news-releases/denunciation-icsid-convention-ecuador>. However, Ecuador has again acceded to the ICSID Convention 2021—see ICSID, News Release, 4 August 2021, 'Ecuador Ratifies the ICSID Convention' <https://icsid.worldbank.org/news-and-events/news-releases/ecuador-ratifies-icsid-convention>

[12] Michael D Nolan and Frédéric G Sourgens, 'Limits of Consent: Arbitration without Privity and Beyond' in Miguel A Fernández Ballesteros and David Arias Lozano (eds), *Liber Amicorum Bernardo Cremades* (La Ley 2010) 873.

[13] Nolan and Sourgens (n 12) 876.

[14] This term is used to describe the existence of the consent of both parties to the dispute. Another term used is 'mutual consent'.

Hence, their analytical framework remains one of private law and awards are based ultimately on a private law theory of contractual nature.[15]

A. Imitating Private Law: Contractual Approaches

A first model considers state consent as an offer to arbitrate. Within this model, further specific nuances are attributed to the state offer, which affect whether or until when the offer remains valid or can be withdrawn. It is also argued that the offer requires a transformation or conversion before the investors' acceptance. Another model imitates a contract for the benefit of a third-party.

1. Unilateral Offer-and-Acceptance Model

The dominant view concerning state consent in international investment law is the 'unilateral offer-and-acceptance model'.[16] This model uses a common law-influenced contract analogy to describe consent.[17] Accordingly, the state's consent contained in the investor-state dispute settlement (ISDS) clause in an IIA creates two legal effects, which differ depending on the respective legal relationship.[18] In the relationship with the other treaty party, the ISDS clause requires the host state to submit disputes with investors of the other treaty party to arbitration. The host state performs this obligation by giving its consent. In relation to the investor, the ISDS clause creates an abstract and general offer to arbitrate.[19] The investor must accept the offer to bind the state. Without the acceptance by the concrete investor, the state offer is not binding by default.[20] Once the parties establish the perfected consent, the principle of *pacta sunt servanda* protects the arbitration agreement from subsequent interference by one of the parties.[21] Under this model investors are advised to explicitly accept the offer early on,[22] even if this

[15] Andrea M Steingruber, *Consent in International Arbitration* (OUP 2012) 61.

[16] Schreuer (n 1) para 851; James Crawford, 'Treaty and Contract in Investment Arbitration' (2008) 24 Arbitration International 351, 360; Gary B Born, *International Arbitration: Law and Practice* (3rd edn, Kluwer 2021) para 1.04[A][7]; Relja Radović, *Beyond Consent: Revisiting Jurisdiction in Investment Treaty Arbitration* (Brill 2021) 57; Andrés Mezgravis, 'The Standard of Interpretation Applicable to Consent and Its Revocation in Investment Arbitration' (2011) 8(2) Transnational Dispute Management 1, 8; Martina Magnarelli, *Privity of Contract in International Investment Arbitration: Original Sin or Useful Tool?* (Kluwer 2020) 41ff, 46ff; Fernando Tupa, *The Dilemma of Consent to International Arbitration in Investment Agreements without a Forum* (Brill 2023) 23. Also portraying this approach, Laurence Boisson de Chazournes, 'Variations around the Notion of Consent in Investment Arbitration' in Samantha Besson (ed), *Consenting to International Law* (CUP 2023) 223, 230ff.

[17] Nolan and Sourgens (n 12) 875–76.

[18] Steingruber (n 12) 230; already rejecting the different legal relationships, *Blue Bank International & Trust (Barbados) Ltd v the Bolivarian Republic of Venezuela*, ICSID Case No ARB 12/20 (13 April 2017) Separate Opinion Christer Söderlung [32]ff.

[19] Steingruber (n 12) 230.

[20] Michael D Nolan and Frédéric G Sourgens, 'The Interplay between State Consent to ICSID Arbitration and Denunciation of the ICSID Convention: The (Possible) Venezuela Case Study' (2007) 5 Transnational Dispute Management 1, 18; Schreuer (n 1) paras 855ff who, however, states that, in his view, withdrawal should only be possible by terminating the IIA.

[21] Georges R Delaume, 'Law and Practice of Transnational Contracts' (Oceana Publications 1988), 363–66.

[22] Schreuer (n 1) para 856.

may have a negative effect on the relationship with the host state.[23] Therefore, the later award is based on a contractual relationship between the parties.

On the one side, the model is simple and practicable. Offer-and-acceptance are universally recognized as basic conditions for the formation of a contract, ie, in this case, an arbitration agreement.[24] In addition, the consideration that the state's consent is only binding if it is accepted by the investor is an advantage of this model. Since the investor's acceptance will certainly coincide with the initiation of the arbitral proceedings, or will be expressly communicated before that time, the date of acceptance can be precisely determined. Accordingly, an arbitral tribunal can certainly determine the relevant point for the existence of a valid offer to arbitrate as compared to other dates, such as eg when the offer 'reached' the investor.[25] In addition, this approach satisfies the requirement of the existence of an arbitration agreement between the disputing parties necessary for all ISDS fora such as Arbitration Rules of the United Nations Commission on International Trade Law (UNCITRAL) or the Stockholm Chamber of Commerce (SCC) Rules.[26]

On the other side, one could criticize the model for overly emphasizing the legal nature from a contractual conception and hence the perspective of requirements set by the ICSID Convention or the institutional arbitration rules. These concerns could be raised in particular because it is not possible to 'reversely' draw a conclusion from the requirements of the ICSID Convention and rules to the legal nature of the state's consent (argumentum e contrario). An IIA, the ICSID Convention, and institutional arbitration rules are independent legal instruments that must be considered separately.[27] Consequently, while the rules of arbitration institutions or the ICSID convention may require an arbitration agreement, an IIA remains a separate legal instrument and the requirements of arbitration institutions or the ICSID convention cannot be read into the IIA. Hence, state consent is provided independently of the ICSID Convention or other institutional arbitration rules, and therefore its legal nature must be assessed independently.

However, such an isolated approach to the legal relationship and correlations between the IIA, the ICSID Convention or arbitration rules would admittedly not be convincing. It is important to remember that the state consent needs to meet the consent requirements of the ICSID Convention and other arbitration rules in order to become

[23] Lars Markert, *Streitschlichtungsklauseln in Investitionsschutzabkommen* (Nomos 2010) 128.

[24] See eg German Civil Code (Bürgerliches Gesetzbuch, BGB) §§ 145ff; French Code Civil art 1113ff; Mindy Chen-Wishart in Hugh G Beale (ed), *Chitty on Contracts*, vol 1 (35th edn, Sweet & Maxwell 2023) 4-001; US Uniform Commercial Code § 2–206; UN Convention on Contracts for the International Sale of Goods (CISG) arts 14ff; 2016 UNIDROIT Principles of International Commercial Contracts arts 2.1.1ff. Although the rules are not always identical due to the procedural nature of an arbitration agreement, private law rules on contract formation can generally be applied by analogy, see Christoph A Kern, 'The Flight from ISDS' in Christoph Benicke and Stefan Huber (eds), *National, International, Transnational: Harmonischer Dreiklang im Recht, Festschrift für Herbert Kronke zum 70 Geburtstag* (Gieseking 2020) 1458.

[25] *Blue Bank International & Trust (Barbados) Ltd v Venezuela*, ICSID Case No ARB 12/20, Award [106ff].

[26] 2021 UNCITRAL Arbitration Rules art 23(1), 2023 SCC Rules art 6.

[27] See eg, *Fábrica de Vidrios Los Andes, CA and Owens-Illinois de Venezuela, CA v Venezuela*, ICSID Case No ARB/12/2, Award (13 November 2017) [259] ('The ICSID Convention ... as an instrument of international ... has a life of its own') [262] ('[T]he conditions for resorting to ICSID arbitration are set out in two separate and wholly independent international legal instruments and both must be satisfied for the Tribunal to have jurisdiction').

operable. Vice versa, state consent that does not fulfil these requirements would ultimately be invalid. Hence, it can be assumed that states—even though they provide consent in an independent IIA—intend to provide consent satisfying all specifications of the possible ISDS fora. A typical IIA contains an ISDS clause which provides the investor with a wide choice regarding arbitral fora. Generally, the respective rules establish the arbitral tribunal's jurisdiction based on an arbitration agreement. Phrases such as 'in accordance with the Rules of Procedure of the SCC' or 'established under the arbitration Rules of Procedure of the UNCITRAL' indicate that the parties to the IIA expressed their intention to fulfil the requirements of these arbitration rules ie, to conclude an arbitration agreement with investors. Hence, both parties to the dispute need to act and satisfy the requirements of the chosen forum.[28] In sum, the approach seems consistent with the intentions of the treaty parties and the parties to the dispute.

2. Firm Offer-and-Acceptance Model

A second approach which seems to be inspired by the conclusion of contracts in civil law jurisdictions is the firm offer-and-acceptance model, which considers that the state offer is binding from the outset and cannot be withdrawn.[29] It is argued that the rights and obligations attached to the 'unqualified consent' should not be dispositive and subject to interference by the state.[30]

However, a binding effect by default does not seem to entirely coincide with treaty practice. While some IIAs explicitly use the term 'irrevocably' with regard to the consent, most of them do not employ this wording.[31] In addition, the conduct of some states in arbitration proceedings also contradicts such a conception. For example, in the arbitral proceedings *Fábrica de Vidrios Los Andes v Venezuela* and *Blue Bank v Venezuela*, Venezuela argued that with the denunciation of the ICSID Convection it withdrew its treaty-based consent to ICSID Convention arbitration.[32] Similarly, Ecuador challenged the tribunal's jurisdiction in *Murphy Exploration v Ecuador*.[33] Also Bolivia took this position from the beginning in *ETI Euro Telecom v Bolivia*.[34] Therefore, the approach should offer a more detailed and nuanced explanation of the reasons behind this binding effect, especially in relation to investors.

[28] In this regard compare *Murphy Exploration and Production Company International v Ecuador*, ICSID Case No ARB/08/4, Award (15 December 2010) [74] and *Magyar Farming Company Ltd, Kintyre Kft and Inicia Zrt v Hungary*, ICSID Case No ARB/17/27, Award (13 November 2019) [214].

[29] Emmanuel Gaillard, 'The Denunciation of the ICSID Convention' (2007) 237(122) New York Law Journal 1, 3; Jeswald W Salacuse, *The Law of Investment Treaties* (OUP 2021) 528.

[30] Gaillard (n 29) 3.

[31] Only about 100 of the approximately 2600 IIAs currently in force attribute consent as 'irrevocable'. Numbers based on a rough search of all IIAs conducted by the *Jus Mundi* platform.

[32] *Fábrica de Vidrios Los Andes, CA and Owens-Illinois de Venezuela, CA v Venezuela*, ICSID Case No ARB/12/2, Award (13 November 2017) [212]ff; *Blue Bank International & Trust (Barbados) Ltd v Venezuela*, ICSID Case No ARB 12/20, Award (26 April 2017) [51a].

[33] *Murphy Exploration and Production Company International v Ecuador*, ICSID Case No ARB/08/4, Award (15 December 2010) [43]–[45], [74].

[34] *ETI Euro Telecom International NV v Bolivia*, ICSID Case No ARB/07/28, Bolivia's Response to Request of Arbitration (29 October 2007).

Arguments to consider offers to arbitrate to be firm by default have also relied on comparisons with the German and US legal systems.[35] It has been argued that the state offer would correspond to an *offerta ad incertas personas*.[36] The binding effect of the offer would cease with the termination period of the IIA and the expiry of the period stipulated in the sunset clause.[37] However, it should be noted that the *offerta ad incertas personas* becomes only irrevocable when it has reached the other party. Hence, before reaching investors, the arbitral *offerta ad incertas personas—like* any offer—can be withdrawn.[38] Determining when the offer reached an investor seems still unclear. Assuming that the offer 'reaches' the investors when the investment is made, the *offerta ad incertas personas* would have a binding effect on those who have already invested but can be withdrawn in relation to investors who intend to invest.

Michael Nolan and Frédéderic G Sourgens tried to combine the unilateral and firm offer models.[39] They suggested that offers are generally not binding unless 'the offeree could reasonably rely on the offer being irrevocable and the offeree acted in reliance on the offer'.[40] They see this solution as providing adequate flexibility and, at the same time, sufficiently protecting investors' legitimate expectations of the stability of the state's jurisdictional undertakings.[41] Strictly speaking, this is not a new approach, but the application of the estoppel principle to state consent. This does not contribute to legal certainty for investors and states.

3. Transformation or Conversion of the Offer

Generally, it remains questionable whether state consent based on an IIA constitutes a valid offer because it is of an abstract and general nature.[42] Hence, a concretized offer could be necessary so that the investor can form an arbitration agreement by acceptance. These concerns are further substantiated when one considers the characteristics of the advanced consent. Many investors who may benefit from the consent may not have invested yet in the territory of the host state. Accordingly, the time of future proceedings, the exact subject matter of the disputes and the corresponding investors are entirely unknown when the state ratifies the IIA.[43] Therefore it is argued that a 'conversion'[44] or 'transformation'[45] is required before investors can accept the offer. This means that the abstract and general state offer transforms into a concrete individual offer in the 'logical second' before the acceptance by the investor.[46] Accordingly, the

[35] Nolan and Sourgens (n 12) 877.
[36] ibid.
[37] ibid.
[38] Joachim Münch, '§ 1029' in Wolfgang Krüger and Thomas Rauscher (eds), *Münchener Kommentar zur Zivilprozessordnung* (6th edn, CH Beck 2022) s 15.
[39] Nolan and Sourgens (n 12) 877–78.
[40] ibid 878; 2004 UNIDROIT Principles art 2.1.4(2)(b).
[41] Nolan and Sourgens (n 12) 878.
[42] Steingruber (n 12) 230.
[43] Although this is an achievement for investors, it poses an almost incalculable risk for host states because, unlike investor-state contracts, they can barely assess the number of potential claims. Furthermore, the states' radius of action has been reduced, as they can only act as defendants—see Schreuer (n 2) 259.
[44] Sornarajah (n 3) 140.
[45] Steingruber (n 12) 230.
[46] ibid; Kern (n 24) 1456.

investor does not accept the general offer contained in the ISDS clause, but an individualized and concretized offer.[47]

However, neither a 'conversion' nor a 'transformation' is necessary. As the mandatory minimum *essentialia*, the state offer contemplates that a dispute between the parties will be bindingly or finally resolved by arbitration.[48] Comparing these elements with the state consent in ISDS clauses, it becomes clear that already the abstract general offer exactly meets the minimum requirement for the formation of an arbitration agreement.[49] Although the parties to the dispute are not expressly determined, they can be determined on the basis of the IIA's definitions (eg investor). The scope of the disputes submitted to arbitration is evident because the IIA specifies categories of investment disputes with the host state. The fact that the investor is entitled to choose different fora is not detrimental since the forum is either explicitly or impliedly selected with the initiation of the proceedings.

4. The Third-Party Beneficiary Model

Some commentators, arbitral tribunals and national courts also referred to the idea of a contract for the benefit of a third-party when dealing with arbitration without privity.[50]

Transferring the contract for the benefit of a third-party to investor-state arbitration assumes that the arbitration agreement is not concluded between a treaty party and the investor but rather between the treaty parties to the IIA.[51] Investors, as a third-party to the treaty, ie, the arbitration agreement, are the beneficiaries. Hence, this model entirely avoids the 'canonical' offer-and-acceptance model as introduced above,[52] but still the award relies on a contractual basis of the perfected consent.

[47] ibid; Bernardo M Cremades, 'Arbitration in Investment Treaties: Public Offer of Arbitration in Investment-Protection Treaties' in Robert Briner and others (eds), *Recht der internationalen Wirtschaft und Streiterledigung im 21. Jahrhundert, Liber Amicorum Karl-Heinz Böckstiegel* (Carl Heymanns 2001) 152ff.

[48] cf eg Born (n 16) § 2.02.

[49] For a different opinion, see Axel Flessner, 'Investitionsschutz und Schiedsrecht—Ein schräges Verhältnis' in Christoph Benicke and Stefan Huber (eds), *National, International, Transnational: Harmonischer Dreiklang im Recht, Festschrift für Herbert Kronke zum 70. Geburtstag* (Gieseking 2020) 1404ff.

[50] To clarify, by the third-party beneficiary model, we do not refer to the idea of a procedural individual right. While the states' consent to arbitration is such a right, this observation cannot explain how the mandatory arbitration agreement is concluded. *Blue Bank International & Trust (Barbados) Ltd v Venezuela*, ICSID Case No ARB 12/20, Separate Opinion Christer Söderlung (13 April 2017) [31]ff; Anuraag Rajagopalan, 'Denunciation of ICSID Convention: Re-Visiting Mr Söderlund's Separate Opinion' (*Kluwer Arbitration Blog*, 31 May 2020) <http://arbitrationblog.kluwerarbitration.com/2020/05/31/denunciation-of-icsid-convention-re-visiting-mr-soderlunds-separate-opinion/>; deliberately left open, *Poland v Saar Papier (Germany)*, Decision of the Federal Tribunal 1P113/2000/mks, 20 September 2000; Kern (n 24) 1459; *Saluka Investments BV v Czech Republic*, Swiss Federal Tribunal (7 September 2006) 4P 114/2006/bie; Helene Bubrowski, *Internationale Investitionsschiedsverfahren und nationale Gerichte* (Mohr Siebeck 2013) 69; W Laurence Craig, 'The Arbitrator's Mission and the Application of Law' (2010) 21 American Review of International Arbitration 243, 257; Alan Scott Rau and Andrea K Bjorklund, 'BG Group and "Conditions" to Arbitral Jurisdiction' (2016) 43 Pepperdine Law Review 577, 587; Yas Banifatemi, 'The Law Applicable in Investment Treaty Arbitration' in Katia Yannaca-Small (ed), *Arbitration under International Investment Agreements: A Guide to the Key Issues* (OUP 2010) 194ff. This assumption in general with regard to IIAs: Richard Happ, 'Beilegung von Streitigkeiten zwischen Investoren und ausländischen Staaten durch Schiedsgerichte' (2006) 15 Internationales Steuerrecht 649, 650; Anne van Aaken, 'International Investment Law between Commitment and Flexibility: A Contract Theory Analysis' (2009) 12 Journal of International Economic Law 507, 520; Anthea Roberts, 'Triangular Treaties: The Extent and Limits of Investment Treaty Rights' (2015) 56 Harvard International Law Journal 353, 353ff.

[51] Rau and Bjorklund (n 50) 587.

[52] See Rau and Bjorklund (n 50) 587 n 39.

The assumption of an 'already-concluded prior arbitration agreement' for the benefit of investors raises two concerns.[53] First, as the arbitration agreement is concluded among the treaty parties, it is necessary that the benefit directly transferred to the investor is really merely the right to initiate arbitration and does not force the investor into arbitration.[54] In particular, the arbitration agreement between the states must not bar the investor's access to domestic courts.[55] Anything else would constitute an inadmissible agreement to the detriment of third-parties. Therefore, and in order to avoid an agreement to the detriment of a third-party, either the benefit must be transferred together with the possibility of a waiver with regard to arbitration[56] or the benefit does not constitute a right but merely something like a 'procedural option to arbitrate'.[57] Whether something like a 'procedural option to arbitrate' exists, seems at least questionable.[58]

Second, a third-party beneficiary arbitration agreement depends on the promisor's will, ie the will of the host state. Therefore, such an understanding of arbitration without privity would have to be reflected in the wording of ISDS clauses. However, these do not contain any wording to that effect. ISDS clauses only address the procedural legal relationship between states and investors and in particular, they do not describe the situation as a single legal relationship under a contract for the benefit of third-parties.[59] In particular, the wording does not reflect a concluded arbitration agreement.

B. Focusing on States: The Public International Law Approach

The other main approach considers the legal nature of consent from the perspective of public international law. Its supporters argue against a contractual nature of the state's consent to arbitrate describing the offer-and-acceptance models as a 'fallacy of false analogies'.[60] Others attribute only 'figurative sense' to the models.[61] The tribunal in *İçkale v Turkmenistan* evaluated the private law theory as 'inaccurate and legally incorrect'.[62]

[53] ibid 587 but differing opinion.
[54] Kern (n 24) 1459.
[55] In German courts, however, that would be the situation, see German Code of Civil Procedure (Zivilprozessordnung, ZPO) § 1032(1).
[56] For UK legislation, see Contracts (Rights of Third Parties) Act 1999 c 31 s 8; Nigel Blackaby and others, *Redfern and Hunter on International Arbitration* (7th edn, OUP 2023) s 2.56. In German civil law such a right of rejection is codified in § 333 of the German Civil Code (BGB); Reinhold Geimer, '§ 1031' in Richard Zöller and others (eds), *Zivilprozessordnung* (35th edn, Ottoschmidt 2024) s 18.
[57] Kern (n 24) 1459.
[58] ibid 1459ff.
[59] See Australia–Hong Kong Investment Agreement (concluded 26 March 2019 and entered into force 17 January 2020), s C as representative of numerous others.
[60] Oscar M Garibaldi, 'On the Denunciation of the ICSID Convention, Consent to ICSID Jurisdiction, and the Limits of the Contract Analogy' in Christina Binder and others (eds), *International Investment Law for the 21st Century: Essays in Honour of Christoph Schreuer* (OUP 2009) 251, 254.
[61] Nolan and Sourgens (n 12) 895.
[62] *İçkale İnşaat Limited Şirketi v Turkmenistan*, ICSID Case No ARB/10/24, Award (8 March 2016) [244].

The public international law theory does not deny that consent is the basic requirement to confer upon an arbitral tribunal the power to adjudicate.[63] However, it uses a different method to reach this conclusion by suggesting that jurisdiction in investment arbitration is based on a mechanism similar to the optional clause declarations under Article 36(2) of the Statute of the International Court of Justice (ICJ): Accordingly, consent can be expressed either by a unilateral act or by an agreement regarding a concrete dispute.[64] In contrast to the private law models, the public international law approach does not require that the parties' consent materializes in the form of an agreement. Instead, the existence of 'arbitral consent'[65] is seen as sufficient and the reciprocal structure of IIAs is considered to be only of formal nature.[66] Thus, the consent of the host state in an ISDS clause constitutes an independent international obligation.[67] As a consequence, the investor's consent to arbitration constitutes a mere 'notification necessary to come within the benefit of the right obtained for it by its home state'.[68] Accordingly, the role of the investor is the most important difference between the public international law approach and the offer-and-acceptance models. For the latter, the investor's act is legally necessary to establish jurisdiction. For the former jurisdiction exists regardless of an act by the investor. In conclusion, there is no privity of contract between the disputing parties according to the public international law approach. Arguably, this could be the true understanding of arbitration without privity.

This assumption is additionally supported by the characteristics that the treaty-based state consent shares with unilateral declarations under Article 36(2) of the ICJ Statute: unilateral declarations express an advance consent to submit all or certain categories of dispute to the ICJ.[69] States that grant such consent expose themselves to a certain degree of unpredictability and vulnerability.[70] Further consent declared under Article 36(2) is generally neither given at the same time, nor in the same document.[71] All these observations also apply to the state consent contained in IIAs. Additionally,

[63] Garibaldi (n 60) 257.

[64] Stanimir A Alexandrov, 'The Compulsory Jurisdiction of the International Court of Justice: How Compulsory Is It?' (2006) 5 Chinese Journal of International Law 29, 35ff. Also discussing this approach, Boisson de Chazournes (n 16) 233ff.

[65] Nolan and Sourgens (n 12) 880; Jesper Lünsmann, *Unilateraler "Consent" im System der Streitbeilegung nach der ICSID Konvention* (Nomos 2017) 99.

[66] Yulia Andreeva, 'Consent to Arbitration as a Unilateral Act of State: In Search for a Non-Conventional Approach towards Treaty Interpretation' in Ian A Laird and Todd J Weiler (eds), *Investment Treaty Arbitration and International Law* (Juris 2010) 65f; Lünsmann (n 65) 283.

[67] Nolan and Sourgens (n 12) 879ff; Ousmane Diallo, *Le consentment des parties à l'arbitrage international* (Graduate Institute Publications 2010) 5ff; Lünsmann (n 65) 98f; Andreeva (n 66) 61. More vaguely in this direction, see Stephan Schill, 'Internationales Investitionsschutzrecht und Vergleichendes Öffentliches Recht: Grundlagen und Methode eines öffentlich-rechtlichen Leitbildes für die Investitionsschiedsgerichtsbark eit' (2011) 71 Zeitschrift für ausländisches öffentliches Recht und Völkerrecht 247, 262.

[68] Reaching the same conclusion, however naming the action by the investor 'acceptance', cf *Waguih Elie Georg Siag and Clorinda Vecchi v Egypt*, ICSID Case No ARB/05/15, Decision on Jurisdiction, and Partial Dissenting Opinion of Francisco Orrego Vicuña (15 April 2007) 62, 64.

[69] Alexandrov (n 64) 35ff.

[70] ibid.

[71] See eg *Temple of Preah Vihear (Cambodia v Thailand)* (Preliminary Objections) [1961] ICJ Rep 17, 31f; Military *and Paramilitary Activities in and against Nicaragua (Nicaragua v United States of America)* (Jurisdiction and Admissibility) [1984] ICJ Rep 392, 412.

the wording of IIAs appears to be consistent with the public international law approach when viewed in isolation. It refers to 'submission' or 'consent'.[72]

However, the public international law approach can be questioned on the basis of two arguments. First, commercial arbitration fora and their rules explicitly require an 'agreement' as a form of consent and thus action by both *disputing* parties.[73] Assuming the International Centre for Settlement of Investment Disputes (ICSID) is a forum that allows for consensual but not necessarily contractual consent of the parties, the legal nature of the host state would be divided and have a dual nature.[74] In other words, if an investor opts for a commercial arbitration forum, an arbitration agreement in the sense of the private models (I.A) is the basis for the jurisdiction of this tribunal.[75] If another investor under the same IIA chooses an ICSID tribunal, this tribunal's jurisdiction is based on a unilateral act. This bifurcation would cause a fragmentation of the rules and effects regarding the consent to ICSID arbitration and non-ICSID arbitration.[76] The rules of interpretation, the need of an acceptance by the investor, the form, as well as the moment of the binding effect of state consent would differ. This could possibly lead to the annulment of awards in one forum and the upholding of awards in the other even though based on comparable facts. Such a legal uncertainty for both the contracting party and the investor should be avoided.

Second, the presented approach ignores the fact that international jurisdiction cannot be established unilaterally, but always requires action by both parties to the dispute.[77] However, the public international law approach deems the consent of the contracting states to the IIA sufficient. Yet, the contracting parties are not the parties of the dispute, ie the host state and the respective investor,[78] whose consent is necessary. To the extent that the public international law theory assumes that the ISDS clause constitutes an independent international obligation and a mere notification by the investor should be sufficient, it is not convincing. It also contradicts contemporary arbitral practice.[79]

C. Combining Private and Public Law: The Dual Nature Approach

Lars Markert suggests a combination of the two approaches mentioned above and ascribes a dual nature to the state consent. He suggests it embodies elements of both arbitration and public international law.[80] According to Markert, it is necessary to

[72] Contra Markert (n 23) 122.
[73] See eg 2021 UNCITRAL Arbitration Rules art 23(1) and 2023 SCC Rules art 6(iv); Markert (n 23) 120.
[74] Markert (n 23) 123. For a detailed analysis of the nature of ISDS in general, see Catharine Titi, 'Investment Treaty Arbitration Caught in the Public-Private Law Divide' (2024) 45(3) Michigan Journal of International Law (forthcoming), also on SSRN <https://papers.ssrn.com/sol3/papers.cfm?abstract_id=4536824>.
[75] ibid (n 23) 119ff.
[76] For clarification, the terms 'ICSID tribunal' or 'ICSID arbitration (agreement)' refer only to arbitrations under the ICSID Convention. Tribunals or proceedings under the ICSID Additional Rules are not included. They are covered by the term 'non-ICSID tribunal' or 'non-ICSID arbitration (agreement)'.
[77] Radović (n 16) 56.
[78] ibid 56ff.
[79] Schreuer (n 1) para 851 fn 1394 with further references.
[80] Markert (n 23) 123.

attribute an arbitral nature to the consent because ISDS clauses refer to the arbitration rules of, inter alia, ICSID, ICC, and SCC, which demand an arbitration agreement as the basis for jurisdiction.[81] Additionally, he also attributes a public international law nature to the state consent, because it is an element of the treaty under public international law.[82] The arbitration clause would therefore constitute a unilateral declaration of submission to all investors, combined with a waiver of sovereign immunity in relation to arbitral jurisdiction.[83]

Markert's classification of consent is not persuasive to the extent that he considers the state's consent as a unilateral declaration of submission to all investors and a waiver of sovereign immunity to arbitral jurisdiction. A declaration of submission to dispute settlement is redundant because this function is performed by the arbitration agreement between the investor and the state. The disputing parties agree to confer the power to adjudicate upon the arbitral tribunal with the arbitration agreement.[84] Also, a waiver of sovereign immunity regarding jurisdictional immunity is not necessary, because ISDS arbitral proceedings do not concern sovereign immunity. State immunity under public international law only applies to foreign courts but not to international arbitral tribunals.[85] Unlike state courts, arbitral tribunals do not exercise state sovereignty and cannot be attributed to a foreign state.[86] The competence of an arbitral tribunal is based on the arbitration agreement which manifests party autonomy. Thus, the arbitration agreement cannot affect state immunity from the outset.[87] Consequently, the state's consent cannot be ascribed as a waiver of immunity concerning arbitration proceedings.

III. Beyond the Private–Public Dichotomy: Determining the Legal Nature of Consent on the Basis of the General Principle of the Closest Connection

Even though one could assume that conclusively public international law governs the arbitration agreement, such general assessment of the applicable law is not sufficient. Aspects such as the nationality of the investor and the capacity of the parties to agree to arbitration are governed by municipal law.[88] Accordingly, depending on the

[81] ibid 119ff.
[82] ibid 120ff.
[83] ibid.
[84] Radović (n 16) 30.
[85] With further references, see Jochen Langkeit, *Staatenimmunität und Schiedsgerichtsbarkeit* (Recht und Wirtschaft 1989) 62ff.
[86] *Société de Grands Travaux de Marseille (France) v East Pakistan Industrial Development Corporation*, ICC Case No 1803, Award (12 December 1972) (1980) Yearbook of Commercial Arbitration 179, 185; *Solel Boneh International Ltd (Israel) and Water Resources Development International (Israel) v Uganda and National Housing and Construction Corporation of Uganda*, ICC Case No 2321, Interim Decision (4 July 1974) (1976) Yearbook of Commercial Arbitration 133, 134; J Gillis Wetter, 'Pleas of Sovereign Immunity and Act of Sovereignty before International Arbitral Tribunals' (1985) 3 Journal of International Arbitration 7, 9f; Sigrid Lorz, *Ausländische Staaten vor deutschen Zivilgerichten* (Mohr Siebeck 2017) 140.
[87] Contra Andreeva (n 66) 72.
[88] Veijo Heiskanen, 'Forbidding Dépeçage: Law Governing Investment Treaty Arbitration' (2009) 32 Suffolk Transnational Law Review 367, 378ff; Masimo V Benedettelli, 'Determining the Applicable Law in Commercial

applicable law, the state's consent could be characterized differently. Therefore, the authors propose to first determine the law applicable to the material validity of the state consent, and second to characterise the legal nature within the applicable legal system. However, in order to determine the applicable law, a conflict of laws rule is necessary. After describing the difficulties regarding conflict of laws rules for investment arbitration agreements (A), the chapter identifies a specific conflict of laws rule covering the perfected consent and hence, the state consent to investor-state arbitration.[89] This rule is introduced in section (B) and follows the principle of party autonomy as well as the conflict of laws principle of the closest connection. Finally, this rule is used to determine the law applicable to the consent, thus revealing its legal nature (C).

A. Determining the Applicable Law to Investment Arbitration Agreements

The determination of the law applicable to the investment arbitration agreement is largely unresolved and has hardly been discussed in literature so far.[90] Most of the approaches proposed to date rely on arguments developed in the context of commercial arbitration. However, these are not suitable for investment arbitration agreements for the following reasons. The conflict of laws of commercial arbitration agreements is based on three widely accepted fundamental principles: party autonomy, the application of the law of the main contract, or the application of the law of the place of arbitration (*lex loci arbitri*).[91] However, these three principles are of limited use for the conflict of laws of investment arbitration agreements. Already in commercial arbitration, an explicit choice of law for an arbitration agreement is rare.[92] This is even more true for investment arbitration.[93] If IIAs contain choice-of-law clauses, these address

and Investment Arbitration: Two Intertwined Road Maps for Conflicts-Solving' (2022) 37(3) ICSID Review 687, 720 fn 144; Andrea K Bjorklund, 'International Arbitration' (2020) 66 McGill Law Journal 91, 94.

[89] When referring to the law of arbitration agreement, this also includes the law applicable to the consent of the host state, because the consent of the host state and the perfected consent are governed by the same law. Also, with a different result, cf Heiskanen (n 88) 393.

[90] With the notable exception of Heiskanen (n 88) 367ff; Christoph H Schreuer, 'Jurisdiction and Applicable Law in Investment Treaty Arbitration' (2014) 1 McGill Journal of Dispute Resolution 1; Julian Scheu and Petyo Nikolov, 'The Setting Aside and Enforcement of Intra-EU Investment Arbitration Awards after *Achmea*' (2020) 36 Arbitration International 253, 260ff; Julian Scheu and Petyo Nikolov, 'Jurisdiction of Tribunals to Settle Intra-EU Investment Treaty Disputes' (2021) 36 ICSID Review 171, 179ff; Carsten Kern, *Schiedsgericht und Generalklausel* (Mohr Siebeck 2017) 73–76; Lünsmann (n 65) 289ff; Michail Risvas, 'International Law as the Basis for Extending Arbitration Agreements Concluded by States or State Entities to Non-Signatories' (2022) 71 International and Comparative Law Quarterly 183.

[91] Other approaches, inter alia, the application of 'substantive principles of private international law' are not explicitly considered in the discussion, because they are not as recognized as the presented default rules or concern other subject matters. On this, see Jan Paulsson, 'May a State Invoke its Internal Law to Repudiate Consent to International Commercial Arbitration?' (1986) 2 Arbitration International 90–103; Emmanuel Gaillard, 'Formation of the Arbitration Agreement' in Emmanuel Gaillard and John Savage (eds), *Fouchard Gaillard Goldmann on International Commercial Arbitration* (Kluwer 1999) 318ff; Julian D Lew, Loukas A Mistelis, and Stefan M Kröll, *Comparative International Commercial Arbitration* (Kluwer 2003) 733ff; Muthucumaraswamy Sornarajah, *The Settlement of Foreign Investment Disputes* (Kluwer 2000) 104ff; Jonathan Mance, 'Arbitration: A Law unto Itself?' (2016) 32 Arbitration International 223–41; Heiskanen (n 88) 367ff, 399ff.

[92] See Born (n 16) para 4.04[A] as representative of numerous others.

[93] Schreuer (n 94) 12; Scheu and Nikolov (n 90) 261.

the substantive law.[94] Additionally, and in the absence of a 'main contract' between the parties to the arbitration, the rationale for applying the law of the main contract cannot be transferred to ISDS. Thus, it is not possible to resort to this law. Therefore, the determination of the law applicable to investment arbitration agreements according to the commercial arbitration approach would lead to the application of the *lex loci arbitri*.[95] For this purpose, however, the determination of the seat of arbitration is decisive. If the seat cannot be located, no *lex loci arbitri* can be determined. ICSID tribunals have no seat due to the transnational character of the proceedings. Articles 62 and 63 of the ICSID Convention only concern the place of hearings, but do not localize a legal seat of an ICSID tribunal. Accordingly, it does not lead to the application of the relevant national *lex loci arbitri*. Thus, the default conflict of laws rules for the law governing commercial arbitration agreements cannot be used for ICSID arbitration agreements. Only if the investor opts for a commercial arbitration forum the *lex loci arbitri* could apply. Consequently, tribunals and scholars differentiate between the conflict of laws rules to ICSID and non-ICSID arbitration agreements, which refer to different applicable laws.

B. The Better Choice—The General Principle of the Closest Connection

However, the just described bifurcated approach has drawbacks. First, the law applicable to the arbitration agreement can only be determined when the investor selects the forum, ie initiates the arbitral proceeding, and if necessary a seat is fixed. This may cause a costly and unnecessary burden on the parties' resources, if the tribunal later declares—based on the applicable law—that no valid consent was given.[96] Second, ICSID and non-ICSID tribunals render contradictory or at least non coherent decisions regarding their jurisdiction. Guided by the bifurcated approach, they apply different bodies of law and consequently consider the identical state consent to be valid or invalid.[97] Therefore, it seems preferable and in the interest of the disputing parties that the law applicable to investment arbitration agreements is uniformly determined, if the parties do not choose it themselves.

[94] In detail and with further references, cf Dafina Atanasova, 'Applicable Law Provisions in Investment Treaties: Forever Midnight Clauses?' (2019) 10 Journal of International Dispute Settlement 396, 399.

[95] See Convention on the Recognition and Enforcement of Foreign Arbitral Awards (concluded 10 June 1958, entered into force 7 June 1959) 330 UNTS 3 art 5(1)(a); Albert Jan van den Berg, *The New York Arbitration Convention of 1958* (Kluwer 1981) 126ff; The closest connection test of the English courts, applied to commercial arbitration cases in which the parties have not chosen the law of the main contract, also directs to the law of the seat, see *Enka Insaat Ve Sanayi AS v OOO Insurance Company Chubb* [2020] UKSC 38 [118]ff.

[96] *Green Power Partners K/S, SCE Solar Don Benito APS v Spain*, SCC Arbitration V (2016/135), Award (16 June 2022) [445].

[97] The arbitral awards rendered in the so-called Spanish renewable energy saga are illustrative examples. Three arbitral tribunals determined three different compositions of law applicable to the consent of the parties: *Green Power Partners K/S, SCE Solar Don Benito APS v Spain*, SCC Arbitration V (2016/135), Award (16 June 2022) [162] ff; *Triodos SICAV II v Spain*, SCC Case No 2017-194, Award (24 October 2022) [315]–[356] (the authors hold an unredacted copy of the award); *Cavalum SGPS, SA v Spain*, ICSID Case No ARB/15/34, Procedural Order No 6 on Spain's Request for Reconsideration of the Tribunal's Decisions on Jurisdiction (31 August 2020 and 10 January 2022) [56]ff.

However, this requires a conflict of laws rule, which can be applied to both ICSID as well as non-ICSID arbitration agreements. In the absence of a choice-of-laws clause in the IIAs, the law applicable to the material validity must be sought in other sources of law.[98] Neither the ICSID Convention nor other arbitration rules contain conflict of laws rules regarding the law applicable to ICSID as well as non-ICSID arbitration agreements.[99] In particular, general public international law does not contain any codified conflict of laws rules regarding the state's consent to arbitration.[100]

In contrast, the use of conflict of laws rules and methods in disputes arising from state conduct, whether between private parties or between states and private parties, is not new in general.[101] International adjudicating bodies have already resorted to conflicts of laws techniques and principles when necessary.[102] Furthermore, in academia it has been already suggested to fill the gap regarding the state consent to arbitration with general principles of conflict of laws by assuming that 'conflict of laws rules are ... an inherent part of every national legal system. An analysis of the relevant conflict of laws rules in comparative law could therefore reveal general principles of conflict of laws.'[103] Of course, a conclusive analysis whether such general principles of conflict of laws exist is beyond the scope of this chapter. However, there are considerable indications that they do, in particular, the principle of the closest connection,[104] because conflict of laws rules always seek the closest connection unless the parties have made an autonomous choice of law. Hence, this is the basic principle behind conflict of laws.[105]

[98] Lünsmann (n 65) 290; see also eg ICSID Convention art 44.

[99] Examples in institutional arbitration rules that only concern the substantive law are ICSID Convention art 42, 2021 ICC Rules art 21, 2023 SCC Rules art 27, or 2021 UNCITRAL Rules art 35; cf a notable exception LCIA Arbitration Rules art 16.4 2020 however, referring to the law of the seat.

[100] Lünsmann (n 65) 290.

[101] Kurt Lipstein, 'Conflict of Laws before International Tribunals' (1941) 27 Transactions of the Grotius Society 142; Kurt Lipstein, 'Conflict of Laws before International Tribunals (ii)' (1943) 29 Transactions of the Grotius Society 51, 62; Kurt Lipstein, *Principles of the Conflict of Laws, National and International* (Martinus Nijhoff 1981) 67ff; sceptical, Christian von Bar and Peter Mankowski, *Internationales Privatrecht*, vol 1 (2nd edn, CH Beck 2003) § 3 Rn 7; Werner Niederer, *Einführung in die allgemeinen Lehren des internationalen Privatrechts* (3rd edn, Polygraphischer Verlag AG 1961) 107ff; *Saudi Arabia v Arabian American Oil Company (Aramco)*, Award (27 August 1958) 27 (1958) International Law Review 117, 156ff, 167.

[102] cf eg *Serbian Loans (France v Kingdom of Serbs, Croats and Slovenes)* (Judgment) [1929] PCIJ Series A, nos 20/21 6, 41; *Saudi Arabia v Arabian American Oil Company (Aramco)*, Award (27 August 1958) 27 (1958) International Law Review 117, 156ff, 167; see, with further references, Lipstein 'Conflict of Laws' (n 101) 142; Lipstein, 'Conflict of Laws (ii)' (n 101) 51.

[103] Lünsmann (n 65) 290 (authors' translation). However, he suggests this only regarding ICSID arbitration agreements.

[104] Lünsmann (n 65) 294, 296ff; Benjamin Hayward, *Conflict of Laws and Arbitral Discretion: The Closest Connection Test* (OUP 2017) 5.28ff.

[105] Talia Einhorn, 'Israel', *International Encyclopedia of Laws: Private International Law* (Kluwer 2022) 39:

> It is a very basic principle of [private international law] that the law of the state with the closest connection to the factual circumstances should, in principle, govern the case. This principle holds true for both codified and uncodified legal systems. In a codified system it is primarily the role of the legislature to design rules that make the law with the closest connection the one that governs the legal relationship, even though there is always need for further refinement done by legal scholars and by the courts. In an uncodified system, it is up to the courts to find out, in an ever evolving process, which law has the closest connection, apply it to case at hand and, then, as the need arises in a subsequent case, refine the rule further.

The widespread use of the closest connection as a connecting factor is also a clear evidence for this.[106]

In conclusion, the law applicable to investment arbitration agreements should be in absence of a choice of the parties, determined by the general principle of the closest connection. This approach not only provides for greater legal certainty, but also increases the (cost-)efficiency of arbitral proceedings. Another advantage of the conflict of laws approach in comparison with the models presented above (II) is that, unlike the models, which are merely imitating legal concepts (eg *offerta ad incertas personas*), the conflict of laws approach gives access to coherent legal systems. At the same time, however, this raises the question of which law the arbitration agreement is most closely connected to.

C. Determining the Law with the Closest Connection to Investor-State Arbitration

In investor-state arbitration, only three legal systems have a connection to the consent of the parties: public international law, host state law, and home state law. The *lex loci arbitri*, ie the law of the seat of the tribunal, is not useful in this uniform conception. It is either excluded from the outset because ICSID tribunals do not have a seat or the seat of a non-ICSID tribunal is determined quasi-arbitrarily.[107]

Public international law could be considered as the legal system with the closest connection because the state consent is contained in an international treaty and the state had to act in its capacity as a sovereign to sign it.[108] Furthermore, the consent is intended to establish the jurisdiction of an international arbitral tribunal—such as under Article 25 of the ICSID Convention—that applies public international law.[109]

However, dispute settlement proceedings between private individuals and the state are typically governed by national law. This is also reflected in the significance of the connection of the arbitration agreement with these systems. The law of the home state of the investor may seem close as it contains the legal rules which allow the investor not only to exist as a juridical person or the law of its nationality if the investor is a natural person.[110] However, the law of incorporation of a company is not necessarily very closely linked to the investor's commercial activities in general and the investment in particular. Moreover, investors sometimes even chose a legal system which may seem favourable from a regulatory perspective, such as tax havens, without any connection

[106] cf Symeon Symeonides, *Idealism, Pragmatism, Eclecticism* (Brill Nijhoff 2021) 228ff with many references to domestic conflict of laws systems.

[107] In the absence of an agreement between the parties, the arbitral institution (2023 SCC Rules art 25(1)) or the arbitral tribunal (2021 ICC Rules art 18(1), 2021 UNCITRAL Rules art 18(1)) determines the seat of the arbitration.

[108] *Occidental Exploration and Production Co v Ecuador* [2005] EWCA Civ 1116 [32]ff; Lünsmann (n 65) 315; Heiskanen (n 88) 373, 393.

[109] Lünsmann (n 65) 303.

[110] cf Schreuer (n 1) paras 1117ff.

to their activities.[111] Hence, the law of the home state is not the law of the closest connection to the arbitration agreement.[112]

Similarly to public international law, the arbitration agreement has several connections to the law of the host state. In many cases, the underlying conflict between an investor and the host state may involve matters of domestic law of the host state (state measures such as expropriations, refusal or withdrawal of licenses, taxation matters).[113] Furthermore, the investment as such might be situated on the territory of the host state, and the choice of the host state is based on the free will as well as the decision of the investor. Apart from substantive rights derived from the IIA—to which the private investor is not a party—the legal framework between the investor and the host state is based on the law of the host state. Since it is assumed that it corresponds with the expectation of the parties and both are familiar with host state law,[114] it is convincing to consider the law of the host state as the applicable law.[115] This applies to the exclusion of the municipal conflict of laws rules.[116] Otherwise these rules may refer to another system of municipal law. In conflict of laws, this situation is known as transmission or *renvoi*. However, in respect to the investment arbitration agreement a *renvoi* would contradict the legal certainty and efficacy of an arbitral proceeding desired by the parties.

Hence, for example, Germany's consent is subject to German law. In the German legal system, the perfected consent of the parties is considered as an arbitration agreement.[117] According to the majority opinion in German law, the conclusion and validity of the arbitration agreement is governed by the rules and principles of substantive contracts based on the German Civil Code (Bürgerliches Gesetzbuch (BGB)).[118] While the German judiciary has not yet specifically decided on the legal nature of the treaty-based consent, at least the Federal Supreme Court (BGH) seems to favour a third-party beneficiary in its *Achmea* decision.[119] Thus, the BGH appears not to share the concerns

[111] Van Harten (n 3) 67ff.

[112] Partially differing opinion based on *dépeçage* Heiskanen (n 88) 393: '[T]he investor's acceptance of that consent is, as a matter of principle, governed by its own proper or personal law.'

[113] For example, the 'Spanish renewable energy saga'. In detail Danae Azaria, 'The Renewable Energy Arbitrations under the Energy Charter Treaty' in Fabri and Stoppioni (n 2) 153.

[114] Hege Elisabeth Kjos, *Applicable Law in Investor-State Arbitration* (OUP 2013) 87.

[115] Same opinion, if making an arbitration agreement subject to public international law was not possible *Occidental Exploration and Production Co v Ecuador* [2005] EWCA Civ 1116 [35]; contra Heiskanen (n 88) 393; contra Kern (n 90) 75ff applying *in favorem validitatis* the law of the host state or the law of the home state.

[116] An in-depth discussion would go beyond the scope of this article, but see Kurt Lipstein, 'Conflict of Laws (ii)' (n 101) 62f; Niederer (n 101) 276.

[117] See inter alia BGH, Beschluss I ZB 2/15, ECLI:DE:BGH:2018:311018BIZB2.15.0, 31 October 2018 ; BGH, Beschluss I ZB 16/21, ECLI:DE:BGH:2021:171121BIZB16.21.0, 17 November 2021; Münch (n 38) s 48.

[118] In German law, arbitration agreements have a dual character, being a substantive contract on a procedural subject matter, see Münch (n 38) ss 12, 15 as representative of numerous others. Contra Sebastian Bertolini, *Die Durchsetzung von ISDS-Entscheidungen in Deutschland* (Dunker & Humblot 2019) 169ff referring to a contract governed by German administrative law.

[119] BGH, Beschluss I ZB 2/15, ECLI:DE:BGH:2018:311018BIZB2.15.0, 31 October 2018, s 17:

> The clause of Article 8(2) of the BIT constitutes an agreement in favour of the investors of the contracting states involved, which is intended to give them the choice whether to initiate arbitration proceedings or proceedings before a state court in the event of an investment dispute against the other contracting state .... Article 8(2) of the BIT thus contains an offer by the contracting states to conclude an arbitration agreement with the investors of the other contracting state, which the respective investor may accept expressly or impliedly. (authors' translation and references omitted)

expressed above (II.A.4), but rather considers the transfer of a 'procedural option to arbitrate' feasible.[120] In another decision, however, the BGH only mentions the 'provision enabling the jurisdiction of an arbitral tribunal'.[121] Nevertheless, it is questionable whether the court itself would feel bound by its decisions just cited, because the decisions focused only on the validity of state consent in intra-EU disputes. To answer this question, the court did not consider it necessary to determine the legal nature of the state's consent in detail. Therefore, it seems equally arguable to base the arbitration agreement on an *offerta ad incertas personas* of the host state. However, this would also require solving the flaws outlined above (II.A.2).

If one prefers the categorization as a third-party beneficiary, the withdrawal of consent is determined by the provisions of the IIA and once the investor has acquired the option to arbitrate, this option can no longer be affected by the contracting states.

In contrast to a third-party beneficiary or an *offerta ad incertas personas*, the unilateral act model would not be feasible under German law. Even though German law permits a unilateral contract (eg § 657 BGB), the German conception of unilateral contracts seems not transferable to an arbitration agreement. At least it would only be applied accordingly. In view of the other possible solutions, however, there is no reason to use this stopgap.

In conclusion, the legal nature and characteristics of state consent in ISDS depend on the respective host state law. Even if this means that the legal nature of state consent differs between host states, it is the most appropriate framework of analysis because it provides consistent solutions to the key problems and challenges of the private law and public law approaches developed so far.

IV. Conclusion

Determining the legal nature of state consent to treaty-based investment arbitration is not seen as a significant practical problem by most commentators and arbitration tribunals. Still, from a doctrinal perspective the determination is neither clear nor undisputed. Having assessed the private law and public international law approaches developed so far and pointed out their systemic flaws, this chapter has shown that the law applicable to state consent should be considered with greater attention. In this regard, the conflict of laws principle of the closest connection leads to convincing results. It is argued that the law of the host state is the legal system with the closest connection to the investment arbitration agreement and hence state consent.

[120] Considering this also to be possible Münch (n 38) s 48.

[121] BGH, Beschluss I ZB 16/21, ECLI:DE:BGH:2021:171121BIZB16.21.0, 17 November 2021, s 21 (authors' translation). However, in a recent decision, the BGH adopts again the approach of an offer. BGH, Beschluss I ZB 43/22, ECLI:DE:BGH:2023:270723BIZB43.22.0, 27 July 2023, s 100.

8

Burden and Standard of Proof on Jurisdiction

Christoph Schreuer

I. Introduction

Questions of burden and standard of proof are of considerable practical importance but have attracted limited attention in academic writings.[1] The difference between the burden of proof and the standard of proof was described by the tribunal in *Rompetrol v Romania* in the following terms:

> the burden of proof defines which party has to prove what, in order for its case to prevail; the standard of proof defines how much evidence is needed to establish either an individual issue or the party's case as a whole. As soon as the distinction is stated in that way, it becomes evident that the burden of proof is absolute, whereas the standard of proof is relative.[2]

Arbitral tribunals have applied several rules regarding the burden of proof concerning facts upon which the parties rely. These rules are well established in international adjudication. The rule most frequently invoked by respondents is that the burden of proof is with the claimant—*actori incumbit probatio*.[3] For instance, the tribunal in *Tokios Tokelės v Ukraine* said:

> The principle of onus *probandi actori incumbit*—that a claimant bears the burden of proving its claims—is widely recognized in practice before international tribunals. The significance of this burden was stated effectively by the tribunal in *Asian Agricultural Products, Ltd v Sri Lanka* (ARB/87/3), which noted that:

[1] See however Mojtaba Kazazi, *Burden of Proof and Related Issues: A Study of Evidence before International Tribunals* (Brill 1996); Gary B Born, 'On Burden and Standard of Proof' in Meg Kinnear and others (eds), *Building International Investment Law—The First 50 Years of ICSID* (Wolters Kluwer 2016) 43; Baiju S Vasani, Timothy L Foden, and Hafsa Zayyan, 'Burden and Standard of Proof at the Jurisdictional Stage' in Katia Yannaca-Small (ed), *Arbitration under International Investment Agreements—A Guide to the Key Issues* (2nd edn, OUP 2018) 312.

[2] *Rompetrol v Romania*, Award (6 May 2013) [178].

[3] *SOABI v Senegal*, Award (25 February 1988) [9.23]; *AAPL v Sri Lanka*, Award (27 June 1990) [56]; *Tradex v Albania*, Award (29 April 1999) [73]–[75]; *Middle East Cement v Egypt*, Award (12 April 2002) [88]–[91]; *Generation Ukraine v Ukraine*, Award (16 September 2003) [19.1], [19.4]; *CSOB v Slovakia*, Award (29 December 2004) [225]–[226]; *Noble Ventures v Romania*, Award (12 October 2005) [100]; *Salini v Jordan*, Award (31 January 2006) [70]–[75]; *Tokios Tokelės v Ukraine*, Award (26 July 2007) [121], [122]. See also Bin Cheng, *General Principles of Law as Applied by International Courts and Tribunals* (CUP 1987) 327–31.

Christoph Schreuer, *Burden and Standard of Proof on Jurisdiction* In: *The Award in International Investment Arbitration*.
Edited by: Katia Fach Gómez and Catharine Titi, Oxford University Press. © Katia Fach Gómez and Aikaterini Titi 2024.
DOI: 10.1093/9780191975936.003.0008

> [a] Party having the burden of proof must not only bring evidence in support of his allegations, but must also convince the Tribunal of their truth, lest they be disregarded for want, or insufficiency, of proof.[4]

Another well-accepted rule is that the burden of proof lies with the party asserting a fact, whether it is the claimant or the respondent.[5] In this respect, the tribunal in *Saipem v Bangladesh* said:

> It is a well-established rule in international adjudication that the burden of proof lies with the party alleging a fact, whether it is the claimant or the respondent.[6]

In some cases, tribunals have shifted the burden of proof.[7] This was done where a party that originally bore the burden of proof had adduced prima facie evidence.[8] The tribunal in *Thunderbird v Mexico* applied this rule and said:

> The Tribunal shall apply the well-established principle that the party alleging a violation of international law giving rise to international responsibility has the burden of proving its assertion. If said Party adduces evidence that *prima facie* supports its allegation, the burden of proof may be shifted to the other Party, if the circumstances so justify.[9]

The standard of proof indicates how much evidence is needed to establish a fact. Rules on the standard of proof vary in different legal cultures and depending on the subject matter addressed. For instance, the standard of proof will be different in criminal matters and with claims for damages.

Typical standards applied by international tribunals in claims for damages are the 'preponderance of probabilities', 'convincing evidence', 'the balance of probabilities' or

[4] *Tokios Tokelės v Ukraine*, Award (26 July 2007) [121], quoting *Asian Agricultural Products Ltd v Sri Lanka*, Award (27 June 1990) [56] (italics original).

[5] *Feldman v Mexico*, Award (16 December 2002) [177]; *Soufraki v UAE*, Award (7 July 2004) [58], [81]; *Thunderbird v Mexico*, Award (26 January 2006) [95]; *Saipem v Bangladesh*, Decision on Jurisdiction (21 March 2007) [83]; *OKO Pankki v Estonia*, Award (19 November 2007) [211]; *Rompetrol v Romania*, Decision on Jurisdiction (18 April 2008) [75]; *EDF v Romania*, Award (8 October 2009) [221], [232]; *Azurix v Argentina*, Decision on Annulment (1 September 2009) [215]; *El Paso v Argentina*, Award (31 October 2011) [625]–[626]; *Oostergetel v Slovakia*, Final Award (23 April 2012) [146]–[148]; *Metal-Tech Ltd v Uzbekistan*, Award (4 October 2013) [237]; *Gavrilović v Croatia*, Award (26 July 2018) [230], [414]; *Venezuela US v Venezuela*, Partial Award (5 February 2021) [221].

[6] *Saipem v Bangladesh*, Award (30 June 2009) [113].

[7] But see the critical remarks on burden shifting in *Rompetrol v Romania*, Award (6 May 2013) [178]–[183].

[8] *AAPL v Sri Lanka*, Award (27 June 1990) [56]; *Middle East Cement v Egypt*, Award (12 April 2002) [94]; *Feldman v Mexico*, Award (16 December 2002) [177]; *Zhinvali v Georgia*, Award (24 January 2003) [311]; *Thunderbird v Mexico*, Award (26 January 2006) [95]; *Soufraki v UAE*, Decision on Annulment (5 June 2007) [109]; *Micula v Romania*, Decision on Jurisdiction (24 September 2008) [76]; *Siag v Egypt*, Award (1 June 2009) [317]; *RosInvest v Russian Federation*, Final Award (12 September 2010) [250]; *Alpha v Ukraine*, Award (8 November 2010) [236]; *Kardassopoulos v Georgia*, Award (3 March 2010) [230]; *Apotex v United States*, Award (25 August 2014) [8.65], [8.67]–[8.68]; *Karkey v Pakistan*, Award (22 August 2017) [497]; *ConocoPhillips v Venezuela*, Award (8 March 2019) [275].

[9] *Thunderbird v Mexico*, Award (26 January 2006) [95].

'the balance of evidence'.[10] In an article on burden and standard of proof, Gary Born has summarized the practice of tribunals as follows:

> It is widely accepted that the standard of proof in relation to the majority of claims and affirmative defences in investment arbitration is the balance of probabilities. This is true both when proving essential requirements of jurisdiction (such as nationality or ownership and control of an investment) and at the merits phase.[11]

Some tribunals have applied distinct standards to prove illegal conduct such as corruption.[12] In *Siag v Egypt* the respondent had argued that the claimants had committed fraud in connection with the acquisition of Lebanese nationality. The tribunal said:

> The standard suggested by the Claimants was the American standard of 'clear and convincing evidence', that being somewhere between the traditional civil standard of 'preponderance of the evidence' (otherwise known as the 'balance of probabilities'), and the criminal standard of 'beyond reasonable doubt'. ... The Tribunal accepts that the applicable standard of proof is greater that [*sic*] the balance of probabilities but less than beyond reasonable doubt. The term favoured by Claimants is 'clear and convincing evidence'. The Tribunal agrees with that test.[13]

In some cases, tribunals have found it unnecessary to rely on rules on the standard of proof because they were able to reach a result based on the evidence before them with 'reasonable certainty'.[14]

II. Burden of Proof and Burden Shifting in Matters of Jurisdiction

Some tribunals dealing with questions of jurisdiction, were content to apply the rule that the claimant bears the burden of proof.[15] For instance, in *Cortec v Kenya*, the tribunal said:

> The Claimants bear the onus of establishing jurisdiction under the BIT and under the ICSID Convention. The onus includes proof of the facts on which jurisdiction

[10] *Kardassopoulos v Georgia*, Award (3 March 2010) [229]; *Pugachev v Russia*, Award on Jurisdiction (18 June 2020) [256].

[11] Born (n 1) 50.

[12] *EDF v Romania*, Award (8 October 2009) [221]; *Liman Caspian Oil v Kazakhstan*, Award (22 June 2010) [422]–[424]; *Libananco v Turkey*, Award (2 September 2011) [125]; *Oostergetel v Slovakia*, Final Award (23 April 2012) [295]–[298], [302]–[303]; *Fraport v Philippines*, Award (10 December 2014) [477]–[481]; *Spentex v Uzbekistan*, Award (27 December 2016) [860]; *Kim v Uzbekistan*, Decision on Jurisdiction (8 March 2017) [544]–[548], [557]; *E energija v Latvia*, Award (22 December 2017) [541]; *Gavrilović v Croatia*, Award (26 July 2018) [224], [226], [228], [233]; *Karkey v Pakistan*, Award (22 August 2017) [490]–[493]; *Sanum v Laos*, Award (6 August 2019) [147]; *Fynerdale v Czech Republic*, Award (29 April 2021) [565]–[575]; *Penwell v Kyrgyz Republic*, Final Award (8 October 2021) [319]–[334].

[13] *Siag v Egypt*, Award (1 June 2009) [325]–[326] (footnote omitted).

[14] *World Duty Free v Kenya*, Award (4 October 2006) [166]; *Metal-Tech Ltd. v Uzbekistan*, Award (4 October 2013) [243].

[15] *Abaclat v Argentina*, Decision on Jurisdiction an Admissibility (4 August 2011) [678]; *InterTrade v Czech Republic*, Final Award (29 May 2012) [136]; *Tulip v Turkey*, Decision on Bifurcated Jurisdictional Issue (5 March

depends. ... the facts on which the Claimants rest the jurisdiction of the Tribunal have to be proven by them at the outset.[16]

In other cases, tribunals required initial proof of the jurisdictional requirements from the claimant. Once the claimant had supplied sufficient initial proof of jurisdiction, the burden shifted to the respondent. According to his practice, the claimant has the initial burden of proving these facts, but the respondent has the burden of substantiating any objections to jurisdiction. This is a consequence of the principle, briefly discussed in the introduction, that the burden of proof lies with the party asserting a fact, whether it is the claimant or the respondent.

Under this practice, a claimant has the burden of demonstrating that the factual prerequisites for jurisdiction are met. But the respondent raising objections to jurisdiction or other preliminary objections bears the burden of proving the facts upon which these objections are based. Therefore, under appropriate circumstances, the burden of proof will shift from the claimant to the respondent.

For instance, in *Rompetrol v Romania* the tribunal described the distribution of the burden of proof on matters of jurisdiction as follows:

> It will be seen that the jurisdictional objection entails issues of fact ... and issues of law .... The issues of fact are ones which the Respondent bears the burden of proving according to the requisite standard, in order to sustain the claims of law it bases on them.[17]

Similarly, in *Pac Rim v El Salvador*, the tribunal said with respect to the burden of proof relating to jurisdiction:

> As far as the burden of proof is concerned, in the Tribunal's view, it cannot here be disputed that the party which alleges something positive has ordinarily to prove it to the satisfaction of the Tribunal. At this jurisdictional level, in other words, the Claimant has to prove that the Tribunal has jurisdiction. Of course, if there are positive objections to jurisdiction, the burden lies on the Party presenting those objections, in other words, here the Respondent.[18]

2013) [48]; *Caratube v Kazakhstan*, Decision on Annulment (21 February 2014) [268]; *National Gas v Egypt*, Award (3 April 2014) [118]; *Emmis v Hungary*, Award (16 April 2014) [171], [173]; *Ampal-American v Egypt*, Decision on Jurisdiction (1 February 2016) paras 216-219; *Blue Bank. v Venezuela*, Award (26 April 2017) [65]–[73]; *Beijing Urban Construction v Yemen*, Decision on Jurisdiction (31 May 2017) [124]; *Besserglik v Mozambique*, Award (28 October 2019) [366]–[367]; *Sevilla Beheer v Spain*, Decision on Jurisdiction, Liability and the Principles of Quantum (11 February 2022) [548].

[16] *Cortec v Kenya*, Award (22 October 2018) [250].

[17] *Rompetrol v Romania*, Decision on Respondent's Preliminary Objections on Jurisdiction and Admissibility (18 April 2008) [75].

[18] *Pac Rim v El Salvador*, Decision on Jurisdiction (1 June 2012) [2.11]; see also [2.13] and [2.15].

In numerous other cases, tribunals found that once the claimant had provided initial proof of the facts supporting jurisdiction, the burden of proof shifted to the respondent who had to adduce evidence in support of its objections.[19]

Burden shifting in matters of jurisdiction has also been applied to the question of the claimant's nationality, which is necessary to establish jurisdiction.[20] In *Soufraki v UAE* the ad hoc committee said:

> Clearly, Mr Soufraki had the burden of proving to the Tribunal that he possessed Italian nationality as of the pertinent dates. This is consistent with general principles of law and has been constantly applied by ICSID tribunals. If he failed to prove his nationality to the Tribunal, the latter could not have jurisdiction to hear the case on the merits. Mr Soufraki had submitted to the Tribunal certificates of Italian nationality, which were *prima facie* evidence of the existence of such Italian nationality. Therefore, it would appear that the burden of proving the contrary should have shifted to the Respondent.[21]

Similarly, the tribunal in *Micula v Romania* said:

> As held by the *Soufraki ad hoc* Committee, if the claimant submits prima facie evidence of his nationality, the burden of proof shifts to the respondent.[22]

The same principle was adopted in *Siag v Egypt*:

> Claimants stated that Mr Siag had provided extensive *prima facie* evidence of his Lebanese nationality, and that accordingly 'the burden of proof is now on Egypt'. The Tribunal agrees with this contention.[23]

These authorities demonstrate that the burden of proof concerning questions that are relevant to jurisdiction will be shifted to the respondent in appropriate circumstances.

[19] *Generation Ukraine v Ukraine*, Award (16 September 2003) [15.7]–[15.9]; *AMTO v Ukraine*, Award (26 March 2008) [64], [65]; *Chevron and Texaco v Ecuador*, Interim Award (1 December 2008) [138]; *Libananco v Turkey*, Award (2 September 2011) [116.3]; *Victor Pey Casado v Chile*, Decision on Annulment (18 December 2012) [121]; *Teinver v Argentina*, Decision on Jurisdiction (21 December 2012) [324]; *Lao Holding v Laos*, Decision on Jurisdiction (21 February 2014) [66], [67], [153]; *Fraport v Philippines II*, Award (10 December 2014) [299]; *von Pezold v Zimbabwe*, Award (28 July 2015) [174]; *Spence v Costa Rica*, Interim Award (25 October 2016) [239]; *Kim v Uzbekistan*, Decision on Jurisdiction (8 March 2017) [180]; *Philip Morris Asia v Australia*, Award on Jurisdiction and Admissibility (17 December 2015) [495], [514]; *Manuel García Armas et al v Venezuela*, Award on Jurisdiction (13 December 2019) [636]; *Capital Financial Holdings v Cameroon*, Award (22 June 2017) [138]; *President Allende Foundation v Chile*, Award (28 November 2019) [264]–[265]; *Eyre and Montrose v Sri Lanka*, Award (5 March 2020) [275]; *Littop v Ukraine*, Final Award (4 February 2021) [325], [326].

[20] *Ambiente Ufficio v Argentina*, Decision on Jurisdiction and Admissibility (8 February 2013) [312]; *Arif v Moldova*, Award (8 April 2013) [356]–[357]; *CEAC v Montenegro*, Award (26 July 2016) [154]–[158]; *Kim v Uzbekistan*, Decision on Jurisdiction (8 March 2017) [209]–[212]. See also the ICJ in *Case concerning Avena and other Mexican Nationals (Mexico v United States of America)* (Judgment) [2004] ICJ Rep 41 [55]–[57].

[21] *Soufraki v United Arab Emirates*, Decision of the ad hoc Committee on the Application for Annulment of Mr Soufraki (5 June 2007) [109].

[22] *Micula v Romania*, Decision on Jurisdiction (24 September 2008) [76].

[23] *Siag v Egypt*, Award (1 June 2009) [317].

In particular, if a claimant adduces plausible prima facie proof of the facts supporting its position, the burden of proof will be shifted to the respondent to make a showing to the contrary.[24]

Some tribunals have noted that questions of burden of proof apply only to questions of fact but not to questions of law. The tribunal in *Westmoreland v Canada* said in this respect:

> The question of burden of proof arises only with respect to matters of fact, where each party has the burden of establishing those facts that they assert. If the Claimant cannot establish, on the balance of probabilities, those facts which are critical to founding jurisdiction, there is no jurisdiction.[25]

III. Preponderance of Arguments

The determination of a tribunal's jurisdiction is governed by special considerations that make it questionable whether rules on the burden and standard of proof are suitable. A tribunal's power to determine its own jurisdiction includes the power to determine its jurisdiction *ex officio*. This is underlined by Rule 41(2) of the ICSID Arbitration Rules:

> The Tribunal may on its own initiative consider, at any stage of the proceeding, whether the dispute or any ancillary claim before it is within the jurisdiction of the Centre and within its own competence.[26]

Therefore, under the ICSID Convention, a tribunal does not depend on an objection to jurisdiction by a party. Even in the absence of an objection or in the face of an insufficiently substantiated objection, a tribunal may consider on its own initiative whether the dispute before it is within the Centre's jurisdiction. Likewise, gaps in the claimant's arguments or evidence to substantiate jurisdiction may be filled by the tribunal.

Similar considerations apply to the provisions of a treaty offering consent to investor-state arbitration. The tribunal's power to examine issues of jurisdiction on its own initiative extends to the interpretation of the treaty's provisions dealing with jurisdiction.[27] In *Metal-Tech v Uzbekistan*, the tribunal stated in this respect:

[24] This process should be distinguished from a practice, developed by tribunals, to subject the facts supporting the merits of the case to a prima facie test at the jurisdictional stage. Under this test, tribunals make a provisional evaluation of the facts supporting the claimant's case to determine whether, if true, they are capable of constituting a violation. See eg *Casinos Austria v Argentina*, Decision on Jurisdiction (29 June 2018) [197]–[213]; Audley Sheppard, 'The Jurisdictional Threshold of a Prima-Facie Case' in Peter Muchlinski, Federico Ortino, and Christoph Schreuer (eds), *The Oxford Handbook of International Investment Law* (OUP 2008) 932; Stephan Schill and others (eds), *Schreuer's Commentary on the ICSID Convention* (3rd edn, CUP 2022) Article 41, [105]–[115].

[25] *Westmoreland v Canado*, Final Award (31 January 2022) [193].

[26] ICSID Arbitration Rule 43(3) of 2022 provides: 'The Tribunal may at any time on its own initiative consider whether a dispute or an ancillary claim is within the jurisdiction of the Centre or within its own competence.'

[27] *See Micula v Romania*, Decision on Jurisdiction and Admissibility (24 September 2008) [65]: 'The Tribunal understands its duty to determine its jurisdiction, including through examination of the jurisdictional requirements, *sua sponte*, if necessary, as it has an obligation to reject a claim if the record shows that jurisdiction is lacking.'

it is the duty of a tribunal established on the basis of a treaty to verify its jurisdiction under that treaty, even if the parties have not objected to it.[28]

The tribunal's authority to examine questions of jurisdiction on its own initiative is designed to avoid awards that exceed the tribunal's powers if the parties fail to make preliminary objections or are unable to substantiate them properly. Tribunals have stressed their power to consider any issues relating to jurisdiction on an *ex officio* basis, and at any stage of the proceedings.[29] At times, tribunals have explicitly satisfied themselves of jurisdictional requirements that were not raised by the parties[30] or have examined belated objections to jurisdiction based on their power to examine them on their own initiative.[31]

In *Vattenfall v Germany II*, the tribunal confirmed that it had the power to examine objections to its jurisdiction *ex officio* at any stage of the proceedings:

> the Tribunal considers that it has broad power to examine issues relating to its jurisdiction on an *ex officio* basis. In this respect, ICSID Rule 41(2) is the basis of a tribunal's power to assess, on 'its own initiative ... at any stage of the proceeding, whether the dispute or any ancillary claim before it is within the jurisdiction of the Centre and within its own competence'.
>
> ... In general, the provision [ICSID Rule 41(2)] is the repository of an ICSID tribunal's broad power to consider any issues relating to its jurisdiction on an *ex officio* basis, and at any stage of the proceedings.[32]

The failure of a party to raise jurisdictional objections cannot serve as a waiver. Under the ICSID Convention, certain jurisdictional requirements are objective and not subject to the parties' disposition. The existence of a legal dispute arising directly out of an investment as well as the Convention's nationality requirements cannot be

[28] *Metal-Tech v Uzbekistan*, Award (4 October 2013) [123].

[29] *Clayton and Bilcon v Canada*, Award (17 March 2015) [342]–[343]; *İçkale v Turkmenistan*, Award (8 March 2016) [239]; *Pac Rim v El Salvador*, Award (14 October 2016) [5.50]; *Infinito Gold v Costa Rica*, Decision on Jurisdiction (4 December 2017) [137]; *Krederi v Ukraine*, Award (2 July 2018) [233], [234]; *Standard Chartered Bank v TANESCO*, Decision on Annulment (22 August 2018) [153]; *Besserglik v Mozambique* (AF), Award (28 October 2019) [307]–[315]; *Green Power v Spain*, Award (16 June 2022) [125].

[30] See eg *SPP v Egypt*, Decision on Jurisdiction I (27 November 1985) [46]–[47]; *AMT v Zaire*, Award (21 February 1997) [5.03]; *Cable TV v St. Kitts and Nevis*, Award (13 January 1997) [5.03]; *Fedax v Venezuela*, Decision on Jurisdiction (11 July 1997) [25]; *Santa Elena v Costa Rica*, Award (17 February 2000) [11]; *Tanzania Electric v IPTL*, Award (12 July 2001) [13]; *CDC v Seychelles*, Award (17 December 2003) [3]–[6]; *MTD v Chile*, Award (25 May 2004) [90]–[97]; *Gas Natural v Argentina*, Decision on Jurisdiction (17 June 2005) [5]–[6]; *Saipem v Bangladesh*, Decision on Jurisdiction and Recommendation on Provisional Measures (21 March 2007) [71]–[74]; *Kardassopoulos v Georgia*, Decision on Jurisdiction (6 July 2007) [108]–[119]; *Ares v Georgia*, Award (28 February 2008) [5.4.3]–[5.4.7]; *Micula v Romania*, Decision on Jurisdiction (24 September 2008) [65]; *AES v Hungary*, Award (23 September 2010) [5.2]–[6.5.5]; *Dan Cake v Hungary*, Decision on Jurisdiction and Liability (24 August 2015) [67]–[79]; *Saint-Gobin v Venezuela*, Decision on Liability and the Principles of Quantum (30 December 2016) [356]–[361]; *Strabag v Libya*, Award (29 June 2020) [210]; *Interocean v Nigeria*, Award (6 October 2020) [180]; *Infinito Gold v Costa Rica*, Award (3 June 2021) [178].

[31] See eg *Zhinvali v Georgia*, Award (24 January 2003) [317], [321], [323], [324]; *Azurix v Argentina*, Decision on Jurisdiction (8 December 2003) [68]; see also *Gruslin v Malaysia*, Award (27 November 2000) [19.7]; *Besserglik v Mozambique*, Award (28 October 2019) [307]–[316], [318]–[324].

[32] *Vattenfall v Germany II*, Decision on the *Achmea* Issue (31 August 2018) [104]–[105].

waived. A tribunal may rely on a party's failure to invoke the non-existence of its consent as an indication of its consent, but it cannot rely on a waiver when it comes to the Convention's objective requirements.[33] Therefore, the failure of a party to carry its burden of proof or its inability to meet the necessary standard of proof for an objection with respect to these objective requirements is not necessarily dispositive. Similarly, provisions of treaties offering consent to arbitration contain objective parameters for jurisdiction which are not subject to waiver.

It follows that when it comes to questions of jurisdiction, the parties' submissions are not necessarily decisive. The tribunal must assure itself of its own jurisdiction and is not bound by the success or failure of the parties to carry their burden of proof or meet a particular standard of proof.

The International Court of Justice (ICJ) as well as some investment tribunals have declined to adopt a method whereby one of the parties carries the burden of proof in matters of jurisdiction. They have adopted a different approach to deciding whether jurisdiction exists which is better suited to the role of international courts and tribunals in determining their jurisdiction. Under this method the decision-maker does not decide on the basis of rules of burden and standard of proof but looks at the preponderance of arguments for or against jurisdiction.

In the *Fisheries Jurisdiction* case before the ICJ, the parties had argued about who should bear the burden of proving jurisdiction. The Court, following earlier decisions, dismissed these arguments and found that it had to make its decision on the preponderance of evidence:

> The Court points out that the establishment or otherwise of jurisdiction is not a matter for the parties but for the Court itself. Although a party seeking to assert a fact must bear the burden of proving it ... this has no relevance for the establishment of the Court's jurisdiction, which is a 'question of law to be resolved in the light of the relevant facts' ...
>
> That being so, there is no burden of proof to be discharged in the matter of jurisdiction. Rather, it is for the Court to determine from all the facts and taking into account all the arguments advanced by the Parties, 'whether the force of the arguments militating in favour of jurisdiction is preponderant, and to "ascertain whether an intention on the part of the Parties exists to confer jurisdiction upon it"'.[34]

Investment tribunals have adopted a similar line of reasoning. The tribunal in *Grand River v United States*, when determining its jurisdiction, felt that there was no need to operate with any rules on burden of proof. It simply examined the entire documentation on jurisdiction that had been put before it by the parties:

[33] *Besserglik v Mozambique*, Award (28 October 2019) [307]–[316], [318]–[324].

[34] *Fisheries Jurisdiction (Spain v Canada)* (Jurisdiction of the Court, Judgment) [1998] ICJ Rep 432 [36], [37], [38]. See also *Border and Transborder Armed Actions (Nicaragua v Honduras)* (Jurisdiction and Admissibility, Judgment) [1988] ICJ Rep 69, 76.

> The Parties differed as to which of them bore the burden of proof on disputed facts bearing on the existence of jurisdiction. Claimants contended that, as the moving party opposing jurisdiction, the Respondent bore the burden of proof. Respondent disagreed, maintaining that the Claimants were obliged to establish the facts required for the Tribunal to have jurisdiction. Nevertheless, both Parties presented extensive evidence to support their positions regarding the application of Articles 1116(2) and 1117(2). For its part, the Tribunal considered all of the extensive documentation produced and did not exclude any evidence on the ground that it was belatedly produced. Accordingly, the Tribunal did not find it necessary to determine which Party had a burden of going forward with the evidence.[35]

More recently, tribunals have confirmed this line of reasoning.[36] In *Çap v Turkmenistan*, the tribunal rejected the notion of a burden of proof in determining its jurisdiction. Rather, it found that it had to weigh all relevant facts and arguments to determine whether it had jurisdiction:

> The Tribunal does not accept that the burden of proof in respect of jurisdiction is on either Party. Rather, the Tribunal must determine whether it has jurisdiction, and the scope of its jurisdiction, on the basis of all the relevant facts and arguments presented by the Parties.
>
> In this respect, in the first instance it is for Claimants to show that the relevant requirements for the Tribunal's jurisdiction are present, including consent to arbitration. Consent cannot be presumed and its existence must be established. By corollary, in this case, where Respondent is challenging jurisdiction, it has to adduce evidence to support its objections. Accordingly, the Tribunal has to weigh the evidence and arguments from both Parties to determine on balance whether it has jurisdiction in this matter.[37]

Similarly, in *WNC v Czech Republic*, the tribunal dismissed the concept of a burden of proof with respect to objections to jurisdiction emanating from the interpretation of the BIT:

> where, as here, the objections arise from the construction of specific provisions of the BIT, the Tribunal must apply the principles of interpretation reflected in the Vienna Convention on the Law of Treaties ('VCLT'). Issues of onus do not come into play and the process of interpretation engaged in by the Tribunal determines the result.[38]

[35] *Grand River v United States*, Decision on Objections to Jurisdiction (20 July 2006) [37].
[36] *See also Clayton and Bilcon v Canada*, Award on Jurisdiction and Liability (17 March 2015) [341]–[344], where the tribunal rejected the concept of a burden of proof on jurisdiction in favour of the tribunal's duty to decide on its jurisdiction *sua sponte*.
[37] *Çap v Turkmenistan*, Decision on Jurisdiction (13 February 2015) [119]–[120].
[38] *WNC v Czech Republic*, Award (22 February 2017) [293].

This approach is confirmed by a series of other recent decisions. In *Itisaluna v Iraq*, the tribunal rejected the concept of a burden of proof with respect to jurisdiction and said:

> As an initial matter, the Tribunal observes that nothing in its analysis turns on any question of burden or standard of proof. These evidential principles address the responsibility of parties to establish the evidential case on which they rely, and typically shift between claimant and respondent to adduce a sufficiency of evidence to establish facts germane to their case. These principles do not operate in respect of contentions of international law addressed to an international tribunal which, as in this case, has a responsibility for determining the content and application of international law. Still less do they operate in respect of legal questions going to the jurisdiction of a tribunal, which a tribunal is required to address *proprio motu*, even if not raised by a party.[39]

In *Addiko v Croatia*, the tribunal relied on the ICJ's judgment in the *Fisheries Jurisdiction* case, quoted above,[40] and said:

> In applying these VCLT principles to interpret a treaty text, no burden of proof applies as between the parties to a particular dispute. The Tribunal must satisfy itself of the correct meaning of the treaty, and this correct reading will not shift based on traditional notions of burden of proof, which exist primarily to define the duty placed on a party to demonstrate or refute a disputed fact.[41]

The tribunal in *Raiffeisen v Croatia*, distinguished between the burden of proving factual allegations and the legal burden of proving jurisdiction. It said:

> neither Raiffeisen nor the Respondent bears the legal burden of proving jurisdiction here. As to the reasons, the Tribunal can do no better than quote the reasoning of the ICJ in the *Fisheries Jurisdiction* Judgment: [quoting the passage reproduced above]
>
> The issue of jurisdiction here turns on the interpretation and application of the relevant articles of the Austria–Croatia BIT in the circumstances presented. This is properly the legal task of the Tribunal.[42]

It appears from these cases that in determining questions concerning a tribunal's jurisdiction, a focus on burden of proof is not the best approach. The ICJ as well as some investment tribunals have discarded the burden of proof approach and have adopted a

[39] *Itisaluna v Iraq*, Award (3 April 2020) [151].
[40] See text to n 34.
[41] *Addiko v Croatia*, Decision on Croatia's Jurisdictional Objection Related to the Alleged Incompatibility of the BIT with the EU *Acquis* (12 June 2020) [200].
[42] *Raiffeisen Bank International v Croatia*, Decision on Jurisdiction (30 September 2020) [93]–[94]; see also [127].

method whereby the weight of evidence and of legal arguments is decisive to establish jurisdiction.

Some decisions may be interpreted to suggest that even under this new approach the rules on the burden and standard of proof may continue to apply to questions of fact, whereas the preponderance of arguments would be restricted to questions of law. This distinction is less than convincing for purposes of deciding a tribunal's jurisdiction. Legal arguments are never subject to rules on burden or standard of proof. They carry a higher or lower degree of plausibility. They need not be proven by a party but are governed by the maxim *iura novit curia*. As the ICJ pointed out in the *Fisheries Jurisdiction* case, a court or tribunal's jurisdiction is a 'question of law to be resolved in the light of the relevant facts'. The court or tribunal will determine its jurisdiction 'from all the facts and taking into account all the arguments advanced by the Parties'.[43] Therefore, the preponderance of arguments that determines jurisdiction combines factual and legal elements.

IV. The Interpretation of Consent

Closely related to the question of the burden and standard of proof for jurisdiction is the interpretation of consent to arbitration. Depending on a tribunal's interpretative approach to an ostensible arbitration agreement, a claimant will have to meet a higher or lower standard of proof for the existence of consent to arbitration.

Some tribunals have been hesitant to assume the existence of consent and have demanded unequivocal evidence. For instance, the Decision on Jurisdiction in *Plama v Bulgaria* stated:

> It is a well-established principle, both in domestic and international law, that such an agreement [to arbitrate] should be clear and unambiguous.[44]

Respondents have invoked this statement to argue for a restrictive interpretation of expressions of consent but have mostly failed. Tribunals have rejected the idea of special rules of interpretation for provisions containing consent to jurisdiction and have distanced themselves from the passage in *Plama* containing the 'clear and unambiguous' requirement.[45]

Some tribunals, however, have suggested that there was a presumption against consent to arbitration, which is a limitation of sovereignty. In *Wintershall v Argentina*, the tribunal said:

[43] *Fisheries Jurisdiction (Spain v Canada)* (Jurisdiction of the Court, Judgment) [1998] ICJ Rep 432 [37], [38].
[44] *Plama v Bulgaria*, Decision on Jurisdiction (8 February 2005) [198].
[45] *Suez, Sociedad General de Aguas de Barcelona and InterAguas Servicios Integrales del Agua v Argentina*, Decision on Jurisdiction (16 May 2006) [64]; *Berschader v Russia*, Award, 21 April 2006 [177] (but see [181]); *Renta 4 v Russian Federation*, Award on Preliminary Objections, Separate Opinion Charles Brower (20 March 2009) [7]; *Garanti Koza v Turkmenistan*, Decision on the Objection to Jurisdiction for Lack of Consent (3 July 2013) [22].

> it is a general principle of international law that international courts and tribunals can exercise jurisdiction over a State only with its consent. The principle is often described as a corollary to the sovereignty and independence of the State. A *presumed* consent is not regarded as sufficient, because any restriction upon the independence of a State (not agreed to) cannot be presumed by courts—See the *Lotus case* (1927), PCIJ, Series A, No. 10, at p. 18.[46]

Similarly, the tribunal in *Tulip v Turkey* stated:

> consent is the cornerstone of all international treaty commitments and that here the provisions of the BIT qualify the state sovereignty of Turkey. Here, Article 8 is a specific and qualified derogation to Turkey's sovereign immunity and the Tribunal accepts that in its interpretation and application there is an inertia against too expansive a construction of the reach of the BIT.[47]

On the other hand, some tribunals have embraced a doctrine of extensive interpretation of expressions of consent to arbitration. In *Tradex v Albania*, the tribunal, after finding that the Albanian Investment Law was an expression of Albania's commitment to the full protection of foreign investment, said:

> It would, therefore, seem appropriate to at least take into account, though not as a decisive factor by itself but rather as a confirming factor, that in case of doubt the 1993 Law should rather be interpreted in favour of investor protection and in favour of ICSID jurisdiction in particular.[48]

Similarly, in *Millicom v Senegal*, the tribunal noted the international trend towards arbitration for dispute resolution in concession agreements and found that there was a presumption in favour of arbitration:

> Even if the expression may appear excessive, we can indeed speak, in case of serious doubts, of a presumption in favour of arbitration.[49]

Despite these isolated cases, the prevailing view is that neither a restrictive nor an extensive interpretation is to be applied to expressions of consent to jurisdiction. In the *Oil Platforms* case in the ICJ, Judge Higgins summarized this principle in the following terms:

> It is clear from the jurisprudence of the Permanent Court and of the International Court that there is no rule that requires a restrictive interpretation of compromissory

[46] *Wintershall v Argentina*, Award (8 December 2008) [160(3)] (emphasis in the original, footnotes omitted).
[47] *Tulip v Turkey*, Decision on Bifurcated Jurisdictional Issue (5 March 2013) [44].
[48] *Tradex v Albania*, Decision on Jurisdiction (24 December 1996) 5 ICSID Reports 43, 68.
[49] *Millicom v Senegal*, Decision on Jurisdiction (16 July 2010) [98].

> clauses. But equally, there is no evidence that the various exercises of jurisdiction by the two Courts really indicate a jurisdictional presumption in favour of the plaintiff.… The Court has no judicial policy of being either liberal or strict in deciding the scope of compromissory clauses: they are judicial decisions like any other.[50]

Most investment tribunals have rejected either a restrictive or an extensive interpretations of consent clauses. In *Amco v Indonesia*, the tribunal was confronted with the argument that consent given by a sovereign state to an arbitration convention amounting to a limitation of its sovereignty should be construed restrictively. The tribunal rejected this contention categorically. It said:

> like any other conventions, a convention to arbitrate is not to be construed *restrictively*, nor, as a matter of fact, *broadly* or *liberally*. It is to be construed in a way which leads to find out and to respect the common will of the parties: such a method of interpretation is but the application of the fundamental principle *pacta sunt servanda*, a principle common, indeed, to all systems of internal law and to international law.[51]

In the tribunal's view, the investor's interest in submitting investment disputes to international arbitration was matched by a parallel interest of the host state: to protect investments is to protect the general interest of development and of developing countries.[52]

In *SOABI v Senegal*, the government's argument was that Article 25 of the ICSID Convention must be given a strict interpretation 'as with any provision derogating from general rules of municipal law'. The tribunal noted that consent to arbitral proceedings was in derogation from the right to have recourse to national courts. Such consent should not be presumed. But it refused to accept the consequence that the interpretation of an expression of consent should be stricter with regard to the consent of a state than with regard to that of an investor. In the tribunal's view, the correct approach, as with any other agreement, was an interpretation consistent with the principle of good faith:

> In other words, the interpretation must take into account the consequences which the parties must reasonably and legitimately be considered to have envisaged as flowing from their undertakings. It is this principle of interpretation, rather than one of *a priori* strict, or, for that matter, broad and liberal construction, that the Tribunal has chosen to apply.[53]

[50] *Oil Platforms (Islamic Republic of Iran v United States of America)* (Preliminary Objections, Judgment, Separate Opinion of Judge Higgins) [1996] ICJ Rep 847 [35].
[51] *Amco v Indonesia*, Decision on Jurisdiction (25 September 1983) [14(i)] (italics original).
[52] At [23].
[53] *SOABI v Senegal*, Award (25 February 1988) [4.08]–[4.10].

The tribunal in *PNG Sustainable Development Program v Papua New Guinea* discussed the question of a presumption for and against jurisdiction in some detail and rejected both approaches. It said:

> In the Tribunal's view, it is well-settled, for good reason, that there is no presumption against the finding of jurisdiction under the ICSID Convention, and no heightened requirement of proof of an agreement to arbitrate. Jurisdictional instruments, whether investment contracts, treaties, or legislation, must be interpreted objectively and neutrally, and not either expansively or restrictively.[54]

A considerable number of other tribunals have also endorsed a balanced approach to the interpretation of consent clauses.[55] Such an approach rejects both a presumption against and in favour of jurisdiction. It also implicitly rejects a heightened or lower standard of proof for jurisdiction.

V. Summary and Conclusions

Tribunals have applied various rules regarding the burden of proof. The most important of these are the rule that the burden of proof is with the claimant and the rule that the burden of proof lies with the party asserting a fact. Where a party that had initially borne the burden of proof adduces plausible evidence, arbitral tribunals have shifted the burden of proof to the other party.

Tribunals have described the required standard of proof variously as the preponderance of evidence, convincing evidence, the balance of probabilities or the balance of evidence. Some tribunals have applied distinct standards to prove illegal conduct such as corruption.

When addressing questions of jurisdiction, many tribunals have applied similar standards. They have applied the rule that initially the claimant bears the burden of proof. Once the claimant had supplied sufficient initial proof of jurisdiction, the burden shifted to the respondent.

It is questionable whether these traditional mechanisms are well-suited for the determination of a tribunal's jurisdiction. A tribunal must determine its jurisdiction *ex*

[54] *PNG Sustainable Development Program v Papua New Guinea*, Award (5 May 2015) [253].

[55] *SPP v Egypt*, Decision on Jurisdiction II (14 April 1988) [63]; *CSOB v Slovakia*, Decision on Jurisdiction (24 May 1999) [34]; *Methanex v United States*, Preliminary Award on Jurisdiction (7 August 2002) [103]–[105]; *Mondev v United States*, Award (11 October 2002) [42], [43]; *Aguas del Tunari v Bolivia*, Decision on Jurisdiction (21 October 2005) [91]; *Duke Energy v Peru*, Decision on Jurisdiction (1 February 2006) [76]–[78]; *Inceysa v El Salvador*, Award (2 August 2006) [176]–[181]; *Noble Energy v Ecuador*, Decision on Jurisdiction (5 March 2008) [195]–[197]; *Renta 4 v Russian Federation*, Award on Preliminary Objections (20 March 2009) Separate Opinion Charles Brower [7]–[9]; *Tza Yap Shum v Peru*, Decision on Jurisdiction (19 June 2009) [37]; *Austrian Airlines v Slovak Republic*, Final Award (9 October 2009) [119]–[121]; *Libananco v Turkey*, Award (2 September 2011) [540]; *Iberdrola v Guatemala*, Award (17 August 2012) [303]; *Daimler v Argentina*, Award (2 August 2012) [174]–[178]; *Churchill Mining v Indonesia*, Decision on Jurisdiction (24 February 2014) [151]; *National Gas v Egypt*, Award (3 April 2014) [119]; *Lighthouse v Timor-Leste*, Award (22 December 2017) [148]; *Alcor v Czech Republic*, Award (2 March 2022) [245].

officio or *proprio motu*. The evidence and arguments submitted by the parties do not necessarily determine the tribunal's decision on its jurisdiction. Moreover, many jurisdictional requirements are objective and not subject to the disposition of the parties. With respect to these requirements, a party's failure to raise a jurisdictional objection cannot be accepted as a waiver.

In recent years, the ICJ and some investment tribunals have discarded principles of burden and standard of proof when determining their jurisdiction. They have adopted a method whereby the court or tribunal looks at the overall evidence for and against jurisdiction and decides on the preponderance of facts and legal arguments. An important aspect of jurisdiction is the parties' consent to arbitration. A few tribunals have adopted presumptions for or against the existence of consent. Most tribunals reject these presumptions thereby implicitly rejecting a higher or lower standard of proof.

9

On the Adjudicative Discretion of Investment Arbitrators

Between *ne ultra petita*, *ne infra petita*, and *jura novit curia*

Attila M Tanzi

I. Introduction

It is a given that the power of international courts and tribunals to adjudicate a dispute depends on the consent expressed by the disputing parties. And it is, again, the consent of the parties which determines the law by which the dispute is decided. In investment arbitration this applies no less than in interstate adjudication, with the specification that the applicants triggering the proceedings complement the consent to arbitration expressed by the state of nationality through the conclusion of applicable investment agreements.

The present chapter primarily illustrates, on the basis of the case law, how the adjudicative power of investment arbitrators in their *ratio decidendi*,[1] much like interstate adjudicators, is constrained by the ability of the parties to impact on the law to be applied to the facts in dispute, in combination with the principle of *ne ultra petita* and its logical legal corollary *ne infra petita*. That is to say that under such principles, the arbitral tribunal is to decide the dispute within the parameters set by the parties, avoiding any overreach, yet fully addressing all claims and counterarguments within the framework of the applicable law.

It will also be shown how these principles may be counterbalanced—according to case-specific circumstances—by the judicial discretion that arbitrators are afforded under the principle of *jura novit curia*. The latter confers on the tribunal the power to rely on any relevant legal arguments, including those that have not been advanced by the parties, in order to decide the case, provided that such arguments fall within the boundaries of the applicable law and the facts in dispute.

The principles in question, which govern adjudicative discretion of investment arbitrators, will be illustrated emphasizing their derivation from interstate adjudication,[2]

[1] See generally Pierre Lalive, 'On the Reasoning of International Arbitral Awards' (2010) 1 Journal of International Dispute Settlement 55. See also, critically, Federico Ortino, 'Legal Reasoning of International Investment Tribunals: A Typology of Egregious Failures' (2012) 3 Journal of International Dispute Settlement 31.

[2] As observed by Eric De Brabandere, also with a view to distinguishing investment treaty arbitration from international commercial arbitration, '[b]eing founded in public international law, investment tribunals and arbitrators are subjected to some specific principles imported from public international litigation', Eric De Brabandere, *Investment Treaty Arbitration as Public International Law: Procedural Aspects and Implications*

Attila M Tanzi, *On the Adjudicative Discretion of Investment Arbitrators* In: *The Award in International Investment Arbitration.* Edited by: Katia Fach Gómez and Catharine Titi, Oxford University Press.
DOI: 10.1093/9780191975936.003.0009

and through their interpretation and application in investment case law. The analysis relies mostly on the case law of the International Centre for Settlement of Investment Disputes (ICSID), since its annulment mechanism offers interestingly objective scrutiny and critical jurisprudential analysis of the adjudicative discretion of arbitral tribunals.

II. *Ne ultra petita* and Its Related Principles

The primary general principle curtailing the arbitrators' adjudicative discretion—so called *ne ultra petita*—constraints such discretion within the four corners of the scope of the dispute before them as determined by the *petitum*, based on the causes of action, within the boundaries of the tribunal's jurisdictional competence and the applicable law, as determined by the parties' consent. In other words, an investment tribunal having jurisdictional competence to entertain a given dispute may not decide on issues other than those that have been submitted to it.

The application of *ne ultra petita* to investment arbitration as 'a derivative of the consent principle'[3] flows from its consistent recognition in interstate case law. As observed by the International Court of Justice (ICJ, or the Court) in *Haya de la Torre*, when interpreting its own decision in the *Asylum* case between Colombia and Peru, 'it is the duty of the Court not only to reply to the questions as stated in the final submissions of the parties, but also to abstain from deciding points not included in those submissions'.[4] In the same vein, in the *Boundary dispute between Argentina and Chile*, the arbitral tribunal affirmed that:

> The competence of international judges is limited by the functions assigned to them by the parties in the case. Their powers are also limited by the extreme claims which the parties put forward in the hearings. To exceed these functions or powers means deciding *ultra vires* and rendering the decision null by reason of *excès de pouvoir*.[5]

It is fully in line with the rationale of the principle in question that the ICJ in *Barcelona Traction* did not address the treatment of shareholders under international

(CUP 2014) 100. See also Thomas W Wälde, 'Procedural Challenges in Investment Arbitration under the Shadow of the Dual Role of the State: Asymmetries and Tribunals' Duty to Ensure, Pro-Actively, the Equality of Arms' (2010) 26 Arbitration International 3; Stephan Wittich, 'The Limits of Party Autonomy in Investment Arbitration' in Christina Knahr and others (eds), *Investment and Commercial Arbitration: Similarities and Divergences* (Eleven 2010) 50ff.

[3] Gerald Fitzmaurice, *The Law and Procedure of the International Court of Justice* (Grotius Publications 1986) 524.

[4] *Request for Interpretation of the Judgment of 20 November 1950 in the Asylum Case (Colombia v Peru)* [1950] ICJ Rep 395, 402.

[5] *Boundary dispute between Argentina and Chile concerning the frontier line between boundary post 62 and Mount Fitzroy*, 21 October 1994 [2006] 22 RIAA 3, 26 [77].

law, confining itself to the treatment of foreign companies, since the former issue had not been raised by the parties.[6]

Ne ultra petita operates jointly with two other general principles of international adjudication in curtailing adjudicative discretion of international courts and tribunals. Namely, *ne infra petita* and *non liquet*. Having regard to the former, one may recall the ICJ statement in the *Continental Shelf* case between Libya and Malta, whereby '[t]he Court must not exceed the jurisdiction conferred upon it by the Parties, but it must ... exercise that jurisdiction to its full extent'.[7] Indeed, as put by Sir Gerald Fitzmaurice, if 'an international tribunal [may] not decide more than it is asked to decide',[8] *a contrario*, it also cannot decide less than it is asked to decide.

In this respect, according to the circumstances of the case, including the state of the law in relation to the facts in dispute, *ne infra petita* may coincide with the prohibition of *non liquet*, whereby, based on the assumption of the completeness of the international legal system,[9] an adjudicator may not fall short of deciding a dispute alleging lack of applicable law governing the disputed facts.

An adjudicative body can also be said to incur *infra petita* when it fails to decide the entirety, or certain aspects, of the dispute, omitting to consider certain facts, including as and when the facts in question have not been clearly defined by the parties. This is a situation of so-called *non licet*.[10] It is a rare but not impossible circumstance. By way of example, such circumstance occurred in the 1988 *Taba* case, concerning the boundary delimitation dispute between Egypt and Israel.[11] Here, Egypt and Israel had requested the arbitral tribunal to identify the line of their border based on the location of a series of telegraph pillars which had been planted during the British Mandate over Palestine (1923–47). The problem concerned the location of the 'last pillar', which had in fact been destroyed in the 1970s. While Israel argued that the tribunal should declare a *non licet*[12]—due to the imprecision on the factual elements in the Special Agreement—in order to avoid such an outcome, and stressing the will of the parties to settle 'fully and finally' their boundary as stated in the *compromis*, the tribunal re-characterized the factual aspects of the dispute by regarding the penultimate pillar as the final pillar, although this could in principle qualify as an *ultra petita* decision.[13]

[6] *Barcelona Traction, Light and Power Company, Limited (Belgium v Spain)* (Second Phase, Preliminary Objections) [1970] ICJ Rep 3, 37 [49].

[7] *Continental Shelf (Libyan Arab Jamahiriya v Malta)* (Merits) [1985] ICJ Rep 3, 24 [19].

[8] Fitzmaurice (n 3) 524.

[9] See Hersch Lauterpacht, 'Some Observations on the Prohibition of "Non Liquet" and the Completeness of the Law' in Frederik Mari van Asbeck (ed), *Symbolae Verzijl, présentées au professeur JHW Verzijl à l'occasion de son LXXX-ième anniversaire* (Nijhoff 1958) 217. See also, for a critical analysis of the traditional view on the prohibition of *non liquet*, Daniel Bodansky, 'Non Liquet and the Incompleteness of International Law' in Laurence Boisson de Chazournes and Philippe Sands (eds), *International Law, the International Court of Justice and Nuclear Weapons* (CUP 1999) 155.

[10] Gerald Fitzmaurice, 'The Problem of Non-Liquet: Prolegomena to a Restatement' in Charles Rousseau (ed), *Mélanges offerts à Charles Rousseau: La communauté international* (Pedone 1974) 96; Prosper Weil, 'Some Observations on the Arbitral Award in the Taba Case' (1989) 23 Israel Law Review 1, 17.

[11] *Case concerning the location of boundary markers in Taba between Egypt and Israel*, 29 September 1988 [2006] 20 UNRIAA 1, 65ff [238]ff. See also Elihu Lauterpacht, 'The Taba Case: Some Recollections and Reflections' (1989) 23 Israel Law Review 443, 468 and Weil (n 10) 25.

[12] *Taba* (n 11) 65 [239].

[13] ibid 66 [242].

The complexity under similar circumstances of the application of the principles in question for purposes of curtailing the scope of the disputed facts emerges all the more in relation to the principle *jura novit curia* in light of the blurred distinction between the disputed facts and the law.[14] This principle will be addressed in the next section.

III. *Jura novit curia* and Its Relation to the Other Adjudicative Principles

While, according to *ne ultra petita*, the mandate of any given international adjudicative body curtails the boundaries of its jurisdictional competence, under *ne infra petita*, within such boundaries, the adjudicator is to exercise its judicial function to the full extent, including *sua sponte*. Against this backdrop, the question naturally arises as to whether and, if so, to what extent an international adjudicator is entitled to decide a case on the basis of legal grounds which have not been invoked, or have been poorly invoked by the parties. Here, the principle of *jura novit curia*, according to which 'the tribunal both knows and will apply the law, whatever the parties say, or omit to say', comes to the fore.[15] As observed by the ICJ in the *Military and Paramilitary Activities in and against Nicaragua* case, '[f]or the purpose of deciding whether the claim is well founded in law ... *jura novit curia* signifies that the Court is not solely dependent on the argument of the parties before it with respect to the applicable law.'[16]

Jura novit curia and *ne infra petita* may complement each other, thus grounding the preservation of the autonomy of the adjudicative function precisely by affording the tribunal the jurisdictional power to apply the applicable law to the facts in dispute to its fullest extent, irrespective of the arguments pleaded by the parties. *Ne ultra petita*, on the other hand, by enhancing the consensual nature of international adjudication, thus the autonomy of the parties, prevents the adjudicator from following—by way of *ratio decidendi*, while keeping free on the *obiter dicta* level—legal arguments which would

[14] See *Brazilian Loans (Brazil v France)* [1929] PCIJ Rep Series A No 21, 93, 124. See also Frédéric G Sourgens, Kabir Duggal, and Ian A Laird, *Evidence in International Investment Arbitration* (OUP 2018); Robert Kolb, 'General Principles of Procedural Law' in Andreas Zimmerman and others (eds), *The Statute of the International Court of Justice: A Commentary* (3rd edn, OUP 2019). The International Law Commission (ILC) observed that in international adjudication '[t]he line between "fact" and "law" is often obscured', and that '[b]ased on *jura novit curia*, the Court can in principle apply any law to any fact, and in theory can evaluate evidence and draw conclusions as it sees appropriate as long as the Court complies with the *non ultra petita* rule); these are all legal matters. Given its judicial function and under *jura novit curia*, the Court needs to sufficiently understand the meaning of each related technical fact in the case at hand', Report of the International Law Commission, GAOR 73rd Session Supplement No 10, UN Doc A/73/10 (2018) 200, n 991. Interestingly, and more generally, the following dialectical view has been advanced: '[t]here is a presumption that the judge knows the law. There is no need, in theory, for the parties to provide him with the materials and information necessary for the decision of questions of law. No similar presumption is possible in relation to questions of fact. *jura novit curia* may be plausible; *facta novit curia* is absurd. Nevertheless ... at the end of the day, decisions of fact are as much for the judge as are decisions on the applicable law', John Anthony Jolowicz, *On Civil Procedure* (CUP 2000) 222.

[15] Fitzmaurice (n 3) 531.

[16] *Military and Paramilitary Activities in and against Nicaragua (Nicaragua v United States of America)* (Merits) [1986] ICJ Rep 14, 24 [29].

re-characterize the dispute as curtailed by the claims of the parties. The principles in point, through their mutual interplay, are key to the proper administration of international justice.

Jura novit curia, in combination with the adage *narra mihi factum dabo tibi ius*,[17] can be said to describe in principle the allocation of responsibilities between the parties and the adjudicator in domestic judicial proceedings, whereby it is primarily for the former to prove the facts and for the latter to apply the law to such facts.[18] In international litigation, though, such distinction is less neat, if only because, as already alluded, the dividing line between the facts and the law appears to be more blurred than in domestic litigation.[19]

The crucial importance of the connection between the law and the facts was also raised by the ICJ in the *Military and Paramilitary Activities in and against Nicaragua* case. Precisely after restating the principle *jura novit curia* as recalled above,[20] the Court observed that '[a]s to the facts of the case, in principle the Court is not bound to confine its consideration to the material formally submitted to it by the parties'.[21] The ICJ further developed its reasoning on the point at issue in *Armed Activities on the Territory of the Congo*, where it stated that it would 'first make its own determination of the facts and then apply the relevant rules of international law to the facts which it has found to have existed'.[22]

In other words, the international adjudicator has the power to look for and appreciate the relevant facts *motu proprio*, as much as it is entitled under *jura novit curia* to look *sua sponte* for the legal arguments which are appropriate in order to decide the dispute, irrespective of what the parties submit. In fact, it is often not only difficult, but even unnecessary, to distinguish between party-produced and court-gathered evidence of the disputed facts, or between appreciations of facts and legal appreciations. As put by Professor Anastasios Gourgourinis, '[c]laims of the parties to the dispute and

[17] *Western Sahara* (Advisory Opinion), Separate Opinion of Judge de Castro [1975] ICJ Rep 127, 138.

[18] See, for all, Friedrich Rosenfeld, '*Iura Novit Curia* in International Law' (2017) 6 European International Arbitration Review 131. On the different configuration of the principle in hand in domestic and international adjudication, see Joe Verhoeven, 'Jura Novit Curia et le juge international' in Pierre-Marie Dupuy and others (eds), *Völkerrecht als Wertordnung: Festschrift für Christian Tomuschat—Common Values in International Law: Essays in Honour of Christian Tomuschat* (NP Engel Verlag 2006) 637ff.

[19] See text to n 14.

[20] See n 16.

[21] *Military and Paramilitary Activities in and against Nicaragua* (n 16) 24 [29]. The Court had considered the matter elsewhere, for example in the *Lotus* case, where it stated that:

> [H]aving arrived at the conclusion that the arguments advanced by the French Government either are irrelevant to the issue or do not establish the existence of a principle of international law precluding Turkey from instituting the prosecution which was in fact brought against Lieutenant Demons, [the Court] observes that in the fulfilment of its task of itself ascertaining what the international law is, it has not confined itself to a consideration of the arguments put forward, but has included in its researches all precedents, teachings and facts to which it had access and which might possibly have revealed the existence of one of the principles of international law contemplated in the special agreement.

The SS Lotus (France v Turkey) [1927] PCIJ Rep Series A No 10, 5, 31

See also *Brazilian Loans* (n 14) 124 and *Nuclear Tests (Australia v France)* [1974] ICJ Rep 253, 263–64 [31]–[32]; *(New Zealand v France)* [1974] ICJ Rep 457, 467–68 [31]–[32].

[22] *Armed Activities on the Territory of the Congo (Democratic Republic of the Congo v Uganda)* [2005] ICJ Rep 168, 200 [57].

relevant facts are closely related with the identification of any given applicable norm', in what is essentially considered as an exercise of 'qualification juridique'.[23]

IV. The Principles in Point in International Investment Arbitration

The above delineated boundaries within which is confined the adjudicative function in inter-state litigation also represent the four corners within which investment arbitrators have to confine themselves in the exercise of their arbitral decision-making function. This naturally flows from the public international law rationale of the investment arbitration system as originally conceived under the ICSID Convention.[24] As stressed by its founding father, Aron Broches, '[t]he parallel if any lays with the International Court of Justice rather than with commercial arbitration'.[25] While for purposes of the present chapter the focus is on the award, the same boundaries here discussed also apply to decisions by annulment committees.

A. *Ne ultra petita*

Interestingly, as it emerges from the *travaux* of the Convention, it was Broches himself, in his capacity as chairman of the Washington Conference, who stressed how '*ultra petita*, namely where the Tribunal would have gone beyond the scope of agreement of the parties or would have decided points which had not been submitted to it', would ground the annulment of the award entailing an excess of power under Article 52(1)(b).[26] In *Enron v Argentina*, concerning the possibility of awarding moratory interest to the claimant lacking a specific request to that effect, the tribunal touched upon the issue in general terms:

> [J]ust as [the Tribunal] must decide a matter that has been duly submitted and petitioned, the same is conversely true that this cannot be done if not requested, as this would amount to an excess of power which, as the Respondent explains, can result in a decision that is *ultra petita* and thus subject to the sanction of an annulment.[27]

In *Compagnie d'Exploitation du Chemin v Gabon*, the tribunal found it necessary to note that a 'revendication a bien été introduite dans la procédure de manière explicite

[23] Anastasios Gourgourinis, 'The Distinction between Interpretation and Application of Norms in International Adjudication' (2011) 2 Journal of International Dispute Settlement 31, 44–45.

[24] Convention on the Settlement of Investment Disputes between States and Nationals of Other States (adopted 18 March 1965, entered into force 14 October 1966) 575 UNTS 159.

[25] Quoted in ICSID (ed), *History of the ICSID Convention: Documents Concerning the Origin and the Formulation of the Convention*, vol II(1) (reprinted, ICSID Publication 2009) 423. For a general analysis of the relationship between the two, see De Brabandere (n 2) esp 15–67.

[26] Quoted in Mark B Feldman, 'The Annulment Proceedings and the Finality of ICSID Arbitral Awards' (1987) 2 ICSID Review 85, 100. Art 52(1)(b) of the ICSID Convention establishes that '[e]ither party may request annulment of the award by an application in writing addressed to the Secretary-General on one or more of the following grounds ... that the Tribunal has manifestly exceeded its powers'.

[27] *Enron Corporation Ponderosa Assets, LP v Argentina*, ICSID Case No ARB/01/3, Decision on Claimants' Request for Rectification and/or Supplementary Decision of the Award (3 October 2007) [42].

et qu'elle a fait l'objet d'un débat entre le Tribunal et les Parties' in order to find that '[l]e Tribunal n'a donc pas statué *ultra petita*'.[28]

Ne ultra petita has been considered within the framework of excess of power, as a ground for annulment in *El Paso v Argentina*,[29] *Continental Casualty v Argentina*,[30] and *SAUR v Argentina*, under Article 52(1)(b) of the ICSID Convention.[31] It has also been addressed as a potentially serious departure from a fundamental rule of procedure (Article 52(1)(d)), although, at least from what it can be inferred from the relevant case law, only to the extent that the violation of *ne ultra petita* essentially stems from a violation of the parties' right to be heard.[32] For instance, in *Vivendi (I)*, the annulment committee, in assessing that the disputed award was not vitiated by 'a serious departure from a fundamental rule of procedure'—in the sense that it 'was in no ... *ultra petita*'—satisfied itself that '[f]rom the record, it [was] evident that the parties had a full and fair opportunity to be heard at every stage of the proceedings'.[33] Moreover, as was the case in *Vivendi (I)*, while not ruling out that, in principle, an award incurring *ultra petita* may fall within a ground for annulment under Article 52(1)(d), never have requests for annulment so framed been upheld by annulment committees.

B. *Ne infra petita*

Annulment committees have also highlighted the legal implication that underlies the relationship between *ne ultra petita* and *ne infra petita*. In *Micula v Romania (I)*, for instance, the committee pointed out that:

> Excess of powers can be committed both by overreach and by default. Awards can be annulled if tribunals either assume powers to which they are not entitled by way of a

[28] 'Si le Tribunal a octroyé un droit non revendiqué et donc aurait éventuellement commis un excès de ses pouvoirs', *Compagnie d'Exploitation du Chemin de Fer Transgabonais v Gabonese Republic*, ICSID Case No ARB/04/5, Decision on Annulment (11 May 2010) [193].

[29] *El Paso Energy International Company v Argentina*, ICSID Case No ARB/03/15, Decision on Annulment (22 September 2014) [138].

[30] *Continental Casualty Company v Argentina*, ICSID Case No ARB/03/9, Decision on Partial Annulment (16 September 2011) [242].

[31] *SAUR International SA v Argentina*, ICSID Case No ARB/04/4, Decision on Annulment (19 December 2016) [167].

[32] Art 52(1)(d) of the ICSID Convention establishes that '[e]ither party may request annulment of the award by an application in writing ... on one or more of the following grounds ... that there has been a serious departure from a fundamental rule of procedure'. See, among others, *Maritime International Nominees Establishment (MINE) v Guinea*, ICSID Case No ARB/84/4, Decision on Annulment (22 December 1989) [5.06]; *Wena Hotels Ltd v Egypt*, ICSID Case No ARB/98/4, Decision on Annulment (28 January 2002) [57]; *MTD Equity Sdn Bhd and MTD Chile SA v Chile*, ICSID Case No ARB/01/7, Decision on Annulment (21 March 2007) [49]; *CDC Group plc v Seychelles*, ICSID Case No ARB/02/14, Decision on Annulment (29 June 2005) [49]; *Azurix Corp v Argentina*, ICSID Case No ARB/01/12, Decision on Annulment (1 September 2009) [49]–[52].

[33] *Compañía de Aguas del Aconquija SA and Vivendi Universal SA v Argentina*, ICSID Case No ARB/97/3, Decision on Annulment (3 July 2002) (*Vivendi (I)*) [85]. As recalled by Aron Broches, a failure to afford a party the opportunity to exercise such a right was envisaged precisely as a ground for annulment consisting of 'a serious departure from a fundamental rule of procedure'. To that end, he argued that one such '"[f]undamental rul[e]" would comprise, for instance, the so-called principles of natural justice, e.g. that both parties must be heard and that there must be an adequate opportunity for rebuttal', 'Observations on the Finality of ICSID Awards' (1991) 6 ICSID Review 321, 331 (quoted from ICSID (n 25) 480). On the relationship between *ne ultra petita* and the right of the parties to the dispute to be heard, see section V.

decision which is *ultra petita* (eg by an excess of jurisdiction), or fail to exercise an existing jurisdiction by way of *infra petita* (eg by omitting to decide over a head of a claim raised by the parties). In this context, a manifest shortfall in the exercise of jurisdiction may constitute a manifest excess of power.[34]

For an award to be found to incur *infra petita*, it must have omitted to address, not just any issue plausibly falling within the scope of the dispute, but one specifically raised before the tribunal. This only apparently obvious point was emphasized in *Gambrinus v Venezuela*, where the committee found that 'the Tribunal cannot be faulted in not addressing the issue of prescription period or limitation when it was not raised specifically as an issue or argued in extenso by the Applicant before the Tribunal'.[35]

An award incurring *infra petita* could, in principle, and according to the specific circumstances of any given case, ground a request for annulment under 'failure to state reasons' (Article 52(1)(e)).[36] The conceptual proximity between *ne infra petita* and this ground for annulment is implicit in the structure of the award which, pursuant to ICSID Arbitration Rule 47(1)(i), 'shall contain the decision of the Tribunal on every question submitted to it, together with the reasons upon which the decision is based'. However, ICSID case law consistently shows that, in order for an omission in the award to qualify as a 'failure to state reasons', it must concern an 'essential' or 'decisive' question.[37]

C. *Jura novit curia*

As to *jura novit curia*, as plainly put by the tribunal in *Metal-Tech v Uzbekistan*, 'when it comes to applying the law, including municipal law, as opposed to establishing facts, the principle *iura novit curia*—or better *iura novit arbiter*—allows it to form its own opinion on the meaning of the law'.[38] As stressed by Christoph Schreuer, 'the annulment-case law has uniformly rejected the idea that the tribunals in drafting their awards are restricted to the arguments presented by the parties'.[39] That is to say that, as colourfully put by Jan Paulsson, 'a tribunal in an investment dispute

[34] *Ioan Micula, Viorel Micula, SC European Food SA, SC Starmill SRL and SC Multipack SRL v Romania (I)*, ICSID Case No ARB/05/20, Decision on Annulment (26 February 2016) [126].

[35] *Gambrinus Corp v Venezuela*, ICSID Case No ARB/11/31, Decision on Annulment (3 October 2017) [199].

[36] *Klöckner Industrie-Anlagen GmbH and others v Cameroon and Société Camerounaise des Engrais*, ICSID Case No ARB/81/2, Decision on Annulment (3 May 1985) [115]–[116]; *MINE v Guinea* (n 32) [5.08]–[5.09]; *Wena v Egypt* (n 32) [57]; *Amco Asia Corporation and others v Indonesia*, ICSID Case No ARB/81/1, Decision on Annulment (16 May 1986) [86]ff.

[37] *Klöckner v Cameroon* (n 36) [114]–[115]; *MINE v Guinea* (n 32) [5.11]–[5.13]; *CDC v Seychelles* (n 32) [50], [56]–[57].

[38] *Metal-Tech Ltd v Uzbekistan*, ICSID Case No ARB/10/3, Award (4 October 2013) [287].

[39] Christoph H Schreuer, 'Three Generations of ICSID Annulment Proceedings' in Emmanuel Gaillard and Yas Banifatemi (eds), *Annulment of ICSID Awards* (Juris Publishing 2004) 30.

cannot content itself with inept pleadings, and simply apply the least implausible of the two'.[40]

In 2010, the annulment committee in *Enron v Argentina* found that—in assessing whether the measures adopted by Argentina in the midst of the 2000s economic crisis were the 'only way' for it to safeguard its essential interests according to the doctrine of the state of necessity as codified under Article 25(1)(a) of the International Law Commission's (ILC) Articles on State Responsibility—the tribunal omitted to address a number of potentially relevant questions entrenched in the legal concept of state of necessity.[41] In particular, the committee found that the award did not deal with the legal definition of 'contribution to the situation of necessity' under Article 25(2)(b).[42] Interestingly, it first read this circumstance through the lens of *ne ultra petita*, as it noted that:

> [T]he parties in their arguments before the Tribunal do not appear to have expressly identified and argued the questions set out above, which would provide an explanation for why the Tribunal did not expressly address them. [A] Tribunal is ... certainly not required to address arguments that have not been put by parties.[43]

The committee then complemented this observation in relation to *jura novit curia* by adding that 'the Tribunal is required to apply the applicable law'[44] and that, accordingly, regardless of the pleadings of the parties, it was the tribunal's duty to elaborate upon the doctrine of state of necessity in order to explain why Argentina's measures were not the 'only way' to safeguard its essential interests and why it could be said that Argentina contributed to the situation of necessity.[45] The award had in fact basically relied on evidence from an economics expert to apodictically reach its conclusions.[46] With extreme rigour, to the extent of nearly associating annulment to appellate competence, the committee found that the tribunal had not applied the applicable law and, even if the parties had not specifically addressed the interpretation and application of Article 25 of the ILC Articles—assuming that the tribunal should have done so *sua sponte*—annulled the award for excess of power[47] and failure to state reasons.[48]

In the annulment proceedings in *Caratube v Kazakhstan*, Caratube claimed that the fact that the tribunal 'used in its Award legal reasoning which had never been argued

[40] Jan Paulsson, 'International Arbitration and the Generation of Legal Norms: Treaty Arbitration and International Law' in Albert Jan van den Berg (ed), *International Arbitration 2006: Back to Basics?* (Kluwer Law International 2007) 879.

[41] *Enron Corporation Ponderosa Assets, LP v Argentina*, ICSID Case No ARB/01/3, Decision on Annulment (30 July 2010) [368].

[42] ibid [392]–[393].

[43] ibid [375].

[44] ibid [376].

[45] ibid [377].

[46] ibid [376].

[47] ibid [393].

[48] ibid [378]. Interestingly, the annulment did not occur here because of a serious departure from a fundamental rule of procedure, although the right to be heard was in fact potentially violated. In this respect, it might be argued that the committee annulled the award due to an evidentiary issue, ie, that the tribunal would have conferred full evidentiary value on a 'legal fact' produced by expert who had no qualification in this respect.

by or disclosed to the parties' entailed a violation of a fundamental rule of procedure, justifying the annulment of the award.[49] The committee rejected this argument and, while conceding that 'tribunals should avoid the parties be surprise[d] by the consideration of legal issues that were not taken into consideration in the proceedings',[50] it also stressed that 'surprise in itself does not give rise to a ground for annulment'[51] and that 'tribunals are entitled, *within certain limits*, to proceed without asking for the parties' views'.[52] Elaborating on such 'limits', the committee specified that such adjudicative freedom may be exercised 'provided that the tribunal's arguments can be framed within the legal framework argued during the procedure and therefore concern aspects on which the parties could reasonably be expected to comment, if they wished their views to be taken into account by the tribunal'.[53]

Subsequent case law adopts the above approach, emphasizing the procedural right of the parties to be heard. In *Quiborax v Bolivia*, for instance, the tribunal noted that:

> When applying the law (whether national or international), the Tribunal is of the view that it is not bound by the arguments and sources invoked by the Parties. The principle *iura novit curia*—or better, *iura novit arbiter*—allows the Tribunal to form its own opinion of the meaning of the law, provided that it does not surprise the Parties with a legal theory that was not subject to debate and that the Parties could not anticipate.[54]

Such a cautious stance has further been adopted in *Daimler v Argentina*,[55] *Vestey Group v Venezuela*,[56] and *Churchill v Indonesia*,[57] and, as will also be shown in section V, it would seem to signal the consolidation of a trend towards the application of *jura novit curia* conditional upon compliance with the parties' right to be heard.

V. Interplay between the Adjudicative Principles in Question and the Right to Be Heard

As anticipated, the case law increasingly appears to address the right of the parties to be heard as the balancing factor between judicial discretion and the parties' autonomy.

[49] *Caratube International Oil Company LLP v Kazakhstan*, ICSID Case No ARB/08/12, Decision on Annulment (21 February 2014) [90].
[50] ibid [95], quoting *Iurii Bogdanov, Agurdino-Invest Ltd and Agurdino-Chimia JSC v Moldova*, SCC Case No 93/2004, Award (22 September 2005) [4.2.2].
[51] *Caratube v Kazakhstan* (n 49) [96].
[52] ibid [95] (emphasis added).
[53] ibid [94].
[54] *Quiborax SA, Non Metallic Minerals SA and Allan Fosk Kaplún v Bolivia*, ICSID Case No ARB/06/2, Award (16 September 2015) [92] (echoing *Metal-Tech v Uzbekistan* (n 38)).
[55] *Daimler Financial Services AG v Argentine Republic*, ICSID Case No ARB/05/1, Decision on Annulment (7 January 2015) [295].
[56] *Vestey Group Ltd v Venezuela*, ICSID Case No ARB/06/4, Award (5 April 2016) [118].
[57] *Churchill Mining and Planet Mining Pty Ltd v Indonesia*, ICSID Case No ARB/12/14, Award (6 December 2016) [236].

As stated in 2002 by the annulment committee in *Wena Hotels v Egypt*, the procedural principle in point:

> [I]ncludes the right [for any party] to state its claim or its defense and to produce all arguments and evidence in support of it [and] has to be ensured on an equal level, in a way that allows each party to respond adequately to the arguments and evidence presented by the other.[58]

While this statement flows from the procedural principle of the equality of arms in relation to the right of defence, for purposes of the adjudicative principles in question, the right to be heard is to be tested against the legal reasoning of the tribunal, which may be found in the award and on which the parties did not have the opportunity to express themselves. Indeed, the *Wena Hotels* committee observed that 'if *iura novit curia* is exercised, an invitation to the parties to comment on the new legal arguments may reduce the risk of errors or mistakes'.[59]

This is plainly in line with the reasoning followed by the very first ICSID annulment committee, in 1984, in *Klöckner v Cameroon*, finding that '[i]t matters little in principle that the Tribunal's legal construction was different from that of one or the other of the parties, so long as the right of each to be heard was respected and ... so long as it remains within the "legal framework" provided by the parties.'[60] Eventually, the committee annulled the award in light of excess of powers considerations. In particular, it found that the tribunal went beyond 'the legal framework provided by the parties' by deciding on the basis of equity without the agreement of the parties, thus, beyond the framework provided by Article 42(1) of the ICSID Convention on the applicable law.[61]

Given different circumstances, the same principle was applied in *Vivendi (I)* to substantiate the rejection of the request for annulment for departure from a fundamental rule of procedure due to an alleged *ultra petita* decision. The committee found that:

> From the record, it is evident that the parties had a full and fair opportunity to be heard at every stage of the proceedings. They had ample opportunity to consider and present written and oral submissions on the issues, and the oral hearing itself was meticulously conducted to enable each party to present its point of view. The Tribunal's analysis of the issues was clearly based on the materials presented by the parties and was in no sense *ultra petita*.[62]

Annulment case law has also relied on the right of the parties to be heard in relation to *jura novit curia*. As the committee in *Perenco v Ecuador* put it, '[i]n case that the tribunal prefers to use a distinct legal framework, or to bring attention to other issues not

58 *Wena v Egypt* (n 32) [57].
59 *Caratube v Kazakhstan* (n 49) [95].
60 *Klöckner v Cameroon* (n 36) [56] (emphasis added).
61 ibid [57]ff.
62 *Vivendi (I)* (n 33) [85].

raised by the parties, the tribunal shall give an opportunity to the parties to comment on such new legal framework'.[63]

This statement suggests that, although the right of the parties to be heard should be guaranteed, generally, it must be a fortiori and more rigidly applied whenever, in deciding the dispute, the adjudicative body is inclined to alter the 'legal framework' provided by the parties. Although these considerations concern the 'legal framework' of the dispute, it cannot be ruled out entirely that an enhanced application of *jura novit curia* would end up curtailing *ne ultra petita*, 'moving' the boundaries of the dispute. As will be illustrated below, this is the more so if one considers that *ne ultra petita* implies *ne infra petita* and that ICSID adjudicative bodies operate under the express obligation to avoid a *non liquet*.

VI. *Ne ultra petita* as Curtailed by *jura novit curia*, *ne infra petita*, and *non liquet*

Article 42(2) of the ICSID Convention provides that '[t]he Tribunal may not bring in a finding of *non liquet* on the ground of silence or obscurity of the law'. *Non liquet*, as it has been illustrated above,[64] ties in with *ne infra petita* and is inextricably linked to *jura novit curia*. The risk of *non liquet* is considered in the abstract by the 'silence or obscurity of the law' applicable to the settlement of the dispute. In practice, however, such risk consists of the circumstance in which the parties fail to assert or clarify the law substantiating their claims. Therefore, in line with Professor Schreuer's interpretation of *non liquet* as embedded in the principle whereby 'the award must deal exhaustively with the dispute',[65] it will be for the arbitrators to assert and clarify the law, possibly even by resorting to a systemic interpretation and application of the relevant general principles of law.[66] The *Vivendi (I)* committee found that '[a]n ICSID tribunal commits an excess of powers not only if it exercises a jurisdiction which it does not have under the relevant agreement or treaty and the ICSID Convention, read together, but also if it fails to exercise a jurisdiction which it possesses under those instruments'.[67]

Also bearing in mind the prohibition of *non liquet*, this passage suggests an affirmative answer to the vexed question whether, next to the obligation to review all of the

[63] *Perenco Ecuador Limited v Republic of Ecuador*, ICSID Case No ARB/08/6, Decision on Annulment (28 May 2021) [127].

[64] See section II.

[65] Christoph H Schreuer and others, *The ICSID Convention: A Commentary* (2nd edn, CUP 2009) 816.

[66] See, in general, Andrea Gattini, 'General Principles of Law and International Investment Arbitration' in Andrea Gattini, Attila Tanzi, and Filippo Fontanelli (eds), *General Principles of Law and International Investment Arbitration* (Brill Nijhoff 2018) and Attila M Tanzi, 'Conclusions: Testing General Principles of Law in International Investment Law: Between Principles and Rules of International Law' in Mads Andenas and others (eds), *General Principles and the Coherence of International Law* (Brill Nijhoff 2019).

[67] *Vivendi (I)* (n 33) [86]. See also *Togo Electricité and GDF-Suez Energie Services v Togo*, ICSID Case No ARB/06/7, Decision on Annulment (6 September 2011) [109]; *Duke Energy International Peru Investments No 1 Ltd v Peru*, ICSID Case No ARB/03/28, Decision on Annulment (1 March 2011) [97]: 'a failure to decide a question entrusted to the tribunal and requiring its decision ... constitute[s] an excess of powers, since the tribunal has ... failed to fulfil the mandate entrusted to it by virtue of the parties' agreement'; *Teinver SA, Transportes de Cercanías SA and Autobuses Urbanos del Sur SA v Argentina*, ICSID Case No ARB/09/1, Decision on Annulment (29 May 2019) [59].

legal arguments and the evidentiary record submitted by the parties, tribunals have also the duty to address elements of *both law and fact* that are relevant to the decision of the dispute but which have not been pleaded by the parties.

As to the elements of law, it has already been illustrated in relation to *Enron v Argentina* that, under extreme circumstances, according to the ICSID Convention, failure to apply the applicable law may be sanctioned with annulment under different grounds, with special regard to manifest excess of power and failure to state reasons.[68] According to a constructive reading of this reasoning, a tribunal that applies legal arguments, or even rules, that have not been pleaded by the parties, cannot be held to incur *ultra petita* when it does so in order to avoid failure to apply the applicable law. By the same token, a tribunal would be bound under *ne infra petita* and *non liquet* to apply such rules and legal arguments within the framework of the applicable law that are necessary to settle in its entirety the dispute before it, even when such rules and arguments have not been pleaded by the parties.

The scope of application of the principles in question can be said to stretch also to the facts of the case and their forensic explanation when this is necessary to settle the dispute. Again, that is so under three counts: namely, *jura novit curia*, *ne infra petita*, and *non liquet*. As to the first count, as observed by the ILC Special Rapporteur on the protection of the atmosphere with regard to the ICJ adjudicative powers, '[*j*]*ura novit curia* ... can enable or even require the Court to consider *factual points* that have not been taken by the parties, by virtue of proper application of international law'.[69] As to the second count, while under Article 43 of the ICSID Convention the tribunal may require the parties to produce evidence, conversely, when facts adduced by the parties are not addressed by the tribunal which would be determinant for its decision, an *infra petita* problem arises. As to the third count, Article 42(2) on *non liquet* refers to cases of 'obscurity of the law'. Such obscurity often depends not so much on the law itself, as on the complexity or the highly technical nature of the disputed facts or on evidentiary issues, shifting the *non liquet* to *non licet*.

Again, the principle of the right to be heard may come to hand to create a fruitful interaction between the arbitrators and the parties in order to clarify such 'obscurities' and justify an 'extensive' application of *jura novit curia* as well as potential departures from *ne ultra petita*.

VII. Concluding Remarks

The above analysis has sought to illustrate how the adjudicative discretion of investment arbitral tribunals—much like interstate international courts and tribunals—is, or should be, exercised within the boundaries set by *ne ultra petita*, *ne infra petita*, *jura*

[68] See text to nn 41ff.

[69] ILC, 'Fifth Report on the Protection of the Atmosphere by Shinya Murase, Special Rapporteur', UN Doc A/CV.4/711 (8 February 2018) 45 (emphasis added).

novit curia. The case law shows not only how international investment arbitrators have applied, on a case-specific basis, each of the three adjudicative principles in question discretely, but also how each such principle generally operates through interaction with the other two, according to the circumstances of any given case. Such interplay aims at catalysing an adjudicative balance between arbitrators' adjudicative discretion and the autonomy of the parties.

Ne ultra petita gives effect to party autonomy—which is foundational of a tribunal's jurisdictional power—effectively making the parties' claims an integral component of the adjudicator's mandate. It flows from this that the support to arbitral discretion and creativity derived from *jura novit curia* is reduced to the minimum. Such limitation, though, can, in turn, be mitigated by *ne infra petita*, let alone the prohibition of *non liquet*, as the case may be.

It appears from the case law that investment arbitrators—in terms akin to interstate adjudicators—may well employ interpretive legal reasoning in coming down to their decision independently from the parties, but only to the extent that this is confined to the rules that have been pleaded by them. Such restrictive statement requires qualification, or exceptions. The first exception operates in the hypothetical and unlikely circumstance in which the rules invoked by the parties are inadequate, or insufficient, to decide the dispute. Here, the prohibition of *non liquet* and/or *ne infra petita* principles would bring *jura novit curia* to the forefront. Second, arbitrators may refer to rules that have not been invoked by the litigants by way of Article 31(3)(c) of the Vienna Convention on the Law of Treaties[70] or equity *infra legem*,[71] provided that the rules in question are incidental to the subject matter of the dispute. Third, interstate and investor-state case law show that, when the judge or arbitrator exercises elements of *jura novit curia*, the procedural rights of the parties, with special regard to the right to be heard, should always be given due consideration. In particular, in such circumstance, seeking post-hearing briefs from the parties based on well-considered written questions should be encouraged. In fact, it would be more than advisable for purposes of enhancing the legitimacy of the award, or shielding it from annulment, where such form of review is available.

[70] (Adopted 23 May 1969, entered into force 27 January 1980) 1155 UNTS 332. Article 31(3)(c) states that, in interpreting a treaty, '[t]here shall be taken into account, together with the context ... any relevant rules of international law applicable in the relations between the parties'.

[71] See, in general, Catharine Titi, *The Function of Equity in International Law* (OUP 2021).

10

Equality of Arms

Lukas Vanhonnaeker

I. Introduction

The phrase 'equality of arms' expresses the mandatory duty of arbitral tribunals, among other adjudicative instances, to treat the parties equally in all aspects of the arbitral procedure.[1] As one of the most fundamental adjudicative principles and a structural component of the idea of justice itself,[2] the roots of the equal treatment principle are intertwined with the concepts of the right to a fair trial and due process and can already be identified in the Magna Carta Libertatum of 1215.[3] Since then, this key principle has been expressed in a plethora of domestic[4] and international arbitration rules.[5] The phrase 'equality of arms', which is often encompassed under notions such as 'procedural fairness' or the 'good administration of justice', made its way into the realm of international arbitration with an early appearance of the principle of equal treatment in an arbitration taking place under the Jay Treaty in 1797.[6] Similarly, domestic or international arbitration rules and conventions provide for equal treatment in arbitration, even if not always using the phrase 'equality of arms'.[7] For example, one of the most important international arbitration instruments, the New York Convention,[8] is widely considered as protecting this key principle by precluding enforcement of an arbitral award falling under its scope of application if a party was not treated equally.[9] Similarly,

[1] See United Nations Commission on International Trade Law (UNCITRAL), *2012 Digest Case Law on the Model Law on International Commercial Arbitration* (United Nations 2012) 98; Gary B Born, *International Commercial Arbitration* (3rd edn, Kluwer Law International 2021) 2336.

[2] HLA Hart, *The Concept of Law* (OUP 1961) 156.

[3] See eg Vincent R Johnson, 'The Magna Carta and the Beginning of Modern Legal Thought' (2016) 85(3) Mississippi Law Journal 621, 639–40; Jane Rutherford, 'The Myth of Due Process' (1992) 72(1) Boston University Law Review 1, 68–69.

[4] See eg English Arbitration Act 1996 s 33(1)(a); French Code of Civil Procedure art 1510; Hong Kong Arbitration Ordinance s 46(2); Swiss Law on Private International Law art 182(3).

[5] See eg 2013 UNCITRAL Arbitration Rules art 17(1); 2006 UNCITRAL Model Law art 18; 2014 London Court of International Arbitration (LCIA) Arbitration Rules art 14.4(i); International Centre for Dispute Resolution (ICDR) Rules art 22(1); 2022 American Arbitration Association (AAA) Arbitration Rules r 33(a).

[6] Bin Cheng, *General Principles of Law as Applied by International Courts and Tribunals* (Grotius Publications 1987) 290, citing *The Betsey* (1797) 4 Int Adj MS 179, 185.

[7] See nn 4 and 5.

[8] Convention on the Recognition and Enforcement of Foreign Arbitral Awards, 10 June 1958, 330 UNTS 3.

[9] While the principle of equal treatment is generally considered to fall under the New York Convention art V(1)(b) and linked to the notion of due process, it has also been included under New York Convention V(2)(b) as a component of procedural public policy. See in this regard Born (n 1) 3839–40; Nigel Blackaby and others, *Redfern and Hunter on International Arbitration* (6th edn, Kluwer Law International/OUP 2015) 356–57; Andrés Jana L, Angie Armer, and Johanna Klein Kranenberg, 'Article V(1)(b)' in Herbert Kronke and others (eds), *Recognition and Enforcement of Foreign Arbitral Awards: A Global Commentary on the New York Convention* (Kluwer Law International 2010) 246–48; George A Bermann, 'Recognition and Enforcement of Foreign Arbitral Awards: The

Lukas Vanhonnaeker, *Equality of Arms* In: *The Award in International Investment Arbitration*. Edited by: Katia Fach Gómez and Catharine Titi, Oxford University Press. DOI: 10.1093/9780191975936.003.0010

as will be analysed in the first section of this chapter, this principle is key in the field of international investment law. It will also be explained why the asymmetries inherent to this field make it even more important to guarantee respect of the parties' equality of arms in investment arbitration (section II). Section III will then survey investor-state arbitration (ISA) cases in which the parties' unequal treatment was raised and section IV suggests ways in which ISA arbitrators could respond to equal treatment concerns.

II. The Concept of Equality of Arms in Investment Arbitration

The principle of equality of arms is prevalent in the realm of investment arbitration. It is provided in the most frequently used arbitration rules in ISA, including Article 18 of the United Nations Commission on International Trade Law (UNCITRAL) Model Law[10] and Rule 3(2) of the ICSID Arbitration Rules, the latter of which provides that '[t]he Tribunal shall treat the parties equally and provide each party with a reasonable opportunity to present its case'.

Additionally, although the principle of equality of arms is not explicitly provided for under the Convention on the Settlement of Investment Disputes Between States and Nationals of Other States (ICSID Convention), it is generally accepted that a sufficiently serious breach of that principle[11] could constitute a cause for annulment of ICSID Convention awards under Article 52(1)(d) of the Convention.[12] The early *Wena Hotels* award recognizes the inclusion of the principle of equality of arms in Article 52(1)(d) in the following terms:

> The Applicant has to identify the fundamental rule of procedure from which the Tribunal departed and it has to show that such departure has been serious.
>
> [Article 52(1)(d)] refers to a set of minimal standards of procedure to be respected as a matter of international law. It is fundamental, as a matter of procedure, that each

Interpretation and Application of the New York Convention by National Courts' in George A Bermann (ed), *Recognition and Enforcement of Foreign Arbitral Awards: The Interpretation and Application of the New York Convention by National Courts* (Springer 2017) 45–46; Reto Marghitola, *Document Production in International Arbitration* (Kluwer Law International 2015) 216.

10 A comparable requirement is provided in 2013 UNCITRAL Arbitration Rules art 17. Furthermore, the failure to provide the guarantee of equal treatment set forth in UNCITRAL Model Law art 18 constitutes a ground for refusing recognition and enforcement of an arbitral award pursuant to Model Law art 36(1)(a)(ii).

11 See eg *Tulip Real Estate and Development Netherlands BV v Turkey*, ICSID Case No ARB/11/20, Decision on Annulment (30 December 2015) [84] and [145]: 'Unequal treatment of the parties may be a sign of lack of impartiality and may amount to a serious violation of a fundamental rule of procedure. However, a finding of this nature would require clear and incontrovertible substantiation.'

12 This article refers to a 'serious departure from a fundamental rule of procedure'. See also *Enron Creditors Recovery Corp Ponderosa Assets, LP v Argentina*, ICSID Case No ARB/01/3, Decision on Annulment (30 July 2010) [197] (the annulment committee deciding that there was no inconsistency 'with the principle of equality of the parties or right of defence'); *Azurix Corp v Argentina*, ICSID Case No ARB/01/12, Decision on Annulment (1 September 2009) [233]–[234] (the annulment committee noting that 'in order to be a 'serious' departure from a fundamental rule of procedure, the violation of such a rule [ie the equality of treatment] must have caused the Tribunal to reach a result substantially different from what it would have awarded had such a rule been observed'); *Giovanni Alemanni and others v Argentina*, ICSID Case No ARB/07/8, Decision on Jurisdiction and Admissibility (17 November 2014) [323].

party is given the right to be heard before an independent and impartial tribunal. This includes the right to state its claim or its defence and to produce all arguments and evidence in support of it. This fundamental right has to be ensured on an equal level, in a way that allows each party to respond adequately to the arguments and evidence presented by the other.[13]

Subsequent tribunals followed suit, with, for example, the *MINE* Annulment Committee which explained with respect to Article 52(1)(d) that:

> even a serious departure from a rule of procedure will not give rise to annulment, unless that rule is 'fundamental'. The Committee considers that a clear example of such a fundamental rule is to be found in Article 18 of the UNCITRAL Model Law on International Commercial Arbitration which provides:
>
> 'The parties shall be treated with equality and each party shall be given full opportunity of presenting his case.'[14]

Investment tribunals, whether constituted under the ICSID Convention or applying arbitration rules such as the UNICTRAL Arbitration Rules, have had many opportunities to emphasize the key importance of the principle of equality of arms and the need to guarantee it, including through provisional measures.[15] The *Pope & Talbot* tribunal, for example, described the principle of equal treatment as an 'overriding principle' under the UNCITRAL Rules.[16] This stance was reaffirmed by subsequent tribunals, with the *Biwater Gauff* tribunal affirming that '[i]t is indeed one of the most fundamental principles of international arbitration that the parties should be treated with equality',[17] and the *Alemanni* tribunal asserting that 'the principle of equality of arms [is] fundamental to the judicial process'.[18]

Yet, despite being consistently referred to as a fundamental concept of adjudication—and notwithstanding the far-reaching consequences that not abiding by it can have with respect to the annulment of an award—the contours of 'equality of arms' remain blurred. When raised in the context of arbitral proceedings, tribunals must use their discretion to assess whether a breach of the parties' equality of arms has materialized and, if so, how to reinstate an equilibrium. One of the difficulties in defining the precise contours of this key principle lies in the

[13] *Wena Hotels LTD v Egypt*, ICSID Case No ARB/98/4, Decision on Annulment (5 February 2002) [56]–[57].

[14] *Maritime International Nominees Establishment (MINE) v Guinea*, ICSID Case No ARB/84/4, Decision on Partial Annulment (14 December 1989) [5.06]; *MTD Equity Sdn Bhd and MTD Chile SA v Chile*, ICSID Case No ARB/01/7, Decision on Annulment (21 March 2007) [49].

[15] *Gavrilović and Gavrilović doo v Croatia*, ICSID Case No ARB/12/39, Decision on Claimants' Request for Provisional Measures (30 April 2015) [192].

[16] *Pope & Talbot Inc v Canada*, UNCITRAL, Award on the Merits of Phase 2 (10 April 2001) [193].

[17] *Biwater Gauff (Tanzania) Ltd v Tanzania*, ICSID Case No ARB/05/22, Procedural Order No 2 (24 May 2005) [9].

[18] *Giovanni Alemanni and others v Argentina*, ICSID Case No ARB/07/8, Decision on Jurisdiction and Admissibility (17 November 2014) [323].

fact that the notion of equality of arms does not mandate strict equality or identical treatment.[19]

For instance, the principle according to which each party must have a reasonable opportunity to present its case is protected under the notion of equality of arms. If one party is afforded the possibility to fully present its case and the other party is limited in the presentation of its own case, the tribunal is not abiding by the principle of equality of arms. However, the principle of equality of arms does not necessarily require giving to the parties more than the opportunity to adequality present their respective case.[20] As such, the parties may be allocated different amounts of time to present their cases.

The decision of the *Azurix* annulment committee highlights the fact that the equality of arms´ principle does not entail identical treatment. When rejecting Argentina's claim that the tribunal did not treat the parties equally with respect to evidence and the production of document-related orders, the Annulment Committee explained that:

> As to Argentina's claim that the Tribunal's Procedural Orders No. 2 to No. 6 did not treat the parties equally, the Committee observes that the fact that a request by one party is allowed while a request by another party is denied does not mean that there has been an inequality in the treatment of the parties ... It is only where it can be shown that a tribunal has applied inconsistent standards in the way that it has treated the requests of the different parties that there can be said to be inequality of treatment.[21]

In fact, strict equality is often difficult to achieve and may be undesirable. For example, if one were to abide by the principle of strict equality, an argument claiming a breach of the principle could be made if the language of the arbitration is an official language of only one of the parties, if the seat of the tribunal is located geographically closer to one party's home jurisdiction, or if one of the parties is granted three more days to prepare its case.

The first two examples illustrate the difficulty of abiding by the principle of strict equality. The third example demonstrates its undesirability and, in some cases, unfairness. Indeed, as observed by Jeffrey Waincymer, in the context of arbitral proceedings, and adjudication more generally, the claimant is free to initiate arbitral proceedings whenever it thinks most opportune and after having taken all the time necessary to prepare its case, provided that statutory limitations are respected. By contrast, once arbitral proceedings are initiated, the respondent will often have to prepare its case under strict and much shorter time limits, thus possibly justifying a different allocation of

[19] See Yves Derains and Eric A Schwartz, *A Guide to the ICC Rules of Arbitration* (2nd edn, Kluwer Law International 2005) 229; Jeffrey Waincymer, *Procedure and Evidence in International Arbitration* (Kluwer Law International 2012) 82; Andrea K Bjorklund and Lukas Vanhonnaeker, 'The Powers, Duties, and Rights of International Arbitrators' in Stefan Kröll, Andrea K Bjorklund, and Franco Ferrari (eds), *Cambridge Compendium of International Commercial and Investment Arbitration*, vol 1 (CUP 2023) 1022–23.

[20] See Born (n 1) 2336.

[21] *Azurix Corp v Argentina*, ICSID Case No ARB/01/12, Decision on Annulment (1 September 2009) [233]; *Tulip Real Estate and Development Netherlands BV v Turkey*, ICSID Case No ARB/11/20, Decision on Annulment (30 December 2015) [85].

time for the preparation of its defence.[22] In addition, it is important to take into account the fact that it may be more difficult and lengthier for some parties to collect evidence and relevant documents than it is for other parties. In the context of ISA, although the state can be seen as the more powerful party, it may be more difficult and burdensome for it to collect the relevant documents from state entities or other official bodies due to complicated internal procedures. Such circumstances should be considered when allocating time and the same goes for the time allocated to the parties to present their case, which should not by default be strictly equal but must take into account the complexity of one's position.[23]

Therefore, equal treatment in ISA, and in adjudication in general, should not be assessed in terms of strict equality but rather in terms of equality of arms which requires 'to consider in detail the circumstances of the parties' respective positions, claims and evidence, and the arbitral process as a whole'.[24] As explained by the *Azurix* annulment committee, '[i]t is only where it can be shown that a tribunal has applied inconsistent standards in the way that it has treated the requests of the different parties that there can be said to be inequality of treatment'.[25] In other words, the principle of equal treatment mandates that neither party is favoured or disfavoured at any step of the arbitration process and that they have been granted the same procedural rights.

III. International Investment Law's Asymmetries and Their Impact on the Principle of Equality of Arms

One of the overall circumstances of a dispute that must be considered when assessing the equality of the parties in a given arbitration is the underlying inequalities or asymmetries in the parties' relationship.[26] Such asymmetries in the parties' underlying relationship are especially pronounced in the context of investment disputes. Although, as explained above, the principle of equality of arms is a fundamental concept of adjudication, it plays an especially important role in the ISA context due to the identity of the disputing parties: a private party (the investor) and a state. More generally, international investment law is characterized by many asymmetries and the equality of arms principle acts as a correcting and rebalancing tool when they lead to unfairness.

A first instance of asymmetry is the fact that investment treaties have traditionally only provided rights for investors and imposed obligations on states.[27] A second type of asymmetry consists, as observed by Thomas Wälde, of the fact that it is '[t]he treaty

[22] See Waincymer (n 19) 82; Bjorklund and Vanhonnaeker (n 19) 1023.

[23] See Derains and Schwartz (n 19) 229.

[24] Born (n 1) 2337.

[25] *Azurix Corp v Argentina*, ICSID Case No ARB/01/12, Decision on Annulment (1 September 2009) [233].

[26] Born (n 1) 2337 ('"equal treatment" must be assessed within the context of the parties' arbitration agreement, which may, like any contract, have elements of inequality').

[27] It is noteworthy, however, that a tendency to 'recalibrate' international investment treaties is in progress. See in this regard Lukas Vanhonnaeker, 'International Investment Agreements: Recalibration in Progress: Regulating Investor Behavior through International Investment Agreements' in Csongor István Nagy (ed), *Global Values and International Trade Law* (Routledge 2021) 229.

states, and not the private claimant, [that] are in the end the masters of the treaty and its procedures'.[28] This asymmetry, which is not found in a typical contractual relationship, has important consequences as it grants states important powers to, when acting jointly, agree on interpretative decisions of the treaty at issue.[29] When the interpretation of a treaty is at stake, this specific asymmetry can have important consequences with respect to the equality of the parties. In this regard, the dissenting arbitrator observed in *Industria Nacional de Alimentos, SA and Indalsa Perú, SA v Peru* that:

> Every case of the interpretation of a BIT by an ICSID Tribunal shares this unusual feature, namely that the Tribunal has to find the meaning of a bilateral instrument, one of the Parties to which (the Respondent) will be a party before the Tribunal, while the other Treaty Party by definition will not. Or, to put the matter the other way round, one of the parties to the arbitration before the Tribunal (but not the other) will have been a stranger to the treaty negotiation ... That circumstance surely imposes a particular duty of caution on the Tribunal: it can clearly not discount assertions put forward in argument by the Respondent as to the intentions behind the BIT and its negotiation (since that is authentic information which may be of importance), but it must at the same time treat them with all due caution, in the interests of its overriding duty to treat the parties to the arbitration on a basis of complete equality (since it is also possible that assertions by the Respondent may be incomplete, misleading or even self-serving).[30]

The asymmetries are most striking in the realm of ISA. First, one can argue that ISA, as a means of settling investment disputes provided under IIAs, is asymmetrical because it can only be triggered by investors.[31] This asymmetry may at first glance appear unfair vis-à-vis the state, particularly when compared to commercial arbitration which empowers both parties to a contract containing an arbitration clause to submit a claim.

[28] Thomas W Wälde, 'Procedural Challenges in Investment Arbitration under the Shadow of the Dual Role of the State: Asymmetries and Tribunals' Duty to Ensure, Pro-actively, the Equality of Arms' (2010) 26 (1) Arbitration International 3, 16.

[29] A significant example of such a power recognized to the states party to a treaty and of its far-reaching consequences consists of the Notes of Interpretation of Certain Chapter 11 Provisions of the North American Free Trade Agreement (NAFTA) Free Trade Commission of 31 July 2001. In these notes of interpretations, Canada, Mexico, and the United States agreed, through the NAFTA Free Trade Commission, on the interpretation of important provisions of the now defunct NAFTA (32 ILM 289 and 605 (1993)), such as its art 1105 on the minimum standard of treatment of investments of investors of another party. These notes of interpretation have been enforced by investment tribunals by application of NAFTA art 1131(2) which provides that '[a]n interpretation by the Commission of a provision of this Agreement shall be binding on a Tribunal established under this Section' (see also NAFTA art 1132).

[30] *Industria Nacional de Alimentos, SA and Indalsa Perú, SA v Peru*, ICSID Case No ARB/03/4, Annulment Proceedings, Dissenting Opinion of Franklin Berman (5 September 2007) [9].

[31] See Gus Van Harten, *Investment Treaty Arbitration and Public Law* (OUP 2008) 98; Ole Spiermann, 'Individual Rights, State Interests and the Power to Waive ICSID Jurisdiction under Bilateral Investment Treaties' (2004) 20 (2) Arbitration International 179. It is noteworthy, however, that this first case of asymmetry exists in the realm of treaty-based investment arbitration by contrast with contract-based investment arbitration in the context of which each party can bring a claim. In addition, in the realm of treaty-based investment arbitration this asymmetry can, to a certain extent, be alleviated by the possibility for states to bring counterclaims. See Andrea K Bjorklund, 'The Role of Counterclaims in Rebalancing Investment Law' (2013) 17(2) Lewis & Clark Law Review 461.

However, by contrast with typical commercial transactions, foreign direct investors are generally not on equal footing with their contractual partner. Rather, as a state, their contractual partner wears two hats: first, as a party to the contract and, second, as regulator.[32]

Taking account of this duality, ISA, and investment protections provided in IIAs more generally, can be understood as an answer to an underlying asymmetry. With respect to ISA more specifically, it can be seen, both 'in terms of objective and function[, as] a specific form of international judicial review of administrative conduct'.[33] As such, ISA constitutes a counterweight to the investor's exposure to the legal regime of the host state as well as to its judiciary which, in states with a weak rule of law, can be politically influenced or even controlled.[34]

Those imbalances that are inherent to international investment law and the dual role of states can have important implications with respect to the parties' equality of arms in ISA. Pierre Lalive explained in this regard that in the context of arbitral proceedings, as a consequence of its 'dual capacity':

> the State often finds it hard to adjust to the 'rules of the game': it sometimes expects or even requests, directly or indirectly, certain procedural privileges, including extension or disregard of time-limits, derogation of ordinary rules of evidence, etc.[35]

Such attempts to derogate from the 'rules of the game' may arise as a consequence of the important political nature of investment disputes. Indeed, in its capacity as government and regulator, it is in the state's interest to avoid at all costs a loss in the context of an investment arbitration. This is because ISA losses may resonate internally as a political failure and embarrassment.[36]

To avoid such failure and embarrassment, the respondent may rely on its inherent state powers to undermine the principle of equality of arms. For example, the state may exercise pressure on arbitral appointees by way of corruption and intimidation, abuse procedural rights as the better-funded party with the aim of exploiting the other party's financial weakness, intimidate a party's counsel, representatives or experts and witnesses, obstruct legal representation, unilaterally lift the confidentiality of the proceedings, or conceal documents.[37]

It is generally assumed that the respondent state is more inclined to engage in such tactics to increase its chances of victory, for example by invoking its own laws to tilt

[32] This unequal position of the investor, which is especially pronounced once the investment is underway in the host state, can lead to a hostage-like position. See Lukas Vanhonnaeker, 'Promoting Successful and Sustainable Foreign Direct Investment through Political Risk Mitigation Strategies—Turning "Obsolescing Bargains" into Mutually Beneficial Arrangements' (2015) 1 Chinese Journal of Global Governance 133.

[33] Thomas W Wälde, 'The Specific Nature of Investment Arbitration' in Thomas W Wälde and Philippe Kahn (eds), *New Aspects of International Investment Law* (Hague Academy of International Law/Nijhoff 2007) 60.

[34] Wälde (n 28) 15–18.

[35] Pierre Lalive, 'Some Threats to International Investment Arbitration' (1986) 1 (1) ICSID Review 26, 37.

[36] See Thomas W Wälde, 'Renegotiating Acquired Rights in the Oil and Gas Industries: Industry and Political Cycles Meet the Rule of Law` (2008) 1(1) Journal of World Energy Law & Business 55.

[37] Wälde (n 28) 21–34.

the balance in its favour. The reason for such an assumption lies in the fact that a respondent state 'controls the levers of government, public, formal, legal or secret; as a result, the state as a rule will not be disturbed by the existing institutions of justice (police, prosecution, courts) as they will be part of its litigation conduct or at least will be persuaded or compelled to tolerate or support it'.[38] However, even if as a consequence of these attributes the state may be the usual suspect when an issue of equality of arms arises in ISA, it does not mean that investors are not in a position to act in a manner that would affect the parties' equality of arms. The best example of this is when deep-pocketed and powerful corporations retain the most experienced counsel to initiate proceedings against less developed states with no experience in the field of investment law and arbitration. The analysis of the case law provided in the next section highlights the circumstances in which the question of the parties' equality of arms was raised in ISA, and demonstrates that states are not necessarily the only parties who may engage in bad faith tactics.

IV. Equality of Arms in ISA Case Law

Equality of arms concerns have been raised with respect to the conduct of both states and investors in ISA proceedings. In particular, they have been raised with respect to alleged threats and harassment by one of the parties. For example, in *Libananco* the claimant alleged acts of surveillance against it by the respondent,[39] while in *Gavrilovic* the claimant unsuccessfully argued acts of harassment on the part of the respondent.[40] Another instance in which tribunals had to assess the parties' equality of arms, such as in the *Methanex* and *UPS* cases, concerns the use of *amicus curiae* submissions as a procedural means to increase costs for the other party.[41] Finally, the question of the parties' equal treatment has arisen in relation to the appointment of the same arbitrator to two tribunals that were considering the same measure—the concern being that the parties' equality of arms would be degraded if the arbitrator used information gained from one arbitration in the other.[42]

In addition to these instances in which ISA tribunals assessed the parties' equal treatment in the context of arbitral proceedings, three distinct sets of issues raising equality of arms concerns can be identified: the parties' right to be heard, a party's refusal to produce documents, and the unlawful gathering of evidence by a party.

[38] ibid 21.

[39] *Libananco Holdings Co Limited v Turkey*, ICSID Case No ARB/06/8, Decision on Annulment (22 May 2013) [213].

[40] *Gavrilović and Gavrilović doo v Croatia*, ICSID Case No ARB/12/39, Decision on Claimants' Request for Provisional Measures (30 April 2015) [52]–[57] and [192]ff.

[41] *Methanex Corporation v United States of America*, UNCITRAL, Decision of the Tribunal on Petitions from Third Persons to Intervene as *amici curiae* (15 January 2001) [24]–[37] (esp [35]–[37]); *United Parcel Service of America Inc v Canada*, UNCITRAL, Decision of the Tribunal on Petitions for Intervention and Participation as *amici curiae* (17 October 2001) [69].

[42] *EnCana Corporation v Ecuador*, UNCITRAL, Partial Award on Jurisdiction (27 February 2004) [44]–[46]. The issue became moot after the arbitrator resigned from the tribunal (*EnCana Corporation v Ecuador*, UNCITRAL, Award (3 February 2006) [10]).

The parties' right to be heard is one of the most important areas in which equality of arms arguments have been presented by parties or assessments made by ISA tribunals. In this regard, many tribunals had the opportunity to highlight the inclusion of that right under the realm of the equal treatment of the parties. The *Wena Hotels* tribunal, for instance, emphasized the importance of the parties' right to be heard and the necessity of ensuring that right on an equal level.[43] This finding was confirmed by subsequent tribunals, such as in the *Tulip* case in which the majority of the annulment committee explained that:

> the lack of a fair hearing would be a serious breach of a fundamental rule of procedure under the ICSID Convention. The right to a fair hearing encompasses a number of matters. In the present case, the focus is on three particular aspects of a fair hearing, namely, the right to be heard, the principle of equality of arms and the duty to give reasons.[44]

In particular, the annulment committee had to consider whether the tribunal's lack of reference to the oral evidence of the parties could constitute a breach of the tribunal's duty to act fairly, to respect the right to be heard, and ensure the parties' equality of arms. The majority of the annulment committee found that no such breach had occurred, holding that the tribunal had merely 'exercise[ed] its judicial function of choosing which evidence it finds relevant and which it does not'.[45]

The question of the right to be heard in connection with the principle of equality of arms was also raised in *ConocoPhillips* in a vigorous dissenting opinion. A core issue raised by the dissenting arbitrator was the fact that the majority found in the *dispositif* of the decision that the respondent had breached its obligation to negotiate in good faith over compensation with the claimant despite the fact that this issue had not been raised in the arbitral proceedings. In particular, the dissenting arbitrator explained that:

> [n]o such claim of bad faith appears in any of the Claimants' submissions, from the Request of Arbitration to the post-hearings briefs. Nor was it raised or contended by any of their Counsel and witnesses in the oral hearings. Nor was it raised by way of question to the Parties from the bench. An utter decision by surprise.[46]

On that basis, in addition to arguing that this finding by the majority was *ultra petita* and *ultra vires*,[47] the dissenting arbitrator noted that from a procedural point of view:

[43] *Wena Hotels LTD v Egypt*, ICSID Case No ARB/98/4, Decision on Annulment (5 February 2002) [56]–[57].

[44] *Tulip Real Estate and Development Netherlands BV v Turkey*, ICSID Case No ARB/11/20, Decision on Annulment (30 December 2015)[145].

[45] ibid [149].

[46] *ConocoPhillips Petrozuata BV, ConocoPhillips Hamca BV, ConocoPhillips Gulf of Paria BV, and ConocoPhillips Company v Venezuela*, ICSID Case No ARB/07/30, Decision on Jurisdiction and the Merits, Dissenting Opinion of Georges Abi-Sab (19 February 2015) [282].

[47] ibid [283].

> [t]he Majority centered its decision on an issue that had not been raised or addressed by the Parties, and to which their attention was not drawn by the Tribunal to illicit their opinion. In particular, the Respondent, who was found responsible for a most serious internationally wrongful conduct on that basis, was not given the opportunity to present its position on the matter. By proceeding in this manner, the Majority committed a serious violation of the procedural rights of the Parties, particularly the Respondent, and of the fundamental principle of even handedness and equality of arms between the Parties; that which constitutes a serious departure from due process.[48]

A second important area in which the question of the parties' equality of arms has been raised in investment arbitration is that of the refusal to produce documents and evidence as well as the withholding of documents. This was the issue at stake in *Pope & Talbot* which involved the respondent state, Canada, refusing to produce certain documents in the course of the discovery process between the parties, arguing that they constituted cabinet confidences under the Canada Evidence Act s 39 and that their disclosure was thus prohibited.[49] The tribunal did not agree with Canada in this regard, finding that the Act and its terms did not apply to a North American Free Trade Agreement (NAFTA) Chapter 11 tribunal and despite not contesting the ruling, Canada nonetheless refused to produce or identify the documents at issue. Even if ultimately the refusal to produce the documents was not prejudicial to the investor, which allowed the tribunal to proceed with the arbitration, the latter deplored Canada's decision, observing that:

> Canada's position could well be a derogation from the 'overriding principle' found in Article 15 of the UNCITRAL Arbitration Rules, under which these proceedings have been conducted, that all Parties should be treated with equality. Moreover, Article 1115 of NAFTA declares that there shall be 'equal treatment among investors of the Parties'. As Canada's refusal to disclose or identify documents in these circumstances is at variance with the practice of other NAFTA Parties, at least of the United States, that refusal could well result in a denial of equality of treatment of investors and investments of the Parties bringing claims under Chapter 11.[50]

A similar issue was raised in *Biwater Gauff* that involved the respondent state, Tanzania, objecting to the request by the claimant to produce certain categories of documents on the basis of public interest immunity provided under Tanzanian law.[51] Adopting a

[48] ibid [284], [285].

[49] *Pope & Talbot Inc v Canada*, UNCITRAL, Award on the Merits of Phase 2 (10 April 2001) [4], [93]. See also *Pope & Talbot Inc v Canada*, UNCITRAL, Decision by the Tribunal on Canada's refusal to produce certain documents (6 September 2000).

[50] *Pope & Talbot Inc v Canada*, UNCITRAL, Award on the Merits of Phase 2 (10 April 2001) [193].

[51] *Biwater Gauff (Tanzania) Ltd v* Tanzania, ICSID Case No ARB/05/22, Procedural Order No 2 (24 May 2005) [8] (the argument of the respondent was based on Article 54(5) of the Tanzanian Constitution's prohibition of the disclosure of any information relating to any advice the President has received or may receive

similar approach to that of the *Pope & Talbot* tribunal, the *Biwater Gauff* tribunal explained that the nature of ISA is entirely different from a national court process[52] and that 'if a State were permitted to deploy its own national law in this way, it would, in effect, be avoiding its obligation to produce documents in so far as called upon to do so by this Tribunal'.[53] The tribunal further explained that acting in that way would permit a state to have recourse to its national laws to avoid its international responsibilities and added that it 'would create an imbalance between the parties, which the Tribunal considers unacceptable. It is indeed one of the most fundamental principles of international arbitration that the parties should be treated with equality.'[54]

The *Caratube* tribunal was also faced with an issue of access to documents and observed that:

> in view of the particular importance of procedural equality between the parties in an arbitration proceeding and that all parties can use and rely on the same evidence, the Tribunal notes with pleasure that, during the hearing, considerable progress and agreement could be reached in the discussion between the Parties and the Tribunal.[55]

Closely related to the question of access to documents, another set of issues which has been analysed by investment tribunals from the angle of the parties' equality of arms, is the question of evidence obtained unlawfully or through coercion. The *Methanex* case stands as a good example as it involved, inter alia, a question surrounding the obtention by the investor of series of documents (the 'Vind Documents') unlawfully 'by deliberately trespassing onto private property and rummaging through dumpsters inside the office-building for other persons' documentation'.[56] In this regard, the tribunal established a direct link between the way in which evidence is

from the Cabinet and section 132 of the Tanzanian Evidence Act 1967 applying to unpublished official records and communications received by a public officer whose disclosure would be prejudicial to the public interest).

[52] ibid.

[53] ibid.

[54] ibid [9]. The tribunal added, relying on *Pope & Talbot*, that 'the only ground which might justify a refusal by the Republic to produce documents to this Tribunal is the protection of privileged or politically sensitive information, including State secrets' [9]. See also *Gran Colombia Gold Corp v Colombia*, ICSID Case No ARB/18/23, Procedural Order No 11 (28 September 2021) [7] ('the Tribunal confirms that for purposes of both schedules, its production orders are understood to apply only to non-privileged material. To avoid subsequent disputes over the scope of applicable privilege, and to maintain equality of treatment as between the Parties').

[55] *Caratube International Oil Company LLP v Kazakhstan*, ICSID Case No ARB/08/12, Decision Regarding Claimant's Application for Provisional Measures (31 July 2009) [100]. In particular, the Respondent agreed that all documents taken by respondent should be preserved by respondent, that the respondent would give the claimant's representatives access to all documents they wish to access, that the claimant's representatives may copy these documents and take these copies out of Kazakhstan to London (ibid [101]). See also *Gavrilović and Gavrilović doo v Croatia*, ICSID Case No ARB/12/39, Decision on Claimants' Request for Provisional Measures (30 April 2015) [223]ff.

[56] *Methanex Corporation v United States of America*, UNCITRAL, Final Award of the Tribunal on Jurisdiction and Merits (3 August 2005) [55].

obtained in the context of ISA proceedings and the cornerstone principle of the parties' equality of arms:

> In the Tribunal's view, the Disputing Parties each owed in this arbitration a general legal duty to the other and to the Tribunal to conduct themselves in good faith during these arbitration proceedings and to respect the equality of arms between them, the principles of 'equal treatment' and procedural fairness being also required by Article 15(1) of the UNCITRAL Rules. As a general principle, therefore, just as it would be wrong for the USA ex hypothesi to misuse its intelligence assets to spy on Methanex (and its witnesses) and to introduce into evidence the resulting materials into this arbitration, so too would it be wrong for Methanex to introduce evidential materials obtained by Methanex unlawfully.[57]

In *Glencore*, the question of coercion with respect to the obtention of documents was at issue. In particular, series of documents which had been obtained by the respondent state in the context of an antitrust investigation were excluded from the arbitral proceedings in a procedural order. The tribunal observed in this regard that:

> the introduction of the Disputed Documents into the record constituted a violation of the international law principle that parties ought to arbitrate fairly, in good faith and with equality of arms; and that under Colombian Law, their introduction would seem to amount to a *desviación de poder*.[58]

The tribunal further observed with respect to coercing evidence and the principle of equality of arms that:

> the obligation to arbitrate fairly and in good faith and the principle of equality of arms precluded Respondent from coercing evidence from Claimants through its administrative powers, and to marshal it thereafter in an investment arbitration. The Tribunal made reference to the general imbalance between claimants, which are normally private companies, and respondent States and explained that if States were allowed to use their wide powers to coerce evidence from claimants, it would create a perverse incentive: States would initiate all types of administrative proceedings against potential claimants in order to improve their litigation positions.[59]

ISA case law addressing the parties' equality of arms with respect to different actions taken by them during arbitral proceedings demonstrates the fundamental importance of this principle. The foundational nature of the principle, coupled with its blurry contours, raises the question: how should tribunals address equality of arms concerns?

[57] ibid [54].
[58] *Glencore International AG and CI Prodeco SA v Colombia*, ICSID Case No ARB/16/6, Award (27 August 2019) [647] (footnotes omitted).
[59] ibid [89].

V. Existing Mechanisms to Ensure the Respect of Equality of Arms

The key importance of the parties' equality of arms in ISA has been repeatedly affirmed by ISA tribunals having to address equal treatment concerns. The foundational nature of the principle requires that arbitrators undertake a proactive role to restore the equality of arms if faced with any behaviour or action from one of the parties which would run against it. Undertaking such a role is, however, no easy task as it entails being cognizant of the needs of the parties and of the hurdles they may face. This includes the fact that a state's or state entity's internal organization may make it more cumbersome to collect evidence and gain access to documents. This difficult exercise was captured by Lalive in the following terms: 'One of the arbitrator's delicate tasks is to reconcile here a need for some flexibility (justified by some of the considerations mentioned above about the particular mechanism of State administration or State-controlled entities) with the fundamental equality of the parties and elementary requirements of justice.'[60]

The key to the intervention of arbitrators to guarantee the parties' equality of arms lies in the concept of arbitrators' inherent powers which finds its roots 'in the common [practice] for judges to identify inherent powers flowing from the essential nature of the judicial office'.[61] In this regard, Waincymer observed that:

> Regardless of the procedure and the law chosen, it is undisputed that the arbitration tribunal shall guarantee a number of principles that constitute the procedural 'magna carta of arbitration'. What are these fundamental standards of international commercial arbitration and where are they to be found? In fact they are the constitutional cornerstones of arbitration proceedings—due process, fairness and the application of the appropriate law or other standard to the substance of the dispute.[62]

Given the fact that the parties' equality of arms must be considered as a principle that is part of the magna carta of adjudication, inherent powers, understood here as the powers to 'conserve the respective rights of the Parties and to ensure that [the] Tribunal's jurisdiction and authority are made fully effective',[63] should be mobilized to ensure its respect. The *Libananco* tribunal stated in this regard: 'the tribunal [does not] doubt for a moment that like any other international tribunal, it must be regarded as endowed with the inherent powers required to preserve the integrity of its own process'.[64]

[60] Lalive (n 35) 37 (footnote omitted).

[61] Waincymer (n 19) 72; Andrea K Bjorklund and Jonathan Brosseau, 'Sources of Inherent Powers in International Adjudication' (2018) 6(2) European International Arbitration Review 1, 18–28.

[62] Waincymer (n 19) 124; Julian DM Lew, Loukas A Mistelis, and Stefan M Kröll, *Comparative International Commercial Arbitration* (Kluwer Law International 2003) 95, 5–68.

[63] *E-Systems, Inc v Iran, Bank Melli Iran*, IUSCT Case No 388 [33].

[64] *Libananco Holdings Co Limited v Turkey*, ICSID Case No ARB/06/8, Decision on Preliminary Issues (23 June 2008) [78].

Yet again, in light of the uncertain content of the notion of 'inherent powers' and the fact specific assessment of whether parties to an arbitration have equal arms, tribunals must exercise careful discretion in relying on their inherent powers. This will especially be the case when the arbitrators' duty to ensure the respect of the parties' right to equal treatment conflicts with another duty, such as conducting arbitral proceedings with expediency. Such conflicting principles may force arbitrators to impose a limit on the number of submissions that the parties are allowed to fill or on the time allocated for hearings, which can impact the parties' right to adequately present their case, although not to the same extent.[65]

VI. Conclusion

Guaranteeing the parties' equality of arms is critical in investment arbitration to ensure fairness. From a more pragmatic viewpoint, ensuring the parties' equality of arms is also important to avoid rendering the arbitration award vulnerable to annulment under Article 52 of the ICSID Convention, or to a refusal to be recognized and enforced under the New York Convention. Although the equal treatment principle is a hallmark of any type of adjudication, the importance of protecting it is more pronounced in ISA. This is due to the inherent asymmetries of international investment law and arbitration, and the potential impact of these asymmetries on the parties' equality of arms. Even though both foreign investors and states can attempt to erode this principle, the state, because of its power as a sovereign entity, is often considered the most likely party to impede the fairness of arbitral proceedings. In the ISA context, states have done so, for example, by relying on their internal laws to interfere with the access to relevant documents and evidence. Considering the importance of the principle of the parties' equality of arms and of the more pronounced vulnerability of that principle in the context of ISA, it is key that arbitrators take it upon themselves, by virtue of their inherent powers, to guarantee the parties' equality of arms.

[65] Bjorklund and Vanhonnaeker (n 19) 1041–42.

PART III

THE CONTENT OF INVESTMENT AWARDS

11

The Relevance of the Facts in Complex Investor-State Arbitration Proceedings

Reflections on the Drafting of Arbitral Awards

Crina Baltag

I. Introduction

This chapter analyses the manner in which facts are approached by arbitral tribunals in the drafting of their awards in the context of investor-state arbitrations. The literature on the topic is scarce, with some publications addressing it either from an interstate dispute settlement perspective, concluding that adjudicators favour a decision on legal grounds and undisputed facts,[1] or from a cultural perspective.[2] Investor-state disputes are complex disputes, which involve heavy factual backgrounds over a span of several years, multiple *dramatis personae*, and various jurisdictions. Two are the main matters highlighted in this context: first, while the record of the case is assembled by the parties, the arbitral tribunal is bound by the rules of evidence, as well as by the rules establishing the manner in which the arbitral tribunal discharges its obligation to state the reasons of its decision and to address the facts of the case; and, second, that the failure of the arbitral tribunal to engage sufficiently in addressing the underlying facts in the final arbitral award may result in the annulment of the award. The present chapter is not a study of the written advocacy skills of arbitrators, nor an anthropological or a sociological study,[3] but it proposes to be a starting point for more in-depth research on the relevance of the facts of the dispute in arbitral tribunals' decisions.

II. Facts *v* Law?

The first step in this analysis is to determine what is understood by 'facts' in investment arbitration. Distinguishing between facts and legal questions is not always a

[1] John Crook, 'Fact-Finding in the Fog: Determining the Facts of Upheavals and Wars in Inter-State Disputes' in Catherine Rogers and Roger Alford (eds), *The Future of Investment Arbitration* (OUP 2009) 313–37, 325.

[2] See also Nigel Blackaby and Maria Julia Milesi, 'Investment Tribunals' Search for the Truth and Its Impact on the Arbitral Award' in Katia Fach Gómez and Catharine Titi (eds), *The Award in Investment Arbitration* (OUP 2024).

[3] See on the broader intersections between arbitration with these disciplines, Emmanuel Gaillard, 'Sociology of international arbitration' (2005) 31 Arbitration International 1.

Crina Baltag, *The Relevance of the Facts in Complex Investor-State Arbitration Proceedings* In: *The Award in International Investment Arbitration*. Edited by: Katia Fach Gómez and Catharine Titi, Oxford University Press.
DOI: 10.1093/9780191975936.003.0011

straightforward exercise. Alexander Orakhelashvili explains that '[f]act is normally understood as something that actually exists, which is much broader than what can be subsumed by the rules and standards accepted as law'.[4] However, as the author observes, the diversity of what is encompassed by the notion of 'facts', including the adoption and implementation of a legal instrument, suggests that it is difficult to adopt a clear-cut differentiation between fact and law.[5]

However, the distinction between 'facts' and 'legal questions' becomes necessary and relevant where, for example, the jurisdiction of adjudicatory bodies is triggered by the existence of particular facts. For example, Article 17(6) of Annex 2 to the World Trade Organization (WTO) Agreement confines the jurisdiction of the WTO Appellate Body to appeals on 'issues of law covered in the panel report and legal interpretations developed by the panel'. Findings of fact by a panel are 'in principle, not subject to review by Appellate Body'.[6]

It is rightly affirmed that while facts commonly do not lead, by themselves, 'to the creation, modification or abrogation of legal rules and rights ... they cannot prevail over established legal rules and titles'.[7] Nonetheless, factual elements are, undoubtedly, included in the rationale of a legal rule, determining the scope of their application.[8] One illustrative example is the rule establishing the jurisdiction *ratione personae* under a relevant international investment agreement (IIA). For this purpose, one can consider the requirements of Article 17 of the Energy Charter Treaty (ECT) referring to the denial of the benefits of the Treaty to a legal entity if citizens or nationals of a third state own or control such entity and if that entity has no substantial business activities in the area of the contracting party in which it is organized.[9] While the ECT does not contain a definition of 'substantial business activities', it is undeniable that this is essentially a factual requirement.[10] With reference to this, the tribunal in *Masdar v Spain* concluded that 'the unchallenged evidence adduced by Claimant, notably as to its standing as a holding company with substantial international assets under its control ... and the similarly unchallenged evidence of Mr. Al Ramahi, is persuasive of the true extent and

[4] Alexander Orakhelashvili, *The Interpretation of Acts and Rules in Public International Law* (OUP 2008) 108.

[5] ibid.

[6] *European Communities—Measures Concerning Meat and Meat Products (Hormones)*, (*United States v European Communities*), WT/DS26/AB/R, Report of the Appellate Body, AB-1997-4 (16 February 1998) [132]: under Article 17(6) of the DSU, appellate review is limited to appeals on questions of law covered in a panel report and legal interpretations developed by the panel. Findings of fact, as distinguished from legal interpretations or legal conclusions, by a panel are, in principle, not subject to review by the Appellate Body. The determination of whether or not a certain event did occur in time and space is typically a question of fact; for example, the question of whether or not Codex has adopted an international standard, guideline, or recommendation on MGA is a factual question. See also, Orakhelashvili (n 4) 108–09.

[7] Orakhelashvili (n 4) 129. But see customary international law, which relies on 'a usual or habitual course of action, a long-established practice', Hans Kelsen, *Principles of International Law* (Lawbook Exchange reprinted 2012) 307; it is deduced from the 'practice and behaviour of states', Malcolm N Shaw, *International Law* (8th edn, CUP 2017) 54.

[8] See Orakhelashvili (n 4) 148.

[9] eg see Turkey–Uzbekistan BIT art 1(2)(b): 'a legal entity constituted or established under the laws and regulations of the State of Contracting Party having its seat together with substantial business activity in the territory of the State of that Contracting Party'.

[10] See Crina Baltag, 'Denying the Benefits of the Energy Charter Treaty: Shifting the Policy or Just the Burden of Proof?' *Columbia FDI Perspectives*, no 331 (16 May 2022).

materiality of the business conducted by Claimant in The Netherlands'.[11] On a similar requirement of 'substantial business activity', but from the perspective of the definition of the notion of 'investor', the 2019 Dutch Model BIT, provides in Article 1(c) that:

> Indications of having 'substantive business activities' in a Contracting Party may include: (i) the undertaking's registered office and/or administration is established in that Contracting Party; (ii) the undertaking's headquarters and/or management is established in that Contracting Party; (iii) the number of employees and their qualifications based in that Contracting Party; (iv) the turnover generated in that Contracting Party; and (v) an office, production facility and/or research laboratory is established in that Contracting Party.[12]

Such indicative elements identified in the Dutch Model BIT are, unquestionably factual elements which serve to establish the application of the legal rule concerning the coverage of investors who are legal entities by the BIT.

Other examples of legal rules essentially being determined by facts are the substantive standards enshrined in IIAs. Article 2(2) of the Hungary–Iran BIT explains the fair and equitable treatment (FET), and full protection and security (FPS) standards as follows: 'Each Contracting Party shall accord at all times in its territory to investments made by investors of the other Contracting Party and to investors with respect to their investments fair and equitable treatment and full protection and security in accordance with paragraphs 3–6.'[13] Article 2(3) of Hungary–Iran BIT then specifies that a breach of the FET may be found where a measure or series of measures constitutes:

> (a) denial of justice in criminal, civil or administrative proceedings; (b) fundamental breach of due process, including a fundamental breach of transparency and obstacles to effective access to justice, in judicial and administrative proceedings; (c) manifest arbitrariness; (d) targeted discrimination on manifestly wrongful grounds, such as gender, race or religious belief; or (e) harassment, coercion, abuse of power or similar bad faith conduct.

As to the FPS, Article 2(4) of Hungary–Iran BIT explains that this 'refers to the Contracting Party's obligations relating to physical security of investors and investments'. Such elements in the definition of FET and FPS require a factual determination in the context of the specific dispute.

The other standards usually incorporated in IIAs—protection against unlawful expropriation, compensation for losses, national treatment (NT), most favoured nation

[11] *Masdar Solar & Wind Cooperatief UA v Spain*, ICSID Case No ARB/14/1, Award (16 May 2018) [254].

[12] Article 1(c) of the 2019 Dutch Model BIT complements art 1(b)(ii) which provides: '"investor" means with regard to either Contracting Party ... any legal person constituted under the law of that Contracting Party and having substantial business activities in the territory of that Contracting Party'.

[13] The Hungary–Iran BIT is a recent treaty, having entered into force on 23 March 2022.

(MFN) treatment, etc—also entail a factual determination in upholding their application to that dispute. NT and MFN, being relative standards of treatment, in the sense that they require a comparator: either a national investor or an investor of a third state, respectively, inherently appeal to facts in establishing their application. Such assessment may be emphasized in the drafting of the provision itself: '[e]ach Contracting Party shall in its territory accord to investors of the other Contracting Party and their investments and returns of investments treatment which is no less favourable than that which it accords, *in like situations*, to its own investors or their investments.'[14] The 'like situations' are understood as fundamentally factual circumstances. In this respect, the tribunal in *SD Myers v Canada* stated:

> The concept of 'like circumstances' invites an examination of whether a non-national investor complaining of less favourable treatment is in the same 'sector' as the national investor. ... From the business perspective, it is clear that SDMI and Myers Canada were in 'like circumstances' with Canadian operators such as Chem-Security and Cintec. They all were engaged in providing PCB [polychlorinated biphenyl] waste remediation services.[15]

From the above, one can conclude that, indeed, 'facts' and 'legal questions' may be separate issues, but most often they appear intertwined. International adjudication, including investment law and arbitration, are a good example of legal rules being essentially triggered by factual circumstances. Jurisdictional and merits questions, including the legal standing of the parties in the dispute, the existence of a breach of the FET clause, etc, must be addressed by the parties and by the arbitral tribunal in its decisions on essentially factual elements.

III. Facts and the Drafting of Arbitral Awards: More than Written Advocacy Skills

As shown above, establishing the facts is a necessary element in the application of the legal rules. The fine line between facts and legal questions, as well as the discretion of the arbitral tribunal in appreciating the relevance of the evidence determining the facts submitted before it, as it will be addressed in this chapter, add to the complexity of these arbitrations.[16] Investment awards are usually very long.[17] Although rarely, arbitral

[14] ibid art 3(1) (emphasis added).

[15] *SD Myers v Canada*, ad hoc arbitration, Partial Award (13 November 2000) [250]–[251].See also, International Law Commission, 'Most-Favoured-Nation Clause. Final Report of the Study Group on the Most-Favoured-Nation clause' (2015) II Yearbook of the International Law Commission, pt 2.

[16] The chapter mainly addresses arbitrations cases before the International Centre for Settlement of Investment Disputes (ICSID), although references may be made to non-ICSID arbitral awards or post-award proceedings.

[17] See *Muhammet Çap and Sehil Insaat Endustri ve Ticaret Ltd Sti v Turkmenistan*, ICSID Case No ARB/12/6, Award (4 May 2021).

awards may appropriately reflect the factual complexity of a case in a concise award, as the sole arbitrator did in *Pantechniki v Albania*, in only twenty-seven pages.[18]

Leaving aside the written advocacy skills of the arbitrators, there is no doubt that arbitral tribunals draft their awards for the purpose of adjudicating the dispute between the parties, ensuring that the issues raised by the parties are addressed, and the award provides a logical, substantiated reasoning which would be uncontested by the parties in subsequent post-award remedies. However, quite often it is stated that in these arbitrations, tribunals also draft their awards in consideration of the transparency of the proceedings and their outcomes. Guillermo Alvarez and Michael Reisman eloquently capture this aspect of investment arbitral awards:

> international investment awards may have a major political impact on an entire country. ... Thus, the reasons requirement, as a control mechanism in other sectors of arbitration, acquires a greater importance in international investment arbitration. Indeed, these considerations should lead to the drafting of awards that are accessible to reasonably intelligent people and are not so recondite that none but a small group of specialists can comprehend them.[19]

This is a compelling reason for arbitral tribunals to reflect the relevant facts in the reasoning of the arbitral awards, as the objective element triggering the application of the legal rules.

While approaching the complexity of the facts in itself raises interesting issues, this is even more challenging in the context of arbitral awards rendered in disputes arising out of similar facts. While most of the arbitral rules and laws refer to the requirement that arbitral awards contain the reasons upon which the award is based, as well as a statement of the facts 'as found by the tribunal', the actual drafting approach of each tribunal may differ. This is also the consequence of the absence of *stare decisis*—doctrine of precedent—in investment arbitration. For example, there are over fifty investment arbitrations against Argentina which rest on similar facts,[20] going back to a 1989 plan for economic recovery, which included the privatization of government-owned industries and public utilities and also the legislative framework pegging the Argentinean peso to the US dollar. Furthermore, in 1998, the economic situation in Argentina started to deteriorate and this culminated in 2000 with the continued appreciation of the US dollar, which triggered the limitations imposed on the transfer of currency abroad and the abolition of the peg of the peso to the US dollar.[21]

[18] *Pantechniki SA Contractors and Engineers v Albania*, ICSID Case No ARB/07/21, Award (30 July 2009); *Emilio Agustín Maffezini v Spain*, ICSID Case No ARB/97/7, Award (13 November 2000).

[19] Guillermo Alvarez and W Michael Reisman, 'How Well Are Investment Awards Reasoned?' in Guillermo Alvarez and W Michael Reisman (eds), *The Reasons Requirement in International Investment Arbitration* (Brill 2008) 2.

[20] See Lucy Reed, 'Scorecard of Investment Treaty Cases Against Argentina Since 2001' (*Kluwer Arbitration Blog*, 2 March 2009) <http://arbitrationblog.kluwerarbitration.com/2009/03/02/scorecard-of-investment-treaty-cases-against-argentina-since-2001/>. See also United Nations Conference on Trade and Development (UNCTAD), Investment Dispute Settlement Navigator <https://investmentpolicy.unctad.org/investment-dispute-settlement> (accessed 29 October 2022).

[21] See in detail, Gebhard Bücheler, *Proportionality in Investor-State Arbitration* (OUP 2015) 21–22.

In *CMS v Argentina*, the arbitral tribunal rendered a decision on jurisdiction, which was followed by an arbitral award, which was ultimately annulled by an ad hoc committee annulling the tribunal's decision on the umbrella clause for failure to state reasons.[22] For the purpose of the decision on jurisdiction, the reference to the underlying facts of the dispute was rather limited, with few paragraphs dedicated to clarifying the context in which the dispute emerged.[23] The factual background is substantially developed in the arbitral award, with the tribunal detailing the context of the privatization plan commenced by Argentina in 1989, as well as Argentina's measures in the period 1999–2002.[24] In addition to the general statement on the facts generating the dispute, the award engages with the relevant factual circumstances when addressing the issues raised by the parties, including whether the claimant had a right to a tariff calculated in US dollars,[25] whether the claimant had a right to the adjustment of tariffs,[26] and to the stabilization mechanism under the license,[27] whether the economic balance of the license was altered in the light of the changing realities,[28] in addition to the breaches of the expropriation, FET, FPS, and umbrella clauses in the Argentina–US BIT. The ad hoc committee found that the tribunal failed to state the reasons in its finding that Argentina has breached the umbrella clause obligation under the Argentina–US BIT. The ad hoc committee explained that 'it is quite unclear how the Tribunal arrived at its conclusion that CMS could enforce the obligations of Argentina to TGN [Transportadora de Gas del Norte]. ... In these circumstances there is a significant lacuna in the Award, which makes it impossible for the reader to follow the reasoning on this point.'[29] On the other hand, the ad hoc committee praised the arbitral tribunal for one of the 'most detailed decisions on damages in ICSID case-law'.[30] The ad hoc committee explained that '[u]nder the title "Remedies", the Tribunal considered the matter in 25 pages' and 'declared itself "persuaded that the cumulative nature of the breaches discussed here is best dealt with by resorting to the standard of [compensation known as the] fair market value"'.[31]

In *El Paso v Argentina*, on similar facts, the arbitral tribunal in its decision on jurisdiction chose to refer to the decision on jurisdiction in *Natural Gas v Argentina*, in relation to the background of the dispute: 'The global economic and financial situation forming the background of the present case has been aptly described by the ICSID Tribunal in *Natural Gas SDG, SA v Argentina*, Decision on Preliminary Questions on Jurisdiction of 17 June 2005.'[32] In contrast with the approach in the decision on

[22] *CMS Gas Transmission Company v Argentina*, ICSID Case No ARB/01/8, Decision on Jurisdiction (17 July 2003); Award (12 May 2005); and Decision on Annulment (25 September 2007).
[23] *CMS Gas Transmission Company v Argentina*, ICSID Case No ARB/01/8, Decision on Jurisdiction, 17 July 2003; Award (12 May 2005) [18]–[21].
[24] *CMS Gas Transmission Company v Argentina*, ICSID Case No ARB/01/8, Award (12 May 2005) [53]–[67].
[25] ibid [127]–[138].
[26] ibid [139]–[144].
[27] ibid [145]–[151].
[28] ibid [152]–[166].
[29] *CMS Gas Transmission Company v Argentina*, ICSID Case No ARB/01/8, Decision on Annulment (25 September 2007) [96]–[97].
[30] ibid [154].
[31] ibid.
[32] *El Paso v Argentina*, ICSID Case No ARB/03/15, Decision on Jurisdiction (27 April 2006) [10].

jurisdiction, the award in *El Paso v Argentina*, takes an expansive approach to the facts of the case, highlighting at the outset that '[t]he facts summarised hereafter are those considered and debated in the Parties' written pleadings and oral arguments'.[33] The tribunal addressed the history and general context of the disputes,[34] the electricity regulatory framework,[35] the hydrocarbon regulatory framework,[36] Argentina's drive to attract foreign investment,[37] and the economic crisis and the measures taken by Argentina in the energy sector.[38] The award was subject to annulment proceedings, with Argentina arguing, among others, that the tribunal failed to state the reasons for its decision.[39] Unlike the ad hoc committee in *CMS v Argentina*, the committee in *El Paso v Argentina* dismissed the application for annulment and explained that 'the Tribunal did express reasons for its decision in a very detailed way'.[40] The two examples of cases show that tribunals have approached the facts of the dispute in a similar manner, although the *El Paso* tribunal took a slightly more detailed approach to the relevant facts. Furthermore, and as will be further addressed in this chapter, the reasoning of the tribunals, which include the facts and legal rules, are a requirement of the arbitral award which can be reviewed at the annulment stage.

Similar to the Argentinean cases, the renewable energy investment arbitrations against Spain, now over fifty,[41] rely on comparable, if not identical, sets of facts and have been brought before arbitral tribunals under the ECT. In 2007, Spain decided to implement a set of measures meant to incentivize investments in renewable energy, in particular, in solar renewable energy investments. Soon afterwards, in 2013, Spain amended the original framework, ending up abolishing the fixed feed-in tariffs.[42] In *Next Era v Spain*, the arbitral tribunal extensively addressed the factual framework in its 'Decision on Jurisdiction, Liability and Quantum Principles',[43] with the award only narrowly referring to relevant factual circumstances, while being limited to the issue of damages and costs.[44] In the annulment proceeding, Spain relied, among others, on the ground in Article 52(1)(e) of the ICSID Convention that the arbitral tribunal failed to state the reasons on which the award was based.[45] While the ad hoc committee rejected

[33] *El Paso v Argentina*, ICSID Case No ARB/03/15, Award (31 October 2011) [48].
[34] ibid [51]–[58].
[35] ibid [59]–[73].
[36] ibid [74]–[80].
[37] ibid [81–[88].
[38] ibid [89]–[120].
[39] *El Paso v Argentina*, ICSID Case No ARB/03/15, Decision on Annulment (22 September 2014).
[40] ibid [235].
[41] See also UNCTAD, Investment Dispute Settlement Navigator <https://investmentpolicy.unctad.org/investment-dispute-settlement> (accessed 29 October 2022).
[42] See more on the ECT renewables arbitrations in Crina Baltag and Stefan Dudas, '*Achmea*, Arbitral Tribunals and the ECT: Modernisation or Regression?' in Crina Baltag and Ana Stanic (eds), *The Future of Investment Treaty Arbitration in the EU: Intra-EU BITs, the Energy Charter Treaty, and the Multilateral Investment Court* (Kluwer Law International 2020) 23–42.
[43] *NextEra Energy Global Holdings BV and NextEra Energy Spain Holdings BV v Spain*, ICSID Case No ARB/14/11, Decision on Jurisdiction, Liability and Quantum Principles (12 March 2019) [93]–[179]. The tribunal explained that the facts presented represent an overview and relevant facts are also addressed by the tribunal when proceeding to the legal analysis of the claims at issue, see [92].
[44] *NextEra Energy Global Holdings BV and NextEra Energy Spain Holdings BV v Spain*, ICSID Case No ARB/14/11, Award (31 May 2019).
[45] *NextEra Energy Global Holdings BV and NextEra Energy Spain Holdings BV v Spain*, ICSID Case No ARB/14/11, Decision on Annulment (18 March 2022).

Spain's submissions in their entirety, it highlighted that the mandate of the committee under Article 52(1)(e) 'does not include a reassessment of the Tribunal's analysis of the evidence and the weight and significance it placed on the evidence', and, in particular, it:

> does not include how the Tribunal determined (1) whether the statements that the Spanish authorities made amounted to guarantees of security; (2) whether the Claimants conducted due diligence; (3) how other tribunals treated the regulatory changes; (4) how to treat the jurisprudence of the Spanish Supreme Court; and (5) whether the assurances were made to a legal entity different from the Claimants.[46]

The committee concluded that 'Spain's claims are more a dissatisfaction with the adequacy, correctness, and quality of the reasons, which, however fair the criticisms might be, would not form the basis for the "*lack of reasons*" ground.'[47] In another Spanish solar energy case under the ECT, *SolEs v Spain*, the tribunal aptly summarized the case theory in one brief paragraph,[48] continuing afterwards with the detailed description of the facts of the case.[49] In the annulment proceeding, Spain challenged the arbitral award also on the ground that the award failed to state reasons, an argument which was rejected in its entirety by the ad hoc committee. In doing so, the committee explained that the tribunal engaged in a detailed account of the case and extensive reasoning. As in the Argentinean cases, there is little difference in the manner in which these two tribunals have relied on the facts of the dispute, with both arbitral tribunals engaging in a detailed account of the relevant facts.

The brief overview of the Argentinean and Spanish investment arbitrations shows that arbitral tribunals address the relevant facts of the case as part of the reasoning of their arbitral awards. This will further be discussed below in the context of the annulment of awards. However, for the purpose of this analysis, it is important to highlight that the record of the case is assembled through the submissions of the parties.[50] Hence, the parties play an important—if not decisive—role in setting the framework within which the resolution of the dispute takes place, and such framework is equally represented by the factual and legal submissions.[51] Furthermore, it is uncontested that culture plays an important part in how facts are considered by an arbitral tribunal. Won Kidane explains that parties themselves may present the facts in a manner in which they would resonate with the members of the arbitral tribunal, 'to help the chances of success for their respective side'.[52]

46 ibid [349].
47 ibid [351] (emphasis in original).
48 *SolEs Badajoz GmbH v Spain*, ICSID Case No ARB/15/38, Award (31 July 2019) [95]: 'This case arises out of Claimant's investments in Spain in PV plants, which use one of several technologies that produce renewable energy.'
49 ibid [96]–[141].
50 Frédéric G Sourgens, Ian A Laird, and Kabir Duggal, *Evidence in International Investment Arbitration* (OUP 2018) 14 ('[n]either the parties, nor the tribunal have a monopoly on the assembly of the record. Rather, party submissions and tribunal decisions have an important role to play').
51 ibid.
52 Won L Kidane, *The Culture of International Arbitration* (OUP 2017) 217.

Nonetheless, beyond the subjectivity of the factual record and the assessment of the arbitral tribunal, there is also an objective element. While arbitral awards in cases arising from similar facts may differ in the way each arbitral tribunal reflects such facts in the arbitral awards, the law ensures that objective significance of the facts of the case is observed.

IV. Facts and Evidence: Discretion of the Arbitral Tribunal in Determining the Relevant Facts

The two preceding sections have immediately emphasized the relevance of facts in the decision of an arbitral tribunal. The complexity of investment disputes and the not always clear distinction between facts and legal questions should be analysed in the context of the applicable legal framework. As mentioned, different arbitration rules, as well as the ICSID Convention, oblige the arbitral tribunal to state the reasons on which the award rests, including a statement of the 'relevant facts'. It is therefore appropriate to analyse the discretion of the arbitral tribunal, in light of the rules of evidence, in determining the relevance of the facts in a particular arbitration. This also emphasizes the inherent limitations and peculiarities of establishing the facts in investment disputes, which may lead to a challenge of the arbitral award, as will be further discussed in this chapter.

Arbitral tribunals do have wide discretion in addressing evidence in international arbitration. Article 9, 'Admissibility and Assessment of Evidence', of the 2020 International Bar Association (IBA) Rules on the Taking of Evidence in International Arbitration, confirms this position: 'The Arbitral Tribunal shall determine the admissibility, relevance, materiality and weight of evidence.'[53]

In the context of ICSID arbitration proceedings, Rule 36 of the 2022 ICSID Arbitration Rules provides similar broad discretion to arbitral tribunals in accessing evidence: 'The Tribunal shall determine the admissibility and probative value of the evidence adduced.' Furthermore, Rule 36 also provides that the burden of proof lies on the party relying on the facts in support of its claim or defence, as well as that the tribunal may call upon a party to produce documents or other evidence it deems necessary.[54] The UNCITRAL Arbitration Rules contain provisions similar to those found in the ICSID Arbitration Rules.[55] Article 27 of the UNCITRAL Arbitration Rules

[53] Although soft law, the IBA Rules are often retained even by judiciaries as guiding principles in addressing issues of the relation between courts and arbitration, therefore they are to be highly considered. See Swedish Supreme Court of 10 May 2012, *Euroflon Tekniska Produkter AB v Flexiboys i Motala AB*, Case No Ö1590–11.

[54] ICSID Arbitration Rules Rule 36(2)–(3). See also ICSID Convention art 43:

> Except as the parties otherwise agree, the Tribunal may, if it deems it necessary at any stage of the proceedings,
> (a) call upon the parties to produce documents or other evidence, and
> (b) visit the scene connected with the dispute, and conduct such inquiries there as it may deem appropriate.

[55] As amended in 2013 and 2021.

provides, among others, that each party shall have the burden of proving the facts relied on, and the arbitral tribunal shall have the discretion to determine the admissibility, relevance, materiality, and weight of the evidence submitted.[56]

The discretion of the arbitral tribunal to appreciate the relevance of the facts presented by the parties is uncontested in arbitral practice. In *Rompetrol v Romania*, the tribunal concluded that it has extensive discretion in deciding which facts are relevant for the particular case and even on drawing adverse inferences appropriate from the failure of a party to produce evidence which was expected to produce:

> A tribunal should possess a large measure of discretion over how the relevant facts are to be found and to be proved—a general principle which finds strong reinforcement in the Arbitration Rules, notably in paragraphs (1) and (3) of [ICSID Arbitration] Rule 34. The overall effect of these provisions is that an ICSID tribunal is endowed with the independent power to determine, within the context provided by the circumstances of the dispute before it, whether particular evidence or kinds of evidence should be admitted or excluded, what weight (if any) should be given to particular items of evidence so admitted, whether it would like to see further evidence of any particular kind on any issue arising in the case, and so on and so forth.[57]

Reflecting such discretion, the arbitral tribunal in *ADC v Hungary* dedicated considerable space in addressing the credibility of factual witnesses. The tribunal held that the witnesses, Huang, Tahy and Onozó, 'gave their evidence in such a way as to give the Tribunal confidence that they could be relied upon. They all had intimate knowledge [of] this matter.'[58] As such, the power of arbitral tribunals in appreciating the evidence submitted to them is uncontested. However, arbitral tribunals should be mindful of the fact that a fine line exists between the discretion of the tribunal in assessing the relevance and weight of the evidence produced and the failure to apply the rules of evidence.[59] ICSID ad hoc committees showed a flexible approach to this: in *CDC v Seychelles*, the ad hoc committee explained that 'a trier of fact may ... find a party's evidence not to be credible' and that this does not amount to a failure to observe the rules of evidence.[60]

Arbitral tribunals are often presented with an inequity in the possibility of submitting the relevant evidence by the parties, and in particular by the claimant investor, because the premises of the claimant's business in the respondent state have been seized or because the claimant and/or its employees were forced to leave the respondent state. Such arguments may be raised in the arbitration proceedings or at the annulment

[56] See also SCC Arbitration Rules art 31(1) ('The admissibility, relevance, materiality and weight of evidence shall be for the Arbitral Tribunal to determine').

[57] *Rompetrol Group NV v Romania*, ICSID Case No ARB/06/3, Award (6 May 2013) [181].

[58] *ADC Affiliate Limited and ADC & ADMC Management Limited v Hungary*, ICSID Case No ARB/03/16, Award (2 October 2006) [250].

[59] See Stephan Schill (ed), *Schreuer's Commentary on the ICSID Convention* (3rd edn, CUP 2022) 1330, para 405.

[60] *CDC Group plc v Seychelles*, ICSID Case No ARB/02/14, Decision on Annulment (29 June 2005) [60].

stage. For example, in *Amco v Indonesia*, Amco argued that it could not submit the evidence, as it was expelled from its business premises. Deciding on the dispute before it in the absence of such evidence would amount to a 'serious departure from a fundamental rule of procedure' and constitute a ground for the annulment of the arbitral award under Article 52(1)(d) of the ICSID Convention.[61] The ad hoc committee in *Amco v Indonesia* rejected this particular contention, noting that the tribunal 'was aware of all these difficulties and took them into account in distributing the burden of proof between the parties'.[62] Nonetheless, such situations only come to confirm the complexity of the facts and of the evidence process before an investment arbitration tribunal. While the tribunal has discretion in determining the relevance of the evidence produced, it is undisputed that presenting such evidence to the arbitral tribunal may not be a straightforward process.

V. Failure in relation to the Facts: Enough to Annul an Arbitral Award?

The Argentinean and Spanish investment arbitrations, besides highlighting the undisputed discretion of arbitral tribunals in assessing the evidence before them, have already advanced another important aspect of the relevance of the facts to the reasoning of the arbitral award. Certain grounds of annulment of the arbitral award under Article 52 of the ICSID Convention would arguably encompass the failure of a tribunal to properly address the factual circumstances. For example, that the tribunal has manifestly exceeded its powers (Article 52(1)(b)) and that that the award has failed to state the reasons on which it is based (Article 52(1)(e)) have already been addressed in this context by ICSID ad hoc committees.[63] Article 52(1)(d), referring to a 'serious departure from a fundamental rule of procedure' could also become relevant. On this latter point, Peter Trooboff explains that the very factual finding considered by a party to be erroneous could constitute the point of annulment under (d), if that party were denied the opportunity to present its arguments on the fact.[64] Christoph Schreuer explains that ad hoc committees have dealt with the following allegations of serious departure from a fundamental rule of procedure, among others: violation of the right to

[61] *Amco Asia Corporation and others v Indonesia*, ICSID Case No ARB/81/1, Decision on Annulment (16 May 1986) [90].

[62] ibid.

[63] In non-ICSID arbitrations, the law at the seat, the *lex loci arbitri*, determines to what extent the failure of an arbitral tribunal to engage with the facts of the case can trigger the set-aside of the award. For example, the Swedish Arbitration Act with the amendments of 2019, refers in s 34(3) to the set-aside of the award if the arbitrators have exceeded their mandate in a manner that probably influenced the outcome. The threshold set by this provision is extremely high, as only such excess of mandate probable to influence the outcome of the case can justify the set-aside of the award. Such ground may be deemed to exist when for example, the award relies on facts or grounds not invoked by a party, see Gisela Knuts, 'Recourse to the Courts against an Arbitral Award' in Annette Magnusson, Jakob Ragnwaldh, and Martin Wallin (eds), *International Arbitration in Sweden: A Practitioner's Guide* (2nd edn, 2021 Kluwer Law International) 327–60, 338.

[64] Peter D Trooboff, 'To What Extent May an ad hoc Committee Review the Factual Findings of an Arbitral Tribunal Based on a Procedural Error?' in Emmanuel Gaillard and Yas Banifatemi (eds), *Annulment of ICSID Awards* (Juris Publishing 2004) 256.

be heard and violation of the rules of evidence.[65] As to the violations of the right to be heard, factual circumstances can play a central role in the substantiation of the ground for annulment. For example, in *MTD v Chile*, Chile argued that

> in holding that there was a lack of fair and equitable treatment, the Tribunal fails to consider or otherwise respond to abundant evidence presented by the Parties with respect to material issues in dispute that would have affected significantly its holding on liability as well as its assessment of compensation. ... Furthermore, there are numerous instances throughout the Award where the Tribunal simply recounts the important arguments presented by each party but never analyses or makes determinations regarding such questions.[66]

In addressing this argument, the ad hoc committee distinguished between Articles 52(1)(d) and 52(1)(e) of the ICSID Convention,[67] at the same time explaining that '[c]onceivably an award might recite the arguments of the parties in such a defective or inaccurate way as to evidence a failure to hear the arguments in the first place. But it cannot be suggested that this was the case here'.[68]

Authors highlight the limited review by ad hoc committees of the tribunal's fact finding. Pierre Mayer identifies two situations depending on the role of the factual finding in the reasoning of the applicant: sometimes it is the way in which the fact was found that is at the centre of the criticism; at other times it is the fact itself which needs a fresh determination in order to decide whether a certain criticism is justified.[69] As explained by the scholar, in circumstances in which the fact itself is under question, possibly framed in the context of the tribunal manifestly exceeding its powers, it is reasonable to accept that annulment committees can review the tribunal's factual findings.[70] However, such review can only be done by observing the following limitations: first, the annulment committee should limit its review to the evidence produced before the arbitral tribunal; second, the annulment committee should not come easily to the conclusion that the tribunal erred in its factual finding.[71] Nonetheless, and as Trooboff highlights, 'the annulment request occurs *after* a full evidentiary hearing.

[65] Schill (n 59) 1316, para 348.

[66] *MTD Equity Sdn Bhd and MTD Chile SA v Chile*, ICSID Case No ARB/01/7, Decision on Annulment (21 March 2007) [56].

[67] But see the drafting history of the ICSID Convention with the Preliminary Draft referring to a 'serious departure from a fundamental rule of procedure, including failure to state the reasons for the award', ICSID, *History of the ICSID Convention, Documents Concerning the Origin and the Formulation of the Convention on the Settlement of Investment Disputes between States and Nationals of Other States, Analysis of Documents*, vol 1 (ICSID 1970) 230.

[68] *MTD Equity Sdn Bhd and MTD Chile SA v Chile*, ICSID Case No ARB/01/7, Decision on Annulment (21 March 2007) [57].

[69] Pierre Mayer, 'To What Extent Can an ad hoc Committee Review the Factual Findings of an Arbitral Tribunal?' in Gaillard and Banifatemi (n 64) 244.

[70] ibid 245. The author takes as an example the case in which the respondent in the arbitration would challenge the jurisdiction of the tribunal based on the fact that the arbitration clause provides for ICC arbitration, rather than for ICSID arbitration (with reference to *Klöckner Industrie-Anlagen GmbH and others v Cameroon and Société Camerounaise des Engrais*, ICSID Case No ARB/81/2).

[71] ibid 249.

Each party has had an opportunity to present a factual basis for its legal claims. ... Thus, the legal issues presented to an annulment panel usually rely upon a fully developed factual record that the tribunal has carefully evaluated and on which the tribunal has made specific findings.'[72] Furthermore, '[a]bsent a serious procedural error in the tribunal's proceedings, neither party should be permitted to litigate further before an *ad hoc* committee if the tribunal has found that the facts presented are not legally sufficient to sustain the allegations made by one of the parties and the defenses of the other'.[73] In *El Paso v Argentina*, the ad hoc committee held that it 'cannot assess the facts and the evidence submitted in the proceedings'.[74]

Concerns with the factual matrix of the dispute as recorded and relied upon by the tribunal in its award would likely become more relevant in the context of Article 52(1)(e) of the ICSID Convention, if the award has failed to state the reasons on which it is based.[75] This ground for the annulment of ICSID awards is understood to cover the absence of reasons in the award, which would be a violation of Article 48(3) of the ICSID Convention;[76] the existence of inconsistent reasoning in the arbitral award;[77] and the existence of inadequate reasoning, which in the practice of ad hoc committees proved to be the most controversial, with committees refusing to adopt this approach as it would lead to an examination of the persuasiveness or correctness of the tribunal's reasoning.[78]

This was the approach of the committee in *SolEs v Spain*:

> in practice, ad hoc committees have considered that a failure to state reasons can arise in varying situations; for example, where: (a) there is a complete absence of reasons for the award or for a given conclusion; (b) there is some apparent reasoning, but a critical lacuna in the explanation, which makes it impossible for the reader to follow the reasoning up to the conclusion; (c) there are contradictory reasons cancelling each other out to the extent that they could not stand together, thereby undermining the basis of the conclusions; and (d) the statement of reasons is unrelated to the issues

[72] Trooboff (n 64) 263. Trooboff further explains that '[t]he annulment proceeding should not permit a party to reargue its case on the ground that the party *could* have presented some other set of facts to the tribunal and that those new facts *could* have supported a legal theory that the tribunal held was not supported by the facts *actually presented*', ibid 264 (emphasis in the original).

[73] ibid 264.

[74] *El Paso v Argentina*, ICSID Case No ARB/03/15, Decision on Annulment (22 September 2014) [213].

[75] According to ICSID, by 2016, '[t]he ground of failure to state the reasons on which the award is based has been invoked by parties in 50 proceedings leading to decisions. The ground was upheld in 8 cases which resulted in 2 full and 6 partial annulments', ICSID, *Updated Background Paper on Annulment for the Administrative Council of ICSID* (5 May 2016), para 108. See also the similar ground relied upon in set-aside proceedings before the courts at the seat of arbitration, in non-ICSID arbitrations, eg *Metalclad v Mexico*, where Mexico sought to have the award set aside before the Supreme Court of British Columbia, relying on the failure of the tribunal to address the issues submitted by the parties.

[76] Charalampos Giannakopoulos, 'Reconceptualizing "Failure to State Reasons" as a Ground for Annulment under Article 52(1)(e) of the ICSID Convention' (2017) 8(1) Journal of International Dispute Settlement 125, 142.

[77] ibid 143. But see the conclusion of the ad hoc committee in *Daimler v Argentina* that 'in reviewing the alleged contradictions, an ad hoc committee must be mindful of the fact that what sometimes may appear as a contradiction may be the result of a compromise reached by a collegiate body to reach a decision', *Daimler Financial Services AG v Argentina*, ICSID Case No ARB/05/1, Decision on Annulment (7 January 2015) [78].

[78] Giannakopoulos (n 76) 144.

before the tribunal, not 'sufficiently pertinent', not 'sufficiently relevant' or 'capable of providing a basis for the decision', 'insufficient, inadequate', or 'frivolous'.[79]

In *MINE v Guinea*, the ad hoc committee concluded that 'the requirement that an award has to be motivated implies that it must enable the reader to follow the reasoning of the Tribunal on points of fact and law'.[80] A similar conclusion was reached by the ad hoc committee in *TECO v Guatemala*: 'It is the view of this Committee that annulment of an award for failure to state reasons can only occur when a tribunal has failed to set out the considerations which underpinned its decision in a manner that can be understood and followed by a reader.'[81]

Nonetheless, in assessing whether the arbitral tribunal has stated reasons, ad hoc committees have looked at whether 'the Award is adequately founded on the applicable law and the relevant facts'.[82] This was also the position of the ad hoc committee in *Lucchetti v Peru*: 'The Committee cannot find in the Tribunal's reasoning any contradiction or lack of precision such as to leave a doubt about the legal or factual elements upon which the Tribunal based its conclusion.'[83] Also, the *Wena Hotels v Egypt* committee stated: 'This requirement [Article 52(1)(e)] is based on the Tribunal's duty to identify, and to let the parties know, the factual and legal premises leading the Tribunal to its decision.'[84] A similar conclusion was reached by the committee in *Soufraki v UAE*, noting that that 'a tribunal may give reasons for its award without elaborating the factual or legal bases of such reasons. So long as those reasons in fact make it possible reasonably to connect the facts or law of the case to the conclusions reached in the award, annulment may appropriately be avoided.'[85] Furthermore, as noted by the *Soufraki v UAE* ad hoc committee, '[l]ack of references supporting a proposition in an award is not, by itself, a ground for annulment, particularly where such documentation is provided by the parties to the case in their memorials and counter-memorials, and relate to well-known propositions'.[86] At the same time, the ad hoc committee in *EDF v Argentina* has highlighted the fine line between addressing whether the arbitral tribunal has stated the reasons for its decision and transforming this assessment into an appeal:

> The requirement to state reasons is an important one but it is equally important that an ad hoc committee is not drawn into using Article 52(1)(e) as a means for conducting

[79] *SolEs Badajoz GmbH v Kingdom of Spain*, ICSID Case No ARB/15/38, Decision on Annulment (16 March 2022) [81].
[80] *Maritime International Nominees Establishment v Guinea*, ICSID Case No ARB/84/4, Decision on Annulment (22 December 1989) [5.08].
[81] *TECO Guatemala Holdings LLC v Guatemala*, ICSID Case No ARB/10/23, Decision on Annulment (5 April 2016) [87].
[82] *CMS Gas Transmission Company v Argentina*, ICSID Case No ARB/01/8, Decision on Annulment (25 September 2007) [85].
[83] *Empresas Lucchetti, SA and Lucchetti Peru, SA v Peru*, ICSID Case No ARB/03/4, Decision on Annulment (5 September 2007) [129].
[84] *Wena Hotels Ltd v Egypt*, ICSID Case No ARB/98/4, Decision on Annulment (5 February 2022) [79].
[85] *Hussein Nuaman Soufraki v United Arab Emirates*, ICSID Case No ARB/02/7, Decision on Annulment (5 June 2007) [128].
[86] ibid.

> an appeal. Article 52(1)(e) empowers a committee to annul an award if there has been a failure to state the reasons on which the award is based; it does not entitle a committee to annul an award because it finds the reasoning unconvincing.[87]

It is, thus, uncontested that a proper reasoned award, delivered according to the requirements of Article 48(3) of the ICSID Convention and Rule 59 of the 2022 ICSID Arbitration Rules, allows parties to have understand the outcome of the dispute. Conversely, an arbitral award which has failed to state the factual and legal reasons for the outcome is likely to be subject to annulment proceedings. The approach of ICSID ad hoc committees appears to be uniform, with issues of factual evidence being often considered under Article 52(1)(e) of the ICSID Convention. Nonetheless, committees appear to be mindful of their role as 'annulment' committees and not as 'appeal' committees when reviewing the discretion of arbitral tribunals in addressing the relevance of the factual evidence submitted to them. Even so, it cannot be contested that the relevance of addressing the complex factual circumstances of the investment disputes is an important element in annulment proceedings.

VI. Conclusions

As eloquently put by Federico Ortino, '[t]he field of international investment law, practically non-existent until the end of the 20th century, is certainly today one of the most active and controversial fields in international law'.[88] Addressing the relevance of facts in the reasoning of investment arbitral tribunals is important: while arbitral tribunals have discretion in determining the relevance of the facts in the dispute, and while important economic and geopolitical events can generate numerous investment arbitrations relying on similar or identical facts, the undisputed issue remains that under the applicable legal framework, arbitral awards must be reasoned—with respect to both the facts and the law—and the failure to provide reasons may result in the annulment of the award.

Given the importance of investment arbitrations, arbitral awards and their reasoning may serve different purposes. As Ortino explains:

> It is useful here to distinguish between arguments in favour of a high level of clarity in the reasoning of investment decisions to strengthen the internal functioning of the system of international investment law and arbitration and arguments in favour of a

[87] *EDF International SA, SAUR International SA and León Participaciones Argentinas SA v Argentina*, ICSID Case No ARB/03/23, Decision on Annulment (5 February 2016) [195], with reference to *Vivendi I (Compañiá de Aguas del Aconquija SA and Vivendi Universal SA v Argentina*, ICSID Case No ARB/97/3, Decision on Annulment (3 July 2002) [64]–[65].

[88] Federico Ortino, 'Legal Reasoning of International Investment Tribunals: A Typology of Egregious Failures' (2012) 3 Journal of International Dispute Settlement 31, 31.

high level of clarity in the reasoning of investment decisions in order to strengthen the legitimacy of the system vis-à-vis external stakeholders.[89]

It is, however, apparent that 'complex high level international dispute ... requires an extensive investigation, and detailed, sophisticated analysis of fact and law (and often multiple laws)',[90] and, as such, the task of arbitral tribunals in determining the relevant facts of the dispute, as well as the legal grounds on which the decision rests, is not an easy task. Dealing with complex facts is not only the challenge of investment arbitration. Counsel and arbitrators in large international commercial arbitrations share similar experience. Large infrastructure projects generate equally complex disputes which rest on facts spanning over several years, and of significant difficulty to be elaborated on and exhaustively reflected in arbitral awards.[91] Similarly, the International Court of Justice (ICJ), has only recently been considering the shift from the traditional approach on the facts, namely deciding the outcome of a case solely relying on undisputed facts,[92] to engaging in examining the complex facts of the case. In the *Armed Activities* case, the ICJ explained that it has to make a determination of the facts and such task necessarily requires an assessment of the evidence before it:

> In accordance with its practice, the Court will first make its own determination of the facts and then apply the relevant rules of international law to the facts which it has found to have existed. ... These findings of fact necessarily entail an assessment of the evidence. The Court has in this case been presented with a vast amount of materials proffered by the Parties in support of their versions of the facts. The Court has not only the task of deciding which of those materials must be considered relevant, but also the duty to determine which of them have probative value with regard to the alleged facts. ... it will identify the documents relied on and make its own clear assessment of their weight, reliability and value.[93]

An analogous approach was taken by the ICJ in the *Bosnian Genocide* case, concluding that '[t]he Court must itself make its own determination of the facts which are relevant to the law which the Applicant claims the Respondent has breached'.[94] In the *Pulp Mills*

[89] ibid 33–34.

[90] Toby Thomas Landau, 'Reasons for Reasons: The Tribunal's Duty in Investor-State Arbitration' in Albert Jan Van den Berg (ed), *50 Years of the New York Convention: ICCA International Arbitration Conference* (Kluwer Law International 2009) 191.

[91] See for example *Grupo Unidos por el Canal, SA, Sacyr SA, Salini-Impregilo SpA, and Jan de Nul NV v Autoridad del Canal de Panama (I)*, ICC Case No 19962/ASM, arising out of the expansion of the Panama Canal.

[92] James Gerard Devaney, *Fact-Finding before the International Court of Justice* (CUP 2016) 1. See also the explanation of the author that '[i]n the past it has been argued that well-reasoned judgments based in the law rather than decided on technical issues of fact have traditionally been perceived as being of a higher prestige and consequently somehow less offensive to the State party on the wrong end of the judgment', ibid 7.

[93] *Armed Activities on the Territory of the Congo (Democratic Republic of the Congo v Uganda)* (Judgment) [2005] ICJ Rep 168 [57]–[59].

[94] *Application of the Convention on the Prevention and Punishment of the Crime of Genocide (Bosnia and Herzegovina v Serbia and Montenegro)*, International Court of Justice, Judgment of 26 February 2007, ICG Reports 2007, para 212. The ICJ acknowledges, however, that many of the allegations before the Court in this case had been subject of the processes and decisions of the International Criminal Tribunal for the former Yugoslavia.

case, the Court acknowledged that it 'needs only to be mindful of the fact that, despite the volume and complexity of the factual information submitted to it, it is the responsibility of the Court, after having given careful consideration to all the evidence placed before it by the Parties, to determine which facts must be considered relevant, to assess their probative value, and to draw conclusions from them as appropriate'.[95]

Engaging with the facts of a case is not only an exercise of the skills of written advocacy, managing to reflect the logical argumentation of the decision of the arbitral tribunal. The reference to the facts of the dispute is a necessary, often compulsory element of an arbitral award, as an expression of tribunal applying the rules of evidence. Furthermore, reflecting the facts on which the decision of the tribunal rests is also a condition of the effectiveness of the arbitral award, given that the absence of the reference to the facts on which the decision rests may trigger the annulment of the award. Suggestions on how to improve the work for the investment arbitral tribunals is provided by John Crook who concludes that in the successful assessment of the 'difficult factual issues in factually complex investor-state cases', the following elements should be observed: 'the willingness and ability of the sorts of arbitrators typically named in significant investor-state cases to probe the record and pursue the facts', 'active involvement by facts-finders in exploring the facts', 'frequent use of live witnesses ad their cross-examination in the presence of the tribunal', and the use of 'other available fact-finding tools, such as recourse to tribunal-appointed experts'.[96]

[95] *Pulp Mills on the River Uruguay (Argentina v Uruguay)* (Judgment) [2010] ICJ Rep 14 [168].
[96] Crook (n 1) 318–19.

12

The Applicable Law in Investor-State Dispute Settlement

*George A Bermann**

I. Introduction

In principle, the applicable law in investor-state dispute settlement (ISDS)—the law governing the merits of a dispute between a state and a foreign investor—is determined by the contract, statute, or treaty under which the arbitration is brought. Contract and statute-based arbitrations present the easiest cases from a choice-of-law point of view. The law applicable to a dispute arising under an investment contract between an investor and a host state, like any contract-based dispute, is governed in principle by the *lex causae*, that is, the law under which the claim arises. A dispute arising under a host state's foreign investment legislation will be governed by the statute itself. Consequently, it is treaty-based ISDS that raises the most serious choice-of-law issues.

II. The Applicable Law under the Investment Treaty

Bilateral investment treaties (BITs) and the investment chapters of free trade agreements (FTAs) invariably contain a clause designating the applicable law. So too do sectoral agreements with investment chapters such as the Energy Charter Treaty (ECT). That clause commonly prescribes as applicable the treaties themselves, international law more generally, and host state law.

Generalizations notwithstanding, it is in all cases essential to examine the text of an investment treaty's choice-of-law provision. For example, while most provisions include host state law as a source,[1] Article 30 of the US Model BIT affirms that claims brought under the treaty are to be determined 'in accordance with this Treaty and applicable rules of international law'.[2] Article 2(6) of the ECT is to the same effect.[3] Both knowingly omit host state law as a source.

* The author gratefully acknowledges the valuable research assistance of R Daniel Knaap, Columbia Law School, class of 2024, in preparation of this chapter.

[1] See, eg, 2019 Netherlands Model BIT art 2(1). For a list of BITs with similar provisions, see Yas Banifatemi, 'The Law Applicable in Investment Treaty Arbitration' in Katia Yannaca-Small (ed), *Arbitration under International Investment Agreements: A Guide to Key Issues* (2018) 490 n 22.

[2] 2012 US Model BIT art 30(2).

[3] ECT, 17 December 1994, 2080 UNTS 100, art 26(6).

George A Bermann, *The Applicable Law in Investor-State Dispute Settlement* In: *The Award in International Investment Arbitration*. Edited by: Katia Fach Gómez and Catharine Titi, Oxford University Press. © Katia Fach Gómez and Aikaterini Titi 2024.
DOI: 10.1093/9780191975936.003.0012

The treaty text typically identifies claims that may be brought under the treaty which include most commonly fair and equitable treatment (FTA), full protection and security (FPS), national treatment, most-favoured-nation treatment (MFN), and expropriation. Likely others will be included, such as the right to an adequate remedy for wrongs,[4] free transfer of capital,[5] various protections (for example, against denial of justice,[6] performance requirements,[7] and nationality requirements for senior management and boards of directors),[8] and publication of laws and decisions.[9] The US Model BIT contains a special choice-of-law provision for claims submitted in connection with 'an investment authorization or an investment agreement'. Such claims are governed by:

(a) the rules of law specified in the pertinent investment authorization or investment agreement, or as the disputing parties may otherwise agree; or
(b) if the rules of law have not been specified or otherwise agreed:
  (i) the law of the respondent, including its rules on the conflict of laws; and
  (ii) such rules of international law as may be applicable.[10]

The institutional rules under which ISDS is conducted also typically contain their own choice-of-law provisions. For example, the Arbitration Rules of the Stockholm Chamber of Commerce (SCC) Arbitration Institute provide:

> The Arbitral Tribunal shall decide the merits of the dispute on the basis of the law(s) or rules of law agreed upon by the parties. In the absence of such agreement, the Arbitral Tribunal shall apply the law or rules of law that it considers most appropriate.[11]

The coexistence of choice-of-law provisions in the investment agreement and the applicable rules of arbitral procedure is potentially problematic since a tribunal cannot be expected to operate under two different sets of applicable law. The problem, however, is illusory. It is largely understood that, in the case of disparities, the sources identified in the applicable BIT, FTA, or sectoral agreement prevail, which is logical in that those are the instruments from which substantive foreign investment rights and obligations derive.

[4] US Model BIT art 5(5).
[5] ibid art 7.
[6] ibid art 5(2)(a).
[7] ibid art 8.
[8] ibid art 9.
[9] ibid art 10.
[10] ibid art 30(2).
[11] SCC Arbitration Rules art 27(1) (2023). Article 27(2) goes on to state that '[a]ny designation by the parties of the law of a given state shall be deemed to refer to the substantive law of that state, not to its conflict of laws rules', while Article 27(3) specifies that '[t]he Arbitral Tribunal shall decide the dispute ex aequo et bono or as amiable compositeur only if the parties have expressly authorised it to do so'.

III. The Applicable Law under the ICSID Convention

The situation under the International Convention for the Settlement of Investment Disputes between States and the Nationals of Other States (ICSID Convention)[12] is in principle no different. The Convention is not the source of substantive investor protections. Rather, it supplies an institutional framework through which claims cognizable under BITs, FTAs, and sectoral agreement such as the ECT may be asserted. Any confusion that might otherwise arise is obviated by the Convention's very choice-of-law provision. Like the rules of many other arbitral institutions, Article 42 of the ICSID Convention specifies that it is a default rule only. Thus:

> The Tribunal shall decide a dispute in accordance with such rules of law as may be agreed by the parties. *In the absence of such agreement*, the Tribunal shall apply the law of the Contracting State party to the dispute (including its rules on the conflict of laws) and such rules of international law as may be applicable.[13]

The rules of law to which the parties will have agreed are precisely those provided for by the instrument from which the investment rights and obligations derive, again the applicable BIT, FTA, and sectoral investment agreement. Notably, the ICSID Convention expressly makes the host state's conflict of law rules part of host state law,[14] thereby adopting *renvoi*.[15] In principle, the applicable law will not be the law of the state that is specified, but rather the jurisdiction to which that state's choice-of-law rules point. When we later examine the scope of application of host state law,[16] we will see that the mention of *renvoi* is inconsequential, since on the issues to which host State law is applicable, that state's conflict of law rules will lead not to a foreign law, but that state's own.

Thus, in ICSID Convention cases, questions of applicable law are far simpler than questions of arbitral jurisdiction. Under the so-called double keyhole approach,[17] in order for an investment treaty arbitration to go forward under the aegis of ICSID, the investment treaty's definition of 'investment' must be met, but so too must the ICSID definition of that term, as set out in Article 25 of the Convention.[18] If a contribution of

[12] ICSID Convention, 18 March 1965, 575 UNTS 159, art 42(1).

[13] ibid art 42 (emphasis added). Article 42(3) goes on to state that '[t]he provisions of [this] paragraph ... shall not prejudice the power of the Tribunal to decide a dispute ex aequo et bono if the parties so agree'.

[14] ibid art 42(1).

[15] See generally Andrew Newcombe and Lluís Paradell Trius, *Law and Practice of Investment Treaties: Standards of Treatment* (Wolters Kluwer 2009) 81.

[16] See nn 145–68.

[17] Rudolf Dolzer, Ursula Kriebaum, and Christoph Schreuer, *Principles of International Investment Law* (3rd edn, OUP 2022) 84; *Beijing Urban Construction Group Co Ltd v Yemen*, ICSID Case No ARB/14/30, Decision on Jurisdiction (31 May 2017) [126].

[18] ICSID Convention art 25(1) ('The jurisdiction of the Centre shall extend to any legal dispute arising directly out of an investment, between a Contracting State (or any constituent subdivision or agency of a Contracting State designated to the Centre by that State) and a national of another Contracting State, which the parties to the dispute consent in writing to submit to the Centre').

capital meets the definition of an investment under a BIT, for example, but not under the ICSID Convention, the claim must be brought, if at all, in some other forum among those that the BIT makes available.

In early ICSID cases, tribunals did not focus particularly on the interaction between host state and international law. Instead, tribunals quickly concluded that the host state's domestic law conformed to international law and thus found it unnecessary to choose between them.[19] As observed by one commentator: 'These instances of a parallel application of domestic and international law, coupled with assurances of their harmony, do not provide much useful information on the interaction of the two legal systems.'[20] An exception was the ad hoc committee's decision to annul the award in the case of *Klockner v Cameroon*.[21] There, the committee found that principles of international law performed at best a 'complementary' or 'corrective' function:

> The arbitrators may have recourse to the 'principles of international law' only after having inquired into and established the content of the law of the State party to the dispute (which cannot be reduced to one principle, even a basic one) and after having applied the relevant rules of the State's law.[22]

This decision effectively relegated international law to a secondary role.[23]

However, this is clearly not how the relationship between international and host state law is viewed today, and the explanation is close at hand. Early ICSID Convention cases happen to have been contract- rather than treaty-based. BITs as such were hardly known. Giving priority to domestic law in purely commercial disputes between a state and a foreign national, such as in a claim for breach of a concession agreement, makes perfect sense, especially since, as so often is the case, the contract itself designates a body of national law as applicable to the claim. It was and remains similarly logical to apply domestic law, notably host state law, in the determination of statute-based claims.

Notions of the applicable law in ICSID cases necessarily changed with the advent of BITs. While national law is suitable to adjudicate contract claims and claims arising under a state's investment protection legislation, international law is the default applicable law in the adjudication of claims arising under an international treaty, itself an international law instrument.[24] This was precisely the position taken

[19] *Adriano Gardella v Côte d'Ivoire*, ICSID Case No ARB/74/1, Award (29 August 1977) ICSID Rep 282, 287 (1993); *Aguaytia Energy LLC v Peru*, ICSID Case No ARB/06/13, Award (11 December 2008 [71]–[74].

[20] Ursula Kriebaum, 'Article 42' in Stephan W Schill and others, *Schreuer's Commentary on the ICSID Convention* (3rd edn, CUP 2022) 884.

[21] *Klöckner Industrie-Anlagen GmbH and others v Cameroon and Société Camerounaise des Engrais*, ICSID Case No ARB/81/2, Decision on Annulment (3 May 1985).

[22] ibid [69].

[23] See, eg, *AGIP SpA v Congo*, ICSID Case No ARB/77/1, Award (30 November 1979) 1 ICSID Rep 306 (1993); *Amco Asia Corporation and others v Indonesia*, ICSID Case No ARB/81/1, Award (20 November 1984) 1 ICSID Rep 413 (1993); *Société Ouest Africaine des Bétons Industriels v Senegal*, ICSID Case No ARB/82/1, Award (25 February 1988) 2 ICSID Rep 164 (1994).

[24] W Michael Reisman and Mahnoush H Arsanjani, 'Applicable Law under the ICSID Convention: The Tortured History of the Interpretation of ICSID Article 42' in Meg Kinnear and others (eds), *Building International Investment Law: The First 50 Years of ICSID* (Wolters Kluwer 2016) 3.

by the tribunal in the first treaty-based ICSID case, *AAPL v Sri Lanka*.[25] There, the tribunal held that 'in the absence of a specific rule provided for in the Treaty itself as *lex specialis*, the general international law rules have to assume their role as *lex generalis*'.[26] Of course, the application of international law to treaty-based investment claims was not left to chance. There is no bilateral or multilateral investment treaty that fails to make international law, whether or not accompanied by host state law, the applicable law.

IV. International Law as Applicable Law

A. Treaty and International Law Generally

As earlier suggested,[27] the law applicable to a claim arising out of an investment treaty necessarily includes the treaty itself. A claimant will invariably assert that the challenged measure breached one or more rights to which the investor was entitled under the treaty. Accordingly, the tribunal will be tasked to interpret the treaty—presumably in accordance with the relevant provisions of the Vienna Convention on the Law of Treaties (VCLT)[28]—and apply it.

Besides the provisions in the applicable investment agreement, tribunals apply, as if gap-fillers, the norms emanating from all sources of international law without restriction, absent clear evidence that the treaty drafters intended otherwise.[29] The authority to do so stems from two main sources. First, the agreement will usually contain

[25] *Asian Agricultural Products Limited v Sri Lanka*, ICSID Case No ARB/87/3, Award (27 June 1990) 4 ICSID Rep 246 (1997).

[26] ibid [54].

[27] See nn 1–3.

[28] Vienna Convention on the Law of Treaties (VCLT), 23 May 1969, 1155 UNTS 331, arts 31–32:

Article 31 General rule of interpretation

1. A treaty shall be interpreted in good faith in accordance with the ordinary meaning to be given to the terms of the treaty in their context and in the light of its object and purpose.
2. The context for the purpose of the interpretation of a treaty shall comprise, in addition to the text, including its preamble and annexes:
   (a) any agreement relating to the treaty which was made between all the parties in connection with the conclusion of the treaty;
   (b) any instrument which was made by one or more parties in connection with the conclusion of the treaty and accepted by the other parties as an instrument related to the treaty.
3. There shall be taken into account, together with the context:
   (a) any subsequent agreement between the parties regarding the interpretation of the treaty or the application of its provisions;
   (b) any subsequent practice in the application of the treaty which establishes the agreement of the parties regarding its interpretation;
   (c) any relevant rules of international law applicable in the relations between the parties.
4. A special meaning shall be given to a term if it is established that the parties so intended.

Article 32 Supplementary means of interpretation

Recourse may be had to supplementary means of interpretation, including the preparatory work of the treaty and the circumstances of its conclusion, in order to confirm the meaning resulting from the application of article 31, or to determine the meaning when the interpretation according to article 31:
   (a) leaves the meaning ambiguous or obscure; or
   (b) leads to a result which is manifestly absurd or unreasonable.

[29] Newcombe and Paradell (n 15) 80.

a provision stating that the tribunal shall decide the dispute in according with the rules of international law that may be applicable.[30] Second, the VCLT requires treaties to be interpreted in light of their context, which includes 'any relevant rules of international law applicable in the relations between the parties'.[31]

B. Sources of International Law

The conventional sources of international law are those enumerated in Article 38(1) of the Statute of the International Court of Justice (ICJ):

(a) international conventions, whether general or particular, establishing rules expressly recognized by the contesting states;
(b) international custom, as evidence of a general practice accepted as law;
(c) the general principles of law recognized by civilized nations;
(d) subject to the provisions of Article 59, judicial decisions and the teachings of the most highly qualified publicists of the various nations, as subsidiary means for the determination of rules of law.[32]

Conventions (or treaties), customary international law (CIL), and general principles of law (GPL) are primary sources of international law, and there is no hierarchy between them (subject to such prioritization principles as *lex posterior derogat legi priori* or *lex specialis derogat legi generali*). The term 'international conventions' is capacious. It will include not only the investment agreement pursuant to which the claim is proceeding, but also other agreements to which the states are parties, such as human rights or international environmental agreements.[33]

CIL emerges where there has been widespread and consistent state practice *and* where that practice is accompanied by a belief that it is required under international law (*opinio juris*).[34] The finding of CIL does not require the participation of all, or even a majority of, countries. Widespread and consistent practice will suffice for a CIL norm to bind all countries.[35] This can be contrasted with regional CIL, where a certain number of states impliedly agree to be bound by a special rule that deviates from the general international law rule.[36]

[30] See, eg, ICSID Convention art 42(1); Chile–South Africa BIT, 12 November 1998, art IX(5); Italy–Eritrea BIT, 26 April 1999, art 7(4)(B).
[31] VCLT art 31.
[32] Statute of the International Court of Justice, 18 April 1946, 33 UST 993, art 38(1).
[33] *Biloune and Marine Drive Complex Ltd v Ghana Investments Centre and Ghana*, UNCITRAL, Award on Jurisdiction and Liability (27 October1989) [60]
[34] *North Sea Continental Shelf Cases* (*Germany v Denmark; Germany v Netherlands*), Judgment [1969] ICJ Rep 3 [74]–[77].
[35] Patrick Dumberry, *The Formation and Identification of Rules of Customary International Law in International Investment Law* (CUP 2016) 392.
[36] ibid 25; *Rights of Passage over Indian Territory* (*Portugal v India*), Judgment [1960] ICJ Rep 6 [39]–[40]; *Asylum Case (Colombia v Peru)*, Judgment [1950] ICJ Rep 266 [276]–[277].

Many CIL rules applicable to ISDS disputes have been codified in BITs and other international investment agreements themselves.[37] Other rules of CIL play what may be called a supporting role, for example, filling in possible lacunae in the treaty, defining undefined terms or aid in the interpretation and application of treaty provisions.[38] Examples include the invocation of state defences under international law,[39] or modalities for ascertaining damages.[40] CIL norms such as the precautionary principle may have relevance for disputes engaging environmental or trade as in defence of a basis measures taken in the public interest. Finally, tribunals have recognized their duty to apply *jus cogens* norms and avoid 'giv[ing] effect to parties' choices of law that are inconsistent with such principles'.[41]

The notion of GPL refers to general legal norms that have been so widely and commonly accepted across legal systems that it may be said to have gained something approaching a consensus (though not necessarily universal acceptance).[42] Though GPL are a primary source of law, they often merely fill gaps where treaty provisions and custom do not in and of themselves suffice.[43] Classic examples include good faith,[44] equity,[45] and fairness[46] and doctrines such as *pacta sunt servanda*.[47] The ICJ has invoked applied on a surprisingly wide range of issues such as the admission of circumstantial evidence,[48] procedural due process,[49] and the proper conception of a limited liability company.[50]

Under Article 38(1)(d) of the Statute, judicial decisions and teachings of 'the most highly qualified publicists' are secondary sources of law; they are not in and of

[37] See, eg, North American Free Trade Agreement, 17 December 1992, 32 ILM 289, ch 11; US Model BIT; Netherlands Model BIT.

[38] *Amoco International Fin Corp v Iran* [1987] IUSCT Rep 189 [112].

[39] *Sempra Energy International v Argentina*, ICSID Case No ARB/02/16, Award (28 September 2007) [378].

[40] *ADC Affiliate Ltd and others v Hungary*, ICSID Case No ARB/03/16, Award (2 October 2006) [483]; *Archer Daniels Midland Co and others v Mexico*, ICSID Case No ARB(AF)/04/5, Award (21 November 2007) [122].

[41] *Methanex Corp v United States*, NAFTA/UNCITRAL, Final Award (3 August 2005) [24]; International Law Commission (ILC), Report on the Work of Its Fifty-Third, UN Doc.A/56/10 (2001).

[42] Charles T Kotuby Jr and Luke A Sobota, *General Principles of Law and International Due Process: Principles and Norms Applicable in Transnational Disputes* (OUP 2007) 87.

[43] See Yilin Wang, 'The Origins and Operation of the General Principles of Law as Gap Fillers' (2022) 13 Journal of International Dispute Settlement 560.

[44] *Canfor Corp v United States*, UNCITRAL, Decision of Preliminary Question (6 June 2006) [182] ('Good faith is also a basic principle in the performance of a treaty by States').

[45] *SARL Benvenuti & Bonfant v Congo*, ICSID Case No ARB/77/2, Award (8 August 1980) [4.64] ('The principle of compensation in case of nationalization ... constitutes one of the generally recognized principles of international law as well as of equity').

[46] *Glencore Finance (Berm) Ltd v Bolivia*, PCA Case No 2016-39, Procedural Order No 2 (Decision on Bifurcation) (31 January 2018) [56] ('Nevertheless, the Tribunal recalls that the overarching principle is the fairness and efficiency of this process as a whole').

[47] *Amco Asia* (n 23) [248] ('The principle *pacta sunt servanda* is a principle of international law').

[48] *Corfu Channel (United Kingdom v Albania)*, Judgment [1949] ICJ Rep 4, 18; *Right of Passage over Indian Territory (Portugal v India)*, Preliminary Objections [1957] ICJ Rep 125, 141–42; *Certain German Interests in Polish Upper Silesia*, Preliminary Objections, PCIJ Ser A No 6, 19 (25 August 1925).

[49] *Application for Review of Judgment No 158 of the United Nations Administrative Tribunal*, Advisory Opinion [1973] ICJ Rep 166, 177, 181, 210; *Application for Review of Judgment No 273 of the United Nations Administrative Tribunal*, Advisory Opinion [1982] ICJ Rep 325, 338–40, 345, 356.

[50] *Barcelona Traction, Light and Power Co, Ltd (Belgium v Spain) (New Application: 1962)*, Preliminary Objections (Second Phase) [1970] ICJ Rep 3, 33–35; *Ahmadou Sadio Diallo (Guinea v Democratic Republic of the Congo)*, Judgment [2010] ICJ Rep 639, 675.

themselves binding but are meant to help determine primary rules of international law. Decisions of international courts and tribunals, while not enjoying binding effect in later cases,[51] can be especially persuasive, and most tribunals do in fact turn to them for guidance.[52] They may actually have even greater effect by contributing to the emergence of GPL, in which case they become binding indirectly.[53]

The list of sources in Article 38 is not exhaustive, however.[54] The ICJ made this clear by recognizing unilateral declarations as a supplemental source of international law.[55] For instance, in the *Bear Creek* case,[56] the dissenting arbitrator Philippe Sands would have held the investor contributorily at fault due to its failure to obtain a social license from the local Aymara people, as required under the International Labor Organization (ILO) Convention 169 on Indigenous and Tribal Peoples. The treaty was binding on Peru at the time and, according to Sands, also imposed obligations on private parties *within* Peru.

V. The Law Applicable to Umbrella Clause Claims

A. The Nature of Umbrella Clause Claims

Umbrella clauses are treaty provisions that typically provide that host states shall observe any obligations they assume vis-à-vis the investor. An immediate question is whether, by virtue of an umbrella clause, a contract claim as such becomes an investment treaty claim subject to arbitration pursuant to the treaty. In *SGS v Pakistan*,[57] the first known decision on the effect of an umbrella clause, the tribunal rejected the notion that an umbrella clause 'elevates' a contract claim to the international plane, converts it into a treaty claim, and subjects it to arbitration under the treaty. It found that proposition to diverge too radically from the starting assumption under general international law that a violation of a contract entered into by a state with an investor of another State is not in itself a violation of international law.[58] More would be required to 'incorporate[e] by reference an unlimited number of State contracts, as well as other municipal law instruments setting out State commitments including unilateral commitments to an investor of the other Contracting Party'.[59] Moreover, the tribunal found

[51] Richard C Chen, 'Precedent and Dialogue in Investment Treaty Arbitration' (2019) 60 Harvard International Law Journal 47.

[52] Newcombe and Paradell (n 15) 102.

[53] See Jan Paulsson, 'International Arbitration and the Generation of Legal Norms: Treaty Arbitration and International Law' (2006) 5 Transnational Dispute Management 1.

[54] Rüdiger Wolfrum, 'Sources of International Law' *in Max Planck Encyclopedia of Public International Law* (OUP 2011) 1471, para 10.

[55] *Nuclear Tests Case (Australia v France)*, Judgment [1974] ICJ Rep 253.

[56] *Bear Creek Mining Corp v Peru*, ICSID Case No ARB/14/21, Partial Dissenting Opinion of Philippe Sands (30 November 2017).

[57] *SGS Société Générale de Surveillance v Pakistan*, ICSID Case No ARB/01/13, Decision on Jurisdiction (6 August 2003).

[58] ibid [167].

[59] ibid [168].

it significant that the umbrella clause was not situated in the treaty alongside the treaty obligations, such as the guarantee of fair and equitable treatment.[60] It also found in such an approach an unacceptable asymmetry. 'The investor would remain free to go to arbitration either under the contract or under the BIT. But the State party to the contract would be effectively precluded from proceeding to the ... forum specified in the contract unless the investor was minded to agree.'[61] However, the tribunal allowed that the result might be different if the umbrella clause were worded and situated in such a way as to suggest that the parties indeed intended to submit their contract disputes to investment treaty arbitration.

This view of umbrella clauses adopted by the *SGS v Pakistan* tribunal represents a restrictive one, which only a minority of other tribunals have followed.[62] More influential has been the award in the case of *SGS v Philippines*,[63] in which the tribunal considered that to refuse in the presence of an umbrella clause to treat breach of contract claims as treaty claims would be in effect to render the clause meaningless. In the tribunal's view, the probable intention of parties to an umbrella clause is that contract claims and claims based on other obligations vis-à-vis an investor are to be assimilated to treaty claims,[64] and that such intention is consistent with the object and purpose of the treaty to create and maintain favourable conditions for investors of one contracting party in the territory of the other.[65] In sum, by virtue of an umbrella clause, a tribunal can exercise jurisdiction over contractual claims related to the investment in question.[66]

This view has gained traction. In *Noble v Romania*,[67] the tribunal held that the umbrella clause transformed 'municipal law obligations into obligations directly cognizable in international law'.[68] As such, it concluded that contractual breaches amounted to treaty breaches, subject to the applicable law of the investment treaty.[69] In *Siemens v Argentina*,[70] the tribunal held that contractual obligations were 'converted by this [umbrella] clause into a breach of the Treaty',[71] and in *BIVAC v Paraguay*,[72] the tribunal

[60] ibid [169].
[61] ibid.
[62] *Joy Mining Machinery Ltd v Egypt*, ICSID Case No ARB/03/11, Award on Jurisdiction (6 August 2004) [82] ('The Tribunal concludes therefore that, even if for the sake of argument there was an investment in this case, the absence of a Treaty-based claim, and the evidence that, on the contrary, all claims are contractual, justifies the finding that the Tribunal lacks jurisdiction'); *El Paso Energy International Co v Argentina*, ICSID Case No ARB/03/15, Decision on Jurisdiction (27 April 2006) [84]; *Pan American Energy LLC and BP Argentina Exploration Co v Argentina*, ICSID Case No ARB/03/13, and *BP America Production Co, Pan American Sur SRL, Pan American Fuegina, SRL and Pan American Continental SRL v Argentina*, ICSID Case No ARB/04/8, Decision on Preliminary Objections (27 July 2006) [113]; *Supervision y Control SA v Costa Rica*, ICSID Case No ARB/12/4, Award (18 January 2017) [282].
[63] *SGS Société Générale de Surveillance SA v Philippines*, ICSID Case No ARB/02/6, Decision on Jurisdiction (29 January 2004).
[64] ibid [115].
[65] ibid [116].
[66] ibid [128].
[67] *Noble Ventures, Inc v Romania*, ICSID Case No ARB/01/11, Award (12 October 2005).
[68] ibid [53].
[69] ibid [54].
[70] *Siemens AG v Argentina*, ICSID Case No ARB/02/8, Award (6 February 2007).
[71] ibid [204].
[72] *Bureau Veritas, Inspection, Valuation, Assessment and Control, BIVAC BV v Paraguay*, ICSID Case No ARB/07/9, Decision Tribunal on Jurisdiction (29 May 2009).

held that the treaty's umbrella clause 'imported into the BIT all of the obligations owed by Paraguay to BIVAC under the Contract'.[73]

B. Applicable Law

Under the approach taken by *SGS v Pakistan*, no question of the applicable law under the investment treaty arises since, as noted, the dispute is not subject to investment treaty arbitration. The dispute will be subject to the law of the contract, in most cases the law the parties designated in a choice of law provision. The answer under the *SGS v Philippines* position is less clear. Arguably, once the contract claim has been elevated to a treaty claim, it is subject to the law that is ordinarily applicable to such claims, viz. the treaty and international law generally. However, even the *SGS v Philippines* tribunal did not take the position. According to it, even though, in the presence of an umbrella clause, a contract claim is properly before the investment arbitration tribunal, the law applicable to that claim remains the law of the contract:

> The basic obligation on the State ... does not mean that the determination of how much money the Philippines is obligated to pay becomes a treaty matter. The extent of the obligation is still governed by the contract, and it can only be determined by reference to the terms of the contract.[74]

This has clearly become the majority view among tribunals.[75]

C. The Effect of Forum Selection Clauses

Although the *SGS v Philippines* tribunal determined that the contract claim at hand had in effect become a treaty claim, it remained to deal with the fact that the contract itself contained a forum selection clause designating the Philippine courts as exclusively competent to decide disputes arising under the contract.[76] The tribunal determined that the 'extent' and 'content' of the claim, though subject to an umbrella clause, remains governed by the terms of the contract,[77] among which figures the contractual

[73] ibid [142].
[74] *SGS v Philippines* (n 63) [127].
[75] *CMS Gas Transmission Co v Argentina*, ICSID Case No ARB/01/8, Decision on Annulment (25 September 2007) [95(c)]; *Continental Casualty Co v Argentina*, ICSID Case No ARB/03/9, Award (5 September 2008); *MTD Equity Sdn Bhd and MTD Chile SA v Chile*, ICSID Case No ARB/01/7, Award (5 May 2004); *Toto Costruzioni Generali SpA v Lebanon*, ICSID Case No ARB/07/12, Decision on Jurisdiction (11 September 2009); *WNC Factoring v Czech Republic*, UNCITRAL, PCA Case No 2014-34, Award (22 February 2017).
[76] The contract in *SGS v Pakistan* also contained a forum selection clause which, according to the tribunal had to be honoured. However, that clause was not crucial to the outcome because the tribunal, as noted, found that the contract claim had not been elevated to the level of a treaty claim, and was therefore not before the investment tribunal in any case.
[77] ibid [128].

forum selection clause. On that basis, it found the claim to be inadmissible.[78] This reasoning was followed in *Bosh v Ukraine*, where the tribunal held that the claimants were bound to the underlying contract's forum selection clause,[79] which required submission of claims to Ukrainian courts, and that the umbrella clause 'did not have the effect of converting "the *extent* or *content* of [contractual] obligations into an issue of international law" '.[80]

While *SGS v Philippines* reflects the dominant view among tribunals of the effect of an umbrella clause on a forum selection clause,[81] not all tribunals have followed it,[82] and the literature is divided.[83] To further complicate matters, one tribunal held that, while domestic law applies to 'the existence and dimensions of the obligation', international law should be applied to whether the obligation has been breached.[84]

D. Attributability under Umbrella Clause Claims

Another issue relating to the law applicable to umbrella clause claims is whether a commercial contract between an investor and a sub-state entity can be attributed to the state. Attribution is, after all, part of international law. It is not the case, however, that tribunals that select domestic law as applicable law reject attribution while tribunals that select international law accept it. For example, both the *Noble v Romania* tribunal, which held that contractual claims become treaty claims by virtue of the umbrella clause,[85] and the *Toto v Lebanon* tribunal, which applied domestic law,[86] were willing to apply international law on attribution to commercial contracts involving sub-state entities.[87]

[78] ibid [154].

[79] *Bosh International, Inc and B&P, LTD Foreign Invs Enter v Ukraine*, ICSID Case No ARB/08, Award (25 October 2012) [258].

[80] ibid [247].

[81] See, eg, *Eureko BV v Poland*, UNCITRAL, Partial Award (19 August 2005) [255]–[257]; *Noble Ventures, Inc v Romania*, ICSID Case No ARB/01/11, Award (12 October 2005) [53]–[55]; *Siemens AG v Argentina*, ICSID Case No ARB/02/8, Award (6 February 2007) [204]; *Ioan Micula and others v Romania*, ICSID Case No ARB/05/20, Final Award (11 December 2013) [417]–[418].

[82] Some tribunals have held that the contract's forum selection clause requires an express waiver of an investor's right to recourse to an investment tribunal. See *Aguas del Tunari, SA v Bolivia*, ICSID Case No ARB/02/3, Decision on Jurisdiction (21 October 2005) [115]; *TSA Spectrum de Argentina, SA v Argentina*, ICSID Case No ARB/05/5, Award (19 December 2008) [58]; *Crystallex International Corp v Venezuela*, ICSID Case No ARB(AF)/11/2, Award (4 April 2016) [481]. See also *Siemens AG v Argentina*, ICSID Case No ARB/02/8, Decision on Jurisdiction (3 August 2004) [174], [180].

[83] Compare Zachary Douglas, *The International Law of Investment Claims* (CUP 2009) 712 (suggesting that, where a contractual forum selection clause and a treaty arbitration clause conflict, the earlier in time should prevail) with Stephen Donnelly, 'Conflicting Forum-Selection Agreements in Treaty and Contract' (2020) 69 International & Comparative Law Quarterly 759 (suggesting that tribunals should decide on a case-by-case basis whether the forum selection clause amounts to a waiver of the investor's right to recourse to an investment tribunal).

[84] *Garanti Koza LLP v Turkmenistan*, ICSID Case No ARB/11/20, Award (19 December 2016) [331]–[332].

[85] *Noble* (n 67) [54].

[86] *Toto* (n 75) [102].

[87] *Noble* (n 67) [82] ('Apart from the fact that there is no reason why one should not regard commercial acts as being in principle also attributable, it is difficult to define whether a particular act is governmental'); *Toto* (n

Not all tribunals, however, are as willing to attribute commercial contracts entered into by sub-state entities to the state. For example, in *Impregilo v Pakistan*,[88] the tribunal, relying on the annulment in the *Compañia de Aguas del Aconquija SA and Vivendi Universal SA v Argentina* case,[89] held:

> Much of Impregilo's argument on this issue rested upon international law principles of state responsibility and attribution. However, a clear distinction exists between the responsibility of a State for the conduct of an entity that breaches a municipal law contract (ie Impregilo's Contract Claims). As noted by the *ad hoc* Committee in its decision on annulment in *Compañia de Aguas del Aconquija and Vivendi Universal v Argentine Republic*, the international law rules on State responsibility and attribution apply to the former, but not the latter.[90]

Although there appears to be a slowly emerging consensus on the law applicable to umbrella clause claims and the effect of those clauses on forum selection clauses, there has been a notable trend toward the elimination of umbrella clauses in newly concluded treaties.[91] Still, in light of sunset clauses and therefore the longevity of investment treaties, umbrella clause claims and the associated questions are likely to come up often in the foreseeable future.

VI. European Union Law as Applicable Law

Of particular interest and some controversy of late is the role of European Union law (EU law) as applicable law in investor-state cases. Awareness of this peaked with the rise of an ever-greater number of so-called intra-EU cases, ie, treaty disputes between a national of one EU member state and another EU member state. The European Commission and the Court of Justice of the European Union (CJEU) have introduced EU law into debates over applicable law in two distinct respects: the law applicable to the validity of the investment treaty invoked and the availability of EU law as a defence to a claim arising out of a treaty or international law more generally.

75) [53] ('the CEPG, with projects funded by the State budget, and in charge of implementing the decisions of the Council of Ministers, exercised Lebanese governmental authority when it entered into the Contract with Toto. As also confirmed by Article 5 of the ILC Draft Articles, its conduct has to be considered as an act of the Lebanese state').

[88] *Impregilo SpA v Pakistan*, ICSID Case No ARB/03/3, Decision on Jurisdiction (22 April 2005).

[89] *Compañia de Aguas del Aconquija SA and Vivendi Universal SA v Argentina*, Decision on Annulment (3 July 2002) [96].

[90] *Impregilo* (n 88) [210].

[91] See Raúl Pereira de Souza Fleury 'Umbrella Clauses: A Trend Towards Its Elimination' (2015) 31 Arbitration International 679.

A. EU Law as the Law Applicable to the Validity of an Investment Treaty

In the landmark *Achmea* judgment, the CJEU held that ISDS provisions in intra-EU BITs are incompatible with the autonomy of EU law. Though the Commission, intervening in many intra-EU proceedings, had advanced a range of legal arguments for treating intra-EU BITs as invalid and unenforceable, the Court in *Achmea* relied specifically on Article 344 of the Treaty on the Functioning of the European Union (TFEU),[92] by which member states undertook not to submit disputes between themselves over the interpretation or application of EU law to any method of settlement other than those provided for in the EU treaties. But the Court placed greatest emphasis on TFEU Article 267,[93] which enables courts and tribunals within the EU legal order to refer questions of the interpretation and validity of EU law to the CJEU when necessary in deciding cases pending before them.[94] The highest national court in a member state to which a case may be brought not only may, but must, make a so-called preliminary reference to the CJEU whenever it finds the meaning or validity of an EU law provision to be unclear or unsettled.[95] But because the Court has long since held that international arbitral tribunals seated in a member state do not qualify as courts or tribunals of that state, within the meaning of Article 267,[96] such tribunals are ineligible to make such references.[97] As a consequence they run the risk, in the eyes of the Commission and CJEU, of misconstruing or misapplying EU law, without any possibility of correction, to the detriment of the uniform understanding of EU law and thereby the EU legal order's autonomy.[98]

In sum, the CJEU determined that, in light of this risk, intra-EU BITs must be viewed as incompatible with the EU Treaties and may not be given effect.[99] In the CJEU's view, due to the invalidity of intra-EU BITs, arbitral tribunals established under those treaties lack jurisdiction and the awards they render are subject to set aside and

[92] ibid [32].

[93] ibid [37], [43]–[49].

[94] Consolidated Version of the Treaty on the Functioning of the European Union 2012 OJ C 326/47, 164, art 267: The Court of Justice of the European Union shall have jurisdiction to give preliminary rulings concerning:

(a) the interpretation of the Treaties;
(b) the validity and interpretation of acts of the institutions, bodies, offices or agencies of the Union;

Where such a question is raised before any court or tribunal of a Member State, that court or tribunal may, if it considers that a decision on the question is necessary to enable it to give judgment, request the Court to give a ruling thereon.

Where any such question is raised in a case pending before a court or tribunal of a Member State against whose decisions there is no judicial remedy under national law, that court or tribunal shall bring the matter before the Court.If such a question is raised in a case pending before a court or tribunal of a Member State with regard to a person in custody, the Court of Justice of the European Union shall act with the minimum of delay. *Achmea* (n 92) [60].ibid, in custody, the CJEU shall act with the minimum of delay.

[95] Case C-416/17 *European Commission v France*, ECLI:EU:C:2018:811 (4 October 2018) [108], [114] (finding for the first time a violation of TFEU art 267(3) by a national court of last instance).

[96] Case C-102/81 *Nordsee Deutsche Hochseefischerei GmbH v Reederei Mond Hochseefischerei Nordstern AG & Co KG and Reederei Friedrich Busse Hochseefischerei Nordstern AG & Co KG*, ECLI:EU:C:1982:107 (23 March 1982) [13].

[97] *Achmea* (n 92) [49].

[98] ibid [42], [49], [58].

[99] ibid [60].

unenforceable.[100] The CJEU later extended this ruling to both intra-EU investment claims arising out of the ECT[101] and intra-EU investment claims arising out of a commercial contract.[102] In the wake of these rulings, EU member state courts have both annulled intra-EU awards[103] and denied their recognition and enforcement.[104]

With one notable and recent exception,[105] investor-state tribunals—both before and after *Achmea*—have uniformly rejected the CJEU's reasoning. In their view, the jurisdiction of an arbitral tribunal is determined exclusively in accordance with the rules and principles of the regime from which it derives its authority and under which they operate, be it a BIT, FTA, or the ECT, almost as if the treaty in question were the tribunal's constitution.[106] Viewed through this lens, the jurisdiction of an intra-EU tribunal to adjudicate a claim falling within the scope of the treaty is not subject to question. For example, the *Eskosol* tribunal determined that a tribunal constituted under the ECT is not bound by principles of EU law (including those expressed by the CJEU in the *Achmea* case), which represents a different international law regime, just as the CJEU is not bound by the decisions of tribunals constituted under the ECT.[107]

B. EU Law as a Defence to Liability

The conflict between an international arbitration agreement and EU law has not only a jurisdictional, but also a substantive dimension. The CJEU and member state courts argue that EU law, as the product of a treaty among the member states, necessarily forms part of international law and is therefore applicable to any issue in BIT, FTA, and ECT proceedings that is properly governed by international law.[108] If EU law constitutes international law, it can supply the substantive legal norm under which an international investment dispute will be decided. Some intra-EU tribunals have accordingly held that substantive protections of EU law should 'apply to the merits of a dispute brought under EU law',[109] and that it is within the 'jurisdiction [of an intra-EU arbitral

[100] ibid.

[101] Case C-741/19 *Moldova v Komstroy LLC*, ECLI:EU:C:2021:655 (2 September 2021) [65]–[66].

[102] Case C-109/20 *Poland v PL Holdings Sàrl*, ECLI:EU:C:2021:321 (6 October 2021) [85].

[103] Cour d'appel [CA] [regional court of appeal] Paris, 10 January 2023, 3/2023.

[104] See, eg, Bundesgerichtshof [BGH] [Federal Court of Justice] 31 October 2018, I ZB 2/15; Cour d'appel [CA] Bruxelles (17th ch), 2016/AR/393, 12 March 2019.

[105] *Green Power and SCE v Spain*, SCC Case No V2016/135, Award (16 June 2022).

[106] See, eg, *UP and CD Holding International v Hungary*, ICSID Case No ARB/13/35, Decision on Annulment (11 August 2021); *Vattenfall AB and others v Germany*, ICSID Case No ARB/12/12, Decision on the *Achmea* Issue (31 August 2018); *RREEF Infrastructure (GP) Ltd and others v Spain*, ICSID Case No ARB/13/30, Decision on Annulment (10 June 2022); *Cube Infrastructure Fund SICAV and others v Spain*, ICSID Case No ARB/15/20, Decision on Annulment (28 March 2022).

[107] *Eskosol SpA in liquidazione v Italy*, ICSID Case No ARB/15/50, Decision on Termination Request and Intra-EU Objection (7 May 2019) [181]–[184].

[108] See, eg, *Electrabel SA v Hungary*, ICSID Case No ARB/07/19, Decision on Jurisdiction, Applicable Law and Liability (30 November 2012) [4.126]; *Jürgen Wirtgen and others v Czech Republic*, PCA Case No 2014-03, Final Award (11 October 2017) [177]; *Eureko BV v Slovakia*, PCA Case No 2008-13 (26 October 2010) [283].

[109] *Antin Infrastructure Services Luxembourg Sàrl and Antin Energia Termosolar BV v Spain*, ICSID Case No ARB/13/31, Award (15 June 2018) [228].

tribunal] to consider EU law to the extent necessary for the resolution of the dispute under *international* law'.[110]

But the difficult question facing tribunals is not whether claimants may invoke investment claims arising under EU law in intra-EU arbitrations. There is no reason why they should not be able to do so. The real issue is whether an EU member state may invoke substantive EU law as a defence to an otherwise valid investment treaty claim. In the many intra-EU disputes that have arisen, the respondent member state, supported by the European Commission, has sought to justify what would otherwise be an investment treaty violation on the ground that the allegedly wrongful measure was taken under compulsion of EU law.

Arbitral tribunals have not reacted uniformly to these assertions. A leading award is *Electrabel SA v Hungary*,[111] in which Hungary, under compulsion of EU law, changed the law that had conferred substantial benefits on the Belgian investor. The Commission had ordered Hungary to make the change because the law as it stood represented an illegal state aid under EU law. The tribunal first recalled that it was operating under the aegis of the ECT and the ICSID Convention, not EU law,[112] and that under Article 26 of the ECT and Article 42 of the ICSID Convention, it was 'placed in a public international law context and not a national or regional context'.[113] On that basis, it held that the validity of the ECT, as applied to intra-EU disputes, is governed by international law, not EU law. Like virtually all tribunals, it saw no reason for questioning the applicability of the ECT to intra-EU disputes or the jurisdiction of tribunals to entertain intra-EU claims.

However, the *Electrabel* tribunal then turned to the relationship between international and EU law from a substantive law rather than a jurisdictional viewpoint. It noted that EU law is a *sui generis* legal order in that it forms part both of the Hungarian legal order and of international law.[114] It based its view that EU law constituted international law on the fact that it is rooted in international treaties, such as the TEU and the TFEU.[115] It also refused in this connection to distinguish between the EU Treaties, on the one hand, and secondary legislation (notably regulations and directives), on the other,[116] and further held that the fact that EU law is also applied within the national legal order of EU member states does not deprive it of its international legal nature.[117]

In fact, the *Electrabel* tribunal discerned no conflict between Hungarian law and Hungary's obligations under the ECT, and Electrabel's claim was accordingly unsuccessful. However, counsel, supposing the tribunal might find them to be incompatible, had thoroughly addressed the question of the relationship between the two bodies of law in the event of a conflict between them. Thus, even though the hierarchical relationship

[110] *9REN Holding Sàrl v Spain*, ICSID Case No ARB/15/15, Award (31 May 2019) [172] (emphasis in the original).
[111] *Electrabel* (n 108).
[112] ibid [4.111].
[113] ibid [4.112].
[114] ibid [4.117]–[4.119].
[115] ibid [4.120].
[116] ibid [4.122].
[117] ibid [4.124].

between the ECT and EU law was irrelevant to the outcome of the case, the tribunal chose to address it. The tribunal began by acknowledging the necessity to find a proper balance between two important and potentially competing values: the treaty-based rights of a foreign investor under international law, on the one hand, and market integration as an essential purpose of EU law, on the other.[118] The tribunal ultimately concluded that, if conflict could not be avoided, priority had to be given to EU law. It so held for at least two reasons. The first, which is peculiar to the ECT as an investment agreement, is that the EU acceded to the ECT in the form of a so-called regional economic integration organization (REIO), which the tribunal understood to mean that the ECT had no application to disputes between investors and states internal to the EU.[119] In a sense, it considered that EU investors could have no legitimate expectation of protection under the ECT against measures taken by an EU member state in compliance with EU law.[120]

The tribunal also reasoned on the basis of a provision of EU law, TFEU Article 351, which provides that agreements that a member state may have entered into prior to accession do not lapse merely because they are inconsistent with EU law (though member states are expected to take action to eliminate the inconsistency).[121] From that provision, the tribunal drew the inference that, while treaties a member state concludes before accession survive, treaties a member state enters into after accession do not.[122] Since Hungary had already acceded to the EU when it subscribed to the ECT, any inconsistency between the ECT and EU law must therefore be resolved in favour of EU law.[123] The result is somewhat surprising in that TFEU Article 307 is law internal to the EU (which is itself an ECT member) and Hungary, and under Article 27 of the VCLT, a state may not invoke its internal law to defeat its obligations under an international treaty.[124] It is further surprising because the ECT contains its own supremacy clause. ECT Article 16 provides that nothing in the ECT shall be construed to derogate from rights established by a prior treaty.[125]

Most tribunals, however, have parted ways with the *Electrabel* tribunal. For example, in the *SolEs Badajoz* case, likewise an ECT dispute, the tribunal stated that:

> even assuming that an EU instrument that is derived from an EU treaty (such as a decision of the European Commission) could be regarded as international law for

[118] ibid [4.113].
[119] ibid [4.142].
[120] ibid [4.141].
[121] ibid [4.180].
[122] ibid [4.188].
[123] ibid [4.187].
[124] Compare ibid [4.189] ('[TFEU Article 351] precludes inconsistent pre-existing treaty rights of EU Member States and their own nationals against other EU Member States') with VCLT art 27 ('A party may not invoke the provisions of its internal law as justification for its failure to perform a treaty').
[125] ECT art 16:

> Where two or more Contracting Parties have entered into a prior international agreement, or enter into a subsequent international agreement, ...
> (1) nothing in ... this Treaty shall be construed to derogate from any provision of such terms of the other agreement or from any right to dispute resolution with respect thereto under that agreement; and
> (2) nothing in such terms of the other agreement shall be construed to derogate from ... this Treaty or from any right to dispute resolution with respect thereto under this Treaty,
> where any such provision is more favourable to the Investor or Investment.

> purposes of Article 26(6) of the ECT, it follows from Article 16 of the ECT that the provisions of [a European Commission] decision could replace an investor protection provision of the ECT as a rule of decision only if the [European Commission] decision contained investor protection provisions that were more favorable to investors than are the provisions of Part III of the ECT. No such provision has been identified in this proceeding.[126]

In these awards, tribunals have also ruled that Article 16 of the ECT, as *lex specialis*, prevails over EU law in the event of conflict between them.[127] Thus, even if EU law is viewed as a species of international law, it cannot operate to lower the level of protection afforded by the applicable treaty or by general international law.

Similarly, in the *RREEF* arbitration, the tribunal held flatly that, in the event of a conflict between the demands of public international law and those of EU law, the former public international law must prevail: 'EU law does not and cannot "trump" public international law.'[128] Other tribunals have reached the same result by distinguishing between general public international law, on the one hand, and EU law, on the other, and finding the notion of 'principles of international law', within the meaning of ECT Article 26(6), to consist of general principles rather than those of a particular treaty regime.[129]

One way in which tribunals have avoided the difficulty altogether is by treating questions of EU law, by definition, as questions of fact rather than law.[130] Under this approach, EU law does not supply the substantive legal norms under which a dispute will be decided, but functions merely as a datum. For example, in *Cube*, the tribunal found:

> While the EU treaties are of course international agreements made within the framework of, and governed by, public international law, they do not thereby become 'principles of international law'.[131] ... Under the provisions concerning the applicable law that are binding on this Tribunal, Spanish law and EU law are relevant only as facts in the light of which the rights and duties of the Parties under the ECT and international law are to be determined. Thus, for example, the provisions on EU law concerning State aid are not applied by this Tribunal, nor does the Tribunal make any decision on their interpretation. They are relevant only as part of the factual matrix, and in this

126 *SolEs Badajoz GmbH v Spain*, ICSID Case No ARB/15/38, Award (31 July 2019) [165].

127 *OperaFund Eco-Invest SICAV PLC and Schwab Holding AG v Spain*, ICSID Case No ARB/15/36, Award (6 September 2019) [329].

128 *RREEF Infrastructure (GP) Ltd and RREEF Pan-European Infrastructure Two Lux Sàrl v Spain*, ICSID Case No ARB/13/30, Decision on Jurisdiction (6 June 2016) [184].

129 Vattenfall (n 106) [133]; *Eskosol* (n 107) [121].

130 *AES Summit Generation Limited and AES-Tisza Erömü Kft v Hungary*, ICSID Case No ARB/07/22, Award (23 September 2010) [7.6.6]; *Micula* (n 81) [328]; *Wirtgen* (n 108) 177]; *Cube Infrastructure Fund SICAV and others v Spain*, ICSID Case No ARB/15/20, Decision on Jurisdiction, Liability and Partial Decision on Quantum (19 February 2019) [160].

131 *Cube* (n 130) [158].

case particularly as part of the factual basis for determinations of how the Claimants could expect to be treated in respect of their power plants in Spain.[132]

Similarly, in the first *Micula v Romania* arbitration,[133] the tribunal noted that 'EU law forms part of the "factual matrix" of the case'.[134]

The prevailing view among tribunals today is not only that intra-EU claims arising under BITs or FTAs are subject to adjudication under those treaties, notwithstanding the opposition to that view of the European Commission and the CJEU, but also that, in the event of an irreconcilable conflict between investment treaty law and EU law, the former must prevail. That said, the fate of an intra-EU award ultimately depends on the seat of arbitration and the place where recognition or enforcement of the resulting award is sought. Post-*Achmea*, intra-EU awards rendered on the territory of a member state have been consistently annulled by the competent member state court[135] and denied enforcement by member state courts to which they are brought for enforcement.[136] However, they have been enforced in courts of states outside the EU, including the United States.[137] What remains to be seen, among other things, is whether an intra-EU award that would otherwise be enforced in the United States might be enforced despite its having been set aside at the seat.[138]

Recently, Spain has begun seeking injunctions in European courts, typically courts of the home state of the investor (notably Luxembourg and the Netherlands) to bar enforcement of adverse ICSID awards. No such relief is needed when the enforcement action is in a member state, since in the wake of *Achmea* the courts of those states decline to enforce such awards in any case. However, matters are different when enforcement is sought outside the EU, as in the *9Ren*,[139] *Antin*,[140] *Cube*,[141] and *NextEra*[142] cases.[143] In response, some of the award creditors have successfully obtained anti-anti-suit injunctions in the DC District Court.[144] It remains to be seen, however, if and when the

[132] ibid [160]. See also *AES Summit* (n 130) [7.6.6]; *Wirtgen* (n 108) [177]; *Eurus Energy Holdings Corporation v Spain*, ICSID Case No ARB/16/4, Decision on Jurisdiction and Liability (17 March 2021) [232].

[133] *Micula* (n 81).

[134] ibid [328].

[135] See n 104.

[136] See n 105. See also Marc Bungenberg, Andrés E Alvarado-Garzón, and Bianca Böhme, 'Recognition and Enforcement of ICSID Convention Awards' in Katia Fach Gómez and Catharine Titi (eds), *The Award in Investment Arbitration* (OUP 2024).

[137] See, eg, *Micula v Romania*, 2022 WL 18356669 (DDC 22 December 2022).

[138] For example, the DC District Court stayed enforcement proceedings until resolution of set-aside proceedings in *Novenergia II—Energy & Environment (SCA) v Spain*, 2020 WL 417794 (DDC 27 January 2020). The *Novenergia II* award has since been set aside, Hovrätt [HovR] [Court of Appeals] 2022-12-13 T 4658-18 (Sweden).

[139] *9Ren* (n 111).

[140] *Antin* (n 109).

[141] *Cube* (n 130).

[142] *NextEra Energy Global Holdings BV, and NextEra Energy Spain Holdings BV v Spain*, ICSID Case No ARB/14/11, Final Award (31 May 2019).

[143] Lisa Bohmer, 'Dispute over Enforcement of Intra-EU ICSID Award against Spain Heats up, as Both Parties to NextEra v Spain Arbitration Seek Anti-Suit Injunctions' *Investment Arbitration Report* (13 January 2023); Damien Charlotin, 'Another ECT Award-Creditor Seeks Anti-Anti-Suit Injunction from US Courts, in Reply to Spain's Efforts to Thwart World-Wide Enforcement of the Award' *Investment Arbitration Reporter* (13 January 2023).

[144] *NextEra Energy Global Holdings BV and NextEra Energy Spain Holdings BV v Spain, 2023* WL 2016932 (DDC 15 February 2023); *9REN Holdings Sàrl v Spain*, 2023 WL 2016933 (DDC 15 February 2023).

CJEU will get involved and, more generally, how the impasses, should they persist, will be overcome.

VII. National Law as Applicable Law

A. Host State Law

Given that investment agreements typically identify both international and host state law as the applicable law in disputes arising under those agreements, attention must be paid to their respective spheres of application. In early case law, host state law was deemed to carry primary weight, with international law serving only filling in gaps or serving a corrective function.[145] Once again,[146] this may be due to the fact that the early ICSID cases entailed contract-based, not treaty-based, claims. It is now assumed that international law and host state law apply conjunctively, though each applies only to issues to which it is applicable. As the ad hoc committee decision in *Wena Hotels v Egypt* put it, where the parties have not reached an agreement on the applicable law, 'each ICSID tribunal should have discretion to decide whether any rules of international law are directly applicable, without any requirement of initial scrutiny into the law of the host State'.[147] However, they 'will not have complete discretion in selecting international and domestic law [as they] will have to identify the questions to which the respective legal systems apply'.[148] In other words, domestic and international law are to be applied in consideration of the legal issues at hand viewed in their proper legal context.[149] As will be clearly seen below, the spheres of application of international law and host state law are indeed radically different.

It goes nearly without saying that the compatibility of a state measure with the applicable treaty is strictly governed by that treaty, supplemented as needed by international law. It would be utterly unworkable for that question to be determined by host state law, as the measure under challenge is precisely a host state measure. Thus, even if host state law contains certain protections against uncompensated expropriation, the

[145] See, eg, *Amco v Indonesia*, ICSID Case No ARB/81/1, Decision on the Application for Annulment (16 May 1986) [19].

[146] See text to nn 19–23.

[147] *Wena Hotels Ltd v Egypt*, ICSID Case No ARB/98/4, Decision on Annulment (8 December 2000, 5 February 2002) [40]. See Emmanuel Gaillard and Yas Banifatemi, 'The Meaning of "and" in Article 42(1), Second Sentence, of the Washington Convention: The Role of International Law in the ICSID Choice of Law Process' (2003) 18(2) ICSID Review 375.

[148] Kriebaum (n 20) 896.

[149] See, eg, *Compañía de Aguas del Aconquija SA and Vivendi Universal SA v Argentina*, ICSID Case No ARB/97/3, Award (21 November 2000); *CMS Gas Transmission Co v Argentina*, ICSID Case No ARB/01/8, Award (12 May 2005); *LG&E Energy Corp, LG&E Capital Corp, and LG&E International Inc v Argentina*, ICSID Case No ARB/02/1, Award (25 July 2007); *Ioannis Kardassopoulus v Georgia*, ICSID Case No ARB/05/18, Award (3 March 2010); *El Paso Energy International Co v Argentina*, ICSID Case No ARB/03/15, Award (31 October 2011); *Vestey Group Ltd v Venezuela*, ICSID Case No ARB.06/4, Award (15 April 2016); *Phillip Morris Brands Sàrl, Philip Morris Products SA and Abal Hermanos SA v Uruguay*, ICSID Case No ARB/10/7, Award (8 July 2016).

question of whether an expropriation occurred will be resolved in treaty-based investment arbitration under international law and not host state law. Unsurprisingly, the situation is otherwise in contract-based and statute-based investment claims, which are subject to the *lex causae*.

That international law alone governs liability under an investment treaty is fully in keeping with the VCLT, according to which a state may not defend against a claim under a treaty by relying on its internal law,[150] including the law pursuant to which the state took the measure whose conformity with the treaty is called into question.[151] The same may be said about all liability-related issues more generally, not least the question of remedies in case of breach.[152] But certain issues that regularly arise in investment arbitration can, by their nature, only properly be governed by host state law rather than international law.

1. The Definition of the Investment at Issue

A vital issue regularly viewed as governed by host state law is the existence, meaning, nature, and scope of a putative investment.[153] This makes eminent sense, for the role of investment treaties is to protect investments, not to determine the content of the investment. There is no contradiction between the notion of 'investment' being governed by the terms of the treaty and international law, on the one hand, and the definition of a particular investment for which protection is claimed being governed by host state law, on the other. In any bilateral or multilateral treaty, it is necessary to establish uniformly the treaty's scope of application. A treaty by which states undertake to protect investments must in principle establish a unitary principle of what constitutes an investment. But investments obviously differ in nature and scope, and it is plainly for host states to determine the dimensions of any given investment.[154] Thus, while an activity or enterprise will be protected under an investment treaty only to the extent that it falls within the treaty's definition of an 'investment', the metes and bounds of that investment, including the investor's rights and obligations in connection with its investment,[155] are in principle a matter of host state law, and it is only the investment as defined by host state law that investment arbitration is meant to protect.[156] The domestic law relevant to the dispute in this respect may be, depending on the circumstances, the law in force at the

[150] VCLT art 27 ('A party may not invoke the provisions of its internal law as justification for its failure to perform a treaty').

[151] Hege Elisabeth Kjos, *Applicable Law in Investor-State Arbitration: The Interplay between National and International Law* (OUP 2013) 5.

[152] Newcombe and Paradell (n 15) 99.

[153] ibid 93–94.

[154] *Barcelona Traction* (n 50) 234 (Separate Opinion of Judge Morelli [translation]) ('There is nothing abnormal in this reference of an international rule to the law of a given State ... In reality, no subordination of international responsibility, as such, to the provisions of municipal law is involved; the point is rather that the very existence of the international obligation depends on a state of affairs created in municipal law, though this is so not by virtue of municipal law but, on the contrary, by virtue of the international rule itself, which to that end refers to the law of the State').

[155] Newcombe and Paradell (n 15) 92.

[156] Christoph Schreuer, 'Interaction of International Tribunals and Domestic Courts in Investment Law' in Arthur W Rovine (ed), *Contemporary Issues in International Arbitration and Mediation: The Fordham Papers* (Brill 2011) 71, 87.

time the investment was made or a later date. To determine this, the place to start is the treaty itself.[157]

2. Lawfulness of the Investment

It follows from what has been said that host state law should also determine whether an investment is lawful, should that become an issue. In fact, it can easily become an issue because many investment agreements specify that, in order to enjoy protection, an investment must be a lawful one,[158] and some tribunals have imposed a requirement of lawfulness on an investment even though the applicable treaty does not so provide.[159] Moreover, the lawfulness of an investment is increasingly viewed as a jurisdictional, not simply a merits, issue. This seems justifiable. It is well established that, unless a tribunal has before it what qualifies an investment, it lacks jurisdiction to decide the dispute surrounding the putative investment.[160] Once the presence of an investment is treated as a jurisdictional issue, it is not a giant step to say that only a lawful investment will count as such. In sum, there is no question that an investment's lawfulness is determined by the law of the state where it is made.

The only possible exception arises when an investor has engaged in corruption. It is unlikely that tribunal will feel bound by the definition of corruption under host state law. There is unquestionably emerging a truly international conception of what does and does not constitute corruption for purposes of an investor's entitlement to redress.[161]

3. Determination of National Territory

Finally, host state law, at least in principle, determines whether an investment was made on that state's territory, as required in order for it to be protected under a treaty, though international law may have something important to say about that.[162] A tribunal will disregard the law of a state in regard to the determination of its territorial boundaries only in the unusual circumstance in which international law or public policy so dictates.[163]

[157] Newcombe and Paradell (n 15) 98.

[158] Zachary Douglas, 'The Plea of Illegality in Investment Treaty Arbitration' (2014) 29 ICSID Review 155, 172–77.

[159] *Saluka Investments BV v Czech Republic*, PCA Case No 2001-04, Partial Award (17 March 2006) [204]; *Plama Consortium Ltd v Bulgaria*, ICSID Case No ARB/03/24, Award (27 August 2008) [138]–[140]; *Fraport AG Frankfurt Airport Services Worldwide v Philippines II*, ICSID Case No ARB/11/12, Award (10 December 2014) [328]; *South American Silver Ltd v Bolivia*, PCA Case No 2013-15, Award (30 August 2018) [469].

[160] CL Lim, Jean Ho, and Martins Paparinskis, *International Investment Law and Arbitration: Commentary, Awards and Other Materials* (2nd edn, CUP 2021) 276.

[161] See generally Domitille Baizeau and Richard H Kreindler (eds), *Addressing Issues of Corruption in Commercial and Investment Arbitration* (ICC 2015).

[162] *Oschadbank v Russia*, PCA Case No 2016-14, Award (26 November 2018), set aside Cour d'appel [CA] [regional court of appeal], Paris, ch 16, 31 March 2021, reversed Cour de cassation [Cass] [Supreme Court for judicial matters] 1e civ, 7 December 2022; *Limited Liability Company Lugzor and others v Russia*, PCA Case No 2015-29, Press Release (PCA 2019).

[163] Newcombe and Paradell (n 15) 97.

In several cases arising under the Ukraine–Russia BIT,[164] Ukrainian nationals had made investments in Crimea prior to Russia's annexation of that region of Ukraine in March 2014. Following the annexation, the Ukrainians initiated claims of expropriation. To defeat the tribunals' jurisdiction to decide those claims, Russia advanced two arguments having a distinct territorial dimension. According to one, whether a claimant is a foreign investor must be determined as of the time the investment is made, the reason being that the sole purpose of a BIT is to induce foreign investment and because the investors were not foreign when they made their investments, they are not entitled to protection under the BIT. Russia argued that the fact that the claimants, though not foreign when they made their investments, had become foreign vis-à-vis the place of investment at the time the alleged violation was committed was of no consequence. In still other words, according to Russia, a country's borders are fixed at the time a BIT is concluded and no account should be taken of territorial changes that might occur thereafter.

Second, Russia argued that even if the claimants could be considered foreign by virtue of the fact that the alleged violation was committed on Russian territory, jurisdiction was still lacking. This was due to the fact that in Russia's view, despite the annexation, Crimea had not become Russian territory. As evidence of that, Russia cited the fact that Ukraine, as well as many other nations, had declared the annexation invalid.

The tribunals properly accepted neither of Russia's arguments. First, they rightly concluded that inducement of foreign investment is not a BIT's sole purpose. BITs likewise have as their purpose protection of investments that are foreign when the alleged breach occurs. In other words, BITs serve not only to induce foreign investments but also to protect investments that are foreign at the time of breach. It did not matter that the Ukrainians had initially made their investment in Ukraine.[165] Even more directly relevant for present purposes was the tribunals' response to the assertion that Crimea had not become Russian territory at the time of the alleged breach. None of the tribunals found it difficult, under the geopolitical circumstances, to consider Russia estopped from disclaiming ownership of Ukraine.[166] The tribunals felt free to determine for themselves that, for purposes of the BIT, Crimea did not, as Russia argued, lay outside the borders of Russia.[167] They independently determined, again strictly for purposes of applying the BIT, that as of 2014 a Ukrainian national whose investment is situated in Crimea after 2014 has an investment situated in Russia and is entitled to protection under of the Ukraine–Russia BIT. The studiously avoided making any pronouncement about the legality or illegality of the annexation.[168] Without exception,

[164] *Oschadbank* (n 162); *PJSC CB PrivatBank and Finland Co Finilon v Russia*, PCA Case No 2015-21, Interim Award (Corrected) (27 March 2017) [195]; *Aeroport Belbek LLC and Igor Valerievich Kolomoisky v Russia*, PCA Case No 2015-07, Procedural Order 11 (21 December 2020); *Stabil LLC and others v Russia*, PCA Case No 2015-35, Award on Jurisdiction (26 June 2017); *Everest Estate LLC and others v Russia*, PCA Case No 2015-36, Press Release on Tribunal's Decision on Jurisdiction (PCA 2017); *PJSC Ukrnafta v Russia*, PCA Case No 2015-34, Press Release (PCA 2016).

[165] *Stabil* (n 164) [189]–[193].

[166] ibid [132]–[134].

[167] ibid [191].

[168] ibid [103].

Russia's attempts to have these awards annulled on jurisdictional grounds among others were unsuccessful. None of the courts allowed Russia, under the circumstances, to be the judge of its own national boundaries.

B. Home State Law: The Nationality of the Putative Investor

There remains one issue to which, not host state law, but rather home state law, is applicable. In order to avail itself of the protection offered by a BIT, a claimant, whether a natural or juridical person, must have the nationality of the host state's co-contracting state.[169] It must, in other words, have the requisite nationality. Otherwise, it is not a qualifying 'investor' under the applicable treaty. Sensibly enough, the question whether a person has the requisite nationality is governed by the law of the state whose nationality is in issue.[170] This does not mean, however, that a tribunal cannot, in a rare circumstance, scrutinize a state's certification of nationality. That has exceptionally occurred.[171]

VIII. Conclusion

Among the ways in which international commercial and investment arbitration differ most saliently is in terms of the law applicable to the merits of a dispute. In commercial arbitration, the applicable law is almost always one body of national law or another, whether the law the parties designated in a contractual choice of law clause or the law a tribunal, in the absence of party choice, considers most appropriate to apply under its preferred choice of law reasoning. Parties can, but rarely do, select international law or non-state law, much less recourse to decision-making *ex aequo et bono*, to govern the merits of their eventual disputes. Only rarely will a tribunal, in the absence of a choice of law clause, have recourse to those sources of applicable law. The applicable law in treaty-based ISDS is distinctly different. The merits of the dispute will, first and foremost, be governed by the terms of the applicable treaty, whether the treaty expressly so provides or not. However, the treaty terms will invariably be supplemented, as needed, by principles of international law.

While national law does not in principle govern the merits of a treaty-based investor-state dispute, it does have particular functions to perform. In principle, whether the claimant has home state nationality, as required under a BIT, will in principle be determined in accordance with home state law. It is highly improbable that a tribunal would look anywhere else to determine whether the claimant has the requisite nationality.

Host state law has a wider scope of application. Most obviously, host state law will determine the contours and content of the property or other right that, in the claimant's

[169] ICSID Convention art 25.
[170] Lim, Ho, and Paparinskis (n 160) 306–7, 316.
[171] ibid 307.

view, has been adversely affected by the challenged measure. Also, generally speaking, in order to earn protection under an investment treaty, an investment must be a lawful one and that too, in principle, is a matter subject to host state law. We may also assume that the host state will have a major voice in determining the metes and bounds of national territory though, as the Crimea cases show, international law may well have something to say on the subject.

Complicating matters somewhat is the umbrella clause by virtue of which states agree in their investment treaties to respect contract and other obligations they have incurred vis-à-vis investors. However, whether or not tribunals regard the contract claim as having been converted into a treaty claim and become subject to adjudication pursuant to the treaty, the parties' contractual and rights and obligations continue to be governed exclusively by the contract, including its choice of law clause if any. Thus, umbrella clauses do not alter the law applicable to the claims they cover. Those claims are fully governed, even in an investor-state proceeding, by the terms of the contract. According to the majority of tribunals, if the contract in question contains a forum selection clause, claims arising under it do not become subject to the jurisdiction of the arbitral tribunal constituted pursuant to the treaty. Under this view, the forum selection clause is entitled to as much respect by a tribunal as any other terms of the contract.

The role of European Union law has come to complicate still further the question of the applicable law in ISDS. The Commission and CJEU do not maintain that EU law governs the merits of claims that are advanced in investor-state arbitration. But they do maintain that a member state may defeat an otherwise valid investment claim on the ground that the challenged measure is mandated by EU law. To that extent that is allowed, EU law will very much have become part of the law applicable in investor-state arbitration. This, as seen, is a proposition that the great majority of intra-EU tribunals have rejected.

Of course, the EU challenge to ISDS, and to intra-EU disputes in particular, is more basic than that. The Commission and CJEU maintain that intra-EU BITs are altogether invalid under EU law, that intra-EU tribunals accordingly lack jurisdiction and that intra-EU awards must be annulled and denied recognition and enforcement. Under this view, intra-EU disputes may only be adjudicated in the national courts of the member states, which in turn may, as necessary, make preliminary references to the CJEU on the proper interpretation of EU law principles applicable to the protection of investors from one member state in the territory of another. In that scenario, the applicable law in intra-EU investment disputes is strictly the law of the EU. The position taken by the EU represents one of the most serious challenges to ISDS, particularly since it rests upon the potentially far-reaching notion of EU law autonomy. At the present time, considerations such as the seat and the place of enforcement of an arbitral award are decisive. This is because courts in the EU are—to put it mildly—vastly more likely than courts outside the EU to accept the EU's thesis.

13

The Interpretation of Exceptions

Ursula Kriebaum and Kilian Wagner

I. Introduction

International investment agreements (IIAs) increasingly include varying types of provisions understood as exception clauses. *Black's Law Dictionary* defines exception as something that is excluded from a rule's operation or alternatively as the retention of an existing right or interest by and for the grantor. In principle, exceptions aim at providing regulatory freedom for states to adopt public policy measures without incurring responsibility. States use exceptions to implement the well-accepted principle of their 'right to regulate' for the public good. They form a mechanism to balance economic interests and other policy objectives. Exception provisions are not a peculiarity of the investment law regime. For example, general and security exception clauses allow measures otherwise in conflict with the law of the World Trade Organization (WTO).[1] Restrictions and limitations allow interferences with human rights obligations under specified conditions and even permit derogations in exceptional situations.[2] The circumstances precluding wrongfulness fulfil a similar function in the absence of a particular treaty regime.[3]

Efforts to modernize investment agreements by taking account of societal concerns have led to a significant increase of provisions expressing the 'right to regulate'. They include declarations, interpretative statements, and exceptions.[4] While proponents of exceptions argue that they provide the necessary leeway for regulatory activity,[5] critics anticipate limits for the 'right to regulate'.[6] The case law shows difficulties in the application of exceptions concerning their effects and their role as a defence in arbitral proceedings.

[1] Susan Rose-Ackerman and Benjamin Billa, 'Treaties and National Security' (2008) 40 New York University Journal of International Law & Politics 437, 462ff.

[2] ibid 472ff; William A Schabas, *The European Convention on Human Rights: A Commentary* (2016) 401.

[3] Rose-Ackerman and Billa (n 1) 443ff.

[4] Catharine Titi, *The Right to Regulate in International Investment Law* (Hart/Nomos 2014) 104.

[5] Jürgen Kurtz, *The WTO and International Investment Law: Converging Systems* (CUP 2016) 175ff.

[6] Barton Legum and Ioana Petculescu, 'GATT Article XX and International Investment Law' in Roberto Echandi and Pierre Sauvé (eds), *Prospects in International Investment Law and Policy: World Trade Forum* (2013) 340, 352–54, 354–56, 361–62; Céline Lévesque, 'The Inclusion of GATT Article XX Exceptions in IIAs: A Potentially Risky Policy' in Roberto Echandi and Pierre Sauvé (eds), *Prospects in International Investment Law and Policy: World Trade Forum* (CUP 2013) 363, 364–67; Andrew Newcombe, 'General Exceptions in International Investment Agreements' in Marie-Claire Cordonier Segger and others (eds), *Sustainable Development in World Investment Law* (Kluwer 2011) 355, 366–69.

Ursula Kriebaum and Kilian Wagner, *The Interpretation of Exceptions* In: *The Award in International Investment Arbitration.*
Edited by: Katia Fach Gómez and Catharine Titi, Oxford University Press.
DOI: 10.1093/9780191975936.003.0013

Section II of this chapter presents key provisions operating as exceptions in IIAs, ie security and general exception clauses as well as provisions that have a similar function by limiting the scope of the treaty or individual provisions thereof. Section III explains the varying approaches of arbitral tribunals when interpreting exceptions. Despite similar wording of some types of exceptions, doctrinal considerations may warrant a different qualification of the legal effects of some provisions. Section IV discusses the blurred line between exception clauses and other increasingly used provisions embodying the 'right to regulate'. Finally, section V provides a summary and conclusions.

II. Types of Exception Clauses

Different types of exception clauses increasingly appear in IIAs. However, exception clauses do not form an essential part of IIAs and only few states have regularly included exceptions in traditional BITs.[7] Unlike the legal framework for investment protection, the spectrum of potential exception clauses varies significantly. Linguistically, the term 'exception' relates to the exception from a rule.[8] The normative effect of successfully invoking clauses understood as exceptions has been a contested matter. It is conceivable to conceptualize exceptions as carve-outs from treaties, derogations from substantive protection standards or justifications of interferences with guaranteed rights.[9] The characterization affects the interpretation and application, availability of other defences, as well as the burden of proof.[10] However, it may be questionable whether the effect of a clause serves as an appropriate parameter to distinguish between exception clauses. Interpretative results reached by a tribunal on a certain clause are not necessarily transferable to clauses in other treaties with different formulations. Interchangeably used designations for exceptions, such as 'non-precluded measures provisions'[11] or 'emergency exceptions' exacerbate interpretative challenges.[12]

Exceptions typically allow the pursuit of public policy objectives, so that an interference with substantive obligations does not amount to or justify a breach. Their objective allows to distinguish between clauses containing general policy goals, such

[7] eg the United States has a long tradition of including security exceptions in IIAs: Kenneth J Vandevelde, *US International Investment Agreements* (OUP 2009) 196ff.

[8] On the functioning of exceptions, see Jaap Hage, Antonia Waltermann, and Gustavo Arosemena, 'Exceptions in International Law' in Lorand Bartels and Federicca Paddeu (eds), *Exceptions in International Law* (OUP 2020) 11.

[9] For these concepts, see Caroline Henckels, 'Scope Limitation or Affirmative Defence' in Bartels and Paddeu (n 8) 363; Jorge E Viñuales, 'Seven Ways of Escaping a Rule—Of Exceptions and Their Avatars in International Law' 65, 66–78.

[10] Viñuales (n 9) 65.

[11] William Burke-White and Andreas von Staden, 'Investment Protection in Extraordinary Times: The Interpretation and Application of Non-Precluded Measures Provisions in Bilateral Investment Treaties' (2008) Virginia Journal of International Law 307; Prabhash Ranjan, '"Necessary" in Non-Precluded Measures Provisions in Bilateral Investment Treaties: The Indian Contribution' (2020) Netherlands International Law Review 473.

[12] Diane A Desierto, *Necessity and National Emergency Clauses: Sovereignty in Modern Treaty Interpretation* (Brill 2012); Andrea K Bjorklund, 'Emergency Exceptions' in Peter T Muchlinski, Federico Ortino, and Christoph Schreuer (eds), *The Oxford Handbook of International Investment Law* (OUP 2008) 549.

as the protection of life, public health, or the environment, and clauses containing security-related goals.[13] Additionally, a nexus requirement typically describes the relationship between the measure in question and the objective pursued. These range from loose formulations like 'for' or 'directed to' to a stricter 'necessary' requirement.[14]

Another possible distinction between different types of exceptions is their scope of application. While general exceptions are usually applicable to the entire treaty,[15] other types of exceptions only concern particular chapters, eg investor-state dispute settlement (ISDS), or certain substantive standards.[16] The following analysis will focus on security (A) and general exceptions (B) as well as similar mechanisms to limit the scope of the treaty or certain substantive standards (C).

A. Security Exceptions

Decisive and rapid action may be required in circumstances affecting a state's security interests even if these acts interfere with investors' rights. At the same time, the investment law regime seeks to protect investors especially under difficult circumstances, including emergencies or armed conflicts. Security exceptions allow for a measure that would otherwise breach substantive standards under certain conditions. William Burke-White and Andreas von Staden describe this effect as a reversion of the risk allocation established by an IIA:[17] 'NPM clauses ["Non-Precluded Measures clauses"] reallocate risks to investors, creating a less favourable legal regime for investors, but giving states considerable freedom of action to respond to exceptional threats'.[18]

States have recognized the need for a security exception for the first time in the negotiations for an international trade organization. Article XXI of the General Agreement on Tariffs and Trade (GATT) was the outcome of these deliberations at the advent of the Cold War.[19] Subsequently, the United States has included security exception in post-war friendship, commerce, and navigation treaties (FCN) which are the predecessors of their IIAs.[20] A number of IIAs follows either the GATT or the FCN model for security exception clauses.

Amid an increasing 'securitization' of international economic relations, the notion of security itself may prove a contentious issue.[21] While most treaties use the terms 'essential security interests' and 'public order', others include 'public security' or 'national

[13] Burke-White and von Staden (n 11) 332–36.
[14] ibid 342.
[15] Titi (n 4) 171.
[16] The prohibition of performance requirements is typically complemented by corresponding exceptions, see eg Agreement between the United States of America, the United Mexican States, and Canada (USMCA) (signed 30 November 2018, entry into force 1 July 2020) art 14.10(3).
[17] Burke-White and von Staden (n 11) 307, 314, 401–03.
[18] ibid 402.
[19] Kenneth J Vandevelde, *The First Bilateral Investment Treaties: US Postwar Friendship, Commerce, and Navigation Treaties* (OUP 2017) 146–54, 509–11.
[20] ibid 507–27.
[21] Benton Heath, 'The New National Security Challenge to the Economic Order' (2020) 129 Yale Law Journal 1020, 1044–45.

security'.[22] The notion of 'security' is dynamic and varies from state to state, subject to societal and technological developments.[23] Nevertheless, the level of discretion for the state in determining its security interests has become a contested affair. Some clauses contain so-called self-judging formulations linked to the nexus requirement, such as 'it considers necessary', to limit the reviewability of a measure.[24] Clauses modelled on Article XXI of the GATT follow this approach. However, they confine the concept of security to certain categories, such as situations of war or other emergencies in international relations.[25] Other security exceptions likewise frame the objective based on specific security-related situations, such as armed conflicts[26] and international peace and security.[27] While most security exceptions apply to the entire treaty, some are standard specific[28] or do not affect the rules on expropriations to provide at least a minimum level of protection in difficult times.[29]

B. General Exceptions

BITs rarely contain general exception clauses. In contrast, free trade agreements (FTAs) with investment chapters increasingly include general exceptions with objectives, such as the protection of life, health, morals, the environment, or natural resources.[30] The structure of Article XX of the GATT and Article XIV of the General Agreement on Trade in Services (GATS)[31] has served as a model subject to alterations concerning

[22] Burke-White and von Staden (n 11) 332.

[23] Benton Heath (n 21) 1031ff; Carlos Esplugues, *Foreign Investment, Strategic Assets and National Security* (Intersentia 2018) 82ff.

[24] Burke-White and von Staden (n 11) 376ff.

[25] General Agreement on Tariffs and Trade 1994 (GATT 1994) (adopted 15 April 1994, entry into force 1 January 1995) 1867 UNTS 187 art XXI reads in the relevant parts:

> Nothing in this Agreement shall be construed to ...
> (b) to prevent any contracting party from taking any action which it considers necessary for the protection of its essential security interests
> (i) relating to fissionable materials or the materials from which they are derived;
> (ii) relating to the traffic in arms, ammunition and implements of war and to such traffic in other goods and materials as is carried on directly or indirectly for the purpose of supplying a military establishment;
> (iii) taken in time of war or other emergency in international relations.

[26] Energy Charter Treaty (Annex I of the Final Act of the European Energy Charter Conference) (signed 17 December 1994, entered into force 16 April 1998) 2080 UNTS 95 (ECT) art 24(3)(a)(ii). See Rudolf Dolzer, Ursula Kriebaum, and Christoph Schreuer, *Principles of International Investment Law* (OUP 2022) 310.

[27] Cyprus–Serbia BIT (signed 21 July 2005, entry into force 23 December 2005) art 13 (Essential Security Interests); Finland–Egypt BIT (signed 3 March 2004, entry into force 5 February 2005) art 14.

[28] Protocol to the Germany-Indonesia BIT (signed 14 May 2003, entry into force 2 June 2007, date of termination 1 June 2017) para (3)(a) Ad art 3 of the BIT.

[29] ECT (n 26) art 24(1).

[30] For studies, see Levent Sabanogullari, *General Exception Clauses in International Investment Law* (Nomos 2016) 54–55; Amelia Keene, 'The Incorporation and Interpretation of WTO-Style Environmental Exceptions in International Investment Agreements' (2017) 18 Journal of World Investment & Trade 62, 64–73; Tobias Ackermann, 'Exception Clauses in International Investment Agreements: A Case for Systemic Integration' in Mesut Akbaba and Giancarlo Capurro (eds), *International Challenges in Investment Arbitration* (Routledge 2018) 37.

[31] General Agreement on Trade in Services (GATS) (adopted 15 April 1994, entry into force 1 January 1995) 1869 UNTS 183 (GATS) art XIV*bis*.

the policy objectives. Moreover, combinations between a security objective and other objectives appear in treaty practice.[32] General exception clauses typically adopt the wording 'nothing in this Agreement shall be construed to prevent'[33] or allow a state to 'adopt or enforce a measure necessary'.[34]

The term 'general' may imply that the exception applies to the whole agreement.[35] FTAs usually include such exceptions in final chapters but also adopt limits for the availability of the general exception. According to Article 28(3) of the Comprehensive Economic and Trade Agreement between the European Union and Canada (CETA), for instance, the general exception only applies to section B on establishment of investments and section C on non-discriminatory treatment of the investment chapter.[36]

EU member states had divergent positions when trying to agree on a common investment policy, as some feared a weakening of investment protection through the introduction of general exception clauses.[37] In the Energy Charter Treaty (ECT), the objectives of protecting 'human, animal or plant life or health' in Article 24(2)(b)(i) of the ECT[38] do not apply to the chapter on investment protection. This exclusion from the investment chapter formed a compromise between states wishing to adopt a WTO-style exception and states that opposed this idea.[39] Moreover, Article 24(1) of the ECT removes the expropriation provisions from the scope of the exception entirely.[40] Limits to the scope of exception clauses are advisable for providing clarity and ensuring that investment protection does not fall below the minimum standard of treatment.

In WTO-style exceptions, the so-called chapeau imposes the prerequisite that 'measures are not applied in a manner which would constitute a means of arbitrary or unjustifiable discrimination'.[41] For some scholars, the inclusion of general exceptions is redundant as many disputes concern such measures. Rather, interpretative approaches for substantive standards would provide sufficient flexibility.[42] Others, however, advocate in its favour to remove the 'right to regulate' from the discretion of arbitral tribunals.[43]

[32] China–Singapore BIT (signed 21 November 1985, entry into force 7 February 1986, date of termination 16 October 2019) art 11 (Prohibitions and Restrictions); Burke-White and von Staden (n 11) 328, 334.
[33] Canada–Ecuador BIT (signed 29 April 1996, entry into force 6 June 1997, date of termination 19 May 2018) art XVII(3); Canada–Peru FTA (signed 29 May 2008, entry into force 1 August 2008) art 2201.
[34] Canada–Serbia BIT (signed 1 September 2014, entry into force 27 April 2015) 18(1)(a) (General Exceptions).
[35] Titi (n 4) 171; Sabanogullari (n 30) 40.
[36] Comprehensive Economic and Trade Agreement between Canada, of the one Part, and the European Union and its Member States, of the other Part (signed 30 October 2016, provisionally applied as of 21 September 2017) (CETA) art 28(3).
[37] Jörn Griebel, 'The New EU Investment Policy Approach' in Marc Bungenberg and others (eds), *International Investment Law: A Handbook* (Nomos 2015) 304, paras 38–40.
[38] ECT (n 26) art 24(2)(b).
[39] Craig S Bamberger, 'An Overview of the Energy Charter Treaty' in Thomas Wälde (ed), *The Energy Charter Treaty: An East–West Gateway for Investment & Trade* (Kluwer Law 1996) 1, 22.
[40] ECT (n 26) art 24(1).
[41] GATT (n 25) art XX; Canada–Peru FTA (n 33) art 2201.
[42] Legum and Petculescu (n 6) 352–56, 361–62; Lévesque (n 6) 364–67; Newcombe (n 6) 366–69.
[43] Sabanogullari (n 30) 40; Kurtz (n 5) 175–80.

C. 'Exceptions' Operating as Treaty Limitations

In addition to general and security exceptions that usually come into play during the assessment of state measures, modern IIAs include provisions operating as restraints to the treaty or substantive standards. The terms used in this category vary significantly and range from carve-outs and reservations for non-conforming measures to exclusions. A complex system of schedules and annexes typically accompanies these mechanisms.[44]

Carve-out provisions typically exclude entire policy fields. The terms reservations and exclusions are used interchangeably[45] and allow to maintain existing or to adopt future acts that otherwise would be inconsistent with the treaty.[46] As also bilateral investment treaties (BITs) include such 'reservations',[47] these clauses have to be distinguished from reservations according to Article 2(1)(d) of the Vienna Convention on the Law of Treaties (VCLT).[48] On the one hand, these mechanisms reflect policy preferences to retain the states' sovereignty over these areas. Most prominently, this concerns taxation measures, public procurement, or cultural industries.[49] Moreover, states intending to ease market access via treaty commitments use carve-outs and reservations to shield vital industries or sectors from these obligations.[50] On the other hand, previous ISDS experiences may influence the subject matters to which a treaty or certain obligations shall not apply. For instance, claims over 'packaging legislation'[51] have influenced the inclusion of carve-outs for tobacco-related measures.[52] Arguably, the vast number of renewable energy disputes may have influenced the shift to a limited protection for subsidies.[53]

[44] UNCTAD, 'Preserving Flexibility in IIAs: The Use of Reservations' in UNCTAD (ed), *UNCTAD Series on International Investment Policies for Development* (UN 2006) 17ff.

[45] ibid 3.

[46] Caroline Henckels, 'Should Investment Treaties Contain Public Policy Exceptions?' (2018) 59 Boston College Law Review 2825, 2828; Andrew Newcombe and Luís Paradell, *The Law and Practice of Investment Treaties: Standards of Treatment* (Kluwer Law International 2009) 506ff.

[47] Canada–Serbia BIT (n 34) art 17.

[48] Vienna Convention on the Law of Treaties (signed 23 May 1969, entry into force 27 January 1980) (VCLT) 1155 UNTS 331 art 2(1)(d): '"reservation" means a unilateral statement, however phrased or named, made by a State, when signing, ratifying, accepting, approving or acceding to a treaty, whereby it purports to exclude or to modify the legal effect of certain provisions of the treaty in their application to that State'; Newcombe and Paradell (n 46) 482–83.

[49] See for instance ECT (n 26) art 21; USMCA (n 16) 32.3; Article 8(2)(3) CETA (n 36), see also Henckels (n 46) 2833–34; Newcombe and Paradell (n 46) 507–08.

[50] Thomas Pollan, *Legal Framework for the Admission of FDI* (Eleven 2006) 174ff.

[51] GATT, *Thailand—Restrictions on Importation of and Internal Taxes on Cigarettes*, Panel Report DS10/R-37S/200, 5 October 1990; Philip *Morris v Uruguay*, ICSID Case No ARB/10/7, Award (8 July 2016); *Philip Morris v Australia*, PCA Case No 2012-12, Award on Jurisdiction and Admissibility (17 December 2015).

[52] See eg Article 29(5) of the Comprehensive and Progressive Pacific Partnership (signed 8 March 2018, entry into force 30 December 2018) (CPTPP); Robert Stumberg, 'Safeguards for Tobacco Control: Options for the TPPA' (2013) 39 American Journal of Law and Medicine 382, discussing states' options for limiting tobacco-related claims in the negotiations for the Trans-Pacific Partnership; Vera Korzun, 'The Right to Regulate in Investor-State Arbitration: Slicing and Dicing Regulatory Carve-Outs' (2017) 50 Vanderbilt Journal of Transnational Law 355, 398–406; Tania Voon, 'Evidentiary Challenges for Public Health Regulation in International Trade and Investment Law' (2015) 18 Journal of International Economic Law 795.

[53] CETA (n 36) arts 8.9(3), (4), 8.15(5). On this provision in general, see Lori Di Pierdomenico, 'Article 8.15 Reservations and Exceptions' in Marc Bungenberg and August Reinisch (eds), *CETA Investment Law: Article-by-Article Commentary* (Beck/Hart/Nomos 2022) 374, paras 59–67; see also Agreement in Principle on

Moreover, such mechanisms allow supplementing certain standards of treatment to limit their application in undesirable situations. For instance, 'exceptions' complement the prohibition of performance requirements for public policy reasons.[54] Likewise, states limit national treatment and most-favoured-nation treatment clauses with respect to preferential treatments mutually granted in regional economic organizations.[55] For example, under the Czech Republic–Azerbaijan BIT, these obligations 'shall not apply to advantages accorded by a Contracting Party pursuant to its obligations as a member of a customs, economic, or monetary union, a common market or free trade area'.[56]

Treaties do not necessarily abandon protection in these matters entirely but adopt counter-exceptions from the general limitations. With respect to taxation measures, so-called clawback provisions are a typical feature to provide a minimum level of protection.[57] For instance, Article 21 of the ECT carves-out taxation measures save to the applicability of the expropriation provision in Article 13.[58]

Overall, the restricting effect of these mechanisms may range between fully retaining sovereignty and limiting the consent to ISDS.[59] As exclusions or reservations shall grant flexibility to the contracting states, the limitations to the treaty or certain standards do not necessarily apply reciprocally between the states. In *Lauder v Czech Republic*, a dispute under the US–Czech Republic BIT, only the United States had made a reservation to the prohibition of arbitrary and discriminatory treatment for the broadcasting sector.[60] Thus, for ascertaining the extent of a state's obligations in certain sectors or policy matters, it is necessary to consult the respective schedules and annexes to a treaty carefully. The obligation fully applied to the Czech Republic and the tribunal found that the measures violated the treaty.[61]

III. The Interpretation of Exception Clauses in Arbitral Practice

The interpretation of exceptions or provisions with a limiting effect may pose a challenging task for tribunals. This has resulted in inconsistencies as to the legal character,

the Modernisation of the Energy Charter Treaty, 24 June 2022, art 17*bis*; EU–Vietnam Investment Protection Agreement (signed 30 June 2019, not yet in force), arts 2.1(3) and 2.2(3).

[54] See n 16.

[55] August Reinisch, 'Most Favoured Nation Treatment' in Bungenberg and others (n 37) para 807, paras 44–45.

[56] Czech Republic–Azerbaijan BIT (signed 17 May 2011, entry into force 9 February 2012) art 4(3).

[57] Kaj Hobér, *The Energy Charter Treaty* (OUP 2020) 367ff.

[58] ECT (n 26) art 21:

> (1) Except as otherwise provided in this Article, nothing in this Treaty shall create rights or impose obligations with respect to Taxation Measures of the Contracting Parties. In the event of any inconsistency between this Article and any other provision of the Treaty, this Article shall prevail to the extent of the inconsistency. ...
>
> (5) (a) Article 13 shall apply to taxes.

[59] Korzun (n 52) 398–401.

[60] See eg *Lauder v Czech Republic*, Final Award (3 September 2001) [220].

[61] ibid [222].

effect, and consequences of invoking exceptions. The increasing use of varying provisions aimed at safeguarding the right to regulate can explain these inconsistencies to a certain extent. A further factor contributing to the inconsistencies of the case law are the litigation strategies of disputing parties that cannot be disregarded for understanding the complexities in the constantly evolving case law. This section will first address the interpretation of security exceptions (A), followed by general exception clauses (B) and the divergent forms of limitations (C).

A. The Interpretation of Security Exceptions

Arbitral practice on security exception clauses predominantly concerns cases arising out of the Argentine financial crisis of 2001/02. Argentina relied on the security exception clause of Article XI of the US–Argentina BIT[62] for defending emergency measures that had severely affected foreign investors. Despite the similar facts of the disputes, the interpretation of the exception by tribunals showed significant differences and has led to a critical assessment in the literature.[63] The relationship between the security exception and the state of necessity as well as the standard of review, in particular an allegedly self-judging effect of the exception, have been the most controversial aspects.

In some of the first cases, *CMS*, *Enron*, and *Sempra*, the tribunals applied the criteria of the state of necessity rule under customary international law[64] when assessing the elements of the exception.[65] Among them, the 'only way criterion' for the nexus requirement created an unsurmountable barrier. Accordingly, these tribunals dismissed Argentina's invocation of the security exception. In contrast, the tribunal in *LG&E* relied on the state of necessity to support its conclusion that the security exception excused Argentina from liability for a certain period of the crisis.[66] The tribunal in *Continental Casualty v Argentina* relied on WTO case law, in particular concerning Article XX of the GATT, when assessing the security exception of the US–Argentina

[62] US–Argentina BIT (signed 14 November 1991, entry into force 20 October 1994) art XI reads: 'This Treaty shall not preclude the application by either Party of measures necessary for the maintenance of public order, the fulfillment of its obligations with respect to the maintenance or restoration of international peace or security, or the Protection of its own essential security interests.'

[63] Jürgen Kurtz, 'Adjudging the Exceptional at International Investment Law: Security, Public Order and Financial Crisis' (2010) 59 International 1 Comparative Law Quarterly 325, 344–47; August Reinisch, 'Necessity in Investment Arbitration: An Unnecessary Split of Opinions in Recent ICSID Cases? Comments on *CMS v Argentina* and *LG&E v Argentina*' (2007) 8 Journal of World Investment & Trade 191, 212–13ff; Stephan Schill, 'International Investment Law and the Host State's Power to Handle Economic Crises: Comment on the ICSID Decision in *LG&E v Argentina*' (2007) 24 Journal of International Arbitration 265, 277–84; Michael Waibel, 'Two Worlds of Necessity in ICSID Arbitration: *CMS* and *LG&E*' (2007) 20 Leiden Journal of International Law 637, 643, 644–47.

[64] Articles on Responsibility of States for Internationally Wrongful Acts (ARSIWA) (2001) UN Doc A/56/10 art 25.

[65] *CMS v Argentina*, ICSID Case No ARB/01/8, Award (12 May 2005) [323–24, 374]; *Enron v Argentina*, ICSID Case No ARB/01/3, Award (22 May 2007) [309, 333, 339]; *Sempra v Argentina*, ICSID Case No ARB/02/16, Award (28 September 2007) [338, 347–51].

[66] *LG&E v Argentina*, ICSID Case No ARB/02/1, Decision on Liability (3 October 2006) [245], [246]–[259].

BIT.[67] Upon weighing and balancing the measures in light of their legitimate aim and in the absence of reasonably available alternatives, it held that the exception applied.[68]

Annulment committees provided more clarity and set the stage for harmonizing the case law on the effect of security exceptions when reviewing these awards. To use the criteria of the customary international law state of necessity rules to interpret security exceptions has two problematic consequences concerning the nature and effect of an exception. First, the circumstances precluding wrongfulness justify an internationally wrongful act and are therefore only relevant after a breach has been established.[69] An exception, terminologically, would prevent the occurrence of a breach in the first place. Second, the 'invocation of a circumstance precluding wrongfulness ... is without prejudice to ... the question of compensation'.[70] Therefore, applying the state of necessity rules would significantly narrow the effect of a security exception. The ad hoc committee in *CMS* distinguished the exception from the state of necessity excuse by qualifying the security exception as a 'threshold requirement'.[71] Accordingly, the substantive obligations will not apply if a measure meets the conditions of the clause.[72] Subsequent tribunals followed this characterization of the legal effect of the security exception in principle.[73] However, elements of Article 25 of the Articles on Responsibility of States for Internationally Wrongful Acts (ARSIWA) retained some relevance for interpretative questions on the nexus requirement.[74]

Respondents have attempted to rely on a 'self-judging' nature of security exceptions, arguing that the state shall be the sole judge to decide whether a measure fulfils the conditions of the clause.[75] Several tribunals followed the dismissal of such an effect by the International Court of Justice (ICJ) in the *Nicaragua* case.[76] For the ICJ, the absence of the prefatory formulation 'it considers necessary' as included in Article XXI of the GATT was decisive.[77] Whether such an effect exists in WTO law has long been unacknowledged. However, the panel in *Russia—Measures Concerning Traffic in Transit* ruled that Article XXI GATT allows examining whether the action taken concerns the elements of subparagraphs (i)–(iii)[78] followed by a good faith

[67] *Continental Casualty v Argentina*, ICSID Case No ARB/03/9, Award (5 September 2008) [192]; Keene (n 30) 81–82.

[68] *Continental Casualty v Argentina* (n 67) [196]–[230].

[69] *Mobil Exploration v Argentina*, ICSID Case No ARB/04/16, Decision on Jurisdiction and Liability (10 April 2013) [1028].

[70] Article 27 ARSIWA (n 64).

[71] *CMS v Argentina*, ICSID Case No ARB/01/8, Decision on Annulment (25 September 2007) [129].

[72] ibid; see also *Sempra v Argentina*, ICSID Case No ARB/02/16, Decision on Annulment (29 June 2010) [200].

[73] *Continental Casualty v Argentina* (n 67) [164]; *Mobil v Argentina*, ICSID Case No ARB/04/16, Decision on Jurisdiction and Liability (10 April 2013) [1060]; *El Paso v Argentina*, ICSID Case No ARB/03/15, Award (31 October 2011) [552], [612].

[74] *Continental Casualty v Argentina* (n 67) [168]; *Mobil v Argentina* (n 73) [1060]; *El Paso v Argentina*, ICSID Case No ARB/03/15, Award (31 October 2011) [552, 613].

[75] See eg *Enron v Argentina* (n 65) [324]; *LG&E v Argentina* (n 66) [208]; see also Burke-White and von Staden (n 11) 381–86.

[76] *Case Concerning Military and Paramilitary Activities in and against Nicaragua (Nicaragua v United States)*, Judgment (Merits) [1986] ICJ Rep 14 [222].

[77] ibid; *CMS v Argentina* (n 65) [371, 373]; *CC/Devas v India*, PCA Case No 2013-09, Award on Jurisdiction and Merits (25 July 2016) [219]; *Deutsche Telekom v India*, PCA Case No 2014-10, Interim Award (13 December 2017) [231].

[78] See n 25.

review.[79] This precludes an entirely 'self-judging' effect of WTO security exceptions. Given the pertinence of Article XXI of the GATT for a number of exceptions in IIAs, arbitral tribunals may take guidance from this interpretation. Indeed, an unlimited self-judging effect of security exceptions would undermine the system of investment protection as states could rely on the exception as they see fit. This would not only reverse the risk allocation established by a treaty but entail the loss of protection to an indeterminate extent. Tribunals in more recent cases have acknowledged the particularities of security interests by granting discretion to the state without second-guessing administrative decisions.[80] The tribunal in *CC/Devas v India* distinguished national security matters from other factual disputes and imposed a heavy burden of proof on the investor, 'such as bad faith, absence of authority or application to measures that do not relate to essential security interests' to bar the application of the clause.[81] However, it remains to be seen how tribunals will address security concerns in the absence of an economic emergency or a traditional military context.[82] In *Michael Anthony Lee-Chin v Dominican Republic*, the respondent invoked a security exception clause in the context of environmental measures. The tribunal rejected a self-judging nature of the clause but concluded 'that environmental measures may be necessary, in certain circumstances, to ensure national security interests'.[83] It found that the underlying measures indeed addressed the deplorable conditions of the investor's landfill and its potential harm to the environment and human health. However, the majority of the tribunal did not see an emergency of 'national scope or impact' and thus rejected the invocation of the clause.[84]

B. The Interpretation of General Exceptions

Whereas general exception clauses operate as a major defence in WTO law, these have only recently found their way into investment arbitration. The WTO Appellate Body qualifies the general exception as an instrument for justifying inconsistencies with

[79] *Russia—Measures Concerning Traffic in Transit*, Report of the Panel, WT/DS512/R (5 April 2019) [7.77], [7.132]; *Saudi Arabia—Measures Concerning the Protection of Intellectual Property Rights*, Report of the Panel, WT/DS567/R (16 June 2020) [7.244], [7.250]–[7.252]; *United States—Certain Measures on Steel and Aluminum Products (Turkey v United States)*, Report of the Panel, WT/DS564/R (9 December 2022) [7.143]; *United States—Certain Measures on Steel and Aluminum Products (Norway v United States)*, Report of the Panel, WT/DS552/R (9 December 2022) [7.116]; *United States—Certain Measures on Steel and Aluminum Products (China v United States)*, Report of the Panel, WT/DS544/R (9 December 2022) [7.128]; *United States—Certain Measures on Steel and Aluminum Products (Switzerland v United States)*, Report of the Panel, WT/DS556/R (9 December 2022) [7.146].

[80] *Deutsche Telekom v India* (n 77) [235]; *CC/Devas v India* (n 77) [245].

[81] *CC/Devas v India* (n 77) [245].

[82] See the recently initiated arbitral proceedings in *Huawei v Sweden*, ICSID Case No ARB/22/2, Request for Arbitration (7 January 2022), which concerns the ban of Huawei's equipment for the 5G network setup allegedly due to security considerations.

[83] *Michael Anthony Lee-Chin v The Dominican Republic*, ICSID Case No UNCT/18/3, Final Award (6 October 2023) [238], [244–46].

[84] Ibid [251], [253–60], [261–65]; Arbitrator Prof Marcelo Kohen disagreed with this qualification: *Michael Anthony Lee-Chin v The Dominican Republic*, ICSID Case No UNCT/18/3, Dissenting Opinion of Professor Marcelo G. Kohen, 9 (August 2023) [43–46].

WTO obligations.[85] However, it may be doubtful whether general exceptions have the same role and legal effect in investment law.[86] In contrast to WTO jurisprudence,[87] arbitral tribunals regularly consider policy objectives when assessing measures against substantive protection standards. However, this could entail problems as to the parallel availability of exceptions and other defences. In *Bear Creek v Peru*, the respondent relied on a provision defining indirect expropriation,[88] the police powers doctrine,[89] and a general exception.[90] The tribunal indicated an exclusive effect of the provision defining indirect expropriation and the general exception. In the view of the tribunal, this barred the application of 'other exceptions from general international law' such as the police powers doctrine.[91]

WTO-style exceptions including a chapeau requirement that prevents the application of a general exception to arbitrary or discriminatory measures may constitute an additional obstacle. If a state breaches substantive standards by arbitrary or discriminatory acts, it is unlikely that such measures will fulfil the conditions of the general exception.[92] The tribunal in *Copper Mesa v Ecuador* assessed the applicability of a general exception clause from the Canada–Ecuador BIT.[93] As it found that the respondent revoked the claimant's concession 'in an arbitrary manner and without due process', the general exception was inapplicable.[94]

Thus far, the legal effect of successfully relying on a general exception remains contested. Formulations similar to security exceptions, such as 'nothing in this Agreement shall be construed to prevent' may indicate a derogation from the treaty[95] or a permission to act without breaching the treaty.[96] However, states have taken different positions on the effect of general exception clauses, subject to their role in proceedings. In *Bear Creek v Peru*, the respondent understood a general exception as a 'carve-out for measures ... that are necessary to protect human life or health'.[97] Likewise, Colombia qualified a WTO-style general exception as a 'carve-out'.[98] Canada took a different position in a non-disputing party submission reconciling it with the interpretation in WTO law. It acknowledged the flexibilities to consider regulatory motives when interpreting substantive standards, with general exceptions only operating as 'an additional tool or a final "safety net"'.[99] According to this perception, general exceptions

[85] Viñuales (n 9) 73–74; Henckels (n 9) 373.
[86] See n 42.
[87] Keene (n 30) 78–81.
[88] *Bear Creek v Peru*, ICSID Case No ARB/14/21, Respondent's Rejoinder on the Merits and Reply on Jurisdiction (13 April 2016) [476]ff.
[89] ibid [431]ff.
[90] ibid [442]–[443].
[91] *Bear Creek v Peru*, ICSID Case No ARB/14/21, Award (30 November 2017) [473].
[92] See the considerations in the literature: Legum and Petculescu (n 6) 352–54; Lévesque (n 6) 366–67.
[93] Canada–Ecuador BIT (n 33) art XVII.
[94] *Copper Mesa v Ecuador*, PCA Case No 2012-2, Award (15 March 2016) [6.66].
[95] Titi (n 4) 171.
[96] Sabanogullari (n 30) 40; Henckels (n 46) 2829, 2838ff.
[97] *Bear Creek v Peru*, Respondent's Rejoinder (n 88) [443].
[98] *Eco Oro v Colombia*, ICSID Case No ARB/16/41, Decision on Jurisdiction, Liability and Directions on Quantum (9 September 2021) [364], [366].
[99] *Eco Oro v Colombia*, ICSID Case No ARB/16/41, Non-Disputing Party Submission of Canada (27 February 2020) [20].

come into play only after a tribunal finds a violation of substantive standards and thus operate as justifications.[100] As some general exception clauses include rather loose nexus requirements, such as 'for' or 'directed to', a teleological approach confirms such a qualification. Otherwise, this would already 'carve-out' any measure in pursuit of the legitimate objectives from the treaty and tremendously curtail investment protection in the context of such regulatory acts.

The approach taken by the tribunal in *Bear Creek v Peru* to first inquire whether an expropriation occurred and then to turn to the general exception clause would suggest an understanding as a potential justification for an otherwise breach of the expropriation provision.[101] Moreover, the tribunal took a restrictive view concerning the exhaustive list of objectives in the general exception. Amid ongoing social unrest, the state had revoked the investor's mining licence. While the decree inter alia referred to the social unrest, the tribunal held that the revocation did not relate to the protection of the exception's objectives 'human, animal or plant life or health'.[102]

In *Eco Oro v Colombia*, the respondent invoked the general exception clause of the Canada–Colombia FTA[103] in a twofold manner, as a jurisdictional objection and a defence on the merits.[104] The tribunal denied a jurisdictional effect from a contextual view, holding that the exception concerned the application of the investment chapter.[105] Substantively, the tribunal construed the general exception as a permission 'ensuring a Party is not prohibited from adopting or enforcing a measure to protect human, animal or plant life and health, provided that such measures are not arbitrary or unjustifiably discriminatory'.[106] However, the tribunal concluded that this does not preclude the obligation to pay compensation for breaches of the agreement.[107]

The case law on general exceptions is still in its infancy. The frequent inclusion of such provisions in 'modernized treaties' suggests a growing relevance in future cases. At the same time, a potentially limiting effect of general exception clauses for regulatory activities under IIAs may have led to Canada's decision to exclude the WTO-modelled general exception from its 2021 Foreign Investment Promotion and Protection Model.[108] Arbitral practice has thus far confirmed existing concerns. One the one hand, the restrictive approach of the *Eco Oro* tribunal deprives the clause of any meaningful effect, as a successful invocation would still require the state to pay compensation.

[100] ibid [22].
[101] *Bear Creek v Peru*, Award (n 91) [473]–[474]; see also Henckels (n 9) 366–67.
[102] *Bear Creek v Peru*, Award (n 91) [475]; Canada–Peru FTA (n 33) art 2201(3).
[103] Canada–Colombia FTA (signed 21 November 2008, entry into force 15 August 2011) art 2201(3).
[104] *Eco Oro v Colombia*, Decision on Jurisdiction, Liability and Directions on Quantum (n 98) [362]–[366]; on case analysis, see Robert Garden, '*Eco Oro v Colombia*: The Brave New World of Environmental Exceptions' (2023) 38 ICSID Review 17; Laura Létourneau Tremblay, 'In Need of a Paradigm Shift: Reimagining *Eco Oro v Colombia* in Light of New Treaty Language' (2022) 23 Journal of World Investment & Trade 915; Güneş Ünüvar, 'A Tale of Policy Carve-Outs and General Exceptions: *Eco Oro v Colombia* as a Case Study' (2023) 14 Journal of International Dispute Settlement 517; Aarushi Gupta, '*Eco Oro v Colombia*: Is GATT Article XX to Be Blamed?' (2023) 89 Arbitration: The International Journal of Arbitration, Mediation and Dispute Management 21.
[105] *Eco Oro v Colombia*, Decision on Jurisdiction, Liability and Directions on Quantum (n 98) [379]–[381].
[106] ibid [829].
[107] ibid; Gupta (n 104) 28–32; Garden (n 104) 21–23; Ünüvar (n 104) 12–16.
[108] Wolfgang Alschner, 'Why Omitting General Public Policy Exceptions from Investment Treaties Is a Setback for the Right to Regulate' (2022) 342 Colombia FDI Perspectives.

Interpreted in this manner a general exception clause would not alter the legal situation established by the treaty. The substantive standards do not prohibit regulatory measures but may require compensation under certain circumstances. On the other hand, to prevent undermining the level of protection guaranteed by the treaty, tribunals will have to strike a balance for general exceptions containing loose nexus requirements. An operation as a 'final safety net' may suit best to meet these demands.

C. The Interpretation of 'Exceptions' Operating as Treaty Limitations

In contrast to security and general exceptions, a number of tribunals had the task to interpret diverse forms of treaty limitations.[109] Most prominently, this concerns carve-outs for taxation measures, which shall retain the states' full sovereignty over fiscal matters.[110] Further disputes concerned other policy fields, such as public procurement,[111] limits for substantive standards,[112] or the ISDS mechanism.[113] While respondents often rely on carve-outs, reservations, and exclusions as an objection to jurisdiction, the subject matter concerned may require substantive considerations.[114]

A number of cases thus far relates to the taxation provision of Article 21 of the ECT.[115] In the *Yukos* cases, the Russian Federation relied on the taxation provision as a jurisdictional objection, arguing that it comprises all sorts of measures related to taxation.[116] The tribunal considered the objection on the merits and concluded that the provision only applies to bona fide taxation measures. A state can thus not rely on the tax carve-out to disguise a measure in fact targeting a certain investor.[117] Hence, in addition to expropriation claims under Article 13 of the ECT, the jurisdiction extends to a good faith review of whether the disputed measure was in fact adopted for taxation. Several tribunals had to apply the taxation carve-out of the ECT in the context of Spain's amended regulatory framework for renewable energies and likewise conducted a good faith review.[118] Understanding the taxation provisions as a carve-out has important implications for the burden of proof. Several tribunals held that there is an assumption that a measure was adopted in good faith, with the claimant having the burden of proof that a

[109] Henckels (n 46) 2833, giving an overview over different types of provisions and case law thereunder.
[110] In general, see Arno Gildemeister, 'Investment Law and Taxation' in Bungenberg and others (n 37) 1677; Hobér (n 57) 357ff.
[111] *ADF v United States*, ICSID Case No ARB(AF)/00/1, Award (9 January 2003) [161]; *UPS v Canada*, ICSID Case No UNCT/02/1, Award on the Merits (24 May 2007) [131–36]; *Mesa Power v Canada*, PCA Case No 2012-17, Award (24 March 2016) [395ff].
[112] *Lauder v Czech Republic* (n 60) [220]; *Lemire v Ukraine*, ICSID Case No ARB/06/18, Award (28 March 2011) [46]–[47]. *Global Telecom v Canada*, ICSID Case No ARB/16/16, Award (27 March 2020) [363–80].
[113] *Global Telecom v Canada*, ICSID Case No ARB/16/16, Award (27 March 2020) [324–36].
[114] *Yukos Universal v Russian Federation*, PCA Case No 2005-04/AA227, Final Award (18 July 2013) [1401]; *RREEF v Spain*, ICSID Case No ARB/13/30, Decision on Jurisdiction (6 June 2016) [197].
[115] Hobér (n 57) 358ff.
[116] *Yukos Universal v Russia* (n 114) [1385]–[1400].
[117] ibid [1433].
[118] Hobér (n 57) 360ff.

measure was adopted for other reasons. The tribunal in *Novenergia II v Spain*, relying on the *Yukos* case held:

> [T]he starting point, or the assumption, should always be that the taxation measure was in fact adopted in good faith. The consequence of this assumption is that the Claimant bears the burden of proving to the Tribunal ... that the measure therefore was enacted mala fide.[119]

An issue that will typically arise in the context of a carve-out is whether the measure at issue concerns the policy area to be excluded. In this regard, taxation measures have to be distinguished from other payments owed to the state, such as certain tariffs or levies, for which the state typically provides particular services in return.[120] Similar problems occurred with respect to the carve-out for public procurement from the national treatment and most-favoured-nation treatment standard under Article 1108(7)(a) of the North American Free Trade Agreement (NAFTA). In the absence of a definition in the investment chapter, tribunals interpreted the term public procurement broadly.[121] In *Mesa Power v Canada*, the claims related to a renewable energy scheme offering feed-in tariffs (FITs) for the purchase of energy, with Canada relying on the procurement 'exception'.[122] The tribunal declined a restrictive reading of the clause[123] and concluded that 'the NAFTA Contracting Parties sought to protect their ability to exercise nationality-based preferences in cases of procurement'.[124] As the FITs fell within this term, the tribunal declined jurisdiction over these claims.[125]

An aspect that has just recently arisen in case law is whether a provision with a limiting effect operates *ex lege* or whether the state has to actively enact the clause before a dispute arises. In *Global Telecom v Canada*, a reservation to the national treatment standard of the Canada–Egypt BIT allowed the states to make or maintain exceptions within the sectors listed in the Annex.[126] The claimant argued that this requires a state to 'exercise its right to make or maintain an exception before such an exception can take effect'[127] by relying on case law on denial of benefits provisions.[128] The tribunal's majority denied such an 'intermediary step to "activate" that right'[129] and found no condition to explicitly set out future non-conforming measures.[130] However, such an

[119] *Novernergia II v Spain*, SCC Case No V2015/063, Final Award (15 February 2018) [521] (footnote omitted); *RREEF v Spain*, ICSID Case No ARB/13/30, Decision on Responsibility and on the Principles of Quantum (30 November 2018) [186]–[188]; *Isolux v Spain*, SCC Case No 2013/153, Award (12 July 2016) [734].
[120] Gildemeister (n 110) paras 21–26; for such distinctions, see *Antaris v Czech Republic*, PCA Case No 2014-01, Award (2 May 2018) [245]–[253]; *Natland v Czech Republic*, PCA Case No 2013–35, Partial Award (20 December 2017) [246], [259].
[121] *ADF v United States* (n 111) [161]–[174]; *UPS v Canada* (n 111) [131]–[136].
[122] *Mesa Power v Canada* (n 111) [378]–[384].
[123] ibid [405].
[124] ibid [419].
[125] ibid [465].
[126] Canada–Egypt BIT (signed 13 November 1996, entry into force 3 November 1997) art IV(2)(d) includes 'the right of each Contracting Party to make or maintain exceptions within the sectors or matters listed in the Annex to this Agreement'.
[127] *Global Telecom v Canada* (n 112) [359].
[128] ibid [357], in particular n 517.
[129] ibid [368]–[369].
[130] ibid [373].

interpretation has also led to criticism, as it leaves the investor in the dark about which future acts are excluded. Assuming that the reservation comprises all future acts with respect to a certain sector virtually reduces investment protection, as it would amount to an entire carve-out of the respective sector.[131]

IV. Exceptions and Other Manifestations of the Right to Regulate

In addition to interpretative issues that have arisen with respect to the different types of exceptions and limitations, several mechanisms prescribing the 'right to regulate' entail difficulties to distinguish these instruments from one another. References to regulatory objectives in the preamble, declarative statements on the right to regulate, non-regression clauses, or interpretative notes are by no means without any effect.[132] However, in the ISDS context the role of these provisions is essentially limited to a means of interpreting the substantive standards in accordance with Article 31 of the VCLT. A tribunal has to consider these when assessing the terms of the treaty in their context and in the light of its object and purpose.[133] Thus, such provisions by themselves do not limit the scope of the treaty, exempt a certain measure, or justify the breach of substantive standards. However, similar formulations of such provisions to exception clauses may pose specific problems. This concerns restatements of the right to regulate as well as provisions distinguishing indirect expropriations from legitimate regulatory activity.

A. Restatements of the Right to Regulate

Declarative expressions of the right to regulate in treaties may take varying forms. The European Union includes articles on 'Investment and Regulatory Measures' in the investment chapters of its treaties, which shall reaffirm the right to regulate 'to achieve legitimate policy objectives, such as protection of public health, safety, the environment or public morals, social or consumer protection or the promotion and protection of cultural diversity'.[134] North American FTAs include provisions with a permissive formulation with respect to regulatory objectives. Article 14(16) of the United States–Mexico–Canada Agreement (USMCA) reads:

> Nothing in this Chapter shall be construed to prevent a Party from adopting, maintaining, or enforcing any measure otherwise consistent with this Chapter that

[131] *Global Telecom v Canada*, ICSID Case No ARB/16/16, Dissenting Opinion of Gary Born (27 March 2020) [38]–[39].

[132] Titi (n 4) 104–22.

[133] VCLT (n 48) art 31(1), (2).

[134] CETA (n 36) art 8.9; EU–Vietnam Investment Protection Agreement (n 33) art 2.2; EU–Singapore Investment Protection Agreement (signed 15 October 2018, not yet in force) art 2.2; see also Stefanie Schacherer, 'Article 8.9 Investment and Regulatory Measures' in August Reinisch and Marc Bungenberg (eds), *CETA Investment Law Article-by-Article Commentary* (Nomos 2022) 236, paras 14–15.

> it considers appropriate to ensure that investment activity in its territory is undertaken in a manner sensitive to environmental, health, safety, or other regulatory objectives.[135]

The formulation '[n]othing ... shall be construed to prevent' resembles the wording of some security and general exception clauses.[136] Moreover, the objectives are similar to general exception clauses. However, the wording 'otherwise consistent with this Chapter' marks a decisive difference, as it requires such measures to comply with the substantive protection standards. Such a provision has been described as 'tautological' as it 'does not provide additional regulatory flexibility'.[137]

In *Infinito Gold v Costa Rica*, the respondent relied on a similar provision of the Canada–Costa Rica BIT. Annex I of the BIT, in addition to limitations for the national treatment and most-favoured-nation standard, includes a comprehensive provision with the heading 'General Exceptions and Exemptions'. Paragraph 1 of this provision includes wording similar to Article 14(16) of the USMCA allowing for measures sensitive to environmental concerns.[138] Paragraph 2 reflects a WTO-style general exception clause, followed by other paragraphs on financial and cultural industries exceptions. Costa Rica invoked paragraph 1 of the clause as an exception arguing that it exempts from liability as the challenged measures aimed 'at protecting the environment from possible negative effects of open-pit mining'.[139] It remains unclear why the respondent did not rely on the WTO-style exception in paragraph 2 but the wording 'sensitive to environmental concerns' may have influenced the decision. By interpreting the ordinary meaning of the terms 'any measure otherwise consistent with this Agreement', the tribunal denied any derogatory effect over substantive standards.[140] It concluded that the provision 'is not a carve-out from the BIT's protections, but rather a reaffirmation of the State's right to regulate'.[141] While such a provision does not limit the state's regulatory leeway, it does not expand it either. However, this shows that not all provisions appearing as an exception in fact operate as such and calls for a deliberate litigation strategy in case a treaty contains several provisions on the 'right to regulate'.

135 USMCA (n 16) art 14.16.

136 See GATT art XXI as quoted in n 25.

137 Newcombe and Paradell (n 46) 509; Titi (n 4) 112–13.

138 Canada–Costa Rica BIT (signed 18 March 1998, entry into force 29 September 1999) annex I.III (General Exceptions and Exemptions) reads:

> 1. Nothing in this Agreement shall be construed to prevent a Contracting Party from adopting, maintaining or enforcing any measure otherwise consistent with this Agreement that it considers appropriate to ensure that investment activity in its territory is undertaken in a manner sensitive to environmental concerns.

139 *Infinito Gold v Costa Rica*, ICSID Case No ARB/14/5, Award (3 June 2021) [762].

140 ibid [772–73].

141 ibid [777].

B. 'Rare Circumstances' in which Legitimate Regulatory Activity Amounts to an Indirect Expropriation

In distinguishing between indirect expropriations and non-compensable legitimate regulatory activity, tribunals have frequently applied the 'police powers' doctrine. Accordingly, non-discriminatory measures adopted in good faith and pursuing a legitimate public policy objective do not necessarily require compensation. The 1961 Harvard Draft Convention on the International Responsibility of States for Injury to Aliens[142] adopted this approach. Moreover, the Third Restatement of the Foreign Relations Law of the United States of 1987 also reflects this consideration.[143]

Starting with the Model BITs of Canada and the United States of 2004, modern IIAs increasingly include provisions defining indirect expropriations combined with a clause reflecting the police powers doctrine. This provision of the Canada Model BITs reads:

> Except in rare circumstances, such as when a measure or series of measures are so severe in the light of their purpose that they cannot be reasonably viewed as having been adopted and applied in good faith, non-discriminatory measures of a Party that are designed and applied to protect legitimate public welfare objectives, such as health, safety and the environment, do not constitute indirect expropriation.[144]

However, the inclusion of such a provision in a treaty is not necessary to consider these elements when assessing regulatory measures that deprive an investment of its value. Many arbitral tribunals have established varying approaches to the police powers doctrine in the absence of such clauses.[145]

The *Casinos Austria v Argentina* case shows a particularly stringent analysis of the rights of host states to exercise their police powers and to regulate. It shows that such an analysis can be done with a classic expropriation definition without any reference to regulatory powers of states.[146] The applicable BIT between Austria and Argentina

[142] Draft Convention on the International Responsibility of States for Injuries to Aliens (1961) 55 American Journal of International Law 548, 562.

[143] American Law Institute, *Restatement (Third) Foreign Relations of the United States*, vol 1 (American Law Institute 1987) (RLA-257), § 712: 'A State is not responsible for loss of property or for other economic disadvantage resulting from bona fide general taxation, regulation, forfeiture for crime, or other action of the kind that is commonly accepted as within the police powers of states, if it is not discriminatory.'

[144] Canada Model BIT 2004 annex B.13(1) Expropriation (c).

[145] See Ursula Kriebaum, *Eigentumsschutz im Völkerrecht: Eine vergleichende Untersuchung zum internationalen Investitionsrecht sowie zum Menschenrechtsschutz* (Duncker & Humblot 2008) 341ff; Catherine Titi, 'Police Powers and International Investment Law' in Andrea Gattini, Attila Tanzi, and Filippo Fontanelli (eds), *General Principles of Law and International Investment Arbitration* (Brill Nijhoff 2018) 323, 334–38, 338–40. For an overview of these approaches, see also *Eco Oro v Colombia* (n 98), Decision on Jurisdiction, Liability and Directions on Quantum [627]–[629]; see, however, the recently rendered award in *Rockhopper v Italy*, ICSID Case No ARB/17/14, Award (23 August 2022) [190–203] in which the tribunal has not considered the policy objective of the disputed measure.

[146] Ursula Kriebaum, 'International Investment Law' in Siobhan McInerney-Langford and Robert McCorquodale (eds), *The Role of International Law in Development* (OUP 2023) 305–38, 327–28.

of 1994 contains a classic expropriation definition without any reference to the regulatory powers of states.[147] The *Casinos Austria* tribunal relied for this purpose on the *Methanex* tribunal and later arbitral awards.[148] It pointed out in this regard, that host states' police powers that imply measures negatively affecting foreign investments without triggering a compensation obligation have long before modern investment treaty arbitration been recognized as part of customary international law.[149] A state's police powers and its right to regulate under customary international law qualify as 'relevant rules of international law applicable in the relations between the parties' in the sense of Article 31(3)(c) of the VCLT.[150] Therefore, tribunals have to take them into account when interpreting the provisions of an investment protection treaty such as the protection against uncompensated expropriation or the fair and equitable treatment clause. This encompasses the right to regulate in the public interest and to enforce these regulations against foreign investors without triggering a duty to pay compensation.[151] This is however only valid for reasonable bona fide, non-discriminatory regulation.[152] Abusive exercise of these rights triggers a violation of international law.[153]

To distinguish between a measure that is covered by the host state's right to regulate and to exercise its police powers, on the one hand, and a measure that is abusive, on the other, tribunals have resorted to rule of law elements albeit without explicitly referring to the concept. These include good faith, non-discrimination, the prohibition of arbitrariness, and proportionality. The Tribunal in *Casinos Austria v Argentina* relied on a long line of cases and held:

> In order to avoid abuse of the host State's regulatory powers, their exercise must be *bona fide* and in line with principles of international investment law, such as good faith, non-discrimination, and the prohibition of arbitrariness, and result in measures whose impact on investments is proportionate to the interest(s) protected.[154]

The *Casinos* tribunal noted that these limits on the rights to regulate and to exercise police powers exist not only in treaty provisions but also have a basis in customary international law.[155]

The formulation 'except in rare circumstances' included in the Canadian Model BIT and a number of modern IIAs to provide for policy space could suggest an exception from a rule with two divergent perceptions.[156] First, this may relate to the general

[147] Argentina–Austria BIT (signed 7 August 1992, entry into force 1 January 1995).
[148] *Casinos Austria v Argentina*, ICSID Case No ARB/14/32, Award (5 November 2021) [331].
[149] ibid [332] n 417.
[150] *Philipp Morris v Uruguay* (n 51) [290]; *Marfin v Cyprus*, ICSID Case No ARB/13/27, Award (26 July 2018, 828; *Casinos Austria v Argentina* (n 148) [332].
[151] *Casinos Austria v Argentina* (n 148) [333].
[152] ibid; see also eg *Philipp Morris v Uruguay* (n 51) [295].
[153] *Casinos Austria v Argentina* (n 148) [333].
[154] *Casinos Austria v Argentina* (n 148) [336]. For case law on proportionality, see eg Ursula Kriebaum, 'Article 8.12 Expropriation' in Bungenberg and Reinisch (n 134) 297, paras 73–84; August Reinisch and Christoph Schreuer, *International Protection of Investments: The Substantive Standards* (CUP 2020) 168–70.
[155] *Casinos Austria v Argentina* (n 148) [336].
[156] Arnaud de Nanteuil, 'Expropriation' in Makane Mbengue and Stefanie Schacherer (eds), *Foreign Investment under the CETA* (Springer 2019) 127, 150. The authors of the present chapter have also used the term exception

rule that legitimate regulatory activity does not constitute an expropriation. However, by considering the elements of the provisions, in 'rare circumstances' such measures amount to an indirect expropriation.[157] Second, one may consider that regulatory measures depriving an investor of its investment necessarily constitute indirect expropriations, except if the measure is non-discriminatory and pursues a legitimate policy objective.[158]

The tribunal in *Bear Creek v Peru* applied the 'factors' of such a provision for the 'identification of an indirect expropriation'.[159] However, it seems that in applying these factors it rather perceived the elements as potential justifications for a taking.[160] By concluding that this provision and the general exception[161] precluded the application of other exceptions, it understood the police powers doctrine to be a different defence.[162]

Nevertheless, the qualification of the 'rare circumstances' as an identification or a clarification rather than an exception not only better relates to tribunals' understanding of the police powers doctrine but also reflects states' understandings in third-party submissions.[163] Already the Annex to the final draft for a Multilateral Agreement on Investment (MAI) included an 'interpretative note' in a footnote to clarify inter alia that the expropriation provision:

> does not establish a new requirement that Parties pay compensation for losses which an investor or investment may incur through regulation, revenue raising and other normal activity in the public interest undertaken by governments.[164]

for such provisions in other writings. See Ursula Kriebaum (n 154) paras 73–93; Kilian Wagner, 'Regulation by Exception—The Emergence of (General) Exception Clauses in International Investment Law?' (2023) 26 Austrian Review of International and European Law 77, 93, 111–12, 115–16. The tribunal in *Eco Oro v Colombia* (n 98), Decision on Jurisdiction, Liability and Directions on Quantum [629] also used the term 'exception' but understood it as a 'reflection or explanation of the factors that are relevant to the expropriation inquiry'; Keene (n 30) 68 understands it as a carve-out.

[157] This appears to be *Eco Oro's* understanding in *Eco Oro v Colombia*, Decision on Jurisdiction, Liability and Directions on Quantum (n 98) [625].

[158] Apparently this was Costa Rica's perception of the 'rare circumstances' provision of the Annex 10-C(4)(b) of the Free Trade Agreement between Central America, the Dominican Republic and the United States of America (CAFTA) (signed 5 August 2004, entry into force 1 March 2006), as Keene (n 30) 83–84 concludes with respect to *Aaron Berkowitz and others v Costa Rica*, ICSID Case No UNCT/13/2, Respondent's Memorial on Jurisdiction and Counter-Memorial on Merits (15 July 2014) [187].

[159] *Bear Creek v Peru*, Award (n 91) [415].

[160] ibid: 'in application of subsection (iii), the character of the measure did not justify the taking'.

[161] See also section II.

[162] *Bear Creek v Peru*, Award (n 91) [473].

[163] See Keene (n 30) 84; *Aaron Berkowitz and others v Costa Rica*, ICSID Case No UNCT/13/2, Non-Disputing Party Submission of the United States of America (17 April 2015) [25]–[31], esp [31]: 'This paragraph is not an exception, but rather is intended to provide tribunals with additional guidance in determining whether an indirect expropriation has occurred'; *Eco Oro v Colombia*, Non-Disputing Party Submission of Canada (n 99) [9]–[11]; *Bear Creek v Peru*, ICSID Case No ARB/14/21, Submission of Canada pursuant to Article 832 of the Canada–Peru Free Trade Agreement (9 June 2016) [3]–[6]; El Salvador in *Aaron Berkowitz and others v Costa Rica*, ICSID Case No UNCT/13/2, Non-Disputing Party Submission of El Salvador (17 April 2015) [22]–[24], understood it as a 'strong presumption created in CAFTA-DR that a State's nondiscriminatory regulatory measures [...] do not constitute an indirect expropriation'.

[164] Multilateral Agreement on Investment Draft Consolidated Text <www.oecd.org/daf/mai/pdf/ng/ng987r1e.pdf> annex 'Package of Proposals for Text on Environment and Labour'.

The tribunal in *Eco Oro* applied the 'rare circumstances' provision of the Canada–Columbia FTA[165] in such a manner by a two-step approach. It first qualified the prohibition of mining activities in an ecological sensitive area as a non-discriminatory regulatory activity to protect the environment.[166] Thereafter, it assessed whether such 'rare circumstances' existed, which would require Colombia to compensate the investor. After considering Eco Oro's investment-backed expectations, the precautionary principle and how Colombia conducted its administrative actions, it confirmed its initial finding in a proportionality analysis:[167]

> In sum, the Challenged Measures were adopted in good faith, are non-discriminatory and designed and applied to protect the environment such that they are a legitimate exercise of Colombia's police powers and do not constitute indirect expropriation.[168]

Understanding these provisions attached to indirect expropriations clauses as giving guidance under which 'rare circumstances' regulatory measures in fact constitute an indirect expropriation better reflects the existing state of international law. This does not extend the regulatory capacity of the state and does not form an exception for measures requiring compensation. For instance, if a measure specifically targets a certain investor, is not adopted or reviewable in a due process of law or the depriving effect is not proportionate to investment-backed expectations, the state has to provide compensation.

V. Summary and Conclusion

The significant increase of exception clauses in investment protection treaties has certainly not provided for more predictability concerning the scope of protection of the treaties. States included them with the aim to preserve regulatory space in certain fields reaching from security in its classical sense to all sorts of public purposes. The exception clauses themselves are not uniform. They reach from very precise clauses that sometimes only repeat what would otherwise already be the law such as exclusion from the treaty protection for measures to implement UN sanctions to very broad security exception clauses. Furthermore, we also find clauses that replicate what the customary international law right to regulate would provide for already. Especially, if several layers of exception clauses seeking to implement regulatory space are included in one treaty, this risks unintended effects when these clauses have to be interpreted. It is unlikely that tribunals will assume that a treaty that has as its stated goal investment protection has no effect at all. Overly general exception clauses will risk having only a limited effect on the interpretation of substantive standards. Unless,

[165] Canada–Columbia FTA (n 103) annex 811(2)(b).
[166] *Eco Oro v Colombia*, Decision on Jurisdiction, Liability and Directions on Quantum (n 98) [642].
[167] ibid [643]–[699].
[168] ibid [699]; see also Garden (n 104) 18–20; Ünüvar (n 104) 5–9.

states want to limit investments in certain sectors or to make them more expensive, caution is also warranted towards exception clauses that exclude certain types of investments from treaty protection. Overall, the increase of exception clauses has certainly made the interpretation of investment treaties more complex and we can already see that some states include fewer exception clauses than they did before, in their last generation of BITs.

14

The Role of Human Rights in Investment Awards

Diane A Desierto

I. Introduction: Human Rights Pathways in International Investment Law

An investor-state arbitral tribunal quaintly likened investment arbitration to 'mechanisms of judicial review found . . . internationally in human rights courts'.[1] Ironically, however, international human rights law has rarely had direct applicability to the laws governing foreign investment. International human rights law only gained direct applicability to foreign investment law through recent deliberate innovations created in new generations of international investment treaties,[2] domestic investment rules and regulations,[3] as well as procedural rules applicable to investment

[1] *Casinos Austria International GmBH and Castinos Austria Aktiengesellschaft v Argentina*, ICSID Case No ARB/14/32, Decision on Jurisdiction (29 June 2018) [273].

[2] See among many others Agreement between the Hungary–San Marino bilateral investment treaty (BIT) (2022), preamble, fourth paragraph ('Seeking to ensure that investment is consistent with the protection of health, safety and the environment, the promotion and protection of internationally and domestically recognized human rights, labour rights, and internationally recognized standards of corporate social responsibility'); United Kingdom–New Zealand free trade agreement (FTA) (2022) art 14(19) (Corporate Social Responsibility); Australia–United Kingdom FTA (2021) ch 13, art 13(19) (Corporate Social Responsibility); Iceland–Liechtenstein–Norway–United Kingdom FTA (2021) ch 3, art 3(4) (Denial of Benefits), para (b) ('A Party may deny the benefits of this Chapter and Chapter 5 . . . . to an investor or service supplier of another Party that is a legal person of that Party, or to a covered enterprise of that legal person, if . . . (b) the denying Party adopts or maintains a measure with respect to the non-Party or the person of the non-Party which is related to the maintenance of international peace and security, including the protection of human rights, and prohibits transactions with that legal person or covered enterprise, or which would be violated or circumvented if the benefits of this Chapter or Chapter 5 . . . were accorded to that legal person or its covered enterprise'); United Kingdom–Cameroon Interim Agreement Establishing an Economic Partnership Agreement (2021) annex IV (Joint Statement of the Parties on the Objectives and Essential and Fundamental Elements of this Agreement), para 5, United Kingdom Ghana Interim Trade Partnership Agreement (2021) preamble, seventh para ('Reaffirming their commitment to the respect of human rights, to democratic principles and to the rule of law, which constitute essential elements of this Agreement, and to good governance, which constitutes a fundamental element of it'); Brazil–India Investment Cooperation and Facilitation Treaty (2020) art 12(2) (Corporate Social Responsibility), paras (b) ('respect the internationally recognized human rights of those involved in the companies' activities') and (e) ('refrain from seeking or accepting exemptions that are not established in the legal or regulatory framework relating to human rights, environment, health, security, work, tax system, financial incentives, or other issues'); EU–Singapore Investment Protection Agreement (2018) preamble, seventh para ('Reaffirming their commitment to the Charter of the United Nations . . . and having regard to the principles articulated in the Universal Declaration of Human Rights').

[3] See for example Revised Investment Agreement for the COMESA Common Investment Area, part four, art 25 (Compliance with Domestic Laws) ('COMESA investors and their investments shall comply with all applicable domestic laws and measures of the host State'), art 29 (Business Ethics and Human Rights):

1. COMESA investors and their investments shall observe the United Nations Guiding Principles on Business and Human Rights with modifications necessary for local circumstances.
2. COMESA investors and investments shall among others:
   (a) support and respect the protection of internationally proclaimed human rights;
   (b) ensure that they are not complicit in human rights abuses;

Diane A Desierto, *The Role of Human Rights in Investment Awards* In: *The Award in International Investment Arbitration*.
Edited by: Katia Fach Gómez and Catharine Titi, Oxford University Press. © Katia Fach Gómez and Aikaterini Titi 2024.
DOI: 10.1093/9780191975936.003.0014

disputes.[4] Much of these ongoing legislative or prescriptive reforms demonstrate a growing consensus about the centrality of the continued performance of host states' international human rights law obligations, well alongside host states' international obligations to foreign investors.[5] These global rule-making and state-driven responses, all designed to intentionally create human rights law pathways into international investment law, have also emerged out of a climate of discontent over the human rights impacts of foreign investment activities within host states.[6]

However, the significant corpus of much of international investment disputes in existing arbitral jurisprudence thus far does not yet reflect the intentional internalization of both the substance and procedure of international human rights law into international investment law.[7] As a result, when one examines the full range of publicly available international investment arbitral awards as of this writing, scarcely any awards speak of the direct applicability of international human rights law as a source of binding law in investor-state disputes. Neither do these arbitral awards remotely approach the complexity of the universality, interdependence, interrelatedness, intersectionality, and multidimensionality of human rights treaty provisions, which often cross-reference to established human rights customary law norms,[8] as well as general human rights principles such as non-discrimination, equality, good faith, among others.[9] Parties and arbitral tribunals have thus been engaging in a 'human rights dialectic'[10] within the strict parameters of international investment law as *lex specialis*, developing interpretive and tactical arbitration strategies to address the demands of *pacta sunt servanda* for both foreign investment obligations as well as international human rights law obligations of host states.[11] Foreign investors, as transnational business enterprises, likewise have

(c) uphold the freedom of association and the effective recognition of the right to collective bargaining;
(d) eliminate all forms of forced and compulsory labour, including the effective abolition of child labour; and
(e) eliminate discrimination in respect of employment and occupation.

Where it is necessary to prioritize actions to address actual and potential adverse human rights impacts, COMESA investors should first seek to prevent and mitigate those that are most severe or where delayed response would make them irremediable.

[4] 2019 Hague Rules on Business and Human Rights Arbitration <www.cilc.nl/cms/wp-content/uploads/2019/12/The-Hague-Rules-on-Business-and-Human-Rights-Arbitration_CILC-digital-version.pdf>.

[5] See among others Erika George and Elizabeth Thomas, 'Bringing Human Rights into Bilateral Investment Treaties: South Africa and a Different Approach to International Investment Disputes' (2018) 27 Transnational Law and Contemporary Problems 403.

[6] See Lorenzo Cotula, 'International Law and Negotiating Power in Foreign Investment Projects: Comparing Property Rights Protection under Human Rights and Investment Law in Africa' (2008) 33 South African Yearbook of International Law 62; Niccolo Zugliani, 'Human Rights in International Investment Law: The 2016 Morocco–Nigeria Bilateral Investment Treaty' (2019) 68 International and Comparative Law Quarterly 761.

[7] See Crina Baltag and Ylli Dautaj, 'Promoting, Regulating, and Enforcing Human Rights through International Investment Law and ISDS' (2021) 45 Fordham International Law Journal 1.

[8] See Brian D Lepard, *Reexamining Customary International Law* (CUP 2017) 231–306.

[9] See among others Fernand De Varennes, 'Equality and Non-Discrimination: Fundamental Principles of Minority Language Rights' (1999) 6 International Journal on Minority and Group Rights 307; Jim Ife, *Human Rights from Below: Achieving Rights through Community Development* (CUP 2012) ch 4.

[10] See Christoph Schreuer and Clara Reiner, 'Human Rights and International Investment Arbitration' in Pierre-Marie Dupuy, Francesco Francioni, and Ernst Ulrich Petersmann (eds), *Human Rights in International Investment Law and Arbitration* (OUP 2009) 82.

[11] See Ursula Kriebaum, 'Human Rights and International Investment Arbitration' in Thomas Schultz and Federico Ortino (eds), *The Oxford Handbook of International Arbitration* (OUP 2020) 150–86.

duties to at least respect human rights law in their respective business operations and activities (also as part of their duty of care).[12] But what is ultimately applied thus far in an investor-state arbitration remains mainly defined within the context of foreign investment law as the applicable substantive law,[13] and international arbitration rules as the applicable procedural rules.[14]

The lingering gaps on the direct applicability of international human rights law in international investor-state arbitration disputes continue to provoke interpretive and strategic responses from parties to these disputes. This chapter maps four prevalent uses of international human rights law in investor-state arbitral jurisprudence: first, as the bases for investment treaty interpretation; second, as a recognized part of applicable law; third, as evidence for substantive arguments on the merits; and fourth, as the bases for non-disputing party submissions. This chapter examines publicly available investor-state arbitral awards from the earliest decisions in the 1970s up to 2022. As the following subsections will show, these four prevalent uses have yet to demonstrate their ultimate effectiveness in realizing international human rights law outcomes within investor-state disputes.

II. Human Rights as Bases for Investment Treaty Interpretation

International human rights law has been argued as a 'relevant rule of international law' to interpret investment treaty provisions, with varying degrees of success. Arbitral tribunals have had little trouble invoking, narrating, or citing to international human rights law and jurisprudence in the course of interpreting expropriation clauses in investment treaties.[15] In *Técnicas Medioambientales Tecmed SA v Mexico*,[16] for example, the arbitral tribunal referred to both European Court of Human Rights as well as Inter-American Court of Human Rights jurisprudence to substantiate its interpretation of

[12] United Nations Guiding Principles on Business and Human Rights, Pillar II (The Corporate Responsibility to Respect Human Rights) <www.ohchr.org/sites/default/files/documents/publications/guidingprinciplesbusinesshr_en.pdf>; *Vedanta Resources PLC and another v Lungowe and others* [2019] UKSC 20 [49–55]; *Okpabi and others v Royal Dutch Shell Plc and another* [2021] UKSC 3 [25].

[13] See for example Jarrod Hepburn, 'Applicable Law in TPP Investment Disputes' (2016) 17 Melbourne Journal of International Law 1, 349.

[14] See Christoph Schreuer, 'Jurisdiction and Applicable Law in Investment Treaty Arbitration' (2014) 1 McGill Journal of Dispute Resolution 1.

[15] See among others *EnCana Corporation v Ecuador*, London Court of International Arbitration, Award (3 February 2006) [176–177]; *Ronald S. Lauder v Czech Republic*, UNCITRAL Final Award (3 September 2001) [200]. See also Frederic Bertrand, 'The Human Right to Property in International Investment Law' (2019) 24 Appeal 45, although one arbitral tribunal did not find international human rights law relevant for the compensation element of expropriation clauses. See *Amco Asia Corporation and others v Indonesia*, ICSID Case No ARB/81/1, Award in Resubmitted Proceeding (31 March 1990) [127]; *Hassan Awdi and others v Romania*, ICSID Case No ARB/10/13, Award (2 March 2015) [464]; *Jan Oostergetel and Theodora Laurentius v Slovakia*, UNCITRAL Final Award (23 April 2012) [95], [320]–[321]; *Anatolie Stati and others v Kazakhstan*, SCC Arbitration V (116/2010), Award (19 December 2013); *Burlington Resources Inc v Ecuador*, ICSID Case No ARB/08/5, Decision on Reconsideration and Award (7 February 2017) [145] and [309]; *Gold Reserve Inc v Venezuela*, ICSID Case No ARB(AF)/09/1, Award (22 September 2014) [634]; *Crystallex International Corporation v Venezuela*, ICSID Case ARB (AF)/11/2, Award (4 April 2016) [658].

[16] *Técnicas Medioambientales Tecmed SA v Mexico*, ICSID Case No ARB(AF)/00/2, Award (29 May 2003) [116] and [122].

the expropriation clause in the investment treaty to also encompass indirect de facto expropriation. In *Spyridon Roussalis v Romania*,[17] however, the arbitral tribunal entertained the possibility that the European Convention on Human Rights could be applied, but chose not to do so in the dispute 'given the higher and more specific level of protection offered by the [bilateral investment treaty (BIT)] to the investors compared to the more general protections offered to them [in the European Convention of Human Rights and its Additional Protocol No 1'.[18] A similar posture of differentiation was taken by the arbitral tribunal in *Quasar de Valores SICAV SA and others v Russia*,[19] which cautioned that:

> human rights conventions establish minimum standards to which all individuals are entitled irrespective of any act of volition on their part, whereas investment-protection treaties contain undertakings which are explicitly designed to induce foreigners to make investments in reliance upon them. It therefore makes sense that the reliability of an instrument of the latter kind should not be diluted by precisely the same notions of 'margins of appreciation' that apply to the former.[20]

However, the record is mixed as to the willingness of arbitral tribunals to consider international human rights law and jurisprudence as relevant rules of international law to interpret other investment treaty provisions, apart from expropriation clauses. Arbitral tribunals have not taken the extreme position that any alleged incompatibility between investment treaty obligations and human rights treaty obligations will result in an automatic hierarchical displacement of the former by the latter.[21] Instead, the greater preponderance of investment arbitration awards thus far demonstrate varying degrees of consideration for (or elaborating some arbitral tribunal analysis of) the human rights treaty obligations of host states of investment.[22] None of these awards speak of affecting human rights outcomes *stricto sensu*.

A few arbitral tribunals nevertheless still expressly delineate the investor-state arbitration claim before them from human rights claims, where the said investor-state arbitral tribunals decline to exercise jurisdiction over any human rights claims.[23] In *Grand*

[17] *Spyridon Roussalis v Romania*, ICSID Case No ARB/06/1, Award (7 December 2011).

[18] ibid [312] ('The Tribunal does not exclude the possibility that the international obligations of the Contracting States mentioned at Article 10 of the BIT could include obligations deriving from multilateral instruments to which those states are parties, including, possibly, the European Convention of Human Rights and its Additional Protocol 1. But the issue is moot in the present case and does not require decision by the Tribunal, given the higher and more specific level of protection offered by the BIT to the investors compared to the more general protections offered to them by the human rights instruments referred above. Consequently Article 10 of the BIT cannot, in its own terms and in the instant case, serve as a useful instrument for enlarging the protections available to the Claimant from the Romanian State under the BIT').

[19] *Quasar De Valores SICAV SA and others v Russia*, SCC Arbitration, Award (20 July 2012).

[20] ibid [22].

[21] *Azurix Corporation v Argentina*, ICSID Case No ARB/01/12, Award (14 July 2006) [254] and [261].

[22] *Impregilo SpA v Argentina*, ICSID Case No ARB/07/17, Award (21 June 2011) [230]; *Blusun SA and Jean-Pierre Lecorcier and Michael Stein v Italy*, ICSID Case No ARB/14/3, Award (27 December 2016) [318].

[23] *Antoine Biloune and Marine Drive Complex Ltd v Ghana Investment Centre and the Government of Ghana*, Awards (27 October 1989 and 30 June 1990) (where the tribunal denied jurisdiction over claims for denial of justice or violation of human rights); *Walam Energy LLC v Kenya*, ICSID Case No ARB/15/7, Award (10 July 2020) [469].

River Enterprises Six Nations Ltd and others v United States of America,[24] claimants (corporation and individuals constituted by members of indigenous peoples or First Nations belonging to the Six Nations of the Iroquois Confederacy or Haudenosaunee) urged the arbitral tribunal to take a broad understanding of 'investment' or 'enterprise' under the North American Free Trade Agreement (NAFTA) Chapter 11 and the obligation to take into account other legal rules under NAFTA arts 102(2), 1131(1), and 1131(2), which, in the view of the claimants meant 'bring[ing] into the process of interpretation human rights norms and customary rules relevant to indigenous peoples'.[25] The NAFTA tribunal rejected the claimants' position, reading narrowly the obligation to take into account other rules of international law in treaty interpretation:

> the Tribunal does not understand this obligation to provide a license to import into NAFTA legal elements from other treaties, or to allow alteration of an interpretation established through the normal interpretive processes of the Vienna Convention. This is a Tribunal of limited jurisdiction; it has no mandate to decide claims based on treaties other than NAFTA.[26]

Other investor-state arbitral tribunals have likewise taken a markedly restrictive position against international human rights law ever compressing relevant rules of international law for the interpretation of investment treaties.[27] The arbitral tribunal in *RosInvestCo UK Ltd v Russia* even went as far as to say that 'since the present context is that of a bilateral [investment] treaty, the Tribunal does not have to take up the questions whether other considerations may justify such an interpretation in the context of a long term multilateral convention or human rights'.[28] The arbitral tribunal in *Mohamed Abdel Raouf Bahgat v Egypt* was blunt:

> this Tribunal is not competent to adjudicate matters concerning human rights . . . when the [BIT] was drafted the States involved had not in mind to cover damages for

24 *Grand River Enterprises Six Nations Ltd and others v United States of America*, ICSID UNCITRAL Award (12 January 2011).

25 ibid [63], [66], [67].

26 ibid [71].

27 *See Antoine Biloune and Marine Drive Complex Ltd v Ghana Investment Centre and the Government of Ghana*, Awards (27 October 1989 and 30 June 1990) (where the tribunal denied jurisdiction over claims for denial of justice or violation of human rights); *The Rompetrol Group NV v Romania*, ICSID Case No ARB/06/3, Award (6 May 2013) [172] ('much of the detailed argument about the application of the specific provisions of the [European Convention of Human Rights] in the jurisprudence of the European Court of Human Rights, interesting and illuminating a sit has been, is beside the point when it comes to the issues under the Netherlands–Romania BIT which form the subject of the dispute before the Tribunal . . . the Tribunal is not competent to decide issues as to the application of the European Court of Human Rights within Romania, either to natural persons or to corporate entities'); *Mondev International Ltd v United States of America*, ICSID Case No ARB(AF)/99/2, NAFTA, Award (11 October 2002) [144]; *Kilic Insaat Ithalat Ihracat Sanayi Ve Ticaret Anonim Sirketi v Turkmenistan*, ICSID Case No ARB/10/1, Award (2 July 2013) [4.3.19], [8.1.21]; *Bernhard Friedrich Arnd Rudiger Von Pezold and Others v Zimbabwe*, ICSID Case No ARB/10/15, Award (28 July 2015) [465] ('The Tribunal is of the opinion that due caution should be exercised in importing concepts from other legal regimes [in this case European human rights law] without a solid basis for doing so. Balancing competing [and non-absolute] human rights and the need to grant States a margin of appreciation when making those balancing decisions is well established in human rights law, but the Tribunal is not aware that the concept has found much support in international investment law').

28 *RosInvestCo UK Ltd v Russia*, SCC Case No V079/2005, Award on Jurisdiction (1 October 2007) [121].

> human rights violations having occurred in connection with infringements on investments . . . [though] the events in [this] case might have warranted an award of moral damages, Claimant has failed to convince the Tribunal of its competence to award such damages under the treaties in question.[29]

By contrast, in *Hesham Talaat M Al-Warraq v Indonesia*,[30] the arbitral tribunal wholly accepted the claimant investor's position that Article 14 of the International Covenant on Civil and Political Rights (ICCPR) should be taken as relevant rules of international law in interpreting a fair and equitable treatment provision in another treaty not subject of the dispute (UK–Indonesia BIT art 3), but which had been applied to the claimant by operation of the most-favoured-nation clause in Article 8 of the Organization of Islamic Conference (OIC) Agreement.[31] The arbitral tribunal extensively discussed the ICCPR as 'a part of teneral international law',[32] and thus relevant to the interpretation of the fair and equitable treatment provision applied in this dispute.[33] Drawing on the substantive fair trial guarantees in the ICCPR, the Tribunal ultimately took the view that:

> denial of justice constitutes a clear violation of the [fair and equitable treatment] standard. Failure to comply with the most basic elements of justice when conducting a criminal proceeding against an investor amounts to a breach of the investment treaty . . . the Claimant was not properly notified of the criminal charges against him, he was tried and convicted *in absentia* and the sentence was not properly notified to the Claimant. The Claimant was not able to appoint legal counsel and was not able to appeal his sentence . . . the Claimant did not receive fair and equitable treatment *as enshrined in the ICCPR*.[34]

In this unique case, the arbitral tribunal fully interpreted the investment treaty provision (eg the fair and equitable treatment standard) from all of the substantive contours of the ICCPR.

Arguably the most famous case where an arbitral tribunal openly enumerated, but ultimately did not completely apply, extensive human rights law in investor-state disputes is *Urbaser SA and others v Argentina*.[35] In this case involving the Argentina–Spain BIT, the arbitral tribunal stressed that it was

> reluctant to share Claimants' principled position that guaranteeing the human right to water is a duty that may be born solely by the State, and never borne also by private

[29] *Mohamed Abdel Raouf Bahgat v Egypt*, PCA Case No 2012-07, Final Award (23 December 2001) [514], [519]–[520].
[30] *Hesham Talaat M Al-Warraq v Indonesia*, UNCITRAL, Final Award (15 December 2014).
[31] ibid [540], [541], [551], [683].
[32] ibid [558].
[33] ibid [556]–[621].
[34] ibid (emphasis added).
[35] *Urbaser SA and others v Argentina*, ICSID Case No ARB/07/26, Award (8 December 2016).

> companies like the Claimants ... international law accepts corporate social responsibility as a standard of crucial importance for companies operating in the field of international commerce. This standard includes commitments to comply with human rights in the framework of those entities' operations conducted in countries other than the country of their seat or incorporation. In light of this more recent development, it can no longer be admitted that companies operating internationally are immune from becoming subjects of international law.[36]

The *Urbaser* tribunal went on to extensively quote from and describe various international human rights instruments (such as the Universal Declaration of Human Rights) as well as actual international human rights treaties (such as the International Covenant on Economic Social and Cultural Rights),[37] observing that 'the [BIT] has to be construed in harmony with other rules of international law of which it forms part, including those relating to human rights'. Because the BIT in this case 'instructs the Tribunal to make its decision on the basis of the BIT and, where appropriate, by reference to one of the two bases other than the host state's domestic law, which are the main sources of international law, i.e. "other treaties in force between the Parties" and "general principles of international law" ... the BIT is not framed in isolation, but placed in the overall system of international law.'[38] From this standpoint, the *Urbaser* tribunal was quite receptive to using international human rights instruments and treaty provisions as 'relevant rules of international law' (within the meaning of Article 31(3)(c) of the Vienna Convention on the Law of Treaties) for the interpretation of the Argentina–Spain BIT. But the *Urbaser* tribunal ultimately did not do so given the facts of this dispute.

However, while the *Urbaser* tribunal declared that it was 'not disputed that the human right to water and sanitation is recognized today as part of human rights and that this right has as its corresponding obligation the duty of States to provide all persons living under their jurisdiction with safe and clean drinking water and sewage services',[39] it nonetheless stressed that:

> none of the provisions of the [Argentina–Spain BIT] has the effect of extending or transferring to the Concessionaire an obligation to perform services complying with the residents' human right to access to water and sewage services ... For such an obligation to exist and to become relevant in the framework of the BIT, it should either be part of another treaty (not applicable here) or it should represent a general principle of international law.... such obligation would be applicable as part of the legal framework of international law in which the investment is integrated in the particular case or, either cumulatively or alternatively, on the basis of the provision on applicable law in Article X(5) [of the Argentina–Spain BIT].[40]

36 ibid [1193] and [1195].
37 ibid [1196]–[1199].
38 ibid [1201].
39 ibid [1205].
40 ibid [1207].

Thus, in rejecting the counterclaim that Argentina filed against the claimants in this dispute,[41] what the *Urbaser* tribunal ultimately emphasized was that

> the investor's obligation to ensure the population's access to water is *not based on international law.* This obligation is framed by the legal and regulatory environment under which the investor is admitted to operate on the basis of the BIT and the host State's laws . . . while it is thus correct to state that the State's obligation is based on its obligation to enforce the human right to water of all individuals under its jurisdiction, this is not the case for the investors who pursue, it is true, the same goal, but on the basis of the Concession [contract] and not under an obligation derived from the human right to water. Indeed, the enforcement of the human right to water represents an obligation to perform. Such obligation is imposed upon States. It cannot be imposed on any company knowledgeable in the field of provision of water and sanitation services. In order to have such an obligation to perform applicable to a particular investor, a contract or similar legal relationship of civil and commercial law is required. In such a case, *the investor's obligation to perform has as its source domestic law; it does not find its legal ground in general international law.*[42]

Thus, while the *Urbaser* tribunal may have recognized international human rights law as potentially relevant rules of international law to interpret investment treaties concluded by states, it still required specific contractual language incorporating such international human rights obligations before the latter could bind foreign investors who are not parties to international human rights treaties.

III. Human Rights as a Recognized Part of Applicable Law

International human rights jurisprudence typically contains reasoning that affirms general or customary rules of international law (such as principles of attribution), and when thus cited by investor-state arbitral tribunals,[43] human rights are largely uncontroversial as part of the applicable law of determining the attribution of state responsibility. This is altogether distinct from situations when international human rights law is applied as *the primary legal obligation* against which the investor-state arbitral tribunal will determine the existence or inexistence of an international breach an internationally wrongful act by a state.[44] Arbitrator Philippe Sands' Dissenting Opinion in *Bear*

[41] ibid [1211]–[1221].

[42] ibid [1210] (emphasis added).

[43] See for example *MCI Power Group LC and New Turbine Inc v Ecuador*, ICSID Case No ARB/03/6, Award (31 July 2007) [82–84]; *Archer Daniels Midland Company and others v Mexico*, Award (21 November 2007) [117]–[118] and [170]–[173]; *UP and CD Holding Internationale v Hungary*, ICSID Case No ARB/13/35, Award (9 October 2018) [217], [219]; *Georg Gavrilovic and Gavrilovic DOO v Croatia*, ICSID Case No ARB/12/39, Award (26 July 2018) [774].

[44] Such as the nexus of human rights law with substantive guarantees of a minimum standard of treatment under customary law, as in *OI European Group BV v Venezuela*, Award (10 March 2015) [489].

Creek Mining v Peru[45] best encapsulates this latter situation, which demonstrates the potential for fully operationalizing human rights as a part of the substantive applicable law within an investor-state dispute. Sands took the view that the evidence before the tribunal

> clearly shows that the [investor's] acts and omissions, in the period before 2008, during 2008, thereafter, and right up until May 2011, contributed in material ways to the events that unfolded and then led to the Project's collapse ... the Project collapsed because of the investor's inability to obtain a 'social license', the necessary understanding between the Project's proponents and those living in the communities most likely to be affected by it, whether directly or indirectly.... .the viability and success of a project such as this, located in the community of the Aymara peoples, a group of interconnected communities, was necessarily dependent on local support.[46]

Dissenting arbitrator Sands cited the *Urbaser* award to substantiate the principle that any bilateral investment treaty 'has to be construed in harmony with other rules of international law of which it forms part, including those relating to human rights',[47] and since in the instant dispute the Canada–Peru Free Trade Agreement's Article 837 directed the tribunal to:

> decide issues in dispute in accordance with this Agreement and the applicable rules of international law ... the Tribunal is entitled to take [International Labour Organization (ILO) Convention No 169 on Indigenous Peoples as] ... a rule of international law applicable to the territory of Peru ... [the] Tribunal is entitled to take [ILO Convention No 169] into account in determining whether the Claimant carried out its obligation to give effect to the aspirations of the Aymara peoples in an appropriate manner, having regard to all relevant legal requirements, including the implementing Peruvian legislation.[48]

In light of the required social license for the investment project in this dispute, which inevitably necessitated compliance with international law applicable to Peru, such as ILO Convention No 169, Sands had little trouble finding that the investor (claimant) in the dispute also materially contributed to the alleged damages from the collapse of the investment project therein.

The arbitral tribunal in *Quiborax SA and others v Bolivia* declined to avail of international human rights law as applicable law in designing reparative relief in investor-state disputes, taking the view that remedies such as some types of satisfaction (eg declaratory judgments, apologies) 'are not transposable to investor-State disputes ...

[45] *Bear Creek Mining v Peru*, ICSID Case No ARB/14/21, Award (30 November 2017) with Dissenting Opinion of Philippe Sands.
[46] ibid [6].
[47] ibid [10].
[48] ibid [11].

[they depend] on the nature of the remedy and of the injury which it is meant to repair.'[49] The arbitral tribunal in *White Industries Australia Limited v India* also drew distinctions between the expected urgency of domestic judicial resolution of human rights, vis-à-vis the understandable ordinary delay of judicial resolution of purely commercial matters.[50] In contrast, the arbitral tribunal in *Strabag SE and others v Poland* conceded in principle that 'human rights violations may be relevant to an investment dispute, and a tribunal constituted under a BIT is competent to decide them.'[51] However, it found that under the facts of the dispute the claimants appeared to be:

> no longer pursuing this claim . . . to maintain a claim under the [European Convention on Human Rights on fair trial rights and right to protection of property under the First Protocol to the European Convention on Human Rights], they would have needed to address the operation of [Article 7(1) of the investment treaty, which provides for the application of more favourable treatment to investors from other present or future mutual international obligations of the Contracting Parties] and the Tribunal's mandate to apply international obligations set forth in other treaties. They also would have had to state in an understandable way how the ECHR's 'protection of property' and 'the right to fair trial' constitute an 'agreement which accords to the Claimants' investments more favourable treatment than is provided for by' the Treaty.[52]

Finally, it should also be noted that there is a line of investor-state arbitral claims postulating claims for moral damages, alleging host state breaches of international human rights law towards foreign investors, which have had variable results.[53] Moral damages were awarded in the *Desert Line v Yemen* case, under conditions that arguably described human rights violations in fact while being silent on breaches of human rights law, with the arbitral tribunal positively finding that there was 'physical duress exerted on the executives of the Claimant . . . malicious and therefore constitutive of a fault-based liability . . . prejudice was substantial since it affected the physical health of the Claimant's executives.'[54] Other tribunals, despite making positive findings of physical injury or some form of denial of due process, restriction on freedom of movement, or some other mistreatment that would ordinarily be tantamount to breaches of human rights law (civil, political, economic, social, or cultural rights), have instead chosen not to award moral damages.[55]

[49] *Quiborax SA and others v Bolivia*, ICSID Case No ARB/06/2, Award (16 September 2015) [554–555].

[50] *White Industries Australia Limited v India*, UNCITRAL, Final Award (30 November 2011) [5.2.15].

[51] *Strabag SE and others v Poland*, ICSID Case No ADHOC/15/1, Partial Award on Jurisdiction (4 March 2020).

[52] *White Industries Australia Limited v India*, UNCITRAL, Final Award (30 November 2011) [5.75].

[53] Contrast the rejection of the moral damages claim in *Adel A Hamadi Al Tamimi v Oman*, ICSID Case No ARB/11/33, Award (3 November 2015) [255]–[256], [390], [398]–[399], [402], with the award of moral damages in *Desert Line Projects LLC v Yemen*, ICSID Case No ARB/05/17, Award (6 February 2008).

[54] *Desert Line Projects LLC v Yemen*, ICSID Case No ARB/05/17, Award (6 February 2008) 290.

[55] *Joseph Charles Lemire v Ukraine*, ICSID Case No ARB/06/18, Award (28 March 2011) [344]–[345]; *Frank Charles Arif v Moldova*, ICSID Case No ARB/11/23, Award (8 April 2013) [590]–[592], [602]–[615].

IV. Human Rights as Evidence for Substantive Arguments on the Merits

Human rights may also provide evidence for substantive arguments on the merits.[56] In the 2019 Final Award in *Stabil LLC and others v Russia*,[57] the arbitral tribunal took into account human rights reports at the United Nations to substantiate the conclusion that the Russian Federation did not provide the required 'prompt, adequate, and effective' compensation for the nationalizations of around 4575 public and private real estate assets took place in Crimea soon after the March 2014 referendum that supposedly justified the annexation decision to 'integrate' Crimea with the Russian Federation.[58] These UN human rights fact-finding reports served as the evidentiary basis for the arbitral tribunal to conclude in *Stabill LLC v Russia* that the Russian Federation's nationalizations of the Claimants' investments 'did not meet any of the four requirements set forth in [the expropriation clause in Article 5 of the applicable investment treaty] for the lawfulness of an expropriation'.[59] Claimants in the *Yukos* arbitrations all drew on European Court of Human Rights rulings to argue that the Russian Federation's tax measures against Yukos shareholders were all imposed in bad faith and in violation of human rights; the arbitral tribunal stated that it

> recognizes that it is not a human rights court. Nevertheless, it is within the scope of the Tribunal's jurisdiction to consider the allegations of harassment and intimidation as they form part of the factual matrix of Claimants' complaints that the Russian Federation violated its obligations under Part III of the [Energy Charter Treaty].[60]

Similarly, the arbitral tribunal in *South American Silver Limited v Bolivia* drew from Bolivia's human rights law obligations in the process of evaluating whether Bolivia's Reversion Decree violated the expropriation clause in the Bolivia–United Kingdom BIT.[61] In particular, international human rights law became relevant for purposes of substantiating the first element of a lawful expropriation (eg public purpose):

> If the protection of life—the quintessential human right—and the need to return to normalcy in a region with an indigenous population that is affected and altered

[56] See *'President Allende' Foundation, Vicor Pey Casado and others v Chile*, PCA Case No 2017-30, UNCITRAL, Award (28 November 2019) [176] ('the Tribunal is of the view that Claimants' references to sources of international law other than the Treaty, i.e. the claims based on the breach of the American Convention on Human Rights, the International Covenant on Civil and Political Rights, the Geneva Convention and customary international law, were framed in the form of arguments, but do not constitute new claims, i.e. new requests for relief'); *Tethyan Copper Company Pty Limited v Pakistan*, ICSID Case No ARB/12/1, Award (12 July 2019) [928]–[929], [932]; *Joseph Houben v Burundi*, ICSID Case No ARB/13/7, Award (12 January 2016); *Rumeli Telekom AS and others v Kazakhstan*, ICSID Case No ARB/05/16, Award (29 July 2008) [710].

[57] *Stabil LLC and others v Russia*, PCA Case No 2015-35, UNCITRAL, Final Award (12 April 2019).

[58] ibid [253]–[254].

[59] ibid [259].

[60] See among others *Yukos Universal Limited (Isle of Man) v Russia*, PCA Case No AA 227, Final Award (18 July 2014) [764]–[765]; *Veteran Petroleum Limited (Cyprus) v Russia*, PCA Case No AA 228, Final Award (18 July 2014) [765].

[61] *South American Silver Limited v Bolivia*, PCA Case No 2013-15, Award (22 November 2018).

> by the Project emerge clearly as motivations in the Reversion Decree, the Tribunal cannot understand that the mere absence of a sacramental formula to expressly refer to human rights or to the protection of the communities may lead to the conclusion that the Reversion was not conducted in a social benefit related to the internal needs of Bolivia. In other words, the premises mentioned in the Reversion Decree as causes for Reversion have been proven and such premises include the protection of human rights—the right to life and the right to peace, both expressly mentioned in the Reversion Decree and the *ayllus* against the difficulties resulting from the Project.[62]

In contrast, in *Copper Mesa Mining Corporation v Ecuador*,[63] while the tribunal was fully receptive of all evidence on the possible applicability of international human rights law, it did not give credence to Ecuador's factual allegations of alleged international human rights violations by the foreign investor, which appeared to just have 'surfaced for the first time after the commencement of this arbitration'.[64] A similar position was taken by the arbitral tribunal in *EDF International SA and others v Argentina*,[65] when it found that while

> the Tribunal does not call into question the potential significance or relevance of human rights in connection with international investment law. However, regardless of any political wisdom in a temporary 'pesification' or provisional freeze of tariffs during the period of crisis, no showing has been made that Argentina was not able to comply with the relevant treaty provisions later . . . no evidence persuades the Tribunal that Respondent's failure to renegotiate tariffs in a timely fashion . . . was necessary to guarantee human rights.[66]

V. Human Rights as Bases for Non-Disputing Party Submissions

Arbitral tribunals have permitted amicus curiae or non-disputing party submissions, especially on human rights questions, but under carefully circumscribed conditions. In *Biwater Gauff (Tanzania) Ltd v Tanzania*, the arbitral tribunal clarified in this dispute that

> it was envisaged that [parties seeking recognition as non-disputing parties] would address broad policy issues concerning sustainable development, environment, human rights and governmental policy. These, indeed, are the areas that fell within the ambit of Rule 37(2)(a) of the ICSID Arbitration Rules. Given the generalized nature of [their] interests and participation, what was not expected was that [they] (a) would consider

62 ibid [561].
63 *Copper Mesa Mining Corporation v Ecuador*, PCA Case No 2012-2, Award (15 March 2016).
64 ibid [5.64].
65 *EDF International SA and others v Argentina*, ICSID Case No ARB/03/23, Award (11 June 2012).
66 ibid [912] and [914].

> themselves as simply in the same position as either party's lawyers, or (b) that they would see their role as suggesting to the Arbitral Tribunal how issues of fact or law as presented by the parties ought to be determined (which is obviously the sole mandate of the Arbitral Tribunal itself).[67]

In *Pac Rim Cayman LLC v El Salvador*, the arbitral tribunal admitted the application of the Center of International Economic Law (CIEL) as a non-disputing party but ultimately did not address much of CIEL's submission, because 'CIEL was not made privy to the mass of factual evidence adduced in this arbitration's third phase . . . the Tribunal's decisions in this Award do not require the Tribunal specifically to consider the legal case advanced by CIEL . . . it would be inappropriate for the Tribunal to do so'.[68]

VI. Conclusion

As the foregoing survey of investor-state arbitral awards from the 1970s to 2022 has demonstrated, international human rights law is not yet the directly applicable substantive law in investor-state arbitral disputes adjudicated in this time period. Consequently, little, if any, is indicated in awards in this period that remotely indicates that investor-state arbitral tribunals are in any way minded to consider adjudicating international human rights law as part of their arbitral function in these complex public–private disputes that generate wider human rights impacts (civil, political, economic, social, cultural, labour, environmental). The four dominant uses of international human rights law in investment awards (eg as bases for investment treaty reinterpretation; as invoked or recognized applicable law within the purview of the host state's regulatory environment; as evidence of substantive arguments on the merits; and as the bases for non-disputing party submissions) capture the continuing gulf between the human rights impacts of foreign investments, and the challenges of those seeking human rights outcomes within the fixed *lex specialis* parameters and procedures of investor-state arbitration. In the August 2022 investment award in *Rockhopper Italia SpA and others v Italy*,[69] the foreign investor claimant was awarded €185 million for the unlawful expropriation that Italy committed after Italy invoked environmental and climate change reasons to cancel the claimant's license to exploit an offshore oilfield near the Italian coastline. The *Rockhopper* tribunal stressed that

> this award is not a 'victory' for one side or the other in that environmental debate, which is of a civic or political character, but rather addresses the legal issue at hand, namely, whether compensation is due to a foreign investor in respect of its investment, based on specific international criteria as contained in a treaty to which Italy was, at

[67] *Biwater Gauff (Tanzania) Ltd v Tanzania*, ICSID Case No ARB/05/22, Award (24 July 2008) [366].
[68] *Pac Rim Cayman LLC v El Salvador*, ICSID Case No ARB/09/12, Award (14 October 2016) [3.29]–[3.30].
[69] *Rockhopper Italia SpA and others v Italy*, ICSID Case No ARB/17/14, Award (23 August 2022).

> the material time, a contracting party... the material and factual circumstances which have led to the final result of this arbitration are both specific and discrete from the environmental considerations which have been argued before the Tribunal.[70]

Human rights law may be increasingly present in investment awards, but they are still not given any full legal impacts and meaningful normative effects in investor-state dispute outcomes.

[70] ibid [10].

15

Counterclaims

Trends and Perspectives

Mohamed S Abdel Wahab[*]

I. Introduction

Generally speaking, counterclaims are claims raised by respondents in the same proceedings in which the principal claim(s) is/are adjudicated. While there is no universally accepted definition of the term 'counterclaim',[1] *Black's Law Dictionary* defines it as '[a] claim for relief asserted against an opposing party after an original claim has been made'.[2] The *Oxford Companion to Law* describes it as a cross-claim that can be conveniently examined and disposed of in a pending action initiated by another party (ie the plaintiff).[3] In investment arbitration, 'counterclaims' mainly denote a procedural mechanism whereby the respondents could bring a claim against the claimants.[4] It is commonly submitted that it is usual that host states are the respondents and foreign investors are the claimants. However, it has recently been observed that host states have in some cases been claimants and foreign investors were the respondents.

Counterclaims initially emerged as an institution of municipal laws.[5] Later on, they were transported into the international law and dispute settlement spheres, to first be integrated into the Rules of Procedure of the International Court of justice (ICJ) and its predecessor, the Permanent Court of International Justice (PCIJ).[6] Unlike defences on the merits,[7] which denote assertions or arguments of fact or law made by the

* The author wishes to thank Dr Alia Al Gazzar, Counsel at Zulficar & Partners Law Firm, who provided assistance with the research, compilation of the reviewed decisions, and the preparation of a preliminary draft of this chapter.

[1] Shabtai Rosenne, *Essays on International Law and Practice* (Brill 2007) 267; Constantine Antonopoulos, *Counterclaims before the International Court of Justice* (Springer 2011) 50.

[2] Bryan A Garner, *Black's Law Dictionary* (9th edn, West 2010) 402.

[3] David M Walker, *The Oxford Companion to Law* (OUP 1980) 298.

[4] Jason Rudall, 'The Tribunal with a Toolbox: On *Perenco v Ecuador*, Black Gold and Shades of Green' (2020) 11 Journal of International Dispute Settlement 491; Michael Waibel and Jake Rylatt 'Counterclaims in International Law' in Romina Pezzot and Silvia González Napolitano (eds), *La solución de controversias en derecho internacional y temas vinculados* (Eudeba 2017) 295.

[5] Harshad Pathak, 'Consenting to Counterclaims under the ICSID Convention' (2019) 19 Pepp Dispute Resolution Law Journal 101; Helene Bubrowski, 'Balancing IIA Arbitration through the Use of Counterclaims' in Armand De Mestral and Céline Lévesque (eds), *Improving International Investment Agreements* (Routledge 2012) 212; Dafina Atanasova and others, 'The Legal Framework for Counterclaims in Investment Treaty Arbitration' (2014) 31(3) Journal of International Arbitration, 359–360; Antonopoulos (n 1) 7, 10.

[6] Antonopoulos (n 1) 7; Bubrowski (n 5) 212–13.

[7] It has been reported that host states often conflate mere defences on the merits with proper legal actions against investors, see eg Anna De Luca 'Counterclaims in Investment Arbitration: Reflections on

Mohamed S Abdel Wahab, *Counterclaims* In: *The Award in International Investment Arbitration*. Edited by: Katia Fach Gómez and Catharine Titi, Oxford University Press. © Katia Fach Gómez and Aikaterini Titi 2024. DOI: 10.1093/9780191975936.003.0015

respondent aiming exclusively at undermining the original claim by discharging the respondent's liability (ie the dismissal of the principal claim),[8] counterclaims exhibit a dual nature. Not only do they represent autonomous claims premised on a cause of action separate from the primary claim, but they also ultimately aim to achieve more than the mere dismissal of the principal claim; they aim to secure an affirmative relief of some sort, such as convicting the claimant for its misconduct.[9]

Counterclaims are further distinguished from set-off claims. While the former seek 'payment or performance—and possibly enforcement—beyond the primary claim',[10] a set-off claim aims at the deduction of monies owed by the claimant to the respondent from the former's claim.[11] Another point of distinction in terms of their value and awarded damages is that while set-off claims are typically capped by the total value of the primary claim, a counterclaim is subject to an independent valuation that may either correspond to or exceed the total value of the primary claim.[12]

In short, a set-off claim functions as a shield, rather than a sword, against the claimant's primary claim. Unlike a counterclaim, whereby the respondent aims to vindicate its interests against the claimant based on a separate cause of action, a set-off claim is protective in nature as it merely intends to avoid 'the unnecessary formalism of performing debts which two parties owe each other'.[13] That being the case, the fate of a set-off claim primarily depends on whether it is advanced autonomously as an independent claim or—as in the majority of cases—it is contingent upon a counterclaim. An illustrative example to an investor-state dispute where the counterclaim in question constituted the exact same basis for the set-off claim; hence the fate of the latter was contingent upon the admissibility of the former is the *Oxus v Uzbekistan* case. The dispute arose out of an alleged misappropriation by the Uzbek government of the claimant's goldfields in Uzbekistan. In response, the Uzbekistan raised several counterclaims, alleging that the claimant had misrepresented the financing of the project, wasted natural resources, breached the

UNCITRAL WG III Reform' (*Kluwer Arbitration Blog*, 2021) <http://arbitrationblog.kluwerarbitration.com/2021/11/05/counterclaims-in-investment-arbitration-reflections-on-uncitral-wg-iii-reform/>.

[8] Jeremy Sharpe and Marc Jacob 'Counterclaims and State Claims' in Christina L Beharry (ed), *Contemporary and Emerging Issues on the Law of Damages and Valuation in International Investment Arbitration title* (Brill 2018) 348.

[9] *Application of the Convention on the Prevention and Punishment of the Crime of Genocide* (*Bosnia & Herzegovina v Yugoslavia*) Dissenting Opinion of Judge Weeramantry [1997] ICJ Rep 290. See also Eva Kalnina and Ankita Godbole, 'Article 46' in Julien Fouret and others (eds), *The ICSID Convention, Regulations and Rules: A Practical Commentary* (Edward Elgar Publishing 2019) 417, para 4.439; Atanasova (n 5) 359; Pathak (n 5) 101.

[10] Sharpe and Jacob (n 8) 349.

[11] ibid; H Elisabeth Kjos *Applicable Law in Investor-State Arbitration* (OUP 2013) 128, n 170; David D Caron and others, *The UNCITRAL Arbitration Rules: A Commentary* (OUP 2006), 409–10. See eg *Ioan Micula, Viorel Micula and others v Romania (I)*, ICSID Case No ARB/05/20, Final Award (11 December 2013) [1278] [1280]–[1281] [1291]; *Desert Line Projects LLC v Yemen*, ICSID Case No ARB/05/17, Award (6 February 2008) [144] [223] [247]–[253].

[12] Sharpe and Jacob (n 8) 363; Caron (n 11) 409–10; Christoph Schreuer and others, *The ICSID Convention: A Commentary* (2nd edn, CUP 2009) 749, para 64.

[13] Klaus Peter Berger, 'Set-Off' *ICC Bulletin* (Special Supplement, 2005) 17ff; Pierre A Karrer 'Jurisdiction on Set-Off Defences and Counterclaims' (2001) 67(2) International Journal of Arbitration, Mediation & Dispute Management.

Special Dividend Agreement, violated currency law, and engaged in self-dealing and related-party transactions.[14]

Having found that it lacks jurisdiction over Uzbekistan's counterclaims,[15] of which the set-off claim constituted part, the tribunal held that 'it cannot rely on a set-off defence in the present arbitration, given that the Arbitral Tribunal does not have jurisdiction over the claims upon which Respondent relies for the purpose of its set-off defence'.[16]

From a policy perspective, while considerations underlying the permissibility of defences on the merits may slightly differ from counterclaims and set-off claims, similar to defences on the merits, which essentially preserve the respondent's right to be heard and present its own case as a general principle of law (ie procedural fairness), counterclaims may also be considered an effective means by which procedural equality could be attained, in so far as it allows for equal treatment of the disputing parties.[17] The admissibility of counterclaims is further said to enhance and promote judicial economy, sound administration of justice, the rule of law, and avoids the risk of inconsistent outcomes.[18]

While the above explains the admissibility of counterclaims in virtually all municipal legal systems and interstate proceedings,[19] the right of host states to submit counterclaims, which have become predominant in investment arbitrations,[20] has only recently gained considerable attention in investment arbitration practice and jurisprudence. This chapter addresses state counterclaims from various perspectives. It analyses state counterclaims in investment treaty practice and jurisprudence, before shedding some light on the latest trend in interventionist approaches to state counterclaims.

II. Counterclaims in Investor-State Arbitration: Towards Rebalancing International Treaty Protection

Owing to the fact that arbitration agreements in contracts typically grant the contracting parties (both the investor and the host state) the right to submit their reciprocal

[14] *Oxus Gold plc v Uzbekistan, the State Committee of Uzbekistan for Geology & Mineral Resources, and Navoi Mining & Metallurgical Kombinat*, UNCITRAL Arbitration, Final Award (17 December 2015) [906]–[913].

[15] ibid [960]–[959].

[16] ibid [972].

[17] Crina Baltag, 'Regime Interaction in Investment Arbitration: Counterclaims' (*Kluwer Arbitration Blog*, 2022) <http://arbitrationblog.kluwerarbitration.com/2022/01/11/regime-interaction-in-investment-arbitration-counterclaims/>; De Luca (n 7); Tomoko Ishikawa, 'Counterclaims and the Rule of Law in Investment Arbitration' (2019) 113 American Journal of International Law 37; Kjos (n 13) 131, 147; Kryvoi Yaraslau 'Counterclaims in Investor-State Arbitration' (2012) 21(2) Minnesota Journal of International Law 218; 174; Bubrowski (n 6) 213–14; Walid Ben Hamida, 'L'arbitrage Etat-investisseur cherche son équilibre perdu: Dans quelle mesure l'Etat peut introduire des demandes reconventionnelles contre l'investisseur prive?' (2005) 7(4) International LFD International 270–01. See also Antonopoulos (n 1) 282, 287, 292.

[18] Pathak (n 5); Kjos (n 13) 128; Yaraslau (n 17); Bubrowski (n 6) 214; Ben Hamida (n 17) 262–63. See also Antonopoulos (n 1) 281.

[19] Antonopoulos (n 1) 1, 10; Kjos (n 13) 128; Arnaud De Nanteuil, 'Counterclaims in Investment Arbitration: Old Questions, New Answers' (2018) 17 Law and Practice of International Courts & Tribunals 375.

[20] Bubrowski (n 6) 218.

claims, contract-based disputes generally do not raise difficulties in investment arbitration.[21] Conversely, many IIAs in force, particularly those of the first generation,[22] impeded the admissibility of counterclaims in treaty-based arbitrations.[23]

This asymmetry which plagues first generation IIAs is twofold: procedural and substantive. The procedural asymmetry of IIAs emerged from the dispute settlement clauses (DSCs) set out in such agreements, which are qualified as 'unilateral' standing offers by host states to arbitrate vesting 'solely' foreign investors with direct access to arbitration so as to resolve their dispute against the host state.[24] There is blatant unfairness and inequality that ensues from granting investors exclusive access to arbitration, which was highlighted by the *SGS* tribunal in the following terms:

> It would be inequitable if, by reason of the invocation of ICSID jurisdiction, the [foreign investor] could on the one hand elevate its side of the dispute to international adjudication and, on the other, preclude the [host State] from pursuing its own claim for damages.[25]

Notwithstanding the above, recent developments demonstrate a shift in the traditional paradigm of perceiving investment arbitration as a mechanism whose sole purpose is to provide a venue for foreign investors to vindicate their rights vis-à-vis host states.[26] One scholar went further to suggest that host states could act as claimants in investment treaty arbitrations.[27] A corollary to such a paradigm shift, or possibly a consequence thereof, is the recently growing number counterclaims submitted by host states in investment treaty arbitrations; a development promoted by scholars as an effective means to remedy the disadvantaged position of host states, and ultimately rebalance the investor-state relationship.[28]

[21] Jean E Kalicki, 'Counterclaims by States in Investment Arbitration' *Investment Treaty News* (14 January 2013) <www.iisd.org/itn/en/2013/01/14/counterclaims-by-states-in-investment-arbitration-2/>; Andrea Bjorkund, 'The Role of Counterclaims in Rebalancing Investment Law' (2013) 17 (2) Lewis & Clark Law Review 461, 462; Mehmet Toral and Thomas Schultz, 'The State, a Perpetual Respondent in Investment Arbitration? Some Unorthodox Consideration' in Michael Waibel and others (eds), *The Backlash against Investment Arbitration* (Kluwer Law International 2010) 589; Pierre Lalive and Laura Halonen, 'On the Availability of Counterclaims in Investment Treaty Arbitration' (2011) 2 Czech Yearbook of International Arbitration 146.

[22] For a further discussion on the distinctive features of new generation IIAs, see text to n 130.

[23] *Hesham Talaat M Al-Warraq v Indonesia*, UNCITRAL, Final Award (15 December 2014) [659] (affirming that '[c]ounterclaims are problematic in investment arbitration because of the 'inherently asymmetrical character' of an investment treaty'). See also Lalive and Halonen (n 21). On the asymmetric nature of investment treaty arbitration, see Stefan Dudas 'Treaty Counterclaims under the ICSID Convention' in Crina Baltag (ed), *ICSID Convention After 50 years: Unsettled Issues* (Kluwer Law International 2016) 385–88.

[24] Gustavo Laborde, 'The Case for Host State Claims in Investment Arbitration' (2010) 1(1) Journal of International Dispute Settlement, 105; Eric De Brabandere, 'Human Rights Counterclaims in Investment Treaty Arbitration' (2017) 50 Revue Belge de Droit International 600; Sharpe and Jacob (n 8) 365; De Nanteuil (n 19) 376; Bjorkund (n 21) 461, 462; Ishikawa (n 17) 194.

[25] *SGS Société Générale de Surveillance SA v Pakistan*, ICSID Case No ARB/01/13, Procedural Order No 2 (16 October 2002) 8 ICSID Review, 302. See also Toral and Schultz (n 21) 578–79.

[26] Bubrowski (n 6) 214; cf Dudas (n 23) 386.

[27] See generally Laborde (n 24) 97.

[28] Bjorkund (n 21) 464–65; Pathak (n 5); Julien Chaisse and Rahul Donde 'The State of Investor-State Arbitration' (2018) 51(1) International Lawyer 47; De Nanteuil (n 19) 376–377. See also generally Bubrowski (n 5).

That said, it is worth noting that the right of host states to file a counterclaim has become generally recognized by virtually all arbitration rules,[29] at least this is the case for the predominant arbitration rules such as those of the Convention on the Settlement of Investment Disputes (ICSID),[30] the United Nations Commission in International Trade Law on (UNCITRAL),[31] the Stockholm Chamber of Commerce (SCC),[32] and the International Chamber of Commerce (ICC).[33] Nevertheless, the success of counterclaims in investment treaty arbitration, so as to lead to the establishment of the investor's responsibility and recovery of damages by host states, remains hinged upon a number of jurisdictional, procedural and substantive questions, which came under close scrutiny in several investment treaty awards, as will be examined in the following sections.

A. Awards on Jurisdiction: 'The Consent Conundrum'

The foundational stone of any arbitral proceedings is the parties' consent, which forms the basis for the adjudicatory power of any arbitral tribunal and is determinative of the extent to which the latter could exercise jurisdiction over a specific claim.[34] Awards on jurisdiction demonstrate a tension between two approaches to ascertaining the parties' consent to endow the tribunal with jurisdiction over counterclaims. The first—predominant—approach involves awards where tribunals relied on their reading of the DSC contained in the IIA, so as to verify that the disputing parties have consented to extend the tribunal's jurisdiction to the host state's counterclaims. This approach has been referred to as 'the doctrine of analysis of presence of consent in the arbitral agreement'.[35] The second approach considers that by merely electing a set of procedural rules that permit counterclaims the disputing parties are deemed to have consented to the submission of counterclaims, which is referred to as 'the doctrine of ipso facto importation of consent'.[36]

The leading example of the first approach is the award in *Roussalis v Romania*.[37] The dispute concerned the claimant's allegation that Romania's measures against him

[29] De Nanteuil (n 19) 374, 378.

[30] See ICSID Convention art 46 and ICSID Arbitration Rules r 48.

[31] See 2010 UNCITRAL Arbitration Rules art 21(3), which reads as follows: 'In its statement of defence, or at a later stage in the arbitral proceedings if the arbitral tribunal decides that the delay was justified under the circumstances, the respondent may make a counterclaim or *rely on a claim for the purpose of a set-off provided that the arbitral tribunal has jurisdiction over it*' (emphasis added).

[32] See SCC Arbitration Rules art 9(1)(iii).

[33] See ICC Rules of Arbitration art 5.

[34] Sharpe and Jacob (n 8) 352; De Nanteuil (n 19) 377; Kjos (n 13) 112; Martin Gronemann and Markus Krajewski, 'The Legal Nature of the Treaty-Based Consent to Investment Arbitration' in Katia Fach Gómez and Catharine Titi (eds), *The Award in International Investment Arbitration* (OUP 2024). See also *Abaclat and others v Argentina*, ICSID Case No ARB/07/5, Dissenting Opinion of Georges Abi-Saab (28 October 2011) [7].

[35] José Antonio Rivas, 'ICSID Treaty Counterclaims: Case Law and Treaty Evolution' in Jean E Kalicki and Anna Joubin-Bret (eds), *Reshaping the Investor-State Dispute Settlement System* (Brill 2015) 798, 808–09.

[36] ibid 798, 802–04.

[37] *Spyridon Roussalis v Romania*, ICSID Case No ARB/O6/1, Award (7 December 2011). See also *Saluka Investments BV v Czech Republic*, UNCITRAL Arbitration, Decision on Jurisdiction over the Czech Republic's Counterclaim (7 May 2004) [24] [39]–[40]; *Sergei Paushok, CJSC Golden East Company and CJSC Vostokneftegaz Company v Mongolia*, UNCITRAL, Award on Jurisdiction and Liability (28 April 2011) [684] [689].

constituted harassment, expropriation, and arbitrary and unreasonable treatment of his investment.[38] Romania submitted a counterclaim whereby it requested the tribunal to hold the investor's company liable for the mismanagement of the business, tax evasion, and fraud and to order it to pay damages.[39] On his part, the claimant objected to the tribunal's jurisdiction over the counterclaim, relying on the language of the Greece–Romania BIT, which limits the jurisdiction of the tribunal to disputes 'concerning an obligation of the latter under this Agreement'.[40]

After referring to Article 46 of the ICSID Convention and the former Article 40 of the ICSID Arbitration Rules, the tribunal noted that counterclaims falling within its jurisdiction shall satisfy two conditions: first, they have to arise directly out of the subject matter of the dispute, and, second, found to be within the scope of the consent of the parties and are otherwise within the jurisdiction of the Centre.[41] To determine the existence and scope of the parties' consent, the tribunal noted that the ICSID Convention only requires that the parties' consent be in writing, hence the question of whether and the extent to which the claimant has accepted Romania's offer to arbitrate in the BIT, which included the consent to arbitrate the counterclaims, has to be determined by reference to the language of the dispute settlement clause laid down in the BIT itself:

> The Convention only required that consent be in writing, leaving the parties otherwise free to choose the manner in which to express their consent. [...] The investor's consent to the BIT's arbitration clause can only exist in relation to counterclaims if such counterclaims come within the consent of the host State as expressed in the BIT.[42]

The tribunal then engaged in an interpretation of Article 9 of the BIT, which included the BIT's dispute settlement clause, so as to stand upon the will of the parties, and in so doing it was guided by the customary rules of treaty interpretation as set out in Article 31 of the Vienna Convention on the law of Treaties 1969 (VCLT).[43] The majority accepted the claimant' argument, finding that the phrase 'disputes ... concerning an obligation of the latter' is clear in limiting the tribunal's jurisdiction to investor's claims pertaining to the obligations of the host state, and accordingly it was held that 'the BIT does not provide for counterclaims to be introduced by the host state in relation to obligations of the investor. The meaning of the "dispute" is the issue of compliance by the State with the BIT'.[44]

The majority further supported the above finding by the fact that the BIT imposes no obligations on investors. The majority further noted that Article 9(4) only refers to the BIT as the applicable law; had the competence of a tribunal been intended to extend to counterclaims submitted by a state, the contracting parties could have made

[38] *Spyridon Roussalis v Romania*, ICSID Case No ARB/O6/1, Award (7 December 2011) [66].
[39] ibid [747]–[754].
[40] ibid [828].
[41] ibid [861]–[863].
[42] ibid [865]–[866].
[43] ibid [867]–[871].
[44] ibid [869].

reference to disputes that are grounded in domestic law.[45] Hence, the majority held that the parties' consent to arbitrate counterclaims is lacking.[46]

Notably, Michael Reisman, one of the arbitrators in the *Roussalis* case, disagreed with the majority's finding,[47] as he was of the view that, by electing to arbitrate under the ICSID Convention, which envisages the possibility of filing ancillary claims, the parties are deemed to have impliedly consented to extend the tribunal's jurisdiction to counterclaims. In other words, according to Reisman, consent to arbitrate counterclaims can be automatically imported through the mere selection of procedural rules that allow for the filing of counterclaims.[48]

Notwithstanding that Reisman's dissent represented the minority opinion in the *Roussalis* case, it has yet been endorsed by the tribunal in the *Antoine Goetz v Burundi* award.[49] While the dispute settlement clause in the Belgium–Burundi BIT was not significantly different from the one applicable in the *Roussalis* case, the tribunal followed Reisman's approach in this case.[50] The tribunal first noted that, as per the applicable BIT, Burundi had accepted that disputes be submitted to arbitration under the ICSID Convention, particularly Article 46 of the Convention and the former Rule 40 of the Arbitration Rules. In light of this, and notwithstanding that the dispute settlement clause contained Belgium–Burundi BIT lacked any reference to counterclaims, the tribunal held that by accepting the offer contained in the BIT without qualification, the claimants had consented to arbitrate counterclaims.[51]

The *Goetz* award triggered jurisprudential division. Proponents of the *Goetz* award's approach relied on some policy considerations that, according to them, militate towards the implied theory approach. In particular, they refer to the policy objectives behind the ICSID Convention, which is to ensure faster, more efficient, and final resolution of investment disputes. To further support the *Goetz* award's approach, they warned against the procedural inefficiency and possible contradictory outcomes that could ensue as a consequence of forcing host state to resort to different fora in order to resolve their counterclaims; all of which oppose the objectives underlying Article 46 of the ICSID Convention.[52]

According to the above, either the silence of the constitutive instrument or its limitative arbitration clauses will have little relevance to the tribunal's jurisdiction over a counterclaim. It rather suffices that the procedural rules agreed upon contain the

[45] ibid [870]–[871].
[46] ibid [872].
[47] See also Charles N Brower and Ahmed Mazlom, 'To Err Is Human, to Dissent Divine' in Fach Gómez and Titi (n 34).
[48] Kalnina and Godbole (n 9) 421, para 4.448. See *Spyridon Roussalis v Romania*, ICSID Case No ARB/O6/1, Declaration of Prof W Michael Reisman (7 December 2011) [872].
[49] *Antoine Goetz & Consorts and SA Affinage des Métaux v Burundi*, ICSID Case No ARB/01/2, Award (21 June 201).
[50] Kalnina and Godbole (n 9) 420, para 4.450.
[51] *Antoine Goetz & Consorts and SA Affinage des Métaux v Burundi*, ICSID Case No ARB/01/2, Award (21 June 2012) [278].
[52] See generally Kalnina and Godbole (n 9) 423, para 4.455.

possibility of presenting counterclaims for the tribunal to enjoy the competence to entertain a host state's counterclaim.[53]

Notwithstanding the jurisprudential support that the *Goetz* award's approach has gained, it remains an 'outlier', since the majority of awards addressing jurisdiction over counterclaims have displayed favouritism to the *Roussalis* majority approach of sourcing the consent of the parties in the language of the relevant investment treaty.[54] For instance, in *Oxus v Uzbekistan*, a dispute that was filed under the UK–Uzbekistan BIT and governed by the 2010 UNCITRAL Arbitration Rules,[55] the tribunal refused to accept the possibility that Article 21(3) of the 2010 UNCITRAL Arbitration Rules confers jurisdiction that does not otherwise exist under the applicable BIT. Instead, it considered that reference to counterclaims in Article 21(3) of the UNCITRAL Arbitration Rules merely indicates that counterclaims *already* falling within its jurisdiction as per the dispute settlement clause contained in the applicable BIT (ie the UK–Uzbekistan BIT) would be admissible.[56] Having relied on the language of the applicable BIT, which in Article 8(1), refers only to 'disputes concerning an obligation of the latter [ie the host state] under this Agreement', the tribunal considered that the parties' consent, and therefore its jurisdiction, to be limited to claims advanced by investors against the host state, to the exclusion of the host state's counterclaims.[57]

Similarly, in *Gavazzi v Romania*,[58] an ICSID tribunal constituted under the Italy–Romania BIT was confronted with a counterclaim filed by Romania whereby it requested the claimants to pay compensation for damages it has endured as a consequence of the claimants' failure to comply with their investment obligations under Romanian law and for the mismanagement of their investment.[59] Supporting its assertion of the tribunal's jurisdiction over its counterclaims, and given that the BIT is silent on whether the filing of counterclaims is permissible, Romania relied on the lack of exclusion of such possibility in the BIT, thereby arguing that such right is presumed.[60] The tribunal rejected Romania's argument, noting that 'no jurisdiction can be inferred by the "spirit" of the BIT' where such jurisdiction is not conferred upon the tribunal by the wording of the BIT in relation to a counterclaim.[61] In deciding that the

[53] See Zachary Douglas 'The Enforcement of Environmental Norms in Investment Treaty Arbitration' in Pierre-Marie Dupuy and Jorge E Viñuales (eds), *Harnessing Foreign Investment to Promote Environmental Protection: Incentives and Safeguards* (CUP 2013) 427.

[54] Kalnina and Godbole (n 9) 423, para 4.454. See also *Karkey Karadeniz Elektrik Uretim AS v Pakistan*, ICSID Case No ARB/13/1, Award (22 August 2017) [1003]–[1016]. *Iberdrola Energía, SA v Guatemala (II)*, UNCITRAL Arbitration, PCA Case No 2017-41, Final Award (20 August 2020) [388]–[391]; *Anglo-American plc v Venezuela*, ICSID Case No ARB(AF)/14/1, Award (18 January 2019) [523]–[528]; *Rusoro Mining Ltd v Venezuela*, ICSID Case No ARB(AF)/12/5, Award (22 August 2016) [627]; *Hesham Talaat M Al-Warraq v Indonesia*, UNCITRAL Arbitration, Final Award (15 December 2014) [660]–[672]; *Inmaris Perestroika Sailing Maritime Services GmbH and others v Ukraine*, ICSID Case No ARB/08/8, Award (1 March 2012) [432].

[55] *Oxus Gold plc v Uzbekistan, the State Committee of Uzbekistan for Geology & Mineral Resources, and Navoi Mining & Metallurgical Kombinat* (UNCITRAL Arbitration, Final Award (17 December 2015) [123] and [125].

[56] ibid [944]–[945].

[57] ibid [947]–[948].

[58] *Marco Gavazzi and Stefano Gavazzi v Romania*, ICSID Case No ARB/12/25, Decision on Jurisdiction, Admissibility and Liability (21 April 2015).

[59] ibid [148].

[60] ibid [149]–[150].

[61] ibid [54].

Italy–Romania BIT does not entitle Romania the right to present counterclaims, the tribunal relied on the language of the BIT, including its preamble, the wording of the dispute settlement clause enshrined in Article 8 of the BIT.[62]

In *Urbaser v Argentina*,[63] the dispute arose out of some measures adopted by Argentina in response to its economic crisis that took place mid-2001, including emergency measures, which the claimants alleged to have obstructed the operation of its water and sewage services concession, thereby constituted treaty violations under the Spain–Argentine BIT.[64] In response, Argentina submitted a counterclaim against the claimant, whereby it requested the tribunal to order the latter to pay damages, plus interests, for their failure to make the necessary investments; thus violating its commitments and obligations under international law based on the human right to water.[65] The claimants challenged the tribunal's jurisdiction over Argentina's counterclaim, relying primarily on the 'asymmetric nature of BITs', which according to them prevents the host state from invoking any right under the applicable treaty by virtue of a counterclaim.[66]

In departure from the *Goetz* award, the tribunal followed the *Roussalis* approach, and it premised its finding of jurisdiction over Argentina's counterclaims on the broad and neutral wording of the specific dispute settlement clause set out in Article X of the Spain–Argentina BIT. By reference to the latter's language, the tribunal found the identity of the claimant and respondent in an investment dispute to be of no significance to the tribunal's jurisdiction. The tribunal further noted that Article X does not exclude the state's ability to sue the investor. Hence, a dispute under the said BIT could be submitted by either party.[67] The tribunal also rejected the claimants' argument that their consent was restricted in scope so as to only cover their claims. The tribunal found that there is no evidence that the claimants' consent contained any restriction in respect of a future counterclaim or any other limitation relating to Article X of the BIT.[68]

In a relatively more recent case, *Tethyan v Pakistan*,[69] Pakistan submitted a counterclaim against the investor, alleging that the latter has violated the Australia–Pakistan BIT in that its investment was not made in accordance with Pakistan's laws and investment policies.[70] Applying the *Roussalis* majority's approach, the tribunal determined the scope of the parties' consent so as to ascertain its extension to counterclaims in general and to non-treaty claims in particular by interpreting the BIT's dispute resolution clause pursuant to the general rules of interpretation set out in Article 31 of the VCLT.[71] The tribunal further supported its reading that the dispute settlement clause clearly

[62] ibid [151]–[153], [155]–[159].

[63] *Urbaser SA & Consorcio de Aguas Bilbao Bizkaia, Bilbao Biskaia Ur Partzuergoa v Argentina*, ICSID Case No ARB/07/26, Award (8 December 2016).

[64] ibid [34].

[65] ibid [36]–[37].

[66] ibid [1117]–[1125].

[67] ibid [1143]–[1144].

[68] ibid [1145]–[1148].

[69] *Tethyan Copper Company Pty Limited v Pakistan*, ICSID Case No ARB/12/1, Decision on Jurisdiction and Liability (10 November 2017).

[70] ibid [1375].

[71] ibid [1416]–[1418].

allows both parties to initiate arbitration proceedings by referring to the expressed intention of the drafters of the ICSID Convention, which is not to provide for a 'one-way street' for investors.[72]

B. The Admissibility Dilemma: 'The Connexity Requirement' or 'The Test of Connectedness'

Unlike the issue of consent, which relates to the jurisdiction of the tribunal, the requirement that the counterclaim is directly connected to the main claim is a matter of admissibility of the counterclaim.[73] Awards addressing the connectedness requirement demonstrate the prevalence of two approaches to determining the connexity (or connectedness) requirement; one is the restrictive (or the so-called rigorous) approach, and the other is the relatively more lenient approach.

The landmark award on the restrictive approach is rendered in *Saluka v Czech Republic*.[74] In implementation of the Czech Republic's reorganization and privatization strategy of the banking sector, IPB was forced to sell its assets to four major Czech commercial banks.[75] As a consequence, the claimant filed arbitration proceedings against the Czech Republic under the 1976 UNCITRAL Rules, alleging that its conduct constituted a discriminatory, unfair, inequitable, and expropriatory treatment in breach of its obligations under the Netherlands–Czech Republic BIT.[76] Not only did the Czech Republic refute the claimant's allegations, but it also submitted various heads of counterclaims against the claimant,[77] which the latter, unsurprisingly, challenged on the basis, inter alia, that the Czech Republic had failed to address (or even establish) that its counterclaims were 'sufficiently connected' to Saluka's claims.[78]

Notwithstanding the fact that the 1976 UNCITRAL Rules, the rules governing the proceedings, contained no requirement to the effect that counterclaims must have a close connection with the primary claim,[79] the tribunal imported the connexity requirement from the case law of the Iran–US Claims Tribunal and ICSID tribunals, describing it as a condition that 'customarily govern the relationship between

[72] ibid [1419].

[73] Atanasova (n 5) 379–80; Lalive and Halonen (n 21). On the distinction between jurisdiction and admissibility, see generally Xuan Shao, 'Environmental and Human Rights Counterclaims in International Investment Arbitration: At the Crossroads of Domestic and International Law' (2021) 24 Journal of International Economic Law 168; Yuval Shany, *Questions of Jurisdiction and Admissibility before International Courts* (CUP 2016) 47–53; Filippo Fontanelli, *Jurisdiction and Admissibility in Investment Arbitration: The Practice and the Theory* (Brill 2018) 104–09.

[74] *Saluka Investments BV v Czech Republic*, UNCITRAL, Decision on Jurisdiction over the Czech Republic's Counterclaim (7 May 2004).

[75] *Saluka Investments BV v Czech Republic*, UNCITRAL, Decision on Jurisdiction over the Czech Republic's Counterclaim (7 May 2004) [10].

[76] ibid.

[77] ibid [45]–[48], [59].

[78] ibid [27], [31].

[79] Article 19(3) of the 1976 UNCITRAL Arbitration Rules, unlike Article 21(3) of the 2010 UNCITRAL Arbitration Rules, required the counterclaim to arise out of the 'same contract' as the initial claim.

a counterclaim and the primary claim to which it is a response', so that 'a legitimate counterclaim' ought to be proximately connected with the primary claim to which it is a response.[80] Notably, the tribunal gave no leverage to the textual variations between Article 19.3 of the 1976 Rules and Article 8 of the BIT on the one hand, and the legal instruments involved in the referenced decisions of the Iran–US Tribunal and ICSID tribunals on the other, holding that the application of the said instruments demonstrates the existence of 'a general legal principle as to the nature of the close connexion which a counterclaim must have with the primary claim', in light of which Article 8 of the Treaty has to be understood and applied. To this effect the tribunal held that:[81]

> Article 19.3 of the UNCITRAL Rules, Articles 25(1) and 46 of the ICSID Convention and Article II(1) of the Iran—US Claims Settlement Declaration, all reflect essentially the same requirement ... The Tribunal is satisfied that those provisions, as interpreted and applied by the decisions which have been referred to, reflect a general legal principle as to the nature of the close connexion which a counterclaim must have with the primary claim if a tribunal with jurisdiction over the primary claim is to have jurisdiction also over the counterclaim ... The Tribunal considers that Article 8 of the Treaty has to be understood and applied in the light of that general legal principle.

That said, when determining the satisfaction of the connectedness requirement in respect of the Czech Republic's domestic law-based counterclaims, the tribunal first acknowledged that such determination, including the nature and extent of the necessary connection, have to be carried out on a case-by-case basis, taking into account the particular circumstances of the case, the relevant treaty provisions and other texts.[82] Exclusively relying on the *Klöckner* tribunal's test, a contract-based investment arbitration, which required the counterclaim and the primary claim to be both 'indivisible' and 'interdependent',[83] the tribunal refused to exercise jurisdiction over the counterclaims, since—according to the tribunal—domestic law-based counterclaims

> cannot be regarded as constituting (to use the language adopted in *Klöckner v Cameroon*, above, paragraph 65) 'an indivisible whole' with the primary claim asserted by the Claimant, or as invoking obligations which share with the primary claim 'a common origin, identical sources, and an operational unity' or which were assumed for 'the accomplishment of a single goal, [so as to be interdependent'.[84]

[80] *Saluka Investments BV v Czech Republic*, UNCITRAL, Decision on Jurisdiction over the Czech Republic's Counterclaim (7 May 2004) [61].
[81] ibid [76].
[82] ibid [59], [62]–[63].
[83] ibid [65], [79].
[84] ibid [79]–[80]. See also Anne Hoffmann, 'Counterclaims' in Meg Kinnear and others (eds), *Building International Investment Law: The First 50 Years of ICSID* (Kluwer Law International 2015) 513; Kalnina and Godbole (n 9) 417, 425, para 4.463.

Similarly, in *Paushok v Mongolia*, another case filed under the 1976 UNCITRAL Rules,[85] Mongolia asserted several counterclaims that were rooted in Mongolian law. The tribunal's task was to determine whether there was a close connection between the counterclaims and the primary claim, or—as put by the tribunal 'whether the counterclaims are matters that are otherwise covered by the general law of Respondent'.[86] Following the reasoning in the *Saluka* award, the tribunal dismissed Mongolia's counterclaim, finding that they do not to constitute 'an indivisible part of the Claimant's claims based on the BIT and international law or as creating a reasonable nexus between the Claimant's claims and the Counterclaims justifying their joint considerations by an arbitral tribunal exclusively vested with jurisdiction under the BIT'.[87]

In line with the *Saluka* and *Paushok* awards, in *Amto v Ukraine*,[88] the tribunal dismissed Ukraine's counterclaims put forward by Ukraine on the basis that it does not share the same legal foundation with the primary claim (ie the Energy Charter Treaty or the ECT). By way of background, the dispute was filed under the Rules of the Arbitration Institute of the Stockholm Chamber of Commerce (SCC). Relying on Article 10 of the SCC rules, Ukraine submitted a counterclaim whereby it requested the tribunal to order the claimant to pay compensation for the non-material injury inflicted upon its reputation as a result of the latter's wrongful allegations.[89] Having found that Ukraine's counterclaim is not premised upon the applicable law as set out in Article 26(6) of the ECT, which refers to the ECT disputes as well as the applicable rules and principles of international law, the tribunal declined jurisdiction over the counterclaim: 'The Respondent has not presented any basis in this applicable law for a claim of nonmaterial injury to reputation based on the allegations made before an Arbitral Tribunal. Accordingly, the Arbitral Tribunal finds that there is no basis for a counterclaim of this nature and it is accordingly dismissed.'[90]

Commenting on the *Amto* award, one scholar explained the outcome to be a consequence of the intrinsic link between the applicable law and the dispute resolution clause in the ECT.[91] Another scholar noted that the outcome reached by the *Amto* tribunal could have been the same had the North American Free Trade Agreement (NAFTA) been applicable, since, as in the ECT, the dispute settlement clause in NAFTA also limits disputes to be submitted to arbitration to those involving claims brought for a violation by a NAFTA Party to the NAFTA obligations, in particular those set out in

[85] *Sergei Paushok, CJSC Golden East Company and CJSC Vostokneftegaz Company v Mongolia*, UNCITRAL, Award on Jurisdiction and Liability (28 April 2011).

[86] ibid [693].

[87] ibid para 686. See also *Sunlodges Ltd, and Sunlodges (T) Limited v Tanzania*, UNCITRAL Arbitration, PCA Case No 2018-9, Award (20 December 2019) [520]–[521]; *Anglo American plc v Venezuela*, ICSID Case No ARB(AF)/14/1, Award (18 January 2019) [529]–[530]; *Oxus Gold plc v Uzbekistan, the State Committee of Uzbekistan for Geology & Mineral Resources, and Navoi Mining & Metallurgical Kombinat*, UNCITRAL Arbitration, Final Award (17 December 2015) [948]–[958]; *Marco Gavazzi and Stefano Gavazzi v Romania*, ICSID Case No ARB/12/25, Decision on Jurisdiction, Admissibility and Liability (21 April 2015) [154]–[162].

[88] *Limited Liability Company Amto v Ukraine*, SCC Case No 080/2005, Final Award (26 March 2008).

[89] ibid [35], [116].

[90] ibid [118]. See also *Muhammet Çap & Sehil In_aat Endustri ve Ticaret Ltd Sti v Turkmenistan*, ICSID Case No ARB/12/6, Award (4 May 2021) [710]–[713].

[91] Bubrowski (n 5) 221.

Chapter 11. In any event, he suggested that the outcome of the *Amto* award in this respect would have been different had the dispute settlement clause in the ECT covered 'a wider category of disputes or provided for investor obligations'.[92]

In short, the restrictive approach places a heavy emphasis on the legal instrument upon which the counterclaim is founded. In essence, this approach not only requires a factual connection between the counterclaim and the primary claim, but also demands that both arise out of the same legal instrument. Based on this line of thought, while treaty-based counterclaims satisfy the connectedness requirement, thus could be held admissible, counterclaims founded upon a contract or domestic law will ipso facto fail to satisfy the said requirement, and should accordingly be dismissed. Such a restrictive approach, particularly the requirement of 'legal connexity', has attracted rigorous criticisms from several scholars.[93] Seeking guidance from ICJ case law, it has been pointed out that the legal and factual connections are 'two factors' that shall be considered, not 'cumulative criteria' that a counterclaim must fulfil.[94]

In contrast with the restrictive approach mentioned above, the second line of awards demonstrates a shift in practice towards a more lenient approach to determining the connectedness requirement. For instance, in *Goetz v Burundi*,[95] the tribunal first distinguished between Article 25 of the ICSID Convention, which requires the dispute to be directly linked with 'an investment', as a matter of jurisdiction on the one hand, and Article 46 of the ICSID Convention governing the admissibility of counterclaims, and which requires the counterclaim to be directly linked with the subject matter of the dispute on the other hand.[96]

As regards the direct connection that the counterclaim shall have with and the subject matter of the dispute, notwithstanding that Burundi's counterclaim concerned an allegation that one of the claimants' banks has failed to respect the operational conditions imposed by virtue of the free zone certificate; that is to say that it was founded upon a legal basis other than the applicable treaty, the tribunal adopted a lenient approach in its assessment of the connectedness requirement, and considered that the counterclaim is 'directly related' to the subject matter to the dispute, thereby holding the counterclaim admissible.[97]

Similarly, in *Inmaris v Ukraine*, the dispute arose out of Ukraine's imposition of a travel ban on a state-owned ship, which was chartered by the claimants.[98] Ukraine submitted a counterclaim requesting the tribunal to award the winter costs that it had incurred in order to maintain the vessel for the remaining duration of the charterparty.[99] Further to confirming its jurisdiction over the counterclaim, owing to the broadly

[92] Yaraslau (n 17).
[93] Atanasova (n 5) 383–84; Hoffmann (n 84) 514; Kalnina and Godbole (n 9) 425, para 4.462.
[94] Shao (n 73) 169.
[95] *Antoine Goetz & Consorts and SA Affinage des Métaux v Burundi*, ICSID Case No ARB/01/2, Award (21 June 2012).
[96] ibid [282]–[283].
[97] ibid [285].
[98] *Inmaris Perestroika Sailing Maritime Services GmbH and others v Ukraine*, ICSID Case No ARB/08/8, Award (1 March 2012) [234].
[99] ibid [431].

drafted dispute settlement clause in the Germany–Ukraine BIT,[100] the tribunal found the requirement of connectedness between the counterclaim and the primary claim to be fulfilled, since the counterclaim constitutes 'a component of the larger dispute that Claimants have consented to submit to this arbitration'.[101]

Also, in *Al-Warraq v Indonesia*, the tribunal held Indonesia's counterclaim to be closely connected both to the investment as well as the subject matter of the primary claims submitted by the claimant.[102] In so deciding, the tribunal focused on factual linkages between the two claims, including the fact that the counterclaim pertained to the same bank bailout, which Indonesia alleged to have resulted from various fraudulent activities committed by the claimant, as well as the same criminal proceedings against the claimant in Indonesia.[103] In *Urbaser v Argentina*, the claimants alleged that Argentina's counterclaim does not satisfy the necessary connection (ie direct relationship) with the main claim since it does not invoke a breach of the Argentina–Spain BIT.[104] The tribunal rejected this objection and found the counterclaim to be admissible based on its manifest factual link with the primary claim, as both concerned the same investment and related to the same concession.[105]

While the tribunal explicitly affirmed that the existence of a factual link between the counterclaim and the main claim was sufficient to extend its adjudicatory power to both claims,[106] yet it added that the legal nexus was also established as Argentina's counterclaim was not exclusively premised upon domestic law, rather, it also invokes a violation of the fundamental right for access to water, which is the very purpose of the investment covered by the BIT.[107]

As put by some scholars, the *Urbaser* tribunal found the legal connection between the counterclaim and the main claim satisfied as the counterclaim concerned 'the very investment that the BIT aimed to protect, even if the legal basis of counterclaim was not the same as the claim, i.e. the BIT'.[108] In light of this, it has been suggested that the *Urbaser* tribunal should be distinguished from the situation articulated by the tribunal in *Paushok*, since, unlike in the latter case where Mongolia founded its counterclaim on domestic law, Argentina premised its counterclaim on the right to water under international human rights law, thereby shielding its counterclaim from risk of dismissal on the basis explained by the *Paushok* tribunals that the arbitration process cannot be instrumentalized to provide the prohibited extraterritorial effect of domestic laws.[109]

[100] ibid [432].
[101] ibid.
[102] *Hesham Talaat M Al-Warraq v Indonesia*, UNCITRAL Arbitration, Final Award (15 December 2014) [667].
[103] ibid [667]–[668].
[104] *Urbaser SA & Consorcio de Aguas Bilbao Bizkaia, Bilbao Biskaia Ur Partzuergoa v Argentina*, ICSID Case No ARB/07/26, Award (8 December 2016) [1126]–[1134].
[105] ibid [1151].
[106] ibid.
[107] ibid.
[108] Kalnina and Godbole (n 9) 428, para 4.470.
[109] Diane Desierto, 'Environmental Protection in International Investment Arbitration: From Defences to Counterclaims' in Edgardo Sobenes and others (eds), *The Environment through the Lens of International Courts and Tribunals* (Springer 2022).

In *Tethyan v Pakistan*, the tribunal was called upon to determine whether Pakistan's counterclaims, which were consecutively premised upon alleged breaches to the applicable BIT, the contract concluded between the investor and the autonomous province of Balochistan, and the mining rules enacted by the latter, arise directly out of the subject matter of the dispute. The tribunal held all three counterclaims to arise directly out of the subject matter of the dispute and therefore satisfy the connectedness requirement required by Article 46(1) of the ICSID Convention and Rule 40(1) of the ICSID Arbitration Rules.[110]

Interestingly, in so far as Pakistan's non-treaty counterclaims are concerned, the tribunal refused to consider that a 'general rule' [exists] pursuant to which there cannot be a sufficient nexus ... between an investor's treaty claims and a host State's non-treaty counterclaims'.[111] For the tribunal, it suffices for the required proximate relationship between the primary claims and the counterclaims to be established that both involve an examination of the same contractual and regulatory instruments.[112]

In conclusion, while the sufficiency of the nexus between counterclaims and primary claims is subject to a case-by-base analysis, recent cases and scholars support the view that ascertaining the satisfaction of the connectedness requirement has to take into account both the factual and legal aspects of the dispute. It is further suggested that both claims need not arise out of the same legal instrument, as proposed by the restrictive approach. Rather, the lenient approach adopts the view proposes that it suffices for the connectedness requirement to be met that the counterclaim pertains to the same factual matrix, investment, or rights and obligations upon which the primary claim is premised.

C. Awards on the Merits: 'The Law Applicable to the Investor's Responsibility and Awarded Damages'

As demonstrated above, even when jurisdiction is established, few counterclaims pass the admissibility hurdle. Similarly, counterclaims in awards on the merits are quite rare.[113] Two reasons can be advanced for the failure of counterclaims, one is factual or evidentiary and the other relates to legal considerations.

Two awards are demonstrative of counterclaims that were dismissed on factual and evidentiary bases. The first is *Inmaris v Ukraine*, where the tribunal found Ukraine's counterclaim to be sufficiently connected with the primary claim. However,

[110] *Tethyan Copper Company Pty Limited v Pakistan*, ICSID Case No ARB/12/1, Decision on Jurisdiction and Liability (10 November 2017) [1415].
[111] ibid [1414].
[112] ibid.
[113] Ishikawa (n 17) 37; Shao (n 73) 159; Hoffmann (n 84) 518. See also Y Lahlou and R Willard, 'The Rise of Environmental Counterclaims in Mining Arbitration' *Global Arbitration Review* (9 June 2021) <https://globalarbitrationreview.com/guide/the-guide-mining-arbitrations/2nd-edition/article/the-rise-of-environmental-counterclaims-in-mining-arbitration>; A Sundararajan, 'Environmental Counterclaims: Enforcing International Environmental Law through Investor-State Arbitration' <www.salzburgglobal.org/fileadmin/user_upload/Documents/Anagha_Sundararajan__Environmental_Counterclaims.pdf> 2.

it ultimately dismissed the same due to Ukraine's failure to establish the claimant's responsibility for the winter costs, which constituted the basis of the counterclaim.[114] Similarly, in *Al-Warraq v Indonesia*, while the tribunal admitted Indonesia's counterclaims, they were finally dismissed on the basis that the established fraudulent acts alleged to have been committed by the claimant were found to have been committed by another shareholder and other entities, which were not parties to the arbitration, thus could not be covered by the counterclaim.[115]

The second reason for counterclaims to fail on the merits pertains to considerations intrinsic to the applicable law. An example to this is *Urbaser v Argentina*.[116] As previously indicated, Argentina put forward a counterclaim against the claimants in which it alleged their failure to provide the necessary investment into the concession, thus violating its commitments and obligations under the international law based on human rights to water.[117] Owing to the broadly drafted and neutral language of the dispute settlement clause set out in Article X of the Spain–Argentina BIT and the manifest factual links between the counterclaim and the primary claim, the tribunal decided to proceed and examine the counterclaim on the merits.[118]

Interestingly, on the merits, the tribunal found that the BIT does not, as a matter of principle, present itself as 'a set of rules defined in isolation without consideration given to rules of international law external to its own rules'.[119] In so deciding the tribunal, primarily, relied on the general rules of interpretation, particularly Article 31(3)(c) of the VCLT, the wording of the dispute settlement clause of the BIT, other treaty provision and Article 42 of the ICSID Convention; thereby it opened the door for importing any relevant rules of international law into the treaty regime as part of the applicable law.[120] As to the relationship between the BIT and international law on human rights, the tribunal rejected the claimants' argument that, as private corporations, they have no commitments or obligations under international human rights law. Referring to the most-favoured-nation clause in the BIT, which entitles the claimants, as investors, to invoke rights emerging from international law, the tribunal found that international human rights rules do impose obligations on investors.[121]

Notwithstanding the openness the tribunal has demonstrated in accepting, as a matter of principle, that investors do bear commitments and obligation under

[114] *Inmaris Perestroika Sailing Maritime Services GmbH and others v Ukraine*, ICSID Case No ARB/08/8, Award (1 March 2012) [432].

[115] *Hesham Talaat M Al-Warraq v Indonesia*, UNCITRAL Arbitration, Final Award (15 December 2014) [669]–[672]. See also *Gustav FW Hamester GmbH & Co KG v Ghana*, ICSID Case No ARB/07/24, Award (18 June 2012) [352]; *Antoine Goetz & Consorts and SA Affinage des Métaux v Burundi*, ICSID Case No ARB/01/2, Award (21 June 2012) [286]–[287].

[116] *Urbaser SA & Consorcio de Aguas Bilbao Bizkaia, Bilbao Biskaia Ur Partzuergoa v Argentina*, ICSID Case No ARB/07/26, Award (8 December 2016).

[117] ibid [36] (last sentence).

[118] ibid [1143]–[1155].

[119] ibid [1192]; see also paras [1188]–[1191], [1200].

[120] See De Nanteuil (n 19) 389–91; Desierto (n 109); Kate Parlett, 'Protection of the Environment in Investment Arbitration—A Double-Edged Sword' (*Kluwer Arbitration Blog*, 22 August 2017) <http://arbitrationblog.kluwerarbitration.com/category/investment-agreements/>.

[121] *Urbaser SA and Consorcio de Aguas Bilbao Bizkaia, Bilbao Biskaia Ur Partzuergoa v Argentina*, ICSID Case No ARB/07/26, Award (8 December 2016) [1193]–[1195]. See also De Nanteuil (n 19) 390.

international human rights law and that the latter constitutes part of the law applicable to the dispute, it stopped there, as it delineated the question of whether the claimants (as investors or a private parties) were bound by an obligation under international law to provide the population with access to drinking water and sanitation services from the question of whether their responsibility for failure to abide by such an obligation could be triggered under the cause of action invoked by Argentina in the present case.[122] In relation to the latter question, the tribunal noted that Argentina itself acknowledges that international law does not provide a cause of action for its counterclaim since it premised its counterclaim against the claimant on the concession contract, not on international law.[123] The tribunal thus narrowed the applicability of the human right to water to instances where such right were incorporated in the concession contract, the law of the host state or the BIT. Failing to establish that the duty to respect the human right to water under international law has been part of the domestic regulatory framework governing the concession long before the concession was granted, the tribunal dismissed Argentina's counterclaim.[124]

Ever since its issuance, the *Urbaser* award has been the object of wide scholarly discussion.[125] While the award was found to be 'groundbreaking' and 'evolutive' owing to its recognition of investors' international human rights obligations,[126] its dismissal of Argentina's counterclaim was disappointing to some, as the outcome affirmed that an investment treaty is insufficient in and of itself to sustain a counterclaim.[127] In this regard, some limited the significance of the *Urbaser* award is its reiteration of the traditional position that states are the only ones to implement—through their domestic law—private actors' obligations under international human rights law, hence the award's recognition of investors' obligations under the said regime is 'more rhetorical than real'.[128]

On a more optimistic note, it was suggested that, notwithstanding the outcome reached in *Urbaser*, there are two scenarios in which a counterclaim could still yield to the establishment of the investor's responsibility. The first is a straightforward one where the counterclaim is based on a contract that contains reciprocal obligations, in which case the tribunal will be bound by the conjunctive application of the contract provisions and the applicable domestic law. The second scenario addresses a hypothetical situation where the counterclaim is unrelated to a contract, but satisfies the jurisdictional and admissibility requirements set out in the applicable treaty. In this case, it is submitted that tribunals could 'apply only domestic law to the counterclaim, absent

[122] *Urbaser SA & Consorcio de Aguas Bilbao Bizkaia, Bilbao Biskaia Ur Partzuergoa v Argentina*, ICSID Case No ARB/07/26, Award (8 December 2016) [1206].

[123] ibid.

[124] ibid [1207], [1210], [1220]–[1221] (footnotes omitted).

[125] See generally Patrick Abel, 'Counterclaims Based on International Human Rights Obligations of Investors in International Investment Arbitration: Fallacies and Potentials of the 2016 ICSID *Urbaser v Argentina* Award' (2018) in Elisa Baroncini and others (eds), *Global Public Goods, Global Commons, Fundamental Values and International Investment Law*, special issue, 1 (1) Brill Open Law 61 <https://doi.org/10.1163/23527072-00101003>.

[126] De Nanteuil (n 19) 391.

[127] Shao (n 73) 161.

[128] ibid. See also De Nanteuil (n 19) 391; Desierto (n 109) 336.

any rule of international law that could be imposed on the investor. Therefore, future evolutions should strive to concentrate on this last point.'[129]

While the above proposition has its rationale, its tolerability by all arbitral tribunals remains doubtful in light of the reasoning provided in the *Urbaser* award. Probably a relevant paradox in this respect are the criteria for the admissibility of a counterclaim vis-à-vis the possibility of its success on the merits, and this was pointed out in relation to the *Urbaser* award. As previously demonstrated, the *Paushok* award reveals that a counterclaim that is founded upon domestic law bears the risk of being deemed inadmissible.[130] Similarly, as indicated above, when assessing the admissibility of Argentina's counterclaim, in addition to the 'manifest factual link' that the *Urbaser* tribunal has relied upon and the fact that it stated expressly that it 'would be sufficient' for the counterclaim to satisfy the required connection with the investor's claim, it further established the 'legal connection' between the said two claims on the basis that Argentina did not plead its counterclaim 'as a matter of domestic law only', but rather involved 'a violation of the fundamental right for access to water'.[131]

By so indicating, the tribunal has effectively asserted that its admissibility of the counterclaim was based, inter alia, on the fact that the latter was not founded exclusively upon domestic law, but was also 'based on a source of law *outside* of domestic law'.[132] Put differently by one scholar, Argentina's counterclaim 'did not trigger the *Paushok* Tribunal's concerns against giving a prohibited extraterritorial legislative effect to the host State's Environmental laws through the use of the host State counterclaim in the investor-State arbitration process'.[133] That being the case, it is utterly contradictory with this approach that a tribunal hinges the success of the counterclaim on the merits upon the integration of the international human rights obligations into the domestic regulatory and contractual framework over the concession.[134]

Not only would the dual threshold, described above, be onerous and reflective of an unnecessarily stringent requirement that fails to consider the existing diversity in regulatory and statutory practices, but it also unreasonably denies—in so far as ICSID disputes are concerned—the relevance of host state law, which constitutes part of the law applicable pursuant to Article 42 of the ICISD Convention.[135]

In any event, two exceptional awards shed more light on the success of counterclaims on the merits; those are the *Perenco* and *Burlington* awards, both of which were rendered in ICSID cases filed against Ecuador. It is worth noting that in neither case had the tribunal adjudicated upon the jurisdictional and admissibility requirements. In

[129] De Nanteuil (n 19) 391.

[130] See text to n 22.

[131] *Urbaser SA & Consorcio de Aguas Bilbao Bizkaia, Bilbao Biskaia Ur Partzuergoa v Argentina*, ICSID Case No ARB/07/26, Award (8 December 2016) [1151].

[132] Desierto (n 109) 336.

[133] ibid.

[134] ibid [336]–[337].

[135] While the UNCITRAL and ICC rules leave the matter of applicable law to be determined by the tribunal, the municipal law of the host state is said to likely be '"appropriate" for most matters relating to disputes about the investment', see Andrea Bjorklund 'Applicable Law in International Investment Disputes' in Chiara Giorgetti (ed), *Litigating International Investment Disputes: A Practitioner's Guide* (Brill 2014) 272–73.

Perenco, the investor had untimely objected to the tribunal's jurisdiction over Ecuador's counterclaim,[136] and, in *Burlington*, the tribunal's jurisdiction was derived from the agreement of the parties.[137]

Since both cases arise from the same factual circumstances and contractual framework, it is only reasonable that one examines the resulting awards in tandem. Starting with *Perenco v Ecuador*, the dispute arose after Ecuador's amendment of its tax laws in 2008, which resulted in the increase of the taxes levied on oil companies. Following the amendment, Perenco (a French investor) started to pay the additional tax to the government, however it later stopped paying it. After seeking to renegotiate its contractual relationship with Petroecuador (a state-owned entity), the President of Ecuador announced that all production sharing contracts (PSCs) would be terminated and substituted by new ones. Petroecuador then eventually took over the operation of the blocks granted to Perenco and the government filed local proceedings against Perenco to collect the allegedly due taxes.

In response, Perenco and its subsidiaries filed arbitration proceedings against Ecuador, claiming that Ecuador's measures breached the two PSCs and constituted an unfair and inequitable treatment as well as an unlawful expropriation under the France–Ecuador BIT.[138] Ecuador brought counterclaims against Perenco, whereby it requested the tribunal to order the latter to pay damages for the environmental harm it caused to the Ecuadorian Amazon and for the infrastructure damage it inflicted upon Blocks 7 and 21 during its operations.[139] In substantiation of its counterclaim, Ecuador asserted that 'its experts had determined the existence of an "environmental catastrophe" in the two oil blocks situated in the country's Amazonian rainforest that had been worked by the consortium under Perenco's operatorship'.[140] It is worth noting in this regard that Ecuador's counterclaim was based exclusively on Ecuadorian law.[141]

Accordingly, the key question for the tribunal to ascertain Perenco's environmental liability pertained to the nature of such liability under Ecuadorian law, noting that the tort liability regime was fault based prior to the 2008 Constitution, but the 2008 Constitution provided for a strict liability regime.[142] The tribunal rejected Ecuador's argument on the retroactive application of the 2008 Constitution (ie the strict liability regime), and decided to consider the applicable law based on the pre- and post-2008 Constitution regimes.[143] In other words, the tribunal adopted what could be referred

[136] *Perenco Ecuador Ltd v Ecuador and Petroecuador*, ICSID Case No ARB/08/6, Interim Decision on the Environmental Counterclaim (11 August 2015) [9], [19]; *Perenco Ecuador Ltd v Ecuador and Petroecuador*, ICSID Case No ARB/08/6, Decision on Perenco's Application for Dismissal of Ecuador's Counterclaims (18 August 2017) [34]–[35].

[137] *Burlington Inc v Ecuador*, ICSID Case No ARB/08/5, Decision on Counterclaims, 7 February 2017 [60]–[61]. See also *Burlington Inc v Ecuador*, ICSID Case No ARB/08/5, Decision on Liability (14 December 2012) [93].

[138] *Perenco Ecuador Ltd v Ecuador and Petroecuador*, ICSID Case No ARB/08/6, Interim Decision on the Environmental Counterclaim (11 August 2015) [4]; *Burlington Inc v Ecuador*, ICSID Case No ARB/08/5, Procedural Order No 1 on Burlington Oriente's Request for Provisional Measures (29 June 2009) [1]–[17].

[139] *Perenco Ecuador Ltd v Ecuador and Petroecuador*, ICSID Case No ARB/08/6, Interim Decision on the Environmental Counterclaim (11 August 2015) [5], [36].

[140] ibid [34].

[141] ibid [36]–[43].

[142] *Perenco Ecuador Ltd v Ecuador and Petroecuador*, ICSID Case No ARB/08/6, Interim Decision on the Environmental Counterclaim (11 August 2015) [354]–[355].

[143] ibid [356]–[358]; Desierto (n 109) 339.

to as the principle of contemporaneity, pursuant to which the strict liability regime established by the 2008 Constitution was applied to any post-20 October 2008 damage, while damages that occurred prior to that time (prior to 20 October 2008) was subject to the fault-based liability regime.[144]

As to the issue of causation under the fault-based regime, the tribunal followed the approach adopted by the Ecuadorian courts prior to 20 October 2008, which employed a 'rebuttable' presumption to the effect that 'the operator engaged in hazardous activity and benefiting therefrom was responsible for any resulting damage'.[145] Considering the evidentiary complexities surrounding the proof of causation in relation to environmental tort, the tribunal decided to take 'regulatory exceedances' as a point of reference for creating a presumption of failure by the operator (ie the investor in that case) to exercise the duty of care.[146]

Upon its review of the evidence, the tribunal acknowledged the difficulty in evaluating environmental damage and compensation based on the expert reports, and it expressed 'doubts about the expert evidence tendered by both Parties', and accordingly decided to appoint an independent expert to assess the damages in accordance with the tribunal's legal and factual findings.[147] After reviewing the evidence submitted by the disputing parties and the reports of the experts, including the independent environmental expert, the tribunal found Perenco liable to pay almost USD 54.5 million to Ecuador in compensation for environmental damages.[148]

Dealing with a similar factual matrix as in *Perenco*, in *Burlington v Ecuador*, the dispute was filed by Burlington Resources Inc (a US corporation) and its subsidiaries against Ecuador under the United States–Ecuador BIT. The claimants contended the legitimacy of the increased tax rate and the eventual termination of the oil licences, arguing that such measures constituted unlawful expropriation under the BIT.[149] Like in *Perenco*, Ecuador submitted a counterclaim, whereby it requested the tribunal to order Burlington to pay compensation for the harm it caused to sections of the Ecuadorian Amazon (ie the environment counterclaim) and the infrastructure of the oil exploration sites (ie the infrastructure counterclaim).[150] Ecuador relied on Ecuadorian tort law and several provisions of the PSCs, yet the tribunal asserted—by reference to Article 42(1) of the ICSID Convention—its discretion to apply 'either

[144] *Perenco Ecuador Ltd v Ecuador and Petroecuador*, ICSID Case No ARB/08/6, Interim Decision on the Environmental Counterclaim (11 August 2015) [359].

[145] ibid [371].

[146] ibid [374], [379].

[147] *Perenco Ecuador Ltd v Ecuador and Petroecuador*, ICSID Case No ARB/08/6, Decision on Claimant's Application for Dismissal of Respondent's Counterclaims (18 August 2017) [31]. See also *Perenco Ecuador Ltd v Ecuador and Petroecuador*, ICSID Case No ARB/08/6, Interim Decision on the Environmental Counterclaim (11 August 2015) [581]–[594]; *Perenco Ecuador Ltd v Ecuador and Petroecuador*, ICSID Case No ARB/08/6, Award (27 September 2019) [423], [897].

[148] *Perenco Ecuador Ltd v Ecuador and Petroecuador*, ICSID Case No ARB/08/6, Award (27 September 2019) [899], [1023(b)].

[149] *Burlington Inc. v Ecuador*, ICSID Case No ARB/08/5, Procedural Order No 1 on Burlington Oriente's Request for Provisional Measures (29 June 2009) [2]–[16].

[150] *Burlington Inc. v Ecuador*, ICSID Case No ARB/08/5, Decision on Counterclaims (7 February 2017) [52]–[53].

municipal or international law depending on the type of issue to be resolved' as well as PSCs, where relevant.[151]

Similar to the *Perenco* award, the tribunal determined the nature of Burlington's tortious liability for environmental damage by reference to Ecuadorian law. In light of the relevant provisions of the PSCs and Ecuador's environmental framework for oil operations, including the 1987 and 2008 Constitution,[152] unlike the *Perenco* tribunal, the *Burlington* tribunal decided to adopt the post-2008 Constitution standard of strict liability on the basis that 'in Ecuadorian law strict liability governed instances of environmental harm at least since the *Delfina Torres* decision was handed down in 2002'.[153] Disagreeing with the *Perenco* award's adoption of the fault-based approach, the tribunal noted that:

> While the Tribunal agrees with the finding in the Perenco Decision that 'an operator can in general be held only to the legal standards that applied to its conduct at the time', it has difficulty following the Perenco tribunal's view that decisions of the Ecuadorian courts have merely 'strengthened the presumptions in favour of a finding of liability in the case of damage caused through hazardous activities'. It finds indeed that these courts have established a strict liability regime for hazardous activities, in particular oilfield operations.[154]

That said, while the *Burlington* tribunal adopted a different standard of liability from that of the *Perenco* tribunal, following the latter, the *Burlington* tribunal took the exceedance of regulatory criteria as a point reference in ascertaining the environmental harm for which the claimants are liable, explaining that:

> [An] oilfield operator could not be considered to have caused environmental harm if permissible limits were observed, since precisely these permissible limits allow determining when a negative impact crosses the threshold of harm. ... In other words, any exceedance of applicable limits triggers extra-contractual civil liability and the ensuing obligation of full restoration back to these limits, independently from parallel administrative liability and possible sanctions.[155]

Having so established, the tribunal relied on the evidence presented by the parties, including expert reports, and applied the said regulatory criteria to the facts of the case before it, ultimately ascertaining that the environmental harm was due to Burlington's actions, which resulted in ordering the latter to pay Ecuador damages in the amount of USD 39,199,373.[156] Similarly, after examining the Ecuadorian regulatory framework

[151] ibid [73].
[152] ibid [159]–[234].
[153] ibid [247]. See also ibid [235]–[246].
[154] ibid [248] (footnotes omitted).
[155] ibid [291]–[292].
[156] ibid [889], [1075].

applicable to the infrastructure counterclaim,[157] based on the available evidence on the damages arising from Bulington's operations,[158] the tribunal granted Ecuador damages in the amount of USD 2,577,119.77.[159]

In sum, while the *Perenco* and *Burlington* awards constitute a shift towards the direct application of host state law in the adjudication of counterclaims,[160] the respective awards have not escaped criticism. The main criticism directed against the awards concerns their divergent approaches on two issues: the interpretation of Ecuadorian environmental law for the purpose of ascertaining the standard of liability and their assessment of expert evidence. Particularly in so far as the first issue is concerned, the divergence between the awards was said to undermine their credibility and threaten the coherence of the domestic legal order, thus calling into question the legitimacy and suitability of investment tribunals to adjudicate domestic law issues,[161] an area that has long been subject to great scepticism by states.[162]

To reduce the risk of potentially inconsistent decisions on domestic laws, the creation has been suggested of a procedural mechanism whereby domestic law issues is referred to domestic courts so as to make preliminary rulings thereupon.[163] Such a suggestion would, however, be counterproductive if one cannot ensure the neutrality and objectivity of domestic courts when making such preliminary rulings. Moreover, this suggestion implies that arbitral tribunals must then fully and automatically defer to findings of local courts, which could be questionable in light of the tribunals' duty to consider the issues in dispute and to make an independent determination thereof taking into consideration all relevant circumstances, including any judgments rendered by national courts.

Be that as it may be, while more coherence and consistency in dealing with domestic law issues counterclaims are indeed welcome and desired, the *Perenco* and *Burlington* awards undoubtedly constitute a significant long-awaited step towards the introduction of counterclaims and the permissibility of their adjudication in investment treaty arbitrations, and they thereby open the gateway towards redressing the commonly perceived inequality and asymmetry in the investment arbitration system. Besides being the two exceptional awards where counterclaims submitted by host states were successful, the high level of coordination that both the *Burlington* and *Perenco* tribunals have committed themselves to so as to avoid the potential risk of double recovery of damages in relation to Ecuador's counterclaims represents a further remarkable and innovative aspect in the said awards.[164]

[157] ibid [919], [931].
[158] ibid [932], [1073].
[159] ibid [1074]–[1075].
[160] Both tribunals have also deferred to Ecuadorian law in determining the awarded damages and accrued interests, see *Perenco Ecuador Ltd v Ecuador and Petroecuador*, ICSID Case No ARB/08/6, Interim Decision on the Environmental Counterclaim, 11 August 2015 [34]; *Burlington Inc v Ecuador*, ICSID Case No ARB/08/5, Decision on Counterclaims, 7 February 2017 [1090]–[1097].
[161] Shao (n 73) 176.
[162] On the critics of investment treaty arbitration in relation to domestic courts, see generally Gabrielle Kaufmann-Kohler and Michele Potestà, *Investor-State Dispute Settlement and National Courts: Current Framework and Reform Options* (Springer 2020) 8–10.
[163] Shao (n 73) 177.
[164] Rudall (n 4) 499–500.

Mindful of the overlap between Ecuador's environmental counterclaim in the *Burlington* proceedings and that in the parallel *Perenco* proceedings,[165] considering that Ecuador made 'a full claim for the alleged environmental harm' in both cases,[166] the *Burlington* tribunal, being the one deciding on Ecuador's counterclaims in the first place, had to tackle the issue of double recovery in its decision on counterclaims. Noting that since the *Perenco* tribunal had not then rendered its decision on Ecuador's environmental counterclaim, the most appropriate way for the *Burlington* tribunal to avoid double recovery was to leave the issue to be dealt with by the *Perenco* tribunal in its final award, stressing that the *Burlington* decision cannot, in any event, be used so as to compensate Ecuador twice for the same damage.[167]

The *Perenco* tribunal has, in turn, dedicated a separate part in its final award to examine the effect of the *Burlington* award on the potential double recovery of damages.[168] At the outset, the tribunal highlighted the divergences between both tribunals in respect of various issues, including their findings on substantive issues pertaining to the standard of liability under Ecuadorian law, technical aspects as well as their evaluation of the expert evidence of contamination.[169] Relying on the findings reached by the independent expert, the *Perenco* tribunal treated the damages awarded in the *Burlington* award as 'a down payment'.[170] Accordingly, the tribunal adjusted the amount awarded for environmental compensation, its final award, so as to avoid double recovery, by subtracting the damages awarded to Ecuador for environmental harm in the *Burlington* award (ie USD 39,199,373) from the amount of damages it found Perenco liable to pay for (ie USD 93,638,890) to arrive at a figure of USD 54,439,517.[171] Similarly, the *Perenco* tribunal denied Ecuador's infrastructure counterclaim for damage caused to the oil exploration blocks, holding that Ecuador had already been fully compensated in respect of the same by virtue of the *Burlington* award.[172]

III. Concluding Remarks: The New Trend Interventionist Approaches to Counterclaims in Investment Treaty Arbitration

As this chapter has demonstrated, to date, only two known counterclaims advanced by host states against investors have been upheld, out of the twenty-five reported investor-state disputes.[173] As previously explained, such an outcome is predominantly attributed

[165] Ecuador acknowledged the substantial overlap between the environmental damages awarded by the *Burlington* tribunal and the recoverable damages found by the independent expert appointed by the *Perenco* tribunal, see *Perenco Ecuador Ltd v Ecuador and Petroecuador*, ICSID Case No ARB/08/6, Award (27 September 2019) [896].

[166] *Burlington Inc v Ecuador*, ICSID Case No ARB/08/5, Decision on Counterclaims (7 February 2017) [1080].

[167] ibid [1086].

[168] *Perenco Ecuador Ltd v Ecuador and Petroecuador*, ICSID Case No ARB/08/6, Award (27 September 2019) [890]–[899].

[169] ibid [897]–[898].

[170] ibid [898].

[171] ibid [899].

[172] ibid [1015], [1023].

[173] De Luca (n 7); Baltag (n 17).

to the fact that the vast majority of first generation IIAs neither spell out the right of host states to bring counterclaims nor do they contain provisions imposing substantive obligations on investors (ie IIAs asymmetries). In addition, provisions establishing the investor's responsibility for compliance with domestic law are absent from a large number of IIAs.[174]

The scarcity of successful counterclaims, coupled with the inconsistency of awards thereon have motivated an increasing move towards the 'interventionist approach', whereby contracting states undertake to intervene so as to resolve the barriers that often impede the success of counterclaims. This approach could take various forms; starting from devising joint interpretation notes, to reforming the existing IIAs, and ending with the inclusion of specific provisions on counterclaims in new IIAs,[175] to achieve the appropriate balance between host states and investors.[176] Affirming the same in respect of IIA reform, the UNCITRAL Secretariat stated that:

> The Working Group may wish to consider devising a framework in which States could raise counterclaims in ISDS, which would reduce uncertainty, promote fairness and rule of law, and ultimately ensure a balance between respondent States and claimant investors. Such framework could also have a positive impact on the duration and cost of the proceedings as well as on a number of other procedural issues.[177]

While joint interpretation notes are not very common, an example of a provision according to which joint interpretation notes by contracting parties are considered part of the law applicable to the dispute can be found in the Rwanda–UAE BIT, which reads: 'A joint interpretation of this Agreement, agreed upon by the Contracting Parties and received in a timely manner in accordance with Article 14, shall be binding on the arbitral tribunal.'[178]

In so far as IIAs reform is concerned, calls for such reforms have commenced since 2002, when countries such as China Cuba, India, Kenya, Pakistan, and Zimbabwe have stressed the need for a direct inclusion of investors' obligations in IIAs, highlighting the importance of 'legally-binding measures aimed at ensuring corporate responsibility and accountability relating to foreign investors, including measures that clearly spell out investors' obligations and the obligations of their home governments'.[179] In line

[174] Sharpe and Jacob (n 8) 366; UNCTAD, 'Review of ISDS Decisions in 2019: Selected IAA Reform Issues' (2021) IIA Issue Note 1 <https://unctad.org/system/files/official-document/diaepcbinf2021d1_en.pdf> 31.

[175] Sharpe and Jacob (n 8) 367–68; De Brabandere (n 24) 610–11; Yulia Levashova 'The Right of Access to Water in the Context of Investment Disputes in Argentina: *Urbaser* and Beyond' (2020) 16 (2) Utrecht Law Review 110; Shao (n 73) 178; Bubrowski (n 5) 228–29; UNCTAD, 'Investment Policy Framework for Sustainable Development' (2015) UNCTAD/DIAE/PCB/2015/5, 19 <http://unctad.org/en/PublicationsLibrary/diaepcb2015d5_en.pdf>.

[176] UNGA, 'Report of Working Group III (Investor-State Dispute Settlement Reform) on the Work of Its Thirty-Fourth Session' (26 February 2018) UN Doc A/CN.9/930/Add.1/Rev1, paras 3–7.

[177] UNGA 'Possible Reform of Investor-State Dispute Settlement (ISDS)—Multiple Proceedings and Counterclaims' (22 January 2020) UN Doc A/CN.9/WG.III/WP.193, para 38.

[178] Rwanda–United Arab Emirates BIT (signed 1 November 2017, entry into force 17 January 2020) art 17(2).

[179] WTO, 'Working Group on the Relationship between Trade and Investment', Communication from China, Cuba, India, Kenya, Pakistan and Zimbabwe: Investors' and Home Governments' Obligations' (19 November 2002), WT/WGTI/W/152, para 9.

with this approach, recent IIAs started to include provisions that either provide for the right of the host state to submit a counterclaim (ie incorporation of consent to arbitrate counterclaims) or impose direct obligations on investors (ie integration of investor's obligations),[180] or both.[181]

IIAs containing an express reference to counterclaims include the COMESA Investment Agreement, which allows member states to bring a counterclaim against an investor for breaches committed by the latter. To this effect, Article 28(9) of the COMESA Investment Agreement reads as follows:

> Member State against whom a claim is brought by a COMESA investor under this Article may assert as a defence, counterclaim ... that the COMESA investor bringing the claim has not fulfilled its obligations under this Agreement, including the obligations to comply with all applicable domestic measures or that it has not taken all reasonable steps to mitigate possible damages.[182]

More importantly, paragraph 4 of the same article explicitly indicates that the parties (ie the host state and the investor) have already given prior consent to the submission of a claim to arbitration under the COMESA Investment Agreement, thus making it difficult for a tribunal to deny jurisdiction over counterclaims for lack of consent.[183] To this effect, this article reads:

> Each Member State consents to the submission of a claim to arbitration under this Agreement in accordance with its provisions. Each investor, by virtue of establishing or continuing to operate or own an investment subject to this Agreement, consents to the terms of the submission of a claim to dispute resolution under this Agreement if he exercises the right to bring a claim against a Member State under this Agreement.

Similar provisions exist in the Model BIT of the Southern African Development Community (the SADC Model BIT).[184] A more expressive approach to the permissibility of counterclaims could be found in the recently negotiated Draft Pan-African Investment Code (Draft PAIC), which provides for the submission of counterclaims in relation to investors' failure to comply with the Code.[185] That said, it should be

[180] Early examples of IIAs containing an express reference to investor's obligation to abide by the laws and regulations of the host state could be found in Article 14 of the Unified Agreement for the Investment of Arab Capital in the Arab States, which establishes the responsibility of investors for 'any breach of the obligations set forth in the preceding paragraph in accordance with the law in force in the State in which the investment is made or in which the breach occurs', see Unified Agreement for the Investment of Arab Capital in the Arab States (signed 26 November 1980, entry into force 22 February 1988). See also the Agreement on Promotion, Protection and Guarantee of Investments among Member States of the Organization of the Islamic Conference (signed 5 June 1981, entry into force February 1988) art 9.

[181] See generally Rivas (n 35) 817–22.

[182] Investment Agreement for the COMESA Common Investment Area (signed 23 May 2007).

[183] Rivas (n 35) 817.

[184] SADC Model BIT (2012) arts 19(2) and 29.

[185] Draft Pan-African Investment Code, African Union Economic Affairs Department (December 2016) <https://au.int/sites/default/files/documents/32844-doc-draft_pan-african_investment_code_december_2016_en.pdf> art 43(2). See also Article 14.11(i) of the March 2015 India Model BIT, which reads 'A Party may

underscored that while the express reference to counterclaims as indicated in the above IIAs has the advantage of allowing the submission of counterclaims in investor-state arbitration proceedings, it does not guarantee the success of such counterclaims both on the admissibility and merits. In so far as admissibility is concerned, particularly when it comes to ICSID disputes, the satisfaction of the conditions set out in Article 46 of the Convention, particularly the connexity requirement, would have to be ascertained. Even assuming that such requirements are satisfied, a cause of action which falls under the competence of the tribunal would still have to be established—a question that is dependent on, and intrinsically linked to whether of the applicable IIA imposes obligations on the respective investor.[186]

Recent developments have indeed demonstrated an increasing move towards the inclusion of investors' obligations in IIAs. Article 13 of the COMESA Agreement, for instance, imposes on investors the obligation to abide by domestic law, as it requires them to 'comply with all applicable domestic measures of the Member State in which their investment is made'.[187] Article 15 of the SADC Model BIT, in turn, puts on investors the duty 'to respect human rights in the workplace and in the community and State in which they are located', and further requires them to 'undertake or cause to be undertaken acts that breach such human rights. Investors and their investments shall not assist in, or be complicit in, the violation of the human rights by others in the Host State, including by public authorities or during civil strife'. Going even further, the Draft PAIC includes a chapter on investor obligations, setting out various duties of investors including corporate governance obligations, sociopolitical obligations, bribery, human rights obligations, and restrictions on the use of natural resources.[188]

It is also worth noting that most recently, in 2022, the Africa Arbitration Academy issued its Model Bilateral Investment Treaty (AAA Model BIT), which represents a great innovation in the areas of investor obligations and state counterclaims.[189] Moreover, the AAA Model BIT opted for a balanced approach to investment protection, by adding a host of obligations to guarantee responsible and credible investment that contributes to the host state's growth and sustainable development. These include investors' compliance with environmental and social assessment screening criteria as per host state's laws,[190] labour, human rights protection, and gender equality policies and regulations,[191] intellectual property and indigenous peoples' and local/ethnic communities'

initiate a counterclaim against the Investor or Investment for a breach of the obligations set out under Articles 9, 10, 11 and 12 of Chapter III of this Treaty before a tribunal established under this Article and seek as a remedy suitable declaratory relief, enforcement action or monetary compensation' (removed in the December 2015 Indian Model BIT) Model Text for the Indian BIT <https://arbitrationlaw.com/sites/default/files/free_pdfs/model_text_for_the_indian_bilateral_investment_treaty.pdf>.

[186] De Brabandere (n 24) 610–11.

[187] See also December 2015 Indian Model BIT (adopted 28 December 2015) art 11; Model Netherlands BIT (adopted 22 March 2019) art 7(1).

[188] See Draft PAIC, ch 4, arts 19–24. See also Section 3 of the Model Netherlands BIT; Argentina–Qatar BIT (signed 6 November 2016, not yet in force) art 12; Iran–Slovakia BIT (signed 19 January 2016, entry into force 30 August 2017) art 10; Morocco–Nigeria BIT (signed 3 December 2016, not yet in force) arts 14 and 19.

[189] AAA Model BIT art 22 (G).

[190] ibid art 9.

[191] ibid art 10.

rights,[192] anti-corruption, anti-money laundering, and counterterrorism financing policies and regulations,[193] corporate governance and prudent practices policies and regulations,[194] and compliance with host state's laws and regulations.[195] Article 16 of the AAA Model BIT also includes a denial of benefits clause to prevent the exploitation of the BIT.

In light of all the above, it is clear that recent years have shown more attempts by contracting states to open the gateway for counterclaims to be adjudicated before investor-state tribunals. By doing so, contracting parties effectively aim at rebalancing IIAs, by reconsidering restrictive approaches under old generation IIAs. However, only the future will tell whether the new generation of IIAs and the recalibration of investor-state obligations will yield to intended outcome and bring about system stabilization to enable both investors and states to legitimately pursue claims and counterclaims before neutral tribunals in proceedings that are more efficient, more inclusive and aligned with best practices in the field of international law.

[192] ibid art 11.
[193] ibid art 12.
[194] ibid art 13.
[195] ibid art 15.

16

Investment Tribunals' Search for the Truth and Its Impact on the Arbitral Award

*Nigel Blackaby and Maria Julia Milesi**

I. Introduction

Arbitration is essentially 'post-factual'. That is to say, the dispute advanced by the parties is based on facts that have already occurred. The parties, however, may have diverse perceptions of the same facts and arbitrators must determine the 'truth' of what occurred.[1] Arbitrators owe it to the parties to deliver an accurate award based on a reasonable view of the facts (obtained through the evidence). Ultimately, the facts tend to be decisive in the outcome of the dispute.

In deciding a dispute, arbitrators will rarely find an absolute truth.[2] Rather, they will focus on the competing views of the parties and try to build a *reasonable* view of the facts of the case based on the balance of probabilities. To this end, arbitrators rely mainly on documentary evidence, witness statements, and expert opinions.[3] While most commonly the parties provide the necessary evidence, the tribunal also has an important 'fact-finding'[4] role to complement the parties' efforts.

The approach that arbitrators take towards fact-finding may vary as a consequence of their legal culture.[5] Broadly speaking,[6] under a common law approach, lawyers are in

* The authors wish to thank Daniela Cala Perez of Freshfields' Washington office for her assistance in the preparation of this chapter. The views expressed in this chapter are personal and do not necessarily reflect the views of Freshfields.

[1] Julian Bickmann, *Fact-Finding in International Arbitration: The Emergence of a Transnational Lex Evidentiae* (Kluwer Law International 2022) 1–8.

[2] An absolute truth is something that is true at all times and places, independent from the specific context.

[3] Arbitrators have discretion to resolve evidentiary matters. See Frédéric G Sourgens and others, *Evidence in International Investment Arbitration* (OUP 2018) paras 4.18–4.21.

[4] Fact-finding is the process of impartial investigation, at the end of which the tribunal will have established the factual basis to which it applies the law. Fact-finding includes 'the pleading of facts, the pre-hearing exchange of documents and other information, potential investigations by the tribunal, as well as the taking of evidence by hearing witnesses or experts or examining documents or other relevant material in the later stages', Bickmann (n 1) 2. See also Crina Baltag, 'The Relevance of the Facts in Complex Investor-State Arbitration Proceedings: Reflections on the Drafting of Arbitral Awards' in Katia Fach Gómez and Catharine Titi (eds), *The Award in International Investment Arbitration* (OUP 2024).

[5] William W Park, 'Arbitrators and Accuracy' (2010) 1 Journal of International Dispute Settlement 25. See also SI Strong, Katia Fach Gómez, and Laura Carballo Piñeiro, *Comparative Law for Spanish–English Speaking Lawyers: Legal Cultures, Legal Terms and Legal Practices* (Edward Elgar Publishing 2016) 369–431.

[6] This summary is not intended to be a comprehensive description, and caution should be exercised to avoid overgeneralization. However, there is just enough uniformity in the general approach to matters of evidence that it is possible to contrast the so-called 'civil law countries' with 'common law countries'. See Nigel Blackaby and Constantine Partasides, *Redfern and Hunter on International Arbitration* (7th edn, OUP 2022) paras 6.79ff.

Nigel Blackaby and Maria Julia Milesi, *Investment Tribunals' Search for the Truth and Its Impact on the Arbitral Award* In: *The Award in International Investment Arbitration.* Edited by: Katia Fach Gómez and Catharine Titi, Oxford University Press.
 DOI: 10.1093/9780191975936.003.0016

charge of gathering and marshalling evidence, as well as examining witnesses. A judge must find the 'truth' through adversarial exchanges between the parties without the right to engage in independent fact-finding exercises. Under this approach, the judge's role is limited to ensure due process. In contrast, under the inquisitorial approach of many civil law countries, the judge takes a more proactive role in the marshalling of evidence.[7] The judge may decide which witnesses he or she wants to hear and which documents to examine. They may also engage their own expert to assist them in their decision-making process.

Because of the international nature of investment arbitration and the different cultures of the members of the arbitral tribunal, a 'hybrid' approach is often applied.[8] Thus, tribunals do not always rely exclusively on the parties' presentation of the case and sometimes take an active fact-finding role, going beyond party submissions.[9] This reflects in part the added responsibility that arbitrators have for an award that is final and usually not subject to review for legal or factual errors unlike a first instance court judgement. In investment arbitration, there is the added burden of deciding matters of public interest which may be broader than the narrower positions advanced by an investor or state in its own respective interest. The tribunal needs to balance those interests with the need to resolve the dispute in a timely and cost-efficient manner while respecting due process.

Against this backdrop, this chapter analyses how tribunals have exercised their fact-finding powers in seeking the 'material truth' of the case, going beyond the parties' submissions, and exploring the impact of that intervention on the resulting awards. We examine examples of where tribunals have refused to be limited to the dispute as presented by the parties by: appointing their own independent expert (II); taking a proactive approach to the production of documents (III); ordering the examination of witnesses not called by the parties (IV); ordering witness conferencing of experts (V); allowing third party submissions (VI); and undertaking their own investigation of criminal allegations (VII).

II. Appointment of Tribunal Experts

Investment arbitration often touches upon topics that require a specific expertise outside of the parties' representatives' know-how. For this, the parties frequently appoint experts 'to obtain any technical information that might guide [the tribunal] in the

[7] Park (n 5) 12; Redfern and Hunter (n 6) para 6.76.

[8] This is specially the case in ICSID arbitrations, which are not subject to the supervision of the courts of a specific legal system. Arbitrators have discretion to resolve evidentiary matters. See Sourgens and others (n 3) para 4(5).

[9] In fact, in international law, arbitrators are expected to take an active role and many modern arbitration rules expect the tribunal to investigate facts and evidence on its own motion. See Bickmann (n 1) paras 2.173, 2.199, 3.55–3.60.

search for the truth'.[10] The matters on which experts can opine are unlimited. We see economists called upon to give evidence on quantum, industry experts called to discuss technical issues relevant to the resolution of the dispute (for example engineers or geologists). Lawyers may be called to give evidence on the applicable law to the dispute, particularly if that legal system has novel aspects or is not one with which the tribunal is familiar.

Although appointed by each party individually, experts must provide their independent opinion on the topics of their expertise. Normally, each party will present its own expert evidence with its pleadings, in the form of expert reports.[11] The other party will then have the right to cross-examine the expert at the final hearing and test their credibility, technical knowledge, and soundness of their opinion.[12] Tribunals may ask questions as well to understand their reports and to contrast them with the opinions of the other party's expert. The adversarial nature of this process can, however, result in conflicting experts addressing different questions and not properly engaging with the other party's evidence—the legendary 'two ships passing in the night'. In these circumstances, some tribunals have sought the assistance of their own appointed expert, as allowed under most arbitration rules.[13] The process of tribunal appointed experts reflects judicial process in many civil law countries where it is the judge who often decides whether an expert is needed and, if so, who to call. Where a tribunal decides to exercise this power, it will usually seek the views of the parties on the qualifications of the expert and the proposed terms of reference, and then establish a shortlist of candidates and ask the parties to confirm the absence of conflicts.[14] The benefit of having a tribunal-appointed expert, however, comes at a price. On the one hand, the expert will not have been exposed to the influence of one or other of the parties during the briefing process, while on the other hand, the expert will not be as familiar with the details of a case as party-appointed experts.[15] In particular, a tribunal-appointed expert who joins an arbitration after a hearing has taken place will be at a disadvantage when compared

[10] *Starrett Housing Corporation, Starrett Systems Inc and others v Iran, Bank Markazi Iran and others*, IUSCT Case No 24, Final Award (Award No 314-24-1) (14 August 1987) [264] (citing *United Kingdom v Albania (Corfu Channel Case)*, 1949 ICJ Rep 4, [20]).

[11] See eg ICSID Arbitration Rules (2022) r 38, UNCITRAL Arbitration Rules (2010) art 27; IBA Rules on the Taking of Evidence in International Arbitration (2020) art 5(1).

[12] During the amendment process, France, later supported by Australia, Chile, and the European Union, requested that 'experts appointed by disputing parties or tribunals should submit a declaration of independence and neutrality disclosing their relations, past or present, direct or indirect, with the disputing parties, their counsel, tribunal members or any third interested party (e.g. insurer or funder)', ICSID, 'Compendium of State and Public Comments on Working Paper #1' (3 August 2018) 289; ICSID, 'Compendium of State and Public Comments on Working Paper #2' (15 March 2019) 107; ICSID, 'Compendium of State and Public Comments on Working Paper #3' (16 August 2019) 29; ICSID, 'Compendium of State and Public Comments on Working Paper #4' (28 February 2020) 33–34. In practice, an expert is expected to make such disclosures and, in any case, the '[t]ribunal will consider an expert's independence in assessing the probative value of the evidence'. Notwithstanding this, it is generally understood and accepted that experts are paid by and may work closely with the party that appoints them. ICSID, 'Proposals for Amendment of the ICSID Rules, Working Paper #2' (vol 1, March 2019), para 249; ICSID, 'Proposals for Amendment of the ICSID Rules, Working Paper #3' (vol 1, August 2019), para 96.

[13] See Redfern and Hunter (n 6) para 6.141.

[14] Nigel Blackaby and Alex Wilbraham, 'Practical Issues Relating to the Use of Expert Evidence in Investment Treaty Arbitration' (2016) 31 (3) ICSID Review 655, 664.

[15] ibid.

to the parties and the tribunal members. Thus, it is preferable for a tribunal to appoint its own expert as early as possible in the proceedings.[16]

During the modernization of its rules in 2022, ICSID proposed the inclusion of an express rule governing tribunal-appointed experts. The rule eventually adopted (Rule 39) expressly establishes that, unless the parties agree otherwise, tribunals can appoint one or more independent experts and the parties have the obligation to provide the tribunal-appointed expert with any type of evidence they may require.[17] The tribunal must give the parties the opportunity to comment on any report issued by its appointed expert.[18]

When the provision was first proposed, Canada, Colombia, Israel, and South Korea voiced their concerns that this provision could be used by the tribunal to assist a party that had failed to meet its burden of proving its own case.[19] In fact, Korea affirmed that '[e]xtensive use of Tribunal-appointed experts may undermine the adversarial system and the principles of burden of proof'.[20] As stated by ICSID in response, the tribunal's power to appoint its own expert, however, should not affect the principles of the burden of proof.[21] It noted, for instance, that a tribunal-appointed expert may shed light on disagreements between the party-appointed experts that an unassisted tribunal lacks the expertise to resolve.

Let's look at two situations where investment tribunals appointed their own damages expert.

A. Respondent 'No-Show'

In the case of *Stabil v Russia*, following Russia's annexation of Crimea, a group of Ukrainian investors initiated an arbitration against Russia for the taking of their gas stations and associated assets in Crimea.[22] The claimants had requested US$47 million in damages, plus interest and costs, on the basis of their damages expert's report.[23] Russia refused to participate in the proceedings, and thus did not put forward an expert to challenge the claim.

The tribunal was faced with a purely one-sided presentation of the alleged loss and did not have the technical expertise to properly test the propositions advanced by the claimants and their expert. It recognized that it had a 'duty to satisfy itself that the claims before it are well founded'. It therefore decided to appoint an expert 'to whom it

[16] ibid.
[17] ICSID Arbitration Rules (2022) r 39.
[18] ibid r 39(5).
[19] Interestingly, Colombia, a civil law country that, in general terms, has followed an inquisitorial approach, advocated for a more limited role of the tribunal, ICSID, 'Comments on Working Paper #1' (n 12) 292; ICSID, 'Comments on Working Paper #2' (n 12) 107–09. Canada, Costa Rica, and the Republic of Korea expressed their concern mostly based on cost concerns.
[20] ICSID, 'Comments on Working Paper #2' (n 12) 109.
[21] See ICSID Arbitration Rules (2022) r 36(2); ICSID, 'Working Paper #3' (n 12) para 102.
[22] *Stabil LLC and others v Russia*, PCA Case No 2015-35, Final Award (12 April 2019) [3], [134]–[140].
[23] ibid [140], [269].

will put specific questions regarding the quantum of the [c]laimants' damages'.[24] The tribunal's expert provided a report upon which the claimants had the opportunity to comment. Further provision was made for a hearing of the independent expert at which the claimants (and the tribunal) could ask questions.[25]

The tribunal's expert identified some adjustments that the claimants' expert's model required, and the tribunal therefore requested its expert to prepare an alternative valuation.[26] The tribunal ultimately decided to rely on the evidence of the claimants' expert as well as its own expert,[27] giving great deference to the opinions of the latter, which overall reduced the damages awarded to the claimants.[28]

In this case, the tribunal felt the need to test the appropriateness of the damages calculation proposed by the claimants' expert, given that it had not been subject to the other party's comments, made the object of a responsive report or tested in cross examination. It therefore got closer to the 'truth' of the loss suffered by the claimants than if it had remained passive.

B. Inability to Bridge the Differences with Confidence

In 2003, Suez (and other related entities) initiated an ICSID arbitration against Argentina for measures enacted in the midst of Argentina's 2002 economic crisis that affected its investment in the Buenos Aires water and wastewater concession. During the procedure, both parties had presented extensive expert reports on quantum that had agreed on the same methodology, the discounted cash flow (or 'DCF') approach. However, the claimants' experts estimated losses in excess of US$1 billion, whereas the respondent's experts utilized radically different inputs and proposed zero damages. Both experts were heard at the final hearing, with extensive cross examination.[29]

Following the final hearing (and no doubt during deliberations), it became apparent that bridging the gap between the parties' radically different positions required in-depth economic expertise that the tribunal did not consider it possessed. As a consequence, the tribunal issued a decision on liability which was to be followed by a separate damages phase. The tribunal noted in its decision that '[g]iven the complexity of [the] case and the extraordinarily voluminous nature of the record', it would appoint an independent financial expert to assist it with the damages valuation.[30] After a complex process of finding a suitable independent expert and agreeing the terms of reference

[24] *Stabil LLC and others v Russia*, PCA Case No 2015-35, Press Report (19 February 2018); *Stabil LLC and others v Russia*, PCA Case No 2015-35, Press Report (24 April 2019); *Stabil* Final Award (n 22) [56].
[25] *Stabil* Press Report 24 April 2019 (n 24).
[26] *Stabil* Final Award (n 22) [269].
[27] ibid [270]ff.
[28] ibid [310], [331]–[332], [339], [344], [350]–[351], [357], [370]–[373], [379]–[382], [385], [395]–[396], [404]–[405].
[29] *Suez, Sociedad General de Aguas de Barcelona SA and Vivendi Universal SA v Argentina*, ICSID Case No ARB/03/19, Award (9 April 2015) [17]. The authors represented the claimants in the dispute.
[30] *Suez, Sociedad General de Aguas de Barcelona SA and Vivendi Universal SA v Argentina*, ICSID Case No ARB/03/19, Decision on Liability (30 July 2010) [272]; *Suez* Award (n 29) [7].

with the parties, the tribunal tasked its expert with preparing a quantum report.[31] The parties were asked to exchange two rounds of pleadings commenting on the report, which adopted a DCF methodology.[32] After a three-day second hearing on quantum, the tribunal issued its quantum decision, awarding the claimants over US$400 million plus interest in damages, representing a substantial reduction when compared to the claimant's original claim based on its own expert recommendations.[33]

In this case, the tribunal exercised caution by nominating its own expert, but the consequent added costs and delays were material, adding several years to the proceeding. While the tribunal's desire to get closer to the 'truth' of the loss may make such an exercise appealing, it could be questioned whether it could not have been done more efficiently by posing new questions to both parties' experts. One method that is now commonly adopted is for tribunals to ask questions of both parties' experts following the final hearing and (often) to agree a joint damages model with inputs that the tribunal can manipulate to reach its conclusion. Indeed, this seems to be the route many tribunals are now following in order to avoid the risk of delay caused by late appointments of tribunal experts.[34]

III. Document Production

Usually, the parties produce at their own initiative the documentary evidence on which they rely, together with their written submissions; the tribunal then decides on the weight of those documents and (if challenged) their admissibility.[35] Additionally, parties may be required to produce documents that they had not voluntarily submitted, through requests made by the other party and/or ordered by the tribunal.[36]

Document production procedures may be influenced by the participants' cultural background.[37] While common law-trained lawyers will be familiar with the process of documentary discovery and may expect similar procedures in an arbitration, the expectation of civil law-trained lawyers will be that a party decides on which evidence it relies (subject to judicial control) given the inquisitorial and judge-led nature of their systems.[38] Illustrative of this are the comments made by some states during the

[31] *Suez* Award (n 29) [8], [10], [12].

[32] ibid [16], [95].

[33] ibid [14], [28]–[34], [89], [105].

[34] See Tobias Zuberbühler and others, *IBA Rules of Evidence: Commentary on the IBA Rules on the Taking of Evidence in International Arbitration* (2nd edn, Schulthess Juristische Medien AG 2022) 154.

[35] This subject to any agreement between the parties and any mandatory requirements at the place of arbitration. See Christoph H Schreuer and others, *The ICSID Convention: A Commentary* (3rd edn, CUP 2022), 913, 941.

[36] Arbitration rules usually recognize broad powers to the tribunal. See eg UNCITRAL Arbitration Rules (2010) arts 17, 27; ICSID Arbitration Rules (2022) rr 36–37; Convention on the Settlement of Investment Disputes between States and Nationals of Other States (opened for signature 18 March 1965, entered into force 14 October 1966) 575 UNTS 159, art 43. In *Asian Agricultural Products v Sri Lanka*, for example, at the end of the hearing, the tribunal requested the parties to produce certain additional documents and information, as well as their respective comments. *Asian Agricultural Products Limited v Sri Lanka*, ICSID Case No ARB/87/3, Final Award (27 June 1990) [11].

[37] Redfern and Hunter (n 6) para 6.91.

[38] Marieke van Hooijdonk and Yves Herinckx, 'The Impact of the IBA Guidelines and Rules on the Search for the Truth in Arbitration' in Luc Demeyere (ed), *Do Arbitral Awards Reveal the Truth?* (Wolters Kluwer 2019). For

amendment process of the ICSID Arbitration Rules. Panama, for example, advocated for the recognition that 'there is no presumption in favor of document production', a suggestion later adopted in the following iteration of the draft rules.[39] For their part, the IBA Rules on the Taking of Evidence in International Arbitration set out a document production procedure that aims at neutralizing cultural differences.[40]

The evolution of the approach of investment tribunals has been noteworthy. In early cases, document disclosure phases were rare. However, it is now standard practice for investment tribunals to include a document production phase, as they recognize that it 'can be helpful for a party to present its case and in the [t]ribunal's task of establishing the facts of the case relevant for the issues'.[41] However, tribunals will weigh this against other considerations like efficiency,[42] proportionality, and the protection of confidentiality.[43]

Rather than focus on a standardized phased document disclosure exercise taking place after the initial exchange of pleadings, certain tribunals have been willing to adopt novel document disclosure rulings to assist them in reaching a better understanding of the 'truth'.

We set out some examples below.

A. *Libananco v Turkey*

Libananco initiated arbitration following Turkey's seizure of two power utility companies. Central to the dispute was the alleged transfer of bearer shares (ie shares in which ownership passes by mere physical transfer) in the companies to the claimant

example, the tribunal in *Caratube v Kazakhstan* noted that 'on one hand, requests and orders regarding the production of documents are today a regular feature of international arbitration, but, on the other hand, the present arbitration is a case also involving Parties domiciled in Kazakhstan which is predominantly a Civil Law country where production of documents is far less used than in Common Law countries', *Caratube International Oil Company LLP v Kazakhstan*, ICSID Case No ARB/08/12, Procedural Order No 2 (26 April 2010) [1.3].

[39] ICSID, 'Comments on Working Paper #3' (n 12) 28; ICSID, 'Proposals for Amendment of the ICSID Rules, Working Paper #4' (vol 1, February 2020) para 86.

[40] IBA Rules on the Taking of Evidence in International Arbitration (2020) art 3. See also foreword, second paragraph ('The IBA Rules of Evidence reflect procedures in use in many different legal systems, and they may be particularly useful when the parties come from different legal cultures').

[41] *Anatolie Stati, Gabriel Stati, Ascom Group SA and Terra Raf Trans Trading Ltd v Kazakhstan*, SCC Case No V 116/2010, Procedural Order No 2 (3 February 2012) [1.5] cited in Award, 19 December 2013 [47]); Esmé Shirlow, 'E-Discovery in Investment Treaty Arbitration: Practice, Procedures, Challenges and Opportunities' (2020) 11(4) Journal of International Dispute Settlement 549. Tribunals are willing to order a party that does not fully comply with its directions regarding disclosure to bear the costs resulting from that failure, *Alverley Investments Limited and Germen Properties Ltd v Romania*, ICSID Case No ARB/18/30, Excerpts of Award (16 March 2022) [481]–[482].

[42] Shirlow (n 41). To this end, the IBA Rules on the Taking of Evidence in International Arbitration (2020) are almost universally recognized as the international standard for an effective document production regime. Redfern and Hunter (n 6) paras 6.93–6.105.

[43] *Caratube* (n 38) [1.4]; *Churchill Mining PLC and Planet Mining Pty Ltd v Indonesia*, ICSID Case No ARB/12/14 and 12/40, Procedural Order No 5 (19 March 2013) [8]. During the amendment process of the ICSID Arbitration Rules, different states voiced their concerns about the cost and duration of discovery, and requested that tribunals be given specific substantive criteria to address document requests. China, for instance, proposed that national security be included as one of the reasons for which states could refuse to produce documents. See eg ICSID, 'Comments on Working Paper #1' (n 12) 284–87; ICSID, 'Working Paper #2' (n 12) paras 242–46.

before the alleged expropriation which was relevant to whether claimant was a qualifying investor under the applicable investment treaty.

A few weeks after the claimant filed its memorial on jurisdiction and merits, Turkey requested the tribunal to order the claimant: to produce documents relating to its ownership of the shares; and to deposit the original share certificates for safekeeping.[44] For Turkey, the claimant had failed to show ownership of the investment, and it wished 'to put the genuineness of Libananco's ownership stake in [the companies] to a form of prior proof' so as to decide whether to lodge a preliminary objection or not.[45] The claimant, for its part, said that Turkey's request should not be allowed until it had formally formulated an objection to jurisdiction.[46] Because of the early stage of the proceedings and taking into account that Turkey's counter-memorial was due soon, to accommodate the petition, the tribunal suspended the timetable until it had issued its decision and fixed a two-day hearing to discuss the request.[47]

At the hearing, the claimant indicated its willingness to submit the requested documents and proposed the appointment of an escrow agent.[48] In light of this proposal, the tribunal concluded that there was no need to rule on the right to a form of 'pre-pleading discovery'; and requested the claimant to appoint an escrow agent, who would take instructions from the tribunal (without being an agent of the tribunal), and who would have immunity in matters connected to holding the share certificates.[49]

The tribunal acknowledged the unconventional timing of the request and that it would have been in a better position to deal with the application if it had known the parties' arguments. It also warned the parties against using document production 'for a mere fishing expedition launched in the hope of uncovering material to serve as the foundation for an argument (preliminary or substantive) not yet formally advanced before it'. To guarantee that the arbitration moved forward efficiently and expeditiously, the tribunal set a deadline for the submission of Turkey's counter-memorial, which it could later modify based on the results of its inspection of the documents.[50]

After the tribunal's decision was issued, but before the shares were handed to the escrow agent, Turkey formally raised certain objections *ratione materiae*.[51] Further, upon production of the documents, the parties produced legal expert reports on the documents.[52] While the tribunal referred to the findings of the parties' experts, it found the reports to be of little assistance.[53] Taking into account the documents produced, as well as the witness statements and other evidence, the tribunal concluded that while certain aspects of the claimant's case were supported, 'in the light of the various

[44] *Libananco Holdings Co Limited v Turkey*, ICSID Case No ARB/06/8, Decision on Preliminary Issues (23 June 2008) [15], [17], [21]–[22], [51]–[53]. Freshfields represented Turkey in this matter.
[45] ibid [29], [62].
[46] ibid [30].
[47] ibid [20], [23].
[48] ibid [63].
[49] ibid [63]–[65].
[50] ibid [70]–[71].
[51] *Libananco Holdings Co Limited v Turkey*, ICSID Case No ARB/06/8, Award (2 September 2011) [23]–[24], [27]–[28], [104].
[52] ibid [351]–[353].
[53] ibid [356]–[358].

inconsistencies, conflicts and changes in the [c]laimant's account of the events that occurred, its final description and account of how it came to own shares in [the two companies] is not persuasive'.[54] Therefore, the tribunal declined to exercise jurisdiction.

B. *Serafin Garcia Armas et al v Venezuela*

In the *Serafin Garcia Armas* case, Venezuela had taken control of the claimants' corporations by force, essentially excluding management from access to accounts or information. As a consequence, the claimants had no access to key documents necessary to prove their losses, such as the companies' accounts. They therefore made a special application to the tribunal for pre-pleading disclosure, noting that their lack of access to the necessary documents was a direct consequence of the wrongful act of the respondent state. The tribunal was sympathetic to the claimants' situation and granted the application, confirming that the circumstances made it necessary to have a document production phase prior to the presentation of the memorial on the merits, in order to ensure due process for the claimants, and suspended the date for the presentation of the memorial until the preliminary document disclosure phase was completed. Once again, the tribunal exercised its powers to ensure a level playing field and to avoid the respondent state from taking advantage of its own wrongful acts.[55]

C. *Glencore v Colombia I*

Glencore and one of its subsidiaries commenced arbitration following the imposition by the Colombian control authorities of fines in relation to an amendment granted by the competent mining authorities to the claimants' mining contract. Colombia alleged that the amendment to the mining contract had been 'procured by corruption, misrepresentation and the concealment of important information'.[56] To support its assertion, Colombia attempted to introduce into the record internal documents that had been seized from the claimant's offices by the state antitrust authority in the context of an unrelated investigation. The claimants argued that these documents were privileged, had been obtained in an irregular manner and were ultimately inadmissible.[57]

For the tribunal, the key was whether admitting such documents would be fair, taking into account 'that the rule that the equality of arms must be respected applied to "the marshalling of evidence"', and that tribunals may exclude evidence for compelling reasons of fairness and equality between the parties. The tribunal refused to

[54] ibid [530]–[536].

[55] *Serafín García Armas and Karina García Gruber v Venezuela*, PCA Case No 2013-3, Final Award (26 April 2019) [29]. Freshfields represented the claimants in this matter.

[56] *Glencore International AG and CI Prodeco SA v Colombia*, ICSID Case No ARB/16/6, Decision on Annulment (22 September 2021) [59]–[61]. Freshfields represented the claimants in this matter.

[57] ibid [67]–[69].

admit the documents as they had been obtained in the context of an unrelated antitrust investigation; it acknowledged that a contrary decision would have created incentives for a state to launch administrative investigations once it became aware of an investment claim in order to engage in 'self-help', rather than rely on the tribunal's authority to order document production.[58] It did, however, leave the door open for Colombia to seek the production of documents or to apply to submit evidence gathered from a criminal procedure.[59]

Subsequently, Colombia sought to introduce the documents through document production requests, and by requesting permission to introduce documents collected by the Colombian General Prosecutor, and was partially successful.[60] Ultimately, the tribunal found no evidence of corruption and found Colombia liable for a breach of the fair and equitable treatment standard and awarded damages.[61] Colombia later sought the annulment of the award on the basis that it had been 'wrongly prevented from admitting into evidence' documents it considered 'critical' to support its objection,[62] but the application for annulment was rejected.[63]

This case shows the power of a tribunal to avoid the abuse by a state party of its unique police powers and to re-establish a level playing field in pursuit of the 'truth'.

IV. Witnesses Called by the Tribunal

The role of fact witnesses is to explain or supplement other evidence presented by the parties, especially on aspects where no documentary evidence is available. The parties usually present written witness statements with their pleadings, and the witnesses can be called by the opposing party or the tribunal to defend their testimony at the final oral hearing.[64]

Each party will indicate by a certain date the names of the other party's witnesses it wishes to cross-examine.[65] This is another area where cultural traditions may have an influence: practitioners from common law countries, who see the hearing as an opportunity to cross-examine the other party's witnesses to disprove their allegations, may choose not to examine any witnesses whose testimony they deem irrelevant. Practitioners from civil law countries, who are used to an inquisitorial approach looking for the 'material truth', may still wish the tribunal to see those witnesses.[66]

58 ibid [82]–[84].
59 ibid [88]–[94].
60 ibid [97]–[110], [133], [141]–[151].
61 *Glencore International AG and CI Prodeco SA v Colombia*, ICSID Case No ARB/16/6, Award (17 August 2019) [1687].
62 *Glencore* Decision on Annulment (n 56) [6], [63], [188]ff. See also ibid [95].
63 ibid [383]–[388], [408]–[415].
64 See IBA Rules on the Taking of Evidence in International Arbitration (2020) art 4.
65 ibid art 8.1.
66 During the amendment process of the ICSID Arbitration Rules, recognizing that 'not all arbitrators and counsel are familiar with the modalities for examination of witnesses', Armenia suggested that ICSID's Secretariat produce and update a practice direction on best practices to be followed by the tribunal, ICSID, 'Comments on Working Paper #3' (n 12) 29.

Tribunals recognize how important it is to see and examine witnesses during a hearing,[67] and they have the power to require the presence of a witness who has not been called by the parties. However, it is usually up to the parties to decide the pool of witnesses, and tribunals rarely summon additional witnesses.[68]

We provide two examples of cases where they nevertheless exercised their power to hear witnesses not called by either party.

A. *OAO Tatneft v Ukraine*

The claimant brought a case against Ukraine for the loss of its shareholding interest in Ukrtatnafta, a Ukrainian oil refining company. It argued that the actions and omissions of Ukraine led a third party (the Privat Group) to gain control over that company. A key event was the takeover of the company by the once chairman of Ukrtatnafta's management board, Mr Ovcharenko. Although he had been dismissed by the company's supervisory board and shareholders, Mr Ovcharenko obtained favourable rulings that he used to enter the company's premises accompanied by armed men in order to be reinstated as chairman. From that position, he aided the Privat Group in taking over the company. During the arbitration, the parties presented eight witnesses to testify on different aspects of the relevant events. Among others, the claimant offered the testimony of a public official, who testified that he was offered a bribe to put an end to a criminal investigation for the appropriation of the company's seal.[69]

The tribunal, *sua sponte*, requested the parties to use their best efforts to secure the appearance and testimony of two additional individuals, not offered as witnesses by either party which might be relevant to the corruption allegation: Mr Ovcharenko's attorney, identified by the claimant's witness as the person who offered the bribe; and Mr Kolomoisky, the head of the Privat Group, which had benefitted from Mr Ovcharenko's actions.[70] The tribunal ultimately relied on Mr Kolomoisky's testimony in the assessment of damages.[71]

B. *Rumeli and Telsim v Kazakhstan*

Rumeli and Telsim entered into a joint venture with Kazakh company Investel for the provision of mobile telecommunications services in Kazakhstan. The claimants argued that once the joint venture had achieved success, Investel's shareholders (who were Kazakhstan officials or with close ties to the president of Kazakhstan) colluded with the

[67] *Vacuum Salt Products Ltd v Ghana*, ICSID Case No ARB/92/1, Award (16 February 1994) [45].
[68] Redfern and Hunter (n 6) para 6.126.
[69] *OAO Tatneft v Ukraine*, PCA Case No 2008-8, Award (29 July 2014) [114], [118].
[70] ibid [37].
[71] See eg ibid [613]–[614].

state to expel the claimants from the joint venture through the termination of the joint venture's investment contract with the state.

To prove the collusion, the claimants referred extensively to acts performed by certain individuals linked to the respondent. For example, the claimants argued that a Mr Kulibayev, executive director of Investel and son-in-law of the president, had acted on behalf of the state when he terminated the contract with the joint venture.[72] The claimants recognized that Mr Kulibayev's testimony could serve to explain the events surrounding the alleged collusion.[73] The claimants also argued that, once the arbitration was underway, an investment group ultimately controlled by the Kazakh state had offered a derisory price for the claimant's interest in the joint venture, which they interpreted as an admission of guilt by the state.[74] The claimants argued that the offer had been made by a Mr Orazbekov. After considering a request by the claimants, the tribunal ordered the respondent to produce these two additional witnesses at the hearing.

Of course, in both cases, the tribunal could only order the appearance of new witnesses who were under the control of one of the parties. However, in investment arbitration the role of the state is key and so tribunals have been willing to assert their authority to obtain testimony from relevant public officials who (for strategic reasons) the respondent state has decided to exclude. Nevertheless, tribunals should be reticent to overuse this power and reserve it for those witnesses whose testimony seems fundamental to determine a key fact.

V. Witness Conferencing

An additional (or alternative) method to the traditional examination of witnesses and experts in sequence, is to place two or more witnesses or experts together to answer questions from the tribunal at the same time.[75] This method is known as 'witness conferencing' or 'hot tubbing'.[76]

While the decision to have witness conferencing or hot-tubbing should be undertaken on a case-by-case basis, it can offer certain advantages,[77] by allowing the tribunal to clarify areas of agreement and disagreement between the witnesses or experts by direct confrontation under their control, thus complementing examination by counsel.[78]

[72] *Rumeli Telekom AS and Telsim Mobil Telekomunikasyon Hizmetleri AS v Kazakhstan*, ICSID Case No ARB/05/16, Award (29 July 2008) [359], [361].

[73] ibid [437], [460].

[74] ibid [430]–[431], [590].

[75] Article 8.4(f) of the IBA Rules on the Taking of Evidence in International Arbitration (2020) expressly refers to this.

[76] Redfern and Hunter (n 6) para 6.193.

[77] Wolfgang Peter, 'Witness "Conferencing"' (2002) 18 (1) Arbitration International 47.

[78] Redfern and Hunter (n 6) para 6.193; Richard Kreindler, 'Benefiting from Oral Testimony of Expert Witnesses: Traditional and Emerging Techniques' in Laurent Lévy and V Veeder (eds), *Arbitration and Oral Evidence*, vol 2 (Dossiers of the ICC Institute of World Business Law, Kluwer Law International; International Chamber of Commerce 2004) 102.

It therefore assists the tribunal in avoiding the risk of evidence that is not directly responsive by forcing witnesses or experts to answer the same questions at the same time.

During the amendment process of the ICSID Arbitration Rules, Qatar requested that witness conferencing be included in the rules.[79] Ultimately, no express provision on the topic was included because, pursuant to Rule 38(3), that provides that '[t]he Tribunal shall determine the manner in which the examination is conducted', the tribunal was considered to have ample powers to make such determination in any event.[80]

Let's look at two examples.

A. Establishing the Right Legal Standard

In *Tennant Energy v Canada*, the claimant had started an arbitration against Canada due to the government's refusal to grant a feed-in tariff contract for a wind power project. A central issue was whether the claimant qualified as an investor at the time of the breach. The claimant argued that before January 2015, when it acquired its shares in Skyway (the investment), it had been the beneficial owner of the shares through an oral trust set up by its principal, Mr Tennant, under Californian law.[81] Both parties produced legal experts on the existence of this trust.

When setting the schedule for the hearing, the tribunal reserved some time for expert witness conferencing, should the tribunal decide that it was needed.[82] The tribunal decided to use this time, and held a conference with the legal experts.[83] The tribunal used the power to ensure a proper confrontation of the respondent's expert's views with the claimant's expert.[84] During conferencing, the experts agreed that the standard of 'clear and convincing evidence' (the relevant standard under Californian law) required a high probability that the trust had been created at the relevant time. Applying that standard, the tribunal concluded in its award that this agreed standard had not been met in the case[85] and concluded that it did not have jurisdiction.[86] In other words, the witness conferencing provided the tribunal with the necessary agreement on the legal test to make its decision.

[79] ICSID, 'Proposals for Amendment of the ICSID Rules, Working Paper #1' (vol 3, August 2018) para 432; ICSID, 'Comments on Working Paper #1' (n 12) 289; ICSID, 'Working Paper #2' (n 12) para 248.

[80] ICSID Arbitration Rules (2022) r 38(1); ICSID, 'Working Paper #1' (n 79) para 432.

[81] *Tennant Energy LLC v Canada*, PCA Case No 2018-54, Final Award (25 October 2022) [124], [129], [131], [362]–[363].

[82] *Tennant Energy LLC v Canada*, PCA Case No 2018-54, Procedural Order No 14 (2 November 2021) [14].

[83] *Tennant Energy LLC v Canada*, PCA Case No 2018-54, Hearing on Jurisdiction Transcript Day 4, 663:21–667:9.

[84] ibid 493:25–494:15; 663:23–664:3.

[85] *Tennant Energy* Final Award (n 81) [369]–[370]; *Tennant Energy* Hearing on Jurisdiction (n 83) 548:8–15; 673:8–674:7.

[86] *Tennant Energy* Final Award (n 81) [400]–[402], [476].

B. Calculation of Damages

In *Occidental v Ecuador II*, Occidental filed for arbitration against Ecuador following the Ecuadorian authorities' decision to terminate a participation contract for a hydrocarbon block.[87] To support their termination decision, the authorities argued that Occidental had improperly transferred a share of its production activity to a Canadian firm, without ministerial approval and in violation of the applicable law.

Following a six-day hearing on quantum, the tribunal informed the parties that it 'ha[d] reached a point in its deliberations where it required the assistance of both parties' experts [...] in order to help the Tribunal assess the proper calculation of damages'.[88] Accordingly, it instructed the parties to produce both experts for consultation to discuss the fair market value of the block. Notably, the tribunal requested the parties' agreement for it to consult with the experts without the presence of counsel.[89] The tribunal ultimately withdrew this request and decided to instead invite the experts 'to confer and produce jointly a report estimating the fair market value of [the] Block ... using the discounted cash flow method'.[90] After the experts produced this report, as well as two supplemental reports addressing the parties' comments, the tribunal held a one-day hearing where it posed questions to the experts.[91] The tribunal relied heavily on the joint expert report to determine the damages.[92]

The respondent sought to annul the award. Among other reasons, it argued that the tribunal's decisions regarding witness conferencing and the preparation of a joint report constituted a serious departure from a fundamental rule of procedure since it did not follow an 'orthodox approach'.[93] While the committee partially annulled the award on other grounds, it rejected the argument that the tribunal's approach had been a procedural breach.[94]

This is an example where the tribunal used a variety of tools including witness conferencing and joint reports to obtain the most useful information for its decision. It is a particularly useful tool in damages analysis where party reports can often fail to engage fully with the other party's case. It enables the tribunal to seek common positions which it can then use as a reliable foundation for its damages decision.

[87] *Occidental Petroleum Corporation and Occidental Exploration and Production Company v Ecuador*, ICSID Case No ARB/06/11, Award (5 October 2012).
[88] ibid [78].
[89] ibid [67], [74], [78]–[79].
[90] ibid [80].
[91] ibid [81]–[88], [91].
[92] *Occidental Petroleum Corporation and Occidental Exploration and Production Company v Ecuador*, ICSID Case No ARB/06/11, Decision on Annulment of the Award (2 November 2015) [564].
[93] ibid [565]–[566].
[94] ibid [569]–[574], [590].

VI. Admission of Non-Disputing Party Submissions

An *amicus curiae* is a non-disputing party that intervenes in the proceedings, with the purpose of assisting the tribunal by providing different perspectives and experiences to those of the parties. In investment arbitration, the admission of *amicus curiae* briefs was later endorsed through amendments to several sets of procedural rules.[95] The possibility to accept (or even solicit) the views of non-disputing parties is an important tool for tribunals judging issues of public policy and regulation that may affect stakeholders who are not parties to the arbitration.

While the admission of *amicus curiae* briefs has been controversial,[96] the practice has taken root in investment arbitration. Canadian and American civil society groups were the first to ask for leave to intervene in North American Free Trade Agreement (NAFTA) cases,[97] and NAFTA's Free Trade Commission endorsed the participation of non-disputing parties.[98] In time, it became an accepted practice to grant suitably qualified civil society groups leave to participate in ICSID proceedings as well.[99] Tribunals usually impose specific restrictions on the participation of non-disputing parties, including limiting the scope of their briefs, their access to the record, and their attendance at hearings.[100] To date, the European Commission is the organization with the largest number of interventions as a non-disputing party.

Below, we discuss examples where tribunals accepted the participation of *amici curiae* despite party opposition and even at their own initiative.

A. *Suez v Argentina*

The ICSID tribunal in this case exercised its general discretion to allow five non-governmental organizations (NGOs), including consumer protection associations, to submit a joint *amicus curiae* brief while refusing to give them access to the case record.[101] The petitioners argued that the case involved public interest matters and

[95] Nigel Blackaby and Caroline Richard, 'Amicus Curiae: A Panacea for Legitimacy in Investment Arbitration?' in Michael Waibel and others (eds), *The Backlash against Investment Arbitration* (Kluwer Law 2010) 254. See eg ICSID Arbitration Rules (2006) r 37(2); ICSID Arbitration Rules (2022) r 67.

[96] Blackaby and Richard (n 95) 257.

[97] See eg *Methanex Corporation v United States of America*, UNCITRAL; *United Parcel Service of America Inc v Canada*, ICSID Case No UNCT/02/1.

[98] NAFTA, 'Statement of the Free Trade Commission on Non-disputing Party Participation', 7 October 2003.

[99] The first tribunal to consider this issue denied the petition made by various NGOs to intervene, *Aguas del Tunari SA v Bolivia*, ICSID Case No ARB/02/3, Letter from the President of the Tribunal responding to Petition (29 January 2003). The tribunal in *Aguas Argentinas*, however, adopted a different approach at the merits phase, *Suez, Sociedad General de Aguas de Barcelona SA and Vivendi Universal SA v Argentina*, ICSID Case No ARB/03/19, Order in Response to a Petition by Five Non-Governmental Organizations for Permission to make an amicus curiae Submission (12 February 2007). Blackaby and Richard (n 95) 262–266; ICSID, 'Working Paper #1' (n 79) 889–90.

[100] See eg *Infinito Gold Ltd v Costa Rica*, ICSID Case No ARB/14/5, Procedural Order No 2 (1 June 2016) [1], [49]; *Biwater Gauff (Tanzania) Ltd v Tanzania*, ICSID Case No ARB/05/22, Procedural Order No 5 (2 February 2007) [55], [68], [71]; *Isolux Netherlands BV v Spain*, SCC Case V2013/153, Final Award (12 July 2016) [34].

[101] *Suez* Order in Response to Petition 2007 (n 99) [25], [27].

requested the tribunal to give them 'timely, sufficient, and unrestricted access to the documents' and to allow them to file an *amicus curiae* brief.[102] While the respondent had no objections, the claimants argued that the case record was confidential.[103]

Neither the ICSID Convention nor the Arbitration Rules at the time authorized or prohibited the submission of *amicus curiae* briefs. The tribunal concluded that since the ICSID Convention gives arbitrators sufficient powers to decide any 'question of procedure', it had the power to admit *amicus curiae* briefs 'from suitable nonparties in appropriate cases'.[104] The tribunal stated that a decision to admit an *amicus curiae* brief should depend on: the appropriateness of the subject matter of the case; the expertise, experience and independence of the non-party; and the procedure for the submission, which must protect the rights of the parties.[105]

In their brief, the NGOs argued that human rights law recognizes the right to water. According to them, Argentina's measures were justified by this rationale.[106] The tribunal rejected the argument, finding no basis under international law to support it, and found Argentina liable.[107]

Following this case, the ICSID Arbitration Rules were revised in 2006 to expressly include the tribunal's power to allow *amicus curiae*. The amendment reflected the approach followed by the tribunal in *Suez*.[108] This shows how the exercise of the tribunal's powers can not only resolve specific situations, but also shape future practice.

B. *Achmea v Slovakia I*

Achmea commenced arbitration against Slovakia based on measures affecting its medical insurance business. The tribunal held Slovakia liable and awarded Achmea €22 million in damages.[109] During the arbitration, Slovakia objected to the tribunal's jurisdiction and argued that investor-state arbitration was incompatible with EU law.[110]

At the jurisdictional hearing, the tribunal discussed (and agreed) with the parties the possibility of approaching the European Commission and the government of the Netherlands (home state of the investor) to comment on the issue.[111] The Netherlands

[102] ibid [7].

[103] ibid [9]–[10].

[104] *Suez, Sociedad General de Aguas de Barcelona SA and Vivendi Universal SA v Argentina*, ICSID Case No ARB/03/19, Order in response to a Petition for Participation as Amicus Curiae (19 May 2005) [9], [14]–[16]; *Suez* Order in Response to Petition 2007 (n 99) [2].

[105] *Suez* Order in Response to Petition 2005 (n 104) [17]; *Suez* Order in Response to Petition 2007 (n 99) [12]–[13], [26].

[106] *Suez* Decision on Liability (n 30) [256], [262].

[107] ibid [262], [265].

[108] *Suez* Order in Response to Petition 2007 (n 99) [14]–[15].

[109] *Achmea BV v Slovakia*, PCA Case No 2008-13, Award (7 December 2012) [352]. This case is mostly known because of the subsequent decision by the Court of Justice of the European Union (CJEU) that found that the Treaty on the Functioning of the European Union precluded investor-state arbitration clauses between two European Union members. However, the CJEU decision was published after the arbitral award was issued.

[110] *Achmea BV v Slovakia*, PCA Case No 2008-13, Award on Jurisdiction, Arbitrability and Suspension (26 October 2010) [57]–[59].

[111] *Achmea* Award (n 109) [22]–[23]; *Achmea* Award on Jurisdiction (n 110) [161], [176]–[182].

argued that the Netherlands–Slovakia BIT remained in force and should be applied, while the European Commission claimed that the arbitration clause was incompatible with EU law.[112] The jurisdictional objection was nevertheless dismissed.[113] The case shows how the perspective of different non-party stakeholders on a relevant legal question may be considered of interest to a tribunal.

VII. Investigation of Corruption Allegations

The fight against corruption is at the top of the international agenda and investment arbitration has not been immune to this.[114] Tribunals have expressly recognized that corruption is contrary to the international public policy of almost all countries,[115] and not surprisingly arbitrators are increasingly called to deal with corruption issues as part of their fact-finding role.[116] Some authors have argued that 'there is no question today that arbitrators are empowered, and indeed have the duty, to investigate and adjudicate corruption issues'.[117] The question, however, is how far can or should they go.

One example of how tribunals have exercised their fact-finding power in relation to corruption allegations is the case of *Metal-Tech v Uzbekistan*.[118] Metal-Tech had entered into a joint venture with two state-owned enterprises to build and operate a molybdenum production plant in Uzbekistan. Metal-Tech's partners eventually filed domestic bankruptcy proceedings leading to the liquidation of the joint venture and the transfer of its assets to the two state-owned enterprises. Consequently, Metal-Tech commenced arbitration proceedings against Uzbekistan.

During the testimony of one of the claimant's witnesses at the hearing, the tribunal became aware that certain consultants engaged by Metal-Tech had received payments of about US$4 million to conduct 'lobbying activities'. The tribunal ordered the parties to produce additional evidence in relation to this newly discovered fact.[119] The tribunal exercised its *ex officio* powers under the ICSID Convention to avoid 'grant[ing]

[112] *Achmea* Award on Jurisdiction (n 110) [161], [189], [193].

[113] ibid [219], [293] ('In any event, the Tribunal has not found it necessary to rest any part of its decision upon the ostensible attitude of either Party to these arbitration proceedings— still less upon that of the Government of the Netherlands or of the European Commission—to the question of the status of the BIT or the existence, continuation or extent of the jurisdiction of the Tribunal').

[114] See eg *Eni International BV, Eni Oil Holdings BV and Nigerian Agip Exploration Limited v Nigeria*, ICSID Case No ARB/20/41, Procedural Order No 4 (7 March 2023) [21] (as argued by the petitioners requesting the tribunal for leave to submit an *amicus curiae* brief).

[115] See eg Emmanuel Gaillard, 'The Emergence of Transnational Responses to Corruption in International Arbitration' (2019) 35(1) Arbitration International 1; *World Duty Free Company v Kenya*, ICSID Case No ARB/00/7, Award (4 October 2006) [157]. International public policy is defined as 'an international consensus as to universal standards and accepted norms of conduct that must be applied in all fora', see ibid [139].

[116] Gaillard (n 115) 1.

[117] ibid 3. See also eg Pierre Mayer, 'Duty and Power of Arbitrators to Investigate and Evidentiary Issues' in Andrea Meier and Christian Oetiker (eds), *Arbitration and Corruption* (Kluwer Law International 2021) 63; Olivier Caprasse and Maxime Tecqmenne, 'The Evidence of Corruption in Investment Arbitration' (2022) 39 Journal of International Arbitration 519.

[118] *Metal-Tech Ltd v Uzbekistan*, ICSID Case No ARB/10/3, Award (4 October 2013).

[119] ibid [86]–[87], [240].

assistance to a party that has engaged in a corrupt act'.[120] After analysing the evidence, the tribunal concluded that corruption had been established to an extent sufficient to violate Uzbekistan law. Therefore, the tribunal rejected jurisdiction based on its own factual investigation into the allegations, despite the fact that respondent had not raised the issue.[121]

VIII. Conclusion

It is clear from the above examples that tribunals have become ever more confident in the exercise of their multiple fact-finding powers and no longer feel bound to render awards purely on the basis of party submissions. The arsenal of powers they wield when properly engaged enables tribunals to get closer to the 'truth' they are seeking to establish, undoubtfully affecting a tribunal's approach to the award. This is particularly important in the field of investment arbitration where there may be policies and issues of public interest beyond the narrower interests of the disputing parties. While not every exercise of a power leads to a determinative revelation, it provides the tribunal with the confidence to make its award knowing that it has had access to the relevant expertise, documents, and stakeholder views. That in turn creates a more secure system and an answer (at least partially) to the ever-louder criticisms raised against investment arbitration.

There are two takeaways from this analysis. First, the importance of tribunals making use of their powers where appropriate to test propositions without being constrained by the presentation of the case by the parties while at the same time recognizing the importance of a fast, cost-effective process. Second, the importance of tribunals making clear in their awards how they have exercised their powers independently of the parties, thereby providing a response to the allegation that investment arbitration is purely a creature of the parties that ignores wider societal interests.

[120] ibid [241], [389]. The need of additional evidence is understandable as some consider that corruption issues require a 'heightened standard of proof'. Sourgens and others (n 3) para 5(33).

[121] *Metal-Tech* (n 118) [372]–[373], [389], [423].

17

The Impact of Expert Legal Opinions

A NAFTA Chapter 11 Case Study

Céline Lévesque and Christian Schmid

I. Introduction

The role of expert legal opinions in investor-state dispute settlement (ISDS) and its reform is all too often overlooked. Yet, expert legal opinions constitute a practice deserving of attention, as demonstrated by recent debates and related treaty drafting evolutions. Recent international investment agreements (IIAs), for example, provide for expert legal opinions to be made public[1] and impose a prohibition on double-hatting not only when acting simultaneously as arbitrator and counsel, but also when acting as arbitrator and party-appointed expert.[2] More generally, expert legal opinions raise issues of independence from the disputing parties, delegation of decision-making powers from tribunals to experts, and due process.

This chapter examines the practice and impact of expert legal opinions in international investment arbitration, in particular in the context of Chapter 11 of the North American Free Trade Agreement (NAFTA).[3] NAFTA Chapter 11 constitutes an ideal basis for a case study, as it was in force from 1994 to 2020[4] and for many years accounted for most cases under a single IIA.[5] As such, it provides an important case

[1] See eg EU–Singapore Investment Protection Agreement (adopted 19 October 2018, not yet in force) Annex 8 art 1.1(c); UNCITRAL Rules on Transparency in Treaty-based Investor-State Arbitration Annex I (2013) (UNCITRAL Transparency Rules) arts 3.1 (mandating the publication of tables listing expert opinions if one was prepared for the proceeding) 3.2 (requiring the publication of the actual expert opinions 'upon request by any person').

[2] See eg Comprehensive Economic and Trade Agreement between Canada, of the One Part, and the European Union and Its Member States, of the Other Part (adopted 29 February 2016, entered into force provisionally on 21 September 2017) OJ L11/23 (CETA) art 8.30.1; Government of Canada, 'Code of Conduct for Investor-State Dispute Settlement under Chapter 9 Section B (Investor-State Dispute Settlement) of the Comprehensive and Progressive Agreement for Trans-Pacific Partnership' (19 January 2019) para 3(d); Agreement between Canada, the United States of America, and the United Mexican States (adopted 30 November 2018, modified 10 December 2019, entered into force 1 July 2020) Can TS 2020 5–6 (USMCA) art 14.D.6.5(c).

[3] North American Free Trade Agreement between the Government of Canada, the Government of Mexico and the Government of the United States (adopted 17 December 1992, entered into force 1 January 1994, superseded 1 July 2020) Can TS 1994 2 (NAFTA).

[4] NAFTA was replaced by USMCA on 1 July 2020 and provides for legacy claims for a period of three years, USMCA Annex 14-C paras 1, 3.

[5] In this regard, it was later overtaken by the Energy Charter Treaty (ECT), Energy Charter Treaty (adopted 17 December 1994, entered into force 16 April 1998) 2080 UNTS 95. See also Energy Charter Secretariat, 'List of Cases' <www.energychartertreaty.org/cases/list-of-cases/>. For a case study outside of the NAFTA context, see José E Alvarez, 'The Search for Objectivity: The Use of Experts in *Philip Morris v Uruguay*' (2018) 9 Journal of International Dispute Settlement 411.

Céline Lévesque and Christian Schmid, *The Impact of Expert Legal Opinions* In: *The Award in International Investment Arbitration*.
Edited by: Katia Fach Gómez and Catharine Titi, Oxford University Press.
DOI: 10.1093/9780191975936.003.0017

pool to assess the extent of the use of expert legal opinions in ISDS, the evolution of the practice through time, and ultimately the opinions' impact on tribunal awards. Methodologically, the case study was conducted in two steps. First, the Italaw database and NAFTA Parties' websites were used to identify the existence of expert opinions.[6] This allowed the identification of nine cases where expert legal opinions were submitted. Second, a review of the awards and the parties' submissions in those cases revealed the existence of additional opinions, many of them not public.[7]

To give a perspective on scale, as of October 2022, forty-six Chapter 11 cases have led to a final award on jurisdiction and/or the merits, a consent award, or a settlement preceded by a tribunal decision (eg *Ethyl v Canada*)[8] that are publicly available.[9] Yet, as mentioned, many of the expert opinions are not public.[10] It is therefore more than likely that additional non-public expert legal opinions exist in other cases beyond the sample of nine cases used in this case study. Indeed, in the course of our research, we became aware of two such cases, which will also be referred to in this chapter.[11]

Further, this chapter focuses on opinions of legal experts as opposed to technical ones, such as experts on scientific matters or quantum.[12] It specifically examines the need for and impact of expert legal opinions on international law in contradistinction to opinions on domestic law. Already a dozen years ago, Andrew Newcombe had noted the oddity of the submission of expert legal opinions on international law, as they are a 'strange case' indeed.[13] Pursuant to the principle of *jura novit curia*, a tribunal is presumed to know the law applicable to the dispute, which should render legal experts on international law unnecessary.[14] Yet, the disputing parties in six of the NAFTA

[6] Italaw, 'Newly Posted Awards, Decisions & Materials' <www.italaw.com> (created and managed by Professor Andrew Newcombe); Global Affairs Canada, 'NAFTA—Chapter 11—Investment' <www.international.gc.ca/trade-agreements-accords-commerciaux/topics-domaines/disp-diff/gov.aspx?lang=eng>; Government of Mexico, 'Comercio Exterior, Solución de Controversias' <www.gob.mx/se/acciones-y-programas/comercio-exterior-solucion-de-controversias?state=published>; US State Department, 'Cases Filed against the United States of America' 2009–2017 <2009-2017.state.gov/s/l/c3741.htm>.

[7] See Annex.

[8] *Ethyl Corporation v Canada*, UNCITRAL Award on Jurisdiction (24 June 1998). The award in *Lone Pine v Canada* was not counted, as it has not been made public as of the date of writing, *Lone Pine Resources Inc v The Government of Canada*, ICSID Case No UNCT/15/2, Award (21 November 2022).

[9] The cases can be accessed through the NAFTA parties' websites. See (n 6).

[10] For example, the two opinions by Rudolf Dolzer in *CPI v Mexico*, see generally *Corn Products International Inc v Mexico*, ICSID Case No ARB(AF)/04/1, Award (18 August 2009).

[11] Legal experts were also relied on in *Windstream v Canada* (two) and *Joshua Dean Nelson v Mexico* (six), but none of their opinions are listed on Italaw or are available via the respective NAFTA government's website, *Windstream Energy LLC v Canada*, PCA Case No 2013-22, Award (27 September 2016); *Joshua Dean Nelson and Jorge Blanco v Mexico*, ICSID Case No UNCT/17/1, Final Award (5 June 2020).

[12] For an overview of the different types of experts and the use of experts in ISDS more generally, see Brooks W Daly and Fiona Poon, 'Technical and Legal Experts in International Investment Disputes' in Chiara Giorgetti (ed), *Litigating International Investment Disputes* (Koninklijke Brill 2014); Güneş Ünüvar, 'Experts: Investment Arbitration', *Max Planck Encyclopedias of International Law* (2021); Nigel Blackaby and Alex Wilbraham, 'Practical Issues Relating to the Use of Expert Evidence in Investment Treaty Arbitration' (2016) 31 ICSID Review 655.

[13] Andrew Newcombe, 'The Strange Case of Expert Legal Opinions in Investment Treaty Arbitrations' (*Kluwer Arbitration Blog*, 18 March 2010) <arbitrationblog.kluwerarbitration.com/2010/03/18/the-strange-case-of-expert-legal-opinions-in-investment-treaty-arbitrations/>.

[14] For the use of the doctrine in international investment law, see generally: Ahmed Sadek El-Kosheri, 'The Different Types of Experts with Special Emphasis on Legal Experts (Jura Novit Curia)' in Albert Jan Van den Berg (ed), *International Arbitration 2006: Back to Basics?* (ICCA/Kluwer Law International 2007) (also distinguishing between international, domestic, and transnational expert legal opinions); Frédéric Gilles Sourgens, *A Nascent Common Law: The Process of Decisionmaking in International Legal Disputes Between States and Foreign*

Chapter 11 cases probed relied on opinions of international law experts, five of which also featured domestic expert legal opinions. Because one of the six cases—*Eli Lilly v Canada*[15]—included opinions on international patent law that did not address or interpret any of the NAFTA Chapter 11 provisions, the case study primarily centres on the remaining cases: *Loewen v United States* (2003), *Methanex v United States* (2005), *CPI v Mexico* (2009), *Merrill & Ring v Canada* (2010), and *Westmoreland v Canada* (2022).[16] This pool of five cases accounts for sixty-four opinions, of which only eighteen are public (pointing again to the issue of transparency). The arbitration in *Loewen v United States* holds the record for most opinions with forty-two opinions by twenty-four experts. In all cases surveyed, the experts were party-appointed (as opposed to tribunal-appointed). While focusing on international law expert opinions, the case study examines both cases with international and domestic expert legal opinions to ascertain whether tribunals treat them differently.

NAFTA Chapter 11 generated many cases as investment treaty arbitration was just developing with cases being initiated in the mid-1990s and first decisions on jurisdiction and merits being rendered respectively in 1998 (*Ethyl v Canada*)[17] and in 1999 (*Azinian v Mexico*).[18] As such, one might expect relatively more expert legal opinions to be submitted in the early years, as many issues had not been decided previously. Some arbitrators in the early cases were also not what would now be called international investment law specialists. Accordingly, this chapter hypothesizes a decrease in expert legal opinions over time, as a highly persuasive (if not binding) NAFTA Chapter 11 jurisprudence developed, at least for core investment law issues as opposed to domestic law ones, on which opinions are expected to remain constant.[19] Overall, the case study reveals that the experts who opined on international law interpreted NAFTA Chapter 11 provisions inter alia by relying on jurisprudence (in and outside of NAFTA)[20] and principles of public international law (including on State responsibility and diplomatic protection),[21] at times differentiating from other areas of international

Investors (Koninklijke Brill 2015); Attila M Tanzi, 'On Judicial Autonomy and the Autonomy of the Parties in International Adjudication, with Special Regard to Investment Arbitration and ICSID Annulment Proceedings' (2020) 33 Leiden Journal of International Law 57; Attila M Tanzi, 'On the Adjudicative Discretion of Investment Arbitrators: Between *ne ultra petita, ne infra petita,* and *jura novit curia*' in Katia Fach Gómez and Catharine Titi (eds), *The Award in Investment Arbitration* (OUP 2024).

[15] *Eli Lilly and Company v Canada*, UNCITRAL ICSID Case No UNCT/14/2, Final Award (16 March 2017).
[16] *Loewen Group Inc and Raymond L Loewen v United States of America*, ICSID Case No ARB(AF)/98/3, Award (26 June 2003); *Methanex Corporation v United States of America*, UNCITRAL, Final Award on Jurisdiction and Merits (3 August 2005); *Corn Products International Inc v United Mexican States*, ICSID Case No ARB(AF)/04/1, Award (18 August 2009); *Merrill and Ring Forestry LP v Canada*, ICSID Case No UNCT/07/1, Award (31 March 2010); *Westmoreland Coal Company v Canada*, ICSID Case No UNCT/20/3, Final Award (31 January 2022).
[17] *Ethyl Corporation v Canada*, UNCITRAL Award on Jurisdiction (24 June 1998).
[18] *Robert Azinian, Kenneth Davitian, & Ellen Baca v Mexico*, ICSID Case No ARB (AF)/97/2, Award (1 November 1999).
[19] See also Newcombe (n 13).
[20] See eg Jan Paulsson, 'Legal Opinion of Jan Paulsson Relating to the Issue of Jurisdiction Ratione Temporis' (26 February 2021) (*Westmoreland v Canada*) (heavily relying on case law).
[21] See eg Christopher Greenwood, 'Second Opinion of Christopher Greenwood' (16 August 2001) (*Loewen v United States*) (on the distinction between the exhaustion of local remedies rule and the doctrine of judicial finality and their application).

law (such as human rights law).[22] Others, in turn, provided opinions on the relevance of GATT/WTO law for the interpretation of NAFTA Chapter 11,[23] or on treaty law itself, for instance in relation to the distinction between interpretation and amendment.[24]

After some preliminary remarks on the legal framework governing expert legal opinions, the chapter presents the findings of the case study under three headings, encapsulating its main findings: (1) the difficulty in assessing the impact of expert legal opinions on awards and the issue of independence; (2) a greater impact of expertise on domestic law compared to international law and the issue of delegation; and (3) the perils of ignoring experts and the issue of due process. The chapter ultimately confirms the study's research hypothesis and concludes with a few comments related to the principle of *jura novit curia* and the potential impact of recent treaty drafting evolutions concerning transparency and double-hatting.

II. The Legal Framework Applicable to Expert Legal Opinions

Like international investment law in general, the legal framework that governs expert legal opinions is highly decentralized. Applicable rules can be found in procedural provisions such as in the International Centre for Settlement of Investment Disputes (ICSID) and the United Nations Commission on International Trade Law (UNCITRAL) Arbitration Rules, as well as in voluntary instruments like the International Bar Association (IBA) Rules on the Taking of Evidence in International Arbitration (IBA Rules).[25] By and large, the latest versions of these rules distinguish party-appointed from tribunal-appointed experts and provide separate provisions for them. However, they do not distinguish between legal and other types of experts. Some IIAs, especially more recent ones, also include provisions on expert opinions, as did NAFTA, featuring rules focused on factual issues and scientific matters (more on this below).[26]

[22] See eg W Michael Reisman, 'Opinion with Respect to the Effect of NAFTA Article 1116(2) on Merrill & Ring's Claim' (22 April 2008) (*Merrill & Ring v Canada*) (inter alia on continuing acts under major human rights instruments).

[23] See eg Claus-Dieter Ehlermann, 'Opinion of Professor Claus-Dieter Ehlermann' (4 November 2002) (*Methanex v United States*) (on the role of the GATT for NAFTA Article 1102).

[24] Robert Jennings, 'Second Opinion of Professor Sir Robert Jennings' (6 September 2001) (*Methanex v United States*) (on the interpretation of the Notes of Interpretation of Certain Chapter 11 Provisions, NAFTA Free Trade Commission, 31 July 2001).

[25] International Centre for Settlement of Investment Disputes, 'ICSID Arbitration Rules' (2022) (ICSID Rules); UNCITRAL Arbitration Rules (as revised in 2010) UN GAOR 65th Session Supp No 17 UN Doc A/65/17 Annex I (2010) (UNCITRAL Rules); International Bar Association, 'IBA Rules on the Taking of Evidence in International Arbitration' (2020) (IBA Rules). For an in-depth review of the applicable rules, which is beyond the scope of this chapter, see Ünüvar (n 12) paras 4ff.

[26] See eg Pacific Alliance–Singapore Free Trade Agreement (adopted 26 January 2022) (PASFTA) art 8.30; USMCA art 14.D.11; Comprehensive and Progressive Agreement for Trans-Pacific Partnership (adopted 8 March 2018, entered into force 30 December 2018) ATS 2018 23 art 9.27; NAFTA art 1133. More examples can be found through the Electronic Database of Investment Treaties (EDIT). See Wolfgang Alschner, Manfred Elsig and Rodrigo Polanco, 'Introducing the Electronic Database of Investment Treaties (EDIT): The Genesis of a New Database and Its Use' (2021) 20 World Trade Review 73.

As for institutional rules, the 2022 ICSID Arbitration Rules include a handful of rules applicable to legal experts in their chapter on evidence. While Rule 36 allows tribunals to call upon disputing parties for evidence in general at any time, Rules 38 and 39 refer specifically to experts and differentiate between party-appointed and tribunal-appointed experts.[27] In this respect, Rules 38 and 39 provide both the disputing parties and tribunals with broad discretion in relying on experts. For example, Rule 38 provides that: 'A party intending to rely on evidence given by a witness shall file a written statement by that witness. The statement shall identify the witness, contain the evidence of the witness, and be signed and dated'.[28] In addition, party-appointed experts may be questioned at hearings, for which Rule 38 also contains provisions.[29] Conversely, the relatively broad discretion accorded to tribunals in appointing experts, who are subject to an independence requirement and may opine 'on specific matters within the scope of the dispute', is moderated by a duty to consult the disputing parties regarding the appointment.[30] Rule 39 further requires the parties to provide tribunal-appointed experts with information and gives the parties the right to make submissions on the opinion.[31]

In contrast to the ICSID Arbitration Rules, the UNCITRAL Arbitration Rules do not clearly differentiate between experts and witnesses. Article 27 gives disputing parties broad discretion in the use of experts, providing that '[w]itnesses, including expert witnesses, who are presented by the parties to testify to the arbitral tribunal on any issue of fact or expertise may be any individual, notwithstanding that the individual is a party to the arbitration or in any way related to a party'.[32] The rules on tribunal-appointed experts are again somewhat more detailed, however. Tribunals may appoint independent experts, who must describe their qualifications and submit a statement of independence, after consulting the disputing parties.[33] While the parties are required to provide experts with relevant information, they can also object to the qualifications, impartiality, or independence of the expert and may interrogate them at hearings.[34] Hence, despite the clearer language in the new ICSID Arbitration Rules, the provisions on experts under ICSID and UNCITRAL are similar, with more comprehensive rules on tribunal-appointed than party-appointed experts.

Apart from these arbitration rules, expert legal opinions are also governed by voluntary instruments such as the IBA Rules, which provide detailed provisions on both tribunal-appointed and party-appointed experts. Article 5, for instance, applies to the

[27] ICSID Rules rr 36(3), 38, 39. The ICSID Additional Facility Arbitration Rules feature identical provisions. See International Centre for Settlement of Investment Disputes, 'ICSID Additional Facility Arbitration Rules' (2022) rr 46(3), 48, 49.

[28] ICSID Rules r 38(1). Although Rule 38 primarily refers to witnesses, paragraph 7 stipulates that it applies *mutatis mutandis* to experts, r 38(7).

[29] ibid r 38(2)–(5),(8).

[30] ibid r 39(1)–(2). Rule 38 also applies to tribunal-appointed experts, see r 39(6).

[31] ibid r 39(4)–(5).

[32] UNCITRAL Arbitration Rules art 27(2) (further adding that 'expert witnesses' may present their statements in writing '[u]nless otherwise directed by the arbitral tribunal'). See also Ünüvar (n 12) paras 17, 68 (calling the fact that an expert who is a party to the arbitration or affiliated with one can act as party-appointed expert a 'significant feature' of the provision).

[33] UNCITRAL Rules art 29(1)–(2).

[34] The ultimate decision regarding objections remains with the tribunal, ibid art 29(2), (3), (5).

latter. Like the explored arbitration rules, it gives disputing parties broad discretion in appointing experts, yet it also features thorough instructions on the actual expert report, which among other things must contain a statement on any relationship between the expert and the parties, descriptions of the expert's qualifications and of the instructions the expert received, as well as a statement of the expert's independence from the parties, counsel, and the tribunal.[35] In addition, Article 5 also contains rules on subsequent opinions and allows tribunals to order party-appointed experts who opined on the same or related issues to meet and confer.[36] On tribunal-appointed experts, the IBA Rules stipulate that tribunals may employ independent experts after consultations with the disputing parties.[37] Like the UNCITRAL Arbitration Rules, the IBA Rules require tribunal-appointed experts to state their qualifications and independence, to which parties may object, and allow experts to request information from the parties.[38] Moreover, they contain detailed rules on the report itself and its dissemination.[39] The more comprehensive IBA Rules are therefore rightly said to fill the procedural gaps left by common arbitration rules.[40]

Finally, legal experts may also be subject to specific provisions found in IIAs. This includes not only the rules on transparency and double-hatting mentioned in the introduction, but also specific articles on experts. In this respect, NAFTA contained an article on tribunal-appointed experts, which applied to factual issues concerning scientific matters and which newer agreements have largely followed.[41] Canada's 2021 Model Foreign Investment Promotion and Protection Agreement (FIPA), for its part, features

[35] IBA Rules art 5(1)–(2). While the IBA Rules do not define 'independence', the Commentary to Article 5 attempts to provide some guidance. It states:

> 'Article 5.2(a) requires disclosure with respect to any and all relationships the expert may have with the parties, their legal advisors and the arbitral tribunal. Article 5.2(c) then requires a statement of the expert's 'independence'. While the former requirement requires disclosure, satisfaction of the latter requirement requires the expert to evaluate any such relationships and attest that he or she is 'independent', for example in the sense that he or she has no financial interest in the outcome or otherwise has relationships that would prevent the expert from providing his or her honest and frank opinion. Receiving payment for services as an expert does not preclude 'independence'. Article 5.2(c) is intended to emphasise the duty of each party-appointed expert to evaluate the case in an independent and neutral fashion rather than to exclude experts with some connection to the participants or the subject-matter of the case'.

See International Bar Association, 'Commentary on the Revised Text of the 2020 IBA Rules on the Taking of Evidence in International Arbitration' (January 2021) <www.ibanet.org/MediaHandler?id=4F797338-693E-47C7-A92A-1509790ECC9D> 21. Regarding the 2010 IBA Rules, Kantor has raised issues regarding the definition of 'independence', noting that '[t]his prescription may conflate "impartiality" and "objectivity" with "independence"' and further adding that '[t]he 2010 IBA Rules do not themselves explain how a party-appointed expert can be "independent" from a party (or counsel) who selects the expert and works in close quarters with that expert to develop the expert evidence for that side'. See Mark Kantor, 'A Code of Conduct for Party-Appointed Experts in International Arbitration Can One Be Found?' 26 Arbitration International 323, 329.

[36] IBA Rules art 5(3)–(4).

[37] ibid art 6(1).

[38] ibid art 6(2)–(3).

[39] ibid art 6(4)–(5). Further provisions include rules on inspections and the evidentiary hearing, which in part also apply to experts. ibid arts 7–8.

[40] Daly and Poon (n 12) 329.

[41] NAFTA art 1133. See eg PASFTA art 8.30; Free Trade Agreement between the Government of the State of Israel and the Government of the Republic of Korea (adopted 12 May 2021; entered into force 1 December 2022) art 9.27; Investment Agreement Between the Government of Australia and the Government of the Hong Kong Special Administrative Region of the People's Republic of China (adopted 26 March 2019, entered into force 17 January 2020) ATS 2020 5 art 33.

a provision regarding tribunal-appointed experts on factual issues more generally, which could include domestic law, according to which tribunals may appoint experts at the request of a disputing party or on their own should the parties not disapprove.[42]

In sum, there exist relatively few rules on party-appointed experts, particularly in applicable arbitration rules, but stricter requirements for tribunal-appointed experts, who are generally required to be independent.

III. The Difficulty in Assessing the Impact of Expert Legal Opinions on Awards and the Issue of Independence

While not unexpected, one of the findings of the case study is how difficult it is to assess the impact of expert legal opinions on tribunal awards. This is ultimately due to the underlying issue of independence, which is raised by the nature of the appointment.[43] In none of the nine NAFTA Chapter 11 cases with expert legal opinions surveyed did tribunals appoint the expert(s). Rather, all were party-appointed experts, who, as demonstrated above, are subject to few rules and who in particular are not required to be independent under the leading arbitration rules.

Consequently, it is generally very difficult to separate and differentiate a disputing party's submission from the opinion of the party-appointed expert it retained.[44] This leads to the question of whom a tribunal is really following if it agrees with an expert. Is it following the actual expert on whose opinion a disputing party's submission is based, or is it following the party who simply had an expert back up its views?

In some instances, legal experts acted more like advocates arguing in support of one side than independent neutrals elucidating the law. One example can be found in *Loewen v United States*, which revolved around the treatment accorded to the Canadian claimant during a trial with a US competitor in the Mississippi courts.[45] The relatively harsh opinions by international law expert Robert Jennings ultimately prompted the United States to note that 'Jennings . . . appear[ed] to view his role as that of an advocate for the claimants (e.g., writing as "we"), rather than as a dispassionate expert'.[46] Furthermore, Robert Jennings' opinion denouncing the 2001 Note of Interpretation by the NAFTA Free Trade Commission in *Methanex v United States*, a case in which a

[42] Government of Canada, '2021 Model FIPA' (2021) <www.international.gc.ca/trade-commerce/trade-agreements-accords-commerciaux/agr-acc/fipa-apie/2021_model_fipa-2021_modele_apie.aspx?lang=eng> (2021 Model FIPA) art 38. The provision notes that 'any factual issue' includes for instance 'the rights of Indigenous peoples'. See also ibid art 32(3) (requiring domestic law to be regarded as a matter of fact).

[43] Kantor, for instance, concludes that 'one can doubt that most experts acting in good faith are ever entirely free from litigation-related pressures, no matter how much they seek to preserve their independence and objectivity'. Kantor (n 35) 334 (further quoting Thomas Wälde, who argued that 'the actual dynamics [of the independence of party-appointed experts] is more complicated and one can not [*sic*] use the binary independence/no independence matrix but rather think of concepts such as "relative independence" and "professionalism"').

[44] See also Ünüvar (n 12) para 52.

[45] *Loewen Group Inc and Raymond L Loewen v United States of America*, ICSID Case No ARB(AF)/98/3, Award (26 June 2003) [3]–[8].

[46] *Loewen Group Inc and Raymond L Loewen v United States of America*, ICSID Case No ARB(AF)/98/3, Rejoinder of the United States of America (27 August 2001) 4 n 1 (specifically referring to his non-public third opinion). See also Robert Jennings, 'The Loewen Claim' (26 October 1998) (*Loewen v United States*).

Canadian methanol producer claimed compensation for losses allegedly caused by a California ban on the use and sale of the methanol-based gasoline additive MTBE, was equally strident.[47] Jennings' expert opinion referred to what he viewed as the 'impropriety' of the interpretation, which even led the disagreeing tribunal to remark that his words were 'rather severe'.[48] While these observations on Robert Jennings' opinions are by far the most illustrative, they are not the only examples where a legal expert opined in a manner more akin to that of an advocate than a dispassionate expert.[49]

Occasionally, tribunals also gave indications that they were, in their own analysis, equating the legal experts with the disputing parties. One instance can be found in *Merrill & Ring v Canada*, which revolved around a claim by a US forestry company that contended that Canada's log export regime violated NAFTA's investment obligations.[50] When presenting its findings on the alleged violation of NAFTA's national treatment provision in Article 1102, the tribunal revisited Canada's 'reading' of the phrase *in like circumstances* and only cited the expert legal opinion by Michael Reisman as a source.[51] Similarly, in *Westmoreland v Canada*, a case in which a US investor claimed compensation for the Province of Alberta's phaseout of coal power plants,[52] the tribunal mentioned the disputing party's position and implicitly referred to the expert opinion of Jan Paulsson by addressing his argument. Indeed, the tribunal rejected 'Westmoreland's submission' that NAFTA Articles 1116 and 1117 should be interpreted without reference to the treaty's scope provision in Article 1101, which was just what the legal opinion of the claimant's international law expert had proposed.[53]

Whether tribunals expressed their views explicitly or not, the issue of independence of the experts remains. As some of these examples demonstrate, many expert legal opinions are not neutral accounts of the law and, indeed, under the current international legal framework, they do not need to be. This apparent interchangeability of expert legal opinions and party submissions raises the question as to why some parties/counsel find it desirable to rely on experts. Part of the explanation may have to do with credibility. For instance, if counsel is not known for his or her public international law expertise, an opinion by a renowned international law professor may give credit to the arguments being made. Another explanation could lie in the format of the report itself,

[47] *Methanex Corporation v United States of America*, UNCITRAL, Final Award on Jurisdiction and Merits (3 August 2005) pt 1 preface [1].

[48] ibid pt IV ch C [5], [18]–[19]. See also Robert Jennings, 'Second Opinion of Professor Sir Robert Jennings' (6 September 2001) (*Methanex v United States*) 6.

[49] Other examples include the opinions by Richard Neely in *Loewen v United States* and Jan Paulsson in *Westmoreland v Canada*. Richard Neely, 'Affidavit' (28 October 1998) (*Loewen v United States*) 7, 10–11, 13–17; Jan Paulsson, 'Legal Opinion of Jan Paulsson Relating to the Issue of Jurisdiction Ratione Temporis' (26 February 2021) (*Westmoreland v Canada*) [32]ff; cf Kathryn Coleman, 'Expert Report of Kathryn A Coleman' (16 December 2020) (*Westmoreland v Canada*) (exemplifying a dispassionate expert report).

[50] *Merrill and Ring Forestry LP v Canada*, ICSID Case No UNCT/07/1, Award (31 March 2010) [1], [25].

[51] ibid [85]. Another example for such an implicit equating with a direct reference to an expert legal opinion by a tribunal occurred *Methanex v United States*. See *Methanex Corporation v United States of America*, UNCITRAL, Final Award on Jurisdiction and Merits (3 August 2005) pt IV ch B [23] n 32 (citing the claimant's submission and noting that the submission is based on two expert opinions).

[52] *Westmoreland Coal Company v Canada*, ICSID Case No UNCT/20/3, Final Award (31 January 2022) [1]–[5].

[53] ibid [197]; Paulsson, 'Legal Opinion' (n 20) [36]ff.

which can allow for a more detailed treatment of some issues and in a style that is not pure advocacy as would be the case of a brief.

Ultimately, the issue of independence not only calls into question the usefulness of legal opinions by party-appointed experts, but it also underscores the importance of new rules on double-hatting that apply to arbitrators who also act as legal experts. In addition to existing codes mentioned in the introduction, the most recent version of the UNCITRAL draft Code of Conduct for adjudicators also seeks to regulate double-hatting and limit multiple roles.[54]

IV. A Greater Impact of Expertise on Domestic Law Compared to International Law and the Issue of Delegation

An assessment of NAFTA Chapter 11 cases further indicates that expert opinions on domestic law had a relatively greater impact on tribunal decisions than their international law counterparts. This makes intuitive sense, as tribunal members obviously cannot be experts on the domestic laws of (all) host countries.[55] The eight NAFTA Chapter 11 cases with domestic expert legal opinions effectively revolved around diverse areas of host-state law. *Bilcon*, in which a US investor challenged Canada's environmental assessment of their proposal to develop a quarry and marine terminal, for example, featured several experts on Canadian environmental and administrative law.[56] Similarly, in *Merrill & Ring* the parties relied on domestic law experts regarding Canadian constitutional and customs law, and in *Loewen* the parties submitted expert opinions on US bankruptcy law, Mississippi law and trial practice, as well as judicial remedies under US law in general.[57]

Whereas fewer international expert legal opinions have been submitted over time, particularly for core investment law issues, domestic law experts have not only been continuously relied upon throughout the years, but they also appear to have been more influential. In this regard, US bankruptcy law expert Kathryn Coleman, for instance, seems to have had a considerable impact on the tribunal's decision in *Westmoreland*. Her analysis of whether the bankruptcy plan of the Westmoreland Coal Company (WCC)—the entity that suffered the purported losses due to the alleged NAFTA

[54] UNCITRAL (Working Group III), 'Possible Reform of Investor-State Dispute Settlement (ISDS): Draft Codes of Conduct and Commentary: Note by the Secretariat' (23 November 2022) A/CN.9/WG.III/WP.223 (advance copy) art 4 <icsid.worldbank.org/sites/default/files/WP_223_advance_copy.pdf>.

[55] See also Ünüvar (n 12) paras 55–57. The practice under NAFTA Chapter 11 has often been for parties to appoint nationals of their country as arbitrators, which is allowed under NAFTA art 1125. However, Canada has not followed this practice uniformly, especially in recent years, having nominated as party-appointed arbitrators nationals of Australia and Spain, for instance.

[56] *Bilcon of Delaware et al v Government of Canada* PCA Case No 2009-04 Award on Jurisdiction and Liability (17 March 2015) [1], [5].

[57] Other cases involved US administrative, constitutional, and corporate law (*Methanex v United States*), Canadian energy law (*Mercer v Canada*), Massachusetts law (*Mondev v United States*), and NAFTA countries' patent law (*Eli Lilly v Canada*). *Mercer International Inc v Government of Canada*, ICSID Case No ARB(AF)/12/3, Award (6 March 2018); *Mondev International Ltd v United States of America*, ICSID Case No ARB(AF)/99/2, Award (11 October 2002).

violations—involved an *arm's-length* transaction, successor liability, and all of WCC's assets proved central to the tribunal's decision that the claimant was not the legal successor of WCC.[58] As the challenged measures thus did not *relate to* the claimant, the tribunal eventually dismissed the claim.[59] In a similar manner, environmental law expert David Estrin appears to have been a major influence in *Bilcon*. In its award, the tribunal's majority extensively refers to Estrin and cites him on key issues, such as whether the approach of the Joint Review Panel (JRP), which evaluated Bilcon's proposal, violated Canadian law, whether Bilcon's undertaking was *in like circumstances* with other projects, and whether it was accorded *less favourable treatment* by Canada.[60] In both *Westmoreland* and *Bilcon*, expert legal opinions on domestic law therefore played a crucial role in the tribunal's decision.[61]

As tribunal members cannot have in-depth knowledge about all relevant areas of a host states' domestic law, the reliance on experts is clearly a beneficial practice. One might argue that the same holds true for both general international law and specialized international law regimes that serve as a gap-filler or backdrop in treaty interpretation.[62] For instance, Article 31(3)(c) of the Vienna Convention on the Law of Treaties of 1969 mandates the consideration of 'any relevant rules of international law applicable in the relations between the parties', thereby making other international law rules potentially relevant to a given dispute.[63] However, the use of international expert legal opinions runs counter to the principle of *jura novit curia*, as the selected tribunal members should be expected to know the pertinent principles of international investment and public international law. It is thus no surprise that recourse to international law experts in investment arbitration under NAFTA Chapter 11 has prompted some criticism, as demonstrated by the following remarks by Canada in *Westmoreland* with respect to the claimant's reliance on expert Jan Paulsson:

> That the Claimant decided to jettison the principle of *jura novit curia* and hire an outside expert . . . speaks to the frailty of the Claimant's legal position. This Tribunal has been charged with the responsibility to construe and apply the terms of NAFTA in accordance with international principles of treaty interpretation and international law, a task for which it is well-qualified. Any legal opinion that purports to provide the

[58] *Westmoreland Coal Company v Canada*, ICSID Case No UNCT/20/3, Final Award (31 January 2022) [222], [226], [230]; Coleman, 'Expert Report' (n 49) [64]ff, [72], [74]; Kathryn Coleman, 'Second Expert Report of Kathryn A Coleman' (9 April 2021) (*Westmoreland v* Canada) [7]ff, [24].

[59] *Bilcon of Delaware et al v Government of Canada* PCA Case No 2009-04 Award on Jurisdiction and Liability (17 March 2015) [236]ff.

[60] ibid [525]ff, [546], [553]ff, [600], [697]ff.

[61] Another example of a case with impactful domestic expert legal opinions is *Loewen v United States*, in which they appear to have affected the tribunal's trial evaluation and analysis of exhaustion of local remedies. *Loewen Group Inc and Raymond L Loewen v United States of America*, ICSID Case No ARB(AF)/98/3, Award (26 June 2003) [55]ff, [209]; Neely (n 49) 6–7 (regarding the threefold trial strategy); *Loewen Group Inc and Raymond L Loewen v United States of America* ICSID Case No ARB(AF)/98/3 Counter-Memorial of the United States of America (30 March 2001) 85 (referring to experts Warren's and Trost's non-public remarks on the effect of bankruptcy proceedings).

[62] See also Ünüvar (n 12) para 58.

[63] Vienna Convention on the Law of Treaties (adopted 23 May 1969, entered into force 27 January 1980) 1155 UNTS 311, art 31(3)(c).

> Tribunal with the answer to the decision its members have been appointed to make is unnecessary.[64]

Canada's comment eventually prompted a response by the expert, who defended his involvement in the arbitration and his independence as follows:

> I observe that Canada suggests that the very introduction of my Opinion is an abandonment of the principle of *jura novit curia* and evidence of the 'frailty' of the Claimant's position. Yet many successful parties have relied on expert opinions. Independent experts unlike advocates do not have an unfettered assignment to make the best possible argument for the party that has engaged them, but are constrained in principle by their declaration of independence and by the realistic constraints of the positions they have taken in the past. Parties who seek my opinion cut short my involvement when I find that the circumstances of their case do not lead me to the conclusions they wish to advance.[65]

Either way, the reality is that not every tribunal member was familiar with the relevant international law rules and principles, especially in the early years under NAFTA. As a result, there are a few examples of NAFTA Chapter 11 cases in which the tribunal readily agreed with or followed an international law expert, whose opinions appeared to have been determinative. The most obvious example is the *Loewen* tribunal's reliance on the opinions of international law expert Christopher Greenwood. The tribunal, for instance, approached the issue of exhaustion of local remedies based on the three questions laid out by Greenwood and followed his arguments that denial of justice is subject to a high threshold and that justice cannot be considered denied if a court decision can still be challenged domestically.[66] Moreover, the tribunal eventually also heavily relied upon Greenwood regarding the effect of NAFTA's waiver requirement on the principle of finality, albeit largely implicitly. In keeping with the expert, the tribunal differentiated between the principles of exhaustion of local remedies and finality, held that major principles like finality cannot be considered to have been tacitly waived, and added that if Article 1121 had done so, it would lead to the unlikely result that NAFTA would become an alternative to domestic judicial review.[67] Ultimately, the use of expert

[64] *Westmoreland Coal Company v Canada*, ICSID Case No UNCT/20/3, Government of Canada Reply Memorial on Jurisdiction (9 April 2021) [44] n 99. Canada also asserted this view in its submission on costs in *Windstream v Canada*. Among other things, Canada argued that Rudolf Dolzer's opinion on NAFTA art 1105 was 'wholly unnecessary' to establish the claim and that Canada should thus not have to cover its costs, further adding that 'since matters of international law are to be pled by counsel and decided by the Tribunal ... expert evidence on international law has no place'. *Windstream Energy LLC v Canada*, PCA Case No 2013-22, Government of Canada Submission on Costs (11 April 2016) [26]–[27], [29]–[30].

[65] Jan Paulsson, 'Second Opinion of Jan Paulsson Relating to the Issue of Jurisdiction Ratione Temporis' (21 May 2021) (*Westmoreland v Canada*) [7] n 2.

[66] *Loewen Group Inc and Raymond L Loewen v United States of America*, ICSID Case No ARB(AF)/98/3, Award (26 June 2003) [129]–[135], [147]–[149], [151]ff.

[67] It ultimately came to the same conclusion as Greenwood, that is that the finality principle had not been waived, ibid [159]–[164]; Christopher Greenwood, 'Opinion of Christopher Greenwood, QC' (26 March 2001) (*Loewen v United States*) [17]–[20], [34], [43], [46], [49]–[50]; Greenwood, 'Second Opinion' (n 21) [34]ff, [41]–[44], [50].

legal opinions in *Loewen* undoubtedly raises questions about the principle of *jura novit curia*. While the number of international expert legal opinions has indeed gone down since then, cases like *Westmoreland* demonstrate that the use of such opinions persists despite this trend and notwithstanding that such opinions appear generally to have had a limited impact on the outcome of the cases.[68]

Another issue that the case study revealed is that the separation between domestic and international law sometimes becomes blurred. On the one hand, some expert legal opinions themselves mix the two spheres of law. Illustrative examples are the domestic expert legal opinions by Richard Neely and Armis Hawkins in *Loewen*, both of whom eventually opined that there was a violation of international law.[69] On the other hand, tribunal members at times conflate international and domestic law issues based on expert opinions. For instance, the majority in *Bilcon* controversially relied on domestic expert legal opinions to justify its decision that Canada had violated the minimum standard of treatment (MST) pursuant to NAFTA Article 1105.[70] The majority even explicitly noted that its decision was based on the domestic law opinions it had received, which drew severe criticism from the dissenting arbitrator Don McRae.[71] While he acknowledged that the legality of Canada's environmental assessment under its local law was indeed in question and that domestic law experts David Estrin and Murray Rankin are both highly respected,[72] he also added the following comment on his colleagues' use of experts:

> However, neither Mr. Estrin, nor Professor Rankin, is an expert on NAFTA, nor did either seek to give an opinion on whether the actions of the JRP constituted a violation of Article 1105. But that is the issue that this Tribunal had to decide. And whether Canadian law has been complied with is a relevant consideration in deciding whether there has been a violation of NAFTA Article 1105, it is not of itself sufficient to establish such a violation.[73]

Regardless of whether the expert opinions are on international or domestic law, the fact that they may have a significant influence on awards raises a related important issue that came to the fore outside of the NAFTA context, namely the risk of a delegation of

[68] In this respect, there have been instances where tribunals clearly rejected the argument of an international law expert. See eg *Westmoreland Coal Company v Canada*, ICSID Case No UNCT/20/3, Final Award (31 January 2022) [211] (rejecting Paulsson's time-bar argument); *Methanex Corporation v United States of America*, UNCITRAL, Final Award on Jurisdiction and Merits (3 August 2005) pt IV ch B [29]ff, [37] (dismissing Jennings' argument regarding the relevance of GATT/WTO law on NAFTA art 1102). See also Paulsson, 'Legal Opinion' (n 20) [32].

[69] Neely (n 49) 3 (opining that the claimant was 'subjected to a complete denial of justice as that term is traditionally used in international law'); Armis Hawkins, 'Statement of Justice Armis E Hawkins' (6 June 2001) (*Loewen v United States*) 31 (noting that '[w]hile [he does] not purport to be an expert on international law, it seems inescapable that this case must come under the prohibitions of NAFTA').

[70] *Bilcon of Delaware et al v Government of Canada* PCA Case No 2009-04 Award on Jurisdiction and Liability (17 March 2015) [588]–[604].

[71] ibid [600].

[72] *Bilcon of Delaware et al v Canada*, PCA Case No 2009-04, Dissenting Opinion of Professor Donald McRae (10 March 2015) [30].

[73] ibid [31] (citations omitted).

decision-making power from tribunals to experts. In *Enron v Argentina*, the tribunal's reliance on expert opinions was ultimately one of the reasons why the award was annulled.[74] The original dispute revolved around Argentina's emergency measures invoked during the economic crisis of the early 2000s and centred on whether the customary principle of necessity precluded the wrongfulness of Argentina's acts. In the annulment proceeding, Argentina inter alia based its challenge on the ground that the tribunal had manifestly exceeded its powers, which may be the case if a tribunal fails to apply the applicable law.[75] The annulment committee eventually found that the tribunal had based its findings on necessity largely on the opinion of the claimants' non-legal expert (an economist) and consequently held that the tribunal had failed to consider key legal issues arising from Argentina's necessity defence and to provide reasons for its decision, which led it to annul the award.[76] While the issue of delegation in *Enron* arose in the context of an opinion by a non-legal expert, the same might occur whenever a tribunal relies on legal experts to such an extent that it fails to apply the law applicable to the dispute.

Finally, the role accorded to domestic law in recent IIAs also has implications regarding the impact of expert legal opinions. Some recent IIAs now instruct tribunals to treat domestic law as matter of fact and require arbitrators to adhere to 'the prevailing interpretation given to the domestic law by the courts or authorities of that Party'.[77] This trend will likely lead to an increase in the reliance on domestic legal experts and may make tribunal-appointed experts more appealing, but tribunals will simultaneously need to be careful not to outsource their legal analysis and to apply the applicable law themselves.

V. The Perils of Ignoring Experts and the Issue of Due Process

In addition to potential issues with independence and delegation of decision-making power, which should lead tribunals to exercise caution in adhering to expert legal opinions, conversely tribunals would be well-advised not to ignore experts altogether or otherwise run afoul of due process. A recent set-aside decision of the award rendered in *Joshua Dean Nelson v Mexico* exemplifies this risk.[78] The original arbitration concerned a US investor in a Mexican telecommunications firm who alleged that Mexico's measures regarding the firm's interconnection rights amounted to an unlawful expropriation and a violation of MST under NAFTA Articles 1110 and 1105, respectively.[79] In the subsequent set-aside proceeding, which was based on the ground that the claimant was unable to present his case, the applicant argued among other things

[74] *Enron Creditors Recovery Corporation (formerly Enron Corporation) and Ponderosa Assets LP v* Argentina, ICSID Case No ARB/01/3, Decision on Annulment (30 July 2010).
[75] ibid [60], [67].
[76] ibid [367]ff, [373]–[378], [392]–[393].
[77] CETA art 8.31(2); 2021 Model FIPA art 32.3.
[78] *Nelson v Mexico*, 2022 ONSC 1193.
[79] ibid [4], [19].

that the tribunal had failed to consider the expert evidence he submitted on Mexican civil and administrative law, both key issues in the arbitration.[80] Specifically, Mr Nelson complained that the tribunal had made no reference to or acknowledgement of his expert in the award, even though it had referred to the respondent's expert.[81]

The Ontario Superior Court of Justice eventually dismissed the application holding that the tribunal had indirectly addressed the expert evidence by citing relevant parts of the claimant's submissions (which themselves reflected the expert opinion) and while providing reasons for its rejection of the claimant's arguments.[82] Yet, the court also noted that a set-aside is warranted where 'minimum standards of due process and substantive fairness are not met'.[83] In line with prior case law, the court noted that this may happen where a tribunal 'ignored or failed to take the evidence or submissions of the parties into account', if this failure is 'sufficiently serious to offend our most basic notions of morality and justice' and if 'it cannot be condoned under the law of the enforcing State', for example when a tribunal fails to provide intelligible reasons on key issues.[84] Accordingly, tribunals should be aware of the risk of set-aside in such circumstances, where ignorance of expert legal opinions combines with a failure to provide reasons.

Under NAFTA Chapter 11, tribunals appear to have dismissed or not engaged with expert legal opinions for a variety of reasons. In some instances, arbitrators disagreed with a specific analysis or an approach proposed by the expert. In this respect, the tribunal in *Westmoreland* rejected Paulsson's opinion that the tribunal should examine NAFTA Articles 1116 and 1117 without regard to the agreement's scope provision in Article 1101, and the tribunal in *Merrill & Ring* eventually decided not to follow Robert Howse's theory of systemic integration in the NAFTA Chapter 11 context and to interpret investment obligations according to GATT concepts.[85] Other tribunals rejected expert legal opinions on the ground that the cases on which they were based were irrelevant or because they disagreed about the facts. For example, the *Westmoreland* tribunal noted that the cases cited by Paulsson in support of his view on jurisdiction *ratione temporis* under NAFTA were not helpful, and the tribunal in *Methanex* appears to have dismissed Ehlermann's contention that methanol and ethanol products are in a competitive relationship because the facts did not support it.[86] Finally, a few tribunals

[80] ibid [2], [50]. A similar argument was made in the annulment proceeding in *Blue Bank v Venezuela*. Lisa Bohmer, 'Analysis: Blue Bank v Venezuela Ad Hoc Committee Upholds Finding That a Trustee Did Not Qualify as Investor Since It Merely Managed the Trust's Assets' *IA Reporter* (Santa Monica, 11 September 2020) (summarizing the Spanish-only decision by the ICSID ad hoc committee).

[81] *Nelson v Mexico*, 2022 ONSC 1193 [50].

[82] ibid [52]–[53], [57].

[83] ibid [33].

[84] ibid [33]–[34], [51]. See also *Consolidated Contractors Group SAL (Offshore) v Ambatovy Minerals SA*, 2017 ONCA 939 [65]; *Corporacion Transnacional de Inversiones SA de CV v STET International SpA*, 1999 CanLII 14819 (ON SC); *Oil Basins Ltd v BHP Billiton LTD & Ors* [2007] VSCA 255.

[85] Paulsson, 'Legal Opinion' (n 20) [36]ff; *Westmoreland Coal Company v Canada*, ICSID Case No UNCT/20/3, Final Award (31 January 2022) [197]; *Merrill and Ring Forestry LP v Canada*, ICSID Case No UNCT/07/1, Award (31 March 2010) [84], [86]ff (citing Howse's non-public expert legal opinion and rejecting the proposal).

[86] Paulsson, 'Second Opinion' (n 65) [17], [19]–[20]; *Westmoreland Coal Company v Canada*, ICSID Case No UNCT/20/3, Final Award (31 January 2022) [210]; Ehlermann (n 23) [46]–[56]; *Methanex Corporation v United States of America*, UNCITRAL, Final Award on Jurisdiction and Merits (3 August 2005) pt IV ch B [28]ff.

also avoided issues raised by experts due to procedural economy or by focusing on the burden of proof. The *Merrill & Ring* tribunal did not find it necessary to decide whether Reisman's or Howse's opinion on NAFTA Article 1116 was to be preferred, since a ruling on the contested time-bar issue was pointless given that damages had not been proved.[87] Likewise, the *Loewen* tribunal held that the claimant failed to demonstrate why it had not found it reasonable to pursue local remedies, thereby similarly circumventing the conflicting opinions of Professors Tribe and Days.[88]

However, while some tribunals rely extensively on expert legal opinions or dismiss them for specific reasons, others merely note that opinions exist.[89] Still others do not even mention some of the opinions submitted to them, which was the case in *Loewen*, *Methanex*, and *Merrill & Ring*.[90] While *Loewen* was an extreme case with its forty-two opinions, a lack of reference in an award to a specific expert's report does not necessarily mean that the evidence was not considered by the tribunal. In any event, despite the lack of referencing, it is still highly unlikely that such awards could be challenged on the basis that the tribunal failed to provide reasons for its decision, not the least because the opinions of key experts are usually reflected in the submissions of the disputing party that relied on them. Leaving less central opinions unaddressed, in turn, will probably not reach the high threshold required to seriously offend basic notions of morality and justice, as interpreted by the court in *Joshua Dean Nelson*. At the end of the day, this set-aside decision nonetheless exemplifies the perils and due process issues that can arise should a tribunal fail to properly engage with expert legal opinions.

VI. Conclusion

What is the impact of expert legal opinions on NAFTA Chapter 11 awards? As this case study has demonstrated, the answer to this question is much more nuanced than straightforward. As it is generally difficult to differentiate expert opinions from party submissions, it is often impossible to assess what impact an expert had on the outcome of an arbitration. Yet, there are a few NAFTA Chapter 11 cases in which experts—primarily domestic law experts such as Coleman in *Westmoreland* but in some instances also international law experts like Greenwood in *Loewen*—appear to have influenced arbitral awards in key respects. What the case study confirms is the hypothesis that more expert legal opinions on international law were submitted in the early years of NAFTA and that there has indeed been a decrease of the practice for core investment

87 *Merrill and Ring Forestry LP v Canada*, ICSID Case No UNCT/07/1, Award (31 March 2010) [267]–[269].

88 *Loewen Group Inc and Raymond L Loewen v United States of America*, ICSID Case No ARB(AF)/98/3, Award (26 June 2003) [210]–[217].

89 For instance, the majority in *CPI v Mexico* only incidentally mentions that the claimant relied on two expert legal opinions by Rudolf Dolzer. *Corn Products International Inc v Mexico*, ICSID Case No ARB(AF)/04/1, Decision on Responsibility (15 January 2008) [82].

90 Examples include the opinions of Darrel Pearson in *Merrill & Ring* and of Robert Hamilton and Ian Sinclair in *Methanex*. Moreover, the *Loewen* tribunal does not mention most expert legal opinions submitted, such as those by William Joel Blass, Charles Fried, Richard Neely, Ian Sinclair, or Elizabeth Warren. This phenomenon also explains the difficulty in uncovering some of the experts' opinions.

law issues with time. Whereas domestic expert legal opinions have been used more constantly throughout the years,[91] international expert legal opinions were submitted in greater numbers early on.[92]

These findings have implications for the *jura novit curia* principle, for double-hatting prohibitions, but also for transparency. First, once a mature state of investment arbitration has been reached, there should really be no need for expert legal opinions on international law.[93] The parties' submissions and the collective knowledge of tribunal members on international law should be sufficient. Second, in this context, the prohibition on double-hatting targeting the simultaneous role of arbitrator and party-appointed expert would be limited in its effect for international law experts (since there would be no or fewer international law experts), while not impeding recourse to experts on domestic law (who would be highly unlikely to serve as a member of investment arbitration tribunals). Third, and relatedly, the obligation to make expert opinions public or available[94] will serve the need of transparency required to enforce the double-hatting ban, but also to ensure that expert opinions are subject to outside scrutiny. More broadly, as this case study demonstrated, most expert legal opinions under NAFTA Chapter 11 are not public and the existence of some is not even mentioned by tribunals in their award. Therefore, recent changes to the rules, such as the use of the UNCITRAL Transparency Rules in some IIAs, will have a significant practical impact.

Overall, the case study revealed some of the issues raised by the practice of expert legal opinions in ISDS and provided examples for each. The three issues discussed in the main parts of this chapter—independence, delegation of decision-making power, and due process—undoubtedly demonstrate that this practice is too consequential to be overlooked. While this case study focused on NAFTA Chapter 11, some of the lessons it contains can be extrapolated to other IIAs, as applicable arbitration rules are largely similar to NAFTA. As such, the impact of expert legal opinions on investment arbitration awards more generally deserves further study.

[91] For example, domestic expert legal opinions have been used both in large and small numbers in early cases like *Loewen* and *Methanex*, respectively, but also in more recent ones such as *Bilcon* and *Westmoreland*. See Annex.

[92] In this respect, there were fourteen such opinions submitted in *Loewen* and nine in *Methanex*, but only two in *CPI*, three in *Merrill*, and two in *Westmoreland*.

[93] Save maybe on some highly specialized areas of law, such as in *Eli Lilly* in relation to international patent law.

[94] See n 1.

ANNEX

Expert Legal Opinions in NAFTA Chapter 11 Cases

Main case pool[1]	Opinions on international law	Names of experts	Public	Opinions on domestic law	Public	Total
Loewen v United States (2003)	14	Robert Jennings David D Caron Richard B Bilder John Y Gotanda Christopher Greenwood Ian Sinclair	5	28	5	42
Methanex v United States (2005)	9	Detlev V Vagts Robert Jennings Ian Sinclair Claus-Dieter Ehlermann	3	2	0	11
CPI v Mexico (2009)	2	Rudolf Dolzer	0	0	n/a	2
Merrill & Ring v Canada (2010)	3	Michael Reisman Robert Howse	1	2	0	5
Westmoreland v Canada (2022)	2	Jan Paulsson	2	2	2	4
Secondary case pool[2]						
Mondev v United States (2002)	0	n/a	n/a	5	0	5
Eli Lilly v Canada (2017)[3]	7	Jay Erstling Daniel J Gervais T David Reed Philip Thomas	7	19	19	26
Mercer v Canada (2018)	0	n/a	n/a	2	2	2
Bilcon v Canada (2019)	0	n/a	n/a	19	17	19
Other cases[4]						
Windstream v Canada (2016)	1	Rudolf Dolzer	0	2	0	3
Joshua Dean Nelson v Mexico (2020)	0	n/a	n/a	13	0	13

[1] The main case pool comprises cases with international expert legal opinions identified via the Italaw database, NAFTA Parties' websites, and case documents.

[2] The secondary case pool comprises the remaining identified cases with expert legal opinions (ie those with domestic expert legal opinions only) and *Eli Lilly v Canada*, which was included because it only featured opinions on international patent law that did not address/interpret NAFTA Chapter 11 provisions.

[3] *Eli Lilly v Canada* and *Bilcon v Canada* featured expert reports by non-jurists who elaborated on legal issues/practice (eg T David Reed). For the purposes of the case study, these reports were regarded as expert legal opinions, as the legal regime governing expert opinions generally neither defines expertise nor requires experts to hold specific professional qualifications; cf Brooks W Daly and Fiona Poon, 'Technical and Legal Experts in International Investment Disputes' in Chiara Giorgetti (ed), *Litigating International Investment Disputes* (Koninklijke Brill 2014) 34; Güneş Ünüvar, 'Experts: Investment Arbitration', *Max Planck Encyclopedias of International Law* (2021) paras 44–45.[4] This category refers to cases with non-public expert legal opinions beyond the sample of nine cases used in this case study, which we came across during our research.

PART IV
AWARD DRAFTING

18

Tribunal Dynamics and Arbitral Deliberations

Yves Derains

I. Introduction

A reflection on 'Tribunal Dynamics and Arbitral Deliberations' implies defining 'tribunal dynamics' and 'arbitral deliberations'. According to the *Oxford Dictionary*, group dynamics relate to 'small groups and the interaction process within them, such as power relations, leadership, decision-making, productivity, cohesion, conformity, co-operation and conflict'. The small group within which the interaction process is to be considered in this contribution is a tribunal and more specifically an arbitral tribunal, since the discussion is about arbitral deliberations in investment disputes.

According to the same dictionary, 'deliberation' indicates 'the process of carefully considering or discussing something'. In procedural law, the concept of deliberation has a technical meaning which relates to a specific stage of the proceedings: when the tribunal analyses the parties' arguments in the light of the evidence before it makes a decision. It applies both to a sole judge or arbitrator and to a tribunal composed of several members. The present chapter will consider only the deliberations of three-member arbitral tribunals, although the deliberations of sole arbitrators would deserve a psychological study.[1]

It would be wrong to deal only with the ultimate exchange of views between the arbitrators before the issuing of the final award since its form and results are largely conditioned by previous deliberations which take place all along the proceedings. Any tribunal is obliged to make several decisions before the case is ready to be finally decided. Some take the form of an award which, as such, requires a deliberation dealing with the full case, in particular as, depending on the arbitrators' decision and the applicable arbitration rules, it may put an end to the case.[2] But a myriad of other decisions, of a procedural or purely administrative nature, are also subject to deliberations.

The president of the tribunal has specific responsibilities in the conduct of the proceedings, in particular that of making sure that the proceedings are cost and time efficient. However, he or she must discharge them in consultation with the co-arbitrators who should not remain passive. As rightly pointed out by Thomas Clay:

[1] On the practical difficulties that sole arbitrators face in their deliberations, see Yves Derains, 'Global Reflections on International Law, Commerce and Dispute Resolution' in *Liber Amicorum in honour of Robert Briner* (ICC Publishing 2005) 221.

[2] For instance, awards on admissibility of the parties' claims, on jurisdiction the validity of the contract, the principle of responsibility, etc.

Yves Derains, *Tribunal Dynamics and Arbitral Deliberations* In: *The Award in International Investment Arbitration*. Edited by: Katia Fach Gómez and Catharine Titi, Oxford University Press. © Katia Fach Gómez and Aikaterini Titi 2024.
DOI: 10.1093/9780191975936.003.0018

> A co-arbitrator must be proactive during the proceedings, give his or her opinion on everything, permanently solicit discussions, intervene during the hearings, closely participate in the drafting of the award even if not responsible for the first draft. In a nutshell, the role of the co-arbitrator is decisive, it is inherent to collegiality, and this justifies his or her remuneration.[3]

The only responsibility that the president discharges alone is that of conducting the hearings. During the hearings, the president must decide multiple procedural 'incidents', such as objections to the questions put to witnesses and experts during their examination. If the decision is not made immediately, the hearing may be stuck, so to speak. Except for very difficult or sensitive issues, the president may not suspend the hearing to consult his or her fellow arbitrators to decide each objection raised by counsel. This would prevent concluding the hearing on the date fixed in the procedural timetable, an unacceptable consequence in the light of the busy agenda of all participants. Moreover, during the hearing, counsel may test the tribunal's capacity to decide quickly with a view to determining whether raising procedural 'incidents' could delay or derail the proceedings. In addition, it would be unfair to the cross-examining counsel to allow a disruption of the flow of his or her cross-examination. Thus, the objection must be immediately sustained or overruled, and no deliberation is allowed. Leaving apart these specific circumstances, and unless there is urgency, any decision must be the object of a deliberation among the members of the tribunal, be it administrative, procedural, or, a fortiori, involving the substance of the case.[4]

The deliberations of investment arbitration tribunals are governed by three basic rules. First, deliberations must take place. Although few national laws, such as French law, expressly requires deliberations,[5] the arbitrators duty of deliberation is based on international public policy.[6] The Swiss Federal Tribunal stated that deliberation 'is an essential operation which must take place even if it is not expressly contemplated by the law'.[7] Likewise, the ad hoc committee in the *Klöckner v Cameroon* ICSID case stressed that the requirement of actual as opposed to apparent deliberations is such a fundamental procedural rule that its breach is a ground for annulment of the award, even if this is not contemplated by Article 52 of the Washington Convention as an autonomous ground annulment.[8] The rationale is that in the absence of deliberation, the decision

[3] Thomas Clay, 'Le coarbitre' in *Mélanges en l'honneur du Professeur Pierre Mayer: Liber Amicorum* (LGDJ 2015) 150 (author's translation).

[4] Most arbitral tribunals' terms of reference provide that '[o]rganizational measures shall be ordered by the President, on behalf of the Arbitral Tribunal, after consultation with the co-arbitrators.' They also provide that '[i]n case of urgency, the President acting alone may extend or modify any procedural time limit.'

[5] French Code of Civil Procedure art 1476. However, this text does not apply to international arbitration, probably because it obliges the arbitrators to fix the date when the results of the deliberations will be communicated, ie the date of issuance of the award. Yet, the obligation to hold deliberations is implicitly extended to international arbitration by art 1479 of the Code.

[6] Christophe Seraglini and Jérôme Ortscheitdt, *Droit de l'arbitrage interne et international* (2nd edn, LGDJ 2019) 865. In this sense, see also, Cass 1ère civ 29 June 2011, Rev arb (2011) 959, note V Chantebout: Matthieu de Boisséson, *Le droit français de l'arbitrage interne et international* (Joly 1990) 801; see also Philippe Fouchard, commentary on the judgment of the Cour de Cassation, 2e civ, 28 January 1981, Rev arb (1982) 425.

[7] Swiss Federal Tribunal, 16 October 2003, P. 959, Rev arb (2004) 695, note L Levy and B Suckli.

[8] Published in (1986) 1(1) ICSID Review 89.

would not be that of the tribunal but that of one or two individuals abusing the power conferred on them as members of the tribunal.

The natural consequence of this first rule is the second one, the collegiality of deliberations. During deliberations, it is essential that all arbitrators be granted a fair opportunity to express their views, including in writing. This is a condition of the very existence of the deliberations. Consequently, the failure to allow an arbitrator to participate in deliberations is a ground for annulment or non-recognition of the tribunal's award.[9]

The third rule is the confidentiality of deliberations.[10] A well-known award underscored that 'it is improper for any party to probe the secrecy of deliberations. That confidentiality, a fundamental element of the arbitral process, is intended to ensure that each arbitrator is able to exercise his or her independent judgment in a collegial context free of any outside influence.'[11] But the rational for the rule is also that leakage to a party on the content of the deliberations before the award is rendered grants an advantage to that party which, for instance, may offer to the other an amicable settlement less beneficial than the expected award. Unfortunately, this occurs sometimes in practice.

In practice, arbitrators are not always playing by the rules. To assume they do would limit the discussion to ideal deliberations, which are the object of the first part of this chapter (II). The reality, with its pathologies, is more complicated and deserves to be presented as well, because its knowledge may allow us to take preventive measures. It is the subject of the second section (III).

II. The Ideal Deliberations

The ideal deliberation has been described as the 'harmonious deliberation' as opposed to the 'pathological deliberation'.[12] As pointed out by an experienced arbitrator, it is a 'process that extends throughout the arbitration proceedings'.[13] It starts informally as soon as the arbitral tribunal is constituted, produces effects known to the parties each time a decision is made and culminates with a final exchange of views among the arbitrators before an award is issued, referred to hereinunder as the deliberation *stricto sensu*.

[9] In 2017, the Spanish Supreme Court confirmed the annulment of an award rendered by two arbitrators who had excluded their third colleague from the deliberations. The two authors of the award were condemned to the restitution of their fees. See Victor Bonnin Reyes, 'The Spanish Supreme Court Confirms the Liability of Two Arbitrators for Excluding Their Colleague' (2017) 8 Newsletter of the ICC Institute of World Business Law.

[10] French Code of Civil Procedure art 1479, which applies to international arbitration pursuant to art 1506(4): 'The Arbitral Tribunal's Deliberations Shall Be Confidential'; *SAS Merial v Klocke*, 2009 Rev arb 352 (Paris Cour d'Appel); *AT&T Co v Saudi Cable Co* (2000) 2 Lloyd's Rep 127, 137 (English Ct App). See also 2020 London Court of International Arbitration Rules art 30(2); 2021 Swiss Arbitration Rules art 44(2).

[11] *Himpurna Ca Energy Ltd v Indonesia*, Interim Award (26 September 1999) and Final Award (16 October 1999), published in (2000) 25 YB Comm Arb 11, 151.

[12] Derains (n 1) 221.

[13] Ugo Draetta, *The Dark Sides of Arbitration* (JurisNet 2018) 89. See also Alexandre de Fontmichel, Martin Donato, and Alexandre Meyniel, 'Vue d'ensemble du régime juridique du délibéré arbitral en droit français de l'arbitrage' (2014) 2 Les Cahiers de l'Arbitrage 208; Jose Maria Alonso, 'Deliberation and Drafting Awards in International Arbitration' in *Liber Amicorum Bernardo Cremades* (La Ley 2010) 133; Derains (n 1) 223.

Two procedural phases before the deliberation *stricto sensu* deserve specific observations. The first is the disclosure of documents; the second is the evidentiary hearing itself. The former often requires a collegial analysis of the substance of the case before it has been fully pleaded by the parties; the latter gives the arbitrators a series of windows for informal exchanges, which in the best of cases may limit the need for the deliberation *stricto sensu*. Two other moments for deliberations are recommended but they remain exceptional: after the first exchange of pleadings and before the evidentiary hearing.

The phase of disclosure of documents may be a significant opportunity of exchange of views among the members of the arbitral tribunal as to the merits of each parties' case. According to Article (3)(3)(b) of the IBA Rules on the Taking of Evidence in International Arbitration of 17 December 2020, a party which requests the disclosure of a document under the control of the other side must state that this document is 'relevant to the case and material to its outcome'. Pursuant to Article (9)(2)(a) of these Rules, the arbitrators may refuse to order such disclosure for 'lack of sufficient relevance to the case or materiality to its outcome'.

Deciding whether a specific document is material to the outcome of a case requires an analysis of the factual and legal issues in dispute, including the allocation of the burden of proof: a requested document is not material to the outcome of the case if the requesting party does not need it to prove its case. This analysis is made by each member of the arbitral tribunal who must perform a study of the substance of case as it stands at this stage of the proceedings. Yet, a collegial decision on each of the specific requests for disclosure cannot be achieved without deliberations among the members of the tribunal.

With a few exceptions, these deliberations are usually made in writing. Each party requesting the disclosure of documents fills a '*Redfern*'[14] or an '*Armesto*'[15] schedule with its respective requests for documents. The other side introduces its objections to each request it does not accept and provides its reasons. Then, the requesting party includes its reply in the document which must be completed by the tribunal decision on each request. The deliberations usually start by the president adding on the document his or her suggested decisions and requesting the co-arbitrators' comments.

Each president has his or her style, but in most cases, the suggested decisions are drafted as they would be notified to the parties when finally adopted, ie, expressed in a very laconic manner, with a minimum of justifications. No justification at all when the request for disclosure is accepted: the word 'granted' is generally considered as sufficient. When the request is denied, only short reasons are provided such as: 'too broad', 'burdensome', 'privileged', 'not material to the outcome the case', as per Article 9 of the IBA Rules on the Taking of Evidence. Very often, two or three of these justifications will be provided to support the denial of only one request: for instance, 'too broad',

[14] Sigvard Jarvin and Corinne Nguyen, *Compendium of International Commercial Arbitration Forms: Letters, Procedural Instructions, Briefs and Other Documents* (Kluwer Law International 2017) 213–20.

[15] Mélanie Riofrio Piché and Sofia de Sampaio Jalles, 'The Armesto Schedule: A Step Further to a More Efficient Document Production' (*Kluwer Arbitration Blog*, 4 April 2020).

'burdensome', and 'not material to the outcome the case'. This way of drafting the decisions contributes to their swift adoption since the object of the agreement of the three members of the tribunal or at least of two of them is the solution, not the reasons for it. It is particularly so when the request for disclosure is granted: each member of the tribunal may have a different motivation for finding that a party must provide a document to its opponent: one may consider that the document is material to the outcome of the case on the basis of a certain understanding of the factual and legal issue, while another arbitrator, with a completely different approach to the case may reach the same conclusion; it is also possible that the third arbitrator will be in favour of the larger possible disclosure in any circumstances, whatever the real impact of the requested document on the outcome of the case. Yet, the decision to grant the request will be unanimous. This artificial unanimity does not occur so easily when requests are dismissed because the reasons for the decision are provided. Real deliberations are often necessary. Their subject may be procedural or substantial.

The alleged confidentiality of documents or their alleged privileged character give rise to animated discussions among arbitrators, where their respective legal background may play a great role. They are very useful because they contribute to a better knowledge by each arbitrator of his or her colleagues' approach to deliberations, in case no deliberations have taken place before on a difficult issue and the arbitrators have no previous experience of deliberating together. If the president is inclined to try to obtain unanimity through lengthy discussions or considering that the acceptance of his or her views by another arbitrator is sufficient, with no regard to the third arbitrator, this is good to know in view of future deliberations. However, deliberations on the characterization of requested documents as material or not to the outcome of the case are even more useful. The disagreement of one or more arbitrators with the president's suggested decision requires a discussion of at least certain aspects of the substance of the case. Such discussions oblige the arbitrators to exchange preliminary views as to the factual and legal issues to be resolved. They educate all the members of the tribunal thanks to observations they had not thought of, contribute to new reflections, to the progressive formation of a common approach of the tribunal to the merits of the case, and, last but not least, to the pencilling of a first decision tree,[16] although a very provisional one since the parties have not pleaded their full case. Whether the decisions on disclosure are taken unanimously or by majority is irrelevant. What matters is the work in common which the first analysis of certain aspects of the merits of the case,[17] unless the tribunal and the parties agree that the arbitrators express their views in this regard before this analysis takes place.

[16] A decision tree is a decision support tool that identifies in logical sequence the decisions to be taken depending on the evidence produced with a list of the possible consequences and the resulting sub-decisions to be made. Such a decision tree is a very elementary one, with no use of algorithms, usually prepared by the president, on the basis of his or her present views on what he or she considers as the more important issues to be resolved in order to reach a decision.

[17] It must be noted that in most cases, nothing filters to the parties of possible different views of arbitrators as to their decisions on the disclosure of documents. There are almost always notified in a procedural order signed by the president on behalf of the full tribunal, with no mention that some of them may have been reached by majority.

The evidentiary hearing is another ideal procedural phase for deliberations, although informal. It gives the arbitrators the opportunity to spend one or two weeks together, while being permanently exposed to the merit of the case, through counsel's opening statements, witnesses, and experts. The breaks, in particular the lunch break, offer a valuable opportunity to informally exchange views on the respective strength of the parties' arguments, the credibility of the witnesses, and the usefulness of the experts' presentations. These exchanges are extremely rich because they allow each member's views to develop and become stronger. The more these views are informally discussed the better, because the free confrontation of ideas generates questions for the witnesses and experts and gives a more structured shape to what the view of the tribunal on some aspects of the merits of the case may be at this stage; finally, it reveals the extent of possible divergences.

The president must take the initiative to engage in informal discussions on the merits of the case in the light of what is heard at the hearing. The president must stress the informality of these exchanges and the fact that nobody will be bound by momentary impressions and views which are necessarily provisional. However, despite the informal character of these exchanges during the evidentiary hearing, the president must make sure that any significant comment on the conduct of the proceedings and a fortiori on the merits of the case expressed in an informal conversation between two members of the tribunal is immediately shared with the third member. Formal or informal, deliberations must be collegial. Otherwise, the exercise is not only contrary to one of the basic rules of deliberations. It is counterproductive if the president and one of the co-arbitrators progressively develop a common view that they do not share with their third colleague because it gives them the false assurance of the soundness of their understanding of the case, and they may be disappointed when formal deliberations take place.

In order to avoid the costs and the delays generated by proceedings where the parties devote useless efforts to present documentary and witness evidence on factual and/or legal issues irrelevant to the outcome of the case, it has been suggested that the arbitrators could establish, with the parties' agreement, after the first exchange of memorials, a preliminary report including a list of the facts to be proved and a list of the legal issues to be decided. This preliminary report is to be discussed with the parties before the phase of disclosure of documents and helps the parties to focus on issues that the arbitrators consider to be essential for their future pleading, without restricting their right to deal with any other issue.[18]

In the cases where this relatively new procedural step is adopted,[19] the preliminary report cannot be drafted without a prior deliberation of the arbitrators. Such deliberation

[18] See Yves Derains, 'Une nouvelle approche de la procédure arbitrale internationale' (2021) 3 Rev arb 629.

[19] The author knows of two cases where the parties have accepted that the arbitrators define the main issues to be resolved after the first exchange of memorials. This procedural step is 'relatively' new because it is not so different from the definition of the list of the issues to be determined that was mandatory in the ICC's terms of reference before the 1998 revision but was made optional because in most cases it can only be superficial at such an early stage of the proceedings.

is a formal deliberation, similar to the deliberation *stricto sensu* but with a different object. It aims at defining problems and not at providing solutions. The arbitrators must analyse the various elements of the case and build one or more decision trees, based on factual hypotheses in the light of the various possible legal problems. Allowing the arbitrators to explain to the parties their understanding of the main aspects of the case so that they may focus on them or correct what they see as misunderstandings of the tribunal is not the sole advantage of this first deliberation. It facilitates the arbitrators' decision in the phase of disclosure of documents where a new deliberation may even be unnecessary.

The evidentiary hearing is organized during a pre-hearing conference where the arbitrators and the parties discuss its practical organization (venue, transcript, interpretation, etc) and establish a schedule for the hearing: allocation of time between the parties, order of examination of the witnesses, experts, etc. In complex cases, there is an advantage in indicating to the parties the issues that the arbitral tribunal wishes to be particularly dealt with.[20] Presenting such issues on behalf of the arbitral tribunal requires a previous deliberation between its members. It is a formal deliberation submitted to the same rules as the deliberation *stricto sensu*. This process is useful even if the arbitrators have submitted to the parties and discussed with them a preliminary report after the first exchange of memorials because the record has been supplemented by further memorials and evidence. New important issues may have appeared, and others may be moot. Such pre-hearing deliberation is commendable, even if the arbitrators have no intention to submit to the parties a list of issues to be dealt with. 'This way, the tribunal can discuss and home in on the main issues which the tribunal should be especially attentive during the hearing.'[21] It is a sound remark, since this it is another opportunity to foster the emergence of a common approach of the arbitral tribunal to the analysis of the case, which will make easier the deliberation *stricto sensu*.

As a matter of principle, the deliberation *stricto sensu* takes place when the parties have presented their written and oral arguments, submitted their documentary evidence and the arbitrators have heard oral evidence. Yet, it is worth preparing it by a deliberation occurring immediately after the evidentiary hearing, even if it has been agreed that the parties would file post-hearing briefs and although the final transcript of the hearing is not available already. It was rightly pointed out that 'the post-hearing deliberation is key'.[22] The arbitrators are fully immerged in the case, they have a fresh memory of the various arguments, they have weighed the witness and expert evidence and remain able to read their own notes taken during the hearing, an exercise which may be less easy some weeks later, in a different environment and with other issues of concern in mind.

However, failing a proper preparation, such a deliberation made in the heat of the moment, is not exempt of risk. Arbitrators who have not already clearly identified the

[20] Draetta (n 13) 107.

[21] Deva Villanúa and Eward Thorn, 'Improving Deliberations and Awards' in *Leadership, Legitimacy, Legacy: A Tribute to Alexis Mourre* (ICC Publishing 2022) 292.

[22] ibid; Draetta (n 13) 108.

main issues of the dispute have often a very superficial view at the end of the hearing, influenced by the last speaker, particularly brilliant counsel, or a very convincing witness. The various deliberations in previous phases of the proceedings reduce such a risk and this is part of their value. Whatever the case, this post-hearing deliberation, which is an introduction to the deliberation *stricto sensu*, will be really fruitful only if it is carefully prepared by the president of the arbitral tribunal. He or she should submit a list of issues to the other members of the tribunal or conduct the discussion with a decision tree, ideally one of those used in previous deliberations, adapted according to the evolution of the case.

This post-hearing deliberation is also a good opportunity for the arbitrators to elaborate a list of questions that they may wish to submit to the parties so that they deal with them in their post-hearing briefs. One needs to stress that the post-hearing deliberations must be planned, otherwise it is probable that some of the arbitrators will have booked flights to go back to their respective homes.[23] Ideally, the morning following the hearing should be kept free to give the three members of the arbitral tribunal a chance to fine-tune their respective positions.

In many cases, the post-hearing deliberation makes the deliberation *stricto sensu* superfluous. It is often so when the arbitrators have deliberated several times during the course of the proceedings, formally or not. After the hearing, they already know the views of each of them and the post-hearing deliberation allows them to check whether they have changed in the light of the new information provided during the hearing. On this basis, the president may have all the elements to prepare a draft award and a further deliberation is unnecessary.

The conduct of the deliberation *stricto sensu* is a model which may be applied, *mutatis mutandis*, to any formal deliberation. In practice, it depends on the experience and preferences of the president, but basic principles should be respected. For the deliberations to be efficient, the president must send in advance a list of issues or a discussion tree, and the discussion must be limited to these issues, unless it appears that the president has forgotten other essential points. Details should be left for the drafting of the award, even it is true that the devil is in the details and that the exercise of drafting the award may reveal elements which should have been taken into account and, in exceptional cases, may change the decision. With this caveat in mind, the deliberation must aim at being final. If many aspects of the case are left unsettled at the end of the deliberation, the danger is that one of the arbitrators changes his or her mind and withdraws agreements given during the meeting. To avoid that danger, minutes of the deliberations must be prepared and sent to each member of the tribunal.

Some arbitrators consider a deliberation as a negotiation, 'not negotiation in the pejorative sense of "horse trading", but in the more noble sense of a quest for a unanimous acceptable solution that does the greatest possible service to justice'.[24] Even with that qualification, a reference to a negotiation is inadequate. The quoted arbitrator admits

[23] Villanúa and Thorn (n 21) 292; Draetta (n 13) 108.
[24] Draetta (n 13) 149.

that the quest for unanimity should not be pushed to the point of pursuing a unanimous decision at all costs.[25] The arbitrators' duty is not to please each other but to render an award enforceable which does the greatest possible service to justice,[26] be it unanimous award, a majority award or an award issued by the president alone, when it is possible under the applicable arbitration rules.[27] More fundamentally, a negotiation implies different interests and some compromise between them. In an ideal deliberation, the three arbitrators may have different convictions, but they have the same interest: to render an award well founded in fact and law. The purpose of the deliberations is a confrontation of the convictions of the members of the tribunal, which allows them to explain their respective analysis with the hope of convincing their colleagues in case of disagreement. There is no give and take as expected in a negotiation. It is precisely to avoid a negotiation between the president and one of the co-arbitrators that this solution exists. As it has been pointed out '[t]his serves, in and of itself, to promote the integrity of decision-making under the ICC Rules'.[28]

Moreover, tribunal presidents should avoid insisting that the award be rendered unanimously, since it may complicate the discussions between the members of the arbitral tribunal. The concept of unanimity is ambiguous as many confuse the position of an arbitral tribunal and the individual position of each of its members. On the one hand, it is applied to situations where the discussions among the arbitrators on the various issues to be determined reveals that each of them shares the same views; on the other hand, an award signed by the three arbitrators with no mention that it is rendered by majority is often described as a unanimous award when it is not. During the deliberations, the members of the arbitral tribunal exchange their respective views on the issues in dispute and may not agree on all of them. However, when two of the arbitrators share the same view on one issue, the third often defers to the majority, because he or she does consider that no matter of principle is at stake. Though this arbitrator does see the issue differently, he or she recognizes that it had been thoroughly analysed and discussed, with his or her view being duly taken into account. Thus, this arbitrator democratically accepts that the majority position is the position of the tribunal on that specific issue. But that position of the full tribunal was reached by majority, even if this is not disclosed to the parties. This decision-making process is followed in many deliberations, and it is not exceptional that an award is signed by the three arbitrators with no indication that it is a majority award, while the different decisions were in fact adopted by different majorities successively formed among the three members of the arbitral tribunal. The award is not rendered by majority because the decisions are the full tribunal's decisions. But not all these decisions reflect the views of each of its members and it would be wrong to write in the award that the arbitral tribunal has decided

[25] ibid.

[26] Derains (n 1) 232.

[27] See 2021 ICC Rules of Arbitration art 32(1): 'When the arbitral tribunal is composed of more than one arbitrator, an award is made by a majority decision. If there is no majority, the award shall be made by the president of the arbitral tribunal alone.' See also Charles N Brower and Ahmed Mazlom, 'To Err Is Human, to Dissent Divine' in Katia Fach Gómez and Catharine Titi (eds), *The Award in Investment Arbitration* (OUP 2024).

[28] Yves Derains and Eric Schwartz, *A Guide to ICC Arbitration* (Kluwer Law International 2005).

unanimously. It is telling that Article 32(1) of the 2021 ICC Rules for Arbitration does not refer to unanimity.[29]

With a view to increasing the efficiency of the deliberations, some presidents ask their co-arbitrators to send in advance a summary of their views as to the main issues in dispute. This has the advantage of better focusing the discussion when the members of the tribunal meet, since it is not necessary to deal in depth with issues which are common ground. There are some pitfalls as well. The main one is that, when an arbitrator has put a position on paper, he or she is less flexible in the discussion and may adopt defensive behaviour to protect a position which is frozen. Another inconvenience is that without the benefit of their colleague's views, each co-arbitrator may ignore significant element of the case in his or her reasoning and their respective summary may be as ships crossing in the night.

When the meeting starts, the president may open the discussion by presenting his or her views. This is reasonable when the co-arbitrators have already submitted a summary in writing of their own position. It does not mean that, when it is not the case, asking the co-arbitrator appointed by the claimant to speak first, then his or her colleague and only after, the president is necessarily a good solution. Reproducing within the tribunal a show comparable to the hearing is not commendable. The risk is to create a useless tension between the two co-arbitrators, who will be tempted to interrupt each other each time they disagree, even on points of detail. It is often preferable that the president present his views first and ask the co-arbitrators whether they share them. This should be done issue by issue, with a discussion of the three arbitrators on each one.

In this regard, the order of discussing the issues must be chosen with care by the president because a logical order, as presented in a decision tree, is not always the best for an efficient discussion. For instance, when it is hardly debatable that the claimant has not proved its alleged damages and the president thinks that the respondent is not liable, the discussion will be largely facilitated if damages are discussed first. Indeed, when it is established that the claimant has suffered no damages, the discussion on liability has lost part of its interest and convincing both co-arbitrators of the absence of liability of the respondent will be easier.

The deliberation *stricto sensu* may be held in person, by video conference or by telephone, although the progress of videoconferencing has made that last solution obsolete. In the absence of previous deliberations of the arbitral tribunal, in particular post-hearing deliberation, an in-person meeting is highly recommended. When the arbitrators are already aware of their respective positions and have had the opportunity to discuss them, a videoconference is suggested to avoid unnecessary costs.

The 2021 ICC Note to the Parties and Arbitral Tribunals on the Conduct of the Arbitration includes the attendance to deliberations among the tasks that a tribunal

[29] See n 27.

secretary may perform.[30] This should not be misunderstood. As has been observed,[31] the presence at the deliberation meetings of the secretary is a great help for the tribunal. He or she takes notes of each arbitrator's views so that that they concentrate on the discussion. Based on such notes, the minutes of the deliberations will be prepared afterwards. The administrative secretary will also help with finding documents on the record and printing them if necessary. But in no case should he or she intervene in the discussion, unless to correct material mistakes, such as the date of a document, the exact name of a witness, the accuracy of his or her statement as reflected in the transcript.

III. Some Aspects of Reality

Arbitrators are human beings and the personality of some of them is sometimes the source of great differences between ideal deliberations and reality. The practice of the arbitrator's deliberation depends, on the one hand, on the partiality or impartiality of each member of the tribunal and, on the other hand, on their level of preparation. For deliberations as described in the first part of this chapter to be efficiently implemented, the three arbitrators must be impartial and reasonably prepared. However, experience shows several combinations of partiality, unpreparedness, impartiality, and preparedness which, too often, dramatically affect the climate and the efficiency of deliberations.

Impartial but unprepared arbitrators may be a time bomb. Because they have a very superficial knowledge of the substance of the case, they have a passive attitude in the various deliberations before the hearing. They agree with all the president's proposals, sometimes without taking the time to really analyse them, especially when they have been sitting with the president in the past and a relation of trust exits between them. This trust may even be an excuse for the lack of preparation. The unprepared arbitrators discover the substance of the case at the hearing and progressively form their opinion. This opinion may lead them to consider that issues which the other members of the tribunal had found irrelevant are essential to the outcome of the case and/or take the view that documents, in relation to which disclosure was not granted by the tribunal, should be on the record. In the best cases, these new conclusions are raised during the informal deliberations during the hearing or in the post-hearing deliberations. But some arbitrators do not hesitate to speak out during the hearing, to the parties' dismay. When such arbitrators have a sound point, as it may happen, the tribunal is bound to ask the parties to discuss in their post-hearing briefs issues which were not dealt with before, sometimes in the light of new evidence. The result of such behaviour is that the parties are taken by surprise, the duration of the proceedings becomes abnormally extended, and the credibility of the tribunal is jeopardized.

[30] ICC Note to the Parties and Arbitral Tribunals on the Conduct of the Arbitration under the ICC Rules of Arbitration (1 January 2021) para 224. See also Claudia Frutos-Peterson, Marat Umerov, and Marija Ozolins, 'The Role of Tribunal Secretaries in the Drafting of Investment Awards' in Fach Gómez and Titi (n 27).

[31] Villanúa and Thorn (n 21) 292.

There is another type of impartial arbitrators, who are very difficult to deal with in deliberations, although they do not directly affect the conduct of the proceedings. They are individuals fully prepared but who cannot make up their mind as to the solution of the dispute or are unable or unwilling to sustain their position in an in-person discussion. Discussing with their colleagues during the hearing and in the post-hearing deliberations, they immediately agree with them or are easily convinced by the majority. However, some days later and ahead of the deliberation *stricto sensu* meeting, they submit a note expressing a dissenting view. When their dissent is discussed in the deliberation *stricto sensu*, they do not oppose strong arguments to the majority and appear to be finally convinced by its views. Yet, back home, they change their position again and send a note expressing their disagreement with the majority. It is obvious that such an attitude makes impossible a fruitful debate among the arbitrators and leads to an award issued by majority.

The situation is worse when presidents behave the same way and have no firm position, even after the deliberation *stricto sensu* is apparently concluded by decisions that the three arbitrators are prepared to accept. Such presidents open the deliberations by signalling that they hesitate between two or three solutions to the dispute and ask their co-arbitrators to indicate which one would have their preference. Long discussions follow and a solution is eventually adopted by the full tribunal or by majority. A draft award is to be prepared by the president on this basis. But the presidents of that category do not like to close the discussion so easily. When they send their draft award, they suggest a new deliberation because they are not fully convinced that, after all, another solution would not have been better. It is difficult for the two co-arbitrators to refuse a new deliberation, which does not create too many problems when the two co-arbitrators were in agreement with the initial solution. But when it had been adopted by majority, it is a disaster, even if both co-arbitrators are impartial. It is not difficult to figure out what happens if it is not the case.

The partiality of one co-arbitrator, or both, aggravates the difficulties to the conduct deliberations, which have just been described. They are no longer the result of the personal character of an individual but of his or her personal interest, disguised. The unprepared partial arbitrators simply endorse all the positions of the party which appointed them; the prepared partial arbitrators do not hesitate to suggest creative and favourable solutions to that party when they consider that it was poorly advised by counsel. Nothing that an experienced and well-prepared president cannot overcome through majority decisions, or, in exceptional cases, decisions rendered by the president alone! But he or she must be alerted to the danger and the sooner the partiality of an arbitrator is discovered, the better.

The situation is more serious when partial co-arbitrators play the role of informant of a party, regularly informing it of the content of the tribunal deliberations. The party informed by one of the arbitrators of the developments of the reasoning of the arbitral tribunal can improperly take advantage of such information to adapt its procedural strategy, an undue advantage over its counterparty. As already mentioned, when this occurs after the closure of debates and before the award is issued by the arbitral tribunal, it confers on the informed party a privileged position in the search for an amicable solution to the dispute. The fear of a possible breach of the principle of confidentiality by one of the members of the tribunal is an impediment to the conduct of deliberations throughout the proceedings as the members of the tribunal must refrain from discussing the merits of the case before it is absolutely necessary in order to make a final decision. The arbitral tribunal is not in a position to cooperate with the parties to help them to focus on the more important issues, as it is unable to form its own view. Each member keeps his or her own opinion to himself or herself and the tribunal has no voice. Yet, the arbitrators cannot avoid discussing the merits in the deliberations *stricto sensu*. The risk of a breach of the principle of confidentiality of deliberations is no longer avoidable, but at least the principle of equality of the parties would have been respected during the procedure.

The negative influence of a partial arbitrator in the deliberations may reach the level of 'arbitral terrorism' by arbitrators who have no other purpose than to obstruct the arbitration through sabotage.[32] The danger becomes very serious as soon as terrorist arbitrators understand that they will not be able to change the view of the majority of the members of the tribunal unfavourable to the party which appointed them. It can materialize in their resignation, which is a form of arbitral suicide. Failing the possibility of having the award rendered by the two 'surviving' arbitrators,[33] they may considerably delay the proceedings. Less dramatically, they may delay the deliberations by not participating, although they cannot do it forever. If one of the arbitrators refuses to deliberate, it is enough that he or she was given the opportunity to express his or her opinion.[34]

Yet the following example, given in conclusion of these reflections on the dynamics of the arbitral tribunal's deliberations, shows that there are no general solutions to overcome the obstacles created by a non-cooperating arbitrator, whatever be the reasons of his or her behaviour. Each case is specific, and the president of the tribunal must treat it as such. In a construction arbitration, one of the arbitrators, Mr X, could not accept that the claimant, which had nominated him, would lose any of its sixty-five claims. The deliberation *stricto sensu* took place in the president's office, at the seat of the arbitration, and started very well because the three first claims were decided in favour of the claimant. The nice atmosphere became chiller and chiller when Mr X understood that the fate of the fourth claim would not be the same. As he was a very competent lawyer and a well-prepared arbitrator, he fought vehemently but, convinced that he would not reverse the situation, he closed his file, left the room, and flew back home, leaving his colleagues with sixty-one unresolved claims. The president was naive enough to believe that he could resume the deliberation and after several telephone conversations, convinced Mr X to participate in a new meeting, at the seat of the arbitration. Unfortunately, Mr X left after the eighth claim.

[32] On the 'terrorist arbitrator', see Derains (n 1) 221.

[33] See 2021 ICC Rules art 15(5), which, under some conditions, allows the two remaining arbitrators to issue the award and cope with this problem.

[34] See Alonso (n 13) 134.

The president was obstinate and wanted to find a solution. He called again Mr X and explained to him that such an important case deserved a deliberation in person rather than by correspondence and, to please him, suggested that the meeting of the last chance takes place in his office. Mr X accepted and, when the twelfth claim was not decided in favour of the claimant, he discovered that he could not leave his own office. The deliberation lasted three days and was completed, based on a draft decision prepared by the president, with a vote by each arbitrator on each issue, including the reasons for it, and with minutes kept. The award was rendered by majority, with a dissenting opinion. This happy ending was possible only because the partial arbitrator was a gentleman with a great sense of hospitality. Otherwise, he would have seen no problem in abandoning his colleagues in a meeting room of his office or in expelling them. With somebody else, a different solution would have been necessary.

With arbitrators with good professional and human qualities, deliberations contribute to the efficiency of the proceedings until the final hearing and allow the rendering of a fair award enforceable at law. But when one or more members of an arbitral tribunal forget or deliberately ignore their duties as arbitrators, deliberations are the 'Achilles heel of the collegiate jurisdiction', as realistically noted by Dominique Hascher.[35]

[35] Dominique Hascher, 'Principes et pratique de procédure dans l'arbitrage commercial international' (1999) 179 RCADI 162.

19

The Role of Tribunal Secretaries in the Drafting of Investment Awards

*Claudia Frutos-Peterson, Marat Umerov, and Marija Ozolins**

I. Introduction

In the world of international arbitration, it is a controversial notion that a tribunal secretary may play a role in the drafting of an arbitral award. In investment arbitration, this notion has also caused turmoil. For years, allegations, anecdotes, and credible non-official information gleaned from arbitration cases lead to an inference that it is not uncommon for arbitrators to delegate certain drafting responsibilities to tribunal secretaries or even assistants. Each time there is reason to believe that the secretary or an assistant has contributed to the drafting of an award, the central questions are: first, just how much the secretary has drafted, and second, whether the award's substance was impacted by the secretary's own judgment.

These questions arise in the context of both investment arbitration and international commercial arbitration, the latter of which has introduced more public scrutiny of the role of tribunal secretaries and assistants in the form of challenges to awards in national courts. In light of these challenges, institutions administering commercial arbitrations have studied or introduced increased regulation and guidance concerning the role of tribunal secretaries. There have been fewer known challenges on the basis of improper delegation of tribunal functions to secretaries or assistants, but there are important lessons to be learned from the experience in the international commercial arbitration space.

In either context, the mention that a fourth person participating in the drafting of an award stirs controversy as to the appropriateness and extent of such participation. Although parties may consent to the use of a tribunal secretary or assistant and may even be provided with terms of reference for their appointment, it is usually unknown to the parties and their counsel exactly what role the secretary or assistant has occupied, whether they fulfilled that role diligently and fairly, and how this might have influenced a particular outcome in the case. This opacity only fuels doubts about the arbitral process's legitimacy, which is already top of mind for both supporters and critics of ISDS alike.

* The views and opinions expressed in this chapter are exclusively the authors' and do not necessarily reflect those of Curtis, Mallet-Prevost, Colt & Mosle LLP, or its clients.

Claudia Frutos-Peterson, Marat Umerov, and Marija Ozolins, *The Role of Tribunal Secretaries in the Drafting of Investment Awards*
In: *The Award in International Investment Arbitration*. Edited by: Katia Fach Gómez and Catharine Titi, Oxford University Press.
 DOI: 10.1093/9780191975936.003.0019

In fact, the tribunal secretary is often critically referred to as the 'fourth arbitrator'.[1] If the role of a secretary is of such concern, it begs the question of why this role is not more of a focus and better defined during the initial stages of an arbitration. The reality is that the parties are focused on the selection of specific individuals as arbitrators, which is in turn informed by a calculation as to the kind of product and result they expect from those particular adjudicators. At the time the arbitrators are chosen and appointed, parties are much less likely to be concerned about the specific role of a future tribunal's secretary or assistant.[2] The scope of a secretary's involvement is not a decisive factor in the process of selecting arbitrators, despite the fact that parties may know that experienced arbitrators with concurrent appointments in multiple cases will probably need assistance in managing several matters at the same time. Often, the involvement of a secretary or assistant cannot even be a factor when appointing arbitrators because the identity of such a person tends to be unknown until after all the arbitrators are appointed and begin communicating with the parties, or even after the arbitrators gain an appreciation for the complexity of a given matter and whether such assistance is required. It is also possible that parties' counsel may refrain at the outset of an arbitration from questioning the scope of tasks that may be delegated to a secretary, given concerns about efficiently resolving preliminary procedural issues and with earning the goodwill of the tribunal in the long run.

Inquiring about the scope of the secretary's role must stop being taboo. The scope of the secretary's tasks should be specifically defined in an initial procedural order or in the tribunal's terms of appointment. Tribunals can and should be sensitive to counsels' unease about questioning the idea and the scope of assistance by a non-arbitrator in the workings of the tribunal. Tribunals should be ready to clarify the precise role they intend the non-arbitrator party-neutrals to play, especially if it is a role that can be perceived by the parties as being potentially impactful, such as drafting the award or its parts. The institutions that appoint secretaries pursuant to their regulations, or as a matter of practice acquiesce to the appointment of a tribunal's assistant in addition to the official secretary to the tribunal as in the case of the International Centre for Settlement of Investment Disputes (ICSID), should encourage and facilitate a transparent delineation of the tasks at the outset of the case.

Generally, parties to an arbitration may have at least a reasonable expectation that the involvement of a secretary tends to enhance the efficiency of arbitral proceedings. From the tribunal's perspective, the arbitrators benefit from getting the tribunal secretary's assistance with organizing the file of the case, day-to-day administrative assistance, and keeping track of and summarizing the submissions, issues, and procedural history of the case. For younger lawyers, assisting an investor-state tribunal is

[1] Constantine Partasides, 'The Fourth Arbitrator? The Role of Secretaries to Tribunals in International Arbitration' (2002) 18 Arbitration International 147.

[2] Even where parties have chosen ad hoc as opposed to institutional arbitration, arbitrators often make use of assistants who may occupy a similar role to that of a tribunal secretary in an institutional arbitration. It should be noted that tribunal members in an institutional arbitration often use their own assistants in addition to a designated tribunal secretary.

seen as a prestigious opportunity to gain valuable practical experience and build their career. Indeed, generations of investment arbitration practitioners have cut their teeth by assisting high-profile arbitrators. In an institutional setting, such as ICSID or the Permanent Court of Arbitration (PCA), being a tribunal secretary is a profession that lawyers can enjoy for decades, with their knowledge, experience, and skills contributing to the workings of investor-state dispute settlement (ISDS). Parties should then anticipate that a secretary or assistant will likely be involved in assisting the tribunal, and should feel comfortable inquiring about their role.

This chapter examines the typical patterns of a tribunal secretary's involvement in an arbitration, including the evolving role of a tribunal secretary as disputes increase in complexity. We then discuss efforts to regulate or prescribe the tasks that may be performed by a tribunal secretary, as well as the risks that follow when parties are not informed about these tasks. Finally, we discuss potential solutions to the controversy over whether or not secretaries should be involved in drafting awards.

II. The Evolving Role of Tribunal Secretaries in International Arbitration

The role of tribunal secretaries has long been evolving. As international disputes dealt with by tribunals have become more complex and significantly more voluminous than those in earlier decades, tribunals call for more support from secretaries and assistants. In line with this demand, in 2015 the Hong Kong International Arbitration Center (HKIAC) launched the first programme of its kind to train tribunal secretaries.[3] Even at the domestic level, some arbitral institutions maintain pre-vetted rosters of secretaries available to assist tribunals, sometimes even requiring tribunals to appoint a secretary from their lists.[4] Several arbitral institutions typically appoint one of their staff counsel as the secretary to a tribunal.[5]

Most institutions require a conflict check for secretaries and assistants just like for the arbitrators themselves.[6] For instance, a lawyer or clerk considered for a role as tribunal secretary, a party-neutral capacity, may be involved as a party representative in another matter which can present a conflict, or have a work or other relationship with a party, legal representative, or funder, which could be seen as a conflict.

Perhaps the leading precedent for the use of secretaries of tribunals is ICSID, which establishes in its recently amended Administrative Regulation 28 that:

[3] HKIAC, 'Tribunal Secretary Training Programme' <www.hkiac.org/arbitration/tribunal-secretaries/tribunal-secretary-training-programme>.

[4] For example, the Centro de Conciliación y Arbitraje de Panamá (CeCAP) organizes an arbitral tribunal secretary training programme and maintains a list of approved individuals available for appointment as tribunal secretaries. CeCAP, 'National and International Arbitration' <https://cecap.com.pa/en/arbitraje-nacional-e-internacional/>. HKIAC also maintains a list of secretaries. HKIAC (n 3).

[5] Eloïse Obadia and Frauke Nitschke, 'Institutional Arbitration and the Role of the Secretariat' in Chiara Giorgetti (ed), *Litigating International Investment Disputes: A Practitioner's Guide* (Brill Nijhoff 2014) 42.

[6] See Annex.

> The Secretary-General shall appoint a Secretary for each Commission, Tribunal and Committee. The Secretary may be drawn from the Secretariat and shall be considered a member of its staff while serving as a Secretary. The Secretary shall:
> (a) represent the Secretary-General and may perform all functions assigned to the Secretary-General by these Regulations or the Rules applicable to individual proceedings or assigned to the Secretary-General by the Convention, and delegated to the Secretary; and
> (b) assist the parties and the Commission, Tribunal or Committee with the proceeding, including the expeditious and cost-effective conduct of the proceeding.[7]

In fact, it could be argued that ICSID in its recent amendment of this Regulation, previously Regulations 25 and 26, has implicitly sanctioned a broader or at least more discretionary role for tribunal secretaries. This is because the prior version of the regulation on secretaries enumerated four main functions of tribunal secretaries,[8] while the amended regulation simplifies and combines these roles while adding the important modifier that the tribunal secretary is empowered to assist tribunals with 'the expeditious and cost-effective conduct of the proceeding'.[9] ICSID confirmed that this modification only reflects existing practice, and was added in order to 'reinforce the importance of timeliness'.[10] One could certainly argue that the use of tribunal secretaries to draft awards is in fact the more expeditious and cost-effective option. The notion of timeliness is also a justification for having the tribunal secretary draft at least parts of the award to assist the arbitrators with rendering the award within the time limits now expressly imposed by the amended ICSID Rules.[11]

During consultations with ICSID member states on the proposed amendments to the ICSID Rules, some states seemed to express concern over the lack of specificity in the proposed Regulation. This included Spain, which inquired as to the process for the Secretary-General to delegate functions to individual tribunal secretaries.[12]

[7] ICSID Convention, Regulations and Rules (2022), Regulation 28.

[8] ibid Regulations 25 and 26.

The Secretary-General shall appoint a Secretary for each Commission, Tribunal and Committee. The Secretary may be drawn from among the Secretariat of the Centre, and shall in any case, while serving in that capacity, be considered as a member of its staff. He shall:

(a) represent the Secretary-General and may perform all functions assigned to the latter by these Regulations or the Rules with regard to individual proceedings or assigned to the latter by the Convention, and delegated by him to the Secretary;
(b) be the channel through which the parties may request particular services from the Centre;
(c) keep summary minutes of hearings, unless the parties agree with the Commission, Tribunal or Committee on another manner of keeping the record of the hearings; and
(d) perform other functions with respect to the proceeding at the request of the President of the Commission, Tribunal or Committee, or at the direction of the Secretary-General.

[9] ibid Regulation 28.

[10] ICSID explained that 'the Secretariat already encourages parties and Commissions, Tribunals and Committees to proceed in an expeditious fashion, and hence the addition reflects existing practice', ICSID Secretariat, 'Working Paper #3: Proposals for Amendment of the ICSID Rules' (16 August 2019) vol 3, 269, para 13.

[11] ICSID Arbitration Rules (2022) r 58 'Timing of the Award'; ICSID Additional Facility Arbitration Rules (2002), r 69 'Timing of the Award'.

[12] ICSID Secretariat, 'Working Paper #2: Proposal for the Amendment of the ICSID Rules' (March 2019) vol 1, 50, paras 35–36.

In response, ICSID noted that '[i]n practice, members of the ICSID Secretariat follow a set of internal best practices which explain the role of ICSID under each rule, and where consultation with team leaders, Deputy Secretaries-General and the Secretary-General are required'.[13] Georgia suggested that 'a Tribunal consult with the parties on the tasks assigned to the Secretary or assistant', while Chile echoed Spain's concern.[14] Pursuant to these comments and inquiries on amended Regulation 28, ICSID noted that it 'will draft an information note for its website with further information about the role of an ICSID Secretary'.[15]

Other institutions have been more specific in enumerating the exact role of a tribunal secretary and how tasks are delegated from the tribunal. For example, in 2017 the London Court of International Arbitration (LCIA) released guidelines on the use of secretaries, with an emphasis on communication and consent as critical safeguards to ensure party understanding of the role of secretaries and to reduce challenges.[16] The LCIA's guidelines now require arbitrators to propose a list of tasks for the tribunal secretary, and parties must expressly consent to those tasks.[17] These guidelines now serve as a 'starting point' for tribunals and parties to discuss the full extent of the secretary's role.[18] Examples of other institutions which have also recently examined the role of secretaries or assistants in the context of an arbitration include the Singapore International Arbitration Centre (SIAC),[19] the British Virgin Islands International Arbitration Center (BVI IAC),[20] and the Australian Centre for International Commercial Arbitration (ACICA), among others.[21] In the Annex, we provide a non-exhaustive summary of various institutional or arbitral rules and their treatment of the use and role of tribunal secretaries in an arbitration.[22]

Even after reviewing the rules of institutions that do address the role of secretaries, the question remains: what *exactly* do tribunal secretaries do? One commentator explains that the secretary 'provides logistical and administrative support for the proceeding and is responsible for the archives of the respective dispute'.[23] The UNCITRAL

[13] ibid.

[14] ICSID Secretariat, 'Compendium of Member State & Public Comments on Working Paper # 2' (15 March 2019), 17 (Chile: 'Recibimos favorablemente el ofrecimiento del CIADI de incorporar información adicional sobre el rol que cumplen las y los Secretarias(os) de los tribunales en la administración de los casos ante el CIADI, y por tanto apoyamos la solicitud de España en ese sentido').

[15] ICSID Secretariat, 'Working Paper #3' (n 10), 269, para 14. As of the time of writing this chapter, no such note has been published.

[16] LCIA, 'Notes for Arbitrators', s 8.2 <www.lcia.org/adr-services/lcia-notes-for-arbitrators.aspx>.

[17] ibid para 71.

[18] The guidelines also require that the parties consent to a tribunal's decision to pay a tribunal secretary and provides proposed hourly rates, ibid para 72.

[19] SIAC, 'Practice Note for Administered Cases on the Appointment of Administrative Secretaries' (2 February 2015).

[20] BVI IAC, 'Arbitration Rules' (2021).

[21] ACICA, 'Guideline on the Use of Tribunal Secretaries' (2017).

[22] See Annex. This table was created by the authors, taking into consideration the main tasks that one can assume are often performed by tribunal secretaries. The institutions, rules, and functions presented in the table are not exhaustive, and the information in this table is up to date as of October 2023.

[23] Obadia and Nitschke (n 5) 42. See also Yves Derains, 'Tribunal Dynamics and Arbitral Deliberations' in Katia Fach Gomez and Catharine Titi, *The Award in International Investment Arbitration* (OUP 2024).

Rules provide that soon after the constitution of the tribunal, the tribunal is to establish the provisional timetable of the arbitration with the input of the parties—a task that tribunal secretaries often assist with.[24]

Anecdotally, a tribunal secretary or assistant often has responsibility for recording and summarizing the procedural history in an arbitration, summarizing the parties' pleadings, reviewing exhibits, researching evidence, cite checking, preparing notes for tribunal members, bringing the tribunal's attention to procedural issues, and attending deliberations of the tribunal. One commentator notes that:

> In practice, ICSID Secretaries have been asked to advise the respective competent body on various procedural matters, and/or to provide guidance as to any relevant law and practice related to a particular issue. Upon request, and at the direction of the president of the respective tribunal, commission, or committee, ICSID Secretaries have also assisted with the drafting of certain aspects of procedural orders, decisions, discontinuance orders, and awards, such as the procedural history, the summary of the facts, as well as the parties' arguments. ICSID Secretaries also assist with the proofreading, editing, and formatting of instruments such as procedural orders, decisions, reports, or awards to be issued by a tribunal, commission, or committee.[25]

In this regard, it could be said that the tribunal secretary is in a position to exert a significant degree of influence over how the tribunal receives and processes information relating to the case.

According to the 2014 Young International Council for Commercial Arbitration (ICCA) Guide on Arbitral Secretaries, typical tasks of tribunal secretary may include: (1) administrative matters; (2) being the channel of communications; (3) organizing meetings and hearings; (4) handling and organizing correspondence, submissions, and evidence for the tribunal; (5) researching questions of law; (6) researching factual evidence and witness testimony; (7) reviewing the parties' submissions and evidence; (8) drafting factual chronologies and memoranda summarizing the parties' submissions and evidence; (9) drafting procedural orders and similar documents; (10) attending the tribunal's deliberations; and (11) drafting parts of interim decisions/awards and the final award.[26]

The first half or so of these tasks (ie (1)–(4)) are not controversial, because their performance does not carry the risk of influencing the arbitrator's judgment on the substance of the dispute. Parties also expect the secretary to execute these tasks, and their execution by the secretary is to a significant degree transparent, that is, it is visible to the parties.

[24] Manuel Indlekofer, *International Arbitration and the Permanent Court of Arbitration* (Wolters Kluwer 2013) 240; Obadia and Nitschke (n 5) 42.
[25] Obadia and Nitschke (n 5) 51–52.
[26] ICCA, 'Young ICCA Guide on Arbitral Secretaries' (2014) ICCA Reports No 1, art 3 <www.arbitration-icca.org/icca-reports-no-1-young-icca-guide-arbitral-secretaries>.

By contrast, the parties do not usually know whether or not the secretary is requested by the tribunal to research questions of law, research factual evidence and witness testimony, or review the parties' submissions and evidence (tasks (5)–(7) above). The way such tasks are actually performed could potentially impact the views of the arbitrators. Nonetheless, the delegation of these tasks to the secretary is not quite controversial or worrying to the parties. The parties may assume that the secretary is asked to undertake this type of review and research under the direction of the tribunal.

Significantly more sensitive to the parties is the question of whether the secretary is requested to perform such tasks as the drafting of factual chronologies and memoranda, summarizing the parties' submissions and evidence, preparation of procedural orders and rulings, participation in the tribunal's deliberations, and drafting parts of arbitral instruments, including the final award (tasks (8)–(11) above). This sensitivity is acknowledged by the International Chamber of Commerce (ICC) in its express prohibition on drafting of awards by a tribunal secretary:

> The tasks entrusted to an administrative secretary shall in no circumstances release the arbitral tribunal from its duty to personally review the file. Under no circumstances may the arbitral tribunal delegate its decision-making functions to an administrative secretary. Nor shall the arbitral tribunal rely on an administrative secretary to perform on its behalf any of the essential duties of an arbitrator.
>
> [...]
>
> A request by an arbitral tribunal to an administrative secretary to prepare written notes or memoranda shall in no circumstances release the arbitral tribunal from its duty personally to review the file and/or to draft any decision of the arbitral tribunal.[27]

In many arbitrations outside of the ICC, however, whether and to what extent the secretary is involved in these aspects is often unknown to the parties. These activities are related to the tribunals' internal workings, deliberations, and the process of the drafting, and are normally beyond the parties' capacity to observe, as these workings of the tribunal are covered by the secrecy of deliberations.[28] The fact that tribunal deliberations are a 'black box' is well known:

> The form of deliberations can certainly be significant to how a tribunal approaches the task of coming to a decision. To counsel, or to an outside observer, this may be something of a 'black box': the tribunal goes off after the hearing, reaches agreement (or does not), and comes back a few months later with a decision. What a tribunal

[27] ICC, 'Note on the Appointment, Duties and Remuneration of Administrative Secretaries' (April 2014) paras 184, 187.

[28] eg ICSID Arbitration Rules (2022) r 34: '(1) The deliberations of the Tribunal shall take place in private and remain confidential (...) (3) The Tribunal may be assisted by the Secretary of the Tribunal at its deliberations. No other person shall assist the Tribunal at its deliberations, unless the Tribunal decides otherwise and notifies the parties.' On the tribunal's deliberations, see also Derains (n 23).

does during that intervening period, however, is significantly more nuanced . . . The approach taken by arbitral tribunals may be much more varied.[29]

Accordingly, any role that a secretary has in the drafting of an award varies from case to case, depending on a number of factors, including the preferences of the tribunal members for a particular arbitration. However, it is not uncommon for tribunal secretaries to attend tribunal deliberations. Where the secretary has been involved in summarizing the parties' submissions on the issues of the case and preparing similar products to facilitate the tribunal's understanding of the parties' positions on the issues, one could say that the secretary is inherently equipped with the necessary knowledge of the case to assist the tribunal in its deliberations and drafting. Whether or to what extent the secretary is in fact requested to provide this assistance often remains unknown to the parties.

III. The Risks Involved When Tribunal Secretaries Assist in Drafting International Arbitration Awards

The way the tribunals proceed with drafting of the award varies from case to case. However, it is generally acknowledged that the practice of involving the secretary in the drafting of the awards does exist,[30] and the extent of the secretary's involvement raises concerns of practitioners and users alike of international arbitration. Where there is no guidance offered by the applicable institution or arbitral rules, there arises a risk that the outcome of such an arbitration could be challenged on the basis of lack of party consent or improper constitution of a tribunal. Although to date no public award has been overturned on this basis, the risk remains and at a minimum parties can expect delays and additional costs should such a challenge be raised. It is therefore in the interests of all sides—regardless of their views on whether or not tribunal secretaries should assist with drafting awards—to define and agree the scope of a secretary's involvement during an arbitration.

There are several known instances where arbitral awards were challenged based on allegations that the tribunal's secretary or the assistant, not the arbitrators themselves, wrote the award or its substantial parts.[31] By and large such challenges have not

[29] Garth Schofield, 'Remarks by Garth Schofield, PCA—A Summary' (2018) 112 ASIL Proceedings of the Annual Meeting 239.

[30] Obadia and Nitschke (n 5) 51–52 ('ICSID Secretaries have also assisted with the *drafting* of certain aspects of procedural orders, decisions, discontinuance orders, and awards, such as the procedural history, the summary of the facts, as well as the parties' arguments. ICSID Secretaries also assist with the proofreading, editing, and formatting of instruments such as procedural orders, decisions, reports, or awards to be issued by a tribunal, commission, or committee', emphasis added).

[31] See eg *Yukos Universal Limited (Isle of Man) v Russia*, PCA Case No 2005-04/AA227, Judgment of the Hague Court of Appeal (18 February 2020); *Veteran Petroleum Limited v Russia*, PCA Case No 2005-05/AA228, Judgment of the Hague Court of Appeal (18 February 2020); *P v Q* [2017] EWHC 194 (Comm); Partasides (n 1); Pierre Tercier, 'The Role of the Secretary to the Arbitral Tribunal' in Lawrence W Newman and Richard D Hill (eds), *Leading Arbitrators' Guide to International Arbitration* (3rd edn, Juris 2014); Benjamin Hughes, 'The Problem of Undisclosed Assistance to Arbitral Tribunals' in Patricia Shaughnessy and Sherlin Tung (eds), *The Powers and Duties of an Arbitrator: Liber Amicorum Pierre A Karrer* (Kluwer 2017). For an analysis of the grounds

been successful, in part due to the great difficulties in proving the allegations.[32] For example, one of the first known challenges to an award based on the actions of a tribunal secretary was made public in the 1990 Paris Court of Appeal Decision in *Compagnie Honeywell Bull SA v Computacion Bull de Venezuela CA*. The appellant challenging the ICC award, Honeywell, argued that the tribunal secretary had 'interfered' during the two-day hearing on the dispute. The Paris Court of Appeal dismissed this element of the appeal because Honeywell had not explained how the secretary's interference was more prejudicial to Honeywell than to the other side.[33]

The legitimacy of a tribunal secretary's role has also come up in the context of procedural orders, most recently where the claimant in *P v Q* challenged three such decisions on the basis of improper delegation of the adjudicative function of the LCIA tribunal to its secretary.[34] The claimant's application turned on an email from the tribunal chairman intended for the secretary but mistakenly sent to counsel, where the chairman asked the secretary for his views on recent correspondence from the claimant. The claimant also pointed to time records of the tribunal secretary and the arbitrators, arguing that the significant amount of time recorded by the tribunal secretary in relation to the three procedural decisions indicated an improper delegation of functions. In dismissing the application, an English court noted that the consideration of the opinions of others, including those of a tribunal secretary, does not automatically preclude an arbitrator from reaching an independent decision based on their own reasoning and due diligence. The court also noted that the parties, in agreeing to the appointment of the secretary, did not seek to limit his permitted involvement in the arbitration or otherwise place any constraints on the tasks that he may perform. However, the court referred to the 'considerable and understandable anxiety in the international arbitration community that the use of tribunal secretaries risks them becoming, in effect, "fourth arbitrators"' and cautioned tribunals to 'avoid involving a tribunal secretary in anything which could be characterised as expressing a view on the substance of that which the tribunal is called upon to decide'.[35]

Perhaps a more prominent discussion of this issue arose in the context of Russia's application to the District Court of The Hague to set aside the tribunal's awards in the *Yukos* proceedings. Russia argued that the arbitrators did not personally fulfil their mandate towards the parties, but rather delegated their decision-making function to an assistant to the tribunal.[36] Among other arguments, Russia stated that international practice defined the role of a tribunal secretary as limited to the carrying out

for challenge of arbitrators and their awards based on the misuse of tribunal secretaries, see J Ole Jensen, *Tribunal Secretaries in International Arbitration* (OUP 2019) chs 7 and 8.

[32] eg J Ole Jensen, 'Secretaries to Arbitral Tribunals: Judicial Assistants Rooted in Party Autonomy' (2020) 11(3) International Journal for Court Administration.

[33] *Compagnie Honeywell Bull SA v Computacion Bull de Venezuela CA*, Paris Court of Appeal, Judgment, 21 June 1990, 1991(1) Rev arb 96.

[34] *P v Q* [2017] EWHC 194 (Comm).

[35] ibid [68].

[36] *Yukos Universal Limited (Isle of Man) v Russia*, PCA Case No 2005-04/AA227, Writ of Summons (28 January 2015), s V [469].

of administrative tasks relating to the organization of the arbitration. Russia pointed to the assistant's hours, which were between 40 to 70 per cent higher than those of any member of the tribunal, and a report from a linguistics expert analysing the writing styles of the assistant and the tribunal members as evidence of improper delegation of substantive analysis and decision-making. The District Court decided the application on other grounds and did not examine this argument, but upon review the Court of Appeal in The Hague did note that the tribunal had failed to fully inform the parties about the nature and extent of the assistant's role.[37]

Another development on this topic comes from Belgium's Court of Cassation, which recently affirmed a ruling by the Brussels Court of First Instance that upheld the drafting of an ICC award by a secretary as a proper delegation of the tribunal's decision-making powers. The Court of Cassation upheld the lower court's finding that the drafting of all or part of the award by an administrative secretary was permissible, as long as the parties agreed to the appointment of the secretary and that the secretary's work was reviewed by an arbitrator.[38] Interestingly, the lower court noted that the secretary had followed specific trainings for arbitral secretaries organized by the ICC, including sessions on drafting enforceable awards, and that the secretary was of relatively young age, which in the court's view reduced the risk of undue influence on the tribunal when compared to a more experienced secretary.[39]

The involvement of tribunal secretaries in drafting awards has also been discussed in numerous publications, conferences, and surveys.[40] The empirical studies and the solicited opinion views on the issue indicate that most users of international arbitration do not endorse an extensive reliance by tribunals on their secretaries for the drafting of awards.[41]

Generally, the practitioners' and scholars' views range from preferring to completely restrict the tribunals from relying on secretaries' drafting, to allowing limited drafting assistance under a close supervision and instruction by the tribunal members (the majority adheres to this view)[42] and permitting and encouraging tribunal secretaries to do more, primarily to facilitate the efficiency of the tribunal's work.[43]

[37] *Yukos Universal Limited (Isle of Man) v The Russian Federation*, PCA Case No 2005-04/AA227, Judgment of the Hague Court of Appeal (18 February 2020) [6.6.14.2].

[38] *European Commission v Emek İnşaat Şti and WTE Wassertechnik*, Brussels Court of Cassation, Judgment (23 April 2023) [6]; *European Commission v Emek İnşaat Şti and WTE Wassertechnik*, Judgment of the Brussels Court of First Instance (17 June 2021) [81], [89].

[39] *European Commission v Emek İnşaat Şti and WTE Wassertechnik*, Brussels Court of First Instance, Judgment (17 June 2021) [83], [85].

[40] eg see n 31; Lacey Young, 'LCIA Revisits Issue of Tribunal Secretaries' *Global Arbitration Review* (26 October 2017) <https://globalarbitrationreview.com/article/lcia-revisits-issue-of-tribunal-secretaries>; White & Case and Queen Mary University of London School of International Arbitration, '2012 International Arbitration Survey: Current and Preferred Practices in the Arbitral Process' <www.arbitration.qmul.ac.uk/media/arbitration/docs/2012_International_Arbitration_Survey.pdf> 43.

[41] See Young (n 40); White & Case and Queen Mary (n 40).

[42] A survey conducted by White & Case and Queen Mary University of London, which surveyed 710 respondents (including private practitioners, arbitrators, in-house counsel, counsel from arbitral institutions, academics, and expert witnesses), indicates that this view is favoured by the participants since 75 per cent of them were of the opinion that tribunal secretaries should be able to prepare 'non-substantive parts of awards', White & Case and Queen Mary (n 40).

[43] These views towards the role of a tribunal secretary were conceptualized in a 2021 publication as, respectively, (1) strict, (2) popular, (3) liberal approaches. Berk Hasan Özdem, 'Entrusting the Secretary to the Tribunal with

These differing views can be heavily influenced by the judicial practice in a given jurisdiction. For example, one London-based practitioner finds the idea of secretaries writing awards 'shocking', while a practitioner based in New York is more used to the idea of prominent adjudicators—such as the US Supreme Court justices—using clerks to write first drafts of their judgments.[44] Regardless of the viewpoint, it is clear that more guidelines and information on this issue is desired from states, other parties, and practitioners alike.[45]

IV. Conclusion with Reflections on Possible Solutions

In the previous parts of this chapter, we have discussed the increased regulation and guidance concerning the role of tribunal secretaries. This activity has thus far largely occurred within the international commercial arbitration space, and may be the result of a series of challenges to commercial arbitration awards based on allegedly improper delegation of authority from a tribunal to a secretary or assistant. While there have been fewer high-profile challenges in the world of investment arbitration, we do know that the vast majority of investment arbitration tribunals use of secretaries or assistants.[46] It is in the best interests of arbitral institutions, tribunals in investment arbitrations, and parties and their counsel to observe the lessons from international commercial arbitration. Doing so could avoid the risks to individual awards and the ISDS system as a whole that result from inadequate attention paid to the role of tribunal secretaries, particularly when it comes to drafting awards. ICSID has indicated that it will provide more guidance on the role of tribunal secretaries, and one could hope this eases concern among stakeholders about which tasks are performed by secretaries and how they are delegated.

the Preparation of the Arbitral Award: Taking the Aim at the Arbitrators Own Assessment of Coût d'Opportunité' (2021) 12 (22) Law & Justice Review 2.

[44] Editorial, 'Are Tribunal Secretaries Writing Awards?' *Global Arbitration Review* (9 November 2012) <https://globalarbitrationreview.com/article/are-tribunal-secretaries-writing-awards>; see also United States Court of Appeals for the Second Circuit, 839 F.2d 37 (2d Cir 1988) [40] ('the work done by law clerks is supervised, approved, and adopted by the judges who initially authorised it. A judicial opinion is not that of the law clerk, but of the judge. Law clerks are simply extensions of the judges at whose pleasure they serve').

[45] ICSID Secretariat, 'Working Paper #2' (n 12) 50, paras 35–36; ICSID Secretariat, 'Compendium of Member State & Public Comments on Working Paper # 2' (n 14); Young (n 40) ('According to a 2012 survey conducted by Constantine Partasides QC of Three Crowns and three young ICCA members, 57% of responders thought the arbitral process would benefit from regulation of arbitral secretaries, with more than 78% saying they were in favor of guidelines reflecting best practice. Following the survey, ICCA's under-40 group Young ICCA produced a set of tribunal secretary guidelines in 2014, addressing issues such as pay and appropriate tasks. In its commentary, it noted that secretaries may go beyond administrative tasks, but that they should be limited in the drafting of awards').

[46] While some commercial arbitration institutions—such as the ICC—have taken the position that tribunal secretaries may not assist with drafting, institutions such as ICSID have not. This is worth noting as ICSID administers the majority of known investment treaty arbitrations and requires the appointment of a tribunal secretary. Between 1987 and 2021, there were a total of 1190 recorded ISDS cases, with 62.4 per cent (743) of those cases being administered by ICSID and 16.7 per cent (199) by the PCA. UNCTAD, 'Investment Dispute Settlement Navigator' <https://investmentpolicy.unctad.org/investment-dispute-settlement> (information correct as of 1 November 2022).

Until more institutions provide such guidelines, the precise scope of services by the secretary should be disclosed by tribunals and agreed by the parties in advance. If the tribunal does not propose defining the scope, and there are no institutional or rules regulations, the scope will not be defined unless the parties request it. Parties may be reluctant to raise the issue, not willing to risk bothering the tribunal early on in the case. Yet, the role of tribunal secretaries should be defined from the beginning by the parties' agreement, just like other important aspects of international arbitration.

It is perhaps trite to emphasize that consent and party autonomy are the building blocks of international arbitration. There is no reason these principles should not be applied to the question of what role tribunal secretaries should play in an arbitration, specifically whether they can assist with drafting of awards. We have seen that attitudes vary widely as to whether or not this is an acceptable practice. The solution—aside from codifying accepted roles through institutional or arbitral rules—is to insist that parties reach agreement on this important topic well in advance of the substance of the arbitration getting underway.

Against this backdrop, the responsibility of the arbitrator must also be remembered. It is well established that certain parts of a tribunal's mandate are non-delegable, such as the duty to exercise its own discretion and judgment in making its decision.[47] A tribunal is responsible for ensuring that the award resulting from the arbitration 'shall be [the arbitrator's] award' and that it has not 'substitute[d] the opinion of another for [its] own'.[48] Meeting this responsibility requires an arbitrator 'to bring his own personal and independent judgment to bear on the decision in question, taking account of the rival submissions of the parties; and to exercise reasonable diligence in going about discharging that function'.[49] The core of what arbitrators owe the parties in an arbitration is the substantive decision, and it is essential that arbitrators protect this function when deciding what to delegate to tribunal secretaries and assistants.

Absent institutional or arbitral rules to this effect, it is up to parties, their counsel, and arbitrators to insist that the important question of whether tribunal secretaries should assist in tasks such as drafting the award or parts of it, be settled at the outset of an arbitration in a clear manner and with the parties' consent. This could take the form of terms of appointment,[50] a procedural

[47] *Whitmore v Smith* (1861) 7 H & N 509, 516; *Continental Materials Corp. v Gaddis Mining* 306 F.2d 952, 955 (10th Cir, 1962).

[48] *P v Q* [2017] EWHC 194 (Comm) [66].

[49] ibid [65].

[50] An example from a recent terms of reference in a confidential arbitration administered by ICSID is as follows:

> The assistant would not duplicate the work done by the ICSID Secretary and would undertake only such specific tasks as are assigned to him by the Tribunal or the President, which may include: assisting the Tribunal or the President in the review of the evidence and of the issues in dispute, including through the review of submissions and evidence, preparation of summaries and/or memoranda; assisting the Tribunal or the President in the preparation and communication of the Tribunal's decisions to the parties on issues of procedure and substance, including by preparing initial drafts of procedural orders and award, under the direction and supervision of the President; providing other support to the Tribunal and the President, at any time, especially during hearings and deliberations, which the assistant may attend.
>
> Under no circumstances would the Tribunal or the President delegate any decision-making functions of the assistant.

order,[51] or advance agreement between the parties. Such discussions should be as routine as those determining party submission timelines and other key functions that predict how an arbitration will unfold. The more parties and arbitrators bring this up affirmatively, the less taboo it will seem going forward. In addition, agreeing and setting forth these guidelines in a procedural order may help avoid the time and expense of a potential challenge based on the use of a tribunal secretary for drafting awards or procedural decisions.

> The assistant would work at all times under the specific instructions and continuous control and supervision of the President. The Assistant would be subject to the same confidentiality obligations as the Members of the Tribunal and would sign a declaration of confidentiality to that effect, which will distributed to the parties by the ICSID Secretariat.

The terms of reference went on to specify the hourly rate for the proposed assistant to the tribunal.

[51] An example from a recent procedural order in a confidential arbitration administered by the PCA is as follows:

> The Tribunal Secretary provided by the PCA shall perform such tasks as are assigned to her or him by the Arbitral Tribunal or the Presiding Arbitrator, including:
>
> i. Assisting the Arbitral Tribunal in the review of the evidence and of the issues in dispute, including through the review of submissions and evidence, preparation of summaries and/or memoranda, and research on specific factual or legal issues;
>
> ii. Assisting the Arbitral Tribunal in the preparation and communication of its decisions to the Parties on issues of procedure and substance, including by preparing initial drafts of procedural orders and awards, under the direction and supervision of the Arbitral Tribunal or its Presiding Arbitrator;
>
> iii. Providing other support to the Arbitral Tribunal or its members, especially its Presiding Arbitrator, at any time, especially during hearings and deliberations, which the Tribunal Secretary may attend.
>
> Under no circumstances shall the Arbitral Tribunal delegate any decision-making functions to the Tribunal Secretary. The Tribunal Secretary will work at all times under the specific instructions and continuous control and supervision of the Arbitral Tribunal.
>
> The Tribunal Secretary shall be subject to the same independence, impartiality and confidentiality obligations as the members of the Arbitral Tribunal.

ANNEX

Arbitral Rules and Institutional Regulations Concerning Tribunal Secretaries and Assistants[1]

	ICSID	PCA[2]	ICC	UNCITRAL	London Court of International Arbitration	Stockholm Chamber of Commerce	Hong Kong International Arbitration Center	Singapore International Arbitration Centre	British Virgin Islands International Arbitration Center	Australian Centre for International Commercial Arbitration	Swiss Arbitration Center
Explicit prohibition on decision-making	—	—	Yes[3]	Yes[4]	Yes[5]	Yes[6]	Yes[7]	—	Yes[8]	Yes[9]	Yes[10]
Explicit prohibition on drafting of awards	—	—	Yes[11]	No[12]	No[13]	—	No[14]	—	No[15]	No[16]	—
Permits assistance with summarizing pleadings, procedural history, research, or similar	Yes[17]	—	Yes[18]	Yes[19]	Yes[20]	—	Yes[21]	—	Yes[22]	Yes[23]	—
Permits attendance to tribunal deliberations	Yes[24]	—	Yes[25]	—	Yes[26]	—	Yes[27]	—	Yes[28]	—	—
Subject to requirements of impartiality and independence	Yes[29]	—	Yes[30]	Yes[31]	Yes[32]	Yes[33]	Yes[34]	Yes[35]	Yes[36]	Yes[37]	Yes[38]
Enumerates tasks that may be performed	Yes[39]	—	Yes[40]	No[41]	Yes[42]	—	Yes[43]	No[44]	Yes[45]	Yes[46]	No[47]
Requires express agreement of the parties for any tasks to be performed /Requires tribunal to consult parties about the same	—	—	No[48]	Yes[49]	Yes[50]	Yes[51]	—	Yes[52]	No[53]	No[54]	Yes[55]

Statement of independence or impartiality required/ Conflict check required	—	—	Yes[56]	No[57]	Yes[58]	Yes[59]	Yes[60]	Yes[61]	Yes[62]	Yes[63]	Yes[64]
Procedure for parties to challenge tribunal secretaries	—	—	—	—	Yes[65]	Yes[66]	Yes[67]	—	Yes[68]	Yes[69]	Yes[70]

1 A response of 'No' indicates that the applicable rules address this issue specifically. A response of '—' indicates that the applicable rules are silent on the issue.
2 The PCA Arbitration Rules 2012 do not include provisions regarding tribunal secretaries and assistants.
3 ICC, 'Note to Parties and Arbitral Tribunals on the Conduct of the Arbitration' (1 January 2021) para 223.
4 UNCITRAL, 'Notes on Organizing Arbitral Proceedings' (2016) para 36.
5 LCIA Rules 2020, art 14.8; LCIA, 'Notes for Arbitrators', s 8.1, para 68.
6 SCC Arbitration Rules, art 24(2).
7 HKIAC, 'Guidelines on the Use of a Secretary', Guideline 3.2.
8 BVI IAC Arbitration Rules (2021), app 3, art 1, para 2(c).
9 ACICA, 'Guideline on the Use of Tribunal Secretaries' (2017) para 12.
10 Swiss Arbitration Center Guidelines for Arbitrators, para 7.
11 ICC, 'Note to Parties and Arbitral Tribunals on the Conduct of the Arbitration' (1 January 2021) para 223.
12 According to the 2016 UNCITRAL Notes on Organizing Arbitral Proceedings, para 36, 'it is recognized that secretaries are not involved and do not participate in the decision-making of the arbitral tribunal, except in certain rare, specialized types of arbitration (for example, where the specific arbitration rules provide that secretaries are expected to provide legal advice)'.
13 LCIA, 'Notes for Arbitrators', s 8.2, para 71(c).
14 HKIAC 'Guidelines on the Use of a Secretary', Guideline 3.4(f).
15 BVI IAC Arbitration Rules (2021), app 3, art 3, para 2(b) allows the secretary to assist the Tribunal in the preparation of initial drafts of awards, under the direction and supervision of the Tribunal.
16 However, the secretary may only draft non-substantive parts of awards. See ACICA, 'Guideline on the Use of Tribunal Secretaries' (2017) para 11.
17 ICSID (Convention) Arbitration Rules (2022) r 34(3).
18 ICC, 'Note to Parties and Arbitral Tribunals on the Conduct of the Arbitration' (1 January 2021) para 224.
19 UNCITRAL, 'Notes on Organizing Arbitral Proceedings' (2016) para 36.
20 LCIA, 'Notes for Arbitrators', s 8.2, para 71(c).
21 HKIAC, 'Guidelines on the Use of a Secretary', Guideline 3.4.
22 BVI IAC Arbitration Rules (2021), app 3, art 3, para 2(e).
23 ACICA, Guideline on the Use of Tribunal Secretaries (2017) para 11.
24 ICSID (Convention) Arbitration Rules (2022) r 34.
25 ICC, 'Note to Parties and Arbitral Tribunals on the Conduct of the Arbitration' (1 January 2021) para 224.
26 LCIA, 'Notes for Arbitrators', s 8.2, para 71(b).
27 HKIAC, 'Guidelines on the Use of a Secretary', Guideline 3.4(e).
28 BVI IAC Arbitration Rules (2021), app 3, art 3, para 2(e).

[29] ICSID Convention, art 10(2); ICSID (Convention) Administrative and Financial Regulations, Regulation 13.
[30] ICC, 'Note to Parties and Arbitral Tribunals on the Conduct of the Arbitration' (1 January 2021) para 220.
[31] UNCITRAL, 'Notes on Organizing Arbitral Proceedings' (2016) para 37.
[32] LCIA Rules (2020), art 14.9, 14.14; LCIA, 'Notes for Arbitrators', paras 74(d), 78, 80.
[33] SCC Arbitration Rules, art 24(3).
[34] HKIAC, 'Guidelines on the Use of a Secretary', Guideline 2.2; HKIAC Administered Arbitration Rules r 13.4.
[35] SIAC, 'Practice Note for Administered Cases on the Appointment of Administrative Secretaries', para 4.
[36] BVI IAC Arbitration Rules (2021), app 3, art 2.
[37] ACICA, 'Guideline on the Use of Tribunal Secretaries' (2017) paras 4, 7.
[38] Swiss Rules of International Arbitration, art 16.3.
[39] ICSID (Convention) Administrative and Financial Regulations, Regulation 28.
[40] ICC, 'Note to Parties and Arbitral Tribunals on the Conduct of the Arbitration' (1 January 2021) para 224.
[41] UNCITRAL, 'Notes on Organizing Arbitral Proceedings' (2016) para 36.
[42] LCIA, 'Notes for Arbitrators', s 8.2, para 71.
[43] HKIAC, 'Guidelines on the Use of a Secretary', Guideline 3.3.
[44] Practice Note for Administered Cases on the Appointment of Administrative Secretaries, para 2.
[45] BVI IAC Arbitration Rules (2021), app 3, art 3.
[46] ACICA, 'Guideline on the Use of Tribunal Secretaries' (2017) para 11.
[47] Swiss Arbitration Center, 'Guidelines for Arbitrators', para 4.
[48] The ICC, 'Note to Parties and Arbitral Tribunals on the Conduct of the Arbitration' (1 January 2021) para 221 states that the arbitral tribunal must make clear to the parties that they may object to the proposed secretary and that an administrative secretary shall not be appointed if a party has raised such an objection. See also paras 224, 226.
[49] UNCITRAL, 'Notes on Organizing Arbitral Proceedings' (2016) para 38.
[50] LCIA Rules (2020), arts 14.10(i) and 14.11; LCIA, 'Notes for Arbitrators', s 8.3, para 74.
[51] SCC Arbitration Rules, art 24(2).
[52] Practice Note for Administered Cases on the Appointment of Administrative Secretaries, para 3.
[53] BVI IA Arbitration Rules (2021), app 3, art 1, para 2(c) indicates that the tribunal shall submit a statement to the parties setting out the scope of the secretary's tasks.
[54] However, the Tribunal shall only proceed with the appointment of the secretary upon the agreement of the parties. See ACICA, 'Guideline on the Use of Tribunal Secretaries' (2017) para 5.
[55] Swiss Rules of International Arbitration, art 16.3. See also Swiss Arbitration Center Guidelines for Arbitrators, para 4.
[56] ICC, Note to Parties and Arbitral Tribunals on the Conduct of the Arbitration (1 January 2021) para 220.
[57] The UNCITRAL, 'Notes on Organizing Arbitral Proceedings' (2016) para 37, indicate that Secretaries are expected to be and remain impartial and independent during the arbitral proceedings. It is the arbitral tribunal's responsibility to ensure this. Some arbitral tribunals do this by requesting the secretary to sign a declaration of independence and impartiality.
[58] LCIA Rules (2020), arts 14.9, 14.14; LCIA, 'Notes for Arbitrators', s 8.3, paras 74(d), 78.
[59] SCC Arbitration Rules, art 24(4).
[60] HKIAC Administered Arbitration Rules, r 13.4; HKIAC, 'Guidelines on the Use of a Secretary', Guideline 2.2.

[61] Practice Note for Administered Cases on the Appointment of Administrative Secretaries, para 4.
[62] BVI IAC Arbitration Rules (2021), app 3, art 1, para 2(b).
[63] ACICA, 'Guideline on the Use of Tribunal Secretaries' (2017) para 4.
[64] Swiss Rules of International Arbitration, art 16.3.
[65] LCIA Rules (2020), arts 10, 14.15; LCIA, 'Notes for Arbitrators', s 8.4, para 80.
[66] SCC Arbitration Rules, art 24(5).
[67] HKIAC, 'Guidelines on the Use of a Secretary', Guidelines 2.7-2.9.
[68] BVI IAC Arbitration Rules (2021), app 3, art 4.
[69] ACICA, 'Guideline on the Use of Tribunal Secretaries' (2017) para 7.
[70] Swiss Rules of International Arbitration, art 16.3.

20

The Reasoned Award

Bruno Simma and Jan Ortgies[*]

All that is necessary is that the arbitrators should set out what, on their view of the evidence, did or did not happen and should explain succinctly why, in the light of what happened, they have reached their decision and what that decision is. This is all that is meant by a 'reasoned award'. (Lord Justice Donaldson)[1]

I. Introduction

When a topic that is the subject of one, or rather two,[2] chapters of a book on the 'Award in International Investment Arbitration', has already been dealt with in countless further treatises and even encyclopaedia entries,[3] and has already been perfectly

* All views and opinions expressed are solely those of the authors and do not represent views or opinions of the Iran–United States Claims Tribunal or the Register of Damages for Ukraine.

1 *Bremer Handelsgesellschaft mbH v Westzucker GmbH (No 2) Westzucker GmbH v Bunge GmbH*, Court of Appeal (1981) 2 Lloyd's Rep 130, 132–33. The quoted sentence, however, was addressed to 'trade arbitrators' that might have had to amend their practices after the introduction of a new arbitration act in the United Kingdom in 1979. Nevertheless, later, the quote appears to have developed a life of its own and been found fitting for a wide range of arbitral reasoning; see Lord Justice Bingham, 'Reasons and Reasons for Reasons: Differences between a Court Judgment and an Arbitration Award' (1988) 4(2) Arbitration International 141, 150ff; Gary B Born, '§23.03 Requirement that International Arbitral Awards Be Reasoned' in Gary B Born (ed), *International Commercial Arbitration* (3rd edn, Kluwer 2021) 3290, 3294; Toby Landau, 'Reasons for Reasons: The Tribunal's Duty in Investor-State Arbitration' in Albert Jan van den Berg (ed), *50 Years of the New York Convention* (Kluwer 2009) 187.

2 See also SI Strong, 'An Empirical Analysis of Legal Reasoning: Comparing Investment Arbitration and International Commercial Arbitration' in Katia Fach Gómez and Catharine Titi (eds), *The Award in International Investment Arbitration* (OUP 2024).

3 eg Bruno Simma and Jan U Ortgies, 'Duty to Give Reasons' in Hélène Ruiz Fabri (ed), *The Max Planck Encyclopedia of International Procedural Law* (OUP forthcoming) <www.mpeipro.com>; Guillermo Aguilar Alvarez and W Michael Reisman, 'How Well Are Investment Awards Reasoned?' in Guillermo Aguilar Alvarez and W Michael Reisman (eds), *The Reasons Requirement in International Investment Arbitration* (Martinus Nijhoff 2008) 1; Bingham (n 1); Born (n 1) 3290; Romain Dupeyré, 'Les limites de l'obligation de motivation: de la concision des sentences arbitrales' (2006) 19 Revue Québécoise de droit international 41; Pierre Lalive, 'On the Reasoning of International Arbitral Awards' (2010) Journal of International Dispute Settlement 55; Landau (n 1) 187; Bart Legum and Jungmin Cho, 'Annulment: International Centre for Settlement of Investment Disputes (ICSID)' in Hélène Ruiz Fabri (ed), *The Max Planck Encyclopedia of International Procedural Law* (OUP 2018); William W Park and Jeremy Bloomenthal, 'Rule 59' Richard Happ and Stephan Wilske (eds), *ICSID Rules and Regulations 2022: Article-by-Article Commentary* (Beck 2022) 597; Eduardo Silva Romero, Audrey Caminades, and Amir A Farhadi, 'Article 48' in Julien Fouret, Rémy Gerbay, and Gloria M Alvarez (eds), *The ICSID Convention, Regulations and Rules: A Practical Commentary* (Edward Elgar Publishing 2019) 495; Hélène Ruiz Fabri and Jean-Marc Sorel (eds), *La motivation des décisions des jurisdictions internationales* (Pedone 2008); Frederick Schauer, 'Giving Reasons' (1995) 47 Stanford Law Review 633; SI Strong, 'Reasoned Awards in International Commercial Arbitration: Embracing and Exceeding the Common Law–Civil Law Dichotomy' (2015) 37 Michigan Journal of International Law 1; SI Strong, *Legal Reasoning across Commercial Disputes—Comparing Judicial and Arbitral Analyses* (OUP 2020); Jeffrey Sullivan and Naomi Briercliffe, 'Article 52(1)E' in Fouret, Gerbay, and Alvarez (n 3) 634; Hugh Thirlway, 'Judgments of International Courts and Tribunals' in R Wolfrum (ed), *The Max Planck*

Bruno Simma and Jan Ortgies, *The Reasoned Award* In: *The Award in International Investment Arbitration*. Edited by: Katia Fach Gómez and Catharine Titi, Oxford University Press. © Katia Fach Gómez and Aikaterini Titi 2024. DOI: 10.1093/9780191975936.003.0020

delineated and described in fewer than four lines by an eminent English Lord, Lord Justice Donaldson, in the case quoted above more than forty years ago, then the drafting of one of those chapters becomes an exercise in humility and, hopefully, precision.

What thus is there to say about the 'reasoned award' in international investment arbitration under the more global header of 'award drafting' that Lord Justice Donaldson has not said already and better? What can we add to further elucidate his four-liner?

II. The Duty to Provide a Reasoned Award

To start with, while this was not always so certain in commercial arbitration, it is fully accepted and agreed that a duty to give reasons for any award, and in fact any (important) decision in an international investment arbitration exists. Award drafting in investment arbitration must lead to a reasoned award. Article 48(3) of the Convention on the Settlement of Investment Disputes between States and Nationals of other States (ICSID Convention), for example, reads: 'The award shall deal with every question submitted to the Tribunal, and shall state the reasons upon which it is based.'[4]

The International Centre for Settlement of Investment Disputes (ICSID) Arbitration Rules of 2022 (ICSID Rules) go even further by requiring that also orders and decisions 'shall indicate the reasons upon which they are made', including even decisions on costs and decisions whether to permit a non-disputing party submission (Rules 27(2), 52(4), 59(1)(j), 67(5)),[5] before, more in line with the ICSID Convention, requiring that the award contain 'the decision of the Tribunal on every question submitted to it, and the reasons on which the Award is based' (Rule 59(1)(i)).

Article 31(2) of the United Nations Commission on International Trade Law (UNCITRAL) Model Law on International Commercial Arbitration of 1985, with amendments as adopted in 2006, reads: 'The award shall state the reasons upon which it is based, unless the parties have agreed that no reasons are to be given or the award is an award on agreed terms under article 30',[6] while Article 34(3) of the UNCITRAL Arbitration Rules prescribes that '[t]he arbitral tribunal shall state the reasons upon which the award is based, unless the parties have agreed that no reasons are to be given'.[7]

Encyclopedia of Public International Law (OUP 2007); Strong 'An Empirical Analysis of Legal Reasoning' (n 2); Hindelang and Nassl (n 9); Karsten Nowrot and Emily Sipiorski, 'Review beyond Annulment: Correction, Additional Awards, Clarification, and Revision' in Fach Gómez and Titi (n 2); Marc Bungenberg, Andrés E Alvarado-Garzón, and Bianca Böhme, 'Recognition and Enforcement of ICSID Convention Awards' in Fach Gómez and Titi (n 2); Giuditta Cordero-Moss, 'Recognition and Enforcement of Non-ICSID Convention Awards' ibid.

[4] Convention on the Settlement of Investment Disputes between States and Nationals of other States (opened for signature 18 March 1965, entered into force 14 October 1966) 575 UNTS 159 (ICSID Convention).

[5] ICSID, 'ICSID Arbitration Rules' (2022) (ICSID Rules). In contrast, International Court of Justice (ICJ) on the reasoning of a decision on costs in *Application for Review of Judgement No. 158 of the United Nations Administrative Tribunal*, Advisory Opinion [1973] ICJ Rep 166 (*UNAT Opinion*) [97], [98].

[6] UNCITRAL, 'Model Law on International Commercial Arbitration' (2006) UN Doc A/61/17, Annex I.

[7] UNCITRAL, 'Arbitration Rules' (2021) (UNCITRAL Rules).

The duty to give reasons is thus firmly rooted in the treaty provisions, rules, and laws applicable to virtually all investment arbitrations worldwide.[8] What is more, the requirement to issue a reasoned award is given further force by indirect means through the annulment procedure at ICSID and the threat of non-recognition and non-enforcement or setting aside of unreasoned awards for investor-state awards stemming from other fora than ICSID.[9]

Under Article 52(1)(e) of the ICSID Convention, it is a ground for annulment of an award 'that the award has failed to state the reasons on which it is based'. Where the law of the seat of an investment arbitration is of relevance and mirrors the UNCITRAL Model Law with a view to the duty to give reasons, a lack of 'sufficient' reasoning would reflect an arbitral procedure not in accordance with the applicable arbitration law, or a violation of the public policy of the seat. That is the case even on the off chance that the parties to such an arbitration had not agreed on rules of arbitration requiring the giving of reasons, or had agreed on rules that are silent on the duty. Such a defect would then open up the award to successful set-aside proceedings under Article 34 of the UNCITRAL Model Law and to the refusal of its recognition and enforcement under Article V(1)(d) or (2)(b) of the New York Convention.

That an award in an investment arbitration must be a reasoned award is thus also firmly assured indirectly, which is remarkable for a type of adjudication that is based on a one-round procedure and very limited review. It means that the giving of reasons is deemed to be of such importance that it is worthy of making the short list of elements to be scrutinized in the limited review of an investment arbitration award.

It is, finally, of note in that regard that under Article 49(2) of the ICSID Convention and Rule 61 of the ICSID Rules, parties that feel that a question was not decided by the tribunal can request the tribunal to rectify that situation. Failure to do so by a party arguably closes the window for that party to have an award annulled on that ground. That is at least if the question is sufficiently separable from the rest of the reasoning of the award not subject to a request under Article 49(2) of the ICSID Convention. However, it appears that most ad hoc committees are quite ready to assume that any such question is linked to the remainder of an award to an extent that the remedy of annulment is open irrespective of whether Article 49(2) of the ICSID Convention was relied on in an orderly and timely manner, or not.[10]

Article 39(1) of the UNCITRAL Rules allows a party to 'request the arbitral tribunal to make an award or an additional award as to claims presented in the arbitral

[8] The options for parties to opt out of the requirement in that regard must be considered rather theoretical. However, an award on agreed terms would not need to be reasoned. See also Gabriel Bottini, 'Consent Awards' in Fach Gómez and Titi (n 2).

[9] See also Steffen Hindelang and Julia Nassl, 'Annulment and Set-aside' in Fach Gómez and Titi (n 2); Bungenberg, Alvarado-Garzón, and Böhme (n 3).

[10] See also Park and Bloomenthal (n 3) 603, para 41; Silva Romero, Caminades, and Farhadi (n 3) 495, paras 4.740–4.745; Sullivan and Briercliffe (n 3) paras 4.1111–4.1113; *MINE v Guinea*, ICSID Case No ARB/84/4, Decision on Annulment (22 December 1989) (*MINE v Guinea*) [5.12], [5.13]; *WENA Hotels Ltd v Egypt*, ICSID Case No ARB/98/4 (2002), Decision on Application for Annulment (28 January 2002) (*Wena v Egypt*) [80], [101]. See also Karsten Nowrot and Emily Spiorski 'Review Beyond Annulment: Correction, Clarification, Interpretation, Additional Award' in Fach Gómez and Titi (n 2).

proceedings but not decided by the arbitral tribunal'. The Article thus provides an option mirroring the one under Article 49(2) of the ICSID Convention.[11]

III. What Is a Reasoned Award in International Investment Arbitration?

But what then makes an award a reasoned award in compliance with the duty to provide such an award? What is the scope of the duty to give reasons in international investment arbitration? The answer is threefold and applies to all decisions in international investment arbitration, not only to awards. First, in principle, Lord Donaldson's four-liner is an apt summary of what constitutes a reasoned award, even though it deals with commercial arbitration, trade arbitration even, and was addressed to trade professionals, laymen in law, more than forty years ago.

Second, what this will mean *in concreto*, for a specific award or decision, will, as so often in law, depend on all circumstances of a case, including the applicable treaty and arbitration agreement, the nature of the decision, the substance, timing, and addressee(s) of the decision, and whether the decision deals with eg law, procedure, or facts.[12] In reviewing those circumstances, the evaluation of whether an award is a reasoned award will then often be couched in terms of 'sufficiency'. That is a criticized term, and to be avoided where more precise language avails itself, but a necessary term once one accepts that the question what a reasoned award is, and what the duty to provide such an award entails, at least in practice, is not a binary one of reasons having been given or not.[13]

Third, given that, as outlined above, investment arbitration awards know a review for lack of reasoning, review decisions will provide the most relevant background as to the scope of what makes an award a reasoned award and what does not. On that third point a few observations can be made.

A. Who Is the Judge of What a Reasoned Award Is in Investment Arbitration?

As a first observation, it is important to recall that both national courts applying set-aside criteria or criteria for non-recognition and enforcement as well as ICSID ad hoc committees will approach existing decisions and reasoning in international investment

[11] On Article 39, see also David Caron and Lee M Caplan, *The UNCITRAL Arbitration Rules: A Commentary* (2nd edn, OUP 2013) 821.

[12] cf also *Tulip Real Estate and Development Netherlands BV v Turkey*, ICSID Case No ARB/11/28, Decision on Annulment (30 December 2015) (*Tulip*) [152].

[13] Sullivan and Briercliffe (n 3) paras 4.1094–4.1099; See also *Hussein Nuaman Soufraki v United Arab Emirates*, ICSID Case No ARB/02/7, Decision on Annulment (5 June 2007) (*Soufraki*) [122], [123].

awards brought before them with great deference and will only formally, not substantially, review the existing reasoning.

The Paris Court of Appeals, just as one example of an important court in that regard, recently considered with a view to an international arbitration award that 'le contrôle du juge de l'annulation ne porte que sur l'existence et non sur la pertinence des motifs de la sentence'.[14] This deference will be even greater when it comes to investor-state cases which are usually decided on the basis of public international law—a field where the expertise in the law more clearly lies with the tribunal as opposed to the domestic court than in cases in which national commercial law is the focus.

ICSID ad hoc committees equally held that 'within the framework of the Convention [the award] is not subject to review on the merits';[15] that a 'Committee does not have the authority to reassess the merits of the dispute or to substitute the Tribunal's determination by its own convictions';[16] and that the substance of an argument is not subject to review.[17] Such committees also held that the 'adequacy of the reasoning is not an appropriate standard of review under paragraph (1)(e)' of Article 52 of the ICSID Convention,[18] and that an ad hoc committee must try to avoid engaging in 'the appreciation of the quality of the reasons'.[19] 'Article 52(1)(e) [of the ICSID Convention] does not allow a committee to assess the correctness or persuasiveness of the reasoning in the award or to inquire into the quality of the reasons.'[20] It is furthermore important that in any such procedure—annulment, recognition, enforcement, or set-aside—the complainant will also bear the burden of proof and will be bound by short deadlines.

The above means de facto that, except for the most extreme scenarios, the tribunal itself, to a large degree, will be the judge of what degree of reasoning its award requires. It also arguably means that a 'reasoned award' and the duty to provide such an award have a wider scope than what is protected by the limited review of such awards. That means that the quality a reasoned award should have exceeds the minimum quality that is protected and thus required by the limited review of investment arbitration awards. Or, in other words, an investment arbitration tribunal, arguably, has a duty to aim higher than the minimum threshold under which an award would be set aside or annulled, if and as applicable.

[14] *Instrubel NV v Ministries of Finance and Economy of Iraq, Salah Al Din intervening, Cour d'appel de Paris*, First Chamber, Judgment of 20 November 2018, No RG 16/10379 (Jonction avec le No RG 16/10381) No Portalis 35L7-V-B7A-BYYUT (*Instrubel v Iraq*); Robert M Hall, 'So What Is an Arbitration "Reasoned Award" Anyway?' (2019) 29 Mealey's Litigation Report: Reinsurance, No 24.

[15] *MINE v Guinea* [4.02].

[16] *Tidewater Investment SRL and Tidewater Caribe, CA v Venezuela*, ICSID Case No ARB/10/5, Decision on Annulment (27 December 2016) (*Tidewater*) [166].

[17] *MINE v Guinea* [6.53].

[18] ibid [5.08].

[19] *Tidewater* [168].

[20] *Impregilo SpA v Argentina*, ICSID Case No ARB/07/17, Decision on Annulment (24 January 2014) (*Impregilo*), [180], [181]. See also Legum and Cho (n 3) paras 3, 5, 46; Thirlway (n 3) paras 43–46.

B. Requirements for an Award to Be Considered 'Reasoned'

That said, from the above, and the wider scholarship on the reasoning of arbitral decisions and the duty to give reasons, as well as from the practice of international arbitration and adjudication, the following can be distilled.

1. Different Decisions Require Different Reasoning

To start with, different decisions require different reasoning. A procedural order will require less exhaustive reasoning than a final award; a decision on costs, the filing of documents, or a timetable, less than a decision on the merits of a case. Granting of a request can sometimes require less reasoning than dismissing a request, and vice versa, etc.

Where the interpretation of a provision is, in fact, to be seen as the result requested and expected from a decision, the reasoning of that decision is its result, and must be particularly thorough. Equally, decisions that affect individuals, while highly unusual, but not unheard of in investment arbitration, would arguably require more exhaustive reasoning than those between professional parties.

Decisions on requests for interim relief or emergency measures will require less reasoning than a final decision in the main proceeding. However, it appears established that such decisions must also make the 'why' of their result clear. The same holds true for oral decisions, though decisions 'from the bench' during a hearing would, depending on all circumstances, often not require reasons or explanations exceeding a sentence or two at all.

Decisions on document production will not normally need to be reasoned or exhaustively reasoned. Especially in the so-called Redfern Schedules, a mere 'dismissed' or 'granted', potentially with a reference to the relevant article in the International Bar Association Rules on the Taking of Evidence in International Arbitration of 2020 will often suffice.[21] Some decisions may not require any reasoning at all: orders on small technical issues not involving substantial questions of law, fact, or procedure, for example, or the well-known Procedural Order No 1.

As is apparent from the above, it is of less relevance how the decision in question is named. An important decision on jurisdiction, an *Achmea*-type decision, for example, or a decision not to hear a witness, or not to allow an assertedly important submission, or any decision seemingly deviating from the ordinary, may very well require more exhaustive reasoning than an award on damages, especially if that award applies simple law or follows purely mathematical principles and leads to an expected result. This is despite the fact that one decision may be merely a procedural order and the other one an award.

[21] IBA, 'IBA Rules on the Taking of Evidence in International Arbitration' (2020).

2. No Need to Address Every Argument or Question or to Refrain from Succinct Dismissals

A reasoned investment award does not mean that a decision needs to entertain and resolve every argument and counterargument of the parties, or that their every request or question needs to be dealt with in the same detail.[22] The requirement to issue a reasoned award does not even oblige a tribunal to base itself on any of the arguments presented as the winning argument (*iura novit curia*; this may be different for 'winning' facts and of course requires a tribunal to tread carefully in order to stay within the scope of the submission to arbitration).[23]

Naturally, a decision should describe the result it reaches in respect of every request relevant for that decision and, as noted above, in respect of every question, that is every 'head of claim',[24] submitted to the tribunal. However, much like national decision-makers, drafters of international investment arbitration awards are free, and in the interest of judicial economy even encouraged, to focus on the relevant arguments and requests and dismiss summarily, also in bulk, irrelevant or, due to the decision, no longer relevant questions and arguments, eg alternative arguments.[25] A reasoned award also does not require that the drafters give the same room to arguments as one or more parties did, although it can of course raise questions if an argument that parties deemed to be central to a dispute is left out of an award without a good reason.

Tribunals also do not have to follow a party's attempt to try every possible argument rather than to develop one or two winning arguments. Generally speaking, a reasoning why a certain avenue was not followed or a certain argument or request was found meritless can also be much more succinct than the elaboration of the argument and analysis that eventually leads to the result, ie the argument that the tribunal picks as the winning argument.

3. No Particular Requirements as to Format, Place, Style, and Structure of the Reasoning

For ICSID awards, Rule 59 of the ICSID Rules mandates that an award contain a brief summary of the proceeding, a statement of the relevant facts as found by the tribunal, a brief summary of the submissions of the parties, including the relief sought, the decision of the tribunal on every question submitted to it, the reasons on which the award is based, and a reasoned decision on costs. According to Eduardo Silva Romero, Audrey Caminades, and Amir Farhadi, the drafting history of Article 48(3) of the ICSID

[22] *MCI Power Group L.C and New Turbine Inc v Ecuador*, ICSID Case No ARB/03/6, Decision on Annulment (19 October 2009) (*MCI v Ecuador*) [67]; Park and Bloomenthal (n 3) 603, para 40; Silva Romero, Caminades, and Farhadi (n 3) paras 4.727, 4.760; Sullivan and Briercliffe (n 3) paras 4.1085ff; *Compañía de Aguas del Aconquija SA and Vivendi Universal SA v Argentina*, ICSID Case No ARB/97/3, Decision on Annulment (20 August 2007, 10 August 2010) (*Vivendi II*), [248].

[23] Fulvio M Palombino, 'Judicial Economy' in Hélène Ruiz Fabri (ed), *The Max Planck Encyclopedia of International Procedural Law* (OUP 2020) para 20. See also Attila M Tanzi, 'On the Adjudicative Discretion of Investment Arbitrators: Between *ne ultra petita, ne infra petita*, and *jura novit curia*' in Fach Gómez and Titi (n 2).

[24] Silva Romero, Caminades, and Farhadi (n 3) paras 4.723, 4.724.

[25] See also Park and Bloomenthal (n 3) 603, para 39; Silva Romero, Caminades, and Farhadi (n 3) para 4.728; *United Mexican States v Metalclad*, 2001 BCSC 664 [121], [122]; Aguilar Alvarez and Reisman (n 3) 1, 12, n 13.

Convention also makes it clear that an ICSID award must identify the applicable law.[26] All of these formal requirements together, to some degree, force a certain structure and minimum content on an award that may go beyond what is necessary just for the purposes of sound reasoning.[27]

However, for the reasoning itself, there are no general rules on the structure, sequence, or the format of the reasons to be given.[28] There is also no mandatory reasoning style to make an award a reasoned award, eg a strict German *Gutachten-* or *Urteilsstil*, or the succinct style of a French judge. An award will also be considered a reasoned award if it deals with too many arguments, does not start with the main argument, or, in terms of sequence of the argument, needlessly addresses the merits before dismissing a request for lack of jurisdiction. *Obiter dicta*, while controversial in the context of judicial reasoning in arbitration, and, if not drafted with the necessary care, liable to exceed the scope of the submission to arbitration, do not undo the qualification of an award as a reasoned award. A reasoning can also not be so long or exhaustive that it would be considered 'too long' for a reasoned award, although such a reasoning of course would carry its own set of problems, and some have even argued that 'motiver trop longuement . . . peut aboutir à ne pas réellement motiver'.[29]

Understandability of a decision in accordance with general rules of logic/syllogism and reasonableness will be decisive in measuring whether an award is a reasoned award.[30] Therefore, a reasoned award or decision can also require a certain degree of inferences to be drawn by its reader or consist of a combination of arguments (and facts) to be found at different places in it. It can consist of a calculation of numbers, a table, a Redfern Schedule, or a reference to an earlier decision of the same or another tribunal/court or the argument of one of the parties together with an expression of agreement by the tribunal.[31] However, a mere combination of copied and pasted elements or references to other documents, or a decision that is clearly not tailored to a case (at all) will likely not suffice. The ad hoc committee in *Wena v Egypt*, for example, stated:

> Neither Article 48(3) nor Article 52(1)(e) [of the ICSID Convention] specify the manner in which the Tribunal's reasons are to be stated. The object of both provisions is to ensure that the Parties will be able to understand the Tribunal's reasoning. This goal does not require that each reason be stated expressly. The Tribunal's reasons may be implicit in the considerations and conclusions contained in the award, provided they can be reasonably inferred from the terms used in the decision.[32]

[26] Silva Romero, Caminades, and Farhadi (n 3) paras 4.756, 4.757; *MINE v Guinea* [5.09].

[27] For a discussion of this minimum content of the award, see Catharine Titi, 'What Is an Award? Concept, Content, Drafting, Effects' in Fach Gómez and Titi (n 2).

[28] See also Silva Romero, Caminades, and Farhadi (n 3) para 4.761.

[29] Gilbert Guillaume, 'Commentaire' in Ruiz Fabri and Sorel (n 3) 91, 93.

[30] See also Park and Bloomenthal (n 3) 605, para 46; Sullivan and Briercliffe (n 3) para 4.1080.

[31] See also Sullivan and Briercliffe (n 3) paras 4.1084ff; *Vivendi II* [249]–[251]; *Tulip* [108]; *Impregilo* [190], [201].

[32] *Wena v Egypt* [81].

The ad hoc committee in *Tidewater* held that '[r]easons may be long or succinct, they may be exhaustive or "baldly stated", they may quote heavily from preceding decisions or ague without referencing any—the difference of style or effort to convince the Parties is no reason to discredit reasons'.[33] In addition, the ad hoc committee in *Vivendi I* stated that 'reasons may be stated succinctly or at length, and different legal traditions differ in their modes of expressing reasons. Tribunals must be allowed a degree of discretion as to the way in which they express their reasoning.'[34]

4. No Duty to Provide Objectively Correct Reasoning

Finally, an incorrectly reasoned award is also a reasoned award. Not only an objectively correct reasoning, or a reasoning that is objectively fully substantiated by the facts and arguments of a case constitutes a reasoning that makes an award a reasoned award. The duty to give reasons in an award is a safeguarding measure to avoid incorrect reasoning. It is meant to make sure that the process of reasoning takes place and that the advantages of that process to the quality of the result of the decision-making materializes. It is not a guarantee of the flawlessness of that result and it is not meant to directly, rather than indirectly, protect against the risk of a flawed reasoning and a flawed decision or award.[35] The ad hoc committee in *MINE v Guinea* even went so far as to state that 'a manifestly incorrect application of the law . . . is not a ground for annulment',[36] while the ad hoc committee in *Vivendi I* stated that '[p]rovided that the reasons given by a tribunal can be followed and relate to the issues that were before the tribunal, their correctness is beside the point in terms of Article 52(1)(e)'.[37]

However, there are of course limits to such freedom. Reasoning is a process of logic/syllogism and common sense that works in steps, starting at a beginning, and leading to a result at the end. Therefore, evidently incorrect assumptions or interpretations of fact and law and obvious errors will cause gaps in the logical structure of a reasoning. Such gaps can then, potentially sooner than later, lead to a decision being so logically flawed, so 'full of gaps', that the logic of the decision could, or even should, be deemed not to work to a degree that equals the absence of reasons, ie to a degree that the decision is incompliant with the requirement to provide a reasoned award.

5. Lack of Reasoning, Contradictory Reasoning, and Frivolous Reasoning

What amount of reasoning would equal no reasoning at all, however, or when exactly flaws or evident errors in the reasoning of a decision equal the inexistence of (that part) of the reasoning is unclear beyond immediately evident cases and will depend on all circumstances of a case. Arguably, a reasoning equals no reasoning when even with good will and deference and the willingness to imply some findings and arguments

33 *Tidewater* [168] (footnote omitted).

34 *Compañía de Aguas del Aconquija SA and Vivendi Universal (formerly Compagnie Générale des Eaux) v Argentina*, ICSID Case No ARB/97/3, Decision on Annulment (3 July 2002) (*Vivendi I*) [64].

35 See also Silva Romero, Caminades, and Farhadi (n 3) para 4.761; *Wena v Egypt*, para 99.

36 *MINE v Guinea* [5.08].

37 *Vivendi I* [64].

and disregard some errors, a person of the relevant higher education is unable to follow the reasoning from the beginning to its most important results—even though that person had access to the record of a case and all information the original decision-maker had, or should have had. Or, in the words of the ad hoc committee in *MINE v Guinea*, when the reader is not 'enable[d] . . . to follow how the tribunal proceeded from Point A to Point B and eventually to its conclusion', independent of whether the reasoning contains errors of fact and law; the reader would not be enabled to do so, the ad hoc committee adds, however, if the reasoning is frivolous or contradictory.[38] Or, in other words, in the words of the ad hoc committee in *Tidewater*, reasoning would equal no reasoning when 'the reasons developed by the Tribunal have [not] enabled the addressees of the Award . . . to understand the process leading to its conclusions'.[39]

In any case, where there is doubt whether a tribunal succeeded in delivering a reasoned award with sufficient and sufficiently clear reasoning, the presumption appears to be that it did.[40] Further arguably, an obvious and serious computational error, that is left intact despite a correction request, would likely have to be seen as making the reasoning on that part of a decision so flawed or 'contradictory' that it would have to be regarded as equal to no reasoning at all.[41]

What, however, contradictions would consist of, outside the evident cases of stating the actual complete ('genuine') opposite to an earlier statement,[42] and when they would constitute a fatal stop to a logical chain, rather than a misstep, is a subjective assessment, open to criticism. The annulment decision in *MINE v Guinea* which otherwise appears to have set the standard for the review of ICSID awards on the ground of lack of a failure to state reasons, for example, was criticized for finding that the reasoning of the original tribunal was contradictory when it may not actually have been *stricto sensu*.[43]

The label 'frivolous' has equally, and rightly, been criticized as not sharp enough and too subjective, and distracting from the test, set out above, of the 'reasonable, attentive and willing reader' that either is able to understand the reasoning of a tribunal or not.[44] This once more shows that, practically speaking, a reasoning

[38] *Mine v Guinea* [5.09], see also [5.08]. See also Silva Romero, Caminades, and Farhadi (n 3) para 4.762 who use the phrase 'devoid of any sense'; Maxi Scherer and Danielle Morris, 'Rule 47—The Award' in Fouret, Gerbay, and Alvarez (n 3) 1234, para 26.53; Legum and Cho (n 3).

[39] *Tidewater* [172]; or in the words of the ad hoc committee in *Impregilo* [180] 'whether the reasoning would [not] allow an informed reader to understand how the Tribunal reached its conclusions'; 'If the reasoning of the Arbitral Tribunal with respect to an award cannot be understood by the parties and an informed reader, the reasons and basis for the award cannot be considered to have been stated' ibid [181].

[40] cf also *Vivendi II* [247](iii).

[41] On a quantum reasoning, see eg *Tidewater* [191].

[42] The first-ever annulment decision, *Klöckner Industrie-Anlagen GmbH v Cameroon and Société Camerounaise des Engrais*, ICSID Case No ARB/81/2, Decision on Annulment (3 May 1985) [116] speaks of 'genuinely contradictory reasons' and is later often quoted in that regard.

[43] It has been observed in that regard that dismissing two damages theories for being too speculative and then eventually applying a third theory also based on hypotheses rather than real values is, *stricto sensu*, not necessarily a contradiction, but may rather indicate a lack of an explanation how that step was reached. Sullivan and Briercliffe (n 3) paras 4.1102–4.1106; *MINE v Guinea* [6.107]; *Tidewater* [170], cf however, also [189]; *Vivendi I* [65]; *Tulip* [109]–[112].

[44] *Tidewater* [169].

equals no reasoning when the ad hoc committee or the set-aside judge finds it so.[45]

In that regard it is notable, for example, that domestic judges dealing with requests to recognize, enforce, or set aside arbitral awards, will often consider only such reasoning as equalling an unreasoned award that displays an actual (near) total lack of reasoning or a reasoning that is so flawed that it de facto equals a (near) total lack of reasoning. Those domestic judges would not soon consider an award including a wrong interpretation or application of law to be an unreasoned award, even if that wrong application would make the reasoning incorrect. Rather, such an outcome would likely be seen as a risk of having subjected oneself to arbitration.

6. Separate, Concurring, and Dissenting Opinions

Finally, it is, accepted that different reasons can lead to the same result and that a majority decision is not (fatally) undermined, often rather strengthened, by separate and concurring opinions that lead to, or accept, the same result (cf Article 48(4) of the ICSID Convention, Rule 59(3) of the ICSID Rules on dissents).[46]

C. Consequences of Not Issuing a Reasoned Award

An award in violation of the duty to issue a reasoned award, or rather an award that lacks reasoning to a degree that reviewing bodies are inclined to step in and find it is not reasoned, will be annulled (ICSID) or set aside, not recognized, and not enforced (UNCITRAL Rules and Model Law) under the applicable rules and laws—subject of course to the request to do so having been filed in a timely and orderly manner.

An annulment or the setting aside of an award could affect the whole decision or only a part of it.[47] That is different for a decision not being an award. If such a decision lacks sufficient reasoning, it will likely only be subject to review and—indirect—consequences once a later award is rendered. This will be done by subjecting that later award to review.

Importantly, as sort of a 'middle-ground' option, ad hoc committees have preserved for themselves the option, rather than to annul an award, to further explain the reasoning of the original tribunal in order to bring it to a standard that makes annulment unnecessary.[48]

Interestingly, and correctly, the ad hoc committee in *Tidewater* observes in that regard that intent or inadvertency is no criterion in the determination of the sufficiency and logic of a certain reasoning. From the point of view of a reviewer of an award,

[45] Some ad hoc committees even argue that they have a degree of discretion under Article 52(3) of the ICSID Convention as to whether an annullable error must lead to annulment; *Vivendi I* [67]; *Vivendi II* [252].

[46] On dissenting opinions, see Charles N Brower and Ahmed Mazlom, 'To Err Is Human, to Dissent Divine' in Fach Gómez and Titi (n 2).

[47] If that is possible under the applicable law and rules and if the part is discernible from the rest of the award.

[48] See for example, *Wena v Egypt* [83]; *Vivendi II* [63]; *Soufraki* [6]; *Tulip* [108].

the reasoning of that award is an objective fact in relation to which it does not matter whether possible flaws in that reasoning stem from deliberate acts of a tribunal or minor or gross negligence.[49]

D. Conclusion on the Contents of a Reasoned Award

In conclusion, a reasoned award is neither subject to a length requirement nor an enemy of judicial economy. The requirement to draft a reasoned award will normally have been complied with when a decision is sufficiently tailored to the facts of a case and the issues it is asked to resolve and when the award makes it sufficiently clear and understandable as a matter of logic why it reached the result it reached. Thus, at the end of the day, what Justice Donaldson told trade arbitrators in commercial arbitration is also sound advice for arbitrators in international investment law.[50]

IV. Advantages and Disadvantages of a Reasoned Award and the Requirement to Produce One

What are then the advantages and disadvantages of a reasoned award and the requirement to produce one?[51]

A. Advantages

1. Rational as Opposed to Arbitrary Decision-Making

For the parties subject to a decision but also from a broader, political perspective, the giving of reasons provides a decision with the (appearance of) rationality and signals that a rational decision-making process, as opposed to arbitrary decision-making, has taken place. Reasons are an essential part of transparency as an overarching, general

[49] *Tidewater* [194].

[50] Compare also Silva Romero, Caminades, and Farhadi, stating that '[a]s a rule, a tribunal's reasoning must: (i) go to matters of fact and law, and (ii) allow the award to meet the low threshold of intelligibility' ((n 3) para 4.755). Or the ad hoc committee in *Wena v Egypt* speaking of 'the Tribunal's duty to identify, and to let the parties know, the factual and legal premises leading the Tribunal to its decision', calling it a 'sequence of reasons' (ibid [79]).

[51] Lists of the advantages and disadvantages of reasoned awards and judicial and administrative decisions, similar to the list in this chapter have been presented many a time in more or less detail and have inspired each other over the years. See eg Simma and Ortgies (n 3); Born (n 1) 3290; Lori F Damrosch, 'Article 56' in Andreas Zimmermann, Karin Oellers-Frahm, Christian Tomuschat, and Christian J Tams (eds), *The Statute of the International Court of Justice: A Commentary* (2nd edn, 2012) OUP 1366, 1368; Hélène Ruiz Fabri, 'La motivation des décisions dans le règlement des différends de l'OMC' in Ruiz Fabri and Sorel (n 3) 103, 120–23; Schauer (n 3) 656–59, Joana Mendes, 'The Foundations of the Duty to Give Reasons and a Normative Reconstruction' in Elizabeth Fisher, Jeff King, and Alison L Young (eds), *The Foundations and Future of Public Law* (OUP 2020) 299, 300; Strong, 'Reasoned Awards in International Commercial Arbitration (n 3) 15–20; Jarrod Hepburn, 'The Duty to Give Reasons for Administrative Decisions in International Law' (2012) 61 International & Comparative Law Quarterly 641, 644; Silva Romero, Caminades, and Farhadi (n 3) paras 4.747–4.754.

principle of international procedural law.[52] This is of particular importance in investment arbitration, which is not the biggest culprit in terms of a lack of transparency at all, but is the first and foremost addressee of allegations of a lack of transparency.

2. Visibility and Retraceability

Reasons are furthermore easier to retrace and understand than mere results and they increase the accountability of the tribunal and the decision-making process. They create visibility on how the task of the decision-maker was discharged and are, for example, proof that the right to be heard was accorded, that arguments and requests were dealt with, and that decision-making took place on the basis of the law, not *ex aequo et bono*.

3. Enabling the Review Process

In making awards (and decisions) more understandable and retraceable, the giving of reasons also deliberately provides attack vectors and material to subject an award to annulment or set-aside proceedings. This is of particular importance since members of the original tribunal would not normally be heard again or be able to explain themselves and their reasoning during the review of their award—their award is thus the only place where they can explain themselves.

4. Acceptance of the Decision

All of the above are important factors of their own, but, arguably, also increase acceptance of a decision. Parties to a process that ends with a reasoned award see that they have been heard and receive an explanation why the result that was reached by that process was indeed reached.

5. Self-Regulation

The duty to provide a reasoned award, however, also has an internal function for the decision-maker. It is a measure of self-regulation, self-control, and quality assurance when a drafter of a decision not only has to determine the result of a decision but also has to develop the (written) reasons for that result. After all, drafting or setting out an argument in detail is a process that will often lead to a more intimate view of the details and the strengths and weaknesses of a case, a particular argument, and an envisaged result. Indeed, the process of drafting will often lead to minor or major amendments to an originally envisaged result. Amendments which would not have been made had only the result, rather than the reasoning leading to it, been expressed in the decision.[53]

[52] Thore Neumann and Anne Peters, 'Transparency' in Hélène Ruiz Fabri (ed), *The Max Planck Encyclopedia of International Procedural Law* (OUP 2019) para 77; Thore Neumann and Bruno Simma, 'Adjudication' in Andrea Bianchi and Anne Peters (eds), *Transparency in International Law* (CUP 2013) 436, 476.

[53] Heinrich von Kleist *Über die allmähliche Verfertigung der Gedanken beim Reden* (1805); Bruno Genevois, 'Comment' in Ruiz Fabri and Sorel (n 3) 97; Bingham (n 1) 143; Strong *Legal Reasoning across Commercial Disputes* (n 3) 280–83.

6. Precedent and ***jurisprudence constante***

The role of international courts and tribunals transcends the cases before them. To some degree that is arguably also the case for tribunals in investor-state arbitrations individually, and in a more anarchic way as a group. Reasoned awards of such tribunals, therefore, create a body of case law that serves as the interpretative guidance for subjects and students of international law worldwide, and for the states and their citizens as to what is lawful behaviour in international investment law. While there is no rule of precedent in international investment law, reasoned awards nevertheless codify a certain *jurisprudence constante* which signals to future tribunals, users, and practitioners of investor-state dispute resolution how a certain treaty provision or problem would likely have to be seen and why. While more erratically and anarchically than in a system of formal precedents, reasoned awards also guard the coherence of the body of case law thus far created. As Frederick Schauer has put it, '[t]he act of giving a reason . . . is an exercise in generalization' in putting a specific result into a more general framework to which the giver of the reasons commits (to a certain degree).[54]

7. Quality and Legitimacy of the Decision-Maker

Finally, a well-reasoned and accessible decision may be an advertisement for a decision-maker or a decision-making body and an institution as a whole. It may increase the trust in the future decisions of a decision-maker, the selection of that decision-maker and the decision-making institution. The giving of reasons can also raise the legitimacy of a decision and the international institution behind it and make non-compliance with the decision and other decisions stemming from that institution (politically) more costly.

It is that last point that is of particular importance for reasoned awards in investment arbitration, given that individual awards and the system as a whole have come under fire from states and civil society. Some have argued in that regard that giving reasons is even more important for investment arbitration than for commercial arbitration. This is not least because investment arbitration is rather a form of state-to-state arbitration, based on the consent of two states, than of commercial arbitration. It involves larger interest groups than two commercial parties, namely whole states and their people, budgets, and policies. In addition, investment arbitration's legitimacy is in dispute.[55] A reasoned award in that view must function as a demonstration or advertisement of quality, thoroughness, cost-efficiency, and reasonableness towards state interests. It must further serve as a shield against the decrease in popularity of that mode of dispute resolution.

[54] Schauer (n 3) 635, 638ff, 648ff.

[55] Landau (n 1) 187.

B. Disadvantages

1. Length and Time Consumption, Tying up of Resources

The most important criticism of the requirement of a reasoned award is that adhering to it may increase the time and other resources a proceeding may consume. This is especially the case when the requirement is paired with the trend of longer and longer submissions that try every possible argument and angle to a case rather than focus on one or two winning arguments, and when it is accompanied by the prevalent fear of arbitrators that their award may be set aside for violations of the right to be heard and other due process violations. Thus, with submissions growing in length, awards and other decisions become longer too, not least due to an anxious overinterpretation of the duty to give reasons. Indeed, too broad an interpretation of the scope of the duty to give reasons in one case may then, in the next case, encourage more of the trying-every-argument and seeing-which-one-works style of pleadings, which already slows down international arbitration considerably.[56]

2. Service Not Asked For

The giving of reasons, while having all the advantages listed above, may also be a service not ordered and desired by the subjects of a decision. Especially professional parties will often be more interested in the result of a process and its final resolution, rather than in the intricate reasoning that might have led to a result (especially when it comes at the cost of longer and more costly procedures). Against this, however, stands the argument that especially states, and state-to-state procedures, require particularly exhaustive arguments to enhance the latter's legitimacy and to allow for the legitimation and post-hoc validation of a sovereign state's willingness to consent to that form of dispute resolution.[57]

3. Needlessly Facilitating Review Processes

As outlined above, it is a deliberate function of a reasoned award that it makes a decision more vulnerable to counter-arguments and review. Where financially solvent parties are involved, however, this has the downside of opening up perfectly valid decisions to an unintended appeals process that clings to every perceived minor flaw in the reasoning as a possible opening to delay the outcome of a process. It would appear in that regard that since the earlier days of investor-state arbitration, the frequency of set-aside and annulment proceedings, while still the exception rather than the norm, has increased more sharply than the number of cases in total.[58]

[56] See also Born (n 1) 3290, 3293.
[57] Landau (n 1) 187; Lalive (n 3) 55.
[58] cf for example ICSID, 'Decisions on Annulment' <https://icsid.worldbank.org/cases/content/tables-of-decisions/annulment>.

4. Overestimation of the Value of Giving Reasons

The fact that many different reasoning can lead to the same result, and that separate and concurring opinions are even an accepted practice, can also be regarded as undermining the argued need for reasoned awards. As with works of art, appreciation of language-based arguments and reasons is by necessity in the eye of the (learned) beholder. Especially in a discourse-based discipline such as the law, there will thus often be no scientifically right or wrong result to a dispute and no two people understanding the same argument and reasoning in the same way. This is a strong argument as to why only the result is important in a decision, especially if no development of the law or new, progressive interpretation of a provision is requested. In addition, there is arguably no better place to hide something than in plain sight and thus the language of law and legal reasoning have often served to hide, rather than to protect from, ill intentions, oversights, delays, arbitrary decisions, etc.[59]

5. Limiting Future Options, Burdening Future Tribunals

Schauer argues that giving reasons, even in a system without binding precedent, creates at least an 'advisory opinion' to oneself and future deciders.[60] In doing so, giving reasons comes at the price of limiting options in future cases to which the reasons of the present case apply, but may not perfectly fit. Having given reasons earlier may also stand in the way of new, rigorous, and case-specific reasoning that could lead to a different result.

In investment arbitration today, tribunals are faced with ever longer submissions on, and overinterpretation of, existing case law and countless references to the latest 'tests' or 'criteria' that another tribunal has read into often clear, or at least sufficiently clear, short, common sense treaty provisions and terms. This will detract many tribunals from subsuming the actual facts of a specific case under the actually applicable law of a case, and from a tailored resolution of that specific case. It might also lead to time-consuming exercises of either (wrongly) applying allegedly relevant case law (rather than the text of the treaty) or dismissing said application with reasons while being faced with ever longer strings of quotes from awards quoting other awards (sometimes even up to a third or fourth iteration of indirect quotation).

Some authors in that regard hint at a duty or responsibility of investment arbitration tribunals to strive for coherence and to contribute to the harmonious development of investment law in order to 'meet the legitimate expectations of the community of States and investors' ie at obligations of a tribunal to the investment arbitration community as a whole and the states submitting to it,[61] that would require such time-consuming exercises at least to some degree. The authors of the present chapter, however, tend to disagree with this position and see this development as a negative aspect (see below).

[59] See also Hélène Ruiz Fabri on the possible lack of visibility of the true *conviction intime du juge* within a decision: Ruiz Fabri (n 51) 103, 125.

[60] Schauer (n 3) 655.

[61] cf eg Landau (n 1) 187, esp 197–99.

V. Evaluation

A. Difference between Commercial and Investment Arbitration

Coming to the evaluation of the difference between commercial and investment arbitration, as a first observation, it appears that what an award must contain and why the reasoning of awards makes sense is very similar, if not even the same, between commercial and investment arbitration.

It is a truism in that regard that, first, a reasoned award should be tailored to the respective parties and the circumstances of an arbitration; second, that parties to an investment arbitration at least on one side differ significantly from parties in a commercial arbitration; and, thirdly, that investment arbitrations, by definition, concern large arbitrations involving large professional firms and legal departments. That, however, in the view of the authors, is no basis to argue that the standard of reasoning for commercial arbitration should be lesser than for investment arbitration, or that in commercial arbitration an arbitrator would not also need to reach the point where in her conviction she has made clear to an average reader why A leads to B and eventually to the result.

At the end of the day, the biggest difference in the scholarship on those different awards might be that for commercial arbitration the demand has long been to produce shorter, more efficient awards whereas for investment arbitration eminent voices demand longer, more exhaustive reasoning.[62]

B. Problems Caused by Reasoned Awards?

As a second observation, it appears futile to evaluate the concept of a reasoned award in international investment arbitration as a black-and-white topic: of course a reasoned award is necessary and obligatory in international investment arbitration and its advantages for legitimacy, understandability, transparency, and accountability clearly outweigh its disadvantages.

Rather, topics related to the idea of a reasoned award merit attention: procedures take too much time, are too cost-intensive, awards are delayed and too long in total but too short when it comes to the actual relevant reasoning for the specific case.

This is a consequence of how investor-state arbitrations are typically conducted today. Tribunals often consist of repeat players, academics or professionals in the field, with a high drive to deliver a good result and be appointed again, but by inclination and profession almost unavoidably more interested in complicated legal problems and legal scholarship, in the views of their colleagues, and the latest hot topics in the community, rather than in the mundane facts and exhibits of a specific case and in a

[62] Aguilar Alvarez and Reisman (n 3) 1; Lalive (n 3) 55; Landau (n 1) 187; as opposed to eg Born (n 1) 3290; Nigel Blackaby and others, *Redfern and Hunter on International Arbitration* (6th edition, OUP 2015) 555, para 9.161.

pragmatic, tailored solution that is unconcerned with how and where it would feature in the Schreuer/Schill commentary.

They are met, on the other side, by (US) law firms ever so willing to throw their awesome workforce at trying every argument and quoting every case they can get their hands on that may be remotely related to the case at hand. Given that apparently once a case was won on a minor, undeveloped, unexpected argument, these firms will forever refrain from picking one or two winning arguments and rather try them all.

This then overwhelms the tribunals: after all, on the receiving end of the work of the law firms is a tribunal of three, and often a drafting president of one, that is supposed to condense and comprehend in record time the work of ten to twenty lawyers and one to three expert firms on each side expressed in documents worth thousands of working hours.

(Institutional) help is thus needed in the drafting of the award. This, however, is a slippery slope, because all that is really important and central to an award, ie the reasons and factual decisions that make an award a reasoned award, must, it is agreed, only stem from the arbitrators themselves. What ICSID or the Permanent Court of Arbitration (PCA) Secretariat thus can deliver are summaries and memos on innocuous parts of the award and innocuous questions. What is more, they have to draft even those parts in an open-ended manner since they are not the decision-makers that think the decision from the end, ie the result. They will, therefore, usually err on the side of inclusion rather than leaving something out lest the part they left out will be the part the tribunal then asks for. This leads to very long documents, 'Working Papers'.[63]

This means that the drafting arbitrators will in the part they draft, ie the reasoned award, highlight the procedural events and arguments of the parties which they deem relevant at that stage, leading to overlaps with earlier parts of the award where procedural history and the submissions of the parties are already set out in great detail. However, as every drafter knows, what once has reached the paper is very hard to delete, and so redundant elements tend to stay and make the award longer.

All of this is further enhanced by the busyness of all actors involved: law firms, arbitrators, and institutions, all trying to thrive in a business that entrusts most of the new cases to the busiest arbitrators, firms, and institutions. All these actors are usually of very high capability, morality, and drive for excellence and correct solutions—always checked by the constant need to demonstrate quality. But with the clock constantly ticking the item on the to-do list that will first move into the 'nice-to-have' column—both on the side of the law firms and consequently also on the side of the tribunals—is perfectly tailoring and shortening a submission, and consequently an award, to

[63] In addition, institutions, unlike arbitrators, are not working alone. Several junior members of staff will provide a first draft, fearing to leave out what more senior colleagues may have wanted to be included, and not knowing the result of the arbitration, not having been privy, of course, to any deliberations or the email correspondence of a tribunal.

perfection. Rather than picking a winning argument and case-specific fact, counsel and tribunals will try all arguments a little bit and shroud the result in familiar themes and quotes of investor-state dispute settlement, famous quotes from the Vienna Convention on the Law of Treaties and from cases of the International Court of Justice (ICJ) and often read references to scholarly books and articles common to many cases. Rather than resolving any disconnect between the necessary administrative parts of a submission or award and the more decisive parts, no 'baby' is killed in the drafting process. As the famous saying goes (attributed to many different famous poets or scientists such as Goethe, Mark Twain, Blaise Pascal, Cicero): I am sorry I wrote you a long letter, I did not have time for a short one.

As another result of the busyness, the drafting of the award will also usually start after the hearing in a case, and will thus have to draft over holes that could have been filled more quickly and in a shorter way, if the drafting had already begun before the hearing and clarifying questions helpful for the drafting could have been asked at the hearing.

This, it is important to state, does not affect the quality of the investment arbitration process and its outcomes in its broad lines. It, however, bloats the process and the resulting product and undermines the usefulness and desirability of reasoned awards and what the duty to provide such awards seeks to protect.

C. Relativity of the Problem

However, before thinking about solutions to the just described problems with reasoned awards and modern investment arbitration, it is important to also view any such criticism with a grain of salt. As it appears, complaining about the awards of today as compared to allegedly much better, more elegant, and to-the-point awards of yore appears to be a favourite pastime of legal scholars and practitioners of any generation, and may thus come with the territory. As Lord Bingham wrote already in 1988:

> It is often said that counsel in argument cite too many cases of peripheral relevance. I sometimes wonder if this disease, like gaol fever, may not have been communicated to the bench. If, of course, a party founds his case on an authority which the court considers irrelevant it will probably be necessary to examine the case in detail to demonstrate that it is irrelevant and why. But it is in my view symptomatic of the tendency towards over-elaboration to which we are all prone that authorities which could without disadvantage have been left out of the argument nonetheless find a place in the judgment.[64]

Howard Holtzmann, in 1994 similarly uttered some oft-quoted concerns about the length of awards of the Iran–United States Claims Tribunal and in particular the

[64] Bingham (n 1) 144–45.

summaries of the facts and the submissions of the parties.[65] In 2006, Romain Dupeyré also offered similar criticism.[66]

This goes to show that, while criticism of modern-day reasoned awards in investment arbitration is important and should be taken into account by practitioners, the situation is not one of impending doom and abhorrent lack of quality. The situation rather is that of a constant process of quality assurance and improvement—a pendulum swinging between important poles of, eg thoroughness, exhaustiveness, brevity, and efficiency—in a high-quality process conducted by committed professionals all over the world.

VI. Way Forward and Solutions

What are then possible adjustments that could improve the reasoning of awards in the future? What improvements could bring the reasoning of individual awards more in line with the theoretical advantages of a reasoned award as described above?

To start with, in 2006, Dupeyré suggested, with a view to commercial arbitral awards, and in parts echoing comments made by Judge Holtzmann, that the summary of party positions and the description of the facts, as well as the citations of other awards and decisions should be limited to what is absolutely necessary for a decision.[67] This of course would be helpful in investment arbitration, too. It should also be acceptable to the school of thought that repeatedly underlines that reasoning in investor-state arbitration must be more thorough and more focused on the field of investment arbitration as a whole, and the interest of third parties therein, than reasoning in commercial arbitration.

Three other factors, however, appear to be of even more importance: first, daring to pick a winner; second, no over-fulfilment of any duty to give reason and any due process rights; and, third, focusing on the case at hand.

If counsel dared to pick winning arguments instead of trying them all, and if tribunals dared to equally pick a winning theory and to dismiss the others outright, and if institutions dared to summarize with results and a winning theory in mind, this would reduce the size of awards considerably, while increasing the depth and the value of their reasoning.

So would putting due process and the duty to give reasons in perspective. As explained, the risk of an award being annulled or set aside is not as high as most arbitrators

[65] Howard Holtzmann's Dissenting and Concurring Opinion to the Award in IUSCT Case No 559-221-1 of 24 August 1994, 30 Iran–US CTR 163, 168–69 'call[s] attention to the Tribunal's growing tendency to write Awards that are overly long and excessively detailed' and warns that '[a]t stake is the efficient use of the Tribunal's limited time, funds and facilities'. However, he does not propose that the legal reasoning of the award should be shortened but rather that the procedural history and the statement of facts should be streamlined to only provide what is necessary for the legal reasoning.

[66] Dupeyré (n 3).

[67] ibid 48–50; Dissenting and Concurring Opinion Holtzmann (n 65).

(subconsciously) fear it is. That is of course no invitation to violate important procedural rights. Rather, their meaning would be strengthened by not overapplying them, ie by dismissing unfounded requests outright without (much) reasoning, by limiting rounds of submissions, and by daring to direct the parties to questions and areas of interest of the tribunal early in the process.[68] Doing so would have great potential to streamline procedures and to heighten the quality of the results and the discourse, while it would, of course, not prevent any party from bringing forward any argument or fact it deems relevant. Nevertheless, tribunals and institutions often feel more comfortable (not least due to time constraints, see above) with letting the back and forth of submissions on every nuance of a case pile up unmanaged and uninterrupted, leading in the end to a much wider, and much less pertinent, area to be ploughed through and dealt with in an award.

Finally, also in investor-state arbitration, operating in the realm of states and affecting their citizens, sometimes directly, should tribunals (and lawyers) dare to focus on the case before them rather than the field as a whole. A case-specific argument, a case-specific fact or exhibit, an oversight of one of the parties, or a procedural mistake, can make for, or be the angle to, a much better, quicker, and useful solution to a case than endless discussions of strings of quotes from allegedly relevant case law and tests and criteria developed therein. Focusing on the facts of a case also foolproofs any award from review as such review is bound to accept a tribunal's factual determinations. It is also what, first and foremost, the parties are interested in receiving from the tribunal.[69] Incidentally, focusing on the specific facts of a case also makes the reasoning tighter and increases its de facto precedential value and thus its fulfilment of the duty to provide a reasoned award.

Contrary to the arguments of Guillermo Alvarez, Michael Reisman, Toby Landau, and Pierre Lalive,[70] or rather, contrary to interpretations thereof, no one but the two parties to an investment arbitration have any entitlement to a resolution of that arbitration and an explanation as to how it was reached. It is not by positioning itself in a way that would interest scholars or practitioners, but by solving the dispute at hand, that a tribunal fulfils its duty in line with its responsibility. Indeed, it is exactly by solving specific disputes that a tribunal contributes to the investor-state dispute settlement community and makes its reasoning, by accident, so to speak, pertinent to future cases.

[68] This has also been raised by Scherer and Morris (n 38) para 26.51.

[69] Compare also Nigel Blackaby, Constantine Partasides, Alan Redfern, and Martin Hunter stating that

> The general practice of arbitral tribunals in international cases is to devote more time and space in the award to giving the reasons for its determination of the legal arguments than to a review of the factual issues. This is not surprising, since most arbitral tribunals in international cases are composed of lawyers. However, it should be borne in mind by such tribunals that what is needed is an intelligible decision, rather than a legal dissertation. The object should be to keep the reasons for a decision as concise as possible, according to the nature of the dispute. The parties want to read the essential reasoning underlying the decision, not a lesson in the law.

Blackaby and others (n 62) 555, para 9.161

[70] Aguilar Alvarez and Reisman (n 3) 1; Lalive (n 3) 55; Landau (n 1) 187.

VII. Conclusion

The result of award drafting in international investment arbitration always has to be a reasoned award. What a reasoned award consists of exactly depends on all circumstances of a case and a decision. What is certain is that a reasoned award will develop its full strength and right of existence when it keeps the purpose and the addressees of a decision at its centre and is drafted with a healthy dose of restraint, succinctness, and common sense; and when it does not lose sight of the importance of judicial—or arbitral—economy. Whether it can do so depends on the input and discipline, and the audacity of all involved in its creation, be it directly or indirectly.

21

To Err Is Human, to Dissent Divine

*Charles N Brower and Ahmed Mazlom**

I. Introduction

Dissenting, minority, separate, individual, *dubitante*, *seriatim*, and concurring (yes, concurring) opinions, respectively, share the common feature of containing disapproval, disagreement, and dissent, to varying degrees. The mere taxonomical classification of an opinion means nothing, absent one dissecting that opinion in its entirety to ascertain the extent and focus of disapproval towards majority reasoning.[1]

Dissents by an adjudicator, be it in international commercial arbitration, investment treaty arbitration, investomercial arbitration,[2] or public international law, are not only crystallized in 'opinion' form. Actions (or rather the lack of action when it comes to refusing to sign an award) such as withdrawal and resignation also constitute forms of dissent.[3] In essence, what all these examples illustrate, is that dissent is inherent, but variable, in a field that is based on resolving disagreement.

While noting the breadth of the scholarly attention that dissenting opinions have received in investment treaty arbitration throughout the past two decades, the co-authors of the present contribution must emphasize that it is an extension of, actually a *réplique* to, the specific debate initiated by Jan Paulsson and Albert Jan van den Berg,[4] and later continued solely by Van den Berg.[5] Thus the focus is on dissenting opinions in investment treaty arbitration, falling under the umbrella of public international law in the broadest sense.[6]

* Views expressed are of the authors alone and cannot be attributed to any of their respective organizations or affiliated institutions.

[1] Albeit not a dissenting opinion in the strict sense, and by no means labelled as such, the Statement of Don Wallace Jr in *Wena v Egypt* expressed disapproval towards the majority in a brief note: 'Professor Wallace concurs in the Tribunal's entire award and is persuaded that compound interest should be awarded. However, he is not persuaded that compounding should be quarterly.' *Wena Hotels Ltd v Egypt*, ICSID Case No ARB/98/4, Award (8 December 2000).

[2] See Charles N Brower, 'Investomercial Arbitration: Whence Cometh It? What Is It? Whither Goeth It?' (2014) International Journal of Arbitration, Mediation and Dispute Management 179.

[3] See Statement by Judge Parviz Ansari Concerning his Reasons for not Signing the Award in Case No 129, in *Sedco, Inc* and *National Iranian Oil Company*, Award No 309-129-3 (7 July 1987) 15 IUSCTR 23, 187 and Explanation for Failure of Judge Sani to Sign Awards in *Chas. T. Main International, Inc* and *Mahab Consulting Engineers, Inc*, Award No 70-185-3 (2 September 1983) 3 IUSCTR 270, 276.

[4] Albert Jan van den Berg, 'Dissenting Opinions by Party-Appointed Arbitrators in Investment Arbitration' in Mahnoush H Arsanjani and others (eds), *Looking to the Future: Essays on International Law in Honor of W. Michael Reisman* (Brill 2011) 821.

[5] Albert Jan van den Berg, 'Charles Brower's Problem with 100 per cent—Dissenting Opinions by Party-appointed Arbitrators in Investment Arbitration' (2015) Arbitration International 381.

[6] See Eric De Brabandere, *Investment Treaty Arbitration as Public International Law* (CUP 2014).

Charles N Brower and Ahmed Mazlom, *To Err Is Human, to Dissent Divine* In: *The Award in International Investment Arbitration.*
Edited by: Katia Fach Gómez and Catharine Titi, Oxford University Press.
DOI: 10.1093/9780191975936.003.0021

Considering that the International Centre for Settlement of Investment Disputes (ICSID) reports that just thirty-seven of 622 ICSID arbitrations concluded since its inception have involved dissenting opinions (amounting to 5.95 per cent), dissenting opinions are not a new phenomenon to investment treaty arbitration, albeit the field in its modern form is still at an early stage when compared with other forms of dispute resolution.[7]

II. Why Dissent?

Dissenting opinions serve a purpose. Considering the competing norms and societal values humanity has faced over the centuries, it would be no surprise if it happened that dissents of today were concurrences of yesterday, or, for that matter, if concurrences of today evolved from earlier generational dissents.[8]

Dissenting opinions inherently oppose conformity and encourage independent thinking, to the extent of creating *dissenting jurisprudence*. In current times, views expressed in dissenting opinions have been considered by tribunals, such as in *Masdar v Spain*,[9] where the tribunal expressly cited the dissenting opinions of an arbitrator in *Charanne*[10] and *Isolux*.[11] This example alone refutes Van den Berg's earlier claim that 'almost no award or decision referred to a dissenting opinion in an earlier case, a fact that contradicts the argument that dissenting opinions contribute to the development of investment law'.[12]

Multiple reasons form the basis of dissents in investment treaty arbitration, including insufficient reasoning,[13] lack of agreement on imperative terms,[14] misapplication or rather lack of application of fundamental (general) principles of law,[15] and insufficient evidence presented.[16]

[7] As per the cases and opinions published on the ICSID case database. This statistic includes only dissenting opinions written separately to accompany the award, and does not include dissenting statements that are included in the body of the award itself. Further, certain awards (and hence, possible dissenting opinions) are not published and made public, which further questions the validity of empirical studies on the topic.

[8] *Plessy v Ferguson*, 163 US 537 (1896) influencing *Brown v Board of Education*, 347 US 483 (1954)—albeit no express reference was made to Justice Harlan's lone dissent—it formed the intellectual substratum in *Brown*.

[9] *Masdar Solar & Wind Cooperatief UA v Spain*, ICSID Case No ARB/14/1, Award (16 May 2018) [404] n 267, [485] n 375, and [492] n 380.

[10] *Charanne BV and Construction Investments Sarl v Spain*, SCC Case No 062/2012, Dissenting Opinion of Guido Santiago Tawil (21 January 2016).

[11] *Isolux Infrastructure Netherlands BV v Spain*, SCC Case No 2013/153, Dissenting Opinion of Guido Santiago Tawil (6 July 2016).

[12] Van den Berg (n 5) 382. See also Laurence Shore and Kenneth Juan Figueroa, 'Dissents, Concurrences and a Necessary Divide between Investment and Commercial Arbitration' (2008) Global Arbitration Review 6; Catharine Titi, 'Investment Arbitration and the Controverted Right of the Arbitrator to Issue a Separate or Dissenting Opinion' (2018) Law and Practice of International Courts and Tribunals 197.

[13] *Industria Nacional de Alimentos, SA and Indalsa Perú, SA (formerly Empresas Lucchetti, SA and Lucchetti Perú, SA) v Peru*, ICSID Case No ARB/03/4, Dissenting Opinion of Franklin Berman (Decision on Annulment) (5 September 2007) [4] and [14].

[14] *Biwater Gauff (Tanzania) Limited v Tanzania*, ICSID Case No ARB/05/22, Concurring and Dissenting Opinion of Gary Born (18 July 2008) [24]–[29].

[15] *Garanti Koza LLP v Turkmenistan*, ICSID Case No ARB/11/20, Dissenting Opinion of Laurence Boisson de Chazournes (Decision on the Objection to Jurisdiction for Lack of Consent) (3 July 2013) [8]–[9].

[16] *Total SA v Argentina*, ICSID Case No ARB/04/1, Individual Opinion (Dissent) of Henri Alvarez (Decision on Liability) (21 December 2010) [72], [88], [107], and [122]. See for a discussion on external factors from a

Albeit an outlier in the strict sense, one 'dissenter', nevertheless entitling his objections 'Individual Concurring Opinion', stated that the claimant may well have recourse to other legal fora, thus explicitly noting a possible intention of the losing party to initiate set aside proceedings.[17] Save certain anomalies, dissenting opinions do not affect the enforceability of awards.[18] They do help clarify where the award itself is going in the future.

Indeed, rather than *increasing* the likelihood of potential challenges to the award, dissenting opinions, by reciting arguments that obviously were rejected by the majority, *reduce* the possibilities of successful challenges, hence non-enforcement.[19] This of course is premised on the assumption that the majority expressly reasoned the award well enough to reject the alternative arguments on a solid foundation. If that were not the case, then a dissenting opinion leading to a challenge proves justified. Saliently, where the dissent addresses a grave procedural failure of the tribunal, and subsequently, the award was then successfully challenged, and not enforced, the dissent has served the purpose of preventing the enforcement of an unjust award.[20]

As empirical studies indicate, not least that of Van den Berg, there is a paucity of evidence that dissenting opinions are cited *extensively* in other investment treaty arbitration awards.[21] Nonetheless, such opinions prove useful in making other arbitrators *think*. It is not only highly inconceivable, but also against the principle of tribunal secrecy and confidentiality, to carry out an empirical study assessing whether dissenting opinions were discussed amongst arbitrators during their deliberations. It is through a nuanced lens on scholarly articles, academic exchanges, and professional conferences that confirm that dissenting opinions are discussed in the investment treaty community. Dissents are thus found in the subconscious of arbitrators, whether that be in a preventive or corrective capacity.

III. Source of Dissent

Upon what foundation do dissents rest, specifically in investment treaty arbitration? Do they stem from the practice in international fora? Is it more than a century of practice that arbitrators from common law countries inherited? Is it the silence of arbitral

legal semiotic perspective, Ruth Breeze, 'Dissenting and Concurring Opinions in International Investment Arbitration: How the Arbitrators Frame Their Need to Differ' (2012) International Journal for the Semiotics of Law 393.

[17] *Mihaly International Corporation v Sri Lanka*, ICSID Case No ARB/00/2, Individual Concurring Opinion by David Suratgar (7 March 2002) [9].

[18] See *F Ltd v M Ltd* (2009) EWHC 275 (TCC) for an international commercial arbitration perspective, and *Klöckner Industrie-Anlagen GmbH and others v United Republic of Cameroon and Société Camerounaise des Engrais*, ICSID Case No ARB/81/2, Award (21 October 1983) for an investment treaty perspective, respectively.

[19] Richard M Mosk and Tom Ginsburg, 'Dissenting Opinions in International Arbitration' in Matti Tupamäki (ed), *Liber Amicorum Bengt Broms* (Finnish Branch of the International Law Association 1999) 280.

[20] ibid.

[21] Van den Berg (n 4) 826.

rules that effectively gave leeway for arbitrators to issue dissents? Should dissents only be issued when arbitral rules expressly give the arbitrator the opportunity to do so?

In both the International Court of Justice (ICJ) and the European Court of Human Rights (ECtHR), there is an established duty by judges to provide a rationale behind their expressed views and the possibility of issuing a separate opinion (both concurring and dissenting) in the ECtHR, and separate or dissenting opinions in the ICJ.[22] Yet, it must be noted that in the Permanent Court of International Justice, for a brief period of time, dissenting opinions were not published and remained internal to the judges.[23]

The Iran–United States Claims Tribunal, whose Tribunal Rules of Procedure were modelled, albeit with certain amendments, on the 1976 UNCITRAL Arbitration Rules, contain provisions on dissenting opinions.[24] Arguably, the vast number of dissenting opinions issued both by judges appointed by Iran and those appointed by the United States played a central role in giving those Rules their prominence in international arbitration.

There is no denying that international fora accept the practice of dissents, and the ICJ has seen a proliferation of such opinions. Considering this well-established practice, dissents constitute a source of international law. Arguably, dissents can be interpreted as a supplementary means of interpretation as per Article 32 of the Vienna Convention on the Law of Treaties (1969) (VCLT) and Article 38(d) of the ICJ's Statute.

IV. Myths behind Dissents

The literature on dissenting opinions continuously stresses that dissents arrived at international fora via the common law tradition. While there is validity to that point, it would be wrong to assume that common law-trained arbitrators blindly follow that practice. Vice versa, to assume that dissents owe nothing to the civil law tradition ignores the tradition of dissent in Europe (whether in the strictly legal sense or as embodied in political and social movements).

For example, the ECtHR, established in 1959 and chiefly composed of member states of the civil law tradition, not only permits separate opinions (both concurring and dissenting), but whose cases have resulted in a fair number of dissents, particularly in especially critical cases.[25] Under the aegis of the Council of Europe the ECtHR thus has been a distinctly functional judicial system, whereas the earlier Universal Declaration of Human Rights had lacked a legally enforcing mechanism at its inception.

Advocates General of the Court of Justice of the European Union (CJEU) also function as quasi-dissenters. Although their opinions are not legally binding, the Advocate

[22] Statute of the International Court of Justice arts 56 and 57. European Convention on Human Rights art 45.

[23] See Edward Dumbauld, 'Dissenting Opinions in International Adjudication' (1942) University of Pennsylvania Law Review 929.

[24] Tribunal Rules of Procedure (1983) art 32(3).

[25] Catherine A Rogers, 'The Politics of International Investment Arbitrators' (2013) Santa Clara Journal of International Law 223, 244. See also Erik Voeten, 'The Politics of International Judicial Appointments: Evidence from the European Court of Human Rights' (2007) International Organization 669.

General in *Achmea*, for example, conveyed views that the CJEU ultimately disregarded, and once the judgement had been rendered the Advocate General's opinion was seen as a form of dissent.[26] Had the CJEU agreed with the reasoning of the Advocate General and not declared that intra-EU BITs are incompatible with EU law, the Advocate General's opinion would have been viewed as a concurrence.[27] This temporal dynamic proves unique to the design of the CJEU, where Advocates General submit their opinions prior to the ultimate judgment of the CJEU.

Contrastingly, in *Komstroy*, the Advocate General's opinion and CJEU judgement were in line with each other, both of them concluding that the Energy Charter Treaty (ECT) cannot be applied to intra-EU ECT disputes as that would be incompatible with the primacy of EU law.[28] Interestingly, an element of dissent arose, not from the Advocate General or the CJEU, but from EU member states as it was held that:

> The Council of the European Union, the Hungarian, Finnish and Swedish Governments and Komstroy are, in essence, of the view that the Court does not have jurisdiction to provide answers to the questions referred because EU law is inapplicable to the dispute at issue in the main proceedings as the parties to that dispute are external to the European Union.[29]

In terms of the ICJ, one commentator has held that the inclusion of Articles 56 and 57, respectively, entailed 'a concession to Anglo-Saxon system'.[30] Then why do ICJ judges who studied and trained in civil law countries issue dissenting opinions as well?

It is simply stereotypical to label an arbitrator that 'belongs' to either a civil or common law jurisdiction as adhering to the respective system as if it were a static and monolithic value set. This approach diverges from the critical thinking skills taught at universities across both sides of the Channel and the Atlantic and underplays the unique values different arbitrators hold in high regard.

Such an approach is no more sensible than assuming that all Dutch lawyers are against judicial review of acts of parliament just because the Netherlands happens to be one of the few states in the world whose constitution prohibits such review.[31] An arbitrator from either legal tradition may have contrary views on dissenting opinions. Judge Learned Hand, a quintessential American jurist notorious for his opposition to dissenting opinions, cannot be compared to Justice Oliver Wendell Holmes, Justice

[26] Opinion of Advocate General Wathelet, Case C-284/16 *Slowakische Republik v Achmea BV* (2017) EU:C:2017:699.

[27] Case C-284/16 *Slowakische Republik v Achmea BV* (2018) EU:C:2018:158.

[28] Opinion of Advocate General Szpunar, Case C-741/19 *République de Moldavie v Komstroy LLC* (2021) EU:C:2021:164.

[29] Case C-741/19 *République de Moldavie v Komstroy LLC* (2021) EU:C:2021:655 [21]. *Komstroy* involved neither an EU investor nor an EU member state—merely the seat of arbitration proved to be Paris. Further, the CJEU conducted no analysis as per the VCLT.

[30] Ram Prakash Anand, 'The Role of Individual and Dissenting Opinions in International Adjudication' (1965) International and Comparative Law Quarterly 788, 796.

[31] Constitution of the Netherlands art 120.

John Marshall Harlan, and Justice Harlan Fiske Stone, who staunchly supported issuing dissenting opinions.[32]

Considering that investment treaty arbitration is a hybrid model of civil and common law elements, it is unsurprising that dissenting opinions not only reflect this hybrid model, but also prove necessary as a means of highlighting seminal differences that may arise among arbitrators from varied legal systems and cultures.

V. Realism and Dissent

The topic of dissenting opinions, as controversial as it is, has attracted empirical interest from scholars and practitioners alike.[33] Yet, empirical studies, by and large, are much needed in identifying any element of causation (as difficult as it might be) between the culture (be it legal or sociological) of an arbitrator and his or her tendency to issue a dissent. Instead, the literature has focused on the common and civil law divide regarding dissenting opinions—which, as illustrated above, has no place in the hybrid system of investment treaty arbitration—rather than on the cultural norms and heritage of an arbitrator, combined, where applicable, with the jeopardy an arbitrator judges she would be in vis-à-vis her home state were she to fail to dissent from an award that is adverse to it.

It is no surprise that in many states around the world freedom of speech is far from being guaranteed, and at worst, when exercised, endangers the life, not only of the speaker, but also of an entire related network. It is these nuanced political elements—if not a collective paranoia—that inhibits citizens, let alone lawyers and judges, from taking stances seen as unfavourable, if not downright hostile, toward the reigning government. Even one of the staunchest critics of dissenting opinions, Van den Berg, agrees that in the rare but real scenario wherein an arbitrator, by failing to dissent from an award against her home country, upon arriving back in her home state would face serious danger, a dissenting opinion proves justifiable, if not necessary.[34]

Hence, when the literature fixates on the *reward* element of issuing dissenting opinions—eg, that dissents encourage reappointments, comfort the losing party that appointed the dissenting arbitrator, and signal to potential future appointing parties that the respective arbitrator takes this particular stance on an investment treaty dispute—focus also has to be trained on the *consequential* nature of dissents. Namely, at the extreme end, the risk posed to arbitrators who are forced by circumstances to dissent.

[32] See William J Brennan, 'In Defense of Dissents' (1985) Hastings Law Journal 427.

[33] Szilárd Gáspár-Szilágyi and Laura Létourneau-Tremblay, 'A Question of Impartiality: Who Are the Dissenting Arbitrators in Investment Treaty Arbitration?' in Freya Baetens (ed), *Identity and Diversity on the International Bench: Who Is the Judge?* (OUP 2020). Gáspár-Szilágyi and Létourneau-Tremblay focus on nationality, gender, education, and professional experience to deduce whether these variables influence an arbitrator issuing a dissenting opinion.

[34] Van den Berg (n 4) 831.

VI. Dissent towards Dissents

Much criticism of dissenting opinions has been channelled towards the claimed lack of certainty that the very existence of dissenting opinions creates. Further, along this line of reasoning, dissents are at odds with the doctrine of *stare decisis*; not that the aforementioned concept is accepted in investment arbitration in the first place.

In response to the claim that dissenting opinions indicate an egoistic, self-centred approach to adjudication in general, it must be noted that dissenting opinions demand a level of courage. In the investment treaty world, a field composed of elite arbitrators, dissents could potentially signal that the arbitrator in question proves 'difficult' and 'unamicable', yet in a field where reputation reigns paramount, the decision by an arbitrator to dissent clearly denotes a deep ideological belief and question of normative justice, that dissenting arbitrators are willing to express views in public—and thus subsequently 'expose' themselves—rather than remain silent and conform to the majority; thus shunning the path of least resistance. Such action contradicts the claim that dissents may constitute an 'escape route'.[35]

Further, the concept that dissenting opinions advance personal ideology and the dissenting arbitrators' perception of how the law should be applied, is no different from the view that majority awards themselves advance personal ideology and arbitrators' leanings towards the 'right' way of applying the law. Whether there is a *duty* by the arbitrator in either case to voice her views remains to be explored, as arguably, judges do have an obligation to articulate their views, as addressed earlier in relation to the ICJ and ECtHR.

In terms of arbitral economy, dissenting opinions do lead to an increase in costs for both parties and may increase the duration of an arbitral proceeding. While these are valid points, the underlying intention of a respectable arbitrator in dissenting will not be to increase the costs and duration of a proceeding. If anything, the reputational harm of dissenting solely based on such concealed motives, once it becomes apparent to the arbitral community, would prove detrimental to future appointments.

Inherently, a dissenting opinion vanquishes the image of a unanimous tribunal. Then again, what purpose does unanimity serve? Is the image of unanimity linked to the prestige of the tribunal? Do parties to an investment arbitration expect unanimity? Considering the adversarial nature of investment treaty arbitration—with its Janus-faced nature of investor versus state—there is no denying the high stakes involved, hence it could be wishful thinking to assume that the arbitral tribunal would act in unanimity.

Even if the adversarial nature of investment treaty arbitration would be downplayed, dissenting opinions are not necessarily the prerogative only of party-appointed

[35] Peter J Rees and Patrick Rohn, 'Dissenting Opinions: Can They Fulfil a Beneficial Role?' (2009) Arbitration International 329, 336.

arbitrators; the President or Chair of a tribunal may, and from time to time does, issue a dissent.[36]

Interestingly, on the point of unanimity, there have been cases where more than one arbitrator dissents in a three-panel investment treaty arbitration.[37] This further stresses that the importance of unanimity in investment treaty arbitration is exaggerated, as even though a majority is required to form an award, this does not impede two arbitrators from issuing dissenting opinions simultaneously.[38]

The Iran–United States Claims Tribunal witnessed many cases in which a Chamber would form a majority even though the party-appointed arbitrator forming the majority with the chamber chairman would disagree with the opinion.[39] Notably, the Iran–United States Claims Tribunal, when sitting as the 'Full Tribunal' of nine judges, could also see eight out of nine judges issuing separate (mainly, concurring in part, dissenting in part) opinions from Iranian, US, and third-country judges alike![40]

Van den Berg initially dismisses the Iran–United States Claims Tribunal from his analysis: 'This contribution does not deal with the Iran–United States Claims Tribunal's awards and decisions because of that tribunal's sui generis circumstances, even though a number of those awards and decisions may be deemed investment disputes.'[41] When it suits his line of argumentation, however, he relies upon Tribunal cases to note, in regard to two concurring opinions, that '[i]t would have been preferable, in my view, if these arbitrators had simply agreed and not issued a "concurring" opinion signalling disagreement'.[42]

It must be understood that all American nationals' claims against Iran were handled by one of three tribunal chambers, each presided over by a third-country judge, flanked by an American judge and an Iranian one, and that Iranian judges regularly would not join the chamber chairman to award anything to an American claimant. Since tribunal awards could be issued only by a majority, when the chamber chairman would find, at least to some degree, for the American claimant, the American judge in that chamber had no choice but to approve what that chairman was willing to award, so that the American claimant would at least receive that much, notwithstanding that the American judge felt it to be (sometimes grossly) insufficient, hence the American judges routinely expressed their displeasure in their opinions in such cases.

[36] *Tokios Tokelés v Ukraine*, ICSID Case No ARB/02/18, Dissenting Opinion of President Prosper Weil (29 April 2004).

[37] See *Total SA v Argentina*, ICSID Case No ARB/04/1, *Impregilo SpA v Argentina (I)*, ICSID Case No ARB/07/17 and *Tokios Tokelés v Ukraine*, ICSID Case No ARB/02/18, respectively.

[38] *Impregilo SpA v Argentina (I)*, ICSID Case No ARB/07/17, Concurring and Dissenting Opinion of Judge Charles N Brower (21 June 2011); *Impregilo SpA v Argentina (I)*, ICSID Case No ARB/07/17, Concurring and Dissenting Opinion of Brigitte Stern (21 June 2011).

[39] Concurring Opinion of Richard M Mosk in *Ultrasystems Incorporated* and *The Islamic Republic of Iran*, Partial Award No 27-84-3 (4 March 1983) 2 IUSCTR 100, 114.

[40] *The Islamic Republic of Iran* and *United States of America*, Partial Award No 604-A15 (II:A)/A26 (IV)/B43-FT (10 March 2020) IUSCTR (forthcoming). See opinions of Barkett, Brower, Fini, Johnson, Kalkhoran, Seifi, Simma, and Van Houtte, respectively.

[41] Van den Berg (n 4) 824, n 11.

[42] ibid 824, n 11, and 833. Continuing, Van den Berg stated: 'The opinions raise doubts as to whether majority awards actually existed', while in a preceding sentence he noted the explicit reason by the arbitrator that 'I concur in the Tribunal's Partial Award. I do so in order to form a majority so that the award can be rendered.'

VII. Investment Treaty Reforms and the Future of Dissents

Considering that investment treaty arbitration rests upon the right to recourse conferred by bilateral investment treaties (BITs) and multilateral investment treaties (MITs)—and in conjunction with arbitral rules that facilitate investment arbitrations—the question remains: if dissenting opinions have received such criticism as is outlined above, why has no BIT or MIT, let alone prominent arbitration rules or arbitration centres, prohibited the issuance of dissenting opinions?[43] On the contrary, the International Chamber of Commerce (ICC), the London Court of International Arbitration (LCIA), and ICSID permit dissenting opinions, either expressly or in practice.[44]

Prohibiting dissenting opinions would impact the authority and impartiality of an arbitral panel, and it would touch upon the right of freedom of expression and transparency in arbitral proceedings. This sentiment proves highly relevant to why national arbitration laws also do not explicitly prohibit dissenting opinions.[45]

As cited by critics of dissents, neither the Hague Convention for the Pacific Settlement of International Disputes (1899),[46] nor the CJEU allow dissenting opinions.[47] Therefore, it would be anachronistic to invoke the former as constituting the advent of investment treaty arbitration in its modern form, and the latter was not moulded to accommodate, let alone serve, investment treaty arbitration in the first place, irrespective of what the more recent changes in the narrative of certain policymakers might imply.[48]

With the plethora of reforms ongoing in different institutions and fora, be it ICSID reforms, discussions in Working Group III of the United Nations Commission on International Trade Law (UNCITRAL WG III), ECT reforms, the EU's trajectory of imposing its dominance over intra-EU investment disputes, and even beyond that to coerce non-member states to submit to its preferred ways and means of dispute resolution, there is no shortage of crisis in international investment arbitration. Despite the alleged lack of legitimacy in the investor-state dispute settlement (ISDS) system, throughout all the major reforms that are occurring, at times in parallel, and at times,

[43] See Patricia Jimenez Kwast, 'Prohibitions on Dissenting Opinions in International Arbitration' in Cedric Ryngaert and others (eds), *What's Wrong with International Law?* (Brill 2015) 128. Notwithstanding the imprecise title of this publication, Article 18(1) of the Rules of Procedure for the *Iron Rhine* arbitration constitutes a rare outlier, and the 'prohibition' came by mutual party consent rather than from institutional arbitral rules or legislation.

[44] ICSID Convention art 48(4). The rules of the ICC and LCIA, respectively, are silent on the matter but permit dissenting opinions in practice.

[45] See Manuel Arroyo, 'Dealing with Dissenting Opinions in the Award: Some Options for the Tribunal' (2008) ASA Bulletin 437.

[46] However, see Article 52: 'Those members who are in the minority may record their dissent when signing.'

[47] Van den Berg (n 4) 823.

[48] Ironically, in terms of investor-state dispute settlement, a communication dated from 2010 held: 'that the Union has not historically been a significant actor in this field'. Commission, 'Towards a Comprehensive European International Investment Policy' COM (2010) 343. Strikingly, in a 2015 communication, the European Commission voiced a more imposing tone as it maintained that: '[t]he EU is best placed—and has a special responsibility—to lead the reform of the global investment regime, as its founder and main actor'. Commission, 'Trade for All, towards a More Responsible Trade and Investment Policy' COM (2015) 497.

vying for influence, no discussions over dissenting opinions have transpired within ICSID, UNCITRAL, ECT, or the EU, respectively.

Does this silence imply an acceptance of, if not a preference for, arbitrators issuing dissenting opinions? As delegations have been by no means shy to express their critique of various elements of ISDS, have dissenting opinions simply slipped under the radar? If anything, the European Commission as the originator, hence the staunchest backer of a Multilateral Investment Court within a broader Investment Court System, has had multiple opportunities to address its stance on dissenting opinions, if any, throughout its unrelenting advocacy of reforms in ISDS.[49] Until now, however, whether in the Comprehensive Economic and Trade Agreement (CETA) text or in other new generation international investment agreements the EU is negotiating, there is no mention of dissents.

This EU radio silence on dissents also prompts the question of who exactly are the audiences of dissenting opinions? Of course, the other arbitrators and the parties to the dispute are the primary intended readership, and the arbitral community follows developments, but what about the public at large? Considering that investment treaty arbitration affects in varying measures the public interest, the audience of dissents also includes the public at large. By no means is it a romanticized notion that an average citizen would become at least broadly familiar with the substance of a dissent, since the implications of both awards and dissenting opinions necessarily are considered by stakeholders, especially in light of the political scrutiny to which investment treaty arbitration has been subjected from the public in the past decade.

VIII. Van den Berg's Problem with 100 Per Cent

Assuming that Van den Berg's claim that 100 per cent of all separate opinions in investment treaty arbitration are produced by the arbitrator appointed by the 'losing' party were to be accurate (which has been shown above not to be accurate), and in his persistent appeal for Judge Brower to engage with that thesis, it should come as no surprise that scholars have already provided a multitude of answers. They include that in the eyes of the 'losing' party dissenting opinions provide comfort, in part by confirming that opposing arguments have been weighed, and that the course of the tribunal could have gone differently.[50] In the view of the co-authors, none of these warrants further explanation.

Indeed, Van den Berg's claim is not a novel notion per se, as already in 1999 Richard Mosk and Tom Ginsburg noted that '[o]ne fear is that if dissenting opinions are explicitly contemplated by arbitral rules, there may then result a situation where there is a

[49] See Charles N Brower and Jawad Ahmad, 'From the Two-Headed Nightingale to the Fifteen-Headed Hydra: The Many Follies of the Proposed International Investment Court' (2018) Fordham International Law Journal 791.

[50] Breeze (n 16) 405.

dissenting opinion issued by the party-appointed arbitrator for the losing side in every arbitral award'.[51]

Notably, objection to dissenting opinions derives from unease shown by commentators on different facets of investor-state arbitration, with the most notable example being Van den Berg's and Paulsson's critique of party-appointed arbitrators, which in their view, leads to 'undesirable' dissenting opinions.[52]

In his latest *réplique*, Van den Berg reiterates his constant calls to Brower that: '[i]t is concluded that none of them provide a satisfactory answer to the fact that 100 per cent of the separate opinions of party-appointed investment arbitrators have been issued by the arbitrator appointed by the party that has lost the case'; that '[t]he most noteworthy aspect of it is that Charles Brower is unable to give a convincing explanation for the fact that 100 per cent of the separate opinions issued in investment arbitrations by party-appointed arbitrators have been rendered by the arbitrator appointed by the losing party'; and that '[t]he Nightingale Article is brilliantly written. Yet, there is an elephant in the room. It does not give an explanation for the fact that 100 per cent of the separate opinions of party-appointed investment arbitrators have been issued by the arbitrator appointed by the party that has lost the case. This is Charles Brower's problem with 100 per cent'.[53]

Time being the great equalizer, has brought an answer. Considering the timeline of the debate starting with Van den Berg's article that came out in 2011,[54] a reply to which Brower and Rosenberg gave in 2013,[55] followed by a response from Van den Berg in 2015,[56] the following two awards break the stalemate.

In *Impregilo v Argentina (I)*, the claimant won the arbitration and the arbitrator appointed by the winning party—Judge Brower—issued a concurring and dissenting opinion.[57] This opinion alone dismantles Van den Berg's thesis; but, considering that the author also observes Van den Berg's admirable point that 'I am unable to respond as I was the presiding arbitrator in that case and I adhere to the principle that one should not discuss cases in which one was involved as an arbitrator',[58] another award will be invoked.[59]

[51] Mosk and Ginsburg (n 19) 274–75.

[52] Noting Van den Berg's vehement opposition towards party-appointed arbitral tribunals, why does he still appear on them? 'My view was that the current method of unilaterally appointing arbitrators may create arbitrators who are dependent in some way on the parties that appointed them. I agreed with Jan Paulsson that the solution might be to replace the method of party-appointed arbitrators with a list-procedure', Van den Berg (n 5) 382.

[53] ibid 381, 383, and 391.

[54] Van den Berg (n 4).

[55] See Charles N Brower and Charles B Rosenberg, 'The Death of the Two-Headed Nightingale: Why the Paulsson–Van den Berg Presumption that Party-Appointed Arbitrators Are Untrustworthy Is Wrongheaded' (2013) Arbitration International 7.

[56] Van den Berg (n 5).

[57] *Impregilo SpA v Argentina (I)*, ICSID Case No ARB/07/17, Concurring and Dissenting Opinion of Judge Charles N Brower (Award) (21 June 2011).

[58] Van den Berg (n 5) 389.

[59] *Impregilo SpA v Argentina (I)*, ICSID Case No ARB/07/17, Concurring and Dissenting Opinion of Judge Charles N Brower (Award) (21 June 2011).

In *Total v Argentina*, the investor won the dispute, and the arbitrator appointed by the winning claimant, Mr Henri Álvarez, issued a dissenting opinion.[60] Again laying rest to Van den Berg's argument that 100 per cent of all dissenting opinions in investment treaty arbitration derive from the 'losing' party.

Turning from Van den Berg's fixation on statistics, he focuses on dissents in the context of 'losing and winning', but provides no indication as to whether his '100 per cent' includes pre-award decisions on jurisdiction, which may fall either way. Indeed, occasionally an arbitrator will issue a dissent to a procedural order, when neither jurisdiction nor the merits have been reached.[61] This was a fairly common occurrence at the Iran–United States Claims Tribunal.[62] In other words, there is no concrete link between dissents and the outcome of an award as dissents can appear at various stages of the arbitral proceedings.[63] Furthermore, dissents have even appeared during ICSID annulment proceedings, in which all three members of the ICSID ad hoc committee considering the matter are appointed, not by any party, but instead by the Chairman of ICSID's Administrative Council from ICSID's Panel of Arbitrators, none of whom may have any connection to the matter under review.[64]

It is thus imperative to weigh the substance and focus of the dissenting opinion. This ranges from objections to the most favoured-nation clause to allocation of costs.[65] In other words, dissenting opinions vary in their scale of dissent.[66] Dissenting opinions are not at all fungible and certainly not all equally drafted.

This strikes Van den Berg's reduction of grouping all dissenting opinions under an umbrella as he notes that 'the fact that 22 per cent [in investment treaty arbitration] compares badly with commercial arbitration, where the percentage is around 8 per cent. It also overlooks the increase of the percentage in investment arbitration, as compared with a decrease in commercial arbitration.'[67] An increase or decrease as compared to a different field of arbitration does not say much; if anything, it hints towards the deficiencies of empirical studies in arbitration. Is an increasing or decreasing trend an authoritative figure of the normative and relative underpinnings these dissents are

[60] *Total SA v Argentina*, ICSID Case No ARB/04/1, Individual Opinion (Dissent) of Henri Alvarez (27 November 2013).

[61] *Mainstream Renewable Power Ltd and others v Germany*, ICSID Case No ARB/21/26, Dissenting Opinion of Antolín Fernández Antuña (Procedural Order No 3, Decision on Bifurcation) (7 June 2022).

[62] See Dissenting Opinion of Judges Holtzmann, Aldrich, and Brower in *The Islamic Republic of Iran* and *United States of America*, Interlocutory Award No ITL 63-A15-FT (20 August 1986) 12 IUSCTR 64.

[63] See *Total SA v Argentina*, ICSID Case No ARB/04/1 and *Tokios Tokelés v Ukraine*, ICSID Case No ARB/02/18, respectively.

[64] ICSID Convention art 52. See *Industria Nacional de Alimentos, SA and Indalsa Perú, SA (formerly Empresas Lucchetti, SA and Lucchetti Perú, SA) v Peru*, ICSID Case No ARB/03/4, Dissenting Opinion of Franklin Berman (Decision on Annulment) (5 September 2007).

[65] For example, the dissenting opinion of Wolfgang Peter dealt with tribunal jurisdiction and with whether the claimants can incorporate into the OIC Investment Agreement (1981), by virtue of its most-favoured-nation treatment clause in Article 8(1), the ICSID arbitration clause in the Iraq–Japan BIT (2012). See *Itisaluna Iraq LLC and others v Iraq*, ICSID Case No ARB/17/10, Dissenting Opinion of Wolfgang Peter (Award) (3 April 2020). Further, for an instance where the dissenting arbitrator dealt exclusively with allocation of costs see *EDF (Services) Limited v Romania*, ICSID Case No ARB/05/13, Dissenting Opinion of Arthur W Rovine (Dissent regarding Costs) (2 October 2009).

[66] cf (n 1) and (n 38).

[67] Van den Berg (n 5) 384.

based upon? Is it possible to justify an increasing or decreasing trend? Is a trajectory in either direction meant to be 'good' or 'bad'? Such statistics discredit the nuanced and complex proceedings behind arbitrations.

A core thesis of Van den Berg's reasoning is that dissents from party-appointed arbitrators are 'undesirable', hence, such invoked statistics do not even specify or support his line of argumentation.[68] To minimize the significance of dissents in international dispute settlement as seen in the well-established practice of the ICJ, Van den Berg notes: '[international dispute settlement] cannot be compared with investment arbitration because in many cases the judges are not appointed by the parties to the case. Thus, International Court of Justice judges cannot be compared with party-appointed investment arbitrators.'[69] If a similar empirical analysis and comparison to a different field—in this case public international law—were to be conducted as per Van den Berg's methodology, why is that ad hoc judges of the ICJ, who are party-appointed, do not always issue dissenting opinions on behalf of the 'losing' party?[70] Do ad hoc judges dissent relatively more or less than their elected counterparts at the ICJ?

In a final, futile attempt, Van den Berg states: 'I propose a temporary stay in dissenting practice by party-appointed arbitrators in investment arbitration until such time as the international arbitration community has been able to address the concerns expressed in my 2009 Article and below.'[71] Despite the call falling on deaf ears, the forwarded arguments above address the concerns expressed and accordingly, would 'lift' the stay, at least one might hope of our debate.[72]

IX. Dissenting Standards

Considering varying legal codes on ethics, one might question whether a code on dissenting opinions would prove beneficial to the development of investment treaty arbitration. It so happens, that there is an *unwritten code*, what might be deemed as practice, of different types of dissenting opinions; a typology of some sort.[73] In light of Alan Redfern's categorization of dissents as either 'good', 'bad', or 'ugly', dissents must meet professional standards that all arbitrators should aspire to attain.[74]

If a code where to be contemplated by reformists, the following considerations deserve further analysis: (1) a draft dissent should be circulated within the tribunal prior to the issuance of an award, (2) a dissent should not be longer than the award itself, (3) dissenters must aim for civility and temperance, (4) dissenters must avoid

[68] Van den Berg (n 4) 830.
[69] ibid.
[70] There have been 125 different ad hoc judges, past and present, as per the official register of the ICJ.
[71] Van den Berg (n 5) 382–83.
[72] Van den Berg, in relation to justifying dissenting opinions, held: 'I admit that it makes me think that one day there might be a first time for me too', Van den Berg (n 4) 835.
[73] Alan Redfern, 'Dissenting Opinions in International Commercial Arbitration: The Good, the Bad and the Ugly' (2004) 20 Arbitration International 223.
[74] ibid.

breaching confidentiality, and (5) dissenters should work as economically as possible, having regard for the fact that it may well increase the length of the time needed for issuance of the award and the fees to be paid by the parties. Such guidelines could also be implemented by arbitral codes of ethics.[75]

A draft dissenting opinion circulated to the tribunal prior to publication proves good practice and stimulates discussion as it offers the first line of critique to the award. Such an approach encourages dialogue and confirms that tribunal members considered thorny questions, and have the opportunity, to reconsider their positions.[76] If anything, an as yet unpublished dissenting opinion would give the tribunal more time to reflect upon the outcome and encourages greater informal flexibility among the arbitrators without a burdensome procedural requirement of some sort being imposed. It also reduces the element of 'surprise' and any animosity that it might spur.[77]

It is common practice that dissenting opinions are published at the time of the award's issuance. Notably, the Iran–United States Claims Tribunal permits the filing of dissenting or concurring opinions after the date of the award,[78] at times, issued at great length after the award.[79] Hence, the timing of issuing a dissenting opinion plays a salient role in what effect the dissenting arbitrator wants to achieve. Circulate a dissenting opinion prior to the final award, and the tribunal seeks to make sure that the final award is a well-reasoned outcome. A dissenting opinion issued simultaneously with the award best highlights the arbitrators' differing views. A dissenting opinion published long after the award denotes a clear dissatisfaction with the ultimate result but also reduces (if not, eliminates) the impact of the dissenting opinion.

A view held by prominent members of the Iran–United States Claims Tribunal is that dissenting opinions not only have enhanced the legitimacy of the Tribunal, but considering that all claims before it have been based on the Algiers Accords—a brief yet seminal declaration covering only fourteen pages—dissenting opinions covered gaps not previously addressed.[80] Ultimately, dissenting opinions shaped the workings of the Tribunal and its effectiveness in administering and resolving disputes. Considering the ramifications of an arbitrator resigning, the detriment to all parties of withdrawal,[81] and the symbolism of an arbitrator not signing the award,[82] dissents are the best alternative to discontent.

[75] Mosk and Ginsburg (n 19) 271–73.

[76] See also Hans Smit, 'Dissenting Opinions in Arbitration' (2004) ICC International Court of Arbitration Bulletin 37.

[77] Van den Berg (n 5) 387.

[78] Mosk and Ginsburg (n 19) 271.

[79] Concurring and Dissenting Opinion of Assadollah Noori in *Frederica Lincoln Riahi* and *The Government of the Islamic Republic of Iran*, Final Award No 600-485-1 (18 September 2003) 37 IUSCTR 11, 305. The Final Award was signed on 27 February 2003.

[80] Charles N Brower and others, *The Iran–United States Claims Tribunal* (2nd edn, Brill Nijhoff forthcoming).

[81] Arbitrations initiated as per the Jay Treaty between Britain and the United States witnessed both parties withdrawing from proceedings, bringing the arbitrations to a halt. See also Charles H Brower II, 'The Functions and Limits of Arbitration and Judicial Settlement under Private and Public International Law' (2008) Duke Journal of Comparative & International Law 259.

[82] The Iran–US Claims Tribunal faced such scenarios where dissent can be expressed without words, to the degree of not taking any action in the first place. See (n 3).

X. Conclusion

A world in which *nemine dissentiente* rules supreme amongst investment treaty tribunals would only lead to conformity, concessions, and the concealment of how arbitrators truly believe justice should be administered. Considering the ramifications that investment treaty awards have not just on the disputing parties, but to the public at large, an arbitrator's decision to dissent seems not so much a right, as it is an obligation to adhere to judicial standards, and—in the gravest of circumstances—a duty to answer.

In the Code of Hammurabi, the laws mention that '[i]f a judge try a case, reach a decision, and present his judgment in writing; if later error shall appear in his decision, and it be through his own fault, then he shall pay twelve times the fine set by him in the case, and he shall be publicly removed from the judge's bench, and never again shall he sit there to render judgement'.[83] Substituting for such points of antiquated proceedings with modernity, while keeping the spirit of the code alive, one can only hope that dissenting arbitrators possess the same bravery, integrity, and foresight their ancient counterparts aspired to reach.

[83] *The Code of Hammurabi* (tr Leonard William King, 11th edn, Encyclopaedia Britannica 1910).

22

An Empirical Analysis of Legal Reasoning

Comparing Investment Arbitration and International Commercial Arbitration

SI Strong

I. Introduction

Commentators have long sought to discern the differences between investment arbitration and international commercial arbitration. The problem is that most analyses are based on anecdotal evidence and doctrinal research,[1] with empirical research focusing exclusively on either investment arbitration[2] or international commercial arbitration.[3] Comparative empirical studies are virtually unknown.[4] This chapter seeks to remedy that situation by conducting a narrowly focused empirical analysis comparing legal reasoning in international commercial and investment disputes. Of course, the task is not without its challenges. Legal reasoning is notoriously difficult to study empirically, and the choice of an appropriate methodology can be a daunting task. One approach involves the use of surveys and interviews to try to understand what motivates a judge or arbitrator, although such results can be subject to errors associated with self-reporting.[5] Another approach involves objective methodologies such as quantitative (coding) analyses of adjudicators' written decisions, although that fails to address the motivations behind a particular reasoning style. The best technique may be to combine both quantitative and qualitative elements in the same study, thereby allowing for a simultaneous cross-check of results, although that may require a book-length work to discuss the various findings.[6]

[1] eg Karl-Heinz Böckstiegel, 'Commercial and Investment Arbitration: How Different Are They Today? The Lalive Lecture 2012' (2012) 28 Arbitration International 577; Anthea Roberts, 'Divergence between Investment and Commercial Arbitration' (2012) 106 Confronting Complexity: Proceedings of the 106th Meeting of the American Society of International Law 297; SI Strong, *International Commercial Arbitration: A Guide for US Judges* (Federal Judicial Center 2012) 3.

[2] eg Daniel Behn, 'Legitimacy, Evolution, and Growth in Investment Treaty Arbitration: Empirically Evaluating the State-of-the-Art' (2015) 46 Georgetown Law Journal 363; Susan D Franck, *Arbitration Costs: Myths and Realities in Investment Treaty Arbitration* (OUP 2019); Susan D Franck, 'Empirically Evaluating Claims about Investment Treaty Arbitration' (2007) 86 North Carolina Law Review 1.

[3] eg Christopher R Drahozal, 'Commercial Norms, Commercial Codes, and International Commercial Arbitration' (2000) 33 Vanderbilt Journal of Transnational Law; SI Strong, *Legal Reasoning across Commercial Disputes: Comparing Judicial and Arbitral Analyses* (OUP 2020); Queen Mary, University of London, School of International Arbitration, Research (containing various empirical studies into international commercial arbitration) <https://arbitration.qmul.ac.uk/research/>.

[4] The author found no such studies during the design phase of this research.

[5] Strong (n 3) 31, 187, 289 (discussing blind spot bias and other cognitive distortions).

[6] ibid 5 (reflecting that type of triangulated analyses).

SI Strong, *An Empirical Analysis of Legal Reasoning* In: *The Award in International Investment Arbitration*. Edited by: Katia Fach Gómez and Catharine Titi, Oxford University Press. © Katia Fach Gómez and Aikaterini Titi 2024. DOI: 10.1093/9780191975936.003.0022

Restrictions of space preclude use of this third type of analysis, so this chapter will pursue an objective analysis of original arbitral awards generated in international commercial and investment settings using the coding method. As novel as this research is, it is not conducted in a vacuum. Instead, it builds off a combined qualitative–quantitative study conducted by the author on legal reasoning in commercial disputes.[7] That research compared legal reasoning across the judicial–arbitral, national–international, common law–civil law divides, and used an expanded form of the current coding analysis as one of several interrelated methodological techniques.[8] The study reflected herein therefore has a strong foundation from which to begin.

This chapter begins by describing the design of the current empirical study, then presents the substantive findings. In so doing, this chapter introduces several new empirical methodologies, including a novel paragraph-counting technique and a citation count analysis of both legal and factual authorities. The discussion concludes by pulling together various strands of analysis and providing ideas for future research.

II. Methodology and Demographics

A. Generating the Data Set

Because empirical research is only as good as its underlying methodology, it is critical to describe how a study was constructed to allow readers to evaluate the legitimacy of the results.[9] One of the most important aspects of a coding analysis involves identification of the sample population. For non-random studies such as this, it is necessary to identify suitably representative samples to analyse, using selection criteria that are not related to the variables under investigation.[10]

Although investment arbitration has become increasingly transparent, the confidential nature of arbitration often makes it difficult to obtain original arbitral awards to serve as the basis for empirical studies. In this case, a number of arbitral institutions were approached to see whether they would allow access to their unpublished awards. Unfortunately, none of the organizations was willing to allow independent scholarly analysis of their original awards.[11] Fortunately, an alternative mechanism was available. When a motion to vacate or enforce an arbitral award is filed in US court, the requesting party must provide a copy of the original award, which is then available as part

[7] ibid.

[8] The coding analysis in that study included international commercial awards, domestic commercial awards, and judicial decisions from the United States, England, and Canada, ibid 298–307. Other methodologies included a major international survey and a series of semi-structured interviews, ibid 26–296.

[9] Lee Epstein and Gary King, 'Building an Infrastructure for Empirical Research in the Law' (2003) 53 Journal of Legal Education 311, 316–17; Susan D Franck, 'Empiricism and International Law: Insights from Investment Treaty Dispute Resolution' (2008) 48 Virginia Journal of International Law 767, 784–95.

[10] The absence of random selection is not necessarily problematic, particularly in small-size studies such as this. Lee Epstein and Gary King, 'The Rules of Inference' (2002) 51 University of Chicago Law Review 1, 113; see also ibid 108 (describing random selection).

[11] Strong (n 3) 298.

of the public docket. A search was therefore conducted of the US federal courts' Public Access to Court Electronic Records (PACER) system, which is searchable through the Bloomberg legal database.[12] The search parameters focused on capturing proceedings that were likely to include an international arbitral award.[13] Ultimately, thirty-two fully reasoned international commercial awards and eight contract-based investment awards were identified as suitable for study.

When designing this study, the decision was made to focus exclusively on investment awards arising out of investment contracts rather than investment treaties. While contract-based investment arbitration operates largely in the shadow of treaty-based proceedings, contract-based investment arbitration remains an important part of the investor-state arbitration regime.[14] It was also believed that combining contract-based investment awards with treaty-based investment awards could create unintended problems with representation, even if the treaty-based awards were limited to those brought to US courts for enforcement under the United Nations Convention on the Recognition and Enforcement of Foreign Arbitral Awards (New York Convention).[15] Now that the methodology is established, it is hoped that future studies can and will focus on comparing treaty-based awards with international commercial awards.

When considering the results of the current analysis, it is important to recognize that the data is based exclusively on awards that were brought to US courts for enforcement or vacatur. This could suggest a possible bias towards US-style arbitration because the awards involved award debtors with assets in the United States or US-based arbitral proceedings. Future studies involving awards from a wider geographic region may be necessary to confirm the findings of this analysis.

B. Generating and Analysing the Coding Criteria

The second key task involved creation of a 'code book' that specified the information to be pulled by the coders from the individual awards. The code book used in the underlying study involved seventy-six different datapoints, though not all matters are reflected in the current analysis for reasons of space.[16]

The coded material was statistically analysed using t-tests and two-tailed z-tests.[17] In all cases, the null hypothesis (H_0) anticipated that the comparative cohorts were the same

[12] US Courts, Public Access to Court Electronic Records <www.pacer.gov/login.html>.

[13] Awards were identified using the search sequence 'award /s enforc! and "New York Convention" or "Convention on the Recognition or Enforcement" or "Panama Convention"' in addition to the relevant date parameters (2003–2005 and 2015–2017), Strong (n 3) 299.

[14] World Bank, 'Spotlight on Contract-Based Disputes at ICSID' <https://icsid.worldbank.org/node/20966>.

[15] Some treaty-based awards, such as those issued under the ICSID Additional Facility, are enforceable under the New York Convention. United Nations Convention on the Recognition and Enforcement of Foreign Arbitral Awards (10 June 1958) 330 UNTS 3; see also ICSID, Additional Facility Rules 2022, art 3.

[16] For the full analysis of commercial decisions and awards, see Strong (n 3) 297–348; see also ibid appendix III (containing the full code book).

[17] T-statistical tests compare the averages (means) of two independent populations (μ_1 and μ_2) along a single variable to determine whether any difference exists other than that attributable to chance, while two-tailed z-statistical tests compare the proportional responses of two independent populations (μ_1 and μ_2) along a single

(H_0: $\mu_1 - \mu_2 = 0$ or, equivalently, $\mu_1 = \mu_2$), while the alternate hypothesis (H_1) was that the comparative cohorts were not the same (H_1: $\mu_1 \neq \mu_2$). A statistical significance was deemed to exist in cases with an alpha (*a1*) level of $p<.05$ or lower.[18] The study reports *a1* levels of $p<.05$, $p<.01$ and $p<.001$.[19]

III. Substantive Findings

A. Amounts in Dispute

The first item to consider involves the amounts in dispute. While no attempt was made to determine whether and to what extent the value of a dispute might affect the complexity of the legal reasoning reflected in the award, one could logically assume that higher-value disputes would lead to longer and/or more detailed analyses.

Figure 22.1 reflects both the average and median amounts of awards included in this study, with damages awarded in foreign currency converted to US dollars as of the date of the award.[20] The chart only reports actual damages awards and excludes matters where the claimant/counterclaimant did not prevail or where the only relief was non-monetary in nature. The figures do not include attorneys' fees, arbitrators' fees, administrative fees, or interest so as to provide a more accurate comparison of the quantum in dispute. The reported amounts also do not incorporate any applicable setoffs but instead combine damages awarded to both claimants and counterclaimants so as to reflect the scope of the dispute overall.

As Figure 22.1 shows, investment awards exceed international commercial awards by a considerable margin. This outcome was not surprising, given conventional wisdom suggesting that investment disputes involve higher sums than commercial disputes.[21] The difference was statistically significant, with a t-test showing a high degree

variable to determine whether any difference exists other than that attributable to chance. T-test statistics were run on Figures 22.1–22.2, 22.6, 22.8, and 22.10 and calculated via Medcalc, see Medcalc <www.medcalc.org/calc/comparison_of_means.php>. Z-test statistics were run on Figures 22.3–22.5, 22.7, 22.9, and 22.11 and calculated via Social Science Statistics. Social Science Statistics <www.socscistatistics.com/tests/ztest/default2.aspx>.

[18] Statistical significance refers to 'the likelihood, or probability, that a statistic derived from a sample represents some genuine phenomenon in the population', Timothy C Urdan, *Statistics in Plain English* (Routledge 2005) 50; see also Epstein and King (n 10) 60.

[19] A *p* value of .05 means there is a 5 per cent likelihood (or less) that the difference between the two populations is attributable to chance, while a *p* level of .01 means there is a 1 per cent likelihood that the difference between the two populations is attributable to chance. *P* levels of .001 are even more robust, meaning that there is a .1 per cent likelihood that the difference between the two populations is random. Robert W Frick, 'The Appropriate Use of Null Hypothesis Testing' (1996) 1 Psychological Methods 379–90.

[20] Currency conversations were made using the following website: <www.xe.com/currencytables/>.

[21] Though no studies were found directly comparing amounts in dispute across the international commercial–investment divide, statistics from various organizations seem to support this view. eg Matthew Hodgson, Yarik Kryvoi, and Daniel Hrcka, *2021 Empirical Study: Costs, Damages, and Duration in Investor-State Arbitration* (British Institute of International and Comparative Law 2021) 26 (noting the average amount claimed by investors between 2017 and 2020 was USD1.1 billion, with a median claim of USD108.5 million); International Chamber of Commerce, Dispute Resolution Statistics 2020 (citing the median amount in dispute for international commercial

Awards—investment	266,075,000 [43,879,000] (391,042,000) 6
Awards—international reasoned	11,646,000 [2,260,000] (21,277,000) 26
	T-test outcome: $p = 0.0015$

Figure 22.1 Size of damages awards in US dollars (averages rounded to the nearest 1000, followed by medians rounded to the nearest 1000 in brackets, standard deviation rounded to the nearest 1000 in parentheses and sample (N) size)

of confidence ($p<.01$) that the difference between the two populations is not attributable to chance.

B. Legal Reasoning

Legal reasoning includes three separate but interrelated elements: legal analysis; factual analysis; and mixed analysis, where facts are applied to the relevant legal standard.[22] Empirical studies of legal decision-making have traditionally focused only on legal analysis, even though recent studies have demonstrated that factual analyses are as important, if not more important, than legal analyses in complex commercial disputes.[23] This chapter therefore seeks to broaden the understanding of arbitral reasoning by measuring and evaluating all three aspects of legal reasoning, using two different methodologies: a paragraph-by-paragraph analysis and a citation count analysis.

C. Paragraph Analysis

One of the most innovative aspects of the current research involves a paragraph-by-paragraph analysis of the two types of arbitral awards. Previous coding studies have focused exclusively on citation counts of legal authorities, providing a somewhat incomplete picture of the reasoning process.[24] The coding team was instructed to count

disputes as USD5.6 million in 2020 and the average amount of USD54.1 million in 2020) <https://iccwbo.org/publication/icc-dispute-resolution-statistics-2020/>.

[22] Strong (n 3) 10, 308.
[23] ibid 9–10, 354.
[24] eg Stephen J Choi and G Mitu Gulati, 'Bias in Judicial Citations: A Window into the Behavior of Judges?' (2008) 37 Journal of Legal Studies 87; Stephen J Choi and G Mitu Gulati, 'Trading Votes for Reasoning: Covering in Judicial Opinions' (2008) 81 Southern California Law Review 735; Jeffrey P Commission, 'Precedent in Investment Treaty Arbitration: A Citation Analysis of a Developing Jurisprudence' (2007) 24 Journal of

	Total paragraphs	Percentage facts	Percentage law	Percentage application
Awards—investment	646.00 [433.00] (632.48) 8	0.35 (0.18) 8	0.11 (0.06) 8	0.10 (0.10) 8
Awards—international reasoned	133.28 [129.00] (89.78) 32	0.29 (0.19) 32	0.07 (0.05) 32	0.15 (0.19) 32
	t-test outcome: $p < 0.0001$	t-test outcome: $p = 0.4249$	t-test outcome: $p = 0.0590$	t-test outcome: $p = 0.4789$

Figure 22.2 Paragraph analysis (averages followed by standard deviation in parentheses and sample (N) size; medians in brackets for total paragraphs only)

the number of paragraphs associated with procedural analyses, parties' arguments, purely legal analyses, purely factual analyses, mixed factual-legal analyses (ie, the application of the law to the facts), and the final disposition of the case (the *dispositif*). In so doing, this study took full account of all aspects of legal reasoning, providing a broader and hopefully more accurate picture of what arbitrators are doing.

Figure 22.2 outlines the total number of paragraphs associated with investment and international commercial awards as well as the percentage of paragraphs dedicated to legal discussions, factual discussions, and mixed discussions in which the facts are applied to the law. The first thing to note is the overall length of the various awards. Not surprisingly, investment awards were considerably longer than international commercial awards, a phenomenon that has long been believed to be true but that has not been conclusively established.[25] The difference in overall length was statistically significant under a t-test analysis at a high degree of probability ($p<0.0001$). This result is consistent with the assumption that higher-value disputes are more likely to be associated with longer awards, since Figure 22.1 shows that investment awards have a higher dollar value than international commercial awards.[26]

Though the length of the award varies significantly between investment and international commercial arbitration, the structure of the awards does not, as measured by the paragraph-by-paragraph analysis. Indeed, a comparison of the percentages of paragraphs dedicated to factual, legal, and mixed analysis showed no statistically significant differences under a t-test calculation. This suggests that international arbitrators are writing in a similar style, regardless of the type of proceeding, even if investment

International Arbitration 129; Joshua B Fischman and David S Law, 'What Is Judicial Ideology, and How Should We Measure It?' (2009) 29 Washington University Journal of Law & Policy 133, 167; W Mark C Weidemaier, 'Judging-Lite: How Arbitrators Use and Create Precedent' (2012) 90 North Carolina Law Review 1091, 1105–06.

[25] Max Bonnell, 'Arbitral Awards: How Long Is Long Enough?' (*Kluwer Arbitration Blog*, 2 September 2022) <http://arbitrationblog.kluwerarbitration.com/2022/09/02/arbitral-awards-how-long-is-long-enough/>.

[26] Figure 22.1.

	Fact percentage higher	Law percentage higher	Two percentages identical	Total
Awards—investment	7 (.88)	1 (.12)	0 (.00)	8
Awards—international reasoned	27 (.84)	2 (.06)	3 (.09)	32
	Two-tailed z-test outcome: $p = 0.82588$	Two-tailed z-test outcome: $p = 0.54850$	Two-tailed z-test outcome: $p = 0.36812$	

Figure 22.3 Comparison of percentage of fact paragraphs to law paragraphs (actual numbers followed by proportion in parentheses)

arbitrators are writing longer awards. This result is consistent with the understanding that a significant number of international arbitrators work in both investment and commercial matters.[27]

The next inquiry compares the length of different sorts of paragraphs. According to Figure 22.3, both international commercial and investment arbitration have a higher average number of paragraphs involving factual issues than paragraphs involving legal issues. However, a two-tailed z-test calculation of the various percentages did not show any statistically significant differences between the two types of arbitration.

This information is useful because it appears to rebut conventional wisdom suggesting that investment arbitration is more formal and perhaps more 'legalistic' than international commercial arbitration.[28] It also demonstrates the central importance of factual analysis in any legal adjudication, a point that was made repeatedly by interviewees and survey participants in the author's earlier study on legal reasoning in commercial settings.[29]

Figure 22.4 compares the percentage of paragraphs dedicated solely to factual analyses to the percentage of mixed paragraphs reflecting the application of the law to the facts. The data here shows that the percentage of fact paragraphs is higher than the percentage of mixed paragraphs for both international commercial and investment awards, again confirming data from interviewees and survey participants in the author's study on commercial disputes noting the importance of factual considerations in arbitration and litigation.[30] Notably, a two-tailed z-test yielded no statistically significant differences between international commercial and investment awards.

The final paragraph analysis compares the percentage of paragraphs dedicated solely to legal analyses to the percentage of mixed paragraphs. As Figure 22.5 shows, the percentage of paragraphs dedicated to the application of law to facts is higher than the percentage of paragraphs dedicated exclusively to the law in both international commercial and

[27] Böckstiegel (n 1) 582.
[28] ibid 585; Roberts (n 1) 298.
[29] Strong (n 3) 354.
[30] ibid.

	Fact percentage higher	Application percentage higher	Two percentages identical	Total
Awards—investment	7 (.88)	1 (.12)	0 (.00)	8
Awards—international reasoned	24 (.75)	8 (.25)	0 (.00)	32
	Two-tailed z-test outcome: $p = 0.44726$	Two-tailed z-test outcome: $p = 0.44726$	Non-number calculation	

Figure 22.4 Comparison of percentage of fact paragraphs to application paragraphs (actual numbers followed by proportion in parentheses)

	Law percentage higher	Application percentage higher	Two percentages identical	Total
Awards—investment	3 (.38)	4 (.50)	1 (.12)	8
Awards—international reasoned	14 (.44)	17 (.53)	1 (.03)	32
	Two-tailed z-test outcome: $p = 0.74896$	Two-tailed z-test outcome: $p = 0.87288$	Two-tailed z-test outcome: $p = 0.27572$	

Figure 22.5 Comparison of percentage of law paragraphs to application paragraphs (actual numbers followed by proportion in parentheses)

investment matters. However, the intensity of the difference is less than that in Figure 22.4, which compared the percentage of paragraphs dedicated to the application of law to facts and the percentage of paragraphs dedicated exclusively to the facts. Nevertheless, Figure 22.5 did not generate any statistically significant difference between international commercial and investment awards under a two-tailed z-test calculation, suggesting that international arbitrators approach legal reasoning in a similar manner, regardless of the type of dispute they are resolving.[31]

B. Citation Count Analysis

As intriguing as the paragraph-by-paragraph analysis may be, it is a somewhat novel methodology.[32] As a result, this study also adopted the more conventional technique of counting citations as a means of evaluating legal reasoning.[33] However, the current

[31] Böckstiegel (n 1) 582.
[32] The methodology was first introduced by the author in the study on legal reasoning in commercial disputes, Strong (n 3) 321–28.
[33] See text to n 24.

analysis improved on traditional citation count methodologies by (1) distinguishing between different types of legal authorities; (2) differentiating between initial and subsequent citations;[34] and (3) counting factual authorities (evidence) in addition to legal authorities.

1. Legal Authorities

The discussion begins with legal authorities. Here, the coding team distinguished between international treaties and conventions; statutes or regulations (including any legislative or administrative enactments); arbitral rules (meaning any institutional or non-institutional rule set for arbitration); judicial decisions (interpreted as decisions from any jurisdiction); arbitral awards (defined as arbitral awards involving matters other than the instant dispute); commentary (such as books, articles and other forms of scholarship); and any other legal authorities not included in the previous categories.[35]

Figure 22.6 shows the average number of legal citations, separated by initial references (meaning the first citations to unique materials within the relevant categories) and subsequent references (meaning citations to materials that had already been mentioned once in the relevant categories). The chart also includes the outcomes of a t-statistical test. During the design phase, it was decided to use a sample (N) size that reflected the number of awards that mentioned that particular type of authority at issue rather than the total number of awards in that particular cohort. This approach was adopted because the absence of a reference to a particular type of authority might have been due to the type of dispute rather than the reasoning style of the arbitrator. For example, the absence of a reference to a statute might simply reflect the absence of a statutory claim.

Figure 22.6 reveals two statistically significant differences between international commercial and investment awards: initial citations to treaties, which was significant at the $p<.05$ level, and initial citations to statutes or regulations, which was significant at the $p<.001$ level. The first of these results is somewhat predictable, since one would expect that investment arbitration to be more likely to be affected by treaties than commercial disputes, even in contract-based investment disputes. The second result is more surprising, since it shows investment treaties having a significantly higher number of citations to statutes or regulations. Further research is necessary to determine the reason behind this result.

The next issue to consider involves the proportion of references to each type of authority within each cohort. This figure was obtained by dividing the number of awards that referred to each type of authority by the total number of awards in that particular cohort.

[34] Subsequent references were calculated regardless of the form of the subsequent citation. In other words, a subsequent citation could include a shortened name of the initial authority or could involve some sort of abbreviation, such as id, ibid, op cit, or loc cit.

[35] Strong (n 3) appendix III. Any reference to the above items was included in the citation count, regardless of whether it was independently cited by the arbitral tribunal or whether it was simply embedded in quoted material.

	Awards—investment	Awards—international reasoned	
Initial treaties	3 [3.00] (2.00) 3	1.38 [1.00] (.96) 13	t-test outcome: $p = 0.0479$
Subsequent treaties	20.67 [4.00] (31.51) 3	9.00 [13.00] (6.89) 5	t-test outcome: $p = 0.4335$
Initial statutes or regulations	7.86 [8.00] (5.37) 7	2.70 [2.00] (2.18) 27	t-test outcome: $p = 0.0004$
Subsequent statutes or regulations	23.00 [14.00] (27.71) 6	9.64 [4.50] (11.48) 14	t-test outcome: $p = 0.1364$
Initial arbitral rules	3.29 [2.00] (2.56) 7	2.48 [1.00] (2.04) 27	t-test outcome: $p = 0.3804$
Subsequent arbitral rules	7.00 [4.00] (6.63) 5	4.25 [4.00] (2.41) 16	t-test outcome: $p = 0.1654$
Initial judicial decisions	6.33 [4.50] (6.09) 6	6.50 [3.50] (6.35) 20	t-test outcome: $p = 0.9542$
Subsequent judicial decisions	5.00 [2.00] (6.08) 3	5.64 [2.00] (9.09) 14	t-test outcome: $p = 0.9100$
Initial arbitral awards	3.60 [4.00] (1.82) 5	4.25 [1.50] (7.23) 8	t-test outcome: $p = 0.8496$
Subsequent arbitral awards	9.50 [9.50] (12.02) 2	6.60 [8.00] (5.32) 5	t-test outcome: $p = 0.6496$
Initial commentary	4.75 [4.50] (2.50) 4	4.50 [3.00] (3.21) 8	t-test outcome: $p = 0.8950$
Subsequent commentary	2.00 [1.00] (1.73) 3	3.00 [2.00] (2.00) 4	t-test outcome: $p = 0.5207$
Initial other authority	3.67 [2.00] (4.13) 6	4.69 [2.00] (5.17) 13	t-test outcome: $p = 0.6777$
Subsequent other authority	13.67 [5.00] (17.67) 3	16.20 [16.00] (11.12) 5	t-test outcome: $p = 0.8082$

Figure 22.6 Average number of legal citations per award (averages followed by medians in brackets, standard deviation in parentheses and sample (N) size)

It is possible that this analysis could be affected by the type of dispute at issue. For example, a statute or regulation cannot be cited as authority unless the claim is based on a statute or regulation. However, the information was nevertheless considered useful as a means of understanding the types of legal materials that are considered persuasive in a particular forum and the likelihood that a judge or arbitrator will discuss an authority in depth, as opposed to merely in passing.

Figure 22.7 provides a somewhat different perspective than Figure 22.6 on the use of legal authority in international arbitral disputes. In Figure 22.7, the only statistically significant difference under a two-tailed z-test involved initial arbitral awards, with investment arbitrators being more likely to cite arbitral awards than international commercial arbitrators. This result appears to confirm the longstanding theoretical understanding of investment arbitration as utilizing a system of 'soft precedent'.[36]

2. Factual Authorities (Evidence)

The investigation then moved to factual authorities (evidence). Since this was the first known attempt to quantify citation rates for evidentiary matters outside the commercial context, care had to be taken when designing the different categories to ensure that they described materials that might be used in all types of international arbitral disputes. It was decided to create a separate category for contracts, since most commercial disputes and all contract-based investment disputes would involve a contract.

Figure 22.8 shows the three different categories of evidentiary materials that were counted: references to contracts, references to written or oral testimony, and references to other evidentiary materials. A distinction was made between initial and subsequent citations, mirroring the technique used in Figure 22.6.

As an initial matter, the figures relating to contract citations were higher than expected in both international commercial and investment settings. This data is consistent with commentary and anecdotal evidence suggesting that international disputes are moving away from a single-contract model towards multi-contract disputes.[37]

Another interesting phenomenon involved witness testimony, which included written and oral testimony taken either before or during the hearing. While it may be useful in the future to distinguish between testimony given by parties, third parties, and experts, it was unknown at the time the study was designed whether the data would support that level of nuance. Having set the foundation with this research, future work in this field can delve further into these issues.

As with Figure 22.6, the sample (N) size used in Figure 22.8 reflects the number of awards that included that particular type of evidence rather than the total number of awards in that particular cohort. This approach was used because the absence of a reference to a particular type of authority might have been due to the type of procedure

[36] Gabrielle Kaufmann-Kohler, 'Arbitral Precedent: Dream, Necessity or Excuse?' (2007) 23 Arbitration International 357, 361–73.

[37] SI Strong, 'Increasing Legalism in International Commercial Arbitration: A New Theory of Causes, A New Approach to Cures' (2013) 7 World Arbitration and Mediation Review 117, 119.

	Awards—investment	Awards—international reasoned	
Initial treaties	3 (.38)	13 (.41)	Two-tailed z-test outcome: $p = 0.87288$
Subsequent treaties	3 (.38)	5 (.16)	Two-tailed z-test outcome: $p = 0.16758$
Initial statutes or regulations	7 (.88)	27 (.84)	Two-tailed z-test outcome: $p = 0.82588$
Subsequent statutes or regulations	6 (.75)	14 (.44)	Two-tailed z-test outcome: $p = 0.11410$
Initial arbitral rules	7 (.88)	27 (.84)	Two-tailed z-test outcome: $p = 0.82588$
Subsequent arbitral rules	5 (.62)	16 (.50)	Two-tailed z-test outcome: $p = 0.52870$
Initial judicial decisions	6 (.75)	20 (.62)	Two-tailed z-test outcome: $p = 0.50926$
Subsequent judicial decisions	3 (.38)	14 (.44)	Two-tailed z-test outcome: $p = 0.74896$
Initial arbitral awards	5 (.62)	8 (.25)	Two-tailed z-test outcome: $p = 0.04236$
Subsequent arbitral awards	2 (.25)	5 (.16)	Two-tailed z-test outcome: $p = 0.53526$
Initial commentary	4 (.50)	8 (.25)	Two-tailed z-test outcome: $p = 0.16758$
Subsequent commentary	3 (.38)	4 (.12)	Two-tailed z-test outcome: $p = 0.09692$
Initial other authority	6 (.75)	13 (.41)	Two-tailed z-test outcome: $p = 0.08186$
Subsequent other authority	3 (.38)	5 (.16)	Two-tailed z-test outcome: $p = 0.16758$
Total	8	32	

Figure 22.7 Proportion of awards per cohort citing legal authority (actual numbers followed by proportion in parentheses)

rather than the personal predilections of the arbitrator. For example, some arbitrators might have proceeded on a documents-only basis without any written or oral testimony.

The t-test analysis showed three statistically significant differences, all at the $p<.05$ level: subsequent witness testimony, initial other documents, and subsequent other documents. The legal literature does not provide any explanation for these differences. Further research into the nature of 'other documents' might shed some light on this issue.

Figure 22.9 considers the proportion of references to each type of factual authority within each cohort so as to better understand the types of factual authorities that are considered persuasive in a particular place or procedure and the likelihood that an arbitrator will discuss an authority in depth, as opposed to merely in passing. This figure

	Awards—investment	Awards—international reasoned	
Initial contract cites	15.50 [7.50] (18.54) 8	7.42 [2.00] (14.62) 31	t-test outcome: $p = 0.1950$
Subsequent contract cites	30.33 [14.0] (34.21) 6	18.81 [9.00] (25.80) 27	t-test outcome: $p = 0.3576$
Initial witness testimony cites	6.00 [4.00] (6.95) 7	10.28 [3.50] (16.24) 18	t-test outcome: $p = 0.5114$
Subsequent witness testimony cites	42.40 [33.00] (41.75) 5	14.50 [7.00] (17.37) 16	t-test outcome: $p = 0.0393$
Initial other document cites	47.50 [17.50] (57.92) 8	15.76 [5.00] (24.65) 21	t-test outcome: $p = 0.0449$
Subsequent other document cites	131.40 [15.00] 192.01 5	12.07 [7.00] (13.31) 14	t-test outcome: $p = 0.0259$

Figure 22.8 Average number of factual citations per award (averages followed by medians in brackets, standard deviation in parentheses and sample (N) size)

was obtained by dividing the number of awards that referred to each type of authority by the total number of awards in that particular cohort.

The results here showed more consistency between international commercial and investment awards than was the case with Figure 22.8. Indeed, a two-tailed z-test analysis did not identify any statistically significant differences between international commercial and investment awards with respect to the proportion of awards citing each type of evidence. This conclusion does not invalidate the findings generated by Figure 22.8 but simply provides a different perspective on the use of evidence by arbitrators, suggesting that the percentage of arbitrators using factual materials is approximately the same across the investment–commercial divide, even if arbitrators cite evidence differently depending on the context in which they find themselves.

Thus far, the analysis has focused separately on legal authorities and factual authorities. The next two calculations make comparisons across the legal–factual divide.

Figure 22.10 reports the total number of legal and factual citations in each cohort and compares the average figures, providing an understanding of the relative importance of legal authorities as compared to factual authorities in each cohort. As the figure shows, the average number of factual citations is higher than the average number of legal citations in both international commercial and investment awards. A t-test analysis showed the difference between the two cohorts was statistically significant at the

	Awards—investment	Awards—international reasoned	
Initial contract cites	8 (1.00)	31 (.97)	Two-tailed z-test outcome: $p = 0.61006$
Subsequent contract cites	6 (.75)	27 (.84)	Two-tailed z-test outcome: $p = 0.53526$
Initial witness testimony cites	7 (.88)	18 (.56)	Two-tailed z-test outcome: $p = 0.10310$
Subsequent witness testimony cites	5 (.62)	16 (.50)	Two-tailed z-test outcome: $p = 0.52870$
Initial other document cites	8 (1.00)	21 (.66)	Two-tailed z-test outcome: $p = 0.05118$
Subsequent other document cites	5 (.62)	14 (.44)	Two-tailed z-test outcome: $p = 0.34212$
Total	8	32	

Figure 22.9 Proportion of awards per cohort citing factual authority (actual numbers followed by proportion in parentheses)

$p<.05$ level for the total number of legal citations and the $p<.01$ level for the total number of factual citations. This suggests that investment arbitration is more 'cite-heavy' than international commercial arbitration.

One of the problems of this particular methodology is that it simply reports where differences occur without describing why those differences arise. As a result, it is unclear whether the difference in this case arises simply because investment awards are longer than international commercial awards (at least according to a paragraph-count analysis)[38] or because investment awards are more densely packed with citations. Further research on awards of similar lengths may be able to resolve that question.

Perhaps the most interesting aspect of Figure 22.10 is the final column, which shows the ratio of legal citations to factual citations in each comparative cohort, using both averages and medians. This figure was obtained by dividing the average number of legal citations in each cohort by the average number of factual citations in the same group.

Although it was not possible to run a statistical analysis on this data, the column reports the relative incidence of legal citations to factual citations in each type of proceeding. Interestingly, despite the higher overall number of citations in investment arbitration, international commercial arbitration showed a higher proportion of legal

[38] Figure 22.2.

	Total legal citations	Total factual citations	Ratio: legal to factual citations
Awards—investment	62.38 [49.00] (54.79) 8	198.25 [129.00] (237.11) 8	.34 [.38]
Awards—international reasoned	27.03 [16.50] (27.87) 32	56.16 [27.00] (62.21) 32	.48 [.61]
	t-test outcome: $p = 0.0133$	t-test outcome: $p = 0.0037$	

Figure 22.10 Comparison of total legal and factual citations (averages followed by medians in brackets, standard deviation in parentheses and sample (N) size)

	Law citations higher	Fact citations higher	Two citations identical	Total
Awards—investment	2 (.25)	6 (.75)	0 (.00)	8
Awards—international reasoned	8 (.25)	24 (.75)	0 (.00)	32
	Two-tailed z-test outcome: $p = 1.0$	Two-tailed z-test outcome: $p = 1.0$	Non-number calculation	

Figure 22.11 Comparison of legal and factual citations (actual numbers followed by proportion in parentheses)

citations to factual citations, suggesting that international commercial awards are more 'legalistic' than investment awards. This is somewhat contrary to the notion that investment arbitration is a more law-intensive procedure than international commercial arbitration due to the former's quasi-public status.[39]

The final chart, Figure 22.11, lists the number of awards in each cohort that had a higher number of legal citations as compared to factual citations and vice versa, using a methodology similar to that used in Figure 22.3. No statistically significant differences between international commercial and investment arbitration arose under a two-tailed z-test analysis. In fact, all of the proportions were identical. While more research would need to be conducted to confirm the data, this result strongly suggests that international commercial and investment arbitrators are operating in a similar manner when it comes to legal and factual citations, at least when the analysis is conducted at a high degree of generality.

[39] Böckstiegel (n 1) 585; Roberts (n 1) 298.

IV. Conclusion

Though the empirical analysis conducted herein is quite short, it nevertheless provides some very useful results. For example, statistically significant differences were found relating to the length of awards, confirming conventional wisdom suggesting that investment awards are longer than international commercial awards[40] and the amount of the awards, confirming that investment arbitration involves higher-value disputes.[41] The study also showed a statistically significant difference relating to the citation of previously published arbitral awards, confirming theoretical research suggesting that a system of soft precedent exists in investment arbitration.[42]

The current analysis also appeared to rebut certain longstanding assumptions, most notably the notion that investment arbitration is more 'legalistic' than commercial arbitration.[43] For example, statistically significant difference arose with respect to the proportion of legal citations to factual citations, with international commercial arbitration showing a higher proportion of legal citations than investment arbitration.[44] The research also rebutted conventional wisdom suggesting that international disputes arise out of a single contract, instead showing that international arbitration is more likely to involve multi-contract disputes.[45]

Findings from this chapter can also be compared to results generated by the larger study of commercial dispute resolution upon which this coding exercise was based.[46] One of the more revolutionary findings of the larger work involved the central importance of factual analyses to judges and arbitrators involved in commercial dispute resolution.[47] The current research seems to suggest the same is true in investment arbitration.[48]

As useful as this study may be, it merely scratches the surface of what is possible in this field. Numerous areas of additional research exist. For example, it would be useful to expand the methodology adopted here to treaty-based arbitration, using either contract-based investment arbitration and/or international commercial arbitration as comparators.[49] Not only would the transparency associated with treaty-based investment arbitration make it relatively easy to compile a good-sized comparative cohort, but the findings might vary significantly. Alternatively, it would be interesting to delve more deeply into various questions generated by this study, such as the nature of 'other document' introduced as evidence or the citation rates of different types of testifying

[40] Figure 22.2.
[41] Figure 22.1.
[42] Figure 22.7.
[43] Figure 22.3.
[44] Figure 22.10.
[45] Figure 22.8.
[46] Strong (n 3) 297–348.
[47] ibid 354.
[48] Figures 22.3–22.4, 22.10.
[49] The coding book for the larger study on which this chapter is based has been published (Strong (n 3) appendix III).

witnesses. Finally, it would be helpful to counterbalance the quantitative research conducted here with qualitative research on the same subject so as to parse out the motivation behind some of the results reported here.[50]

Though investment arbitration and international commercial arbitration are not equal in all things and in all ways, they are equally important means of resolving cross-border disputes. Hopefully, this chapter has provided some insights into the various ways the two processes operate.

[50] The earlier study on commercial disputes published a survey instrument and interview script that could be adapted for this purpose, ibid appendices I–II.

PART V
REVIEW AND ENFORCEMENT

23

Annulment and Set-Aside

Steffen Hindelang and Julia Nassl

I. Introduction

Regardless of whether investor-state dispute settlement (ISDS) is governed by the Convention on the Settlement of Investment Disputes between States and Nationals of Other States (ICSID Convention[1] or ICSID regime) or not (non-ICSID regimes) (together ISDS regimes), the award is *not* the final say—review mechanisms, albeit with considerable differences, exist under both ICSID and non-ICSID regimes.

Finality, understood as the enforceability of an award without any further possibility of revision or review,[2] is intrinsically linked to the commonly cited key features of ISDS—efficiency, distance from national legal systems, or even delocalization (supranational neutrality), and relative ease and speed. It can be said that finality acts as a shield that protects the award from domestic interference (and connected delays) as soon as it leaves the international arbitral realm.

Unlike in (compulsory) domestic judicial proceedings, in the context of ISDS, some words are in order to explain the necessity of review mechanisms.[3] Indeed, one could argue that when parties submit a dispute to international arbitration, they accept the arbitral tribunal's final decision in return for the benefits of ISDS. But only at first glance do such systemic choices militate against *any* review mechanism, especially in the context of ISDS, where private interests are inseparably entangled with public interests.

ISDS, or international arbitration more generally, is arguably a 'creature of contract'.[4] From this perspective, it is the interests of the contracting parties that determine the contours of the finality of an award.[5] Beyond the concept of consent and to add a

[1] Convention on the Settlement of Investment Disputes between States and Nationals of Other States (adopted 19 March 1965, entered into force 14 October 1966) 575 UNTS 159.

[2] See, eg, Daniel A Redfern, 'ICSID—Losing Its Appeal?' (1987) 3(2) Arbitration International 98, 99.

[3] See Elihu Lauterpacht, *Aspects of the Administration of International Justice* (Grotius Publications 1991) 99; Christian J Tams, 'An Appealing Option? The Debate about an ICSID Appellate Structure' in Christian Tietje and others (eds), *Essays in Transnational Economic Law, No 57* (Institut für Wirtschaftsrecht, Forschungsstelle für Transnationales Wirtschaftsrecht, Juristische Fakultät der Martin-Luther-Universität Halle-Wittenberg 2006) 8.

[4] See W Michael Reisman, 'The Breakdown of the Control Mechanism in ICSID Arbitration' (1989) 4 Duke Law Journal 739, 745.

[5] See W Michael Reisman, *Nullity and Revision: The Review and Enforcement of International Judgments and Awards* (Yale UP 1971) 31; International Law Commission (ILC), Documents of the Fifth Session Including the Report of the General Assembly, 2 Yearbook of the International Law Commission, UN Doc A/CN.4/SER.A/1953/Add.1 (1953) 202 <http://legal.un.org/ilc/publications/yearbooks/Ybkvolumes(e)/ILC_1953_v2_e.pdf>. But see also Tai-Heng Cheng, 'The Role of Justice in Annulling Investor-State Arbitration Awards' (2013) 31 Berkeley Journal of International Law 236, 238 (stating that the link between a narrow understanding of finality and encouraging foreign investment, until now, remains 'folklore of the international arbitration community').

Steffen Hindelang and Julia Nassl, *Annulment and Set-Aside* In: *The Award in International Investment Arbitration.*
Edited by: Katia Fach Gómez and Catharine Titi, Oxford University Press.
DOI: 10.1093/9780191975936.003.0023

sociolegal layer, review mechanisms are said to be designed in such a way as to maintain the parties' 'confidence in the efficiency and fairness'[6] of the dispute resolution mechanism. Bringing these two layers together, this would mean that only those ISDS awards rendered within the parties' (abstract) consent and in accordance with a fair process can be considered binding on them, or 'legitimate'. Under such a conceptualization and in line with party autonomy, review mechanisms translate into a safeguard of party consent and formal legitimacy of the process.

Party consent as a leitmotif of ISDS review mechanisms has important implications for both the standard and subject of review as well as allocation of review competence. First, and this addresses questions of standard and subject of review, review is designed to guard the interests of the contractual parties, to preclude decisions made outside the bounds of party consent and fair process, or in other words, by an arbitral tribunal committing *excès de pouvoir*.[7] Second, and here we are dealing with the issue of allocation of review competence, to uphold practical effectiveness of any such review mechanism, the power to decide on nullity or rectification of an award must lie with a body separate from the adjudicating one, as leaving this decision to the parties or the deciding tribunal would open the doors to abuse or lack of accountability.[8]

Put differently, review mechanisms fulfil the function of reconciling finality of an award with other policy considerations such as 'procedural integrity' or 'substantive correctness'. Which policy considerations are deemed relevant and how they relate to the finality of an award depends on the specific configuration established by the applicable review mechanism. In ISDS, two avenues for an award to be subjected to review coexist.[9] Awards rendered under the ICSID Convention are exclusively subjected to annulment under Article 52(1) of the ICSID Convention and other narrow remedies provided for in the Convention. This is confirmed by Article 53(1) of the ICSID Convention which states: 'The award shall be binding on the parties and shall not be subject to any appeal or to any other remedy except those provided for in this Convention.' Conversely, non-ICSID awards, ie, awards rendered under, among others, the ICSID Additional Facility Rules, the United Nations Commission on International Trade Law (UNCITRAL) Arbitration Rules, or the International Chamber of Commerce (ICC) Rules of Arbitration, are subject to control by the state courts at the seat of arbitration.[10]

[6] eg Reisman (n 4) 744.

[7] The concept of *excès de pouvoir* traces back to the Roman concept of *arbiter nihil extra compromissum facere potest*. The transplantation of this concept to public international legal thought is commonly attributed to de Vattel, see Emer de Vattel, *Le Droit des gens, ou principes de la loi naturelle, appliqués à la conduite et aux affaires des nations et des souverains*, vol 1 (1758) II.18, 329, cited by Vladimir Balaš, 'Review of Awards' in Peter Muchlinski and others (eds), *The Oxford Handbook of International Investment Law* (OUP 2008) 1131.

[8] See also Aron Broches, 'Observations on the Finality of ICSID Awards' (1991) 6(2) ICSID Review 321, 324 ('Since inter-state arbitration typically takes place outside any institutional or conventional framework which provides for a review of allegedly improper or invalid awards, the losing party has in practice often been the final judge, and the "binding" effect of an arbitral award was thus emptied of most of its meaning').

[9] Investment treaties typically authorize an investor to choose between different procedural avenues, see, eg, Energy Charter Treaty art 26(4).

[10] See New York Convention on the Recognition and Enforcement of Foreign Arbitral Awards (1958) art V.1(e) (New York Convention) (authorizing set aside 'by a competent authority of the country in which, or under the law of which, that award was made').

This chapter follows these two paths in ISDS, comparing and contrasting, to the extent possible here, how the different review mechanisms uphold finality as a key property of an award while catering for other policy concerns. Accordingly, this chapter proceeds in three steps. Section II probes into annulment under Article 52 of the ICSID Convention, dissects its governing rules and how these rules are implemented by the ad hoc committees as guardians of both the arbitral process and the finality of awards. Section III contrasts the insights gained from the discussion of the 'ISDS tailor-made' review mechanism with those for non-ICSID awards under domestic arbitration laws at the seat of arbitration, and their application by domestic courts. Section IV reflects on the overall increase in the number of challenges to awards in recent years and what this means for finality before concluding.

II. Finality in the Context of the ICSID Convention: The Tightrope Walk between different Shades of Legitimacy

The often-proclaimed 'self-contained' character of the ICSID regime is not an end in itself, but a corollary to its envisaged overarching objective of facilitating access to justice for foreign investors in order to promote foreign investment.[11] Key properties of the regime such as efficiency, supranational neutrality, and relative ease and speed, are intrinsically conducive to these objectives.

Since (also) the ICSID regime requires the cooperation of national jurisdictions to enforce its awards, it must accommodate a certain degree of 'permeability', while maintaining its autonomy from domestic jurisdictions.[12] Instead of relying (only) on the voluntary cooperation of a respondent state to implement an award, the drafters of the ICSID Convention opted for a tight framework that makes enforcement quasi-automatic if the conditions stipulated in the Convention are fulfilled[13] and excludes remedies other than those allowed for in the Convention, in particular 'domestic review takeovers'.[14]

At the same time, the necessity to reconcile finality with (other) considerations of justice was acknowledged and an internalized review mechanism—under Article 52(1) of the ICSID Convention—integrated. The drafters opted for annulment as the preferred avenue to pierce finality in very confined lines, which is reflected both in the limited subject and standard of review (Articles 52(1) and 53(1) of the ICSID

[11] The attainment of this objective is, however, debated. Mary Hallward-Driemeier, 'Do Bilateral Investment Treaties Attract FDI? Only a Bit ... and They Could Bite' in Karl P Sauvant and Lisa E Sachs (eds), *The Effect of Treaties on Foreign Direct Investment: Bilateral Investment Treaties, Double Taxation Treaties, and Investment Flows* (OUP 2009); Axel Berger and others, 'Do Trade and Investment Agreements Lead to More FDI? Accounting for Key Provisions inside the Black Box' (2013) 10 International Economic Policy 247; Saad Ahmad, Ben Liebman, and Heather Wickramarachi, 'Disentangling the Effects of Investor-State Dispute Settlement Provisions on Foreign Direct Investment', US International Trade Commission, Office of Economics, Working Paper 2022-11-A, November 2022.

[12] It is this dependency on external means which, according to some commentators, casts doubt on whether the ICSID regime can be truly described as 'self-contained', see, eg, Tams (n 3) 8.

[13] ICSID Convention art 54(1); but see art 55.

[14] ibid arts 52, 53(1), also art 26.

Convention) and in the deliberate exclusion of any appeal-like function (Article 53(1) of the ICSID Convention).

Annulment plays an ambivalent role within the ICSID regime: On the one hand, it upholds the formal integrity of proceedings, tribunals, and awards—both in advance and retrospectively—in order to instil acceptance of and trust in the ICSID regime, ie, legitimacy, and to facilitate compliance with the award at the domestic level. On the other hand, along with annulment comes the ability to attack the finality of the award, which poses a challenge to a key feature of ISDS and hence has the potential to undermine its very *raison d'être*.

The exercise of this role turns from ambivalent to problematic when ad hoc committees transgress their limited mandate and seek to turn annulment into some sort of appeal. Appeal differs from annulment both in terms of result—annulment can only void, while appeal can modify—and subject of review—annulment focuses on the legitimacy of the decision-making process, while appeal focuses on the substantive correctness.[15] Put differently, when an ad hoc committee performs appeal-like functions, it allows the finality of the award to be pierced by considerations of substantive correctness that the ICSID Convention sought to exclude.

In what follows we will briefly substantiate the premise that annulment is designed to reconcile finality (only) with formal integrity of the process, the award, and the tribunal—both in terms of its institutional set-up (A) and the rules governing annulment (B). Ad hoc committees have repeatedly ignored this limited balancing exercise, in particular by introducing considerations of substantive correctness into the equation. Therefore, in a third step, we will analyse the balancing practice in which ad hoc committees have engaged, the interpretive approaches underlying this practice (C.1 and C.2), and potential ways out of the (to be asserted) interpretative meandering (C.3).

A. The Actors: Ad hoc Annulment Committees and the Governing Bodies under the ICSID Regime

Effective review mechanisms require the establishment of a body separate from the parties and the adjudicating tribunal. By conferring exclusive review jurisdiction (Article 52(3) of the ICSID Convention) on 'system-inherent' but separate bodies—the ad hoc annulment committees—the contracting states agreed to relinquish their review powers to a delocalized and supranational neutral body.[16] Ad hoc committees were designed to be equal to arbitral tribunals. Neither structurally—both derive their power from party consent—nor normatively—ad hoc committees are tasked with

[15] For this conceptual distinction of appeal and annulment, see, eg, David D Caron, 'Reputation and Reality in the ICSID Annulment Process: Understanding the Distinction Between Annulment and Appeal' (1992) 7(1) ICSID Review 23, 23ff. See further Julien Chaisse, 'The Appeal in International Investment Arbitration' in Katia Fach Gómez and Catharine Titi (eds), *The Award in International Investment Arbitration* (OUP 2024).

[16] See Albert Jan van den Berg, 'Should the Setting Aside of the Arbitral Award Be Abolished?' (2014) 29 (2) ICSID Review 263, 283ff; Redfern (n 2) 98, 99.

resolving a specific legal question in a specific case rather than advancing some sort of an *acquis communautaire* of international investment law—are they superior to each other.[17] Non-ICSID regimes, in contrast, leave the finality of the award (more) 'vulnerable' to domestic discretion and potential re-politization.[18] In the politically sensitive ambit of protection of foreign investment, the involvement of (typically) a third state at review level runs counter to the objective of an efficient, speedy, and especially depoliticized adjudication process.

Supranational neutrality is obtained not only on an institutional, but also on a personal level. ICSID's arbitral tribunals are party-appointed which time and again has cast considerable doubt as to the independence and impartiality of the arbitrators.[19] Conversely, it is the chairman of the Administrative Council, the president of the World Bank, who selects the arbitrators to sit in the ad hoc committee from the so-called Panel of Arbitrators—composed of persons designated by the contracting states and the chairman[20]—without consultation with the parties. This is a case in point that the governing bodies of the ICSID Convention retain a tangible level of control over the annulment proceedings, particularly in terms of *who* is tasked with the delicate exercise of reconciling finality and formal integrity.[21] It is a means of informally instilling personal (dis)continuity in the ad hoc committees, which may be beneficial for the consistency of the decision-making, but also a probate remedy against transgressive annulment practices.[22] As commentators such as David Caron have pointed out, the changes in annulment practice can be linked to changes in the composition of the ad hoc committees, namely the appointment of former World Bank president Aron Broches.[23]

Not only a public law perspective criticizes such 'backroom appointment processes' as they do little to alleviate concerns about the independence and impartiality of ISDS adjudicating bodies.[24] Even apologists of the ISDS regime as it stands today oppose the alienation of the ad hoc committees from the disputing parties in general and the predominant role of the World Bank in particular.[25] This explains well why the activities

[17] See *Burlington Resources Inc v Ecuador*, ICSID Case No ARB/08/5, Decision on Liability (14 December 2012).

[18] Van den Berg (n 16) 283ff.

[19] See ICSID Convention art 38 of which follows *e contrario* that party-appointment of the members of the arbitral tribunal is the norm (stipulating an appointment by the chairman only in absence of a timely appointment by the parties).

[20] ICSID Convention arts 12–16. See also art 52(3) (providing for strict exclusion of members of the ad hoc committees if they have been a member of the tribunal rendering the award, if they are of the same nationality as one of the disputing parties or the members of the tribunal rendering the award, or if they have been appointed to the Panel of Arbitrators by either of the states concerned).

[21] It is remarkable that in annulment proceedings in intra-EU disputes the majority of ad hoc committee members seem to be of non-EU member state background, see, eg, *Eiser Infrastructure Limited and Energía Solar Luxembourg Sàrl v Spain*, ICSID Case No ARB/13/36, Decision on Annulment (11 June 2020), *InfraRed Environmental Infrastructure GP Limited and others v Spain*, ICSID Case No ARB/14/12, Decision on Annulment (10 June 2022), or *Infrastructure Services Luxembourg Sàrl and Energia Termosolar BV (formerly Antin Infrastructure Services Luxembourg Sàrl and Antin Energia Termosolar BV) v Spain*, ICSID Case No ARB/13/31, Decision on Annulment (30 July 2021), with two members from a non-European jurisdiction. See also ICSID Secretariat, 'Updated Background Paper on Annulment' (World Bank 2024) para 45 (pointing out that 'nationality but also legal tradition … serve as a crucial safeguard against potential biases and conflicts of interest').

[22] Paul Friedland and Paul Brumpton, 'Rabid Redux: The Second Wave of Abusive ICSID Annulments'(2012) 27 American University International Law Review 727, 759.

[23] Caron (n 15) 48.

[24] Redfern (n 2) 99.

[25] ibid.

of ad hoc committees are under heightened scrutiny and scholarship is fast to warn of the system spinning out of control when ad hoc committees touch the limits of their competence or even transgress it. However, it should not be forgotten that the link back to the institutional context of the World Bank has at least two valid motives. First, it is a compromise that reconciles both host states and investors with the availability of a review mechanism under the auspices of a supposedly neutral entity. Second, the partial centralization of the ICSID regime enables its executive bodies, the Administrative Council, and the Secretariat, to informally safeguard the functionality and key properties of the ICSID regime, amongst them the finality of awards. Possible interventions go beyond appointment policy: Some commentators have suggested that the Administrative Council may even have the power to issue guidelines or interpretative notes to call on the ad hoc committees to uphold the finality of awards.[26] Arguably, the publication of the Background Papers on Annulment in 2012, 2016, and, most recently, in March 2024, while merely descriptive, was also intended to nudge ad hoc committees to adhere to the finality of awards and treat annulment as the exceptional remedy it was contemplated as.

B. The Rules: Scope and Standard of Review

Under the ICSID Convention, it is Article 52(1) that determines which policy considerations are capable of interfering with the finality of an award. It does so by setting out five grounds for annulment: an improper constitution of the tribunal (lit a), a tribunal's manifest excess of power (lit b), corruption by one of the tribunal's members (lit c),[27] a tribunal's serious departure from a fundamental rule of procedure (lit d), and the award's failure to state reasons (lit e). Already the ordinary meaning of the terms of the provision shows that the grounds do not allow for piercing the finality of the award for considerations other than those relating to the 'fundamental integrity of the ICSID arbitral process in all its facets'.[28] Particularly, they do not provide for scrutinizing the substantive integrity of the award, ie, its correctness in the sense of compliance with substantive rules, and consistency. Hence, ad hoc committees cannot label an award as 'incorrect' and remit the dispute back to an arbitral tribunal for rectification. Instead, only if a lack of formal integrity is established can they lift the award's finality by depriving it of its legal effect. This strictly binary choice is a key distinction from an appeal, which allows the award to be modified and thus parts of the award or the prior deliberation process to be salvaged.

[26] This was deemed a valid measure under ICSID Convention art 6, see Friedland and Brumpton (n 22) 759.

[27] As of 31 December 2023, this ground has not been dealt with in any decision on annulment, see ICSID Secretariat (n 21) para 103.

[28] See *Alapli Elektrik BV v Turkey*, ICSID Case No ARB/08/13, Decision on Annulment (10 July 2014) [32]; *Hussein Nuaman Soufraki v United Arab Emirates*, ICSID Case No ARB/02/7, Decision on Annulment (5 June 2007) [20].

The only relevant antipodes to finality are the formal integrity of the proceedings, of the tribunal, and of the award. The fact that the grounds for annulment were carefully designed as to exclude questions of substantive correctness from piercing finality is further corroborated by the drafting history: proposals that would have allowed for a review on substantive grounds were consistently rejected.[29]

The strictly bipolar balancing process between finality and formal integrity thus established is not only guaranteed by the wording of Article 52(1) of the ICSID Convention itself—qualifiers such as 'manifest', 'serious', 'fundamental', or 'failure' imply a high standard of review—[30] but even more so by Article 53(1) of the ICSID Convention which contrasts annulment with appeal. While the grounds for annulment limit the *standard of review* to safeguarding the award from a 'general compliance control', it is the rejection of any appeal-like function that precludes the merits of the award from being the *subject of review*;[31] ad hoc committees must take the award as it is without considering the adequacy or sufficiency of the reasoning underlying the award.[32]

This two-prong safeguard of finality in the post-award phase is rarely ever disputed—at least *in abstracto*. The updated Background Paper on Annulment of the ICSID Secretariat found that ad hoc committees unanimously concur that, inter alia:

> the grounds listed in Article 52(1) are the only grounds on which an award may be annulled; (2) annulment is an exceptional and narrowly circumscribed remedy and the role of an ad hoc Committee is limited; (3) ad hoc Committees are not courts of appeal, annulment is not a remedy against an incorrect decision, and an ad hoc Committee cannot substitute the Tribunal's determination on the merits for its own.[33]

This assessment is based on a panoply of annulment decisions in which the ad hoc committees routinely introduce their analysis of the grounds for annulment with a chapeau that acknowledges their constrained capability to review,[34] and reaffirmed in

[29] eg ICSID, *History of the ICSID Convention*, vol II (World Bank 1968) 340, 517; ibid (vol II-2) 851ff; Nikolaos Tsolakidis, 'ICSID Annulment Standards: Who Has Finally Won the Reisman v Broches Debate of Two Decades Ago?' in Jean E Kalicki and Anna Joubin-Bret (eds), *Reshaping the Investor-State Dispute Settlement System* (Brill Nijhoff, 2015) 833.

[30] See eg, *Maritime International Nominees Establishment v Guinea*, ICSID Case No ARB/84/4, Decision on Annulment (22 December 1991) (*MINE*) [4.06]; Redfern (n 2) 98, 102, 103. Neither the limited grounds for annulment nor the distinction between annulment and appeal argue a priori for or against a restrictive or extensive standard of interpretation. Instead, the customary rules of interpretation, as reflected in Article 31 of the Vienna Convention on the Law of Treaties, 1155 UNTS 331, require an interpretation that takes into account the ordinary meaning of the terms of ICSID Convention art 52(1), its context, and its object and purpose, see, eg, *Eiser Infrastructure Limited and Energía Solar Luxembourg Sàrl v Spain*, ICSID Case No ARB/13/36, Decision on Annulment (11 June 2020) [126].

[31] See Tsolakidis (n 29) 26.

[32] See Eric A Schwartz, 'Finality at What Cost? The Decision of the Ad Hoc Committee in *Wena Hotels v Egypt*' in Emmanuel Gaillard and Yas Banifatemi (eds), *Annulment of ICSID Awards* (Juris Publishing 2004) 84. For general remarks on the conceptual distinction of appeal and annulment, see also *Arbitral Award Made by the King of Spain on 23 December 1906 (Honduras v Nicaragua)*, Judgment [1960] ICJ Rep 192, 214.

[33] ICSID Secretariat (n 21) paras 77ff; see also *Perenco Ecuador Limited v Ecuador* ICSID Case No ARB/08/6, Decision on Annulment (28 May 2021) (*Perenco*) [55].

[34] See also Caron (n 15) 26ff.

more recent annulment decisions that explicitly reference the Background Paper to buttress their self-constraint. Yet, despite this ubiquitous emphasis on finality, one must not forget that annulment involves a complex balancing exercise, the implementation of which may—intentionally or by error—undermine attempts to prevent ad hoc committees from exceeding their mandate.

C. The Law in Action: Functional Transgressions at Cost of Finality

1. Appeal-like Functions through Extensive Interpretation

The distinction between annulment and appeal, undisputed *in abstracto*, has proved susceptible for *errata* and abuse when applied concretely. Time and again, ad hoc committees have upset the balance between finality and reviewability established by the ICSID Convention by succumbing to the temptation to address questions of substantive correctness, despite mantra-like self-confirmations to the contrary. Word and deed do not confirm each other, and repeated assumptions of appeal-like functions cast doubt on the effectiveness of the two-prong safeguard provided by Article 52(1) and 53(1) of the ICSID Convention.

Assumption of appeal-like functions appears in, painting with broad strokes, two ways: first, ad hoc committees interpret the scope and standard of review extensively as to accommodate questions of substantive correctness under Article 52(1) of the ICSID Convention. In these instances, the transgression of competence and function has direct implication both for the finality of the concrete award—its legal effect is extinguished (in disregard of the grounds for annulment)—and for the legality and legitimacy of the ICSID regime as such—the consent of the parties as manifested in the grounds for annulment is blatantly ignored. Second, and arguably more subtly, ad hoc committees assert that an award is wrong on the merits, while conceding that this is not sufficient to annul the award.[35] While such *obiter* considerations do not encroach upon the finality of the award, the ad hoc committees do exceed their function and undermine the very legitimacy of the award.[36]

Both blatant and more subtle transgressions rely on an extensive interpretation of Article 52(1) of the ICSID Convention and thus of the functions of the ad hoc committees, which has repeatedly sparked fears of erosion of ICSID's review mechanism. To substantiate the claim of erosive effects beyond the individual award, first, the prefix 'ad hoc' is misleading insofar as it may be misunderstood to imply that effects of ad hoc committee decisions remain strictly limited to the specific case. Ad hoc

[35] *CMS Gas Transmission Company v Argentina*, ICSID Case No ARB/01/8, Decision on Annulment (25 September 2007) [125]–[136]; *Fraport AG Frankfurt Airport Services Worldwide v Philippines*, ICSID Case No ARB/03/25, Decision on Annulment (23 December 2010) [112]. See also Christoph H Schreuer, 'From ICSID Annulment to Appeal Half Way Down the Slippery Slope' (2011) 10 Law and Practice of International Courts and Tribunals 211, 223ff.

[36] See Schreuer (n 35) 225.

committees and arbitral tribunals regularly use (not uncontroversially) topoi, such as '*jurisprudence constante*' or 'persuasiveness', to align with previous decisions. This approach can be said to reduce contingency and increase coherence in (annulment) decision-making; however, it is problematic if it reduces contingency and increases coherence of decisions outside the scope and mandate of the ICSID Convention. *Amco I* is a prime example as it overtly embraces the (misled) rationale of *Klöckner I*.[37] Such (self-propelling) extensive interpretation must not be confused with evolutionary interpretation. The latter presupposes that a term's meaning has changed as a result of the intention of the parties, not through a change of opinion of an adjudicating body. Current reform attempts of states outside the context of the ICSID regime that have the integration of appeal-like functions at their core—just see the recent works in the context of the UNCITRAL Working Group III on 'Investor-State Dispute Settlement Reform'—accentuate a static understanding by the contracting states of annulment in the ICSID Convention, which does *not* include appeal-like functions. What is more, and this relates to the second component of the erosive effects mentioned at the beginning of this paragraph, a de facto anticipation of reform 'by interpretation' regardless of actual party consent, does not only contradict the objective pursued by the reform attempts, ie, to relegitimize ISDS in light of waning acceptance and trust in the system, but this 'interpretative approach' undermines legal certainty and stability, and has the potential to further erode the ICSID regime.

2. Interpretive Meandering under Article 52(1) of the ICSID Convention

Christoph Schreuer's often cited grouping of annulment decisions into generations conveniently placed the approaches of the ad hoc committees on a timeline.[38] He suggested a linear trajectory towards an ever more balanced interpretation of Article 52(1) of the ICSID Convention—a process of calibration, of ICSID's review mechanism finding 'its proper place' in the institutional configuration.[39] In his analysis, Schreuer identified three generations. The first generation consisting of *Klöckner I* and *Amco I*, the second of *MINE*, *Klöckner II*,[40] and *Amco II*,[41] and the third of *Wena*[42]

[37] See *Amco Asia Corporation and others v Indonesia* (*Amco I*), ICSID Case No ARB/81/1, Decision on Annulment (16 May 1986) [44]: 'The absence, however, of a rule of *stare decisis* in the ICSID arbitration system does not prevent this ad hoc Committee from sharing the interpretation given to Article 52 (1)(e) by the *Klöckner I* ad hoc Committee [*Klöckner Industrie-Anlagen GmbH and others v Cameroon and Société Camerounaise des Engrais*, ICSID Case No ARB/81/2, Decision on Annulment, 3 May 1985]'.

[38] Christoph H Schreuer, 'Three Generations of ICSID Annulment Proceedings' in Emmanuel Gaillard and Yas Banifatemi (eds), *Annulment of ICSID Awards* (Juris Publishing 2004) 17, 17. But see also ICSID Secretariat (n 21) para 118 (showing that the ICSID Secretariat itself works with a different 'generational' delineation practice, in light of the merely quantitative nature of its assessment).

[39] ibid 37. But compare Schreuer's optimistic account with Schwartz (n 32) 84 (criticizing that concern for finality has been pushed to the extreme at cost of the guarantees of the arbitral process). See also *CDC Group plc v Seychelles*, ICSID Case No ARB/02/14, Decision on Annulment (29 June 2005) [35]; *MTD Equity Sdn Bhd and MTD Chile SA v Chile*, ICSID Case No ARB/01/7, Decision on Annulment (21 March 2007) [52]–[54].

[40] *Klöckner Industrie-Anlagen GmbH and others v Cameroon and Société Camerounaise des Engrais* (*Klöckner II*), ICSID Case No ARB/81/2, Decision on Annulment (17 May 1990).

[41] *Amco Asia Corporation and others v Indonesia (Amco II)*, ICSID Case No ARB/81/1, Decision on Annulment (17 December 1992).

[42] *Wena Hotels Ltd v Egypt*, ICSID Case No ARB/98/4, Decision on Annulment (5 February 2002) (*Wena*).

and *Vivendi I*.[43] The respective generations were formed because of the significant discrepancies in the interpretation of Article 52(1) of the ICSID Convention and the perception of the assumed role of the ad hoc committees within the ICSID regime. The decisions in *Klöckner I* and *Amco I* are characterized by the fact that the respective ad hoc committees assumed de facto appeal functions by basing their decisions on purported substantive incorrectness of the awards in question. Both proceedings were followed by resubmissions (and re-annulment), feeding the fear of never-ending arbitration cycles. The ad hoc committees in both *Klöckner I* and *Amco I* pierced the finality of the award by relying on Article 52(1)(b)—ie that the tribunal manifestly exceeded its powers—and Article 52(1)(e)—ie that the award failed to state the reason on which it is based.[44] Because of their vagueness, these two grounds particularly invite ad hoc committees to engage in a detailed analysis of the arbitral tribunal's findings on the merits.[45] The two first decisions illustrate the 'confusion' that these two grounds for annulment can instil and their indeterminacy tempted both ad hoc committees to solidify their assessment with formulating 'concretizing principles' with regard to the respective grounds for annulment.[46] These *obiter* remarks, arguably, left the door wide open for potential future challenges in the form of an appeal and catalysed the widespread scholarly criticism.[47]

The second and third generation of annulment decisions followed and were overall characterized by a more restrictive interpretation of Article 52(1) of the ICSID Convention.[48] The decision of the ad hoc committee in *MINE* is commonly referred to as a turning point and a 'salutary shift' as it strongly rejected the assumption of appeal-like functions. Its self-restraint, perhaps instilled by a certain appointment policy of the chairman of the Administrative Council,[49] becomes particularly apparent in the ad hoc committee's analysis of Article 52(1)(e) of the ICSID Convention when it rejected the interpretation that the provision required the statement of *adequate* reasons.[50]

[43] *Compañia de Aguas del Aconquija SA and Vivendi Universal SA v Argentina* (*Vivendi I*), ICSID Case No ARB/97/3, Decision on Annulment (3 July 2002).

[44] Unlike the decisions in *Klöckner I* and *Amco I* suggest, ICSID Convention art 52(1)(b) covers refusal to apply the proper law, but not *error in iudicando*; in addition, the nature of such excess must be manifest. Under ICSID Convention art 52(1)(e) annulment is warranted if the reasons are *insufficient*, but not if they are *inadequate*.

[45] Tsolakidis (n 29) 834ff.

[46] The 'hair trigger standard'—regarding the question whether an ad hoc committee has discretion not to annul an award—or the presumption of the validity of an award (*in favorem validates sententiae*) are examples of interpretations developed—some may say 'invented'—by *Klöckner I*, which until today spark debate among both scholarship and ad hoc committees. See Anthony Sinclair, 'Article 53' in Stephan W Schill (ed), *Schreuer's Commentary on the ICSID Convention* (3rd edn, CUP 2022) 599ff and 625.

[47] The most cited critical reflections stem from Reisman and Broches who strongly disagreed, inter alia, over what the two decisions meant for the future of ICSID's review mechanism. While Reisman painted an apocalyptic picture of the control system having spun out of control, Broches considered the first two decisions part of the system's calibration process, see Reisman (n 4) 787; Broches (n 8) 380. See also for an updated account of the debate, Tsolakidis (n 29) 828 (urging for a reconsideration of conceptual reflections of Reisman and Broches to arrive at a more consistent interpretational approach).

[48] The trajectory towards a more restrictive interpretation was not strictly linear, particularly the decisions in *Mitchell* and *MHS* provided backlashing momentum, see *Patrick Mitchell v Congo*, ICSID Case No ARB/99/7, Decision on Annulment (1 November 2006) and *Malaysian Historical Salvors v Malaysia*, ICSID Case No ARB/05/10, Decision on Annulment (16 April 2009).

[49] See Caron (n 15) 48 (suggesting that especially the appointment of Broches brought the critical turn). See also Juan Fernández-Armesto, 'Different Systems for the Annulment of Investment Awards' (2011) 26(1) ICSID Review 128, 146.

[50] *MINE* (n 30) [5.09].

However, uncertainty remained about the terms of the mandate of an ad hoc committee in general and about the correct interpretative approach towards Article 52(1)(b) and (e) of the ICSID Convention in particular. Hence, after vocal criticism of the first years of the operation of the annulment mechanism had worn off, a new wave of decisions appeared which were perceived as overstepping the scope of the ICSID annulment mechanism.[51] Some commentators were forced to revisit their earlier optimistic assessment, now painting a darker picture.[52] In the 2010s, the rulings in *CMS*,[53] *Sempra*,[54] *Enron*,[55] *Helnan*,[56] and *Vivendi II*[57] diverged from the previous restrictive approach, leaving functional constraints behind. *Enron* and *Sempra* were criticized because, similarly to *Klöckner I* and *Amco I*, they examined the merits when seeking to distinguish between *error in iudicando* and non-application of law under Article 52(1)(b) of the ICSID Convention.[58] Like *CMS*, *Helnan* assumed an appeal-like function in a more subtle way, by not overturning the finality of the award, but still pointing out issues of substantive correctness.[59] In *Vivendi II*, the ad hoc committee addressed the procedural issue of impartiality of one of the arbitrators under Article 52(1)(a) and (d) of the ICSID Convention, given her extra-procedural ties to the claimants' shareholders.[60] While the ad hoc committee arguably identified an error of the tribunal which may (or must) lead to annulment, it refrained from actually annulling the award, contenting itself with 'reprimanding' the arbitrator for her conduct in an *obiter*; the 'reprimand' is certainly something not within the ad hoc committee's mandate.[61]

In response to the new 'interpretive meandering', in 2012, the ICSID Secretariat published a Background Paper on Annulment. Despite its descriptive nature and the fact that it addresses the contracting states, it has provided guidance to which subsequent ad hoc committees have repeatedly referred.

For more recent annulment decisions, issued since 2015, not only does the empirical evidence suggest a more restrictive approach, as the number of (partially) annulled awards has remained stable despite the still increasing number of annulment

[51] See Friedland and Brumpton (n 22) 759. On reasoning requirements, see Bruno Simma and Jan Ortgies, 'The Reasoned Award' in Fach Gómez and Titi (n 15).

[52] Schreuer (n 35) 211ff.

[53] *CMS Gas Transmission Company v Argentina*, ICSID Case No ARB/01/8, Decision on Annulment (25 September 2007).

[54] *Sempra Energy International v Argentina*, ICSID Case No ARB/02/16, Decision on Annulment (29 June 2010).

[55] *Enron Creditors Recovery Corp Ponderosa Assets, LP v Argentina*, ICSID Case No ARB/01/3, Decision on Annulment (30 July 2010).

[56] *Helnan International Hotels A/S v Egypt*, ICSID Case No ARB/05/19, Decision on Annulment (14 June 2010).

[57] *Compañia de Aguas del Aconquija SA and Vivendi Universal SA v Argentina*, ICSID Case No ARB/97/3, Decision on Annulment (10 August 2010).

[58] For a comprehensive account, see Tsolakidi (n 29) 844ff.

[59] *Helnan International Hotels A/S v Egypt*, ICSID Case No ARB/05/19, Decision on Annulment (14 June 2010) [45], [57] (The ad hoc committee annulled parts of the reasoning of the tribunal without annulling the dispositive of the award). See also Lucy F Reed and Giorgio Francesco Mandelli, 'Ad hoc or ad arbitrium? An Audit of Recent ICSID Annulment Decisions' in Arthur W Rovine (ed), *Contemporary Issues in International Arbitration and Mediation: The Fordham Papers* (OUP 2011) 70, 75.

[60] See *Compañia de Aguas del Aconquija SA and Vivendi Universal SA v Argentina*, ICSID Case No ARB/97/3, Decision on Annulment (10 August 2010) [222]–[30].

[61] ibid [232].

proceedings initiated.[62] A more consistent approach, in line with the object and purpose of the ICSID Convention in general and the balance between finality and formal integrity contained therein, seems to be gaining traction.

Since 2015, the ad hoc committees in *Occidental Petroleum*,[63] *TECO*,[64] *Tidewater*,[65] *Venezuela Holdings BV*,[66] and *Perenco*[67] have interpreted and applied Article 52(1) of the ICSID Convention as to (partially) piercing finality. To provide a brief overview of the particularities of these annulment decisions, the ad hoc committee in *Tidewater* narrowed down the relevant test for asserting the sufficiency of giving reason under Article 52(1)(e) of the ICSID Convention to whether a reasonable, attentive and willing reader would understand the arbitral tribunal's motivation or not.[68] In *TECO*, the ad hoc committee found, inter alia, a breach of the right to be heard under Article 52(1)(d) of the ICSID Convention, as the tribunal denied accrued interest on historical damages based on a concept of unjust enrichment that was not part of the 'legal framework' established by the parties.[69]

It appears from the above that ad hoc committees have recently upheld a more self-restrained approach to addressing substantive issues in an award.[70] As exemplified also by the decision in *Eiser*,[71] ad hoc committees are more effectively discharging their legitimacy-building and legitimacy-preserving role without overstepping their mandate.[72] In this case, the annulment decision was based on the failure of one of the arbitrators to disclose his relationship with one of the experts in the underlying arbitration. The ad hoc committee found this scenario to warrant annulment both under Article 52(1)(a)—improper constitution of the tribunal—and 52(1)(d) of the ICSID Convention—a serious departure from a fundamental rule of procedure. Both grounds are less susceptible for re-examination of the merits,[73] but some commentators spotted

[62] See ICSID, 'Annual Report 2023' <https://icsid.worldbank.org/sites/default/files/publications/ICSID_AR2023_ENGLISH_web_spread.pdf>, 34.

[63] *Occidental Petroleum Corporation and Occidental Exploration and Production Company v Ecuador*, ICSID Case No ARB/06/11, Decision on Annulment (2 November 2015).

[64] *TECO Guatemala Holdings LLC v Guatemala*, ICSID Case No ARB/10/23, Decision on Annulment (5 April 2016).

[65] *Tidewater Investment SRL and Tidewater Caribe, CA v Venezuela*, ICSID Case No ARB/10/5, Decision on Annulment (27 December 2016).

[66] *Venezuela Holdings BV and others v Venezuela*, ICSID Case No ARB/07/27, Decision on Annulment (9 March 2017).

[67] *Perenco Ecuador Limited v Ecuador*, ICSID Case No ARB/08/6, Decision on Annulment (28 May 2021).

[68] *Tidewater Investment SRL and Tidewater Caribe, CA v Venezuela*, ICSID Case No ARB/10/5, Decision on Annulment (27 December 2016) [168]ff.

[69] *TECO Guatemala Holdings LLC v Guatemala*, ICSID Case No ARB/10/23, Decision on Annulment (5 April 2016) [189]–[190].

[70] See ICSID Secretariat (n 21) para 118 (showing a declining percentage rate of annulments: while the rates for 1971–2000 and 2001–2010 are 13 and 8 per cent, respectively, the rate for 2021–2023 is 5 per cent).

[71] *Eiser Infrastructure Limited and Energía Solar Luxembourg Sàrl v Spain*, ICSID Case No ARB/13/36, Decision on Annulment (11 June 2020).

[72] But see Anthony Sinclair, 'Article 52' in Schill (n 46) 132 (criticizing that the ad hoc committee accepted for itself the role determining the independence and impartiality of a challenged arbitrator despite the Convention providing a procedure for the co-arbitrators to decide such challenge).

[73] The role of an ad hoc committee would have only been limited if the question of impartiality had already been decided by the arbitral tribunal, see *EDF International SA and others v Argentina*, ICSID Case No ARB/03/23, Decision on Annulment (5 February 2016) [132]; *Suez, Sociedad General de Aguas de Barcelona SA and others v Argentina*, ICSID Case No ARB/03/19, Decision on Argentina's Application for Annulment (5 March 2017) [214].

yet another variety of an alleged competence creep vis-à-vis the tribunal and to the detriment of the finality of the award in the ad hoc committee's interpretation.[74] In their reading, and in line with the argument made by the claimants in *Eiser*,[75] Article 52(1)(a) of the ICSID Convention would only capture irregularities at the *initial* stage of formation of the tribunal.[76] For subsequent irregularities, in particular for disqualification of an arbitrator, revision according to Article 51 of the ICSID Convention was supposedly the only available remedy as it is arguably considered less intrusive on the finality of the award: the Tribunal could resume its deliberations with a newly appointed arbitrator.[77] The ad hoc committee rejected any suggestion of an exclusive relationship between annulment and revision, primarily since the connection between arbitrator and expert only surfaced after the award's publication.[78] It accentuated that the 'exceptional nature of the annulment remedy may be among those that inform the role of annulment committees'[79] and that annulment was accordingly 'designed purposefully to confer a limited scope of review'.[80] Precluding an ad hoc committee, however, from scrutinizing the impartiality and independence of an arbitrator, which the ad hoc committee righteously deemed to be a significant risk to the legitimacy and integrity of the arbitral proceedings,[81] amounted, according to the ad hoc committee, to effectively depriving it of the mandate with which it was entrusted by the ICSID Convention. This once again reflects the complexity of the task assigned to ad hoc committees, also acknowledged in the most recent Background Paper on Annulment,[82] precisely because of the still controversial mandate of ad hoc annulment committees.[83] While annulment is an exceptional remedy with the potential to compromise finality, it must retain its function as a guardian of the formal integrity of the ICSID regime and overcome the finality of an award when Article 52(1) of the ICSID Convention so requires. In other words, if concerns about finality are taken to an extreme, legitimacy will suffer and parties will be less likely to support the process.[84]

[74] See also Sinclair (n 72) 132.
[75] *Eiser Infrastructure Limited and Energía Solar Luxembourg Sàrl v Spain*, ICSID Case No ARB/13/36, Decision on Annulment (11 June 2020) [64]ff.
[76] Saar A Pauker and Benny Winston, 'Eiser v Spain—Unprecedented Annulment of an ICSID Award for Improper Constitution of the Tribunal' (2021) 22(2) Journal of World Investment & Trade 313, 318ff.
[77] Sinclair (n 72) 132.
[78] *Eiser Infrastructure Limited and Energía Solar Luxembourg Sàrl v Spain*, ICSID Case No ARB/13/36, Decision on Annulment (11 June 2020) [170].
[79] ibid [175].
[80] ibid [172].
[81] ibid [175].
[82] ICSID Secretariat (n 21) para 116.
[83] Perhaps unsurprisingly, the interpretation of one's mandate is also a source of controversy in the deliberations of the ad hoc committee members. For a recent example, see *Agility Public Warehousing Company K.S.C.P v Republic of Iraq*, ICSID Case No. ARB/17/7, Decision on Annulment (8 February 2024) [105]ff, [119] and Partial Dissent by Jacomijn J van Haersolte-van Hof (25 January 2024) [9]ff. (considering the conclusion of the majority that the tribunal's approach of interpreting the relevant national laws 'shield[ed]' questions of consistency of the national laws with the BIT 'from review' to effectively amount to 'second-guess[ing] a tribunal's analysis or evaluat[ing] the persuasiveness or even correctness of the underlying decision').
[84] See Schwartz (n 32) 85 (sharing the concerns vis-à-vis the *Wena* annulment decision). See also Reed and Mandelli (n 59) 81 (sharing the concerns vis-à-vis the *Vivendi II* annulment decision).

3. Interpretative Safeguards against Functional Transgressions

Schreuer's grouping of annulment decisions has the advantage of illustrating the wave-like development of practice in time stamps, which also confirms the contextuality of the decision-making of ad hoc committees. It helps, furthermore, to identify the degree of responsiveness to criticism, especially through the ICSID Secretariat's appointment policy and non-authoritative administrative measures such as the publication of the Background Papers on Annulment of 2012, 2016, and 2024. Coherence in annulment practice is achieved primarily through interpretative approaches that preserve the object and purpose of the ICSID Convention in general and the enshrined balance between finality and formal integrity in particular. In this context, the often repeated statement that Article 52(1) of the ICSID Convention neither argues for or against an expansive or a restrictive interpretation should not be forgotten. In concrete terms, this means that a restricted scope of review—ie the exclusion of the examination of the merits—has no bearing on the question of the standard of review—ie the question of the interpretation of the grounds for annulment.[85] Such an approach ensures that the limited scope of review in the ICSID regime is neither unduly restricted nor abused.

i. *Finality of the award in non-ICSID contexts: (Un)Conditional deference*

To juxtaposition the review regime(s) of non-ICSID awards with ICSID-awards necessarily entails a simplification. As such, there is no homogeneous regime of setting aside non-ICSID awards. The setting-aside of non-ICSID awards is governed by the national arbitration law at the seat of arbitration. Nonetheless, the fact that many national arbitration laws, by and large, are aligned to the UNCITRAL Model Law[86] conditions a considerable convergence between the domestic setting aside regimes. For the purposes of this chapter, the cursory analysis will therefore be limited to contrasting annulment under Article 52(1) with Article 34(2) of the UNCITRAL Model Law.

Article 34(2) of the UNCITRAL Model Law stipulates the following grounds to set aside an award:

> (i) a party to the arbitration ... was under some incapacity; or the said agreement is not valid under the law to which the parties have subjected it or, failing any indication thereon, under the law of this State; or (ii) the party making the application was not given proper notice of the appointment of an arbitrator or of the arbitral proceedings or was otherwise unable to present his case; or (iii) the award deals with a dispute not contemplated by or not falling within the terms of the submission to arbitration, or contains decisions on matters beyond the scope of the submission to arbitration, provided that, if the decisions on matters submitted to arbitration can be separated from those not so submitted, only that part of the award which contains decisions on matters not submitted to arbitration may be set aside; or (iv) the composition of the

[85] See Tsolakidis (n 29) 852.

[86] United Nations Commission on International Trade Law, UNCITRAL Model Law on International Commercial Arbitration (UNCITRAL Model Law) of 1985, with amendments as adopted in 2006, UN Doc A/40/17, Annex I.

arbitral tribunal or the arbitral procedure was not in accordance with the agreement of the parties, unless such agreement was in conflict with a provision of this Law from which the parties cannot derogate, or, failing such agreement, was not in accordance with this Law; or (b) the court finds that: (i) the subject matter of the dispute is not capable of settlement by arbitration under the law of this State; or (ii) the award is in conflict with the public policy of this State.

Compared to Article 52(1) of the ICSID Convention, there are similarities, but there are two striking differences: first, like Article 52(1) of the ICSID Convention, Article 34(2) of the UNCITRAL Model Law only introduces considerations of formal integrity as antipodes of finality—with one exception, and this addresses the first difference, Article 34(2) of the UNCITRAL Model Law allows for setting aside if an award is contrary to the public policy of the state at the seat of arbitration. As public policy is commonly understood to refer to both procedural and substantive aspects, this ground allows for a substantive review of the challenged award, albeit under a high threshold.[87] The second difference relates to the wording of Article 34(2) of the UNCITRAL Model Law which, thanks to its greater accuracy, leaves less leeway for interpretive meandering.

ii. De facto challenges to finality: 'Inflationary' use of review mechanisms

It goes without saying that 'overzealous' review bodies would put the finality of an award at jeopardy. But the reality of recent review practice suggests that a threat may come from another direction (as well). According to recent datasets on initiated setting aside and annulment proceedings, the rendering of an arbitral award is increasingly marking the beginning of yet another procedure (albeit one that rarely amounts to a true peripeteia), rather than the ultimate end of ISDS proceedings.

As of 31 December 2023, of the approximately 434 awards rendered under the ICSID Convention, 189 have been or are still subject to annulment proceedings,[88] with a dramatic increase in the last decade.[89] Similar observations can be made for setting aside proceedings of non-ICSID[90] awards.[91] The increase in review proceedings is not

[87] The concept of public policy is, notoriously, rather vague, but it is widely recognized that it limits scrutiny to a review of combability with core values of a legal order. Accordingly, domestic courts, so far, were more hesitant so set aside (investment arbitration) awards on this ground. Note also, that recent judgments of the European Court of Human Rights (ECtHR) that turned *ordre public* into a bottleneck to enforce human rights in Court of Arbitration for Sport cannot be extended effortlessly to the context of ISDS as the latter is 'compulsory', see ECtHR, *Semenya v Switzerland*, Application No 10934/21, Judgment (11 July 2023).

[88] ICSID Secretariat (n 21) paras 32, 117. According to the survey, of the 194 annulment proceedings registered (including annulment proceedings after resubmission), only 23 ended in the full or partial annulment of the award. Forty-two proceedings were discontinued and 27 were still pending, as of 31 December.

[89] ICSID Secretariat (n 21) para 34: Seventy-nine per cent of all annulment proceedings have been instituted since January 2011. While ICSID arbitration has experienced an overall growth, the increase in annulment proceedings is not proportionate. See also ICSID, 'Annual Report 2023', 34 (illustrating an increase disproportionate to the overall increase in annulment proceedings).

[90] Here, we refer to awards rendered under other arbitration rules, eg, UNCITRAL 387, ICC 23, the Stockholm Chamber of Commerce (SCC) 56 or the ICSID Additional Facility.

[91] As of 31 December 2022, approximately 139 set-aside proceedings have been initiated, of which 25 led to a full or partial setting aside of the award, see UNCTAD, Investment Dispute Settlement Navigator <https://investmentpolicy.unctad.org/investment-dispute-settlement/>.

matched by an increase in the number of awards annulled or set aside, and hence empirics are in line with the finding that the competent review bodies have returned to (or continue to apply) a restrictive approach when it comes to piercing the finality of an award.[92] Yet, this 'zero-sum game' (or actually a 'negative-sum game' when it comes to costs among others), ie., arbitral proceedings are prolonged without the party seeking annulment actually obtaining the relief sought, raises new concerns. The costs are not only economic but also systemic, as the *raison d'être* and perceived attractiveness of ISDS—the relatively quick, cheap, and easy resolution of disputes over foreign investment—is undermined.[93] The 'inflationary' number of requests for review of awards is arguably no longer just a symptom of the often cited legitimacy crisis of ISDS (in an increasingly ISDS-adverse climate), but its cause and accelerator.

The review mechanisms, as they stand today, are expressions of a practice of legitimization by procedure. This contrasts sharply with the legitimation practices of and within the domestic sphere in state courts, where the procedure has primarily a serving function and the review or an adjudicative decision, as a matter of the rule of law, involves both substantive and formalistic considerations. Under this conceptualization of legitimization, annulment and setting aside, which do not purport to ensure the substantive correctness of an awards, appear inherently 'deficient'.

An arbitral award, however, is legitimate if the decision-making process complied with rules of competence and procedure and thus remained within the contractual constraints envisaged by the (contracting) parties in the applicable legal framework. Under such conceptualization, annulment and setting aside are necessary, but also sufficient review mechanisms in ISDS, since substantive correctness does not form a constitutive element of an award's legitimacy at all (ICSID regime) or only to a very limited extent (non-ICSID regime). Annulment and setting aside are hence (exclusively or largely) *formalistic* and *autonomous* legitimation practices, *formalistic* in the sense that they underscore the legitimacy of an award independently of its substantive correctness, *autonomous* in the sense that they do not (or only to a very limited extend) integrate exogenous interests.

III. Conclusion

In the contemporary global legal landscape, there exists a pressing political imperative to reevaluate and reform the ISDS regime, including its review mechanisms. The discourse surrounding this necessity is both robust and far-reaching, reflecting the critical need for addressing the deficiencies inherent in the current ISDS regime.

[92] See ICSID Secretariat (n 21) para 33.

[93] See Reisman (n 4) 804 (citing ICSID, Administrative Council, Annual Meeting, Berlin, Federal Republic of Germany [December 1988] 3: 'However, if parties dissatisfied with awards regularly seek annulment such a practice may put in doubt the features which make ICSID arbitration an attractive means of settling investment disputes—namely its speed, comparatively low cost, and its effectiveness').

One of the prominent propositions for reform involves the implementation of appellate structures within the ISDS regime. These proposed structures represent a paradigm shift from the existing review mechanisms. They promise to realign the concept of finality with a broader array of interests. In essence, the introduction of appellate mechanisms would recalibrate the shades of legitimacy within ISDS, taking into account not only the formal integrity of the decision-making process, the tribunal, and the award but also the substantive correctness of the award itself. In other words, the reconciliation of finality with other interests would be significantly reconfigured.

Arguably, formalized appeal structures may help overcoming the oscillation of current review mechanisms between annulment/set-aside and de facto appeal which seem to operate under the constant threat, or at least suspicion of a latent transgression of their mandate, undermining the legitimacy of the ISDS regime. However, there are other costs associated with appeals mechanisms, such as an additional layer of complexity or potential political influence in the process of appointing adjudicators. When it comes to finality, the loss may only be in theory, but in real-world terms, and prima facie counterintuitively, finality may not end up worse off, as current practices of annulment/set-aside have already pushed the boundaries.

24

Review beyond Annulment

Correction, Additional Awards, Clarification, and Revision

Karsten Nowrot and Emily Sipiorski

I. Introduction

As a rule, an investment arbitration tribunal is so-called *functus officio* from the moment when the arbitral award is rendered. Consequently, the function of arbitrators in settling the investment disputes normally ends at this stage. In particular, they do not enjoy any competence to revisit the award they have rendered; a legal effect that is also referred to as the principle of finality of awards.[1] Underlying this normative perception are a number of motives, among them the desirability of ending the investment dispute at issue and, albeit closely related, concerns about potential delays, uncertainties and costs resulting from ongoing discussions among the parties concerning the correctness, the completeness as well as the interpretation of the arbitral award.[2]

However, also in the present context the well-known saying applies that there is no rule without exceptions. Indeed, all of the major arbitration rules that are of relevance in the realm of international investment arbitration foresee certain exceptions to the rule of *functus officio* by permitting the parties to request the tribunal to, among others, correct errors, address omissions, and clarify ambiguities in the award. These remedies are ultimately based on the recognition of the human inability to completely avoid mistakes, unintended omissions, or ambiguities in the award and thus deficits that entail the potential to complicate the enforcement or even to compromise the validity of the award. Moreover, in the context of ICSID, they are also motivated by the desire to avoid the necessity for annulment should an additional fact of significance become available shortly after the rendering of an award.

In this chapter, the different types of these so-called post-award remedies, namely requests for correction and rectification (II), requests for additional awards and supplementary decisions (III), requests for interpretations (IV) as well as requests for revision of the award (V), will be introduced and assessed. In addition, and adopting a more overarching perspective, this chapter will also draw attention to and address a

[1] See also Catharine Titi, 'What Is an Award? Concept, Content, Drafting, Effects' in Katia Fach Gómez and Catharine Titi (eds), *The Award in Investment Arbitration* (OUP 2024).

[2] See thereto also eg *Gold Reserve v Venezuela*, ICSID Case No ARB(AF)/09/1, Decision regarding the Claimant's and Respondent's Requests for Corrections (15 December 2014) [35]–[36]; Anthony Sinclair, 'Article 49' in Stephan W Schill and others (eds), *Schreuer's Commentary on the ICSID Convention* (3rd edn, CUP 2022) para 24.

Karsten Nowrot and Emily Sipiorski, *Review beyond Annulment* In: *The Award in International Investment Arbitration.*
Edited by: Katia Fach Gómez and Catharine Titi, Oxford University Press. © Katia Fach Gómez and Aikaterini Titi 2024.
DOI: 10.1093/9780191975936.003.0024

number of challenges that may arise in connection with recourse by parties to these post-award remedies in the practice of investment arbitration (VI).

II. Correction and Rectification of an Award

All major international arbitration rules and regimes commonly used in international investment arbitration include provisions allowing the parties to formally ask the tribunal to correct certain formal and technical errors in its awards. Requests for correction or rectification are recognized for example in Article 49(2) of the ICSID Convention, Rule 72(2) of the 2022 ICSID Additional Facility Arbitration Rules, Article 38(1) of the 2021 UNCITRAL Arbitration Rules, Rule 31.1 of the 2017 Investment Arbitration Rules of the Singapore International Arbitration Centre (SIAC), Article 36(2) of the 2021 International Chamber of Commerce (ICC) Arbitration Rules, Article 27.1 of the 2020 Arbitration Rules of the London Court of International Arbitration (LCIA), as well as in Article 47(1) of the 2017 Arbitration Rules of the Arbitration Institute of the Stockholm Chamber of Commerce (SCC).

The overarching purpose of the post-award remedy of rectification is to correct miscalculations and other unintentional mistakes of a clerical, arithmetical, or similar kind in an award that have occurred during drafting and that have the potential to distort the outcome of an arbitral proceeding as intended by the tribunal, thereby possibly even giving rise to challenges as to the legal validity of the award in question. Correcting respective errors is thus aimed at avoiding a situation where the parties find themselves obliged to honour an award that orders a relief that the tribunal did not want to grant. Consequently, the correction remedy serves to ensure that the actual (and original) intentions of the tribunal members—and not the errors that they may have unintentionally made in the process of finalizing the written version of their decision—find their manifestation in the award.[3]

Equally important is the perception of what is not a legitimate purpose of a request for correction. General agreement exists that it is not the purpose of this remedy to initiate a reconsideration and alteration of the intentions of the tribunal by asking it to reevaluate issues that it has already decided in the award, to serve as an appeal and substantive review of the decision or, however closely related, to function as a means to revisit and modify or otherwise affect the merits of the award.[4] Nevertheless, this perception should not lead to the conclusion that correcting an error under this remedy could never have an impact on the outcome of the award. Quite to the contrary, for example rectifying a false number or a wrong mathematical calculation of an amount clearly changes the substance of the decision. Such scenarios are also covered by the

[3] See also eg *Watkins v Spain*, ICSID Case No ARB/15/44, Decision on Rectification (13 July 2020) [37]; David D Caron and Lee M Caplan, *The UNCITRAL Arbitration Rules* (2nd edn, OUP 2012) 811–12.

[4] *Victor Pey Casado and others v Chile*, ICSID Case No ARB/98/2, Decision on Rectification of the Award (6 October 2017) [49]; Caline Mouawad and Cedric Soule, 'Article 49' in Julien Fouret and others (eds), *The ICSID Convention, Regulations and Rules: A Practical Commentary* (Edward Elgar Publishing 2019) paras 4.813, 4.833.

scope of application of the motion for rectification since such a correction 'would not mean that the tribunal has changed its decision. Rather, it would only mean that the tribunal had incorrectly expressed its decision in the first place'.[5]

Applying these standards in arbitral practice, investment arbitration tribunals have for example rectified errors related to their own wrong reference to certain decrees,[6] to incorrect factual descriptions,[7] to omissions in the respondent's list of representatives,[8] to misidentifications of witnesses,[9] to misquotations from a submission made by a party,[10] to arithmetical mistakes in the determination of the value of future cash flows,[11] to incorrect names of products[12] as well as to the use of wrong terminologies in the summary of facts and contentions.[13] On the contrary, investment tribunals have rejected requests for correction for example in situations where, according to the tribunal's perception, the requesting party intended to subsequently change the methodological approach in the calculation of quantum,[14] to achieve an adjustment in costs,[15] to subsequently raise a claim to post-award interests,[16] or to initiate a re-evaluation of the evidence by the tribunal.[17]

The competence to revisit the award and correct respective errors therein is only bestowed upon the investment tribunal which rendered the decision. As a consequence, requests for correction are in principle not available to the parties in case the original tribunal, for example due to the death of one of its members, cannot be reconvened anymore. Nevertheless, certain exceptions from this rule appear to be accepted in investment arbitration practice, in particular in situations where the post-award proceedings have already commenced prior to the original tribunal becoming unavailable and both parties have consented to their continuation.[18]

As far as the circle of actors entitled to initiate a correction of the award is concerned, most relevant arbitration rules, like Article 38(2) of the 2021 UNCITRAL Arbitration Rules, not only foresee that the parties may request the rectification but in addition also allow the tribunal itself to correct the award *sua sponte* within a certain time frame after rendering the award. The only major exception is Article 49(2) of the

[5] Andrew N Vollmer and Angela J Bedford, 'Post-Award Arbitral Proceedings' (1998) 15 Journal of International Arbitration 37, 39.

[6] See eg *Victor Pey Casado* (n 4) [52].

[7] *Philip Morris and others v Uruguay*, ICSID Case No ARB/10/7, Decision on Rectification (26 September 2016) [29]–[30].

[8] *Noble Ventures v Romania*, ICSID Case No ARB/01/11, Rectification of Award (19 May 2006) [2] and [7].

[9] *Santa Elena v Costa Rica*, ICSID Case No ARB/96/1, Rectification of Award (8 June 2000) [8].

[10] *Victor Pey Casado* (n 4) [53]–[54].

[11] *Antin Infrastructure Services v Spain*, ICSID Case No ARB/13/31, Decision on Rectification of the Award (29 January 2019) [32].

[12] *Philip Morris* (n 7) [26].

[13] *Maffezini v Spain*, ICSID Case No ARB/97/7, Rectification of the Award (31 January 2001) [8]ff.

[14] *Watkins* (n 3) [42]ff.

[15] *Antin Infrastructure Services* (n 11) [39].

[16] *Enron v Argentina*, ICSID Case No ARB/01/3, Decision on Claimant's Request for Rectification and/or Supplementary Decision of the Award (25 October 2007) [42]ff.

[17] *Ickale Insaat v Turkmenistan*, ICSID Case No ARB/10/24, Decision on Claimant's Request for Supplementary Decision and Rectification of the Award (4 October 2016) [143].

[18] For respective examples, see *Antin Infrastructure Services* (n 11) [3]–[11]; and *Mercer International v Canada*, ICSID Case No ARB(AF)/12/3, Supplementary Decision (10 December 2018) [1]–[4]; see also Sinclair (n 2) paras 35–37.

ICSID Convention. Nevertheless, also in the context of ICSID arbitration proceedings, it is rightly recognized in practice that, once a request has been made by a party, the tribunal may not merely rectify the errors explicitly invoked by the requesting party but enjoys the competence to correct other related errors in order to ensure 'that the total outcome of the Award is correct'.[19] Moreover, while many arbitration rules, like Article 38 (1) of the 2021 UNCITRAL Arbitration Rules, grant to the tribunal a certain discretion to decide whether the requested correction is justified and should thus be made,[20] this does not apply—at least based on the wording of the English-language version of the provision ('shall')[21]—to requests for rectification under Article 49(2) of the ICSID Convention[22] as well as under Rule 72 of the 2022 ICSID Additional Facility Arbitration Rules. However, these different approaches in arbitration rules are at best of merely limited relevance in practice, since also under those normative frameworks that qualify rectification decisions as discretionary, this discretion is clearly very much limited by the overarching obligation of every arbitral tribunal to render a coherent and accurate award;[23] and thus an award also devoid of errors.

As already implied by its characterization as a 'post-award' remedy, the request for correction is in principle only applicable to awards. Whereas under arbitration rules like Article 34 (1) of the 2021 UNCITRAL Arbitration Rules or Article 26 (1) of the 2020 LCIA Arbitration Rules the tribunal may make various separate awards on different issues at various times of the proceedings with the remedy of correction being available in respect of all of them,[24] the ICSID Convention recognizes only one type of awards, namely the final decision of the tribunal which disposes of the case.[25] Admittedly, a certain exception is stipulated in Article 52(4) ICSID Convention, extending the scope of application of the remedies available under Article 49(2) also to annulment decisions of ad hoc committees. Moreover, also for example the award of a newly constituted tribunal in a resubmitted case in accordance with Article 52(6) ICSID Convention can legitimately give rise to a request for rectification.[26] Nevertheless, it follows from this finding that as a rule this remedy is not available as far as other decisions of investment tribunals like those on jurisdiction or on provisional measures are concerned. That said, this verdict should not lead to the conclusion that an investment tribunal is legally prevented from correcting errors occurring in its preliminary orders or decisions while the arbitration proceedings are still pending. During still ongoing arbitration proceedings, a party is in principle always entitled to request a correction of a decision and the investment tribunal can respond to this request—or even act on its own initiative—by rectifying respective errors based on the general competences bestowed upon it

[19] *ConocoPhillips and others v Venezuela*, ICSID Case No ARB/07/30, Decision on Rectification (29 August 2019) [30]; see also Sinclair (n 2) para 30.
[20] Caron and Caplan (n 3) 814.
[21] See, however, on the differences in the equally authentic French and Spanish texts of Article 49(2) ICSID Convention, Mouawad and Soule (n 4) para 4.834.
[22] *Ickale Insaat* (n 17) [116]; Sinclair (n 2) para 47.
[23] Generally, on this obligation, Caron and Caplan (n 3) 801.
[24] Vollmer and Bedford (n 5) 45–46.
[25] Titi (n 1).
[26] Sinclair (n 2) para 27.

under provisions like Article 44 of the ICSID Convention or Rule 37 of the 2022 ICSID Additional Facility Arbitration Rules.[27]

As to the procedural rules applicable to motions for corrections, three central aspects common to most international arbitration rules seem to be particularly worth highlighting. First, the arbitration regimes foresee that a party must make a request within a certain time limit—ranging from twenty-eight days after the award was received in the case of Article 27.1 of the 2020 LCIA Arbitration Rules to forty-five days after the award was rendered in accordance with Article 49(2) of the ICSID Convention and Rule 72(2) of the 2022 ICSID Additional Facility Arbitration Rules. Second, as for example stipulated in Article 38(1) of the 2021 UNCITRAL Arbitration Rules, the request must be notified to the other party. Moreover, already in light of the fact that the right to be heard constitutes a fundamental rule of procedure,[28] implied in this requirement is also the right of the other party to comment on this request;[29] an additional legal entitlement that is sometimes—as for example evidenced by Article 47(1) of the 2017 SCC Arbitration Rules—also explicitly stipulated. Third, most if not all major arbitration rules provide for a time limit for the respective decision of the tribunal—from twenty-eight days after receipt of the request in accordance with Article 27.1 of the 2020 LCIA Arbitration Rules to sixty days under Rule 61(7) of the 2022 ICSID Arbitration Rules and Rule 72(8) of the 2022 ICSID Additional Facility Arbitration Rules.

Almost all international arbitration rules—among them Article 49(2) of the ICSID Convention and Article 38(3) of the 2021 UNCITRAL Arbitration Rules—explicitly stipulate that the tribunal's decision on the request for rectification shall become part of the award.[30] Finally, it seems worth mentioning in the context of investment arbitration proceedings under the ICSID Convention that a tribunal does not have the power to order a stay of enforcement of the award pending its decision on the request for rectification—or supplementation—under Article 49(2) of the ICSID Convention.[31]

III. Additional Award and Supplemental Decision

Another post-award remedy frequently foreseen in investment arbitration rules concerns the competence of the tribunal to render an additional award or a supplemental decision at the request of a party on claims or questions that were submitted in the course of the arbitral proceedings but not decided by the tribunal in the award. The remedy is, among others, stipulated in Article 39(1) of the 2021 UNCITRAL Arbitration Rules, Article 49(2) of the ICSID Convention, Rule 72(2) of the 2022 ICSID Additional Facility Arbitration Rules, Article 36(3) of the 2021 ICC Arbitration Rules, Article 48

[27] ibid para 28.
[28] Generally on this perception see eg *Fraport v Philippines*, ICSID Case No ARB/03/25, Decision on Annulment (23 December 2010) [197]ff.
[29] See also eg *Gold Reserve* (n 2) [40]ff; Sinclair (n 2) para 33.
[30] On the procedural consequences see Vollmer and Bedford (n 5) 47; Sinclair (n 2) para 97.
[31] *Watkins* (n 3) [66]–[74]; Sinclair (n 2) para 40.

of the 2017 SCC Arbitration Rules, Article 27.3 of the 2020 LCIA Arbitration Rules, as well as in Rule 31.3 of the 2017 SIAC Investment Arbitration Rules.

This type of post-award remedy is aimed at removing and filling an analytical gap in the award by addressing and thus rectifying the omission of any claims made by a party during the proceedings that were—unintentionally and thus inadvertently—not dealt with by the arbitral tribunal but should have been decided. It thus allows the parties to request the tribunal to complete the award.[32] This remedy is closely connected to the tribunal's general obligation to in principle deal in the award with every claim submitted to it by the parties: a requirement that is for example explicitly stipulated in Article 48(3) of the ICSID Convention. Moreover, it clearly also relates to the tribunal's overarching duty to ensure that the parties receive a valid and enforceable award, in particular taking into account that—outside the context of ICSID arbitration proceedings—domestic courts in many countries are likely to set aside an arbitral award for reasons of incompleteness if it fails to address all relevant claims made by a party, thus rendering it invalid and unenforceable.[33]

Nevertheless, tribunals and academics have also frequently and rightly stressed the limits of this remedy, bearing in mind its object and purpose. In particular, a request for an additional award or a supplemental decision is neither intended to serve as 'a door to revise the Award, or to introduce new arguments, or to present new claims',[34] nor as a means that would permit a party to require the tribunal to rule on a claim that it had already deliberately considered as irrelevant or inappropriate for the dispute at issue.

Against this background, it seems appropriate and useful to adopt a three-step approach when assessing the merits of a request by a party for an additional award or a supplemental decision in international investment arbitration proceedings.[35] In an initial step the tribunal has to determine whether the claim at issue was actually presented—explicitly or at least impliedly[36]—by the party in the course of the prior proceedings. In accordance with the explicit wording of provisions like Article 39(1) of the 2021 UNCITRAL Arbitration Rules, and otherwise based on the object and purpose of this post-award remedy, a tribunal can in this regard only decide claims that have in fact been submitted to it.[37] Once the tribunal has found that the claim or question has indeed been presented in the course of the proceedings, it needs to determine—in a second step—whether it has already dealt with this claim and rendered a decision in this regard in its award. In the affirmative, the arbitral tribunal will—and must—reject the request for an additional award or a supplementary decision, bearing in mind that it is not the purpose of this remedy to initiate a process of reconsideration and thus a potential revision of the award.[38]

[32] On this perception see eg *Pacc Offshore Services v Mexico*, ICSID Case No UNCT/18/5, Decision on Claimant's Application for an Additional Award and on the Applicable Interest Rate (9 May 2022) [37], [41]; Caron and Caplan (n 3) 821–22.

[33] Caron and Caplan (n 3) 821, 823.

[34] *Pacc Offshore Services* (n 32) [37].

[35] For a similar finding, see eg Mouawad and Soule (n 4) para 4.815.

[36] The sufficiency of an implied claim was recognized eg in *Victor Pey Casado* (n 4) [59]–[61].

[37] *Pacc Offshore Services* (n 32) [37]; *Ickale Insaat* (n 16) [107]–[114]; Caron and Caplan (n 3) 824.

[38] For an application of this second step in arbitral practice, see eg *Mercer International* (n 18) [18]–[25].

Only if the tribunal comes to the conclusion that it has not addressed the submitted claim or question in its award, the need arises—in a third and final step—to assess whether it should deal with and decide the question on the basis of an additional award or a supplemental decision. Most, if not even all, relevant arbitration rules grant to the tribunal discretion to decide whether the request for an additional award is justified.[39] This also applies to requests for supplementary decisions in accordance with Article 49(2) of the ICSID Convention.[40] The discretion enjoyed by investment tribunals is most certainly limited by their general obligation to ensure the completeness, validity, and enforceability of the award. Nevertheless, tribunals have also constantly—and rightly—held that the principle of exhaustiveness, as for example stipulated in Article 48(3) of the ICSID Convention, applies to claims and questions that are of relevance in the case at issue, in the sense that they may affect the outcome of the dispute. However, the principle does not require the tribunal to deal with every argument presented by the parties, in particular if it considers them to be devoid of any impact on the award or to be for other reasons irrelevant or inappropriate for the dispute at issue.[41]

In light of these findings, a request for an additional award or a supplementary decision is likely to succeed in practice basically only where an investment arbitration tribunal has unintentionally and thus inadvertently 'forgotten' to address a claim in its award; therefore it will not succeed in cases where the tribunal has intentionally and deliberately chosen not to deal with a submitted question that it considered irrelevant.[42] Consequently, a tribunal has for example decided to supplement its award upon finding that, although the respondent had claimed post-award interest on its legal costs, the tribunal had unintentionally omitted to decide on this claim in the award.[43]

On the contrary, in situations where the omission to address a claim or question in the award is based on a deliberate choice of the investment arbitration tribunal—at least in the context of proceedings under the ICISD Convention—a request for annulment of the award pursuant to Article 52 of the ICSID Convention seems in fact to be the more promising procedural option, in particular as far as the losing party is concerned. Although apparently not supported by the *travaux préparatoires* of the ICSID Convention,[44] ad hoc committees have frequently and in principle rightly recognized the direct availability of a request for annulment of the award for a party based in particular on an alleged failure to state reasons pursuant to Article 52(1)(e) of the ICSID Convention. This applies in particular to cases where the tribunal has deliberately omitted to decide a submitted claim and where the need for a reconsideration of the reasoning supporting the award arises as a result of a respective supplemental decision.[45] Against this background, the availability of requests for supplementary

[39] See eg Caron and Caplan (n 3) 823; *Pacc Offshore Services* (n 32) [37].

[40] *Railroad Development Corporation v Guatemala*, ICSID Case No ARB/07/23, Decision on Supplementation and Rectification of the Award (18 January 2013) [39]; Mouawad and Soule (n 4) para 4.814.

[41] See eg *Standard Chartered Bank v Tanzania*, ICSID Case No ARB/10/12, Award (2 November 2012) [273].

[42] *Pacc Offshore Services* (n 32) [37]; Caron and Caplan (n 3) 823; Sinclair (n 2) paras 49–50.

[43] *Pac Rim Cayman LLC v El Salvador*, ICSID Case No ARB/09/12, Decision on the Respondent's Request for a Supplementary Decision (28 March 2017) [1.16]–[1.19].

[44] For further details in this regard see eg Mouawad and Soule (n 4) paras 4.803ff, 4.831.

[45] See thereto eg Sinclair (n 2) paras 50, 85ff.

decisions pursuant to Article 49(2) of the ICSID Convention seems to be first and foremost a suitable remedy for the successful party that wants the tribunal to address and decide on a particular—and previously omitted—claim, but for understandable reasons does not seek to annul the award.[46]

In the same way as remedies for correction of awards, only the investment tribunal that has rendered the award or—in the case of Article 39(1) of the 2021 UNCITRAL Arbitration Rules—issued the termination order enjoys the power to make an additional award or a supplementary decision. However, contrary to the post-award remedy of correction, most relevant arbitration rules foresee that only the parties to the dispute may request a supplementary decision. Therefore, the tribunal itself in general is not bestowed with the competence to issue additional awards or supplementary decisions *sua sponte*. An exception to this rule is provided by Article 27.4 of the 2020 LCIA Arbitration Rules. At the same time, it has rightly been stated in the literature that under other arbitration rules, a tribunal that becomes aware of an omission is expected to notify the parties of this fact in light of its general obligation to ensure the completeness, validity, and enforceability of the award.[47]

As already indicated by the wording of the relevant provisions, the request for an additional award or a supplementary decision is mostly only permitted with regard to awards. Only Article 39(1) of the 2021 UNCITRAL Arbitration Rules explicitly recognizes the possibility to use this remedy also as far as termination orders are concerned. In the latter scenario, the tribunal in fact often does not render an additional award but rather, in the absence of any prior award in the course of the proceedings, the first award in this connection. This is also indicated by the wording of this provision ('an award or an additional award'). Furthermore, as already implied by the term 'additional award', eg see Rule 31.3 of the 2017 SIAC Investment Arbitration Rules, these decisions usually do not become part of the original award or termination order. Rather, they qualify as independent awards. The main exceptions are supplementary decisions pursuant to Article 49(2) of the ICSID Convention and Rule 72(9) of the 2022 ICSID Additional Facility Arbitration Rules that become part of the previously issued award.

All major arbitration rules stipulate that a party is required to make the request within a specific time frame—ranging from twenty-eight days following the receipt of the award pursuant to Article 27.3 of the 2020 LCIA Arbitration Rules to forty-five days after the award was rendered under Article 49(2) of the ICSID Convention and Rule 72 (2) of the 2022 ICSID Additional Facility Arbitration Rules. Furthermore, the request must also be notified to the other party, as for example explicitly provided for in Article 39(1) of the 2021 UNCITRAL Arbitration Rules, with the party also being entitled to comment on the request. This is a fundamental rule of procedure that is for example explicitly enshrined in Article 48 of the 2017 SCC Arbitration Rules. Finally, all relevant arbitration rules also provide for a time limit for the tribunal's decision on the request for an additional award or supplementation—ranging from forty-five days after

[46] On this perception, see also already Mouawad and Soule (n 4) para 4.832; Sinclair (n 2) para 50.
[47] Caron and Caplan (n 3) 823.

receipt of the request pursuant to Rule 31.3 of the 2017 SIAC Investment Arbitration Rules to sixty days after receipt of the request in accordance with, for example, Rule 61(7) of the 2022 ICSID Arbitration Rules and Article 39(2) of the 2021 UNCITRAL Arbitration Rules.

IV. Interpretation of the Meaning and Scope of an Award

Where a dispute exists between the parties as to the interpretation of the award, arbitral rules provide a mechanism for the award to be further clarified by the tribunal. Article 50 of the ICSID Convention permits parties to indefinitely seek interpretation of the meaning and scope of an award.[48] A similar provision exists under other arbitral rules of relevance to investment law, including UNCITRAL, SIAC, and the SCC rules, providing that parties may request the interpretation of an award within thirty days of its issuance.[49] Notably, the LCIA Arbitration Rules do not provide provisions on interpretation and instead are limited to correction and additional awards.

This interpretation provision ensures that ambiguous awards, while not factually or legally incorrect, can be clarified, providing for a consistent and reasonable application of the award. These provisions have been drafted similarly to Article 60 of the Statute of the International Court of Justice, which ensures that the court has the final word on the interpretation of its decision.[50] This possibility for interpretation reaffirms the tribunal's duty to produce a 'coherent, accurate, and complete award'.[51] In this sense, it applies to interpretation of an existing award and matters within that award.[52] In order for the provision to be activated, there must be clear evidence of a difference of interpretation by the parties. Essentially, the difference in interpretation could lead to conflicting applications of the award in the process of enforcement.[53] The *Wena Hotels v Egypt* tribunal indicated in its decision on interpretation that two conditions were required for bringing a request for interpretation: 'first, there has to be a dispute between the original parties as to the meaning or scope of the award; second, the purpose of the application must be to obtain an interpretation of the award'.[54]

[48] See also ICSID Additional Facilities Arbitration Rules (2022) art 72(2) (providing that the interpretation request be made within forty-five days of the award).

[49] UNCITRAL Arbitration Rules (2021) art 37; UNCITRAL Model Law on International Commercial Arbitration (1985, amended 2006) art 33(1)(b); SIAC Investment Arbitration Rules (2017) r 31.4; SCC Arbitration Rules (2017) art 47.

[50] Statute of the International Court of Justice (ICJ) art 60. See for example, *Case Concerning the Temple of Preah Vihear (Cambodia v Thailand)*, Request for Interpretation of the Judgment of 15 June 1962 [2013] ICJ Rep 281, para 55; see also *Factory at Chorzów (Germany v Poland)*, Interpretation of Judgments Nos 7 and 8, Judgment No 11 [1927], PCIJ Rep, Series A No 13, 21 (indicating that interpretation only applies where the decision 'has acquired the force of res judicata, and can only have binding force within the limits of what was decided in the judgment construed').

[51] Caron and Caplan (n 3) 801.

[52] See for example, *Marvin Roy Feldman Karpa v Mexico*, ICSID Case No ARB(AF)/99/1, Correction and Interpretation of the Award (13 June 2003) [10].

[53] See inter alia *Asylum Case (Colombia v Peru)*, Request for Interpretation of the Judgment of 20 November 1950 [1950] ICJ Rep 395, 403.

[54] *Wena Hotels Ltd v Egypt*, ICSID Case No ARB/98/4, Decision on the Application by Wena Hotels Ltd for Interpretation of the Arbitral Award (31 October 2005) [76].

Within the investment arbitration context under the ICSID Rules, the request for interpretation must be made to the Secretary-General;[55] that request is then passed onto the tribunal. Where possible, the original tribunal should be reconvened to make the interpretation decision.[56] However, if even one member of the original tribunal cannot return to the matter, the entire tribunal needs to be reconstituted in accordance with the Convention.[57] This does not exclude the possibility of reappointment of original members of the tribunal; some commentators consider such reappointment to be beneficial on account of his or her existing knowledge of the facts and reasoning of the decision—namely to 'expedite proceedings and their involvement in the drafting of the award will help to explain its meaning'.[58]

Unlike the right of the parties to seek correction of an award—and the subsequent power of the tribunal to render that correction—the right to request an interpretation of the scope and meaning of the award has no time barriers under the ICSID Convention, pursuant to Rule 69(3) of the ICSID Arbitration Rules. The decision to not include a time limit was discussed extensively during the negotiation of the Convention, with the conclusion that 'an award might impose a continuing obligation over a long period and that questions of interpretation might arise at any time during that period'.[59] The tribunals' authority over the award is thus indefinitely extended and should be acknowledged with respect to the importance of this provision. Notably, the *Wena Hotels v Egypt* request for interpretation was brought three and a half years after the award was issued. [60] In contrast, in *ATA Construction v Jordan*[61] the request for interpretation was made within months of the decision. The timing of the request was made necessary by the nature of the request which dealt with the restoration of an arbitration agreement between the investor and a state-owned enterprise and thus impacted ongoing court proceedings.[62]

The approach in ICSID regarding the time limit differs from other arbitration rules. In particular both UNCITRAL and SIAC rules include a 30-day limit to the possibility to seek an interpretation.[63] The use of these rules for commercial arbitrations may justify—and even require—the imposition of a time limit for the interpretation phase, ensuring that the dispute has been definitively settled and business may continue.[64]

[55] ICISD Arbitration Rules (2022) r 69(1).

[56] ICSID Convention art 51(2).

[57] ibid arts 37(2)(a) and 51(3).

[58] Anthony Sinclair, 'Article 50' in Schill and others (n 2) para 49; see eg *Wena Hotels* (n 54) [8] (where one member of the original tribunal was reappointed).

[59] Sinclair (n 58) para 28. See also, Andreas Kulick, 'Article 60 ICJ Statute, Interpretation Proceedings, and the Competing Concepts of Res Judicata' (2015) 28 Leiden Journal of International Law 73, 75.

[60] *Wena Hotels* (n 54) [1].

[61] *ATA Construction, Industrial and Trading Company v Jordan*, ICSID Case No ARB/08/2, Decision on Interpretation and Provisional Measures (7 March 2011) [1].

[62] Proceedings were initiated but discontinued in *Standard Chartered Bank (Hong Kong) Limited v Tanzania Electric Supply Company Limited (Tanesco)*, ICSID Case No ARB/10/20, Award (12 September 2016); *Victor Pey Casado* (n 4).

[63] Caron and Caplan (n 3) 805 (acknowledging the debate regarding the time-limit under the UNCITRAL Rules with proposals for three years as well as proposals for shorter periods to limit uncertainty).

[64] See generally Caron and Caplan (n 3) 803.

Moreover, the non-applicant party has the opportunity to respond to the request for interpretation,[65] ensuring that the two contradictory interpretations are well understood by the tribunal—thus elucidating the interpretative misunderstanding. Finally, expressly under the UNCITRAL Rules, the interpretation decision becomes part of the award.[66] The same procedures regarding, for example, the need for a majority decision and a decision in writing are respected, and the decision must be issued in 120 days under the ICSID Arbitration Rules.[67]

Requests for interpretation under the Additional Facilities Rules have been more prevalent. For example, in *ADM v Mexico*, following the correction of the award pursuant to Article 57 of the ICSID Arbitration (Additional Facilities) Rules, one of the claimants requested interpretation to clarify which companies were included in the definition of claimants for the purposes of the award.[68] This was important for payment of the award to the correct party.

As another example demonstrating possible misuse of the interpretation function, in *Feldman v Mexico*, the tribunal refused to issue an interpretation of the award and considered the claimant's request to be 'effectively ... seeking a new award'.[69] A similar conclusion was made in *Minnotte and Lewis v Poland* where the tribunal denied the request for interpretation, considering it a request to alter the decision.[70] Interim decisions, namely interpretation of procedural orders[71] or bifurcated jurisdictional decisions, do not fall under the scope of Article 50 of the ICSID Convention; instead Article 44 of the Convention or Rule 35 of the Additional Facilities Rules are used to interpret decisions that are not final.

V. Revision of an Award on the Basis of New Facts

While an award cannot be modified, when new facts become available after the award has been rendered, a request can be made to the tribunal for revision—with certain time restrictions. Under Article 51 of the ICSID Convention, this request must be brought to the tribunal within ninety days of discovery of that new fact and no more than three years after the date of the final award. That fact must have previously been unknown to both parties as well as the tribunal, and it must be something that normal diligence would not have uncovered during the initial proceeding.[72]

65 ICSID Arbitration Rules r 72 (3).

66 Caron and Caplan (n 3) 804 (noting, however, that '[w]hether the interpretation is enforceable as part of the award is ultimately determined under the governing national arbitration law').

67 ICSID Arbitration Rules r 72 (5).

68 See inter alia *Archer Daniels Midland Company and Tate and Lyle Ingredients Americas, Inc v Mexico*, ICSID Case No ARB (AF)/04/5, Decision on Requests for Supplementary Decision, Interpretation and Correction of the Award (10 July 2008) [11] (referencing arts 55 and 56 of the ICSID Arbitration Additional Facilities Rules).

69 *Feldman* (n 52 [8]–[10]).

70 *David Minnotte and Robert Lewis v Poland*, ICSID Case No ARB (AF)/10/1, Decision on the Request for Interpretation of the Award (22 October 2014) [12].

71 See eg *Waste Management, Inc v Mexico II*, ICSID Case No ARB(AF)/00/3, Award (30 April 2004) [13] (denial of the request for interpretation based on lack of finality of the award).

72 *Continental Shelf Case (Tunisia v Libya)* [1985] ICJ 192, 206 [27].

The inclusion of this possibility for revision varies in other arbitral rules. Under the UNCITRAL Arbitration Rules, Article 38(1) provides the possibility for correction of an award based on an 'omission', with no reference to new facts. The SCC Arbitration Rules limit post-award remedies to correction and interpretation.[73] The SIAC Investment Arbitration Rules provide for correction, interpretation, and additional award on issues presented but not dealt with in the decision; revisions based on new facts are not expressly included.[74]

Article 51 of the ICSID Convention applies to 'awards', thus implying the final and binding nature of the decision which is to be reconsidered.[75] This strict interpretation was maintained in the *ConocoPhillips* decision where the majority found that it lacked the discretionary power under Article 44 of the ICSID Convention to reconsider a previous decision on liability.[76] The dissenting opinion of Georges Abi Saab in that decision provided for a broader interpretation,[77] and was followed by other tribunals.[78] Such intervention prior to the rendering of the final award may be an implied necessity with respect to the time limits of the provision.[79] Namely, a newly discovered fact must be submitted to the tribunal within 90 days of discovery. This implies that in the case of a bifurcated jurisdictional award, where a new decisive fact has been discovered, waiting until the final award has been issued may result in the time limit being exceeded, thus undermining the intention of the provision to ensure a just conclusion to the dispute. If the reconsideration were not allowed, the new fact would therefore need to be submitted as part of an annulment hearing, extending the process unnecessarily.

Several criteria must be met in order for the new fact to be considered.[80] First, the applicant's request for revision must be based on a fact. Second, that fact should be decisive for the award. Third, the fact must have been unknown to both the applicant and the tribunal at the time the award was rendered. Fourth, while the fact must have been unknown, it must not have arisen after the conclusion of the award. Finally, the ignorance of the fact must not have been a result of negligence in the party's discovery process. This application must also meet the two-tiered time limitations: namely, that the

[73] SCC Arbitration Rules art 47.

[74] SIAC Investment Arbitration Rules r 31.

[75] This provision does not apply to ad hoc tribunals, including annulment tribunals. Benjamin Remy, 'Article 51' in Fouret and others (n 4) paras 4.885ff.

[76] *ConocoPhillips v Venezuela*, ICSID Case No ARB/07/30, Decision on Respondent's Request for Reconsideration of the Tribunal's Decision of 10 March 2014 (10 February 2016) para 23; see also inter alia *Perenco Ecuador Ltd v Ecuador and Empresa Estatal Petróleos del Ecuador (Petroecuador)*, ICSID Case No ARB/08/6, Decision on Ecuador's Reconsideration Motion (10 April 2015) [81]–[87]; *Compañía de Aguas del Aconquija and Vivendi Universal SA v Argentina*, ICSID Case No ARB/97/3 (Resubmitted Case), Decision on Jurisdiction (14 November 2005) [71]–[78]; *CMS Gas Transmission Company v Argentina*, ICSID Case No ARB/01/8, Award (12 May 2005) [126].

[77] *ConocoPhillips v Venezuela*, ICSID Case No ARB/07/30, Decision on Respondent's Request for Reconsideration of the Tribunal's Decision (10 March 2014) Dissenting Opinion of Georges Abi-Saab (10 February 2016).

[78] *Quiborax SA and Non Metallic Minerals SA v Bolivia*, ICSID Case No ARB/06/2, Award (16 September 2015) [130]ff; *Standard Chartered Bank* (n 62) [318]; *Burlington Resources Inc v Ecuador*, ICSID Case No ARB/08/5, Decision on Reconsideration and Award (7 February 2017) [104]–[105].

[79] Remy (n 73) paras 4.883–4.884.

[80] Anthony Sinclair, 'Article 51' in Schill and others (n 2) para 7.

application be made within ninety days of the discovery of the fact and no more than three years after the conclusion of the award.[81]

In investment arbitration, there is a wide scope of what is considered a fact. For example, domestic law is typically considered by the tribunal as a 'fact'. A domestic Supreme Court case was the basis for the request in *Victor Pey Casado*.[82] The decisive nature of the fact is the most common ground for dismissal of revision requests. In both the *ConocoPhillips*[83] and part of the *Burlington*[84] request, the applicants failed to meet this threshold, thus preventing the consideration of the new fact. This limitation regulates to some extent the number of applications brought under this provision[85]—ideally preventing abuse of process. The burden of proof regarding the new fact rests on the applicant for all aspects, including that the ignorance was not due to negligence.[86]

Under the ICSID Convention, the same tribunal should be convened, where possible, to consider these new facts and their impact on the original award.[87] Where that is not possible, a new tribunal must be convened again in accordance with Rule 38 of the ICSID Arbitration Rules. This—as with other post-award decisions—does not exclude the possibility of members of the original tribunal being reappointed.

Essentially for this issue of revision, the tribunal can determine whether a stay of enforcement should be issued during its determination of those new facts.[88] This is of particular relevance because the new fact will necessarily have a substantial impact on the outcome of the award if it meets the threshold of Article 51 of the ICSID Convention.

The purpose of this provision is to ensure that justice is maintained within the sphere of the final and binding nature of arbitration pursuant to Article 53 of the ICSID Convention. Rather than giving such finality no room for manoeuvre, the provision allows space for factual revisions. Essentially, this excludes any newly discovered legal issue, which would open the argumentative nature of the dispute—possibly enabling a never-ending litigation or encouraging abuse of process. The possibility of raising this new fact also rests on a decidedly high threshold,[89] as a prevention to such abuse.

VI. Conclusion: Post-Award Remedies and some Additional Complications

Post-award remedies disrupt one of the fundamental attributes of the arbitral process, namely its *res judicata* nature.[90] In this sense, these provisions should not be understood

[81] ibid.
[82] *Victor Pey Casado* (n 4).
[83] *ConocoPhillips* (n 74) [156].
[84] *Burlington Resources* (n 76) [124]–[125].
[85] Marie Louise Seelig and Anna Tevini, 'Revision Proceedings under the ICSID Convention: Suggestions for a Possible Interpretation of the Prerequisites of Article 51 of the ICSID Convention' (2010) 26 Arbitration International 467, 472.
[86] ibid 477.
[87] ICSID Convention art 51(3); ICSID Arbitration Rules r 70.
[88] ICSID Convention art 51(4); ICSID Arbitration Rules r 73.
[89] ICSID Convention art 51(1).
[90] Seelig and Tevini (n 85) 471.

as appeal mechanisms, but instead as a contribution to achieving closure in the arbitral process. Post-award remedies are quite straightforwardly limited to final awards. This is key to not only the finality of the award but the overall intention to respect *res judicata*. Of the remedies discussed above, only Article 51 of the ICSID Convention regarding discovery of a new and relevant fact applies not only to final but also to interim awards, namely jurisdictional or liability awards. But it should be kept in mind that tribunals are also divided in this matter. Despite the disrespect to some extent to the finality of the award, this exception in fact only further supports the overall intention that such remedies could prevent unnecessary resort to annulment.

There is, however, also a decided risk when it comes to reopening an already-concluded award, namely the misuse of the mechanism to abusively bring forward an unfounded request with the intention of extending the litigation process or attempting to obtain a more favourable decision. In cases in which such abuse has been identified, and as a mechanism for preventing further abuse, the party bringing the request for correction or interpretation may be responsible for the costs of that proceeding, particularly where unsuccessful.[91]

A further complication is the extension of the tribunal's power. This may be of concern in the post-award proceedings where the original tribunal is called upon to decide the matter. While this serves an important purpose in maintaining the integrity of the award, it also prolongs the authority of the tribunal. The concern, less centred on the parties, relies on the integrity of the arbitral tribunal as well as the arbitrators' continued neutrality even after the award has formally been rendered. Such neutrality is not expressly required of them once their mandate has terminated.

Overall, these post-award remedies serve to uphold the goals of *res judicata* and the finality of award, while also ensuring that certain mistakes can be quickly rectified rather than persist until annulment. They further have an overarching role in maintaining the integrity of the process.

[91] *Minnotte and Lewis* (n 70) [17]; *Feldman* (n 52) [15].

25

The Appeal in International Investment Arbitration

*Julien Chaisse**

I. Introduction

The question of appeal in investment arbitration holds significant importance in the broader context of the award in international investment arbitration. As the ultimate outcome of the arbitration process, the award carries implications for the parties involved, investor-state relations, and overall stability of the international investment regime. However, concerns regarding legal consistency, accuracy, and legitimacy have spurred discussion on the need for an appellate mechanism to ensure fairness and effectiveness. This chapter delves into the specific question of appeal in investment arbitration, examining its potential to address these concerns and to enhance the quality and integrity of arbitral awards.

The debate surrounding appeal in investment arbitration has divided scholars and practitioners into two camps.[1] On the one hand, there are those who prioritize finality in arbitration, while the other group emphasizes the importance of consistency and correctness in decision-making.[2] Although appeals are a common remedy in litigation, international arbitration lacks an appellate mechanism. Parties to international arbitration can only challenge an award before courts on limited procedural grounds as the right of appeal is excluded from national arbitration laws and major arbitral institution rules.[3]

* The author would like to express appreciation to Wenzhu Zhang and Dyuti Pandia for their valuable research assistance. The author also acknowledges the advice and input received from discussions at various events with Jose Antonio Rivas, Ian A Laird, Divij Kumar, Jaemin Lee, Threcy Joboy Lawrence, and Kehinde Olaoye, which proved to be quite insightful for earlier drafts. Special thanks are extended to the book editors Catharine Titi and Katia Fach Gomez for their helpful feedback on the final chapter, which greatly contributed to its improvement. The views expressed in this chapter belong solely to the author.

[1] This question was posed by Sir Eli Lauterpacht in his seminal work. See Eli Lauterpacht, *Aspects of the Administration of International Justice* (CUP 1991).

[2] See eg Christoph Schreuer and Andrea de la Brena Melendez, 'Does ISDS Need an Appeals Mechanism?' (2020) 17 Transnational Dispute Management 1, 6; Rowan Platt, 'The Appeal of Appeal Mechanisms in International Arbitration: Fairness over Finality?' (2013) 30(5) Journal of International Arbitration 531; Ian Laird and Rebecca Askew, 'Finality versus Consistency: Does Investor-State Arbitration Need an Appellate System' (2005) 7 Journal of Appellate Practice and Process 285; Noam Zamir and Peretz Segal, 'Appeal in International Arbitration—An Efficient and Affordable Arbitral Appeal Mechanism' (2019) 35 Arbitration International 79, 93.

[3] Lin Jacobsen, 'ISDS Control Mechanisms (Annulment and Setting Aside)' in Julien Chaisse, Leila Choukroune, and Sufian Jusoh (eds), *Handbook of International Investment Law and Policy* (Springer 2020) 4.

Julien Chaisse, *The Appeal in International Investment Arbitration* In: *The Award in International Investment Arbitration*.
Edited by: Katia Fach Gómez and Catharine Titi, Oxford University Press. © Katia Fach Gómez and Aikaterini Titi 2024.
DOI: 10.1093/9780191975936.003.0025

Within the context of investor-state dispute settlement (ISDS), the proposal for an appellate mechanism has emerged as a potential solution for addressing inconsistencies and ensuring the accuracy of awards.[4] The concept of an appeal facility administered by the International Centre for Settlement of Investment Disputes (ICSID) has gained attention with specific features and rules outlined. However, alternative systems, such as relying on preliminary rulings, have also been suggested to reduce divergent interpretations of the ISDS.

Operating within a conceptual framework aimed at addressing concerns related to the consistency, predictability, accuracy, and legitimacy of ISDS awards, this chapter critically analyses the need for an appellate mechanism within the ISDS regime. Drawing on evidence from discussions within the United Nations Commission on International Trade Law (UNCITRAL) Working Group III, positions of different countries, and existing investment agreements, this article presents a persuasive argument for the implementation of an appellate mechanism. The analysis explores the distinctions between a pure appeals mechanism and the concept of the Multilateral Investment Court (MIC) or bilateral investment courts, evaluating their respective roles, implications for adjudicator selection, and the potential to enhance coherence and legitimacy in ISDS. Additionally, specific issues, such as the scope and standards of review, enforcement considerations, and integration of an appeal procedure, were examined.

The findings of this chapter underscore the fundamental implications of an appellate mechanism for the future development of international investment arbitration. By addressing critical issues, such as legal consistency, accuracy of decisions, and diversity of arbitrators, an appellate mechanism can offer a pathway to rectify manifest errors of fact and law, ultimately enhance the overall quality and fairness of arbitral awards. However, careful design and implementation are essential to ensure the effectiveness, independence, and legitimacy of such mechanisms. By striking the right balance and adopting appropriate safeguards, the envisioned appellate mechanism can serve as a powerful tool to advance the objectives of international investment arbitration.

In the subsequent sections, this chapter delves deeper into the suggested system of appeal and explore its advantages and disadvantages. It distinguishes between setting aside an award and reviewing it, shedding light on the absence of a genuine review mechanism in international investment arbitration. Additionally, existing non-judicial appellate procedures, such as JAMS (formerly Judicial Arbitration and Mediation Services), will be examined alongside a discussion of the approaches of different arbitration laws to appellate mechanisms. Furthermore, a comparison is made between pure appeal mechanisms and an investment court system, highlighting the relevance of dispute settlement provisions in EU trade agreements. By analysing these key aspects,

[4] International Centre for Settlement of Investment Disputes, *Background Paper on Annulment for the Administrative Council of ICSID* (World Bank 2012) para 75. See also Vanina Sucharitkul, 'From Arbitration to the Investment Court System (ICS): Comparing CETA, EVIPA, and TTIP' in Chaisse, Choukroune, and Jusoh (n 3) 13; Yuwen Li, 'The Notion and Development of International Investment Court' ibid 9.

this chapter aims to provide a comprehensive understanding of the appeal debate within international investment arbitration.

II. Interrogating the Appeal Concept: Cross-Pollination from Domestic Legal Systems to International Investment Law

Within various legal systems, the opportunity for parties to seek an appeal after the issuance of an award has been recognized as an important right. This allows parties to request a higher authority to reconsider the decision made by the initial tribunal, particularly in cases where there are concerns about legal interpretation errors or inadequate reasoning provided by the tribunal. However, the use of appeals can also be subject to abuse, as some parties may attempt to exploit the process of seeking a favourable outcome by requesting a reconsideration of the original award.

This part of the chapter delves into the fundamental concept of an appellate mechanism within the arbitration context, highlighting its benefits and limitations in the arbitration process. It argues that the introduction of appellate bodies can contribute to the stability and predictability of arbitration proceedings. Moreover, it addresses significant concerns associated with the current ISDS system, specifically the absence of an appeal mechanism. It explores the issue of frivolous requests for annulment, wherein parties seek reassessment of a tribunal's decision with the aim of overturning the award solely because it does not align with their interests. Additionally, it examines the distinction between the annulment of awards and appeals and the active role played by annulment committees, which has narrowed the gap between the two processes on certain grounds.

A. Examining the Pillars of Appeal: Transparency, Fairness, and Correctness in Domestic Legal Systems

The principle of appeal in arbitration is multifaceted and is subject to debate. While arbitration awards are not immediately effective and often rely on enforcement by the award-winning party, the introduction of an appeal system offers another layer of review. This is seen by some as a means of rectifying errors, ensuring consistency, and encouraging broader participation in arbitration. However, the effectiveness of such an appeal system has been questioned, particularly regarding the implied assumption that appeal judges hold superior judgement over the original arbitrators. Therefore, the concept of appeal within arbitration is fraught with complexities and nuances, which make its implementation a matter of intricate deliberation.

It is crucial to understand that the effectiveness of arbitration awards is not automatic. This means that even when the winning party anticipates the loser's compliance with the award, the latter may refuse to pay the stipulated amount. The onus for enforcing the award thus falls on the party that emerged victorious in arbitration.

Failure to enforce an arbitral award frequently results in an award of little or no value.[5] Appeals enable parties in high-stakes disputes to obtain an additional arbitrator if they believe that a final award contains errors. Additionally, a substantive review is expected to persuade additional parties who consider arbitration too risky to enter the market.[6] Consistency and precision are key considerations for appeal. It is assumed that appeals would ensure that laws are applied consistently and would allow predictable outcomes for greater stability.

However, this proposition does not remain unchallenged. Sir Eli Lauterpacht, for instance, challenges the underpinnings of the appeal system by stating

> the mere fact that one person has been set in a position to pass judgment on the verdict of another does not give the second decision a greater quality than the first. ... [T]he concept of appeal also reflects another unarticulated assumption, namely, that those to whom appeal lies are as judges in some way better than, or superior to, those whose judgment is being reviewed. If that element of superiority is lacking, appeal ... is merely the substitution of one person's view of the situation for that of another.[7]

The concept of an appeal within arbitration, which is largely seen as a tool to ensure consistency and accuracy and to stimulate broader participation, is also subject to critique. The effectiveness and value of an appellate mechanism, as questioned by critics such as Lauterpacht, hinge largely on the inherent assumption of the superiority of judgment in the appellate stage. The dynamism of this discourse underscores the complexity and nuances of implementing the appellate mechanisms in arbitration.

B. Deconstructing the Controversy: The Role of Appeals in Investment Law and ISDS

Appeals help maintain the consistency of a dispute settlement system by promoting predictability. While party autonomy is an important consideration when resorting to arbitration, predictability (through appeals or otherwise) assists parties in understanding how their conduct is likely to be perceived in the case of a future dispute and helps them structure their investment relationship (duties and obligations) accordingly. Additionally, it provides an additional review layer, which is key to fairness in adjudication. Thus, to ensure the coherence and consistency of the ISDS system, an appellate body must be established to review flagrant errors in the interpretation and application

[5] Leonardo Borlini and Stefano Silingardi, 'Enforcement of Investment Arbitration Awards' in Chaisse, Choukroune, and Jusoh (n 3).

[6] Irene M Ten Cate, 'International Arbitration and the Ends of Appellate Review' 44 New York University Journal of International Law & Politics 1109.

[7] Eli Lauterpacht, *Aspects of the Administration of International Justice* (Grotius 1991) 109, 111.

of treaty law.[8] In contrast lies the principle of finality, which requires that international arbitral awards be irrevocable and is a primary reason parties choose arbitration.[9]

While the ICSID system is self-contained, any international arbitration proceeding conducted outside the ICSID system invariably involves national law. While an award made by an ICSID tribunal is enforceable in all contracting states, a party seeking to enforce an award made outside the ICSID system will almost certainly invoke the New York Convention, which requires all contracting states to recognize and enforce awards[10] made by other contracting states.

Within this framework, a system of *stare decisis* would promote stability, certainty, reliability, uniformity, convenience, and expediency.[11] One of the biggest drawbacks of investment arbitration is that each tribunal relies on different criteria, and that the decision of one tribunal plays little or no role in assisting another tribunal, even while determining a similar set of facts or questions of law. An example of such an inconsistency is that of the *Lauder* arbitrations, where different tribunals reached different conclusions despite the facts being the same.[12] The case dealt with expropriation, and the conflicting approaches taken by the tribunals not only revealed the difficulties that plague tribunals when deciding on such issues but also resulted in unpredictability and uncertainty, leading to a lack of uniformity in the understanding of expropriation.[13]

Owing to this, one of the biggest concerns around the current ISDS mechanism that stands today is its inability to provide an appellate mechanism to allow appeals against grossly erroneous decisions that may have unfathomable ramifications on the public interest. Although the ICSID rules allow for the annulment of awards or the UNICITRAL rules permit the setting aside of arbitral awards by national courts, this is not a sufficient mechanism to rectify poor-quality awards as their grounds are highly restricted. This is because set-aside or annulment of awards involves a nullification of the award altogether, bringing the parties back to where they were prior to the institution of arbitration. This is an extremely undesirable situation because it leads to additional costs and a prolonged duration of subsequent legal proceedings that must be undertaken by the parties.[14] Furthermore, Article 52 of the ICSID Convention does

[8] Margie-Lys Jaime, 'Could an Appellate Review Mechanism "Fix" the ISDS System?' (*Kluwer Arbitration Blog*, 11 February 2021) <http://arbitrationblog.kluwerarbitration.com/2021/02/11/could-an-appellate-review-mechanism-fix-the-isds-system/>.

[9] Rowan Platt, 'The Appeal of Appeal Mechanisms in International Arbitration: Fairness over Finality?' (2013) 5 Journal of International Arbitration 531.

[10] Convention on the Recognition and Enforcement of Foreign Arbitral Awards (adopted 10 June 1958, entered into force 7 June 1959) 330 UNTS 3 art XII (New York Convention). See Leonard Quigley, 'Accession by the United States to the United Nations Convention on the Recognition and Enforcement of Foreign Arbitral Awards' 70(7) Yale Law Journal 1049; James van R Springer, 'The United Nations Convention on the Recognition and Enforcement of Foreign Arbitral Awards' (1969) 3 International Lawyer 320.

[11] Jeffery Commission, 'Precedent in Investment Treaty Arbitration: A Citation Analysis of a Developing Jurisprudence' (2007) 24 Journal of International Arbitration 132.

[12] *Ronald S Lauder v Czech Republic*, Final Award (3 September 2001) and *CME Czech Republic BV v Czech Republic*, Partial Award (13 September 2001).

[13] Deepu Jojo Sushama, 'Appellate Structure and Need for Legal Certainty in Investment Arbitration' (*Kluwer Arbitration Blog*, 1 May 2014) <http://arbitrationblog.kluwerarbitration.com/2014/05/01/appellate-structure-and-need-for-legal-certainty-in-investment-arbitration/?print=print>.

[14] Christian Tietje and others, 'The Impact of Investor-State-Dispute Settlement (ISDS) in the Transatlantic Trade and Investment Partnership' (Reference MINBUZA-2014.78850, 2014) <www.eumonitor.eu/9353000/1/j4nvgs5kjg27kof_j9vvik7m1c3gyxp/vjn8exgvufya/f=/blg378683.pdf> 112,

not address concerns regarding inconsistent awards rendered in investment arbitration cases.

The current state of the annulment mechanism is illustrated in *CMS Gas Transmission Co, Argentina.*[15] In this case, the ad hoc committee holds

> Throughout its consideration of the Award, the Committee has identified a series of errors and defects. The Award contained manifest errors of law. It suffered from lacunae and elisions. All this has been identified and underlined by the Committee. However, the Committee is conscious that it exercises its jurisdiction under a narrow and limited mandate conferred by Article 52 of the ICSID Convention. The scope of this mandate allows annulment as an option only when certain specific conditions exist. As stated already (paragraph 136 above), in these circumstances the Committee cannot simply substitute its own view of the law and its own appreciation of the facts for those of the Tribunal.[16]

In these circumstances, the importance of having an appellate mechanism in place is further emphasized, since even if the annulment committee wants to step in and help rectify at least part of the award, it is unable to do so.[17] Conversely, it has been argued that the existence of an appellate mechanism may add to the existing disadvantages within international investment arbitration, since it puts into question the finality of arbitral decisions,[18] and increases the costs and delays proceedings, which are already too slow and too expensive.[19] Any losing party would be tempted to appeal and persuade the second tribunal of the correctness of its position, and as a result, the proceedings would become lengthier and more expensive.[20] However, at this juncture, the credibility of ISDS hinges on the stability and predictability it provides to both investors and states which can be ensured to an extent with the establishment of an appellate mechanism.

Over the years, there have been several discussions about the establishment of an appellate mechanism in ISDS. One such instance is that of ICSID considering the idea of an ICSID Appeals Facility in a 2004 working paper. Following a series of meetings in 2005, it was concluded that it would be premature to establish an ICSID Appellate Mechanism. The working paper indicated that the rationale behind establishing an

[15] *CMS v Argentina*, ICSID Case No. ARB/01/8, Decision on Annulment (25 September 2007).

[16] ibid [158].

[17] Barton Legum, 'Options to Establish an Appellate mechanism for Investment Disputes, in Appeals Mechanism in International Investment Disputes' in Karl P Sauvant and others (eds), *Appeals Mechanism in International Investment Disputes* (OUP 2008) 232.

[18] David Gaukrodger and Kathryn Gordon, 'Investor-state dispute settlement: A scoping paper for the investment policy community' OECD Working Papers on International Investment No 2012/3 <www.oecd.org/daf/inv/investment-policy/WP-2012_3.pdf> 53.

[19] Karl Sauvant, 'The Evolving International Investment Law and Policy Regime: Ways Forward' in *Policy Options Paper, International Centre for Trade and Sustainable Development (ICTSD) and World Economic Forum* (2016) <www3.weforum.org/docs/E15/WEF_Investment_Law_Policy_regime_report_2015_1401.pdf>.

[20] Gabrielle Kaufmann-Kohler, 'Arbitral Precedent: Dream, Necessity or Excuse?' (2007) 23(3) Arbitration International 368. See also Jeffery P Commission, 'Precedent in Investment Treaty Arbitration a Citation Analysis of a Developing Jurisprudence' (2007) 24 Journal of International Arbitration 47.

appellate review framework for investment arbitration is to ensure consistency and correctness in the awards made by diverse arbitral tribunals so that parties can have the opportunity to rectify manifest errors in the interpretation and application of treaty law.[21] This is bound to improve the quality of investment awards while simultaneously ensuring consistency and uniformity within ISDS, thereby moving towards a precedent-based system.

Further, in 2004, the ICSID discussion paper, with some caveats, noted that an ICSID Appellate Mechanism would 'foster coherency and consistency in the case law emerging *under* investment treaties'.[22] One of the reasons behind this consideration was the established success of the Appellate Body of the World Trade Organization (WTO), despite minor hiccups along the way during the Trump presidency, coupled with the perceived legitimacy crisis and inherent institutional shortcomings bedevilling ICSID.[23] As noted by the United Nations Conference on Trade and Development (UNCTAD), the concerns that underscore the current ISDS system include, a 'deficit of legitimacy and transparency; contradictions between arbitral awards; difficulties in correcting erroneous arbitral decisions; questions about the independence and impartiality of arbitrators'.[24] Consequently, there is a need for an appellate mechanism.[25]

The impact an appellate body would have on the ISDS system is undeniable for the current state of affairs. An appellate mechanism would ensure that a tribunal exercises more caution in determining a dispute and lead tribunals to resort to existing awards as precedential value. The appellate mechanism could indicate its stance on matters that brought before it, and those that are regarded as correct would be considered a precedent, while those that are not would be rectified. By adhering to such a process, the appellate mechanism would not only be able to remove existing inconsistencies but also ensure a stable and predictable arbitral process.[26]

Arbitral tribunals in treaty-based arbitrations are currently asked to interpret a broad range of standards as may be included in agreements, including principles and standards under public international law. However, ISDS may be based on a contract or domestic legislation, and the concerns are not the same in nature. These

[21] David D Caron, 'Reputation and Reality in the ICSID Annulment Process: Understanding the Distinction between Annulment and Appeal' (1992) ICSID Review 40.

[22] See Asif H Qureshi, 'An Appellate System in International Investment Arbitration?' in Peter Muchlinski, Federico Ortino, and Christoph Schreuer (eds), *The Oxford Handbook on International Investment* (OUP 2008) 1165–67.

[23] UNCTAD, 'Denunciation of the ICSID Convention and BITs: Impact on Investor-State Claims' UNCTAD International Investment Agreement Issues Note 2 <https://unctad.org/system/files/official-document/webdiaeia20106_en.pdf> 1–2.

[24] UNCTAD, 'Reform of Investor-State Dispute Settlement: In Search of a Roadmap' (2013) <https://unctad.org/system/files/official-document/webdiaepcb2013d4_en.pdf>. See also Katia Yannaca-Small, 'Improving the System of Investor–State Dispute Settlement' Working Papers on International Investment Number 2006/1 (2006) <www.oecd.org/daf/inv/investment-policy/WP-2006_1.pdf>, 3 (outlining the challenges to investor–state arbitration and potential reform options).

[25] Erin E Gleason, 'International Arbitral Appeals: What Are We so Afraid of?' (2007) 7(2) Pepperdine Dispute Resolution Law Journal 271–72 (noting the merits of an appellate system).

[26] cf *SGS Société Général de Surveillance SA v Philippines*, ICSID Case No ARB/02/6, Award (11 April 2008) (holding that the umbrella clause elevated contractual obligations to international law obligations) with *SGS Société Général de Surveillance SA v Pakistan*, ICSID Case No ARB/01/13, Award (6 August 2003) (holding that umbrella clause did not elevate contractual obligations to international law obligations).

considerations would justify reserving the appellate mechanism for ISDS based on the treaties. Additionally, the appellate mechanism should have the authority to grant or deny an appeal based on the ICSID Convention's annulment grounds. If the appellate tribunal determines that an appeal is wholly without merit or is frivolous, it should be dismissed, as per Rule 41 of the ICSID Arbitration Rules.[27] The tribunal should consider all relevant factors before deciding whether to order the appellant to provide security for costs. Additionally, the tribunal can also consider setting a fixed percentage of the security for cost amounts to prevent frequent resorts to/potential misuse of this provision. Nonetheless, the order of security for costs should not impair the appellant's ability to pursue its claim, as this would be unjust.

C. A Critical Examination of the Set-Aside vs Appeal Dichotomy: Towards a More Effective Dispute Resolution Framework

ICSID does not have an appellate facility, although an aggrieved party may apply to an annulment committee against the award.[28] Annulment is only possible on a limited number of fundamental grounds. In the case of the ICSID Convention, these grounds are mentioned exhaustively under Article 52(1).[29] An annulment constitutes an exception to the paramount principle of finality and is regarded as an exceptional remedy only for dealing with extraordinary situations. It was included to provide relief for gross violations of the fundamental principles stipulated within the Convention. The annulment of an award implies complete censure of the tribunal. The annulment only attempts to protect the legitimacy of the decision process. It is not concerned with the substantive correctness of the award, but only checks whether the principles stipulated have been adhered to during decision-making.[30] However, an annulment committee does not *check* the decisions arrived at by the tribunal. An ad hoc committee under the ICSID Convention is only empowered to annul an award. It cannot remand or replace

[27] 'Manifest Lack of Legal Merit', as defined in ICSID Arbitration Rules (2022) r 41, is a provision that allows a party to object if they believe a claim is clearly and unequivocally without legal merit. According to this provision, such an objection can relate to the claim's substance, the jurisdiction of ICSID, or the competence of the tribunal. The rule 41 procedure is designed to swiftly address claims that are evidently without legal merit to ensure an efficient arbitration process. A party must file a written objection no later than forty-five days after the constitution of the tribunal, outlining the grounds for the objection, along with a statement of the relevant facts, law, and arguments. The tribunal then sets time limits for submissions regarding the objection and must render a decision within sixty days. See Julien Chaisse, 'Delays Expected but Duration of Delays Unpredictable: Causes, Types, and Symptoms of Procedural Applications in Investment Arbitration' (2021) 37(4) Arbitration International 863.

[28] See ICSID Convention art 52.

[29] ibid art 52(1) provides:

> Either party may request annulment of the award by an application in writing addressed to the Secretary-General on one or more of the following grounds: (a) that the Tribunal was not properly constituted; (b) that the Tribunal has manifestly exceeded its powers; (c) that there was corruption on the part of a member of the Tribunal; (d) that there has been a serious departure from a fundamental rule of procedure; or (e) that the award has failed to state the reasons on which it is based.

See also Steffen Hindelang and Julia Nassl, 'Annulment and Set-aside' in Katia Fach Gómez and Catharine Titi (eds), *The Award in International Investment Arbitration* (OUP 2024).

[30] A comparative analysis of these mechanisms is published in Freya Baetens 'Keeping the Status Quo or Embarking on a New Course? Setting Aside, Refusal of Enforcement, Annulment and Appeal' in Andreas Kulick (ed), *Reassertion of Control over the Investment Treaty Regime* (CUP 2016).

the award for its own. Therefore, the result of a successful annulment application is a nullification of the original decision. Therefore, annulment is fundamentally different from and narrower in scope than an appeal.

In the ICSID Convention, grounds for annulment are carefully limited. This is indicated through the use of terms such as 'manifest', 'serious', and 'fundamental'. The ad hoc committee in *Amco II* stated that:

> It is incumbent upon Ad Hoc Committees to resist the temptation to rectify incorrect decisions or to annul unjust awards.[31] Article 52(1) of the ICSID Convention stipulates watertight grounds for the annulment.[32] Thus, a. annulment is predicated on the fact that the tribunal was not properly constituted; b. the tribunal has manifestly exceeded its powers; c. there was corruption on the part of a member of the tribunal; d. there has been a serious departure from a fundamental rule of procedure; and e. the award has failed to state the reasons on which it is based. Thus, the grounds for annulment are limited to procedural irregularity and do not extend to 'substantive errors.[33]

It has become common practice for ad hoc committees to underline their limited role during the annulment process. In particular, the committees lay down the differences between annulment and appeal at the beginning of every decision.[34] The annulment grounds were highly restricted and narrow in scope.[35] Often, committees reject the suggestion that the grounds for annulment should be interpreted either extensively or restrictively.[36] While some committees have exercised restraint during the

[31] *Amco v Indonesia*, Resubmitted Case, ICSID Case No ARB/81/1, Decision on Annulment (3 December 1992) [1.18].

[32] An ICSID award that was subjected annulment procedure, *Klöckner v Cameroon*, ICSID Case No ARB/81/2, Decision on Annulment (3 May 1985) [69], [112]. For an argument for faithful adherence to the restrictive terms of annulment by the annulment committee, and the denunciation of annulment on other grounds except as provided by ICSID Convention art 52 see, Paul Friedland and Paul Brumpton, 'Rabid Redux: The Second Wave of Abusive ICSID Annulments' (2011–12) 27 American University International Law Review 727.

[33] Andrea Kupfer Schneider, 'Error Correction and Dispute System Design in Investor-State Arbitration' (2013) 5 Yearbook of Arbitration & Mediation 197.

[34] *MINE v Guinea*, ICSID Case No ARB/84/4, Decision on Annulment (22 December 1989) [5.04], [5.08]; *Wena Hotels v Egypt*, Decision on Annulment (5 February 2002), ICSID Case No ARB/98/4 [18]; *Vivendi v Argentina*, Decision on Annulment (3 July 2002), ICSID Case No ARB/97/3 [62], [63], [64]; *CDC v Seychelles*, ICSID Case No ARB/02/14, Decision on Annulment (29 June 2005) [34]–[37]; *Mitchell v DR Congo*, ICSID Case No ARB/99/7, Decision on Annulment (1 November 2006) [19], [20]; *Soufraki v UAE*, ICSID Case No ARB/02/7, Decision on Annulment (5 June 2007) [20–25]; *Repsol v Petroecuador*, ICSID Case No ARB/01/10, Decision on Annulment (8 January 2007) [38]; *MTD v Chile*, ICSID Case No ARB/01/7, Decision on Annulment (21 March 2007) [31]; *CMS v Argentina*, ICSID Case No ARB/01/8, Decision on Annulment (25 September 2007) [43], [44], [135], [136], [158]; *Rumeli v Kazakhstan*, ICSID Case No ARB/05/16, Decision (25 March 2010) [70]; *Sempra v Argentina*, ICSID Case No ARB/02/16, Decision on Annulment (29 June 2010) [73], [74]; *Enron v Argentina*, ICSID Case No ARB/01/3, Decision on Annulment (30 July 2010) [63]–[65]; *Vivendi II v Argentina*, ICSID Case No ARB/97/3, Decision on Annulment (10 August 2010) [247]; *Fraport v Philippines (I)*, ICSID Case No ARB/03/25, Decision on Annulment (23 December 2010) [76].

[35] Christoph Schreuer, 'From ICSID Annulment to Appeal: Halfway Down the Slippery Slope' (2009) 10 Law and Practice of International Courts and Tribunals 211.

[36] *MINE v Guinea (II)*, ICSID Case No ARB/84/4, Decision on Annulment (22 December 1989) [4.05]; *Amco v Indonesia*, ICSID Case No ARB/81/1, Decision on Annulment (17 December 1992) [1.17], [1.18], [7.55]; *Vivendi v Argentina*, ICSID Case No ARB/97/3, Decision on Annulment (10 August 2010) [62]; *CDC v Seychelles*, ICSID Case No ARB/02/14, Decision on Annulment (29 June 2005) [33]; *Mitchell v DR Congo*, ICSID Case No ARB/99/7, Decision on Annulment (1 November 2006) [19]; *Soufraki v UAE*, ICSID Case No ARB/02/7, Decision on Annulment (5 June 2007) [21].

process,[37] it is said that others have shown an unprecedented level of activism in reviewing ICSID awards.[38] This is sometimes attributed to the increasing number of annulment requests and the tendency of some committees to expand their view of their function. In 2010, ICSID ad hoc committees made eight annulment decisions.[39] Four of these decisions led to annulment of the respective awards.[40] In four cases the awards survived.[41]

Annulment is not an appeal, and in the drafting history of the ICSID Convention, the Legal Committee confirmed that even a manifestly incorrect application of the correct law would not be a ground for annulment.[42] However, some ad hoc committees have taken the view that gross or egregious misapplication or misinterpretation of the proper law may amount to non-application,[43] and therefore constitute a ground for annulment, whereas others deem this approach to be bordering on an appeal.

Thus, while the intention behind allowing for annulment and appeal may overlap to some extent, the two review mechanisms nonetheless differ in their scope of enquiry. In the context of national juridical system, an appeal has a more far-reaching scope than the remedy of annulment under the ICSID framework as it currently stands. An appeal enquires into both 'the legitimacy of the process of decision and the substantive correctness of the decision'.[44] Having the opportunity to appeal erroneous awards is crucial for establishing predictability and consistency within the relevant regime. By contrast, annulment within the ICSID arbitration system is limited in scope, primarily focusing on whether the arbitral decision was derived from a legitimate process, regardless of any errors of law or fact. As a result, as long as the award maintains legitimacy within the annulment procedure, errors of law or facts do not have an impact on its validity. This is an inherent defect in the annulment procedure under the ICSID Convention and is bound to cause injustice to an aggrieved party that genuinely intends to correct the blatant misapplication of law by tribunals. Accordingly, the creation of an

[37] Christoph Schreuer, 'Three Generations of ICSID Annulment Proceedings' in Emmanuel Gaillard, Yas Banifatemi (eds), *Annulment of ICSID Awards* (JurisNet 2004) 17–42.

[38] Antonio Crivellaro, 'Annulment of ICSID Awards: Back to the "First Generation"?' in L Levy and Yves Derains (eds), *Liber Amicorum—Mélanges en l'Honneur de Serge Lazareff* (Pedone 2011) 145.

[39] *Compagnie d'Exploitation du Chemin de Fer Transgabonais v Gabonese Republic*, ICSID Case No ARB/04/5.

[40] *Sempra v Argentina*, ICSID Case No ARB/02/16, Decision on Annulment (29 June 2010); *Enron v Argentina*, ICSID Case No ARB/01/3, Decision on Annulment (30 July 2010); *Fraport v Philippines (I)*, ICSID Case No ARB/03/25, Decision on Annulment (23 December 2010). In *Helnan v Egypt*, ICSID Case No ARB/05/19, Decision on Annulment (14 June 2010), the annulment did not affect the award's *dispositif* but only an aspect of the reasoning.

[41] *Rumeli v Kazakhstan*, ICSID Case No ARB/05/16, Decision on Annulment (25 March 2010); *Compagnie d'Exploitation du Chemin de Fer Transgabonais v. Gabonese Republic*, ICSID Case No ARB/04/5, Decision on Annulment (11 May 2010); *Sociedad Anónima Eduardo Vieira v. Chile*, ICSID Case No ARB/04/7, Decision on Annulment (10 December 2010). In *Vivendi II v Argentina*, ICSID Case No ARB/97/3, Decision on Annulment (10 August 2010) (the ad hoc committee came close to annulling the award but eventually upheld it).

[42] ICSID, *Background Paper* (n 4) [73]; ICSID, *Updated Background Paper on Annulment for the Administrative Council of ICSID* (World Bank 2016) [72].

[43] *Sempra v. Argentina*, ICSID Case No ARB/02/16, Decision on the Argentine Republic's Application for Annulment of the Award (29 June 2010) [174].

[44] David D Caron, 'Reputation and Reality in the ICSID Annulment Process: Understanding the Distinction between Annulment and Appeal' (1992) 7 ICSID Review 40; *Klockner v Cameroon*, ICSID Case No ARB/81/2, Second ad hoc Committee Decision on Annulment (17 May 1990) [4] (noting that excess of powers under the second ground of art 52(1) entailed excess jurisdiction).

appellate mechanism within the ISDS regime would ensure a more robust substantive and procedural review of the awards.

III. The Role and Impact of Appellate Mechanisms in International Dispute Resolution Systems

The evident success of the WTO dispute settlement system stands as a testament to the potential effectiveness of an appellate mechanism within ISDS.[45] The WTO appellate system, widely lauded for instilling greater predictability in the settlement of world trade law disputes through the implicit recognition of precedential value, has set a benchmark for international dispute resolution.[46] The success of the WTO Appellate Body should encourage the setting up of an appeals facility within the ISDS to review and improve the arbitration process with the body of case law which it can generate.[47] The jurisprudence generated by the WTO Appellate Body is impressive in both quality and quantity, and ISDS can definitely attempt and emulate the same.[48]

This trend is not limited to the WTO alone, as regional institutions like the Association of Southeast Asian Nations (ASEAN),[49] the Central America–Dominican Republic-United States Free Trade Agreement (CAFTA–DR)[50] have recognized the importance of integrating an appellate system.[51] In a broader legal context, the presence of appellate mechanisms in traditional judicial systems serves two crucial

[45] According to Dispute Settlement Understanding (DSU) art 3(2), dispute settlement in the World Trade Organization (WTO) 'serves to clarify the existing provisions of those agreements in accordance with the customary rules of interpretation of public international law'.

[46] The WTO dispute settlement system does not operate on a strict doctrine of precedent like some domestic legal systems, especially common law systems. However, the decisions of the WTO Appellate Body do carry significant persuasive weight. While WTO panel and Appellate Body reports are binding only on the parties to the dispute, in practice, these reports tend to be treated with a degree of respect and are often looked upon for guidance in subsequent disputes. This practice adds a layer of predictability to the system, as parties can look at prior decisions to gauge how similar issues might be treated in the future. That said, each dispute is examined on its own merits, and while past decisions may be consulted, they do not bind future panels or the Appellate Body in the strict sense of precedent. However, for consistency's sake, departures from previous interpretations or findings are usually done with careful consideration.

[47] Yenkong Ngangjoh-Hodu and Collins C Ajibo, 'ICSID Annulment Procedure and the WTO Appellate System: The Case for an Appellate System for Investment Arbitration' (2015) 6 Journal of International Dispute Settlement 308.

[48] Although some argue that the ICSID context differs from the WTO's interconnected treaty law framework, it has been argued that an appellate system could bolster the predictability, legitimacy, and fairness of ICSID rulings. Drawing from the WTO's successful appellate body, scholarship advocates for a similar mechanism within ICSID, suggesting it would improve the quality of awards and balance the interests of different stakeholders in investment disputes. This scholarship underscores the critical need for evolution in the investment arbitration ecosystem. See eg Donald McRae, 'The WTO Appellate Body: A Model for an ICSID Appeals Facility?' (2010) 1(2) Journal of International Dispute Settlement 371; Yenkong Ngangjoh-Hodu and Collins C Ajibo, 'ICSID Annulment Procedure and the WTO Appellate System: The Case for an Appellate System for Investment Arbitration' (2015) 6(2) Journal of International Dispute Settlement 308.

[49] Association of Southeast Asian (ASEAN) Enhanced Disputes Settlement Mechanism, where there is also the possibility of appeal, see ASEAN Protocol on Enhanced Dispute Settlement Mechanism, Adopted by the Economic Ministers at the 10th ASEAN Summit in Vientiane (29 November 2004).

[50] See Dominican Republic–Central America Free Trade Agreement (United States of America, Costa Rica, El Salvador, Guatemala, Honduras, Nicaragua, and Dominican Republic) annex 10F 'Appellate Body or Similar Mechanism'.

[51] Yet, it is worth noting that thus far, there has not been concrete proof indicating that these systems have generated decisions via their respective appellate bodies.

purposes: rectifying errors and contributing to the development of legal principles, particularly in common law jurisdictions. Such mechanisms ensure the uniformity of law, coherence of jurisprudence, and reduction in future mistakes.

This part of the chapter discusses the role and impact of appellate mechanisms in international dispute resolution systems. It begins with an examination of the JAMS Optional Arbitration Appeal Procedure and explores its process, implications, and associated issues as a non-judicial arbitral appeal mechanism. Subsequently, it delves into alternative appellate models, shedding light on the reviewing regime under the UNCITRAL Model Law, and emphasizes the need for an appellate-style review mechanism to address errors in the application of facts or law. It also highlights the divergent approaches between different countries and the two prominent models of arbitration laws, namely French law and English law.

A. Assessing the Effectiveness of the 2013 JAMS Optional Arbitration Appeal Procedure

After taking cognizance of the fact that parties are deterred from choosing arbitration because of the lack of any merit-based appeal process, several major arbitration institutions in the United States have attempted to resolve this concern by adopting rules that provide an appeal facility within arbitration.[52]

In the last two decades, the International Institute for Conflict Prevention and Resolution (CPR Institute), the American Arbitration Association (AAA), and JAMS have introduced rules permitting parties to opt into a mechanism for appealing an adverse award before a panel of appellate arbitrators. The parties may agree to the JAMS Optional Appeal Procedure at any time.[53] The Appeal Panel typically consists of three JAMS neutrals with significant appellate experience and provides for the same standard of review that the first-level appellate court in the jurisdiction would apply for an appeal of the trial court decision. The Optional Arbitration Appeal Procedure, without delay, will be completed within twenty-one days.

The major highlights of the JAMS Optional Arbitration Appeal Procedure are as follows. First, Rule 22 provides an optional expedited arbitration procedure for cases involving less than USD5 million, in which parties can choose a process that limits disclosure. Any party may include a request for such a procedure in its arbitration agreement (JAMS International Arbitration Rules (JIAR) art 22(1)). If the request is accepted, arbitration will be conducted in under six months.[54] Second, Rule 3 of JIAR provides for emergency relief procedures. A party in need of emergency relief prior to the appointment of a tribunal may notify JAMS and other parties of the basis for such

[52] Jessica E. Sabbat, 'Non-Judicial Appeals from Arbitration Awards: A Way to Alleviate Concerns about the Finality of Arbitration' (2018) 33 Mealey's International Arbitration Report 1.

[53] JAMS, 'JAMS Optional Arbitration Appeal Procedures' (June 2003) <www.jamsadr.com/appeal/>.

[54] ibid art 22.

relief. JAMS will appoint an emergency arbitrator within 24 hours of the application.[55] Third, Rule 32 authorizes a tribunal to grant interim relief that it deems 'necessary', through a partial or interim award, and may include injunctive relief, protective measures to conserve property, and 'measures to secure the payment of any award that might be rendered'.[56] Fourth, Rule 7 provides for consolidation of disputes and joinder of third parties. Rule 7.1 gives discretion to the administrator to include, after consulting with the parties to all proceedings and with the arbitrators, that the new case will be referred to the tribunal already constituted for the existing proceedings. Rule 7.2 provides for disputes arising out of or in connection with multiple contracts to be consolidated into a single arbitration. Rule 7.3 is invoked if a third party seeks to participate in an arbitration already pending.[57] According to Rule 34.1, after the tribunal has heard the dispute, they have three months to give their final decision. This decision should be made within nine months from the date of the initial preliminary conference.[58] There is also a unique *mediator in the reserve* policy, which states that if the parties agree to use the mediator at any point throughout the proceedings, the mediator will be available to help in settlement negotiations. The parties will not be charged for the reserve mediator's appointment unless they opt to use the mediator's service.[59]

This mechanism may have affected the entire arbitration procedure. Unlike a court case in which the parties are familiar with precedents, an arbitration proceeding introduces an element of unpredictability. Another layer of variability enters the arbitral process when an appeal is added. The disagreement may then be decided by two previously unknown conflict-resolution bodies rather than by one. Second, despite the unpredictability, appeals raise the likelihood that the ultimate award will be based on good legal and factual grounds, based on the work of the two panels. Additionally, a party with the knowledge that it would appear in the same matter before two independent panels, the composition of which is unknown, has an even stronger motivation to prepare a plausible, easier-to-sell legal strategy. However, the appellate process can occasionally alter the procedures because the arbitrators in the first instance, concerned about their own image, may soften their judgment and adopt a less controversial option or make an inescapable conclusion to disincentivize the filing of an appeal and avoid an award reversal. In terms of the appellate tribunal, appeal arbitrators may be hesitant to review and reject what a peer has done, because of friendship, temperament, or other factors.

Arbitral appellate tribunals have different compositions, and arbitrators sitting in one case may not be aware of and are normally not constrained by how other appeal arbitrators decide a similar disagreement, so expecting consistency between the two conclusions is absurd. While it is true that arbitral appellate tribunals vary in their approaches and perspectives, the core benefit to users lies in the content and methodology

[55] ibid art 3.
[56] ibid art 32.
[57] ibid art 7.
[58] ibid art 34.
[59] Robert B Davidson and Matthew Rushton, 'Overview: JAMS' (2021) Global Arbitration Review 66, 70.

of these approaches. Users who find value in a particular tribunal's method of handling cases might see this as an opportunity to gain fresh insights and strategies. It is essential, however, to understand exactly which aspects of the approach are being appreciated—whether it is the tribunal's thoroughness, its interpretative nuances, or its ability to consider alternative viewpoints.

B. Insights from Alternative Appellate Models: Advancing Coherence and Predictability in Dispute Resolution

Until the 1980s, arbitration laws across jurisdictions were different for setting aside awards. With the introduction of the 1985 UNCITRAL Model Law (Model Law), this has changed considerably. The Model Law proved to be successful and was implemented in more than sixty states. Although the UNCITRAL Arbitration Rules were originally intended for international commercial arbitration, they are presently used in several investor-state arbitrations. In international commercial arbitration, as in most investment arbitration cases, the only permissible review is by a domestic court in the place of arbitration. The standard of review under Model Law art 34(2), is limited to six grounds: invalidity of the agreement to arbitrate; lack of notice to a party or other inability to present the case; inclusion in the award of matters outside the scope of submission; irregularity in the composition of the tribunal or arbitral procedure; non arbitrability of the subject matter; and violation of domestic public policy.[60]

This type of review does not extend to the review of errors of law or the application of facts to the law. However, this is not an appellate-style review. This has become a generally accepted principle. The determination of the place of arbitration, or the *lex loci arbitri*, thus, becomes critical to the determination of judicial review and enforcement.[61] If one is going to ask a domestic court to review an international arbitral decision, the claimant particularly wants to be sure that it will receive a fair hearing. Of course, this can encourage forum shopping.[62]

Furthermore, practice indicates that not every violation will result in refusal of enforcement or set-aside. The violation must have a substance and not be *de minimis*. As a result, certain courts have recognized that they have a so-called discretionary power to enforce an award, notwithstanding the presence of a ground for set-aside. This does not imply that the grounds for setting aside an award are the same across jurisdictions. The implementation of the Model Law is not uniform, and states have taken the liberty of deviating in certain respects. For example, Egypt added to the grounds for set-aside

[60] UNCITRAL, 'UNCITRAL Model Law on International Commercial Arbitration' (1995) GA Res 40/72, 112th Plenary Meeting (hereinafter UNCITRAL Model Law), the UNCITRAL Model Law has been incorporated in its entirety into the Commercial Arbitration Act 1985 (Canada).

[61] For a complete discussion of these issues, see Noah Rubins, 'Judicial Review of Investment Arbitration Awards' in Todd Weiler (ed), *NAFTA Investment Law and Arbitration: Past Issues, Current Practice, Future Prospects* (Brill 2004) 359.

[62] The reason is that, typically, it is the claimant in an investor-state arbitration that chooses the arbitration rules under which the arbitration will operate. For example, see NAFTA art 1120.

the ground that 'the arbitral award failed to apply the law agreed upon by the parties to govern the subject matter in dispute'.[63] The normal judicial remedy for a successful challenge under the Federal Arbitration Act in the United States is to vacate the award, not replace it, or re-adjudicate the matter.[64] The court may order a rehearing by the arbitrators at its discretion,[65] but this adds to the time it takes for the dispute to be resolved on the merits.[66] An expedited initial arbitral instance, subject to a possible appellate review, may be an available alternative in some disputes. While such an arrangement may be challenging to implement in practice, it serves to balance the needs of parties who seek a satisfactory award while also curtailing the length of the proceedings.

In moving from a broader, global perspective to give the examples of three national laws, first, a key contrast emerges between the Model Law and French law, the latter of which invokes the all-encompassing concept of 'mandate' (mission) as a ground for setting aside an award.[67] English law, meanwhile, zeroes in on the concept of 'misconduct' of the arbitrator as a basis for setting aside an award, a practice mirrored in India as well.[68] However, under English law, if a court challenge is successful, the court can only set aside the award, declare it null and void, or remand it to the tribunal.[69] Users of appellate procedures generally have needs that are diametrically opposed to those of users of expedited procedures, for whom time is paramount.

IV. Appellate Mechanisms as Vanguard for Reform in Investment Dispute Resolution

The discussion surrounding the introduction of an appellate mechanism in international investment arbitration is gaining momentum, particularly in the context of ongoing reform efforts of the ISDS system within UNCITRAL Working Group III. The options under consideration include the establishment of an MIC to review arbitral awards. While different states hold varying positions on these reform options, a balanced approach that ensures both the finality and correctness of awards is crucial.

[63] See Ibrahim Shehata, '25 Years of Model Law Arbitration in Egypt' (2019) 37(3) ASA Bulletin 631; Samia S Rashed, 'The UNCITRAL Model Law and Recent Developments in Egypt' (1988) 3(1) ICSID Review 126.

[64] Federal Arbitration Act 1925 s 16(a) (US).

[65] ibid s 16(b).

[66] See eg *Tempo Ahin Corp v Bertek Inc*, 1997 WL 580775 (rehearing before the same arbitrators); *Montes v Shearson Lehman Bros*, 128 F.3d 1456, 1464 (11th Cir 1997) (remanding to a new arbitration panel).

[67] The 'all-encompassing concept of "mandate" (mission)' refers to the idea that an arbitrator's authority, or the scope of his or her tasks, is defined by a comprehensive and overarching framework. In many arbitration contexts, the 'mandate' of an arbitrator specifies what they are empowered to do, and any action or decision taken outside this mandate might be seen as exceeding their jurisdiction or authority. In the context of French law as described, invoking the concept of 'mandate' as a ground for setting aside an award suggests that if an arbitrator exceeds or deviates from the comprehensive framework of their assigned task (or 'mission'), their decision could be invalidated.

[68] Alexander J Bělohlávek, 'Procedural Irregularities and Arbitrator Misconduct during Proceedings' in Larry A DiMatteo, Marta Infantino, and Nathalie M-P Potin (eds), *The Cambridge Handbook of Judicial Control of Arbitral Awards* (CUP 2020) 54.

[69] Arbitration Act 1996 s 68(3) (England).

Implementing an appellate mechanism should not undermine the finality of awards but rather enhance the consistency and correctness of awards. It is a step towards addressing concerns related to the lack of coherence, predictability, and correctness of arbitral awards, as well as the impartiality, independence, and diversity of decision-makers.[70] While it may not resolve all concerns about ISDS, an appellate mechanism holds the potential to significantly improve the quality and credibility of the arbitration process. By reviewing manifest errors of fact and law, an appeal mechanism can exercise greater control over tribunal decisions and establish a more reasonable and standardized regime. The need for consistency in treaty interpretation is particularly important given the varied provisions found in bilateral investment treaties.[71]

This part explores the connection between appellate mechanisms and the MIC or bilateral investment courts, highlighting their distinct features and roles within the ISDS landscape. It examines how investment courts have been implemented in various EU trade agreements and delves into the ongoing deliberations of UNCITRAL Working Group III, which has also proposed an appellate mechanism as a potential solution. By critically analysing these reform options, we can pave the way for a more effective and equitable investment dispute resolution framework.

A. A Comparative Analysis of an Appellate Mechanism and Investment Courts

A pure appeal mechanism and an MIC have been conceptualized to address the same concern voiced against ISDS: the lack of consistency, predictability, and accuracy of awards rendered by ISDS tribunals. However, the difference between the two models lies in the extent of the proposed reform. A pure appeals mechanism in ISDS may almost fall within the incremental reform bucket (retaining ISDS with modifications), while the proposal for an MIC clearly advocates for systemic reform, completely overhauling the ISDS regime as it stands.

Unlike the domestic context, where there is generally no possibility of resubmitting to a new court a case that has already been decided, in investment arbitration an award that has been annulled or set aside may be resubmitted to a new tribunal. Just as in the domestic context, where the remand of the issue to the lower instance is the general rule in some jurisdictions, an appeal tribunal in the arbitration context may be able to modify or reverse the legal findings and conclusions of the first tribunal with or without the need to remand the issue to the original tribunal. Resubmission to a new tribunal will not be possible. This would also avoid additional costs, resulting in a

[70] Jeffrey Kucik and Sergio Puig, 'Towards an Effective Appellate Mechanism for ISDS Tribunals' (2023) World Trade Review 3.

[71] Thomas Schultz, 'Against Consistency in Investment Arbitration' in Zachary Douglas, Joost Pauwelyn, and Jorge E Viñuales (eds), *The Foundations of International Investment Law: Bringing Theory into Practice* (OUP 2014) 297.

second arbitration. For example, the EU–Singapore Investment Protection Agreement provides that

> If the appeal is well founded, the Appeal Tribunal shall modify or reverse the legal findings and conclusions in the provisional award in whole or in part. The Appeal Tribunal shall refer the matter back to the Tribunal, specifying precisely how it has modified or reversed the relevant findings and conclusions of the Tribunal.[72]

The EU–Vietnam Investment Protection Agreement provides that:

> If the Appeal Tribunal finds that the appeal is well founded, the decision of the Appeal Tribunal shall modify or reverse the legal findings and conclusions in the provisional award in whole or part. Its decision shall specify precisely how it has modified or reversed the relevant finding s and conclusions of the Tribunal. Where the facts established by the Tribunal so permit, the Appeal Tribunal shall apply its own legal findings and conclusions to such facts and render a final decision. If that is not possible, it shall refer the matter back to the Tribunal.[73]

The pure appeal mechanism proposed by China and a few other states retains the arbitral tribunal constituted by investors and host states as the adjudicator of the first instance.[74] Simultaneously, it envisages the creation of an appeals body that reviews the awards of the first-instance tribunal on its merits.[75] Under the pure appeals mechanism, parties continue to constitute the arbitral tribunal, that is, the first-instance tribunal. However, the appeal body is proposed to be a multilateral, permanent, and quasi-judicial, much like the WTO Appellate Body.

The MIC is a full-blown two-tiered court proposed by the EU and its member states. The MIC entails a two-tier court system consisting of a tribunal of first instance (TFI) and an appellate tribunal (AT). The TFI is an alternative to the existing ISDS mechanism of investor-state arbitration and is a judicial, central, and permanent body that will resolve disputes between investors and states. The adjudicators who are part of the TFI will act as full-time judges and will not receive any financial benefit from either party.[76] The AT will function as a review body, and there will be no other review of the decisions of the TFI, including annulment or set-aside proceedings, both at the

[72] The European Union and Singapore negotiated a free trade agreement and an investment protection agreement. The EU–Singapore trade and investment protection agreements were signed on 19 October 2018. The text of the EU–Singapore Investment Protection Agreement ('EUSPA') is available at <https://trade.ec.europa.eu/doclib/press/index.cfm?id=961>.

[73] EUSPA.

[74] Nikos Lavranos, 'The ICS and MIC Projects: A Critical Review of the Issues of Arbitrator Selection, Control Mechanisms, and Recognition and Enforcement' in Chaisse, Choukroune, and Jusoh (n 3) 5.

[75] Marc Bungenberg and August Reinisch, 'Standalone Appeal Mechanism: Multilateral Investment Appeals Mechanism (MIAM)' in Marc Bungenberg and August Reinisch (eds), *Bilateral Arbitral Tribunals and Investment Courts to a Multilateral Investment Court: European Yearbook of International Economic Law* (Springer 2020) 197.

[76] Yuwen Li, 'The Notion and Development of International Investment Court' in Chaisse, Choukroune, and Jusoh (n 3) 15.

domestic level and through international ad hoc mechanisms.[77] However, if the enforcement of an award is sought in a state which has not acceded to the instrument creating the MIC, awards are proposed to be enforced under the New York Convention.[78]

Therefore, the primary difference between the pure appeals mechanism and MIC is the differing roles played by the parties in appointing their adjudicators. In the pure appeals mechanism, the parties appoint their adjudicators in the first instance, but they do not have any say in the appointment of adjudicators in the MIC, even in the first instance.

While Working Group III has not made a conclusive choice in favour of either of the above mechanisms, the UNCITRAL Secretariat has proposed a draft provision for an Appellate Mechanism in a working paper dated 12 November 2020. This draft provision envisages a pure appeal mechanism with a first-tier ISDS tribunal appointed by parties.[79]

CETA provides for the incorporation of the EU Investment Court System (ICS), a bilateral court. The objective of the system is to increase transparency and enhance the precedent-based system in the ISDS.[80] The ICS system also provides for an appellate mechanism wherein, if the second tribunal judges that there are some mistakes in the original decision, it would give the first instance tribunal an opportunity to amend its decision. Furthermore, either party may decide to appeal on the grounds of errors in the application or interpretation of the applicable law and manifest errors in the appreciation of facts within 90 days of the delivery of the award. The appellate tribunal has the power to uphold, modify, or reverse the award.[81] The EU Singapore Free Trade Agreement (EUSFTA) and the EU–Vietnam Free Trade Agreement (EUVIPA) also contain an appellate mechanism.[82]

EU agreements that contain an ICS do not explicitly mention the investment courts as permanent bodies, but there are varying opinions suggesting that the intention is to judicialize ISDS. The Commission anticipates that the introduction of an appellate mechanism will enhance legitimacy by strengthening independence, impartiality, and predictability of ISDS.

[77] Marc Bungenberg and August Reinisch, 'From Arbitral Tribunals to a Multilateral Investment Court: The European Union Approach' in Julien Chaisse, Leila Choukroune, and Sufian Jusoh (eds), *Handbook of International Investment Law and Policy* (Springer 2020) 31.

[78] For a criticism, see Catharine Titi, 'The European Union's Proposal for an International Investment Court: Significance, Innovations and Challenges Ahead' (2017) 14(1) Transnational Dispute Management 1 (advance publication 25 May 2016) 25–27.

[79] UNCITRAL, 'Possible Reform of Investor-State Dispute Settlement (ISDS)' UN Doc A/CN.9/WG.III/WP.202, 12 November 2020.

[80] Thanapat Chatinakrob, 'Possible Reforms of ISDS: Some Considerations on the ICS in CETA' (*Cambridge International Law Journal Blog*, 29 January 2019) <http://cilj.co.uk/2019/01/29/possible-reforms-of-isds-some-considerations-on-the-ics-in-ceta/>.

[81] Editorial, 'ISDS to Become ICS: New Name but Still Flawed' (*Better Finance*, 5 October 2016) <https://betterfinance.eu/article/isds-to-become-ics-new-name-but-still-flawed/>.

[82] Shilpa Singh Jaswant, 'Analyzing Features of Investment Court System under CETA and EUVIPA: Discussing Improvement in the System and Clarity to Clauses' (*Kluwer Arbitration Blog*, 8 February 2019) <http://arbitrationblog.kluwerarbitration.com/2019/02/08/analyzing-features-of-investment-court-system-under-ceta-and-euvipa-discussing-improvement-in-the-system-and-clarity-to-clauses/>.

In conclusion, a comparative analysis of appellate mechanisms and investment courts provides valuable legal lessons for reforming investment dispute resolution. This underscores the need to address concerns related to the consistency, predictability, and accuracy of the awards rendered by ISDS tribunals. The proposal for a pure appeals mechanism, while retaining ISDS with modifications, seeks to tackle these concerns. It allows parties to select a 'first-instance' arbitral tribunal while establishing a multilateral appellate body. On the other hand, the multilateral investment court advocates for more comprehensive and systemic reform, completely overhauling the existing ISDS regime. The key distinction lies in the extent of reform and the role played by the parties in appointing adjudicators. The pure appeals mechanism maintains party autonomy in tribunal selection, whereas the MIC establishes a permanent and independent court structure for both the first-instance and appellate stages. These comparative lessons underscore the importance of addressing issues related to consistency, predictability, and independence in resolving investment disputes. The choice between a pure appeal mechanism and a multilateral investment court depends on the desired level of reform and the balance between party autonomy and institutionalized decision-making. Regardless of the chosen approach, introducing an appellate mechanism holds great potential for enhancing the quality and legitimacy of the arbitration process. This contributes to a more robust and effective investment dispute resolution system that inspires confidence among investors and promotes fair and equitable outcomes.

B. Engaging with the Appeal Debate: Insights from the UNCITRAL Working Group III on ISDS Reform

ISDS has faced criticism from various quarters, including states, international organizations, and civil society groups, who have called for reform.[83] The member states of UNCITRAL in its 50th session tasked Working Group III with the objective of assessing the legitimacy of the existing ISDS regime.[84] To realize this objective, Working Group III would have to identify the concerns posed by the existing ISDS regime, assess whether reforms were desirable to address the identified concerns, and come up with solutions in case reform was desirable.[85]

In November 2018, Working Group III identified six broad concerns that were commonly raised to challenge the legitimacy of the ISDS regime: (1) excessive legal costs, (2) duration of proceedings, (3) legal consistency, (4) accuracy of decisions,

[83] Malcolm Langford and others, 'Special Issue: UNCITRAL and Investment Arbitration Reform: Matching Concerns and Solutions', (2020) 21(2–3) Journal of World Investment & Trade 167, 169.

[84] UNCITRAL, 'Report of Working Group III (Investor-State Dispute Settlement Reform) on the Work of Its Thirty-Fourth Session (Vienna, 27 November–1 December 2017)' UN Doc A/CN.9/930/Add.1/Rev.1, 26 February 2018.

[85] See United Nations, 'Report of the United Nations Commission on International Trade Law, Fiftieth Session' (3 July–21 July 2015), Official Records of the General Assembly, Seventy Second Session, Supplement No 17, UN Doc A/72/17, paras 263–64.

Table 25.1 Positions on appellate mechanisms in international investment arbitration

Countries	Position with respect to an appellate mechanism
EU member states, Canada, and Mauritius	In support of an appeal mechanism, but in the form of an MIC.
China	In support of a pure appeal mechanism, retaining ISDS tribunals as first-tier adjudication.
Bahrain	Against an appeals mechanism, proposes a joint interpretative committee to ensure consistency and accuracy.
Japan, USA, and Russia	Have opposed the MIC and are in favour of more incremental reforms.

Source: Elaborated by the author from various public official sources

(5) arbitral diversity, and (6) arbitral independence and impartiality.[86] Once this was done, Working Group III resolved in April 2019 that reform would be necessary and desirable to address these concerns.[87] Working Group III is currently in the third phase of negotiation, that is, to determine solutions to address these concerns and reform the ISDS regime.

The third phase has been characterized by competing strategies by different states towards reform; some states have advocated for an incremental approach—to retain ISDS as it exists and adopt reformations that slightly modify the status quo—whereas a few others have advocated for a systemic reform that favours international dispute resolution mechanisms for investment disputes, while restructuring dispute resolution mechanisms.[88] There are a few nations that are pushing for a paradigm shift—to do away with international dispute resolution mechanisms between states and investors– and prefer national courts, ombudsmen, and state-to-state arbitration (see Table 25.1).

Lessons can be drawn from the positions taken by different countries regarding the appeal mechanisms in international investment arbitration. On the one hand, the support from EU member states, Canada, and Mauritius for an appeal mechanism in the form of an MIC highlights the growing recognition of the need for systemic reform in the ISDS system. On the other hand, China's advocacy for a pure appeal mechanism, retaining arbitral tribunals as first-tier adjudication, reflects a preference for comparatively more incremental reforms. Bahrain's opposition to an appeal mechanism and proposal for a joint interpretative committee emphasizes the importance of ensuring consistency and accuracy. The opposition from Japan, the United States, and Russia to the MIC suggests a preference for more gradual reforms, rather than a complete overhaul. These positions underscore the complexity and diverse perspectives surrounding

[86] UNCITRAL, 'Possible Reform of Investor-State Dispute Settlement (ISDS)' UN Doc A/CN.9/WG.III/WP.149, 5 September 2018.

[87] UNCITRAL, 'Report of Working Group III (Investor-State Dispute Settlement Reform) on the Work of Its Thirty-Seventh Session', UN Doc A/CN.9/970, 9 April 2019.

[88] Anthea Roberts, 'Incremental Systemic, and Paradigmatic Reform of Investor-State Arbitration' (2018) 112(3) American Journal of International Law 410.

the design and implementation of an effective appellate mechanism for the resolution of investment disputes.

In the 38th session of Working Group III, several delegations observed that the existing ISDS mechanisms for reviewing arbitral awards were limited, and that an appeal mechanism was necessary to increase the consistency and coherence of the ISDS framework.[89] Pursuant to the discussions in the 38th session, the UNCITRAL Secretariat prepared a working paper addressing the mechanics of an appellate mechanism, potential enforcement issues, and draft provisions. The Working Paper considered the scope of the review in the appeal process, the decisions that could be subject to an appeal, the effect of appeals, the ideal caseload for an appellate body, and possible issues that could arise at the enforcement stage (including the difficulty of integrating an appeal procedure into the ICSID Convention, given the express wording of Article 53).[90]

The working paper has proposed a consolidated draft provision regarding the appellate mechanism, which merits consideration. Notably, this provision refers to Article VI(1) of the New York Convention, raising concerns that it may inadvertently create a double standard. This double standard could potentially allow the appellant to strategically argue for the most advantageous provision or combination thereof, thereby undermining the objective of consistency in the appellate process. Commentators have suggested that the provision enumerates the grounds for review instead of making a bare reference to the New York Convention to avoid duplication.

Building on the foundational insights of the working paper, the Working Group commenced an in-depth exploration of the subject of an appellate mechanism in international investment arbitration during its 38th session in 2020. These initial discussions blossomed into more nuanced deliberations in 2021, when the focus shifted towards sculpting draft provisions for the appeals system while also addressing issues concerning the enforcement of decisions made via this proposed mechanism. In pursuit of a well-rounded approach, the Working Group acknowledged the necessity for a detailed analysis of the multifaceted components of an appellate mechanism. This includes elements such as an ad hoc appeal system, a permanent standalone appellate body, and an appeal mechanism intertwined within a standing system.

Following the 44th session, it became evident that the Working Group was making conscious strides towards outlining potential regulations for the functioning of an appellate mechanism.[91] This reflective endeavour also extended to the discussion of the implementation of this reform element, encompassing the exploration of potential

[89] Andrew Cannon and Helif Laufer, 'Update on the Future of ISDS: Working Group III UNCITRAL Discussions of January 2020' (*HSF Public International Law Notes*, 13 February 2020) <https://hsfnotes.com/publicinternationallaw/2020/02/13/update-on-the-future-of-isds-working-group-iii-uncitral-discussions-of-january-2020/>.

[90] Andrew Cannon and Caitlin Eaton, 'Update on the Future of ISDS: UNCITRAL Working Group III Publishes Draft Working Papers' (*HSF Public International Law Notes*, 2 November 2020) <https://hsfnotes.com/publicinternationallaw/2020/11/02/update-on-the-future-of-isds-uncitral-working-group-iii-publishes-draft-working-papers/>.

[91] UNCITRAL, 'Possible Reform of Investor-State Dispute Settlement (ISDS): Appellate Mechanism' (Note by the Secretariat), UN Doc A/CN.9/WG.III/WP.224, 17 November 2022 <https://uncitral.un.org/sites/uncitral.un.org/files/media-documents/uncitral/en/wp_224-e.pdf>.

pathways to both establish an appellate mechanism and constitute an appellate tribunal. The group also casts light on possible implementation models. One such proposal is an ad hoc mechanism in which an appellate tribunal is constituted on a case-by-case basis. Alternatively, a standing mechanism can be employed to create a permanent tribunal for continuous utility.[92] Notably, certain existing investment treaties have already established bilateral permanent appellate mechanisms. Meanwhile, other treaties introduced the possibility of negotiations aimed at the inception of a multilateral appellate mechanism.

During this comprehensive contemplation on the introduction of an appellate mechanism, the Working Group did not lose sight of the mechanism's relationship with the existing arbitration system. This involves engaging with the complex issues of annulment, recognition, and enforcement of awards. The last critical factor recognized by the group is the establishment of the temporal scope of the appellate mechanism, indicating that the Working Group's reflective journey continues to drive the development of a robust, practical, and fair appellate mechanism in international investment arbitration.[93]

Overall, the positions taken by different countries highlight the varying perspectives on the need for systemic reform and preferred approaches to appellate mechanisms. The support for an appeal mechanism in the form of an MIC reflects recognition of the need for comprehensive reform, while the advocacy for a pure appeal mechanism demonstrates diverse preferences. Opposition to the MIC suggests a preference for more gradual changes. Discussions within the Working Group have shed light on the mechanics and provisions of an appellate mechanism, including the scope of review, enforcement issues, and potential integration with existing arbitration systems. The exploration of different implementation models, such as ad hoc and standing mechanisms, contributes to the understanding of practical considerations for establishing an effective appellate tribunal. Additionally, the attention given to the relationship between the appellate mechanism and the annulment, recognition, and enforcement processes ensures a comprehensive approach.

V. Conclusion

This chapter delved into the significant legal problem surrounding the absence of a well-defined and universally accepted appellate mechanism in international investment arbitration. The lack of such a mechanism raises concerns about the consistency, predictability, and legitimacy of investment dispute resolution. This problem is of utmost importance in the field of international investment law, as it directly impacts

[92] UNCITRAL, 'Report of Working Group III (Investor-State Dispute Settlement Reform) on the Work of Its Forty-Fourth Session (Vienna, 23–27 January 2023)' UN Doc A/CN.9/1130, 7 February 2023.
[93] UNCITRAL, 'Possible Reform of Investor-State Dispute Settlement (ISDS) Appellate Mechanism and enforcement issues', UN Doc A/CN.9/WG.III/WP.202, 12 November 2020.

the rights and obligations of investors and states, coherence of legal interpretations, and overall credibility of the arbitration process. Addressing this problem is crucial to enhancing the effectiveness and fairness of international investment arbitration.

This chapter shows that the development of an appellate mechanism within the international investment arbitration structure requires careful deliberation and tailored approach. An ideal system must facilitate the revision of initial tribunal findings and conclusions without necessitating referral to a new tribunal. The definitive scope of an appeal, especially concerning errors in treaty interpretation, has yet to be decided, and clarity is needed in determining the understanding of 'law' and 'fact' within ISDS context.

Moreover, the development of an appellate mechanism demands reconsideration of the annulment grounds of the ICSID Convention, according to Article 52. It is crucial to integrate the appeal option into the ICSID system while considering its relationship with the New York Convention. Efforts are being made by UNCITRAL Working Group III to explore the scope and standards of review for the appellate mechanism. However, care must be taken to avoid duplications and potential double standards that could stem from referencing both the ICSID and the New York Conventions.

Furthermore, the introduction of an appellate mechanism should not be seen as a standalone solution to all the challenges faced in international investment arbitration. While it can address concerns related to legal consistency and accuracy, it is essential to recognize that it is just one piece of the puzzle. Other issues, such as the diversity of arbitrators, cost and duration of proceedings, and transparency, also require attention and potential reforms. A comprehensive approach that takes into account all these aspects will contribute to a more robust and effective investment arbitration system.

Nevertheless, uncertainty remains concerning the standard for an appellate review, the authority of the appellate tribunal to examine prior evidence, and the potential for case remands. These uncertainties, if left unaddressed, could lead to an increase in appeals, prolonging the time and cost of proceedings. In considering security for costs, tribunals must also be mindful of the potential for denial of justice, making it crucial to adopt a balanced approach that accounts for the interests of all stakeholders.

Ultimately, the introduction of an appellate mechanism in international investment arbitration represents a critical step towards enhancing the fairness, predictability, and legitimacy of the arbitration process. By providing a means to review and correct potential errors in the application and interpretation of the law, it can contribute to the development of a more coherent and consistent body of jurisprudence. It is through thoughtful and informed discussions, collaboration among stakeholders, and the incorporation of best practices from different legal systems that a well-designed appellate mechanism can be established, leading to a more robust and trusted international investment arbitration framework.

26

Recognition and Enforcement of ICSID Convention Awards

Marc Bungenberg, Andrés E Alvarado-Garzón, and Bianca Böhme

I. Introduction

One of the most important features of international (investment) arbitration is the high enforceability of arbitral awards. This high enforceability is essentially achieved through two international conventions: the Convention on the Recognition and Enforcement of Foreign Arbitral Awards (1958 New York Convention),[1] and the Convention on the Settlement of Investment Disputes between States and Nationals of Other States (ICSID Convention).[2] This chapter deals with the enforcement of arbitral awards rendered pursuant to the ICSID Convention.

The ICSID Convention was adopted in 1965 and has 158 contracting states as of October 2023.[3] The vast majority of international investment agreements (IIAs) refer to arbitration under the ICSID Convention as one of the possibilities for investor-state dispute settlement (ISDS). Its popularity is demonstrated by the fact that out of 2,584 mapped IIAs at the United Nations Conference on Trade and Development (UNCTAD) Investment Policy Hub, 2,191 refer to the International Centre for Settlement of Investment Disputes (ICSID) as a forum for the resolution of investor-state disputes.[4] The ICSID caseload statistics further evidence this high popularity: as of 30 June 2022, ICSID registered 804 cases under the ICSID Convention.[5]

The ICSID regime for recognition and enforcement of arbitral awards rendered under the ICSID Convention is certainly one of the main reasons for the high popularity of this dispute resolution mechanism. The ICSID Convention contains a unique enforcement system, which is largely insulated from domestic court review. The enforcement of ICSID awards may, in principle, not even be refused on the ground of the enforcing state's public policy. While the losing party's primary obligation is to voluntarily comply with the award, enforcement mechanisms constitute a safeguard in

[1] Convention on the Recognition and Enforcement of Foreign Arbitral Awards (adopted 10 June 1958, entered into force 7 June 1959) 330 UNTS 3 (New York Convention).
[2] Convention on the Settlement of Investment Disputes between States and Nationals of Other States (adopted 18 March 1965, entered into force 14 October 1966) 575 UNTS 159 (ICSID Convention).
[3] See the list of signatory and contracting states <https://icsid.worldbank.org/about/member-states/database-of-member-states>.
[4] See <https://investmentpolicy.unctad.org/international-investment-agreements/iia-mapping>.
[5] See ICSID, 'The ICSID Caseload—Statistics: Issue 2022-2' 30 June 2022 <https://icsid.worldbank.org/sites/default/files/publications/The_ICSID_Caseload_Statistics_2022-2_ENG.pdf> 9.

Marc Bungenberg, Andrés E Alvarado-Garzón, and Bianca Böhme, *Recognition and Enforcement of ICSID Convention Awards* In: *The Award in International Investment Arbitration.* Edited by: Katia Fach Gómez and Catharine Titi, Oxford University Press.
 DOI: 10.1093/9780191975936.003.0026

the event of non-compliance. However, there is an increasing trend of award debtors refusing to comply with their ICSID awards and opposing enforcement procedures before domestic courts, which warrants a reassessment of the enforcement mechanisms provided under the ICSID Convention.

After outlining the system for the recognition and enforcement of ICSID awards (II), this chapter will illustrate the current challenges that ICSID awards face at the stage of enforcement (III). These challenges are divided in three questions or themes: first, the differentiation between 'recognition', 'enforcement', and 'execution' under the ICSID Convention (A); second, the role of domestic courts and the opposition to enforcement of ICSID awards (B); and, third, the prospect of enforcement of ICSID awards rendered by permanent court structures (C). The final section will conclude (IV).

II. Enforcement of Arbitral Awards under the ICSID Convention

A fundamental obligation of the contracting states to the ICSID Convention is to 'abide by and comply with the terms of the award', as enshrined in Article 53(1) thereof. This obligation begins immediately for both the investor and the respondent host state upon the rendering of an ICSID award.[6] No further steps are needed since ICSID awards are 'self-executing'.[7] Only in the event that a disputing party does not voluntarily abide by and comply with the terms of the rendered award, enforcement may be sought by either the investor or the host state to apply the necessary pressure for payment.[8]

Under the ICSID Convention, there are two alternative avenues for the enforcement of awards. The first avenue can be found in Article 27(1), which generally prevents contracting states from giving diplomatic protection or bringing international claims in respect of disputes which they consented to submit to arbitration under the ICSID Convention. Only in case of non-compliance with an award, Article 27(1) of the ICSID Convention explicitly foresees a revival of this avenue for enforcement, thus enabling investors to ask their home state for diplomatic protection. If the investor's home state agrees to grant diplomatic protection, it may bring a claim against the defaulting host state before the International Court of Justice in accordance with Article 64 of the ICSID Convention. But up to now this has never happened.

The second avenue for the enforcement of ICSID awards can be found in Article 54(1) of the ICSID Convention, which requires each contracting state 'to recognize an award rendered pursuant to [the] Convention as binding and enforce the pecuniary obligations imposed by that award within its territories as if it were a final judgment of a court of that State'. The obligations contained in Article 54 of the ICSID Convention

[6] Stanimir Alexandrov, 'Enforcement of ICSID Awards: Articles 53 and 54 of the ICSID Convention' (2009) 6(1) Transnational Dispute Management 1, 3. See also Catharine Titi, 'What Is an Award? Concept, Content, Drafting, Effects' in Katia Fach Gómez and Catharine Titi (eds), *The Award in Investment Arbitration* (OUP 2024).

[7] Alexandrov (n 6) 4.

[8] Anna Stier, 'Enforcement of ICSID Awards—A Walk in the Park?' in Richard Happ and Stefan Wilske (eds), *ICSID Rules and Regulations 2022* (Beck 2022) para 8.

are twofold: the recognition of an award as binding and the enforcement of pecuniary obligations as a final court judgment. The recognition of an award refers to 'the formal confirmation that it is authentic, and that it has the legal consequences provided by law'.[9] A recognized award is thus confirmed as binding or *res judicata*, which generally allows the award to be treated as a valid title for execution under domestic law.[10] For that purpose, it suffices to submit a copy of the award certified by the ICSID Secretary-General to the specifically designated ICSID member states' court or authority.[11]

While all kinds of awards must be recognized as binding, only those imposing pecuniary obligations must also be enforced by the contracting states, ie be subject to proceedings initiated to force compliance of the award by the debtor, which may include the attachment of assets in execution of the court judgment.[12] Even though this explanation helps to differentiate the concepts of 'recognition' and 'enforcement', it leaves room for interpretation as to how they differ from 'execution', a term equally used in Article 54 of the ICSID Convention.[13] What can be said with certainty is that contracting states must equally recognize non-pecuniary remedies, such as specific performance,[14] whereas only pecuniary remedies may be subject to enforcement proceedings.

Article 53 of the ICSID Convention imposes the obligation to comply with an award *only* on the disputing parties, whereas the obligation contained in Article 54 to recognize and enforce awards applies generally to *all* contracting states.[15] The latter bear an obligation under Article 54 of the ICSID Convention to recognize and enforce ICSID awards whether or not they or any of their nationals had been parties to the dispute.[16] Moreover, whereas Article 27 of the ICSID Convention only provides for an alternative enforcement avenue against defaulting host states, Article 54 of the ICSID Convention allows *both* investors and host states to seek enforcement before the national courts of each of the currently 158 contracting states.

The most outstanding feature of the enforcement avenue under Article 54 ICSID Convention is the unusually high standard it embodies. It provides that an award imposing pecuniary obligations must be enforced within the territory of the contracting states 'as if it were a final judgment of a court of that State'. This means that the contracting states are prevented from imposing more onerous requirements on the enforcement of ICSID awards than for the enforcement of final domestic judgments in the sense of a national treatment obligation.[17] By putting ICSID awards on the same

[9] August Reinisch, 'Article 54' in Stephan Schill and others (eds), *Schreuer's Commentary on the ICSID Convention*, vol 2 (3rd edn, CUP 2022) 1485.

[10] ibid.

[11] Aron Broches, 'Awards Rendered Pursuant to the ICSID Convention: Binding Force, Finality, Recognition, Enforcement, Execution' (1987) 2(2) ICSID Review 287, 326; Reinisch (n 9) 1485.

[12] *Total SA v Argentina*, ICSID Case No ARB/04/01, Decision on Stay of Enforcement of the Award (4 December 2014) [95].

[13] Section III.A deals with this problem in more detail.

[14] Christoph Schreuer, 'Non-Pecuniary Remedies in ICSID Arbitration' (2004) 20(4) Arbitration International 325, 325ff.

[15] Reinisch (n 9) 1474; Broches (n 11) 288.

[16] Broches (n 11) 317.

[17] George A Bermann, 'Understanding ICSID Article 54' (2020) 35(2) ICSID Review 311, 314.

footing as final national court judgments, Article 54 of the ICSID Convention ensures the disputing parties the highest level of enforceability that is currently possible under public international law.[18]

In most cases, national rules will allow enforcing courts to merely ascertain the award's authenticity without re-examining the ICSID tribunal's jurisdiction or reviewing the award on the merits.[19] However, enforcement may also be resisted in those countries where national rules provide for an exceptional refusal to enforce a final judgment.[20] As a result, Article 54 of the ICSID Convention establishes an extraordinarily high international standard for enforcement without implementing a fully automatic mechanism.

The negotiating history of the ICSID Convention shows that this high standard was not immediately agreed upon among the participating state delegations.[21] During the negotiations, different options were discussed, such as borrowing the grounds to refuse enforcement provided in Article V of the 1958 New York Convention, including a self-standing defence of public policy, or treating ICSID awards as domestic awards.[22] The solution that was finally adopted goes beyond these proposals by equating ICSID awards to final local judgments. This result can be at least partially attributed to the founding Secretary-General of ICSID, Aron Broches, who intended that the enforcement obligation be as unconditional as possible.[23] It can be considered a remarkable success under international law that domestic courts cannot rely on the grounds of the 1958 New York Convention to refuse the enforcement of ICSID awards. As a result, domestic courts faced with the enforcement of ICSID awards have regularly rejected the application of grounds for the refusal of enforcement such as public policy.[24]

Yet, recent state practice shows that this strong enforcement mechanism is increasingly being questioned.[25] Numerous domestic courts have encountered fierce opposition to enforcement of ICSID awards due to different grounds that will be analysed below. Notably, Article 54 was originally incorporated into the ICSID Convention to give host states a remedy against defaulting *investors*, since states were believed to voluntarily abide by and comply with the terms of any award rendered against them.[26] It was thought that their own reputation in the international community and the fallback

[18] ibid; ICSID, *History of the ICSID Convention*, vol II-1 (World Bank 1968) 242.

[19] Reinisch (n 9) 1499.

[20] Edward Baldwin, Mark A Kantor, and Michael Nolan, 'Limit to Enforcement of ICSID Awards' (2006) 23(1) Journal of International Arbitration 1, 2.

[21] Stier (n 8) para 12.

[22] Broches described the discussions over Article 54 ICSID Convention as an 'onslaught in [the] Committee, by representatives who wanted the Convention to permit refusal of enforcement either on all the grounds on which such refusal may be based under the 1958 New York Convention or, as a minimum, on the ground of conflict with the public policy of the forum, especially as related to enforceability in "third" States'. See Broches (n 11) 316ff.

[23] Bermann (n 17) 326.

[24] See for instance *SOABI v Senegal*, Cour de Cassation, Chambre Civile 1, France, Judgment (11 June 1991); *Kardassopoulos v Georgia*, Oberlandesgericht Frankfurt am Main, Germany, Judgment (20 November 2012) [reported by Andreas Kulick and Julian Scheu, 'Germany' in Julien Fouret (ed), *Enforcement of Investment Treaty Arbitration Awards* (2nd edn, Global Law and Business 2021) 395].

[25] Stier (n 8) para 8.

[26] ICSID (n 18) 10ff and 177.

option of diplomatic protection under Article 27 ICSID Convention would suffice to guarantee their compliance. In fact, during the negotiating history of the ICSID Convention, the question of enforcement against the host state was even considered to be merely 'academic', thus without any practical relevance.[27] Today, numerous questions relating to the enforcement of ICSID awards have obtained significant practical relevance due to the increasing state practice of refusing the enforcement of ICSID awards at the domestic level. The following section discusses these open questions in detail.

III. Open Questions Regarding the Enforcement of ICSID Awards

A. Differentiation between 'Recognition', 'Enforcement', and 'Execution'

Since arbitral tribunals cannot force compliance of their awards, the ICSID Convention entrusted domestic courts with this task. In the span of one single provision (Article 54), the ICSID Convention refers to the terms 'recognition', 'enforcement', and 'execution', whose definitions may vary depending on their context and the legal system that employs them. In broad terms, 'recognition' and 'execution' may be construed consistently across different jurisdictions: through 'recognition', a domestic court gives legal effect to an arbitral award (*res judicata*) in the particular legal system, whereas by means of 'execution', a court orders the attachment, garnishment, conveyance, or sale of the debtor's assets to satisfy the award.[28]

Yet, the concept of 'enforcement' presents certain terminological challenges. It may be used interchangeably with the terms 'recognition' or 'execution', but it may also describe an intermediate process before execution, whereby the award is transformed into a national judgment (*exequatur*). In other cases, 'enforcement' has been understood to describe the entire process from giving legal effect to an award until the satisfaction of the debt.[29] This has created discrepancies on the interpretation of 'enforcement' in Article 54 of the ICSID Convention.

Some authors have considered that the concepts of 'enforcement' and 'execution' in the English version must be construed as having an identical meaning as the equally official versions of the Convention in Spanish and French.[30] They posit that the English

[27] ibid 304. Broches later recognized that 'he might have been overly sanguine as to compliance by governments with awards rendered against them'. See Broches (n 11) 302.

[28] See on this Olga Gerlich, 'State Immunity from Execution in the Collection of Awards rendered in International Investment Arbitration: The Achilles' Heel of the Investor-State Arbitration System?' (2015) 26 American Review of International Arbitration 47, 55; Ben Juratowitch, 'Waiver of State Immunity and Enforcement of Arbitral Awards' (2016) 6(2) Asian Journal of International Law 199, 217; Josefa Sicard-Mirabal and Yves Derains, *Introduction to Investor-State Arbitration* (Kluwer Law International 2018) 250.

[29] Juratowitch (n 28) 218.

[30] Christoph H Schreuer and others, *The ICSID Convention: A Commentary* (2nd edn, CUP 2009) art 54, paras 64ff; Salim Moollan and Lucas Bastin, 'Article 54' in Julien Fouret, Rémy Gerbay, and Gloria M Álvarez (eds), *The ICSID Convention, Regulation and Rules: A Practical Commentary* (Edward Elgar Publishing 2019) para 4.1350.

version of the ICSID Convention alludes to 'enforcement' in Article 54(1)–(2) and 'execution' in Articles 54(3) and 55. In contrast, the equally official versions in Spanish and French refer to a single concept throughout those provisions: 'ejecución' and 'exécution'. Accordingly, those authors suggest that under the ICSID Convention, the terms 'enforcement' and 'execution' should not be differentiated.

Other authors postulate a distinction between 'enforcement' and 'execution', whereby the former entails the transformation of an award into a domestic judgment (worthy of execution), whereas the latter is the subsequent coercive step through attachment, garnishment, conveyance, or sale of the debtor's assets to satisfy the award.[31] This latter option was recently favoured in Australia. In the enforcement proceedings of the *Antin Infrastructure* award,[32] the Federal Court of Australia considered the distinction between enforcement and execution under the ICSID Convention. The court held that there was an automatic recognition and enforcement of awards with pecuniary obligations (transformation into a domestic judgment), whereas execution was a posterior phase (post-judgment), in which the domestic rules on sovereign immunity were applicable.[33]

In reaching this conclusion, the court firstly held that the Convention's object and purpose was to facilitate enforcement.[34] Second, by assessing the Convention's preparatory material, the court found 'the language of enforcement and execution is used loosely and at times interchangeably in the debates, which is perhaps not surprising given that the original languages of the participants varied considerably and the participants themselves also changed from time to time'.[35] However, the court stressed that in the discussions over sovereign immunity, the understanding of 'execution' as a later stage (post-judgment) was predominant.[36] As such, a difference between enforcement and execution was conceivable. Finally, the Australian court held that the terms 'exécution' and 'ejecución' in the respective French and Spanish versions of the Convention should be construed in some places as enforcement and in some others as execution—otherwise the drafters' intention to limit sovereign immunity to the post-judgment phase would be undermined.[37] This understanding was confirmed on 12 April 2023 by the High Court of Australia.[38]

The relevance of this terminological dilemma lies in the application of domestic rules with respect to enforcement/execution. Pursuant to Article 54(3) of the ICSID Convention, '[e]xecution of the award shall be governed by the laws concerning the execution of judgments in force in the State in whose territories such execution is sought'. Should execution and enforcement have an identical meaning, Article 54(3) of

[31] Bermann (n 17) 317. Similarly, Stefan Kröll, 'Enforcement of Awards' in Marc Bungenberg and others (eds), *International Investment Law: A Handbook* (CH Beck/Hart/Nomos 2015) 1484–85.

[32] *Infrastructure Services Luxembourg Sàrl and Energia Termosolar BV (formerly Antin Infrastructure Services Luxembourg Sàrl and Antin Energia Termosolar BV) v Spain*, ICSID Case No ARB/13/31, Award (15 June 2018).

[33] *Eiser Infrastructure Ltd v Spain* [2020] FCA 157, Case Nos 601 and 602 of 2019, Judgment (24 February 2020) [98].

[34] ibid [114]ff.

[35] ibid [121].

[36] ibid [126]ff.

[37] ibid [136]ff.

[38] *Spain v Infrastructure Services Luxembourg SàrL* [2023] HCA 11, Judgment (12 April 2023) [38]ff.

the ICSID Convention's *renvoi* to domestic laws would open the door for any remedies existing against the enforcement/execution of judgments. This would contradict the drafters' explicit intent to limit the domestic courts' revision of ICSID awards.

Yet, Article 55 of the ICSID Convention sheds some light on the meaning of execution by stating that '[n]othing in Article 54 shall be construed as derogating from the law in force in any Contracting State relating to immunity of that State or of any foreign State from execution'. This recalls the concept of immunity from execution, which embodies rules restricting the domestic courts' powers of attachment, garnishment, conveyance, or sale of assets of another sovereign state.[39] The purpose and use of the state property is usually determinative of whether immunity from execution applies.[40] Immunity from execution is thus limited to the assets in question. This is precisely the caveat preserved by the ICSID Convention under Articles 54(3) and 55 thereof as advanced by the Federal Court and the High Court of Australia.

Indeed, ICSID awards have been subject to domestic rules on immunity from execution. For instance, when the award creditors of the *AIG* award[41] sought execution in the United Kingdom against the property of Kazakhstan's central bank, the English High Court of Justice considered that the funds in question helped to stabilize fiscal policy, thus being immune from execution.[42] This had nothing to do with the obligation to enforce an award under Article 54 of the ICSID Convention, but rather pertained to the nature of the assets from which the award creditor sought payment.

As such, the distinction between enforcement and execution under Article 54 of the ICSID Convention is to be preferred. Only under this understanding, Article 54(3) is consistent with Article 55 of the ICSID Convention reflecting a *renvoi* to domestic laws exclusively for the purpose of immunity from execution. Otherwise, broadly construing the terms of enforcement and execution as synonyms could suggest that any other ground of refusal of enforcement under domestic law could operate by means of Article 54(3) of the ICSID Convention.

B. Domestic Courts and the Opposition to Enforcement of ICSID Awards

As mentioned above, the ICSID Convention does not provide for any grounds for the refusal of recognition and enforcement of ICSID awards. In fact, some implementing statutes in domestic jurisdictions, for instance in the United States,[43] explicitly excluded the application of the 1958 New York Convention from the enforcement of ICSID

[39] Juratowitch (n 28) 219.

[40] August Reinisch, 'European Court Practice Concerning State Immunity from Enforcement Measures' (2006) 17(4) European Journal of International Law 803, 807.

[41] *AIG Capital Partners, Inc and CJSC Tema Real Estate Company Ltd v Kazakhstan*, ICSID Case No ARB/01/6, Award (7 October 2003).

[42] *AIG Capital Partners Inc and CJSC Tema Real Estate Company Limited v Kazakhstan* [2005] EWHC 2239 (Comm) [11] and [57]ff.

[43] 22 US Code §1650a—Arbitration Awards under the Convention.

awards. Yet, compliance with ICSID awards has found increasing resistance over the last years. Notably, the European Union (EU) and its member states have spearheaded an opposition to the enforcement of ICSID awards, where the underlying dispute involves an issue of EU law. In practice, this has created two different regimes for the enforcement of ICSID awards: one regime within the EU, where awards arising out of EU law-related disputes cannot be enforced, and another regime outside the EU, where domestic courts continue to enforce ICSID awards irrespective of the underlying dispute. The *Micula* case[44] exemplifies these contrasting regimes.

On 11 December 2013, the tribunal in *Micula v Romania* rendered an award ordering the respondent to pay damages for the breach of the fair and equitable treatment standard contained in the bilateral investment agreement between Romania and Sweden.[45] On 26 May 2014, the EU Commission issued an injunction requesting Romania to suspend any compliance with the award as it might constitute unlawful state aid under EU law.[46] Since then, the award creditors have sought enforcement in multiple jurisdictions. In Sweden, the Stockholm District Court refused the enforcement of the award stating that the EU law principle of sincere cooperation prevented the court from circumventing the EU Commission's injunction by means of enforcement.[47] Courts in Belgium, Romania, and Luxembourg[48] have also refused to enforce the *Micula* award considering that its enforcement would be in breach of EU law.

By contrast, the enforcement efforts of the *Micula* award outside the EU were more successful. In 2017, when the United Kingdom was still an EU member state, the English High Court stayed the enforcement of the award.[49] However, the Supreme Court of the United Kingdom overturned the stay in 2020, allowing its enforcement.[50] The Court considered that the duty of sincere cooperation was not a valid ground to stay enforcement under Article 54 of the ICSID Convention.[51] In the United States, the District Court for the District of Columbia held that it could only revise the authenticity of the award but it could not revise the merits of the ICSID award nor the jurisdiction of the tribunal rendering such award.[52] This was upheld by the US Court of Appeals for the District of Columbia in 2020.[53]

Additionally, since the *Achmea* decision by the Court of Justice of the European Union,[54] the EU has been adamant in its opposition to the enforcement of arbitral awards arising out of intra-EU investment disputes (ie disputes between an EU member

[44] *Ioan Micula, Viorel Micula, SC European Food SA, SC Starmill SRL and SC Multipack SRL v Romania [I]*, ICSID Case No ARB/05/20.

[45] *Ioan Micula, Viorel Micula, SC European Food SA, SC Starmill SRL and SC Multipack SRL v Romania [I]*, ICSID Case No ARB/05/20, Award (11 December 2013).

[46] EU Commission, Decision C (2014) 3192, 26 May 2014.

[47] *Nacka Tingsrätt, Micula and others v Romania*, Stockholm District Court, Case No A 2550-1, Judgment (23 January 2019).

[48] Cour de Cassation, Luxembourg, Case No CAS-2021-00061, Judgment No 116/2022 (14 July 2022).

[49] *Micula and others v Romania* [2017] EWHC 31 (Comm), Judgment (20 January 2017).

[50] *Micula and others v Romania* [2020] UKSC 5, Judgment (19 February 2020).

[51] ibid [101].

[52] *Micula v Romania*, 404 F Supp 3d 265 (DDC 2019) Case No 17-cv-02332 (APM), Memorandum Opinion (11 September 2019).

[53] *Micula v Romania*, US Court of Appeals for the District of Columbia, No 19-7127, Judgment (19 May 2020).

[54] Court of Justice of the European Union, Case C-284/16, ECLI:EU:C:2018:158, Judgment (6 March 2018).

state and an investor of another member state). This opposition is far-reaching, concerning both ICSID and non-ICSID awards. In enforcement proceedings before US courts in the cases of *Masdar v Spain*,[55] *Watkins v Spain*,[56] *InfraRed v Spain*,[57] the EU Commission and Spain (the award debtor in the abovementioned cases) objected to the enforcement of the respective ICSID awards arguing that arbitration agreements in intra-EU investment disputes were invalid under EU law. This reasoning recalls the ground for refusal of enforcement for lack of a valid arbitration agreement under Article V(1)(a) of the 1958 New York Convention. Yet, a similar ground for refusal of enforcement does not exist under the ICSID Convention. The EU Commission and EU member states have also referred to the doctrine of *forum non-conveniens* and international comity in a plea for refusal of enforcement of the respective ICSID awards, which do not find support in the ICSID Convention either.

The EU and its member states thereby suggest the incorporation of grounds for refusal of enforcement in direct contradiction to the ICSID Convention. This may be necessary within the EU, where the primacy and autonomy of EU law would override any conflict with the ICSID Convention. It is, however, problematic from a systemic point of view as it brings a diverging application of the ICSID Convention in different states, ultimately undermining the finality of the award, and the Convention's object and purpose.[58]

Interestingly, the EU and its member states have recently reshaped the argument on the invalidity of the arbitration agreement for intra-EU investment disputes primarily as an issue of immunity from jurisdiction. In the enforcement proceedings before the US District Court for the District of Columbia of the *Cube Infrastructure* award[59] and the *Hydro Energy* award,[60] the EU Commission and Spain requested the dismissal of the application for recognition and enforcement arguing immunity from jurisdiction.[61]

[55] *Masdar Solar & Winde Cooperatief UA v Spain*, US District Court for the District of Columbia, Civil Action No 1:18-cv-2254, Proposed Brief for the European Commission on behalf of the EU as amicus curiae in support of Spain (3 May 2019).

[56] *Watkins Holdings Sàrl & Watkins (Ned) BV v Spain*, US District Court for the District of Columbia, Civil Action No 1:20-cv-01081-TFH, Brief for the European Commission on behalf of the EU as amicus curiae in support of Spain (4 January 2021); *Watkins Holdings Sàrl & Watkins (Ned) BV v Spain*, US District Court for the District of Columbia, Civil Action No 1:20-cv-01081-TFH, Spain's Reply Memorandum of Points and Authorities in Support of its Motion to Dismiss, or Stay, the Petition (22 February 2021).

[57] *InfraRed Environmental Infrastructure GP Limited and others v Spain*, US District Court for the District of Columbia, Civil Action No 1:20-cv-00817-JDB, Brief for the European Commission on behalf of the EU as amicus curiae in support of Spain (16 February 2021).

[58] Bermann (n 17) 339.

[59] *Cube Infrastructure Fund SICAV and others v Spain*, ICSID Case No ARB/15/20, Award (26 June 2019).

[60] *Hydro Energy 1 Sàrl and Hydroxana Sweden AB v Spain*, ICSID Case No ARB/15/42, Award (5 August 2020).

[61] *Cube Infrastructure Fund Sicav and others v Spain*, US District Court for the District of Columbia, Civil Action No 1:20-cv-01708-EGS, Motion to Dismiss the Complaint (6 May 2022); *Cube Infrastructure Fund Sicav and others v Spain*, US District Court for the District of Columbia, Civil Action No 1:20-cv-01708-EGS, Brief for the European Commission on behalf of the EU as amicus curiae in support of Spain (13 May 2022); *Hydro Energy 1 Sàrl, and Hydroxana Sweden AB, v Spain*, US District Court for the District of Columbia, Civil Action No 1:21-cv-02463-RJL, Memorandum of Law in Support of Spain's Motion to Dismiss the Petition or Stay Proceeding (24 February 2022); *Hydro Energy 1 Sàrl, and Hydroxana Sweden AB, v Spain*, US District Court for the District of Columbia, Civil Action No 1:21-cv-02463-RJL, Brief for the European Commission on behalf of the EU as amicus curiae in support of Spain (17 March 2022).

Immunity from jurisdiction refers to the restriction of domestic courts to adjudicate matters involving another sovereign state.[62] This has played a minor role in the enforcement of investment awards given that consent to arbitration is generally considered as a waiver to immunity from jurisdiction with respect to court proceedings in relation to the respective arbitration.[63] Otherwise, a state could agree to arbitration but subsequently block any enforcement attempt by simply resorting to immunity from jurisdiction.[64] In the United States, § 1605(a)(6) of the Foreign Sovereign Immunities Act (FSIA) provides that a foreign state is not immune from jurisdiction of the US courts in actions related to an arbitration agreement or an award rendered thereunder.

However, in the enforcement proceedings of the *Cube Infrastructure* award and the *Hydro Energy* award, the EU Commission and Spain argued that arbitration agreements in intra-EU investment disputes do not fall under § 1605(a)(6) of the FSIA as they are invalid from the outset. In accordance with this rationale, no waiver to immunity from jurisdiction under §1605(a)(6) of the FSIA would apply.[65] While the core of the argument continues to be the invalidity of arbitration agreements for intra-EU investment disputes, its new focus on sovereign immunity is noteworthy. By this means, the EU Commission and Spain have not only managed to do away with non-existing grounds for the refusal of recognition and enforcement of ICSID awards, they also found statutory support for their claim of immunity from jurisdiction. Yet, whether the US District Court for the District of Columbia would follow such argument remains to be seen.

C. Permanent Court Structures

Under a number of recent investment agreements, notably those concluded by the EU and its member states, traditional investor-state arbitration is replaced by a permanent

[62] Reinisch (n 40) 803; Peter-Tobias Stoll, 'State Immunity' in Rüdiger Wolfrum (ed), *Max Planck Encyclopedia of International Law* (OUP 2011) para 13.

[63] Georges R Delaume, 'Judicial Decisions related to Sovereign Immunity and Transnational Arbitration' (1987) ICSID Review 403, 405; Borzu Sabahi, Noah Rubins, and Don Wallace Jr, *Investor-State Arbitration* (2nd edn, OUP 2019) para 23.17.

[64] Emmanuel Gaillard and John Savage, *Fouchard Gaillard Goldman on International Commercial Arbitration* (Kluwer Law International 1999) 391 ('it would be absurd to conclude that a state could agree to submit disputes to arbitration despite its immunity from jurisdiction, but that it could subsequently prevent the award from becoming enforceable by simply relying on that immunity'); Juratowitch (n 28) 209: ('If a state does not wish to consent to arbitration, it need not do so. If it does not wish to waive its state immunity by agreement in advance of a dispute arising, it need not do so. But when in consenting to arbitration it waives its state immunity, that is an exercise of its sovereignty the terms of which it should not be permitted to revoke if it later does not like the result of the process to which it consented').

[65] *Cube Infrastructure Fund Sicav and others v Spain*, US District Court for the District of Columbia, Civil Action No 1:20-cv-01708-EGS, Motion to Dismiss the Complaint (6 May 2022); *Cube Infrastructure Fund Sicav and others v Spain*, US District Court for the District of Columbia, Civil Action No 1:20-cv-01708-EGS, Brief for the European Commission on behalf of the EU as amicus curiae in support of Spain (13 May 2022); *Hydro Energy 1 Sàrl, and Hydroxana Sweden AB, v Spain*, US District Court for the District of Columbia, Civil Action No 1:21-cv-02463-RJL, Memorandum of Law in Support of Spain's Motion to Dismiss the Petition or Stay Proceeding (24 February 2022); *Hydro Energy 1 Sàrl, and Hydroxana Sweden AB, v Spain*, US District Court for the District of Columbia, Civil Action No 1:21-cv-02463-RJL, Brief for the European Commission on behalf of the EU as amicus curiae in support of Spain (17 March 2022).

investment court system (ICS). One may find these permanent court structures, for instance, in the EU–Canada Comprehensive Economic and Trade Agreement (CETA), the EU–Singapore and EU–Vietnam Investment Protection Agreements, and the EU–Mexico Agreement in principle. The ICS envisaged in those agreements stands out for a number of special features, combining both elements of arbitration and judicial adjudication.[66]

In essence, the ICS introduces a two-tier system, which is composed of a tribunal of first instance and an appellate mechanism. The stages of a proceeding before the ICS can be divided into four: consultations, determination by the tribunal of first instance, determinations by the appellate mechanism, and enforcement of the final award.[67] An important cornerstone of the ICS is the permanence of the members of the tribunal of first instance and the appellate mechanism.[68] Under CETA, the tribunal of first instance will be composed of fifteen members that are appointed by the CETA Joint Committee for a five-year term.[69] They must possess the qualifications required for appointment to judicial office in their jurisdiction, or be jurists of recognized competence.[70] These requirements are typical for members of international courts and tribunals. In fact, the requirements included in CETA were drawn from the Statute of the International Court of Justice. There are no comparable requirements included in the ICSID Convention for the members of ICSID tribunals—they are not even required to have knowledge of public international law.[71]

Another special feature of the ICS is the selection process of the division that will hear a particular case. The president of the tribunal of first instance will appoint the members of the division hearing a case on a rotational basis, ensuring that the composition of the division will be random and unpredictable.[72] This appointment method significantly deviates from arbitration, where the disputing parties usually select the arbitrators. The innovative approach by the ICS is aimed at reducing moral hazard, ie the fear that arbitrators exhibit a predisposition towards the party that appointed them.[73]

However, the most distinctive feature of the ICS is the establishment of an appellate mechanism with broad review powers.[74] The grounds for appeal go beyond the limited ground for annulment that can be found in Article 52(1) of the ICSID Convention

[66] August Reinisch, 'Will the EU's Proposal Concerning an Investment Court System for CETA and TTIP Lead to Enforceable Awards?—The Limits of Modifying the ICSID Convention and the Nature of Investment' (2016) 19 Journal of International Economic Law 761, 762.

[67] Jin Woo Kim and Lucy M Winnington-Ingram, 'Investment Court System under EU Trade and Investment Agreements: Addressing Criticisms of ISDS and Creating New Challenges' (2021) 16 Global Trade and Customs Journal 181, 182.

[68] Marc Bungenberg and Bianca Böhme, 'Friends or Foes? The Interplay between the ICSID and Permanent Investment Courts' in Happ and Wilske (n 8) para 6.

[69] CETA art 8.27(5).

[70] ibid art 8.27(4).

[71] Colin Brown, 'Article 8.27: Constitution of the Tribunal' in Marc Bungenberg and August Reinisch (eds), *CETA Investment Law: Article-by-Article Commentary* (Nomos 2022) 600, 605.

[72] CETA art 8.27(7).

[73] Elsa Sardinha, 'The New EU-led Approach to Investor-State Arbitration: The Investment Tribunal System in the Comprehensive Economic Trade Agreement (CETA) and the EU–Vietnam Free Trade Agreement' (2017) 32(3) ICSID Review 625.

[74] CETA art 8.28.

or in national arbitration laws.[75] The ICS essentially incorporates the grounds for annulment provided in Article 52(2) of the ICSID Convention and adds two substantive grounds: errors in the application or interpretation of the applicable law and manifest errors in the appreciation of facts, including the appreciation of relevant domestic law.[76] This broad appellate review on issues of law and fact is incompatible with Article 53(1) of the ICSID Convention, which provides that awards 'shall not be subject to any appeal or to any other remedy' except those provided under the Convention.

This deviation could be understood as an *inter se* modification of Article 53(1) of the ICSID Convention in accordance with Article 41 of the Vienna Convention on the Law of Treaties (VCLT).[77] Pursuant to Article 41(1) of the VCLT, two or more parties of a multilateral treaty may agree to modify the treaty in their *inter se* relations. These *inter se* modifications are allowed as long as they are not prohibited under the relevant treaty, and as long as they do not affect the enjoyment of the rights of the non-modifying treaty parties nor relate to a provision, derogation from which is incompatible with the effective execution of the object and purpose of the treaty as a whole.

Article 53(1) of the ICSID Convention prohibits appellate review of ICSID awards, but it does not prohibit an *inter se* modification that overrides this prohibition.[78] Moreover, since the appellate review would only concern those cases brought under the treaty establishing an ICS, it would—in principle—not affect the enjoyment of the rights of non-modifying treaty parties. Finally, considering that the ICSID Secretariat itself considered in 2004 allowing ICSID awards to be subjected to appellate review,[79] it appears reasonable to conclude that the ICS would be compatible with the object and purpose of the ICSID Convention in this regard.[80]

However, even though the special features of the ICS, including the establishment of an appellate mechanism, are generally unproblematic in the *inter se* relations of modifying states, they may effectively hinder the enforcement of ICSID awards in non-modifying ICSID members.[81] Those agreements providing for an ICS express the clear intention of utilizing ICSID's strong enforcement mechanism. To that end, they provide that the decisions rendered by the ICS shall qualify as awards rendered under

[75] Bungenberg and Böhme (n 68) para 8. See also Julien Chaisse, 'The Appeal in International Investment Arbitration' in Fach Gómez and Titi (n 5).

[76] CETA art 8.28(2).

[77] Since the VCLT (1980) came into existence after the ICSID Convention (1965), it is only applicable to the extent that it is considered customary international law. See Marc Bungenberg and Anna Holzer, 'Article 8.41: Enforcement of Awards' in Bungenberg and Reinisch (n 70) 907.

[78] Albert Jan van den Berg, 'Appeal Mechanism for ISDS Awards: Interaction with the New York and ICSID Conventions' (2019) 34 ICSID Review 156, 170.

[79] See ICSID Secretariat, 'Possible Improvements of the Framework for ICSID Arbitration', Discussion Paper, October 2004.

[80] Bungenberg and Böhme (n 68) para 22.

[81] Similarly, Freya Baetens, 'The European Union's Proposed Investment Court System: Addressing Criticisms of Investor-State Arbitration While Raising New Challenges' (2016) 43 Legal Issues of Economic Integration 367, 382; Reinisch (n 66); Jin Woo Kim and Lucy M Winnington-Ingram, 'Investment Court System under EU Trade and Investment Agreements: Addressing Criticisms of ISDS and Creating New Challenges' (2021) 16 Global Trade and Customs Journal 181, 189; Michele Potestà, 'Investment Arbitration, Challenges and prospects for the Establishment of a Multilateral Investment Court: Quo Vadis Enforcement' (2018) Austrian Yearbook on International Arbitration 157, 163.

the ICSID Convention.[82] While the contracting parties to agreements providing for an ICS may commit to recognize its decisions as ICSID awards, they cannot force non-modifying ICSID members to do the same. ICSID members are merely bound under Article 54(1) of the ICSID Convention to recognize and enforce awards that were 'rendered pursuant to [the] Convention'.

Accordingly, modifying ICSID members would have to hope for the goodwill of non-modifying states to enforce ICS decisions as ICSID awards, even though they were rendered in a proceeding they did not agree to.[83] However, it is just as possible that the domestic courts of a non-modifying ICSID member refuse enforcement of an award that was not rendered in the way prescribed by the ICSID Convention. ICSID members have effectively renounced their sovereign right to review ICSID awards against their own notions of *ordre public*.[84] They could be hesitant to voluntarily dispense with this right in case of 'awards' rendered pursuant to a modified ICSID procedure.

The ICS included in EU investment agreements is only of a transitional nature and is meant to be replaced by a Multilateral Investment Court (MIC) in the future. This reform proposal is still being discussed in the United Nations Commission on International Trade Law (UNCITRAL) Working Group III.[85] The MIC is envisaged to have a similar structure as the ICS: a two-tier mechanism with a tribunal of first instance and an appellate mechanism, both equipped with tenured, highly qualified adjudicators who apply high rule of law standards.[86] Due to these parallels, it might be reasonable for the MIC to abstain from relying on the ICSID enforcement mechanism to avoid the risks of legal uncertainty described for the ICS. Alternatively, an MIC could provide for a self-standing enforcement mechanism, taking the high standard of the ICSID Convention as a guiding example.

IV. Conclusion

ICSID's facilitated enforcement system has for long been regarded as a unique example of an extraordinarily high standard under public international law that is applicable in over 160 jurisdictions. However, this chapter has shown that ICSID's enforcement system faces several challenges today. Without doubt, the biggest challenge is the increasing opposition to enforcement before domestic courts. An obligation under public international law is only effective as long as states voluntarily comply with it. Even though voluntary compliance with ICSID awards is still the norm, we

[82] See eg CETA art 8.41(6).

[83] Bungenberg and Böhme (n 68) para 26. See also Marc Bungenberg and Anna Holzer, 'Potential Enforcement Mechanisms for Decisions of a Multilateral Investment Court' in Günez Ünüvar and others (eds), *Permanent Investment Courts: The European Experiment* (Springer 2020) 75, 80ff.

[84] Richard Happ and Sebastian Wuschka, 'From the Jay Treaty Commissions towards a Multilateral Investment Court: Addressing the Enforcement Dilemma' (2017) 6 Indian Journal of Arbitration Law 123.

[85] See Note by the UNCITRAL Secretariat, 'Standing Multilateral Mechanism: Selection and Appointment of ISDS Tribunal Members and Related Matters', 8 December 2021, A/CN.9/WG.III/WP.213 <http://undocs.org/en/A/CN.9/WG.III/WP.213>.

[86] Bungenberg and Böhme (n 68) para 31.

can observe how its enforcement system is increasingly called into question. Just recently, ICSID urged Spain to abide by its obligations under the ICSID Convention and to comply with ICSID awards.[87] The failure of some states to abide by their obligations under the ICSID Convention sets a negative precedent for other states and creates legal uncertainty for investors. But this is not the only challenge that ICSID awards are facing today. The terminological debate over the meanings of 'recognition', 'enforcement' and 'execution' creates additional legal uncertainty about the exact scope of ICSID members' obligations under Article 54 of the ICSID Convention. Finally, the creation of permanent court structures under EU investment agreements and the possible establishment of an MIC could further aggravate the situation, leading to serious risks of non-enforcement. These challenges should be taken seriously in order to preserve the integrity and effectiveness of the enforcement system for ICSID awards.

[87] See eg 'CIADI insta a España a que cumpla laudos de renovables' (*CIAR Global*, 24 April 2023) <https://ciarglobal.com/ciadi-insta-a-espana-a-que-cumpla-laudos-de-renovables/>; Alberto Sanz, 'El Banco Mundial exige España que pague los pleitos millonarios de las renovables' *Voz Populi* (25 April 2023) <www.vozpopuli.com/economia_y_finanzas/banco-mundial-exige-a-espana-que-pague-los-pleitos-millonarios.html>.

27

Recognition and Enforcement of Non-ICSID Convention Awards

Giuditta Cordero-Moss

I. Introduction

It is not uncommon for investment disputes to be resolved under rules that are designed for commercial arbitration. Many investment treaties permit the investor to initiate arbitration under rules such as the Arbitration Rules of the United Nations Commission on International Trade Law (UNCITRAL), the International Chamber of Commerce (ICC), or the Arbitration Institute of the Stockholm Chamber of Commerce (SCC) as an alternative to the International Centre for Settlement of Investment Disputes (ICSID) arbitration. These rules were originally meant to govern commercial disputes. In 2020, about 45 per cent of known investment awards had been rendered under arbitration rules equally available to commercial and investment disputes.[1]

If the investor decides to initiate arbitration under such rules instead of under the ICSID Convention, the procedure will be treated as if the dispute was commercial. This implies that, in addition to being regulated by the chosen arbitration rules, the procedure is subject to the arbitration law of the country in which the arbitral tribunal has its seat.[2] The substance of the dispute, to the contrary, will be decided according to the law designated by the instrument (treaty, agreement, or legislation) creating jurisdiction for investment disputes. This means that, often, the substance will be decided under public international law, or under a combination of national law and public international law. From a procedural point of view, however, investment disputes initiated under the UNCITRAL Rules will be treated as a regular commercial ad hoc arbitration, whereas investment disputes initiated under institutional rules will be treated as regular commercial arbitration under the rules of the selected institution.

Given the importance that the share of investment disputes subject to commercial arbitration rules has assumed and is expected to continue assuming, some commercial arbitration rules have been adjusted to cater for the specific aspects of investment

[1] See Giuditta Cordero-Moss and Daniel Behn, 'Arbitration and the Development of Law' in Stefan Kröll, Andrea Bjorklund, and Franco Ferrari (eds), *Cambridge Compendium of International Commercial and Investment Arbitration* (CUP 2023) nn 26–28. For a discussion of the overlap between commercial and investment arbitration rules, see Catharine Titi, 'Investment Treaty Arbitration Caught in the Public–Private Law Divide' (2024) 45(3) Michigan Journal of International Law (forthcoming).

[2] See, for more details, Giuditta Cordero-Moss, *International Commercial Contracts* (2nd edn, CUP 2023) s 5.1.2.

Giuditta Cordero-Moss, *Recognition and Enforcement of Non-ICSID Convention Awards* In: *The Award in International Investment Arbitration*. Edited by: Katia Fach Gómez and Catharine Titi, Oxford University Press.
DOI: 10.1093/9780191975936.003.0027

arbitration. For example, in 2012 the ICC adjusted its arbitration rules in respect, among other things, to the constitution of the arbitral tribunal;[3] UNCITRAL developed rules on transparency, that were incorporated into the UNCITRAL Arbitration Rules in 2013;[4] and the Vienna International Arbitral Centre (VIAC) issued in 2021 a set of Rules for Investment Arbitration.

These adjustments, however, do not have an impact on the issue that interests us here: the enforcement of the award. Arbitral awards rendered under rules for commercial arbitration are enforceable under the regime applicable to commercial awards—irrespective of whether the dispute was commercial or whether it was a dispute between an investor and a state. In this chapter, I will deal with some issues that may be particularly relevant to recognition and enforcement of investment awards. Space constraints made it necessary to be selective in the choice of issues.

II. Basis for Recognition and Enforcement, with a Focus on the New York Convention

Commercial arbitral awards are enforceable under the 1958 New York Convention on the Recognition and Enforcement of Foreign Arbitral Awards. This means that, if the losing party does not comply with the award voluntarily, the winning party may present the award to the enforcement court of any state where the New York Convention is in force,[5] and the court will have to recognize and enforce the award after having carried out a rather restricted, mainly formal review of its enforceability.

In article VII, the New York Convention permits courts to apply their own enforcement regime, if it is more favourable to arbitration than the Convention regime. France is one of the countries in which courts have made use of this possibility—particularly when the award has been set aside in its country of origin. Annulment in the country of origin is one of the grounds for refusing enforcement under the New York Convention;[6] under French law, however, enforcement may not be refused on this ground, because foreign awards are deemed to be part of an autonomous, international system, and thus not subject to the jurisdiction of the courts in the country of origin.[7] Annulment in the country of origin, therefore, does not have a bearing on the enforceability of the award under French law—French courts apply their own enforcement regime, which, in this respect, is more favourable to arbitration than the regime under the New York Convention.

[3] See the ICC Arbitration Commission Report on Arbitration Involving States and State entities under the ICC Rules of Arbitration, 2016, containing comments and recommendations <https://iccwbo.org/news-publications/arbitration-adr-rules-and-tools/icc-arbitration-commission-report-on-arbitration-involving-states-and-state-entities-under-the-icc-rules-of-arbitration/>.

[4] See UNCITRAL Arbitration Rules art 1(4).

[5] The status of the Convention is available on the UNCITRAL webpage. This webpage lists also the reservations made by each state <https://uncitral.un.org/en/texts/arbitration/conventions/foreign_arbitral_awards/status2/>.

[6] There is some case law regarding investment awards, see Cordero-Moss (n 2) s 5.4.10.

[7] However, French courts have the authority to set aside awards rendered on the French territory, even though the dispute is international, see French Code of Civil Procedure arts 1518ff; Christophe Seraglini and Jérôme Ortscheidt, *Droit de l'arbitrage interne et international* (2nd edn, LGDJ 2019) 988ff.

The New York Convention applies to enforcement of *foreign* awards. If the award is rendered in the same country in which enforcement is sought, enforcement will be subject to domestic arbitration law. To a large extent, domestic arbitration law has been harmonized by the UNCITRAL Model Law,[8] which has been adopted in eighty-five states.[9] The Model Law applies to international arbitration; however, several countries have adopted it also for domestic arbitration. In these states, enforcement of awards rendered in the same country will be subject to the same regime as enforcement of foreign awards.

If the Model Law has been faithfully adopted, this implies that the regime will be the same as under the New York Convention—which the Model Law has implemented, without substantial differences, in Article 36. Under the Model Law, the grounds for refusing enforcement laid down in Article 36 have been replicated in Article 34, which is applicable to annulment of awards rendered in the same state where the court is located. Given the intentional correspondence between grounds for setting aside an award and grounds for refusing enforcement, case law on annulment is relevant also to enforcement (unless the circumstances suggest otherwise). In the following, therefore, I will refer to case law without distinguishing between the two phases of judicial control.

At the time of writing, the New York Convention is in force in 172 states. Recognition and enforcement of an award may be sought in any of these states, as long as the award was rendered in another Convention state. Should enforcement require that the court seizes the award debtor's assets in order to satisfy the award creditor out of the proceeds, it is necessary that the enforcement court has jurisdiction over the award debtor's assets—in other words, the enforcement court must be in a country in which the award debtor has assets. However, not all awards necessarily contain an order to pay that needs enforcement: an award may ascertain that a certain contract was properly fulfilled, that one party is liable, that a party's rights were not infringed, etc. Furthermore, a party may simply be interested in the recognition of the award to avoid new claims on the same issue that already was decided in the arbitration. While the presence of assets in the territory is a prerequisite for enforcement when the award orders a transfer of values, it is not necessary otherwise. The New York Convention does not require a connection between the dispute or the award debtor and the court's country where recognition/enforcement is requested. Therefore, any court in a Convention state has to recognize and enforce arbitral awards rendered in another Convention state, irrespective of whether the award debtor is registered in that country, has assets there or there is another connection with the dispute.[10] However, this is not uncontroversial.[11]

[8] 1985 UNCITRAL Model Law on International Commercial Arbitration, revised in 2006.

[9] See the list of countries that adopted the Model Law <https://uncitral.un.org/en/texts/arbitration/modellaw/commercial_arbitration/status>.

[10] See, for example, the Dutch Supreme Court in *Sonera v Çukurova* and *NRSL v Kompas*, respectively ECLI:NL:HR:2015:1194 (1 May 2015) and ECLI:HR:2015:107717 (April 2015); the Canadian Supreme Court in *Chevron Corp v Yaiguaje*, 2015 SCC 42 No 35682.

[11] See the Irish decision *Yukos Capital SARL v OAO Tomskneft VNK* [2014] IEHC. See also Linda Silberman and Aaron D Simowitz, 'Recognition and Enforcement of Foreign Judgements and Awards: What Hath Daimler Wrought' (2015) New York University Law Review 344.

III. The Law Applicable to Court Control, with a Focus on Legal Capacity, Validity of the Arbitration Agreement, and Public Policy

Under the New York Convention, the enforceability of an award has to be measured against specific criteria, that are laid down in Article V. For some of these criteria, it is specified which law has to be applied to verify whether the conditions for enforceability are met. Article V(1)(a) refers, as a first ground to refuse enforcement, to the lack of legal capacity of the parties to the arbitration agreement 'under the law applicable to them'.

Legal capacity is, therefore, to be ascertained under the law applicable to each of the parties, quite irrespective of the law that the parties may have chosen to govern their legal relationship or the law that otherwise is applicable to the merits of the dispute. This implies that the arbitral tribunal needs to exercise separate choices of law for each of the parties' legal capacity: if the tribunal only considers the law that governs the contract, the award risks being refused enforcement under Article V(1)(a).

Thus, an SCC award rendered in a dispute between a Norwegian company and Ukraine was annulled by the Svea Court of Appeal for having applied Swedish law (that had been chosen by the parties to govern the contract) to determine whether the contract had been signed in a manner that could bind Ukraine.[12] The decision was based on the Swedish Arbitration Act as it was before it was revised in 1999. The version prevailing today, however, does not present changes that would lead the court to take a different position regarding the specific question of the law applicable to the capacity of a party to enter into the arbitration agreement and the invalidity of the award if such a law had been violated.[13] This corresponds to Article V(1)(a) of the New York Convention and applies also to enforcement.

As a second ground for refusing enforcement, Article V(a)(1) refers to invalidity of the arbitration agreement. Under this provision, if the parties have not chosen the applicable law, the arbitration agreement is subject to the law of the place of arbitration (the *lex arbitri*). The question is whether the parties may be deemed to have made a choice of law specifically for the arbitration agreement, when this is incorporated as a clause in the larger contract regulating the parties' legal relationship, and this larger

[12] *State of Ukraine* v *Norsk Hydro* ASA, Svea Hovratt, T 3108-06 (17 December 2007), see ITA Monthly Report, Kluwer Arbitration (2008) 6 (5). Appeal not allowed, decision dated 2 June 2008, Case no T 339-08.

[13] The legal incapacity to enter into the arbitration agreement is a ground of invalidity of the award according to Article 34(1) of the 1999 Swedish Arbitration Act, see the preparatory works: SOU 1994:81 77 and proposition 1998/99:35, 48, as well as Lars Heuman and Sigvard Jarvin, *The Swedish Arbitration Act of 1999, Five Years on: A Critical Review of Strengths and Weaknesses* (JurisNet 2006) 237ff. In the new Act, the invalidity is no longer 'absolute', which means that it must be raised by the interested party as a defence within a certain term, see 1999 Arbitration Act art 34(1), as explained in proposition 1998/99:35, 138ff. Earlier, under Article 20(1) of the old Arbitration Act, incapacity to enter into the arbitration agreement was considered as an absolute ground of voidness, ie, the award became void automatically, and the voidness could not be affected by the lapse of time. Under the new provision, incapacity is a defence that needs to be raised by a party within a given term.

contract contains a clause choosing the law applicable to the relationship regulated therein. Under the prevailing separability doctrine,[14] the arbitration clause is an independent contract, and the general choice of law that the parties may have made for the commercial relationship does not affect the arbitration agreement. Failing a choice specifically covering the arbitration agreement, therefore, under the New York Convention this latter is subject to the *lex arbitri*.

This position was earlier adopted also by the UK Supreme Court. In *Dallah v Pakistan*,[15] it applied French law to the issue of whether a non-signatory could be deemed to be bound by the arbitration agreement, because the arbitration agreement chose Paris as the seat of the arbitration.[16] The UK Supreme Court later modified its position on the separability of the arbitration agreement.[17] The Court admitted that an arbitration clause may more readily than other clauses be governed by a different law; however, it found that there is a presumption that the parties, by choosing a governing law for the contract, have intended that law to apply to all clauses of the contract, including the arbitration clause.

An example of the impact of the *lex arbitri* on the validity of the arbitration agreement, and therefore of the award, is recent case law on intra-EU investment disputes. The Court of Justice of the European Union (CJEU), as well as a number of courts of EU member states, have recently applied EU law to exclude arbitration agreements in investment disputes between investors and host states, when both parties belonged to EU member states (section VIII of this chapter).

The other grounds for refusing enforcement laid down in the first paragraph of article V either make no reference to a specific law, suggesting that the standard must be deemed to be autonomous (Article V(1)(b) on the right to be heard), refer to the arbitration agreement, suggesting that party autonomy has primacy (Article V(1)(c) on excess of power), or make reference to the *lex arbitri* (Article V(1)(d) on the composition of the arbitral tribunal and the procedure, and Article V(1)e) on the validity of the award).

By containing a specific choice-of-law rule, referring to autonomous standards, or to the arbitration agreement, the first paragraph of Article V aims to ensure that the

[14] See, for more details and references, Cordero-Moss (n 2) s 5.4.2.a.

[15] *Dallah Real Estate and Tourism Holding Co v Ministry of Religious Affairs*, Pakistan [2010] UKSC [46].

[16] It may be interesting to point out that the UK Supreme Court refused to enforce this award, because it found that, under French law, Pakistan could not be deemed bound by the arbitration agreement. However, the French courts, which had been called upon to decide on the validity of the same award, applied French law in a way that led to the opposite outcome and confirmed the award, Paris Court of Appeal, Case No 09-28533 (17 February 2011).

[17] *Enka Insaat Ve Sanayi AS v OOO Insurance Company Chubb* [2020] UKSC 38, *Kabab-Ji SAL (Lebanon) v Kout Food Group (Kuwait)* [2021] UKSC [48]. The Law Commission of England and Wales, however, in its Final Report on the Review of the Arbitration Act 1996 dated 5 September 2023, recommends a reversal of this case law and the codification of a rule according to which the choice of law made by the parties for the contract does not apply to the arbitration clause unless it specifically refers to it.

grounds for refusing enforcement are applied according to the same criteria (the designated applicable law, the autonomous standard, or the parties' agreement), irrespective of which court or courts are involved.

This uniformity, however, is not necessarily achieved in full, as the law applicable to each of the parties[18] and the law applicable to the arbitration agreement are determined on the basis of conflict rules that may vary from country to country. Each court will apply its own conflict rules, and as a result the law designated as applicable may be different from court to court. Furthermore, different courts may apply the same law differently, as shown in the diverging application of French law in the *Dallah* case.

On the contrary, the second paragraph of Article V does not even have the ambition of designating a single applicable law. Under this paragraph, the court may refuse enforcement if the dispute was not arbitrable (Article V(2)(a)), or if enforcement would infringe public policy (Article V(2)(b)). Both arbitrability and public policy are to be evaluated according to the law of the court.

This means that, if enforcement of an award is sought in different countries, the arbitrability of the dispute and the award's compatibility with public policy will be verified under the law of each of these countries. The grounds for refusing enforcement laid down in the second paragraph relate to such fundamental principles that contracting states, when they drafted the New York Convention, were not willing to abdicate their authority and accept that conformity with an autonomous or a foreign system would suffice to enforce the award. The importance of these parameters is confirmed by the circumstance that arbitrability and conflict with public policy may be considered by the court on its own motion, while the grounds laid down in the first paragraph need to be raised by a party.

Admittedly, in some countries, notably in France, enforcement may be refused if the award conflicts with 'international public policy'. In the discourse on international arbitration, this is sometimes deemed to be a reference to a non-national standard.[19] However, what is meant is '*French* international public policy': not a public policy that relies on international sources, but that part of the national public policy that French courts may have regard to when the dispute before them is international.[20]

The need for adding the term 'international' arises because, in France, the concept of 'public policy' is quite broad. Public policy, in the domestic context, is intended to correspond to those mandatory rules, also known as overriding mandatory rules or *lois de police*, that are deemed to be so important that they shall be applied even in international disputes and without taking into consideration the general choice-of-law rules. This is too broad a scope to be compatible with Article V(2)(b). As will be seen

[18] For references on the conflict rule for legal capacity, see Cordero-Moss (n 2) ss 4.5.2(d) and 5.4.3.

[19] Pierre Lalive, 'L'ordre public transnational et l'arbitre international' in *Liber Fausto Pocar* (Giuffrè 2009) 599–611. This approach is confirmed also in some of the case law eg *Allsop Automatic Inc v Tecnoski snc*, Court of Appeal of Milan (4 December 1992) XXII Yearbook of Commercial Arbitration 725 (Italy).

[20] See, among many others, Paris Court of Appeal, Case No 18/18708 (5 October 2021).

in section VI below, it is only fundamental principles that can qualify as public policy under this provision. Therefore, if the term 'public policy' is, in some legal traditions such as the French, used in a broad sense when it is applied domestically, it must be restricted when it is used in the context of Article V(2)(b). Adding the term 'international' is a way of restricting the broad scope of domestic public policy. In other legal systems, such as under the UNCITRAL Model Law and the New York Convention, it is not necessary to add the term 'international', because 'public policy', also in the domestic context, is interpreted narrowly.[21] In these systems, therefore, the term public policy coincides with the understanding of public policy under Article V(2)(b).

The public policy of the *lex fori* may contain a principle according to which, under certain circumstances, violation of the applicable (foreign) law may be deemed to be immoral. In this case, this could be a basis for applying Article V(2)(b) to an award which violates foreign law. The basis for the refusal would not be the infringement of the foreign law, but the *lex fori* principle according to which, under certain circumstances, infringement of foreign law is immoral.

If recognition and enforcement are sought against a foreign state, the principles of comity and reciprocity may also be relevant, as long as they are part of the court's own legal system. In these cases too, therefore, the basis for public policy is the court's own system. A US District Court applied the principle of reciprocity to refuse recognition and enforcement of an award against a foreign state.[22] The Court affirmed that the doctrine of international comity generally does not prevent recognizing and enforcing awards against foreign states, but it found that it would be against public policy to recognize and enforce an award ordering the foreign state to permit the other party commercialization of hydrocarbons produced under a production sharing agreement. The Court found first that the US Foreign Sovereign Immunities Act does not mention that specific performance is one of the remedies allowed against foreign states. Furthermore, the Court found that it would be against US public policy to enforce an order of specific performance against a foreign state, which would create a reciprocal situation in which a foreign court could enforce a order against the US.

Irrespective of whether the public policy is qualified by the term 'international' or not, therefore, the public policy that is relevant under Article V(2)(b) is the public policy of the enforcing court (of the *lex fori*).[23] While the *lex fori* determines what constitutes a fundamental principle in that country, the New York Convention regulates the conditions for and effects of exercising the public policy defence; and these have to be interpreted autonomously, as section VI explains.[24]

[21] For further references, see Cordero-Moss (n 2) s 5.4.9(b) and Giuditta Cordero-Moss, 'Article V(2)(b)' in Herbert Kronke and others (eds), *Recognition and Enforcement of Foreign Arbitral Awards: A Global Commentary on the New York Convention* (2nd edn, Wolters Kluwer forthcoming) s B(2).

[22] *Hardy Exploration and Production (India) Inc v India*, District Court for the District of Columbia, Civ Act No 2016-0140 (7 June 2018) (United States).

[23] For a discussion of the so-called truly international public policy, see Cordero-Moss (n 2) s 5.4.9(d).

[24] For more references, see ibid s 5.4.9(a) and Cordero-Moss (n 21) s B(1).

IV. Restrictive Scope of Judicial Control

The list of grounds for refusing enforcement contained in Article V of the New York Convention is exhaustive. The grounds for refusing enforcement being so few, the number of awards not voluntarily complied with by the losing party, and that therefore are brought to court for enforcement, is rather low (but increasing).[25] For the same reason, the rate of success for defences against enforcement is rather low, too.[26]

Judicial control in the recognition and enforcement context is not an appeal. It is aimed at ensuring that an award was rendered in accordance with due process principles, that it is based on the consent of the parties, and that it does not infringe upon fundamental principles—it is not aimed at ensuring that the award is correct. Nevertheless, it may occur that an award containing an obvious error, if it remains uncorrected, is deemed to be affected by a procedural irregularity.[27]

V. Intensity of Court Control, with a Focus on Jurisdiction, Public Policy, and Arbitrability

The fact that the enforcement court may not review the award on the merits does not mean that the court may not re-evaluate issues that already have been considered by the arbitral tribunal. The purpose of the court evaluation, however, will not be to verify whether the arbitral tribunal was accurate or came to a correct result. The purpose will be to make sure that none of the conditions for refusing enforcement is met.

The court has, for example, the power to refuse enforcement if the arbitral tribunal did not have jurisdiction, or if enforcing the award would infringe public policy. To assess whether this power is to be exercised, the court needs to ascertain whether the award is based on adequate jurisdiction, or whether the award is compatible with public policy. The arbitral tribunal may already have evaluated these issues; the question that arises is what effects the tribunal's evaluation has for the court's assessment.

Elsewhere, I have analysed the court's authority to independently review the arbitral tribunal's jurisdiction.[28] It is uncontroversial that the court is not bound by the tribunal's own conclusions on jurisdiction and can evaluate the issue irrespective of the tribunal's conclusion. This is notwithstanding that, for the pre-award phase, various doctrines aim to enhance the autonomy of arbitration and minimize the courts' intervention in respect of the issue of jurisdiction. According to the *Kompetenz-Kompetenz*

[25] About 76 per cent of corporate counsel participating in a survey had experienced that the award had been voluntarily complied with: Monique Sasson and others, 'Empirical Research of National Courts Vacatur and Enforcement of International Commercial Arbitration Awards' (2022) 29 Journal of International Arbitration 301.

[26] The overall rate of enforcement is 73 per cent, ibid 307.

[27] In *Ducat Maritime Ltd v Lavender Ship Management Incorporated* [2022] EWHC 766 (Comm), where there was an obvious calculation mistake in the award, a party initiated the procedure to have the mistake corrected, the arbitral tribunal recognized the mistake, but refused to correct it.

[28] Cordero-Moss (n 2) s 5.3.3.(b)(i).

doctrine, enshrined in Article 16 of the UNCITRAL Model Law, an arbitral tribunal has the competence to decide on its own competence. An even clearer priority to the arbitral tribunal's evaluation of its own competence is given by the French theory of the *effet négatif de la compétence-compétence*. According to Article 1448 of the French Code of Civil Procedure, courts must refer the dispute to arbitration whenever they are seized with a dispute which is subject to an arbitration agreement and are only allowed to make a cursory review of the arbitration agreement. In the post-award phase, however, neither the Model Law nor the French Code of Civil Procedure are deemed to prevent courts from independently evaluating whether the award was within the scope of the arbitral tribunal's jurisdiction—even though the tribunal has already evaluated that very matter. This may result in a different outcome from the one to which the tribunal came and may lead to refusing enforcement of the award.[29] The enforcement court, therefore, may independently make the evaluations that are necessary for the application of Article V of the New York Convention. This applies not only to the issue of jurisdiction, which may be raised under letters (a) and (c) of Article V(1), but also in respect of the other grounds listed in Article V.

In respect of one defence, however, this approach is not uncontroversial: when the basis for resisting enforcement is public policy. The prevailing approach is that the court may independently evaluate the issue, just like in the case of the other grounds (so-called maximalist approach).[30] French courts have developed the opposite, the minimalist approach.[31] They interpret the criteria for applying the public policy defence so restrictively (violation must be flagrant, actual and concrete, see section VI), that they exclude an independent evaluation by the enforcement court, if the arbitral tribunal has already considered the issue.

Elsewhere, I have criticized the minimalist approach.[32] States have accepted to lend juridical effects to arbitral awards and to grant arbitration a large autonomy under the New York Convention, on condition that they could maintain the possibility to control that the fundamental principles of their own system are not breached, as argued in section III. Delegating to the arbitral tribunal the evaluation of whether public policy is infringed means that the states are not capable of exercising this control. This in turn may erode the trust and legitimacy on which arbitration depends to preserve its position as an effective method for resolving disputes. This may, consequently, lead to a restriction of the scope of arbitrability.

That the possibility of exercising control on the application of important policies is linked to the arbitrability of disputes was already shown in the *Mitsubishi* case of 1985.[33] The US Supreme Court decided to permit arbitration of a dispute involving

[29] *Renta4 v Russian Federation*, Svea Court of Appeal, Case T-9128–14 (18 January 2016); UK Supreme Court, *Dallah* [2010] UKSC 46; Swiss Supreme Court decision No 4A_564/2020.
[30] For references, see Cordero-Moss (n 2) s 5.3.3.(b)(ii).
[31] *Thalès Air Defence v Euromissile*, Paris Court of Appeal, 1e ch (18 November 2004) (2005) Revue de l'arbitrage 751.
[32] Cordero-Moss (n 2) s 5.3.3(b)(iii).
[33] *Mitsubishi Motors Corp v Soler Chrysler-Plymouth, Inc*, 473 US 614, 628 (1985).

issues of competition law, because courts would still be able to have a 'second look' in the phase of enforcement. This decision initiated an era of arbitration-friendliness and continued expansion of the scope of arbitrability that runs the risk of being reversed if the 'second look' is deprived of any significance—as the minimalist theory considers.

A reversal of the generous attitude to arbitrability is detrimental to arbitration, as courts under the New York Convention may refuse enforcement of awards on the ground that are not arbitrable under the courts' own law. As there is no autonomous standard on arbitrability, courts may be relatively readily inclined to reverse this approach. There are some examples of court decisions excluding the arbitrability of disputes arising out of contracts of commercial agency due to the desire to ensure an accurate application of the provisions protecting the commercial agent, that particularly under EU law are deemed to be necessary for the achievement of the internal market.[34] The rationale is that choosing arbitration, or choosing a court outside the EU, may endanger the effective enforcement of EU law. A comparable development can be seen in respect of intra-EU investment disputes, as developed in section VIII.

Today there is a climate of increasing mistrust against arbitration, particularly against investment arbitration.[35] It does not seem that arbitration can be promoted by insisting on a minimalist approach to court control—quite the contrary. As a matter of fact, in the context of corruption and economic crime, the minimalist theory seems to have been abandoned in its country of origin, France. In the past few years, numerous French court decisions, including one by the Supreme Court,[36] have been based on an independent evaluation of whether the claim was tainted by corruption, without having regard to the evaluation of the same issue that was made by the arbitral tribunal.

Another reason for criticizing the minimalist theory is that the public policy that may have been evaluated by the arbitral tribunal is not necessarily the same public policy that will be evaluated by the enforcement court. A court may refuse enforcement if the award conflicts with the public policy 'of that country' (ie of the enforcement court), as explained in section III. If the award is sought to be enforced in more than one country, each enforcement court will evaluate the compatibility of the award with its own public policy. If the arbitral tribunal's evaluation were to bind all these courts, it must be assumed that there is one public policy that is uniform in all these countries. This, however, contradicts the wording of the New York Convention.

[34] For references, see Cordero-Moss (n 2) s 5.4.8(c).

[35] Suffice it to refer to the works of the UNCITRAL Working Group III (Investor-State Dispute Settlement Reform)—see, among others, 'Possible Reform of Investor-State dispute Settlement (ISDS)', Note by the Secretariat at Its Thirty-Fourth Session, Vienna, 27 November–1 December 2017, UN Doc A/CN.9/WG.III/WP.142. For further references, see Giuditta Cordero-Moss, 'The Alleged Failure of Arbitration to Address Due Process Concerns: Is Arbitration under Attack?' in Axel Calissendorff and Patrik Schöldström (eds), *Stockholm Arbitration Yearbook* (2021).

[36] *Belokon v Kyrgyzstan*, Cass Civ 1ère, Case No 17-17.981 (23 March 2022). For more references, see Cordero-Moss (n 2) s 5.3.3.(b)(2).

VI. Court Control Is Not an Appeal, with a Focus on Public Policy

Courts may independently evaluate some issues that have already been decided by the arbitral tribunal. This, however, applies within the restricted scope of judicial control—which means that the court will evaluate the issues that are necessary to determine whether there is a basis for refusing enforcement of (or for annulling) an award. The court is not concerned with other aspects of the award, such as whether the arbitral tribunal correctly interpreted the contract or applied the law, and may not review the merits of the dispute.

In particular, evaluating whether enforcing an award violates public policy is not the same as reviewing the award on the merits. Elsewhere, I have extensively discussed the criteria that need to be respected to refuse enforcement on the ground of conflict with public policy.[37] These criteria may be summarized as follows: that the court would have reached a different result is irrelevant to the evaluation of public policy. Likewise, it is irrelevant whether the law has been complied with in all its technicalities. In itself, an error of law does not infringe public policy—not even if the error was made in the application of a mandatory or even of an overriding mandatory rule of the court's law. It is only the fundamental principles of society that are relevant to public policy: not the technical formulation of the law, but the underlying principles. And it is not sufficient that they are not applied correctly: they must have been infringed in such a serious way that the result of enforcing the award would be unacceptable. Often, therefore, public policy is defined by reference to concepts such as a sense of justice and socio-economic values, rather than by reference to legal provisions.

Furthermore, it is irrelevant that the award applies a principle or a foreign law that abstractly is unacceptable in the court's system. It is the result of enforcing the award that is relevant: if the award applied a law under which corruption is legal, and this law is unacceptable under the court's public policy, the award may nevertheless be enforceable—for example, because corruption was not proved in the specific case. It is, thus, the actual result of enforcing the award that must be evaluated to verify whether this enforcement would infringe upon fundamental principles.

In this evaluation, the court is not restricted to considering only the specific actions that the award orders the parties to carry out. A great number of arbitral awards order one party to pay money. Transfer of money from one party to another, in itself, is seldom an action that can seriously violate fundamental principles. If the court's evaluation were limited to the effects of recognizing and enforcing the order to pay, isolated from the basis for ordering the payment, the public policy defence would not be applicable, for example, to awards ordering payments under a contract based on corruption or with an illegal object.

[37] Cordero-Moss (n 2) s. 5.4.9; Cordero-Moss (n 21).

Whether effecting the payment ordered by the award infringes fundamental principles or not rather depends on the basis on which the payment has been ordered. If the award puts the winning party in the same position as if the contract had been executed, it is a substitute for contract performance. If performing the contract had been against public policy, also enforcing the award that substitutes performance would be against public policy. Therefore, the basis for the award may be relevant to public policy, such as when the illegality of the contract is invoked as defence against a claim that a breach of contract had occurred. If a party invokes as a defence that the contract was not enforceable, for example alleging that the contract was tainted by corruption, an award disregarding the defence and ordering damages for breach of contract is equivalent to an award ordering to perform an illegal action (assuming that the allegations are correct).

This is the same rationale that underlies an EU Commission Decision against Romania in the *Micula* case.[38] The Micula brothers had made an investment in Romania taking advantage of certain tax benefits that Romania had introduced to encourage foreign investment. Later, Romania acceded to the EU, and the tax benefits were repealed, as they violated EU rules on state aid. An ICSID award ordered Romania to compensate the investors for the loss that the new tax rules had caused.[39] The EU Commission found that payment under the award amounted to illegal state aid, just like the tax benefits that it was meant to compensate for. The General Court later annulled the Commission's decision on the basis that the Commission lacked competence, as well as because Romania had repealed advantages that had been granted prior to Romania's accession to the EU. [40] However, the rationale that the award was a substitute for illegal state aid, and thus itself was illegal, was not criticized. Similarly, the Paris Court of Appeal stayed the enforcement of an award against Malaysia, holding that awarding damages based on the restitution value of a disputed territory is a substitute for restitution, which in turn would infringe on Malaysia's sovereignty.[41]

That the basis for the award is relevant to the public policy evaluation is not inconsistent with the requirement that the violation must actually flow from recognition and enforcement of the award, and that it is the result that must be unacceptable. On the one hand, it is true that recognition and enforcement of an award in many cases simply means that one party transfers a sum of money to the other party and that this, in itself, does not seriously violate any fundamental principles. On the other hand, however, the transfer of money is not the only result of the recognition and enforcement. Another result is that the court is contributing to the implementation of an award that, as was seen above, is a substitute for a conduct that in turn may infringe public policy.

[38] EU Commission Decision No 2015/1470 on State Aid (30 March 2015).
[39] *Iorel Micula and others v Romania*, ICSID Case No ARB/05/20, Final Award (11 December 2013).
[40] Cases T-624/15, T-694/15, and T-704/15.
[41] *Heirs of the Sultan of Sulu v Malaysia*, Paris Court of Appeal, Case No 22/04007 (12 July 2022).

VII. Incidental Questions and Jurisdiction, with a Focus on Corruption

The jurisdiction of the arbitral tribunal is generally based on the parties' arbitration agreement. In investment arbitration, jurisdiction can be based on investment legislation or on investment treaties, but both parties' consent is still necessary as a basis for jurisdiction. The state's consent will then be embodied in the legislation or the treaty, and can be deemed to be a firm offer to arbitrate. The investor will be deemed to have accepted the offer when it initiates arbitration. Thus, also in investment arbitration the tribunal's jurisdiction is based on the terms of the arbitration agreement—more specifically, on the terms of the offer to arbitrate as it is formulated in the relevant legislation or treaty.

The arbitral tribunal's powers are limited to the scope determined in the arbitration agreement, and usually arbitration agreements only refer to disputes arising in connection with a specific legal relationship between the parties. This has prompted some commentators to question that arbitral tribunals have a power to decide on a claim deriving out of a contract tainted by corruption.[42] If an arbitral tribunal renders an award without having jurisdiction, the award may be refused enforcement under Article V(1)(a) or (c) of the New York Convention. However, it is questionable whether this is relevant in this context.

Admittedly, often corruption constitutes a crime, and an arbitral tribunal does not have the power to decide criminal law issues. This, however, does not affect the arbitral tribunal's jurisdiction when the issue of corruption is dealt with incidentally. Generally, the issue of corruption is not the direct object of the claim, but arises as an incidental question in the course of a dispute regarding the enforcement of the parties' rights and obligations or the protection of the investment.

The tribunal does not rule on the incidental question but simply considers it as an assumption, and solely for the purpose of deciding the claim. If a defendant argues that the claim (for example, for breach of contract) is not enforceable because the contract is invalid as it was tainted by corruption, the arbitral tribunal will determine whether the claim is enforceable. As an assumption for determining the claim's enforceability, it will be necessary to consider the allegations of corruption—but the purpose will be to determine the enforceability of the claim, and the award will not impose criminal law sanctions on the basis of its incidental examination of the corruption issue. The award will rule on the validity of the contract and its breach. Apart from this, the consideration of the incidental question will not have any legal effects—because the incidental question is not the object of the tribunal's decision. As long as the claim is within the tribunal's scope of jurisdiction, therefore, the power of the arbitral tribunal is unaffected by the presence of a non-arbitrable incidental question.[43]

[42] For references and more extensive reasoning, see Giuditta Cordero-Moss, 'Corruption and Arbitration: Arbitrability, Jurisdiction, Admissibility or Merits?' in Antonio Crivellaro and others (eds), *Liber Amicorum Bernardini* (Brill forthcoming).

[43] Confirming that issues of corruption are not be considered as issues of jurisdiction, but issues of merits, see *Cengiz v Libya*, Paris Court of Appeal, Case No 18/27648 (25 May 2021); *Nurol v Libya*, Paris Court of Appeal,

In investment arbitration, however, the issue of corruption is sometimes deemed to affect the arbitral tribunal's jurisdiction. This is particularly so when the dispute is based on an investment treaty that explicitly grants protection only to investments made in compliance with the host state's laws. The logic is that the treaty, including also the offer to arbitrate, only covers legal investments. An investment that is tainted by corruption is illegal, and therefore not protected by the treaty and not included in the offer to arbitrate.

This would be parallel to other prerequisites for the applicability of the treaty, such as the requirement that the investor be a national of a contracting state, that the investment falls within the treaty's definition of protected investment, or that the claims fall within the scope of the offer to arbitrate.

The bilateral investment treaty (BIT) between the United Kingdom and the Russian Federation, for example, refers to arbitration disputes on the quantification of the compensation payable in case of unlawful expropriation, but excludes disputes on whether there has been an unlawful expropriation. An investment award rendered by an arbitral tribunal under the rules of the SCC retained jurisdiction when an investor who had acquired some shares in Yukos claimed that the Russian Federation had breached its obligations under the treaty. The award applied the most-favoured-nation clause contained in the treaty and thus applied broader jurisdiction clauses that may be found in other treaties ratified by the Russian Federation. The Svea Court of Appeal in Stockholm confirmed a decision by the District Court that had found that a most-favoured-nation clause may not be used to extend the scope of arbitral jurisdiction determined in the treaty, and set aside the award.[44] A similar decision was taken by the Svea Court of Appeal in respect of an award based on the Spain–Russia BIT.[45] Similarly, an illegal investment will fall outside the scope of the investment treaty, if legality is part of the definition of protected investment. The arbitral tribunal, therefore, will not have jurisdiction and the award may be refused enforcement.

The next question is whether jurisdiction can be restricted by a non-written requirement of legality. A parallel with commercial disputes suggests the opposite: also under national contract law, like for investment protection, the legal system only affords protection to interests that are enforceable. Courts and arbitral tribunals are expected to enforce claims that are legal. Should an unenforceable or illegal claim be brought to court or arbitration, it will be dismissed. However, it will be dismissed on the merits, not because the illegality of the claim, as an implicit requirement, affects the court's or the tribunal's jurisdiction.[46]

Case No 19/19834 (28 September 2021); *Abouk Halil v Senegal*, Paris Court of Appeal, Case No 19/21625 (12 October 2021).

[44] Case No T 24891-07, 9 November 2011, confirmed by the Svea Court of Appeal, Case T-10060-10 (5 September 2013).

[45] *Renta4 v Russian Federation*, Svea Court of Appeal, Case T-9128-14 (18 January 2016).

[46] See, for example, the Hague Court of Appeal, stating that the Energy Charter Treaty does not assume the legality of the investment to be applicable, Hague Court of Appeal, Case No 200.197.079/01, Judgment (18 February 2020).

VIII. Incidental Questions and Arbitrability, with a Focus on Intra-EU Investment Awards

If an arbitral tribunal renders an award on an issue that was not arbitrable, the award may be refused enforcement under Article V(2)(a) of the New York Convention. National law may restrict the parties' ability to submit to arbitration disputes between themselves. Often, disputes are deemed to be arbitrable if they are on commercial matters, or on areas on which the parties enjoy freedom of contract—thus excluding issues where an award could affect third-party interests (such as security interests or the existence and validity of intellectual property rights). Areas in which the public interest is relevant are not arbitrable, for example criminal law issues.

However, as long as issues on these areas are considered incidentally, the arbitrability of the dispute is not affected. An arbitral tribunal is empowered to consider, in their totality, the laws that govern the dispute, as long as the decision remains within the sphere of private law. It does not matter for instance if party autonomy is not allowed (such as for issues of intellectual property), if the issue has a public policy dimension (such as implications of criminal law), or it is subject to overriding mandatory rules (such as competition law). As long as these issues have consequences for the parties' rights and obligations towards each other, and the dispute submitted to arbitration concerns these rights and obligations, the tribunal is empowered to consider them.

A party may allege that it is not in breach of contract because the contract was invalid as a consequence of violation of competition law or of criminal law. These areas of the law are not arbitrable. However, the arbitral tribunal may, even must, determine whether the contract was valid or not. The issues of competition or of criminal law are mere incidental issues: they are not finally decided with effects for third parties, they are simply considered in the course of the determination of the contractual issue—has there been a breach of contract or not? The decision will have *res iudicata* effect only in this respect.

Today, this is not controversial. Earlier, however, the non-arbitrability of an incidental question may have been deemed to affect the arbitrability of the principal claim, especially in connection with disputes involving questions of competition law.[47] Competition law contains, as is known, overriding mandatory provisions; moreover, special bodies have the authority to impose fines and otherwise sanction the violation of these provisions. Hence, the question has been debated as to whether an arbitral tribunal has jurisdiction over disputes involving matters of competition law. A commercial arbitral tribunal is not a competition law authority with powers of public law. Therefore, if one party to a licence agreement requests an arbitral tribunal to impose a fine on the other party because the licence agreement or that party's actions violate competition law, the arbitral tribunal must decline jurisdiction. However, if that party

[47] See the comments made in the preparatory works to the Norwegian Arbitration Bill (NOU 2001:33, 51ff) and to the Swedish Arbitration Act (SOU 1994:81, 86).

requests the arbitral tribunal to rule on the contractual consequences of that violation, the arbitral tribunal has jurisdiction: the tribunal may evaluate whether competition law has been violated and may decide on the consequences that that violation has for the parties. For example, it may decide that a certain contractual clause is invalid due to its conflict with competition law, and that therefore non-compliance therewith by one party does not constitute default under the contract.

That an incidental issue of competition law does not affect the arbitrability of the principal claim was decided in the United States in the *Mitsubishi* decision of 1985, mentioned in section V above. The Supreme Court found that conformity with public interests related to competition law could be ensured by exercising judicial control over the award, the so-called second look doctrine. The same balance can be found in *Eco Swiss*, a decision rendered by the EU Court of Justice in 1999.[48] This decision established that competition law amounts to public policy in EU law, and that therefore an award that violates EU competition law may be refused recognition and enforcement under the New York Convention. The arbitrability of disputes involving competition law issues was not questioned.

In order to avoid any doubts on the jurisdiction of an arbitral tribunal over the contractual and private law aspects of the dispute, even if the dispute also involves matters that are regulated by overriding mandatory rules, some modern arbitration laws have expressly confirmed this approach. The Norwegian Arbitration Act, s 9.2, expressly specifies that a dispute is arbitrable under Norwegian law even if it relates to competition law, as long as the tribunal is requested to decide on the civil law effects of the competition law. The same rule is also to be found in the Swedish Arbitration Act, s 1.3. One might wonder whether the legislators have intended to exclude the arbitrability of the civil effects of any other regulatory provision such as patent law, since they have expressly mentioned only the civil law effects of competition law. The report on the Norwegian bill, however, specifies that there was no intention of excluding the arbitrability of the civil law consequences of other rules, rather a desire to confirm that aspect specifically for competition rules, which have often been the subject of disputes internationally.[49] So long as the issue is incidental, and the tribunal only considers it as a step in the decision of the (arbitrable) principal claim, therefore, the arbitrability of the dispute is not affected.

The same reasoning may apply, for example, to a claim for compensation for unlawful expropriation upon cancellation of tax benefits amounting to state aid. The tribunal will not reverse the decision to cancel the tax benefits, nor will it impose changes on the regulation of state aid (the tribunal does not have the power to do so). It will determine whether cancellation amounts to unlawful expropriation, and its decision will be limited to the legal consequences between the parties of the infringement of investment protection (the tribunal has the power, and the duty, to do so).

[48] Case C-126/97 *Eco Swiss v Benetton*, Judgement (1 June 1999).
[49] Report on the Bill on Arbitration, NOU 2001:33, comment on s 2-1(2) (which became s 9.2 in the Act).

A parallel reasoning may be carried out for disputes involving issues of corruption: as long as the claim is arbitrable, for example a claim for reimbursement of damages as a consequence of breach of contract (or a claim for compensation for, eg, unlawful expropriation), arbitration is not excluded by the simple fact that a defence invoking the contract's invalidity assumes an incidental evaluation of whether the contract was tainted by corruption.[50]

The arbitrability of competition law issues was, as mentioned, confirmed by the *Mitsubishi* and by the *Eco Swiss* decisions, and was linked to the courts' second look. This reasoning applies within the EU to all disputes in which issues of EU law need to be considered as incidental questions. EU law has a mechanism designed to ensure the uniform application of EU law: under Article 267 of the Treaty on the Function of the European Union (TFEU), courts of member states submit to the CJEU requests for preliminary rulings on the interpretation of EU law. This is meant to ensure a uniform application of EU law by the various state courts. Arbitral tribunals may not request preliminary rulings; however, arbitral awards are subject to court control, and the controlling court may request preliminary rulings if an issue of EU law is relevant. Through court control, therefore, the uniformity of EU law is ensured even when the dispute is subject to arbitration. This approach was confirmed by the CJEU in the *Achmea* case, as far as commercial arbitration is concerned.[51] Thus, the CJEU endorses the arbitrability of commercial disputes, even when they involve issues of EU law—on the assumption that the maximalist theory applies, see section V.

However, in the same *Achmea* case, the CJEU denied arbitrability of investment disputes between investors belonging to a state which is a member of the EU, and host state members of the EU, so-called intra-EU investment disputes. One of the reasons for denying arbitrability of intra-EU investment disputes is the alleged lack of an effective method to control the uniform application of EU law when the issue is determined by an arbitral tribunal.[52]

The *Achmea* approach was later confirmed in *Komstroy*, which regarded a dispute under the Energy Charter Treaty,[53] in *PL Holding*, which regarded an ad hoc arbitration agreement with a scope corresponding to the arbitration agreement laid down in the BIT between Sweden and Poland, [54] and in *Micula*, in which the arbitration agreement contained in the BIT between Sweden and Romania was deemed to have been replaced by the judicial remedies contained in the EU treaties.[55] This CJEU case law was followed by the courts of numerous EU member states, which resulted in a number of investment awards being annulled,[56] and it is expected that requests for enforcement

[50] For references, see Cordero-Moss (n 42) ss 4 and 5.
[51] Case C-284/16 *Slowakische Republik (Slovak Republic) v Achmea BV*, Judgment (6 March 2018) [54].
[52] ibid.
[53] Case C-741/19 *Moldova v Komstroy LLC*, Judgment (2 September 2020).
[54] Case C-109/20 *Poland v PL Holdings Sàrl*, Judgement (26 October 2021).
[55] Case C-638/19 *European Commission v European Food SA and others*, Judgement (25 January 2022).
[56] Paris Court of Appeal, *Republic of Poland v CEC Praha and Slot Group AS*, Case No 49/2022 (19 April 2022); Paris Court of Appeal, *Republic of Poland v Strabag SE and others*, Case No 48/2022 (19 April 2022); Bundesgerichtshof, Decision, I ZB 2/15 (31 October 2018); Bundesgerichtshof, Decision, I ZB 16/21 (17 November 2021) in relation to the arbitration *Raiffeisen Bank International AG and Raiffeisen Bank Austria dd*

would equally be refused. US courts, on the contrary, have declined to follow the CJEU policy on intra-EU awards, and have enforced the award in the *Micula* case,[57] particularly considering that the EU General Court found that the *Achmea* doctrine did not apply to facts that predated the state's accession to the EU.[58]

The CJEU denies arbitrability of intra-EU investment disputes, but it allows arbitrability of commercial disputes and of investment disputes with parties from states outside of the EU. The arguments that are used to distinguish these situations are not convincing. The CJEU argues that commercial and non-intra-EU investment disputes are arbitrable because the arbitral tribunal, in these cases, only incidentally considers issues of EU law.[59] In particular, this means that the tribunal does not have the power to rule beyond the scope of the treaty, nor to amend the legislation that it may find in conflict with the treaty. This, however, is a description that applies to any tribunal who considers EU law as an incidental issue—also to intra-EU investment tribunals. It is, therefore, not a basis to distinguish between intra-EU investment arbitration and other forms of arbitration or investment litigation.

Furthermore, the CJEU considers that intra-EU investment tribunals only have limited access to the mechanism laid down in Article 267 of the TFEU: it is only when the *lex arbitri* permits court control, that preliminary rulings may be requested.[60] This, however, applies to all non-ICSID awards, and is therefore not a basis to distinguish investment and commercial arbitration.

The only convincing[61] basis for distinguishing intra-EU investment disputes from other investment disputes is that intra-EU investment arbitration does not fit in the EU system of division of powers between member states and the Union. The principle of mutual trust requires that member states assume that all other member states comply with EU law, including its fundamental rights that would be the EU equivalent of investment protection. It is only the CJEU that has the competence to evaluate the proper application of EU law, and investment arbitration tribunals do not fit into this exclusive competence.[62] Third states, to the contrary, are not covered by the principle of mutual trust and the consequent exclusive competence of the CJEU on EU law. Therefore,

v Croatia, PCA Case No 2020-15; Lithuanian Supreme Court, *Republic of Lithuania v ICOR, Vilniaus Energija, Litesko, Veolia Energie International SA*, Civil Case No e3K-3-121-916/2022 (18 January 2022).

[57] *Micula v Romania*, 404 F Supp 3d 265 (DDC 11 September 2019), affirmed by the US Court of Appeals for the District of Colombia, Case No 19–7127, 2020 US App LEXIS 16008 (DC Cir 19 May 2020).

[58] Cases T-624/15, T-694/15, and T-704/15.

[59] Case C-284/16 *Slowakische Republik (Slovak Republic) v Achmea BV*, Judgment (6 March 2018) [54]; Case C-741/19 *Moldova v Komstroy LLC*, Judgment (2 September 2020), as well as Opinion 1/17 *Comprehensive Economic and Trade Agreement between Canada and the European Union* [2019] EU:C:2019:341 [119], [120]–[127].

[60] Case C-284/16 *Slowakische Republik (Slovak Republic) v Achmea BV*, Judgment (6 March 2018) [35]–[37], [45], [49], [53]; Case C-741/19 *Moldova v Komstroy LLC*, Judgment (2 September 2020) [51]–[53], [57], [58], [63]; Case C-109/20 *Poland v PL Holdings Sàrl*, Judgement (26 October 2021) [44], [45].

[61] For an analysis of other grounds that are laid down in *Achmea*, see Giuditta Cordero-Moss, '*Achmea*'s Distinction between Investment and Commercial Arbitration' in Axel Calissendorff (ed), *The Future of Arbitration in Europe* (Stockholm Centre for Commercial Law Skriftserie 2020) 17–28.

[62] Case C-284/16 *Slowakische Republik (Slovak Republic) v Achmea BV*, Judgment (6 March 2018) [34]; Case C-109/20 *Poland v PL Holdings Sàrl*, Judgement (26 October 2021) [46], [52].

investment arbitration involving parties from third states does not conflict with the division of powers internal to the EU.[63]

This argument, however, is not applicable to the distinction between intra-EU investment disputes and commercial disputes, at least not when investment disputes are subject to the same procedural rules as commercial disputes (that is, to non-ICSID disputes). As was explained above, court control is available to the same extent irrespective of whether the dispute is commercial or investment.[64] If court control is sufficient to safeguard the CJEU competence on EU law when the dispute is commercial, it must be sufficient also for investment disputes that are carried out under rules for commercial arbitration.

IX. Conclusion

This chapter analysed selected issues arising in connection with the enforcement of investment awards rendered under rules of arbitration designed for commercial arbitration. Since enforcement of these awards is subject to the New York Convention, courts may exercise a certain control. While under the New York Convention courts may not review the merits of the award, they may evaluate issues that have already been decided by the arbitral tribunal. The court's evaluation is not to be seen as an appeal, but as an independent evaluation of whether certain procedural or fundamental principles have been complied with—such as the legal capacity of the parties, the validity of the arbitration agreement, public policy, and arbitrability.

[63] Opinion 1/17 *Comprehensive Economic and Trade Agreement between Canada and the European Union* [2019] EU:C:2019:341 [128]ff.

[64] Case C-284/16 *Slowakische Republik (Slovak Republic) v Achmea BV*, Judgment (6 March 2018) [35]–[37], [45], [49]; Case C-741/19 *Moldova v Komstroy LLC*, Judgment (2 September 2020) [51]–[53], [57]ff, 63; Case C-109/20 *Poland v PL Holdings Sàrl*, Judgement (26 October 2021) [44], [45]; Opinion 1/17 *Comprehensive Economic and Trade Agreement between Canada and the European Union* [2019] EU:C:2019:341 [130]–[135].

PART VI
CROSS-CUTTING ISSUES

28

The Investment Award in a Historical Perspective

Valentina Vadi

I. Introduction

International investment awards are of considerable importance not only for the settlement of a specific dispute but also for the progressive development of international (investment) law. In fact, investment awards are a 'subsidiary means for the determination of the rules of law' as provided in Article 38 of the Statute of the International Court of Justice.

The continuing legal and historical significance of investment awards makes them a timely and topical issue to investigate. International investment law, once considered an 'exotic and highly specialized' domain, is now becoming mainstream.[1] The field has become a key area of international law due to economic globalization and the rise of foreign direct investments. Investment arbitration, or the procedure for resolving disputes between foreign investors and host countries, has evolved into a well-developed field of study in its own right. While valuable scholarly work on investment arbitration has boomed in the past decades,[2] only recently have scholars focused on the history and theory of the field.

International legal historians and international lawyers have mined small episodes, often discovered by chance, while seeking insights into major themes of international legal history.[3] They have investigated individual cases,[4] material

[1] International Law Commission, Fragmentation of International Law: Difficulties Arising from the Diversification and Expansion of International Law, Report of the Study Group (Martti Koskenniemi) UN Doc. A/CN.4/L.682, 13 April 2006 [8].

[2] See eg Katia Fach Gomez, *Key Duties of International Investment Arbitrators: A Transnational Study of Legal and Ethical Dilemmas* (Springer 2019); Katia Yannaca-Small (ed), *Arbitration under International Investment Agreements: A Guide to the Key Issues* (2nd edn, OUP 2018); Walter Mattli and Thomas Dietz (eds), *International Arbitration and Global Governance: Contending Theories and Evidence* (OUP 2014); Michael Waibel and others (eds), *The Backlash against Investment Arbitration: Perceptions and Reality* (Kluwer Law International 2010).

[3] See eg Doreen Lustig, *Veiled Power—International Law and the Private Corporation 1886–1981* (OUP 2021) (weaving together five in-depth case studies: Firestone in Liberia, the Industrialist Trials at Nuremberg, the Anglo-Iranian Oil Company, Barcelona Traction and the emergence of the international investment law regime); VV Veeder, 'From Florence to London via Moscow and New Delhi: How and Why Arbitral Ideas Migrate' (2013) 4 Journal of International Dispute Settlement 139, 156 (narrating historical case studies to discuss the migration of ideas across legal systems); Jan Paulsson, *Denial of Justice in International Law* (CUP 2005) 10 (discussing some historical background).

[4] Ignatio de la Rasilla and Jorge E Viñuales (eds), *Experiments in International Adjudication—Historical Accounts* (CUP 2019); Jason Yackee, 'Investor-State Dispute Settlement at the Dawn of International Investment Law: France, Mauritania, and the Nationalization of the MIFERMA Iron Ore Operations' (2019) 59 American Journal of Legal History 71; Jason Yackee, 'The First Investor-State Arbitration? The Suez Canal Dispute of 1864

Valentina Vadi, *The Investment Award in a Historical Perspective* In: *The Award in International Investment Arbitration*.
Edited by: Katia Fach Gómez and Catharine Titi, Oxford University Press.
DOI: 10.1093/9780191975936.003.0028

objects,[5] the lives and works of individuals, institutional developments,[6] military history events, and hidden materials buried in archives.[7] While the turn to history is new, and its potential is only gradually unfolding, the history of international investment law is certainly growing.[8]

Finding a precise starting point for the history and theory of international investment law is controversial. Choosing a specific point of departure can be unrealistic, overly simplistic, and politically charged because it risks favouring one worldview over another. There is growing awareness that the history of the law governing foreign investments cannot be reduced to single pieces of domestic law; rather, just as multiples histories of international law coexist, multiple histories of international investment law must be investigated and narrated.[9]

Several methods can be selected for writing histories of international investment law: scholars have used contextual approaches (historically contextualizing given legal instruments), critical approaches (questioning received assumptions and comparing different voices and views over given legal historical data), or postcolonial approaches (assuming that the origins of international investment law are rooted within the processes of colonialism) to write histories of international investment law. Global (expressing a new interest in comparative and connected histories),[10] institutional (focusing on the history of relevant institutions), and biographical (focusing on the life and work of international investment law scholars, practitioners, and adjudicators) histories are also valuable approaches.[11]

This chapter contributes to the emerging literature on the history of international investment law by focusing on investment awards and taking a long-term global historical perspective. It thus investigates the historical developments in the use of arbitration to settle international and transnational disputes involving foreign investment. It looks into ideas, rules, or principles found in canonical texts or that can be deduced from relevant events or practices. The chapter's underlying assumption is that 'international

and Some Reflections on the Historiography of International Investment Law' in Stephan W Schill, Christian J Tams, and Rainer Hofmann (eds), *International Investment Law and History* (Edward Elgar Publishing 2018) 70.

[5] Jessie Hohmann, 'Opium as an Object of International Law: Doctrines of Sovereignty and Intervention' in Christina Binder, Mary E Footer, and August Reinisch (eds), *International Law and Select Proceedings of the European Society of International Law* (Hart Publishing 2014) 277.

[6] Antonio R Parra, *The History of ICSID* (2nd edn, OUP 2020); Taylor St John, 'Enriching Law with Political History: A Case Study on the Creation of the ICSID Convention' in Schill, Tams, and Hofmann (n 4) ch 10.

[7] Felipe Ford Cole, 'Race and the History of International Investment Law' (2022) University of Chicago Law Review <https://lawreviewblog.uchicago.edu/2022/03/02/cole-investment/>.

[8] Jenrique Fahner, 'The Contested History of International Investment Law' (2015) 17 International Community Law Review 373; Kate Miles, *The Origins of International Investment Law: Empire, Environment, and the Safeguarding of Capital* (CUP 2013); Charles Lipson, *Standing Guard: Protecting Foreign Capital in the Nineteenth and Twentieth Centuries* (University of California Press 1985).

[9] Martti Koskenniemi, 'Histories of International Law: Significance and Problems for a Critical View' (2013) 27 Temple International and Comparative Law Journal 215.

[10] Sebastian Conrad, *What Is Global History?* (Princeton UP 2017); Maxine Berg (ed), *Writing the History of the Global: Challenges for the Twenty-First Century* (British Academy 2013).

[11] See Ignatio de la Rasilla, *International Law and History—Modern Interfaces* (CUP 2021)(discussing these various approaches).

investment law has a longer history' than is commonly assumed and that 'this history is fundamental to understanding its development'.[12]

When mapping the history of international investment law, the adoption of multiple perspectives and different scales of analysis is particularly appropriate because 'there is no single international legal history; rather, a plurality of international legal histories can be narrated depending on the selected research questions, perspectives, and scales of analysis'.[13] Micro- and macro-histories are complementary and mutually reinforcing: micro-histories focus on the details, whereas macro-histories explore the big picture.[14] Understanding long-term or macro-historical trends and processes in the history of international law necessitates long-term or macro-historical perspectives. Both historians and international lawyers have previously used this long-term perspective.[15] Although not novel, this method aims to provide a bird's-eye view of a variety of complex histories of the interactions between merchants and governments.

Thus, this chapter examines investment awards from a historical standpoint. This chapter is not 'the' history of international investment awards. Rather, it provides 'a' (more or less comprehensive) history of such awards through a series of significant precedents and developments, demonstrating how a consolidated turn to history could enrich the discipline of international investment law and arbitration. This research can help us understand not only the past, but also the present and future directions of investment arbitration. It can also contribute to a better understanding of the contribution of international investment arbitration to international dispute resolution and, more broadly, international peace.

II. Arbitration in Antiquity

Arbitration has a long history and has been used since antiquity.[16] According to Greek mythology, on the summit of mount Ida in Greece, the prince Paris arbitrated a beauty contest among Juno, Athena, and Venus. When Eris, the goddess of strife, threw the golden apple of discord dedicated to the most beautiful goddess into a party, the three attendant goddesses started a quarrel. Paris chose Venus for his fateful award, because she bribed him with the love of the most beautiful woman in the world, Helen of Sparta.[17] Following that momentous award, Paris of Troy kidnapped Helen from her husband King Menelaus of Sparta; and the Achaeans (an ancient Greek population) fought the legendary Trojan War to reclaim Helen. Whether or not the Trojan War

[12] Hélène Ruiz Fabri and Edoardo Stoppioni (eds), *International Investment Law—An Analysis of the Major Decisions* (Hart Publishing 2022).

[13] Valentina Vadi, 'Perspective and Scale in the Architecture of International Legal History' (2019) 30 European Journal of International Law 53.

[14] Valentina Vadi, 'The Power of Scale: International Law and Microhistories' (2018) 46 Denver Journal of International Law and Policy 315.

[15] Fernand Braudel, *La Méditerranée et le Monde Méditerranéen à l'Époque de Philippe II* (Armand Colin 1949); David J Bederman, *International Law in Antiquity* (CUP 2009).

[16] Paula Hodges, 'Keynote Speech by Paula Hodges QC' (2016) 18 Arbitral Women Newsletter 6.

[17] See, *ex multis*, Sandro Botticelli's painting *Il giudizio di Paride* [1485–88], Fondazione Giorgio Cini, Venice.

actually occurred is open to debate; however, as vividly described in Homer's *Iliad*, many consider it historical fact rather than an epic poem. The control of the eastern Aegean Sea was likely the cause of the conflict with the Trojans as the Achaeans sought new territories, either as merchants or as potential conquerors.[18]

Certainly, arbitration prominently featured in ancient Greek laws, providing a more flexible procedure than trial.[19] The historians Thucydides (460–400 BC), Polybius (*c* 200–*c* 118 BC), and Plutarch (46–199 AD) narrate that ancient Greek city-states often submitted their disputes to arbitration. For instance, according to Polybius, after the Battle of Leuctra fought on 6 July 371 BC, when the Thebans claimed the hegemony of the Hellenic peninsula, uncertainty prevailed in the country. On the one hand, the Spartans refused to acknowledge their defeat, trying to retain the hegemony they had previously gained after the Peloponnesian war (431–404 BC). On the other hand, the Thebans did not fully believe their unexpected victory. Reportedly, the Achaeans arbitrated the dispute establishing the new borders.[20] Whether this arbitration really took place remains debated; it certainly did not prevent the Theban leader Epaminondas (*c* 410–362 BC) from invading the Peloponnese twice in the following years.[21]

In parallel, the statesman Demosthenes (384–322 BC) refers to a law governing arbitration among private citizens.[22] In both types of arbitration, the parties could select the arbitrator and the resulting award had a final character.[23] Ancient literary works attest that arbitration was common practice. In *The Arbitration* (Epitrepontes), a comedy written by the playwright Menander (*c* 342–291 BC), an arbitrator (Smikrines) had to settle a dispute between two shepherds.[24] One of them (Daos) found an abandoned child and gave the foundling to another shepherd (Syriskos). However, while Daos wished to keep the valuable token found along with the child for himself, Syriskos argued that the token should stay with the child. After their speeches, the arbitrator decided in favour of Syriskos, and Daos handed over the token. The comedy depicts a typical arbitration. It features all of the necessary components of this dispute resolution mechanism, such as the signing of an arbitration agreement, the selection of an arbitrator, public order, and, last but not least, an award.[25] However, in the comedy, the arbitrator's award was quickly rendered irrelevant: the gradual discovery of the identities of the baby's parents resolved multiple strands of conflict along the way.

Foreign investments have a long history as well. The Phoenician civilization, which flourished in what is now Lebanon, Israel, and Palestine, developed an extensive

18 Barry Strauss, *The Trojan War: A New History* (Simon & Schuster 2006).

19 Edward M Harris, 'Trials, Private Arbitration, and Public Arbitration in Classical Athens' in Cinzia Bearzot and others (eds), *Athenaion Politeiai tra Storia, Politica, e Sociologia* (Edizioni Universitarie di Lettere, Economia, Diritto 2018) 213; Remo Martini, *Diritti Greci* (Zanichelli 2005).

20 John Buckler, 'The Alleged Achaean Arbitration after Leuctra' (1978) 53 Symbolae Osloenses85, 85–86 and 90–91; M Cary, 'The Alleged Achaean Arbitration after Leuctra' (1925) 19 Classical Quarterly 165–66.

21 Buckler (n 20) 94.

22 Anna Magnetto, *Gli Arbitrati Interstatali Greci* (Scuola Normale Superiore 1997); Sheila L Ager, *Interstate Arbitrations in the Greek World 337–90* (University of California Press 1997).

23 Derek Roebuck, *Ancient Greek Arbitration* (Arbitration Press 2001).

24 Alan H Sommerstein, *Menander: Epitrepontes* ('The Arbitration') (Bloomsbury 2021).

25 Piotr Nowaczyk, 'Arbitration Is as Old As Mankind' (27 April 2021) <www.globallawexperts.com/NewsArticle.aspx?PID=2726>.

maritime trade and investment network that lasted millennia (from 1200 BC to 330 BC), making it the dominant commercial power for much of classical antiquity.[26] The Phoenicians built ports, warehouses, markets, and settlements on the Mediterranean Sea's shores in Cyprus, Malta, Sicily, Sardinia, and the Balearic Islands, as well as on North Africa's fertile coasts and the mineral-rich Iberian Peninsula. Phoenician entrepreneurs used to do business in foreign communities by settling there and owning and controlling value-added activities in more than one country.[27] If a promise to pay or deliver goods according to an agreement was not kept, Phoenician settlers could be held liable for the debts of their fellow citizens and expelled.[28] Arbitration facilities were established at ports and markets to facilitate and expedite the resolution of disputes.[29] The Phoenician's complex mercantile network was an early example of what the French historian Fernand Braudel (1902–85) referred to as a 'world economy', that is, an economically interconnected region of the world capable of providing for most of its own needs and dominated by a specific city at different times in history.[30] Phoenician trade and investments, which extended from the Atlantic to the Assyrian Empire, also aided in the exchange of cultures, ideas, and knowledge between major centres of civilization such as Greece, Egypt, and Mesopotamia.

III. The Arbitral Award under Roman Law

While interstate arbitration was an important feature of Hellenic diplomacy, Rome was, occasionally, the arbiter of international disputes 'but never the party seeking arbitration'.[31] While arbitration fostered a sense of community within the wider Hellenic world, as well as a sense of equality among the diverse members of that world, Rome preferred to use other dispute resolution methods in international relations. If an alleged wrong occurred, it requested compensation; and if the other state did not comply, it declared war. Even when Rome agreed to hold arbitrations between disputing parties, it frequently attempted to use it to 'exten[d] her own influence'.[32] Reportedly, 'such disputes were referred to the Senate, which decided the general issue, but sometimes left particular points to a third party with local knowledge for settlement'.[33]

[26] David Collins, *An Introduction to International Investment Law* (CUP 2017) 6.

[27] Karl James Moore and David Charles Lewis, 'Multinational Enterprise in Ancient Phoenicia' (2000) 42 Business History 17.

[28] Taco Terpstra, *Trade in the Ancient Mediterranean: Private Order and Public Institutions* (Princeton UP 2019) ch 2.

[29] Nowaczyk (n 25).

[30] Fernand Braudel, *Civilization and Capitalism, 15th–18th Century*, vol 3 (tr Siân Raynolds, University of California Press 1992).

[31] Edward Bispham, '*Roma Iudex*. Interstate Arbitration and Rome's Mediterranean Hegemony' in *L'Imperium Romanum en Perspective. Les Savoirs d'Empire dans la République Romaine et leur Héritage dans l'Europe Médiévale et Moderne* (Institut des Sciences et Techniques de l'Antiquité 2014) 231.

[32] ibid 231 and 240.

[33] Adrian N Sherwin-White and Antony Spawforth, 'Roman Arbitration' in *Oxford Classical Dictionary* (OUP 2016).

Under domestic Roman law, the parties could opt out of the legal process and refer their dispute to an arbitrator (*arbiter ex compromisso*) to settle.[34] Any 'good man' (*bonus pater familias*) could have been called upon to perform such duty.[35] Although Roman jurists and sources do not describe the arbitral procedure, that is, how arbitration worked in practice, some information can be derived from epigraphic sources that record actual arbitrations, how they were procedurally handled, and how they led to final arbitral awards.[36] Such inscriptions show that disputes could arise between public bodies or communities (*res publicae*), private parties, or even private parties and public bodies.[37] The language of the arbitration could be chosen by the parties. Several arbitrations on boundary disputes between different Dalmatian communities for example took place in provincial languages during the first century, even though the final awards were written in Latin.[38]

The main benefits of arbitration under Roman law were its confidentiality and speed. On the one hand, arbitration did not have to reveal business transaction secrets (*secreta negotii*).[39] On the other hand, the arbitral proceedings were conducted orally, making the procedure 'accessible, understandable, and adaptable to the needs and desires of the disputing parties'.[40]

The arbitrator had to declare the final award orally in presence of both parties or, if they were absent, in presence of their legal representatives.[41] The award was the final and binding determination of parties' rights and obligations: 'It had to finally end all disputes, differences, and uncertainties between the disputing parties'.[42] All arbitral tribunals were formed on an ad hoc basis; they were not permanent tribunals and they ceased to exist as soon as the award was issued.[43] A senior magistrate, the *praetor*, then monitored the enforceability of the award and could apply measures of enforcement.

IV. The Middle Ages and the Renaissance

For a long time, international lawyers hypothesized the existence of a medieval *lex mercatoria*, a law merchant created by traders for traders that was the same everywhere and at all times.[44] Such a romantic view of a medieval *lex mercatoria* influenced the emergence of the modern *lex mercatoria* doctrine after the Second World War,

[34] Peter G Stein, 'Arbitration Under Roman Law' (1974) 41 Arbitration: The International Journal of Arbitration, Mediation, and Dispute Management 203.
[35] Derek Roebuck and Bruno de Loynes de Fumichon, *Roman Arbitration* (Holo Books 2004).
[36] Ivan Milotić, 'An Outline of the Arbitral Procedure in Roman Law' (2013) Forum Historiae Juris 1, 4.
[37] ibid 14.
[38] ibid 6.
[39] ibid.
[40] ibid 7.
[41] ibid 15.
[42] ibid 4.
[43] ibid 15.
[44] Harold J Berman and Colin Kaufman, 'The Law of International Commercial Transactions (*Lex Mercatoria*)' (1978) 19 Harvard International Law Journal 221; Harold J Berman, *Law and Revolution: The Formation of the Western Legal Tradition* (Harvard UP 1983) 333.

because 'the proponents of the modern *lex mercatoria* doctrine used the concept not only as historical evidence, but also as the basis of theoretical and political claims of *lex mercatoria* as an autonomous legal system'.[45]

However, historians have questioned the immutable and universal existence of such a law merchant, highlighting the existence of a variety of legal systems and merchants' rights (*iura mercatorum*).[46] In fact, there were various types of foreigners in the Middle Ages, including merchants, pilgrims, diplomats, soldiers, and students, to name a few. Depending on the circumstances and convenience, sovereigns granted various concessions and differential treatment to each of these types of foreigners.[47] Therefore, historians have investigated and compared various practices and institutions in different locations.[48] By 'overcom[ing] the dogma of a widespread and uniform *lex mercatoria* ... [t]he perspective broadens'; the loss of a clear pattern is offset by the gain of previously suppressed colourful details.[49]

Arbitration was certainly used in a variety of different contexts.[50] Sovereigns and other prominent figures have been called upon to arbitrate international disputes since antiquity. This practice continued into the Middle Ages, when arbitration was widely used to settle interstate disputes. As the popes became increasingly involved in European power politics, they were regularly called upon to act as arbitrators.[51] The Republic of Venice also frequently used arbitration to settle international disputes.[52]

Throughout the Middle Ages, merchants benefitted from certain jurisdictional or procedural privileges including 'the right to have disputes adjudicated according to a more summary procedure'.[53] They often preferred arbitration to domestic courts.[54] For example, because the Ottoman Empire was a pluralistic and multi-ethnic society, it was tolerant of non-Muslim foreigners, who were granted the freedom to practice their religion, as well as 'the autonomy to live in accordance with their customs and to apply their own laws'.[55] Furthermore, the Sultan granted specific concessions, known

[45] Mert Elcin, *Lex Mercatoria in International Arbitration* (EUI 2012) 3.

[46] Albrecht Cordes, 'The Search for a Medieval *Lex Mercatoria*' Oxford University Comparative Law Forum 5 <ouclf.law.ox.ac.uk>; Oliver Volckart and Antje Mangels, 'Are the Roots of the Modern *Lex Mercatoria* Really Medieval?' (1999) 65 Southern Economic Journal 427.

[47] Tiziana Ferreri, 'Regime Giuridico dello Straniero e Albinaggio: il Contributo della Canonistica alla *Scientia Iuris* dell'Età Intermedia' (2019) 16 Historia & Ius 1, 7.

[48] See eg Regina Grafe and Oscar Gelderblom, 'The Rise and Fall of the Merchant Guilds: Re-thinking the Comparative Study of Commercial Institutions in Premodern Europe' (2010) 40 Journal of Interdisciplinary History 477.

[49] Cordes (n 46).

[50] Derek Roebuck, *Early English Arbitration* (Arbitration Press 2008).

[51] Giorgio Balladore Pallieri and Giulio Vismara (eds), *Acta Pontificia Juris Gentium Usque ad Annum MCCCIV* (Vita e Pensiero 1946).

[52] Fabrizio Marrella, *Alle Origini dell'Arbitrato Commerciale Internazionale. L'Arbitrato a Venezia tra Medioevo ed Età Moderna* (CEDAM 2001); Andrea Savio, 'Il Ruolo di Mediatore. Venezia tra Autoctoni e Forestieri: i Morlacchi nel Secondo Cinquecento in Istria' (2014) 22 Acta Histriae 265–68 (narrating the mediation Venetian authorities played between local communities and Slavic migrants in Istria in the second half of the sixteenth century).

[53] Emily Kadens, 'The Medieval Law Merchant: The Tyranny of a Construct' (2015) 7 Journal of Legal Analysis 251–89, 253.

[54] ibid 280.

[55] Mariya Tait Slys, *Exporting Legality—The Rise and Fall of Extraterritorial Jurisdiction in the Ottoman Empire and China* (Graduate Institute Publications 2014) ch 3.

as capitulations, to non-Muslims conducting business within his territories in order to make them more appealing for trade. Foreigners were generally granted jurisdictional privileges and immunities as a result of these capitulations.[56] Foreign representatives, such as consuls, could settle cases among foreigners. Thus, the Ottoman capital, Istanbul, had large communities of merchants from Genoa, Venice, and Florence, as well as Iberian Jews and Armenians in the early sixteenth century.[57] Suleiman the Magnificent (1494–1566) signed a 1535 treaty with Francis I of France (1494–1547) to grant traders reciprocal commercial privileges.[58]

Merchant communities, also known as trade diasporas, played an important role in economic growth in Europe during the early modern period.[59] As 'nations of socially interdependent, but spatially dispersed communities',[60] they served not only an economic but also a political function as cultural brokers.[61] Such trading communities 'often centred around a *fondaco* (from the Greek *pandocheion* by way of the Arabic *funduk*), a combination between a warehouse and inn', where foreign merchants were allowed to live, to trade, and to pray, subject to local supervision and taxation all along the Mediterranean basin.[62]

For instance, foreigners could not own real estate in Venice.[63] Rather, different fondaci hosted foreign merchants in the city. The most important were those for the Turks (now hosting the Museum of Natural History) and the Germans (the *Fondaco dei Tedeschi*, now hosting a department store).[64] The Fondaco dei Tedeschi was established in the early thirteenth century next to the Rialto bridge, then Venice's financial centre and housed several hundred northern traders.[65] All the merchants arriving from the territories of the Holy Roman Empire had to reside there. They would find lodging on the upper floors and storage facilities for their goods, mainly precious metals but also fur, wool, and leather, in the building. The frescoed decoration of the building's facade demonstrates that the settlement of commercial disputes was deemed essential to the prosperous and peaceful relations between foreign traders and locals: painted by Titian (*c* 1488–1576) and Giorgione (1478–1510), it depicted Justice.

[56] Tijl Vanneste, *Intra-European Litigation in Eighteenth-Century Izmir—The Role of the Merchants' Style* (Brill 2022) ch 1.

[57] Maurits H Van den Boogerts, 'Merchants and Global Connections' in Shirine Hamadeh and Çiğdem Kafescioğlu (eds), *A Companion to Early Modern Istanbul* (Brill 2021) 233.

[58] Sarah M Alshahrani, 'What Should We Know about the Origins of International Investment Law?' (2020) 48 International Journal of Legal Information 122, 124.

[59] Francesca Trivellato, *The Familiarity of Strangers: The Sephardic Diaspora, Livorno, and Cross-Cultural Trade in the Early Modern Period* (Yale UP 2009).

[60] Victor N Zakharov, Gelina Harlaftis, and Olga Katsiardi-Hering (eds), *Merchant Colonies in the Early Modern Period* (Brill 2012).

[61] Dario Dell'Osa and Stella Lippolis, 'Ragusan Trade Diaspora and the Commerce of Grain in Sixteenth Century: A Network-Institutional Approach' (2021) Business History.

[62] Sophus A Reinert and Robert Fredona, 'Merchants and the Origins of Capitalism', Harvard Business School Working Paper 18-021 (2017) 1, 6.

[63] Maria Fusaro, 'Politics of Justice/Politics of Trade: Foreign Merchants and the Administration of Justice from the Records of Venice's Giudici del Forestier' (2014) Mélanges de l'École Française de Rome—Italie et Méditerranée Modernes et Contemporaines 126, para 14.

[64] Ennio Concina, *Fondaci—Architettura, Arte, e Mercatura tra Levante, Venezia, e Alemagna* (Marsilio 1997).

[65] Reinert and Fredona (n 62) 6.

The judges for foreigners ('giudici del forestier') had jurisdiction over disputes between foreigners and the Republic, Venetian citizens and foreigners, and foreigners themselves.[66] However, foreigners did not have the automatic right to use such a dispute settlement mechanism; rather, the mechanism operated only on the basis of international agreements between Venice and other polities.[67] In other words, Venice granted this privilege to foreigners only when it suited its own commercial interests and submitted the politics of justice to the politics of trade.[68]

V. Modern Period (from the Seventeenth to the Mid-Twentieth Centuries)

In the modern period, the exploration of distant lands and civilizations led to a sharp rise in global trade flows, diplomacy, and cultural interactions. The movement of people, goods, and ideas intensified dramatically during the Age of Exploration. Cartography and navigational instrument advancements resulted in a new mapping of the globe and a new worldview. The world's seas and oceans served as links in dense webs of commercial and cultural exchange, allowing for greater interaction among different polities. Nonetheless, many non-Europeans saw the Age of Exploration as the arrival of foreigners from previously unknown continents, the spread of diseases that decimated populations, and exploitation, conquest, and war. A new international order emerged that increasingly appeared as a competitive and violent stage on which states could grow, decline, and even vanish.[69] Therefore, the age demanded a thorough examination of how the law of nations governed global trade, cultural diversity, and the world's oceans.[70]

Historically, international law did not include clear-cut rules condemning colonization. Whereas conquest has been known to all historic eras, usually entailing alien rule and subjection, colonialism went beyond the mere seizure of foreign land instead involving the partitioning of the world among Spain, Portugal, and other powers like Britain, France, and the Netherlands.[71] Colonization took various forms as each conquering nation 'elaborated its specific colonial law'.[72]

On the one hand, 'colonization proliferated and started to acquire features of an ideology ... marked by a belief in the anthropological, cultural, and political superiority of the European powers and their people' in the nineteenth century.[73] Under imperial rule, it resulted in the exploitation of natural, cultural, and human resources.

[66] Fusaro (n 63).
[67] ibid para 10.
[68] ibid para 20
[69] Valentina Vadi, *War and Peace—Alberico Gentili and the Early Modern Law of Nations* (Brill 2021) 273.
[70] Anthony Anghie, *Imperialism, Sovereignty, and the Making of International Law* (CUP 2004) 14.
[71] Jörn Axel Kämmerer, 'Colonialism' in *Max Planck Encyclopedia of Public International Law* (OUP 2018) para 1.
[72] ibid para 17.
[73] ibid para 1.

Colonialism changed geographical spaces and physical landscapes by preventing 'rural communities from practicing their centuries-old subsistence farming methods' which led to deforestation, environmental degradation, and, in some cases, desertification.[74] The colonial paradigm of natural exploitation entailed a shift towards overspecialization, agriculture intensification, and long-chain models where food was sold over great distances. Such specialty and intensity of agricultural production disrupted traditional lifestyle, reduced biodiversity, and affected soil fertility, thus reducing colonies' ability to withstand crises.[75] Cultural artifacts were removed from the civilizations that produced them and placed in Western museums.[76]

Many communities were 'categorized and treated as inferior, "uncivilised", and incapable of self-government'.[77] According to Luigi Nuzzo, '[t]he territory of the colony was neither part of the territory of the metropole nor part of a foreign state, but floated somewhere between the two'.[78] When colonial powers enacted colonial laws to govern the populations of their overseas territories, these domestic laws treated colonial populations differently than citizens[79] and markedly differed from metropole law. While some native legal traditions were accommodated by colonial law, the latter also contained many special norms and authoritarian rules.[80] In other words, colonial laws developed unjust legal, political, and economic orders.

On the other hand, the colonizers limited the use of international law, as they had traditionally conceived it, 'to the Christian nations or to countries whose civilizations [they] sufficiently respected' or for various reasons they had failed to conquer.[81] As a result, they maintained diplomatic ties with the African nations bordering the Mediterranean Sea, the Middle East nations, and—starting in the 1840s—Persia (present-day Iran), Siam (now Thailand), China, Korea, and Japan. They typically used diplomacy and force to protect their assets in uncolonized countries.[82]

For instance, China had become the dominant culture of East Asia and a major civilization in the centuries preceding its encounter with the West. Nonetheless, during the nineteenth and early twentieth centuries, it signed unequal treaties with various Western powers (including the British Empire, France, the German Empire, and the United States), the Russian Empire, and the Japanese Empire.[83] The treaties, which

[74] Anurasha Varanasi, 'How Colonialism Spawned and Continues to Exacerbate the Climate Crisis' Columbia Climate School News, 21 September 2022 <https://news.climate.columbia.edu/2022/09/21/how-colonialism-spawned-and-continues-to-exacerbate-the-climate-crisis/>; Antony Anghie, 'The Heart of My Home: Colonialism, Environmental Damage, and the Nauru Case' (1993) 34 Harvard International Law Journal 445.

[75] Valentina Vadi, *Cultural Heritage in International Economic Law* (Brill 2023) 239.

[76] Jos Van Beurden, 'How to Break the Deadlock in the Debate about Colonial Acquisitions?' in Valentina Vadi and Hildegard Schneider (eds), *Art, Cultural Heritage, and the Market—Ethical and Legal Issues* (Springer 2014) 165.

[77] Fuad Zarbiyev, 'Decolonization and International Law' (2021) 10 Global Challenges.

[78] Luigi Nuzzo, 'Colonial Law' in *European History Online* (EGO) (Leibniz Institute of European History 2012) 8.

[79] Martti Koskenniemi, 'Colonial Laws: Sources, Strategies, and Lessons?' (2016) 18 Journal of the History of International Law 248, 248.

[80] Nuzzo (n 78) 8.

[81] ibid 3.

[82] Alshahrani (n 58).

[83] Dong Wang, *China's Unequal Treaties: Narrating National History* (Lexington Books 2005).

were frequently signed after a military defeat or the threat of an invasion, contained one-sided terms that required China to cede land, pay reparations, open treaty ports, give up tariff autonomy, legalize the trade in opium, and grant extraterritorial privileges to foreign nationals. Therefore, China regarded such treaties as unequal because they were imposed on it after a war rather than negotiated by nations treating one another as equals, and because they infringed on China's sovereign rights.[84]

For example, British traders and the East India Company had been exporting and smuggling opium into China since the seventeenth century. However, the illicit trade increased significantly in the 1820s, despite imperial decrees that had forbidden opium on moral grounds.[85] Chinese authorities even wrote to Queen Victoria (1819–1901) in an effort to voice their displeasure with the lack of respect that foreign traders showed for their country's law, after making numerous, unsuccessful appeals to foreign powers to stop their illegal commerce.[86] When local officials finally seized and destroyed foreign opium stocks in Canton (currently Guangzhou), they were accused of damaging Great Britain's 'governmental property', igniting the infamous Opium Wars.

According to the terms of the Treaty of Nanking (now Nanjing), which was signed after the First Opium War (1839–42), China paid the British an indemnity, ceded the territory of Hong Kong, and granted British traders, who were previously only permitted to trade at one port, permission to trade at five ports, including Shanghai.[87] British citizens in China were granted extraterritorial rights under supplementary treaties. Accordingly, they were not subject to Chinese law and jurisdiction; rather, they were subject to the English common law and the jurisdiction of their own consuls. The regime of extraterritoriality exempted not just British diplomats but also British citizens from Chinese law and jurisdiction without granting the Chinese in the West reciprocal privileges.[88] Such concessions also included a most-favoured-nation clause, which guaranteed Britain all privileges granted to any other foreign power by China.[89]

The Treaty of Tientsin (now Tianjin), which followed China's defeat by Britain and France in the Second Opium War (1856–60), gave foreigners permission to travel in China's interior and spread their faith, opened the Yangtze River to Western navigation, and legalized the trade of opium.[90] Since the 1930s, China has renegotiated all of these treaties on equal terms, reaffirming its tariff autonomy and withdrawing extraterritoriality. The British returned Hong Kong's sovereignty to China in 1997.

Nowadays, 'international law has ... facilitated the accession to independence of a significant number of former colonies', thus delegitimizing colonialism and promoting

[84] Immanuel Hsu, *The Rise of Modern China*(OUP 1970) 239.

[85] Tait Slys (n 55) ch IV.

[86] ibid.

[87] Treaty of Nanking (now Nanjing), signed on 29 August 1842, ratifications exchanged on 20 June 1843, *London Gazette* 7 November 1843, 3597; Kenneth Pletcher, 'Unequal Treaty', *Encyclopedia Britannica* (2019); John Darwin, *After Tamerlane: The Global History of Empire* (Allen Lane 2007) 271.

[88] Li Chen, 'Law, Empire, and Historiography of Modern Sino-Western Relations: A Case Study of the Lady Hughes Controversy in 1784' (2009) 27 Law and History Review 1, 1.

[89] Supplementary Treaty of Bogue (now Humen), signed 8 October 1843, 95 Consolidated Treaty Series 323.

[90] Treaty of Peace, Friendship, and Commerce, between Great Britain and China, signed at Tientsin (now Tianjin) 26 June 1858, ratifications exchanged at Peking (now Beijing) 24 October 1860.

decolonization. Nonetheless, the field is still 'largely shaped by the "colonial matrix", perpetuates an unequal distribution of power and resources, and has even retained some of its colonialist vocabulary ("*terra nullius*", "civilized nations", etc.)'.[91] Therefore, the question of whether it has redeemed itself remains open.

The impact of colonization can still be felt today in how the world is perceived, understood, and governed.[92] For example, by encouraging the adoption of uniform rules mainly based on Western models, several international treaties still presuppose a technical, non-cultural understanding of law. This approach undervalues the international community's rich cultural diversity and raises the question of whether uniform rules can function at all in the Global South.

Some scholars have identified colonial legacies in international rules governing the protection of foreign investments.[93] Kate Miles, for examples, traces the origins of international investment law to the quest for imperial control over the resources and peoples of the colonized world. Miles claims that the 'history of colonialism, the calculated, often brutal, use of force, and the manipulation of legal doctrines to acquire commercial benefits ... drove the construction of international investment law' from the seventeenth to the mid-twentieth centuries.[94] According to this viewpoint, international law was solely concerned with protecting investors, while host countries were unable to invoke the rule of international law to address damage caused by foreign investors.[95] Similarly, Anthony Anghie contends that the economic exploitation and cultural subordination that accompanied colonialism were foundational to the discipline of international investment law.[96]

Certainly, the contemporary language of international investment treaties derives from earlier treaties including treaties of friendship, commerce, and navigation (FCN treaties) that were concluded from the eighteenth century onwards. They were eventually concluded between, on the one hand, a European country and, on the other, third countries after being initially concluded primarily among European countries. These treaties aimed to facilitate trade, navigation, and investment between the states involved and outlined the treatment each country owed the nationals of the other.[97] FCN treaties typically granted most-favoured-nation treatment, national treatment, and fair and equitable treatment, and required compensation in case of expropriation.[98] They also extended to political and military concerns and often ensured freedom of worship and movement.

[91] Zarbiyev (n 77). See also Walter Mignolo and Catherine Walsh, *On Decoloniality—Concepts, Analytics, Praxis* (Duke UP 2018) 10.

[92] Ralf Michaels, 'Das rechtliche Erbe der Kolonialzeit' (2021) 4 Max Planck Forschung 16.

[93] See generally Miles (n 8).

[94] ibid 32.

[95] ibid.

[96] Anghie (n 70).

[97] Andreas Paulus, 'Treaties of Friendship, Commerce, and Navigation' in *Max Planck Encyclopedia of Public International Law* (OUP 2011) para 1.

[98] Wolfgang Alschner, 'Americanization of the BIT Universe: The Influence of Friendship, Commerce, and Navigation (FCN) Treaties on Modern Investment Treaty Law' (2013) 5 Goettingen Journal of International Law 455, 457; Kenneth J Vandevelde, 'A Brief History of International Investment Agreements' (1995) 12 University of California Davis 157, 158–59.

The United States adopted a long series of FCN treaties, mainly to secure economic and political support from more powerful states. The state viewed its early FCN treaties as essential to its own success as an independent nation.[99] The first treaty of this type that the US concluded with France was also the first international instrument to formally recognize the independence of the United States. With time, these treaties' priorities changed. The United States sought to add increasingly specific property protection clauses in its FCN treaties as the volume and scope of its investments overseas increased.[100]

However, these treaties lacked methods of enforcement or dispute resolution. Therefore, diplomacy and military force were the primary means of protecting foreign capital. Nonetheless, public and private actors responded to the increasingly complex entanglements of interests by setting up transnational arbitration mechanisms in concession agreements. The relationship between the state on the one hand and foreign investors on the other was never an easy one, and arbitration was used 'to navigate novel and complex disputes'.[101]

For instance, several concession agreements signed by Ecuador and foreign companies at the end of the nineteenth century included investor-state arbitration as the dispute settlement mechanism.[102] Ecuador needed international investments and technology transfers in order to develop a modern railway system due to the gigantic proportions of the plan and the geographic challenge of building a railway 3000 metres above sea level. The project thus had a significant ambition as it aimed to foster political and economic integration, modernization, and social development.[103] Ecuador thus signed concession contracts which generally required the completion of a given railway segment within a decade and granted exploitation rights for a period of nearly a century. These concession contracts generally provided for arbitration to resolve disputes between the parties.[104]

VI. The Twentieth Century

Early disputes were brought before mixed claims commissions, bodies consensually established to settle claims between citizens of different states, between citizens of one state and citizens of another state, or between the states themselves.[105] Later, the

[99] John F Coyle, 'The Treaty of Friendship, Commerce, and Navigation in the Modern Era' (2013) 51 Columbia Journal of Transnational Law 302, 307.

[100] ibid 307.

[101] Francis Calvert Boorman, 'Developments in the History of Arbitration: A Past for the Present? (2022) 4 Amicus Curiae 109, 124.

[102] Hernán Pérez Loose, 'Algunos Precedentes Históricos del Arbitraje Privado-Público' (2018) 22 Juris Dictio 19, 20.

[103] ibid 24.

[104] ibid 21.

[105] Frédéric Mégret, 'Mixed Claim Commissions and the Once Centrality of the Protection of Aliens' in de la Rasilla and Viñuales (n 4) ch 6; Annelise Riles, 'The View from the International Plane: Perspective and Scale in the Architecture of Colonial International Law' (1995) 6 Law and Critique 39. See also *Benson Robert Henry (United States) v Great Britain (Fijian Land Claims)* (1923) 6 RIAA 100–04 (discussed by Riles).

Permanent Court of International Justice, and its successor, the International Court of Justice, received referrals for more disputes.[106] The resulting jurisprudence has had a substantial impact on the evolution of international (investment) law; and certain pivotal decisions remain significant today.

The *Neer* case exemplifies the enduring legacy of this diverse jurisprudence.[107] In this instance, armed men killed US citizen Paul Neer who worked as a mine superintendent in Mexico. After his death, his wife and daughter, L Fay H and Pauline E Neer, sought US diplomatic protection, claiming that Mexican authorities lacked due diligence in their investigations. Although the claim was dismissed, the case helped define the customary law minimum standard of treatment, or the floor below which state behaviour would be unacceptable to the international community. Such a standard continues to protect investors from egregious/shocking misconduct.

Most disputes relied on customary law or general principles of international law as treaty law was scarce at the time. In the *Goldenberg* case, for example, the German–Romanian Commission held that respect for foreign private property was one of the general principles of international law (*principes généraux admis par le droit des gens*).[108] If state authorities could seize foreign private property for public purposes (*motifs d'utilité publique*) during a war, they still had to pay fair compensation (*indemnité equitable*).

Other awards used equity to settle investor-state disputes, confirming the state's authority to expropriate foreign property upon payment of compensation.[109] For instance, in a 1920 case involving Portugal's expropriation of religious properties previously held by French, British, and Spanish citizens, the arbitral tribunal generally upheld Portugal's measures while requiring compensation and determining its amount based on equity (*ex aequo et bono*). More intriguingly, equity enabled the arbitrators to find novel answers to specific legal problems: for example, the arbitral tribunal decided that Ms Marie-Joséphine Dupé would continue to own a women's college while the building maintained its educational vocation. If the building changed its intended use, it would then become public Portuguese property and Ms Dupé would receive compensation.[110]

International economic law was increasingly codified in a number of treaties over the course of the twentieth century. Multilateral treaties such as the General Agreement on Tariffs and Trade governed international trade,[111] and bilateral investment treaties gradually governed foreign direct investments.[112] Three main factors led to this codification process. First, there was a growing understanding of how international

[106] The *ELSI* case, one of the few investment disputes brought before the International Court of Justice, concerned the breach of an FCN treaty. See *Elettronica Sicula SpA (ELSI) (United States of America v Italy)*, Judgment [1989] ICJ Rep 15.

[107] *L F H Neer and Pauline Neer (USA) v Mexico*, US–Mexico Claims Commission (1926) 4 RIAA 60–66.

[108] *Affaire Goldenberg (Allemagne contre Roumanie)* (1928) 2 RIAA 901, 909.

[109] *Affaire des Propriétés Religieuses (France, Royaume-Uni, Espagne contre Portugal)* (1920) 1 RIAA 7.

[110] For more on the use of equity in the settlement of international disputes, see generally Catharine Titi, *The Function of Equity in International Law* (OUP 2021).

[111] General Agreement on Tariffs and Trade, 30 October 1947, 55 UNTS 194.

[112] Coyle (n 99) 310.

trade and investments could foster peaceful and prosperous relations among nations. Second, there was disagreement about how to achieve political, economic, and cultural decolonization. While political decolonization was mainly accomplished through independence movements and the collapse of colonial empires, the question of how to address economic disparities caused by colonialism as well as counter cultural hegemony was more contentious. Former colonies advocated permanent sovereignty over natural resources,[113] a New International Economic Order to end economic colonialism,[114] and the adoption of the Charter of Economic Rights and Duties of States.[115] Fearing that massive foreign direct investments would undermine their sovereignty, newly independent countries demonstrated hostility towards foreign direct investments and implemented significant nationalization programmes. Iran and Libya, for example, nationalized the petroleum sector in 1951 and 1955, respectively. Third, as nationalizations increased, former imperial powers recognized the need for a regime to protect foreign investments.

Bilateral investment treaties (BITs) have given investors direct access to an international arbitral tribunal since the 1960s. The arbitration model is intended to depoliticize disputes.[116] Investor-state arbitration insulates investment disputes from power politics and diplomatic relations between states.[117] By allowing foreigners to sue governments directly, host countries hoped to enhance their credibility and, as a result, encourage foreign direct investment. It is debatable whether the ratification of BITs in general and the inclusion of investor-state dispute settlement in IIAs has contributed to attract foreign direct investment.[118]

The depoliticization of investment disputes is said to benefit all three: foreign investors, host countries, and home countries.[119] First, foreign investors no longer have to rely on the vagaries of diplomatic protection; instead, they can file direct claims and make strategic choices about how the arbitral proceedings are conducted.[120] In this regard, investor-state arbitration can help foreign investors gain access to justice[121] by providing a neutral forum for the resolution of investment disputes.[122] Such access is viewed as necessary to render meaningful the more substantive investment treaty provisions. Second, the depoliticization of investment disputes protects the host state by minimizing foreign state meddling in its internal affairs.[123] It prevents or limits adverse

[113] GA Res 1803 (XVII), Permanent Sovereignty over Natural Resources, 14 December 1962.

[114] GA Res, Declaration on the Establishment of a New International Economic Order, 1 May 1974.

[115] Charter of Economic Rights and Duties of States, GA Res 3281 (xxix), UN GAOR, 29th Sess, Supp No 31 (1974) 50.

[116] Ibrahim FI Shihata, 'Towards a Greater Depoliticization of Investment Disputes: The Role of ICSID and MIGA' (1986) 1 ICSID Review 1, 5.

[117] Sergio Puig, 'No Right without a Remedy: Foundations of Investor-State Arbitration' (2013–14) 35 University of Pennsylvania Journal of International Law 829, 848–53.

[118] Jason Webb Yackee, 'Bilateral Investment Treaties, Credible Commitment, and the Rule of (International) Law: Do BITs Promote Foreign Direct Investment?' (2008) 42 Law & Society Review 805.

[119] Anthea Roberts, 'Triangular Treaties: The Extent and Limits of Investment Treaty Rights' (2015) 56 Harvard International Law Journal 353, 390.

[120] Puig (n 117) 844.

[121] Francesco Francioni, 'Access to Justice, Denial of Justice, and International Investment Law' (2009) 20 European Journal of International Law 729.

[122] Puig (n 117) 846.

[123] Roberts (n 119) 389–90.

diplomatic, economic, and sometimes military pressure from powerful states whose nationals believe they have suffered harm.[124] Third, the depoliticization of investment disputes also protects the home state by removing the need for it to get involved in investor-state conflicts.[125]

Certainly, negotiators of the relevant agreements could not have foreseen the growing use of investment arbitration. They probably believed that the creation of such a dispute settlement mechanism would encourage states to abide by the rules. However, as arbitral tribunals have been used more than initially anticipated, focus has shifted to the distributional effects of arbitral awards.[126] Arbitral tribunals have reviewed host-state conduct in key sectors and many of their awards have determined the boundary between two conflicting values: the legitimate need for state regulation in the pursuit of the public interest on the one hand, and the protection of private interests from state interference on the other.

VII. Concluding Remarks

Contemporary investment arbitrations take place in various locations and concern investments in the Arctic, Americas, Africa, Asia, and Europe.[127] They are conducted by different arbitral tribunals under different international investment treaties and concern various matters and claims. They address questions concerning the organization of economic life and often relate to fundamental state interests and values. Because of the impact they may have on the lives of local communities, exploring the history of arbitration and of resulting awards is fascinating as such scrutiny enables 'to uncover the long-standing and complex relationship between the state and merchants'.[128]

One might legitimately question the relevance of studying ancient norms and awards, given that there is no binding precedent in international (investment) law. Nonetheless, the study of previous awards is useful because patterns of consistent use can and do influence subsequent awards. In fact, while investment arbitrations are not binding on each other, they have become an important source of international investment law. In fact, 'lawyers and arbitrators have introduced history into their debates'.[129] As our understanding of the history of investment arbitration is developing, this chapter has illuminated some areas of this history that have thus far been neglected.

[124] Joost Pauwelyn, 'At the Edge of Chaos? Foreign Investment Law as a Complex Adaptive System' (2014) 29 ICSID Review 372, 404.

[125] Roberts (n 119) 390.

[126] Manfred Elsig, Rodrigo Polanco, and Peter Van den Bossche, 'Introduction—International Economic Dispute Settlement: Demise or Transformation?' in Manfred Elsig, Rodrigo Polanco, and Peter Van den Bossche (eds), *International Economic Dispute Settlement—Demise or Transformation?* (CUP 2021) 1–10.

[127] See eg *Peteris Pildegovics and SIA North Star v Kingdom of Norway*, ICSID Case No ARB/20/11, Request for Arbitration (18 March 2020).

[128] Anne-Charlotte Martineau, 'A Forgotten Chapter in the History of International Commercial Arbitration: The Slave Trade's Dispute Settlement System' (2018) 31 Leiden Journal of International Law 219, 220.

[129] Boorman (n 101) 109.

This examination can provide new perspectives on the past, present, and future of investor-state arbitration and hopefully encourage future research in the field.

International investment awards can be a force of good, in preventing international conflicts and wars. At the same time, they may have obvious flaws. Much work remains to be done to right historical wrongs and make international dispute resolution a more integrated and coherent system that can better serve the public interest.

29

Empirical Dimensions of Investment Awards

Rodrigo Polanco

I. Introduction

The goal of this chapter is to provide an empirical analysis of final awards in investor-state arbitration, using descriptive statistics that include both internal and external elements. Internally, it looks at the number of awards and time to draft them, the number of arbitrators, applicable arbitral rules and treaties, language, length, and outcome of final awards, including the presence of dissenting opinions, the amount of damages awarded in successful cases, and the distribution of costs. We also analyse some external elements of the award, such as the types of claimants and respondents, their geographical distribution and development status, and the economic sector of the investor. Additionally, we examine some background information about the age, gender and nationality of arbitrators, and the transparency of awards.

This chapter is divided into three sections. Following the introduction, section II describes the data set used for this chapter and the methodology used to collect and analyse the data. Section III provides information on the internal elements of the award, and section IV on its external elements, both based on the data and the methodology described. We close with a brief conclusion.

II. Data and Methodology

Our study builds upon existing literature and databases on investor-state dispute settlement.

The data was collected from two primary sources: the UNCTAD Investor-State Dispute Settlement (ISDS) database, which as of October 2022, included information on 1190 treaty-based investor-state arbitration cases (809 of them concluded),[1] and the case database of the International Centre for Settlement of Investment Disputes (ICSID), which on the same date, includes documents and procedural information on 925 cases.[2]

[1] UNCTAD, 'Investment Dispute Settlement Navigator' (October 2022) <https://investmentpolicy.unctad.org/investment-dispute-settlement>. Unless indicated otherwise, all the awards cited in this chapter are available on the UNCTAD ISDS Navigator.

[2] ICSID, 'Cases Database' (October 2022) <https://icsid.worldbank.org/cases/case-database>.

Rodrigo Polanco, *Empirical Dimensions of Investment Awards* In: *The Award in International Investment Arbitration*.
Edited by: Katia Fach Gómez and Catharine Titi, Oxford University Press.
DOI: 10.1093/9780191975936.003.0029

Based on those sources, we compiled a data set complemented by the information freely available in other databases and websites, as well as on paid subscriptions, such as the UNCITRAL Transparency Registry,[3] Investment Arbitration Reporter (IA Reporter),[4] Jus Mundi,[5] the Permanent Court of Arbitration (PCA),[6] Investor-State Law Guide (ISLG),[7] the International Energy Charter,[8] and Juris Arbitration Law.[9] We also reviewed the governmental websites of the respondent states.

In this work, we study final investment awards, understood as the final decision taken in a treaty-based investor-state arbitration.[10] The total number of final awards examined was 552. In compiling this data set, we did not consider decisions taken in arbitration proceedings that were still pending, as their status is either incomplete or susceptible to change.[11] However, we can point out that partial awards and other decisions are publicly available in at least sixty-three more cases. Still, their content does not substantially change the conclusions provided in this chapter, particularly concerning language and length of awards, as well as gender, age, and nationality of arbitrators.

It is also important to note that in this study, we only focus on the awards issued in treaty-based investor-state arbitrations. We have not included arbitral investment awards under contracts or domestic law, as information about them is not consistently available (with the notable exception of the ICSID website), or it has not been recently updated (as it was until 2019 in the PITAD database).[12]

However, the award is not always a single document, and often includes a separate decision on jurisdiction and a decision on merits. In some cases, it may also be decided separately on the amount of the compensation, or costs. Our analysis considers all these decisions as part of the 'award'. We did not examine intermediate decisions (for example, on provisional measures) and procedural orders, which arbitral tribunals commonly issue.

Based on the abovementioned information compiled in a data set, we use descriptive statistics to portray internal and external elements of the award. We consider that an element is 'internal' when it can be found directly in the text of the award (eg the award's length). Conversely, we qualify certain elements concerning awards as 'external' when the data needs to be complemented with information not found in its text (eg arbitrator's age).

[3] UNCITRAL Transparency Registry <www.uncitral.org/transparency-registry/registry/index.jspx>.
[4] IA Reporter <www.iareporter.com/>.
[5] Jus Mundi <https://jusmundi.com/en>.
[6] PCA, 'Cases' <https://pca-cpa.org/en/cases/>.
[7] ISLG <https://new.investorstatelawguide.com/>.
[8] International Energy Charter <www.energychartertreaty.org/cases/list-of-cases/>.
[9] Juris Arbitration Law <https://arbitrationlaw.com/>.
[10] See Catharine Titi, 'What Is an Award? Concept, Content, Drafting, Effects' in Katia Fach Gómez and Catharine Titi (eds), *The Award in Investment Arbitration* (OUP 2024).
[11] According to UNCTAD methodology, a case remains pending if it remains to be decided on jurisdiction, liability (merits), or compensation. For example, if a state is found to have breached one or more IIA obligations (liability) but no award on damages has been issued yet, UNCTAD (n 1).
[12] Daniel Behn and others, 'PITAD Investment Law and Arbitration Database: Version 1.0, Pluricourts Centre of Excellence, University of Oslo' (31 January 2019) <https://pitad.org/index#static/about_pitad>.

III. Internal Elements of the Award

We consider internal elements, those that are contained directly in the text of the award (applicable treaties and arbitral rules, number of arbitrators, language, length, and outcome), or in the arbitral proceedings (number of awards and time to draft them).

A. Number of Awards and Duration

The first treaty-based investor-state arbitration award was issued in 1990, in the *AAPL v Sri Lanka* case, after twenty-nine months of proceedings which started in 1987.[13] Since then, the number of awards issued yearly has increased progressively, with a peak of fifty-eight awards issued in 2019.

The time required by an arbitral tribunal to issue an award has increased over time, but with a high degree of variation across cases. Counting the number of months from the initial date of the constitution of the tribunal[14] until the final award (which is the time during which the arbitrators perform their work), the duration averages forty months, with a minimum of four months[15] and a maximum of 134 months (see Figure 29.1).[16] This outcome is consistent with the findings of prior research,[17] although, in this study, we only focus on the time frame to issue the award and not on the subsequent annulment or judicial review process.

Prior research has detected that cases lost by claimants on jurisdictional grounds take less time than those decided on the merits.[18] Along the same lines, we have found that the proceedings' length is longer on average when the case is decided in favour of the investor (forty-six months) than when it is decided in favour of the state (thirty-five months). This difference is primarily explained by the cases won by the state at the jurisdictional phase.

Most awards are contained in a single document (352 cases, representing 64 per cent of the data set). Bifurcation with separate decisions on jurisdiction and merits is found in 156 cases (around 28 per cent of the data set). Three or more decisions on other fundamental aspects of the dispute are scarce, like those concerning the interpretation of awards (nine cases) or separately determining costs (four cases). Other additional

[13] *Asian Agricultural Products Ltd (AAPL) v Sri Lanka*, ICSID Case No ARB/87/3, Award (27 June 1990).

[14] Arbitrations conducted under the 2017 Arbitration Rules of the Stockholm Chamber of Commerce (SCC), the time was counted since the case was referred to the tribunal after the advance payment on costs pursuant to Article 22 of the SCC Arbitration Rules.

[15] In *RSM Production Corporation and others v Grenada*, ICSID Case No ARB/10/6, and *OKKV (OKKB) and others v Kyrgyz Republic*.

[16] In *Suez, Sociedad General de Aguas de Barcelona, SA and Vivendi Universal, SA v Argentina (II)*, ICSID Case No ARB/03/19.

[17] Matthew Hodgson, Yarik Kryvoi, and Daniel Hrcka, '2021 Empirical Study: Costs, Damages and Duration in Investor-State Arbitration' (June 2021) <https://www.biicl.org/documents/136_isds-costs-damages-duration.pdf>; José Manuel Álvarez Zárate and others, 'Duration of Investor-State Dispute Settlement Proceedings' (2020) 21 Journal of World Investment & Trade 300.

[18] Álvarez Zárate and others (n 17).

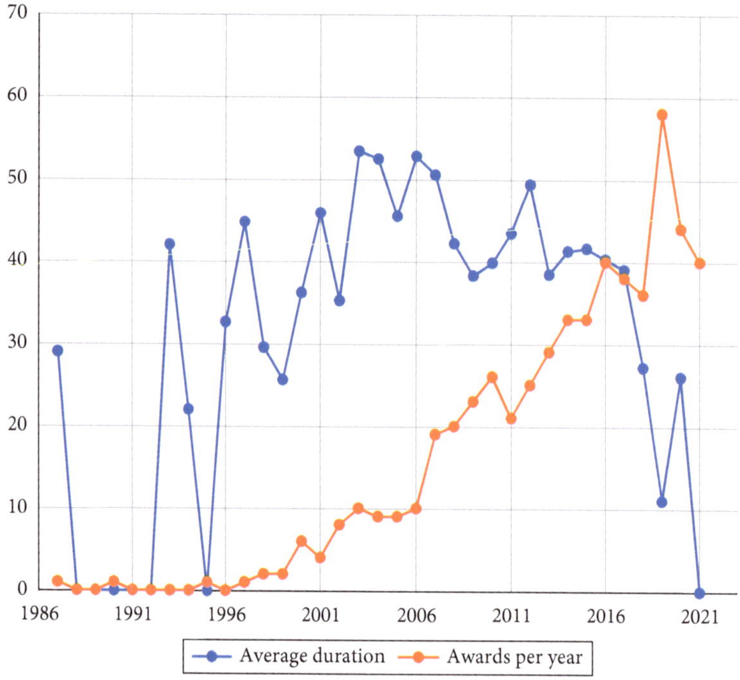

Figure 29.1 Awards per year and their average time frame
Source: Author's elaboration based on UNCTAD (n 1).

decisions may refer to topics such as the quantum of compensation, the rectification of awards, and preliminary objections to arbitration.

B. Number of Arbitrators, Applicable Rules, and Applicable Treaties

The overwhelming majority of awards are issued by a tribunal composed of three arbitrators (543 cases), which is how tribunals are nearly always constituted.[19] However, exceptionally, awards are made by sole arbitrators.

Up to now, we know of nine awards issued by a single arbitrator in treaty-based investor-state arbitration. Notably, three have been brought by the same natural persons against Moldova.[20] Disputing parties seem to rely on the traditional set-up of three arbitrators, with each party appointing at least one of them, even though the

[19] Rudolf Dolzer, Ursula Kriebaum, and Christoph Schreuer, *Principles of International Investment Law* (OUP 2022) 401.

[20] *Philippe Gruslin v Malaysia* (II), ICSID Case No ARB/99/3 (Gavan Griffith); *Iurii Bogdanov, Agurdino-Invest Ltd and Agurdino-Chimia JSC v Moldova* (I) (Giuditta Cordero Moss); *Malaysian Historical Salvors, SDN, BHD v Malaysia*, ICSID Case No ARB/05/10 (Michael Hwang); *Pantechniki SA Contractors & Engineers v Albania*, ICSID Case No ARB/07/21 (Jan Paulsson); *Yury Bogdanov v Moldova* (III), SCC Case No 114/2009 (Bo GH Nilsson); *Yuri Bogdanov and Yulia Bogdanova v Moldova* (IV) SCC Case No 091/2012 (Bengt Sjövall); *Inversión y Gestión de Bienes, IGB, SL and IGB18 Las Rozas, SL v Spain*, ICSID Case No ARB/12/17 (Rodrigo Oreamuno Blanco); *Kristof De Sutter, Peter De Sutter, DS 2 SA and Polo Garments Majunga SARL v Madagascar* (I) (Bart Legum); *Robert Rogers, Ronald Rogers and Dream House v Egypt*, PCA Case No 2019-27 (Nabil Antaki).

average duration of a sole arbitrator's proceeding is notably shorter (an average of fifteen months, compared to forty months in regular cases).

Following the general trend of applicable arbitral rules in these cases, 50 per cent of the existing awards have been issued in proceedings following ICSID Arbitration Rules (276 cases) and 31 per cent under UNCITRAL Arbitration Rules (172 cases). They are followed from a considerable distance by ICSID Additional Facility Arbitration Rules (44 cases, 8 per cent), Arbitration Rules of the Stockholm Chamber of Commerce (SCC) (38 cases, 7 per cent), and ICC Rules of Arbitration (15 cases, 3 per cent).

The overwhelming majority of existing awards result from arbitrations brought under bilateral investment treaties (BITs), representing 81 per cent of the total (449 cases). Yet the international investment agreements (IIAs) that have been applied more frequently are the Energy Charter Treaty (74 cases, 13 per cent) and the North American Free Trade Agreement (NAFTA) (40 cases, 7 per cent).

According to UNCTAD, among the breaches of IIAs provisions alleged and found, we find, in the first place, fair and equitable treatment, international minimum standard of treatment (including denial of justice claims) in 168 awards; indirect expropriation (73 awards); direct expropriation (44 awards); arbitrary, unreasonable, or discriminatory measures (40 awards); full protection and security, or similar standards (24); and umbrella clauses (20 awards).[21]

C. Language

Awards follow the language of the proceedings, which in the large majority of the cases is English: 57 per cent of the awards are only available in English (314 cases), and additionally, we also find several awards are both in English and Spanish (114 cases, 21 per cent). A few are also available in French (nine cases) and Russian (one case). Awards in a language other than English—or without an English translation—are truly exceptional. In our data set, we find 31 in Spanish, 10 in French, and 3 in Russian, which in total only represent around 8 per cent of known awards.

As it has been pointed out in prior research, English is definitely the lingua franca of investor-state arbitration and international arbitration in general.[22] However, looking at the universe of known awards, we can find other factors that may also explain this language choice.

First, an important number of claimants are from home states where the official language is English. We find in our data set 194 cases, representing 35 per cent of awards. In only 42 cases, both claimants and respondents share English as one of their common

[21] UNCTAD (n 1).

[22] Andrea K Bjorklund and others, 'The Diversity Deficit in International Investment Arbitration' (2020) 21 Journal of World Investment & Trade 410; Daniel Greineder, 'Arbitrators Don't Speak Esperanto: The Difficulties and Dominance of English as a Procedural Language in Arbitration' (*Kluwer Arbitration Blog*, 7 November 2021) <http://arbitrationblog.kluwerarbitration.com/2021/11/07/arbitrators-dont-speak-esperanto-the-difficulties-and-dominance-of-english-as-a-procedural-language-in-arbitration/>.

official languages. In contrast, claimants come from French, Spanish or Russian-speaking countries in only 44, 39, and 11 cases, respectively.

Second, English is often chosen as a common language when both parties have a different language, particularly for disputes involving not Spanish or French-speaking parties. If both parties have a common language, the awards and the proceedings will often be in that language. For example, that happened in *Convial Callao v Peru*, where both parties had the Spanish language in common, even if only one of the arbitrators was a native Spanish speaker (Eduardo Zuleta).[23] However, sharing a common language is not always a guarantee that arbitration will be in that language. See, for example, *Al-Kharafi v Libya and others*, where both parties and all tribunal members are Arabic speakers. However, the award is publicly available in English.[24] Likewise, in *Almasryia v Kuwait*, the common language of the parties is Arabic, but the award and the proceedings are in English, which is not the mother tongue of any of the arbitrators.[25] The same happens in *Agility v Iraq*.[26] Likewise, in *Manolium-Processing v Belarus*, both parties were Russian speakers, but the award and the proceedings were conducted in English, as only one of the arbitrators was fluent in Russian (Stanimir Alexandrov).[27] One plausible explanation behind this is probably to improve the chances of enforcement of awards in other jurisdictions.

Third, the language of the arbitrators seems to be the leading issue. For example, in *Eutelsat v Mexico*, the language of the proceedings and the award is Spanish, which was the language of the defendant and the three arbitrators (even though the claimant was French).[28] In *LESI v Algeria*, the award is available in French, which is the arbitrator's language but not that of the parties (Italian and Arabic).[29] In *MMEA and AHSI v Senegal*, the award is in French, the common language of the respondent and all the tribunal members (although claimants are from the Netherlands and the United Kingdom).[30]

Fourth, an English translation is often provided even if the award is in another language. For example, in *Olguin v Paraguay*, both the Decision on Jurisdiction and the Award, initially written in Spanish, were translated into English, although both parties and the majority of the tribunal were Spanish speakers (except for Brazilian Francisco Rezek).[31] However, translations are not always available. For example, in *Pey Casado and Allende Foundation v Chile*, the decisions on the original proceeding were issued in both French (the language of the majority of the arbitral tribunal's members) and Spanish (the common language of the disputing parties). However, often an English

[23] *Convial Callao SA and CCI—Compañía de Concesiones de Infraestructura SA v Peru*, ICSID Case No ARB/10/2, Award (21 May 2013).

[24] *Mohamed Abdulmohsen Al-Kharafi & Sons Co v Libya and others*, Award (22 March 2013).

[25] *Almasryia for Operating and Maintaining Touristic Construction Co LLC v Kuwait*, ICSID Case No ARB/18/2, Award (1 November 2019).

[26] *Agility Public Warehousing Company KSC v Iraq*, ICSID Case No ARB/17/7, Award (22 February 2021).

[27] *OOO Manolium-Processing v Belarus*, PCA Case No 2018-06, Award (22 June 2021).

[28] *Eutelsat SA v Mexico*, ICSID Case No ARB(AF)/17/2, Award (15 September 2021).

[29] *LESI, SpA and Astaldi, SpA v Algeria*, ICSID Case No ARB/05/3), Award (12 November 2008).

[30] *Menzies Middle East and Africa SA and Aviation Handling Services International Ltd v Senegal*, ICSID Case No ARB/15/21, Award (5 August 2016).

[31] *Eudoro Armando Olguín v Paraguay*, ICSID Case No ARB/98/5, Award (26 July 2001).

translation of such decisions was provided. A significant change occurred in the second annulment proceeding, where all publicly available decisions were written in English and French, not in Spanish.[32] The award in the related case *Pey Casado and others v Chile* is only available in English, although the languages of the proceedings allegedly were English, Spanish, and French (although none of the arbitrators was a native Spanish speaker).[33]

Finally, sometimes the language choice is difficult to explain. In *Heemsen v Venezuela*, the chosen language was Spanish, even though the claimant was German and only one of the arbitrators was a native Spanish speaker.[34] Likewise, in *EuroGas and Belmont v Slovakia*, the award and the proceedings are in English (the common language of US and Canadian claimants), even though all arbitrators are French speakers.[35] Similarly, in *Cyprus Popular Bank v Greece*, the award and proceedings were in English, but both parties were Greek speakers, while most of the tribunals were non-native English speakers.[36]

All or some of these reasons could play a role in determining the language of the award. However, here we need a couple of important caveats: using the 'formal' nationality of claimants can be deceptive on occasions, especially concerning legal entities, which can engage in nationality planning and even become foreign investors in their own country.[37] Lastly, international arbitrators are often fluent in several languages, so judging the choice of language for the proceedings solely based on their mother tongue may be misleading.

D. Extension

If we analyse the length of awards per year, we can conclude that they have become increasingly protracted, with a peak of 252 pages on average in the decisions made in 2014 (see Figure 29.2).

Currently, the largest known award is in the *Tethyan Cooper v Pakistan* case (629 pages),[38] which, together with the decisions on jurisdiction and liability and the decision on the respondent's application to dismiss the claims in the same case, makes a total of 1141 pages.[39] In contrast, the shortest award seems to be the one in *Swembalt v*

[32] ICSID, Case Details, *Víctor Pey Casado and President Allende Foundation v Chile*, ICSID Case No ARB/98/2 <https://icsid.worldbank.org/cases/case-database/case-detail?CaseNo=ARB/98/2>.

[33] *President Allende Foundation, Víctor Pey Casado and Coral Pey Grebe v Chile*, PCA Case No 2017-30, Award (28 November 2019).

[34] *Enrique Heemsen and Jorge Heemsen v Venezuela*, PCA Case No 2017-18, Award (29 October 2019).

[35] *EuroGas Inc and Belmont Resources Inc v Slovakia*, ICSID Case No ARB/14/14, Award (18 August 2017).

[36] *Cyprus Popular Bank Public Co Ltd v Greece*, ICSID Case No ARB/14/16, Award (15 April 2021).

[37] Rodrigo Polanco, *The Return of the Home State to Investor-State Disputes: Bringing Back Diplomatic Protection?* (CUP 2019) 275.

[38] *Tethyan Copper Company Pty Limited v Pakistan*, ICSID Case No ARB/12/1, Award (12 July 2019).

[39] In *Georg Gavrilovic and Gavrilovic doo v Croatia*, ICSID Case No ARB/12/39, the award dated 26 July 2018 has formally 757 pages, but almost half of the text is made of annexures including spreadsheets. Similarly, the award in *Bernhard von Pezold and others v Zimbabwe*, ICSID Case No ARB/10/15, dated 28 July 2015 has a total of 647 pages, but more than 300 pages are copies of the procedural orders in the same case.

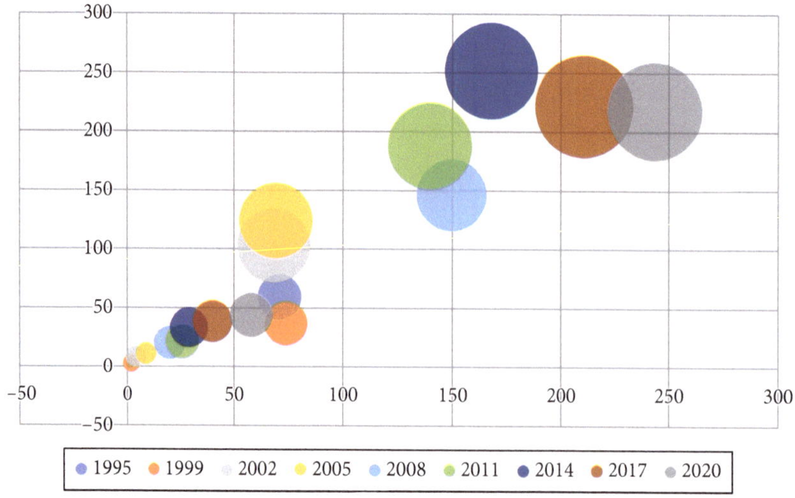

Figure 29.2 Extension of awards per year
Source: Author's elaboration based on UNCTAD (n 1).

Latvia, with seventeen pages.[40] Between both extremes, there is an average of 182 pages, without considering 102 cases where the full length of the awards remains unknown.

E. Outcome

UNCTAD reports that by the end of 2021, of 809 concluded cases, 302 have been decided in favour of the state (37 per cent), 230 in favour of the investor (29 per cent), 20 in favour of neither party (liability found, but no monetary compensation for damages is awarded, 3 per cent), 100 have been discontinued (12 per cent), and 157 were settled (19 per cent).[41] But if we just focus on the outcome embedded in the final arbitral award, from the total 552 studied for this chapter, 55 per cent have been decided in favour of the state (302 cases), 42 per cent in favour of the investor (230 cases), and 3 per cent in favour of neither party (20 cases), as seen in Figure 29.3.

When the claimant wins, it does both on jurisdictional grounds and on merits, the latter meaning that tribunals found that the respondent state breached one or more provisions of the applicable IIA and awarded monetary compensation or non-pecuniary relief. When the respondent state is successful, it can be due to preliminary objections to arbitration, at the jurisdictional phase, or on merits (the tribunal found that the respondent state did not commit any breach of the applicable IIA). The latter is the most

[40] *Swembalt AB, Sweden v Latvia*, Decision by the Court of Arbitration (23 October 2000).
[41] UNCTAD (n 1).

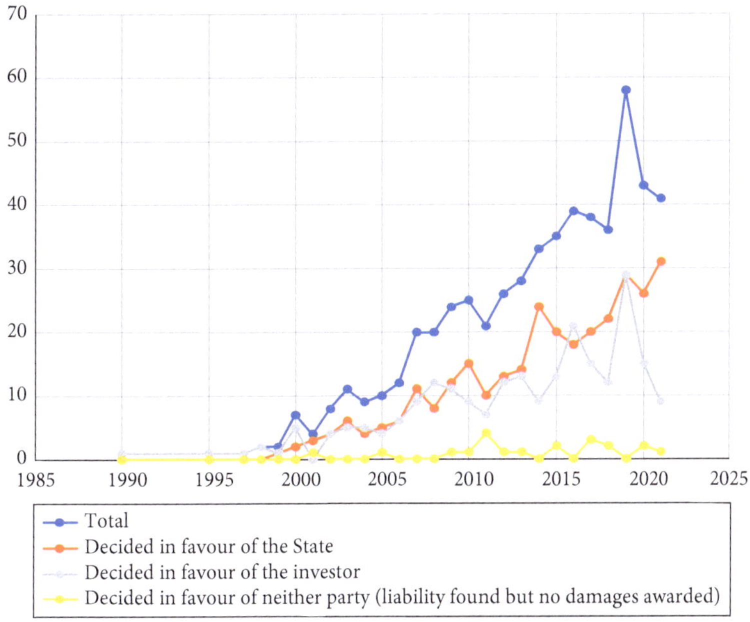

Figure 29.3 Outcome of awards per year
Source: Author's elaboration based on UNCTAD (n 1).

common situation, with a few cases when arbitration is terminated after a decision on jurisdiction (twenty-three cases)[42] or preliminary objections (four cases).[43]

But success can be relative, especially if we compare the amounts initially claimed by the investor and those finally awarded by the arbitral tribunal. In awards where information is available, UNCTAD reports a significant difference between both sums. For example, in more than 217 cases, claimants have sought compensation for USD500 million or over, but such compensation has been granted only in sixteen cases. Those amounts do not include interest, legal costs, or the costs of the arbitration.[44]

Yet more detailed research on this topic has found a rising trend in the amount of compensation awarded in ISDS, and pointed out a lack of complete information concerning the adjusted amount of damages and the real financial liability of the respondent state.[45] The problem is compounded by the fact that not all awards are available, as explained later in

[42] See for example, *Italba Corporation v Uruguay*, ICSID Case No ARB/16/9, Award (22 March 2019); *Christian Doutremepuich and Antoine Doutremepuich v Mauritius*, PCA Case No 2018-37, Award on Jurisdiction (23 August 2019); and *Recalvi SL v Dominican Republic*, PCA Case No 2019-22, Award on Jurisdiction and Admissibility (20 September 2021).

[43] *Pac Rim Cayman LLC v El Salvador*, ICSID Case No ARB/09/12, Decision on the Respondent's Preliminary Objections under CAFTA arts 10.20.4 and 10.20.5 (2 August 2010) and Decision on the Respondent's Jurisdictional Objections (1 June 2012); *Corona Materials, LLC v Dominican Republic*, ICSID Case No ARB(AF)/14/3, Award on the Respondent's expedited preliminary objections in accordance with Article 10.20.5 of the DR–CAFTA (31 May 2016); *Cem Cenzig Uzan v Turkey*, SCC Case No 2014/023, Award on Respondent's Bifurcated Preliminary Objection (20 April 2016); *Almasryia for Operating & Maintaining Touristic Construction Co LLC v Kuwait*, ICSID Case No ARB/18/2, Award on the Respondent's Application under Rule 41(5) of the ICSID Arbitration Rules (1 November 2019).

[44] UNCTAD (n 1).

[45] Susan D Franck, 'Empirically Evaluating Claims about Investment Treaty Arbitration' (2007) 86 North Carolina Law Review 1; Hodgson, Kryvoi, and Hrcka (n 17); Jonathan Bonnitcha and others, 'Damages and ISDS Reform: Between Procedure and Substance' (2021) 14(2) Journal of International Dispute Settlement 213–41.

this chapter. Additionally, the fact that countries do not always lose in ISDS, or they do in amounts much lower than those claims, does not ponder the financial impact that such an award can have in developing countries, particularly in least-developed countries (LDCs).

Overall, examining the number of awards issued per year, there has been a clear spike in the last decade, with an average of forty awards yearly.

F. Dissenting and Concurring Opinions

The large majority of awards are issued unanimously by three arbitrators (78 per cent of the total). In our dataset we find a total of 137 dissenting opinions (considering both partial and complete dissent in a 2:1 split) in 123 awards (22 per cent of the total). Thirty-two concurring opinions appear in 30 awards (5 per cent of the total). This analysis is obviously not applicable to sole arbitrators. However, dissenting opinions have become slightly more common in recent years (around 2.5 per cent more in the past five years, compared to a prior study).[46]

When there is a dissent, it is usually shorter than the award. One of the few exceptions is the famous dissent of Thomas Wälde in *Thunderbird v Mexico*, which almost doubles the size of the award (135 *v* 74 pages).[47] Another impressive case is Jürgen Voss's dissent in *Lemire v Ukraine (II)*, which has 173 pages, while the award has only 107.[48] Other examples include the dissenting opinion of Keith Highet in *Waste Management v Mexico*, which is three pages longer (30 pages) than the award (27 pages),[49] and the 47-page dissenting opinion of Pascal Dévaud in *Almasryia v Kuwait*. This case was dismissed by the majority of the tribunal for manifest lack of legal merit under Rule 41(5) of the ICSID Arbitration Rules in a 27-page long decision.[50]

Dissents are usually issued as separate documents, but on rare occasions, they are in the same text of the award. For example, in *Total v Argentina*, the award includes both the dissenting opinion of Henri Alvarez (in paragraphs 21–24) and the dissent of Luis Herrera Marcano (in paragraph 262).[51]

Prior studies have concluded that there is no significant correlation between the dissenters and their nationality, gender, appointment by the investor or the state, and the number of dissents written, and our findings confirm such conclusions.[52] The 'great

[46] Rodrigo Polanco Lazo and Valentino Desilvestro, 'Does an Arbitrator's Background Influence the Outcome of an Investor-State Arbitration?' (2018) 17 Law & Practice of International Courts and Tribunals 18, 37. On dissenting opinions, see also Charles N Brower and Ahmed Mazlom, 'To Err Is Human, to Dissent Divine' in Fach Gómez and Titi (n 10).

[47] *International Thunderbird Gaming Corporation v Mexico*, Award (26 January 2006) and Separate Opinion of Thomas Wälde.

[48] *Joseph Charles Lemire v Ukraine*, ICSID Case No ARB/06/18, Award (28 March 2011) and Dissenting Opinion of Jürgen Voss.

[49] *Waste Management, Inc v Mexico*, ICSID Case No ARB(AF)/98/2, Award (2 June 2000) and Dissenting Opinion of Keith Highet.

[50] *Almasryia v Kuwait*, Award (1 November 2019) and Dissenting Opinion of Pascal Dévaud.

[51] *Total SA v Argentina*, ICSID Case No ARB/04/1, Award (27 November 2013).

[52] Szilárd Gáspár-Szilágyi and Laura Létourneau-Tremblay, 'A Question of Impartiality: Who Are the Dissenting Arbitrators in Investment Treaty Arbitration?' in Freya Baetens (ed), *Identity and Diversity on the International Bench: Who Is the Judge?* (OUP 2020).

dissenter' until now is Charles N Brower, with a total of 16 dissenting and concurring opinions, followed by Brigitte Stern (with 13) and Santiago Torres Bermúdez (with 9), Philippe Sands (with 7), Georges Abi-Saab, Horacio Grigera Naón and Francisco Orrego Vicuña (with 6 each), Marcelo Kohen and Raúl Vinuesa (with 5 each). The dissenting arbitrator is often appointed by the losing party (in around 60 per cent of the cases), but not always. Approximately 20 per cent of dissenting, separate, and concurring opinions, are issued by the arbitrator appointed by the winning party. In only four cases, the dissenter has been the tribunal's president. In the rest of the cases, the dissents have been issued in pending, discontinued, or settled cases, or decided in favour of neither party (liability found but no damages awarded).

G. Costs

The applicable arbitration rules influence the allocation of costs in treaty-based investor-state arbitration awards. However, tribunals have considerable flexibility in applying these rules.[53] Under the ICSID Convention, the tribunal shall, except as the parties otherwise agree, assess the expenses incurred by them in connection with the proceedings. The tribunal must also decide how and by whom those expenses, the fees, and expenses of the members of the tribunal and the charges for the use of the facilities of the Centre shall be paid.[54] The UNCITRAL Arbitration Rules provide that the cost of arbitration shall, in principle, be borne by the unsuccessful party or parties. However, the tribunal may apportion costs between the parties if it determines that that apportionment is reasonable, taking into account the circumstances of the case.[55]

ISDS tribunals tend to award costs by adopting allocations that range between three approaches. The first is based on the principle 'losing party pays costs'. However, this approach is minoritarian in the universe of known ISDS awards (72 cases, representing around 13 per cent of the total). A second approach considers that costs should be apportioned in equal shares, and each party should bear its own costs ('full split'). We find this approach in a significant number of cases (223 awards, representing around 40 per cent of the total). A third approach, which is also very common, is to resort to the principle 'costs follow the event', according to which costs are apportioned based on the relative success of the parties' positions ('partial split').

When costs are partially split, solutions vary depending on the tribunal's weight on various circumstances, including the parties' conduct in the arbitration and other

[53] See Susan D Franck, 'Costs—Risks and Reality' in Susan D Franck (ed), *Arbitration Costs: Myths and Realities in Investment Treaty Arbitration* (OUP 2019) 181–230; Susan Franck and Bailey Roe, 'The Cost Award' in Fach Gómez and Titi (n 10); Noam Zamir, 'The Issue of Costs: How Much Does ISDS Cost and Who Bears the Cost?' in Julien Chaisse, Leïla Choukroune, and Sufian Jusoh (eds), *Handbook of International Investment Law and Policy* (Springer 2020); Hodgson, Kryvoi, and Hrcka (n 17).

[54] ICSID Convention art 61(2).

[55] UNCITRAL Arbitration Rules art 42(1).

parameters.[56] For example, in *Carrizosa v Colombia*, the tribunal considered several circumstances that it should take into account, including the outcome of the dispute, the reasonableness of the parties' costs, and the parties' procedural conduct.[57] But such assessment can change along the proceedings. In *Pey Casado and President Allende Foundation v Chile*, there was a different split in the award of the original proceeding (one-quarter to be borne by the claimant and three-quarters by the respondent)[58] than in the award of the resubmission proceeding (three-quarters to be borne by the claimants and one-quarter by the respondent).[59] Usually, tribunals differentiate between the costs of the procedure and the costs of the defence. The former are generally easy to ascertain. The latter are assessed based on the overall reasonableness of the costs claimed and the level of success regarding the substantial and procedural parts of the parties' claim. The tribunal has a lot of freedom to determine the different shares between the parties.[60]

In a few cases, costs are also granted with interest. For example, in *Casinos Austria v Argentina*, the tribunal determined that full reparation of the claimants in the sense of Article 38 of the International Law Commission Articles on State Responsibility required that interest be also added to the proceedings' costs from the date the award was rendered. The tribunal adopted the same interest rate as that adopted for the amount of damages awarded, that is, 4 per cent per annum compounded annually, with interest running from the date of the award until full payment thereof.[61]

When awarded, costs are supposed to compensate the expenses incurred by the parties in the arbitral proceedings. However, there is at least one case when costs were used for another purpose. It has been reported that in *Spentex v Uzbekistan*, the award issued by a majority of the tribunal (August Reinisch and Stanimir Alexandrov) 'urged' Uzbekistan to make a substantial donation to a United Nations anticorruption fund (USD8 million), taking into consideration the host state's own role in the corruption at issue in this case. The failure to make such a payment would lead to an adverse cost order in the case, which otherwise would be substantially reduced.[62]

IV. External Elements of the Award

We consider external elements, those not contained in the text of the award, requiring additional data to study them, such as information about claimants and respondents

[56] *Orascom TMT Investments Sàrl v Algeria*, ICSID Case No ARB/12/35, Award (31 May 2017) [583]; *Transban Investments Corp v Venezuela*, ICSID Case No ARB/12/24, Award (22 November 2017) [183].

[57] *Astrida Benita Carrizosa v Colombia (II)*, ICSID Case No ARB/18/5, Award (19 April 2021) [233], [234].

[58] *Víctor Pey Casado and President Allende Foundation v Chile*, ICSID Case No ARB/98/2, Award (8 May 2008).

[59] *Víctor Pey Casado and President Allende Foundation v Chile*, ICSID Case No ARB/98/2, Award (13 September 2016).

[60] See for example, *Autobuses Urbanos del Sur SA, Teinver SA and Transportes de Cercanías SA v Argentina*, ICSID Case No ARB/09/1, Award (21 July 2017) [1140].

[61] *Casinos Austria International GmbH and Casinos Austria Aktiengesellschaft v Argentina*, ICSID Case No ARB/14/32, Award (5 November 2021) [610].

[62] Luke Eric Peterson and Vladislav Djanic, 'In an Innovative Award, Arbitrators Pressure Uzbekistan—under Threat of Adverse Cost Order—to Donate to UN Anti-Corruption Initiative; also Propose Future Treaty-Drafting Changes that Would Penalize States for Corruption' (*Investment Arbitration Reporter*, 22 June 2017).

(geographical distribution and development status), the investor (types and economic sector), arbitrators (age, gender, and nationality), as well as the award's publication.

A. Claimants and Respondents

1. Economic Sector

According to UNCTAD, investment disputes come primarily from the tertiary economic sector (representing 70 per cent of all known cases), while they are less present in the primary and secondary sectors (representing 16 per cent and 14 per cent, respectively, of all known cases).[63] However, if we examine the economic sectors involved in the awards that are publicly available, we find a more nuanced picture, with each of those three sectors representing approximately one-third of all the awards (see Table 29.1 below).

Empirical research has shown that ISDS cases tend to arise in economic sectors with a high level of government intervention. For instance, they cover natural resource industries like gas, oil, and mining, as well as industries that rank high with respect to the 'public interest' and are hence highly regulated, such as telecommunications.[64] Bauerle Danzman argues that foreign investors in infrastructure, extractive industries, and utilities are more likely to file claims because investments in these sectors are more politically contentious and, therefore, are more susceptible to government interference or investment treaty/contract breaches.[65] Indeed, according to ICSID's caseload statistics (2022), investors in oil, gas, and mining have filed the most ISDS cases with ICSID since 1966, accounting for one-quarter of the total number of cases.[66]

2. Geographic Distribution

According to UNCTAD data, the region where more final awards have been issued in treaty-based investor-state arbitration is Europe, with 202 cases representing 36 per cent of all cases. It is followed by America with 175 cases (32 per cent of the total, with 151 awards from Latin America and the Caribbean), Asia with 109 cases (20 per cent of the total), and Africa with 65 (12 per cent of the total).[67] Only one case with a final award, concerns a country from Oceania.[68]

When it comes to the home state region of the claimants, the distribution is not even. The large majority of claimants in available final awards come from Europe (330 cases, 60 per cent of the total, with only 27 from Eastern Europe). It is followed by claimants from America (154 cases, 28 per cent of the total, but only 20 claimants come from

[63] UNCTAD (n 1).

[64] Roberto Echandi, 'The Debate on Treaty-Based Investor-State Dispute Settlement: Empirical Evidence (1987–2017) and Policy Implications' (2019) 34 ICSID Review 32.

[65] Sarah Bauerle Danzman, 'Contracting with Whom? The Differential Effects of Investment Treaties on FDI' (2016) 42 International Interactions 452.

[66] The ICSID Caseload Statistics 2022-2 (2022) <https://icsid.worldbank.org/sites/default/files/publications/The_ICSID_Caseload_Statistics_2022-2_ENG.pdf>.

[67] UNCTAD (n 1).

[68] *Philip Morris Asia Limited v Australia*, PCA Case No 2012-12, Award (17 December 2015).

Table 29.1 Claimants in existing awards per economic sector

Sector	No of awards
Primary Sector	107
Agriculture, forestry, and fishing	24
Crop and animal production, hunting and related service activities	16
Forestry and logging	4
Fishing and aquaculture	4
Mining and quarrying	83
Mining of coal and lignite	7
Extraction of crude petroleum and natural gas	35
Mining of metal ores	28
Other mining and quarrying	11
Mining support service activities	2
Secondary Sector	104
Manufacturing	104
Manufacture of food products	26
Manufacture of beverages	4
Manufacture of tobacco products	6
Manufacture of textiles	5
Manufacture of paper and paper products	1
Manufacture of coke and refined petroleum products	5
Manufacture of chemicals and chemical products	10
Manufacture of basic pharmaceutical products and pharmaceutical preparations	16
Manufacture of rubber and plastics products	2
Manufacture of basic metals	10
Manufacture of electrical equipment	2
Manufacture of machinery and equipment n.e.c.[a]	4
Manufacture of motor vehicles, trailers, and semi-trailers	3
Manufacture of other transport equipment	8
Other manufacturing	2
Tertiary	112
Electricity, gas, steam, and air-conditioning supply	94
Electricity, gas, steam, and air-conditioning supply	94
Water supply; sewerage, waste management, and remediation activities	18
Water collection, treatment, and supply	12
Sewerage	6

Source: Author's elaboration based on UNCTAD (n 1).

[a] n.e.c. stands for not classified elsewhere

Latin America and the Caribbean) and Asia, with 73 cases (13 per cent of the total). Only seven known final awards were brought from African claimants.[69]

3. Level of Development

Some studies on claimants' nationalities in ISDS have focused on their home states' development levels, concluding that claimants primarily come from developed economies or 'high-income' countries where investors have more financial and legal resources to resort to investment arbitration.[70] In a similar study, Wellhausen examined investors' home states in 676 cases from 1990 to 2014, noting that ISDS claimants come from a wide range of at least 73 countries, with the United States, Netherlands, and the United Kingdom being the most frequent home states for ISDS claimants.[71] Available awards corroborate this conclusion. In 483 of them, claimants come from developed economies (87 per cent of the data set), in contrast with 75 cases (13 per cent of the data set) coming from developing economies (including LDCs).

However, in a study encompassing 855 treaty-based ISDS cases filed from 1987 to 2017, Roberto Echandi pointed out that among low-to-middle-income countries, investors from Ukraine, Jordan, India, and Egypt have taken up most of the ISDS cases. In upper-to-middle-income countries, Turkish investors frequently resort to ISDS arbitration, followed by Russian, Mauritian, and Chinese investors.[72]

In a more recent report, UNCTAD found that, although developing country investors are increasingly active in bringing ISDS cases, most cases are still filed by developed country investors, accounting for approximately 75 per cent out of the 68 public treaty-based ISDS cases in 2021. Most of these claimants are from the United States, followed by France, the Netherlands, and the United Kingdom. Overall, investors from the United States, the Netherlands and the United Kingdom have filed the most ISDS cases from 1987 to 2021.[73] That said, investors from EU member states (including the UK)[74] have brought 629 cases since 1987, more than tripling those brought by US investors, with 204 cases in total.[75]

The picture is more balanced if we analyse the development level of respondent states. In 320 awards (58 per cent of the data set), respondent states are developing economies (including LDCs), and in 232 awards (42 per cent of the data set), they are developed economies. The number of cases brought against developing countries is larger if we consider pending, discontinued, and settled cases.

[69] UNCTAD (n 1).

[70] Franck (n 45). See also David Gaukrodger and Kathryn Gordon, 'Investor-State Dispute Settlement: A Scoping Paper of the Investment Policy Community', OECD Working Papers on International Investment, No 2012/3 <www.oecd.org/daf/inv/investment-policy/WP-2012_3.pdf>. Thomas Schultz and Cédric Dupont, 'Investment Arbitration: Promoting the Rule of Law or Over-Empowering Investors? A Quantitative Empirical Study' (2014) 25 European Journal of International Law 1147.

[71] Rachel L Wellhausen, 'Recent Trends in Investor-State Dispute Settlement' (2016) 7 Journal of International Dispute Settlement 117.

[72] Echandi (n 64).

[73] UNCTAD, 'Facts on Investor-State Arbitrations in 2021: With a Special Focus on Tax-Related ISDS Cases' (2022), IIA Issues Note Issue 1, July 2022, 1–15.

[74] We included UK investors for the total number of cases brought by EU investors, as UK investors have not brought any treaty-based ISDS cases since the UK withdrew from the EU on 2 February 2020.

[75] UNCTAD (n 1).

Finally, it should be noted that although claimants can be both natural and legal persons, most claims come from corporations. According to a 2012 OECD study based on a limited sample of cases, around 15 per cent of ISDS cases were brought by individuals or groups of individuals.[76] Using the total number of publicly available awards, our research shows a slightly higher percentage of 18 per cent (100 cases).

B. Arbitrators

1. Nationality

The large majority of ISDS arbitrators who have issued the awards that are publicly known are nationals of the United States or of a selected group of eight Western European countries (United Kingdom, France, Germany, Switzerland, Spain, Sweden, Italy, and Belgium). Another important group have Canadian or Australian nationality. It is noteworthy that three Latin American countries have nationals who are frequently appointed (Mexico, Argentina, and Chile—although the latter is mainly due to the appointments of the late Francisco Orrego Vicuña). Finally, Bulgarian nationality is also relevant, but primarily driven by the high number of appointments of Stanimir Alexandrov.

In 304 cases (representing 55 per cent of the known awards), the award has been issued by an arbitral tribunal composed exclusively of arbitrators from developed countries. A mix of two arbitrators from developed economies and one from a developing country is found in 193 awards (35 per cent of the cases), while one arbitrator from a developed economy and two from developing economies are present in just 42 awards (7 per cent of the cases). Only sixteen awards have been issued by an arbitral tribunal entirely composed of arbitrators from developing countries (3 per cent of the cases).

Minor variations are found depending on whether the appointment has been made by the claimant, by the respondent, or if the arbitrator is appointed as president. It is also interesting to note that only a few arbitrators are dual nationals (around 8 per cent of the sample).[77]

Considering the members of ad hoc committees in annulment proceedings in these cases, the situation changes a bit. Only 20 have been entirely composed of members from developed countries (18 per cent of the total), 51 with a mix of two members from developed economies and one from a developing one (47 per cent of the total), 30 with the reverse combination of one member from a developed economy and two from developing economies (27 per cent of the total), and only nine wholly composed by members of developing countries (8 per cent of the total).

[76] Gaukrodger and Gordon (n 70).

[77] Polanco Lazo and Desilvestro (n 46) 30.

2. Age

Age seems to be a sensitive issue for several ISDS arbitrators. It is often not displayed in their professional curricula, but based on information collected on a prior study[78] complemented with the information currently available on open sources, we obtained the year of birth of around 70 per cent of the arbitrators that issued awards in treaty-based investor-state arbitration.

From that group, the average age of ISDS arbitrators at the moment of issuing the award is 66 years old, with some minor variations. For example, the small group of female arbitrators is generally younger than the predominant male arbitrators. Obtaining the missing information from the remaining 30 per cent is unlikely to change the average, as other available information (eg year of studies) allows us to infer an approximate age.

If we consider the individual age of arbitrators at the moment of making the award, the range goes from 32 to 92 years, with a median of 67 years old. The situation is not different if we examine the ICSID annulment proceedings; the median age goes down to 65 years old.

3. Gender

There is a critical gender gap in ISDS arbitration. The overwhelming majority of arbitrators that have issued the currently available awards are male (around 90 per cent), with only 10 per cent female. Within that group are two remarkable women who represent the large majority of female appointments (Brigitte Stern and Gabrielle Kaufmann-Kohler, who also figure prominently in an elite group of the top twenty-five ISDS arbitrators).[79]

The first known appointment of a woman in a treaty-based investor-state arbitration is that of Carolyn Lamm (US). The appointment was made by the respondent in *ADF v USA*, as a member of the arbitral tribunal constituted on 11 January 2001. In that case, the award was issued on 9 January 2003.[80]

In 401 cases (representing 72 per cent of the known awards), the award has been issued by an arbitral tribunal composed exclusively of male arbitrators. A mix of two male arbitrators and one female is found in 135 awards (24 per cent of the cases), while an alternative of one male arbitrator and two female arbitrators is present in just 19 awards (3 per cent of the cases).

Up to now, there has not been a publicly available award issued by a full three-female arbitral tribunal. Yet, as a sole arbitrator, *Giuditta Cordero Moss* (Norway) made the award in *Bogdanov v Moldova (I)*.[81]

The situation is not different if we examine the ICSID annulment proceedings, where from a total of 428 members of ad hoc committees that have been appointed, 344 are male (80 per cent of the total), and 84 are female (20 per cent of the total).

[78] ibid.
[79] ibid 27–28.
[80] *ADF Group Inc v United States of America*, ICSID Case No ARB(AF)/00/1, Award (9 January 2003.
[81] *Iurii Bogdanov, Agurdino-Invest Ltd and Agurdino-Chimia JSC v Moldova* (I), Award (22 September 2005).

C. Annulment or Set-Aside

A limited number of awards have gone under follow-up proceedings of annulments or set-aside.[82] Among them, only a handful have been successful, as the majority of awards have been upheld either by members of the ad hoc committee (in the case of ICSID annulments) or by national courts (in case of awards issued under UNCITRAL and other arbitral rules), as seen in Table 29.2 below.

Only six ICSID cases have been resubmitted after an annulment. All of them have been decided in favour of the investor, and are included in the data set of final awards examined in this chapter.[83]

D. Publication of Awards

An important limitation of this research is the availability of investment awards. Although rules about ISDS transparency have improved over the years, in the absence of a specific treaty obligation (eg a particular IIA provision, or applicable arbitration rules), if both parties to the dispute do not agree on the publication of the dispute, the award remains confidential.[84] For example, even under the recently amended ICSID Arbitration Rules (2022), the Centre shall publish the awards (or their redacted version) only with the parties' consent. Consent to publish shall be deemed to have been given if no party objects in writing to such publication within sixty days after the dispatch of the document. Absent consent of the parties, the Centre shall publish excerpts of the awards considering previous comments received by the parties.[85] In contrast, the UNCITRAL Rules on Transparency in Treaty-based Investor-State Arbitration, which concerns the publication of awards, shall apply to a treaty-based investor-state arbitration initiated under the UNCITRAL Arbitration Rules if the treaty is concluded on or after 1 April 2014, unless the state parties to the treaty have agreed otherwise.[86]

In fact, from the 552 cases examined, 105 awards (around 21 per cent of the known treaty-based investor-state arbitration cases) are not available either totally or partially (105 awards): within that percentage, 14 are available only as excerpts,[87] 3 only have

[82] See also Steffen Hindelang and Julia Nassl, 'Annulment and Set-Aside' in Fach Gómez and Titi (n 10).

[83] These are *Compañía de Aguas del Aconquija SA and Vivendi Universal SA (formerly Compañía de Aguas del Aconquija, SA and Compagnie Générale des Eaux) v Argentina (I)*, ICSID Case No ARB/97/3; *Víctor Pey Casado and President Allende Foundation v Chile*, ICSID Case No ARB/98/2; *Enron Creditors Recovery Corporation (formerly Enron Corporation) and Ponderosa Assets, LP v Argentina*, ICSID Case No ARB/01/3; *Sempra Energy International v Argentina*, ICSID Case No ARB/02/16; *Mobil Cerro Negro Holding, Ltd, Mobil Cerro Negro, Ltd, Mobil Corporation and others v Venezuela*, ICSID Case No ARB/07/27; *TECO Guatemala Holdings, LLC v Guatemala*, ICSID Case No ARB/10/23.

[84] William Kenny, 'Transparency in Investor State Arbitration' (2016) 33 Journal of International Arbitration 471.

[85] ICSID Arbitration Rules (2022) r 62.

[86] UNCITRAL Rules on Transparency in Treaty-based Investor-State Arbitration art 1.

[87] *Patrick Mitchell v Democratic Republic of the Congo*, ICSID Case No ARB/99/7; *Ahmonseto, Inc and others v Egypt*, ICSID Case No ARB/02/15; *Liman Caspian Oil BV and NCL Dutch Investment BV v Kazakhstan*, ICSID Case No ARB/07/14; *Alapli Elektrik BV v Turkey*, ICSID Case No ARB/08/13; *Inmaris Perestroika Sailing*

Table 29.2 Awards annulment and set-aside proceedings

ICSID annulment	No of cases	Review by national courts	No of cases
Award upheld	65	Award upheld	65
Award entirely annulled	5	Award entirely annulled	18
Award partially annulled	10	Award partially annulled	4
Discontinued	25	Discontinued	4
Pending	35	Pending	22
Total	**140**	**Total**	**113**

Source: Author's elaboration based on UNCTAD (n 1).

available decisions on jurisdiction[88] or responsibility,[89] and 98 remain confidential. Although the decision to make an award public largely depends on the disputing parties, sites such as the IA Reporter have resorted to domestic procedures of freedom of information legislation to access such documents, although they have not always been successful in obtaining the award. Based on that experience, they have reported that, for example, Poland sits on one of the largest national caches of known but unpublished investment treaty awards and decisions.[90]

V. Conclusion

Awards in treaty-based investor-state arbitration appeared for the first time a bit more than thirty years ago. While they were relatively short and straightforward decisions in the beginning, they have become lengthier and more complex. Although they have undergone some significant changes, certain trends remain from earlier years, like the fact that they are primarily written in English, by an arbitral tribunal comprised of three male arbitrators from developed economies.

Maritime Services GmbH and others v Ukraine, ICSID Case No ARB/08/8; *H&H Enterprises Investments, Inc v Egypt*, ICSID Case No ARB/09/15; *Nova Scotia Power Incorporated v Venezuela (II)*, ICSID Case No ARB(AF)/11/1; *Marco Gavazzi and Stefano Gavazzi v Romania*, ICSID Case No ARB/12/25; *Inversión y Gestión de Bienes, IGB, SL and IGB18 Las Rozas, SL v Spain*, ICSID Case No ARB/12/17; *Marfin Investment Group Holdings SA, Alexandros Bakatselos and others v Cyprus*, ICSID Case No ARB/13/27; *Krederi Ltd v Ukraine*, ICSID Case No ARB/14/17; *B3 Croatian Courier Coöperatief UA v Croatia*, ICSID Case No ARB/15/5; *State General Reserve Fund of the Sultanate of Oman v Bulgaria*, ICSID Case No ARB/15/43; and *Cascade Investments NV v Turkey*, ICSID Case No ARB/18/4.

[88] *Suez, Sociedad General de Aguas de Barcelona, SA and Interagua Servicios Integrales de Agua, SA v Argentina*, ICSID Case No ARB/03/17, Decision on Jurisdiction (16 May 2006); *Longreef Investments AVV v Venezuela*, ICSID Case No ARB/11/5, Decision on Jurisdiction (12 February 2014).

[89] *Corn Products International, Inc v Mexico*, ICSID Case No ARB(AF)/04/1, Decision on Responsibility (15 January 2008); *Suez, Sociedad General de Aguas de Barcelona, SA and Interagua Servicios Integrales de Agua, SA v Argentina*, ICSID Case No ARB/03/17, Decision on Liability (30 July 2010).

[90] Luke Eric Peterson, 'Poland Wins Investment Treaty Arbitration with EU Investor; Government Sits on Growing Cache of Unpublished Rulings' (*Investment Arbitration Reporter*, 7 February 2012).

But these awards are also experiencing changes. Female arbitrators, as well as tribunal members from developing countries, have been increasingly appointed in these cases, so we should detect a shift in the authorship of awards in the coming years, although still much more diversity is needed. Arbitrators' age may not be a decisive factor, but future studies could consider whether there are differences between awards written by tribunals composed of arbitrators from different generations.

Concerning costs, the initial approach of arbitral tribunals largely was to consider that each party should bear its own costs. We now see an evolution in shifting this burden more to the losing party, using the principles 'costs follow the event' and 'losing party pays costs'. Finally, rules on transparency in ISDS have increased the publicity and access to investment awards. However, around one-fifth of known awards in treaty-based ISDS remain confidential.

30

Gender and Investment Awards

Patricia Nacimiento and Andrés E Alvarado-Garzón

I. Introduction

In its broadest consideration, diversity encompasses issues of age, language, ethnicity, country of origin, legal background, and certainly gender. In the law profession in particular, gender diversity appears somehow unbalanced: the number of women entering into law schools and working as associates in law firms has been as numerous as (or sometimes higher than) men over the last decades.[1] However, at upper or leading positions in law firms, universities, the judiciary, or even in companies, the number of women starkly decreases, which is often attributed to invisible barriers also known as glass ceiling. Unfortunately, in international arbitration, the story is not different. The arbitration community in general is often depicted as a small group of homogeneous people with a usually limited access for new entrants.[2] While many initiatives have been introduced to rebalance the scales[3] and studies have shown a piecemeal progress in gender diversity in international arbitration,[4] further commitments are necessary to ensure that women are represented equally with men in this field.

This is also true for investment arbitration. This brings about the discussions on the legitimacy of investment treaty arbitration, which have put the entire system under scrutiny for around half a decade. In fact, the issue of diversity has not gone unnoticed by the United Nations Commission on International Trade Law (UNCITRAL), whose Working Group III serves as a forum for all discussions on the reform of investor-state dispute settlement (ISDS). In this forum, delegations of different countries brought up the lack of diversity and have expressed their support 'for diversifying and expanding the pool of arbitrators qualified to serve as arbitrators in ISDS cases'.[5] Gender diversity is certainly a crucial part of these discussions.

[1] Caroline Dos Santos, 'Diversity in International Arbitration: A No-Woman's Land?' (2018) 3 Beiträge zu aktuellen Themen an der Schnittstelle zwischen Recht und Betriebswirtschaft 1, 2.

[2] Some scholars describe the arbitration community as an 'invisible college', see Susan D Franck and others, 'The Diversity Challenge: Exploring the Invisible College of International Arbitration' (2015) 53(3) Columbia Journal of Transnational Law 429.

[3] See for instance, the Equal Representation in Arbitration (ERA) pledge of 2015, or the Equal Representation for Expert Witnesses (ERE) pledge of 2021.

[4] See, for instance, Taylor St John and others, 'Glass Ceilings and Arbitral Dealings: Explaining the Gender Gap in International Investment Arbitration' (2017) PluriCourts Research Paper <https://papers.ssrn.com/sol3/papers.cfm?abstract_id=3782593>.

[5] UNCITRAL, 'Report of Working Group III (Investor-State Dispute Settlement Reform) on the Work of Its Thirty-Fifth Session' UN Doc A/CN.9/935 (14 May 2018) para 72.

Patricia Nacimiento and Andrés E Alvarado-Garzón, *Gender and Investment Awards* In: *The Award in International Investment Arbitration*. Edited by: Katia Fach Gómez and Catharine Titi, Oxford University Press.
DOI: 10.1093/9780191975936.003.0030

Against this backdrop, this chapter will firstly contextualize the discussion of gender diversity in investment arbitration (II). This will follow a deductive reasoning, starting from the general discussions on the legitimacy of ISDS (A), going through the narrower issue of diversity (B), until the specific issue of gender diversity (C). Subsequently, this chapter will specifically assess the (potential) effects of gender diversity on investment awards (III). Finally, some conclusions are presented (IV).

II. Contextualizing Gender Diversity in Investment Arbitration

A. Legitimacy of ISDS

Investment treaty arbitration has suffered from a 'legitimacy crisis'[6] or 'backlash'[7] because of some concerns surrounding its functioning. Criticisms cover issues such as alleged partiality of arbitrators given their repeated appointments, inconsistency of decisions, the asymmetry in access to the dispute settlement mechanism, and concerns about global governance and accountability. This has led different states to discuss possible reform options at UNCITRAL since 2017.[8] In this forum, with respect to the repeated appointment of arbitrators, different state delegations have expressed their support for diversifying the pool of candidates to serve as arbitrators.[9] Diversity thus appears as a legitimacy concern within the broader spectrum of ISDS reform. The discussions on broadening diversity in ISDS have unfortunately lagged behind.

B. Diversity in International Arbitration

Diversity in international arbitration has a multifaceted nature. It may pertain to diversity of arbitrators, expert witnesses, counsel, or tribunal secretaries. Yet, diversity of arbitrators has a direct and immediate impact on the investment award since arbitrators are ultimately in charge of rendering it. For many years, the archetype of an international arbitrator has remained a 'fifty-three year-old man who was a national of a developed state and had served as arbitrators in ten arbitration cases'.[10] Perhaps in more pejorative words, arbitrators are described as 'pale, male, stale'.[11]

[6] On this, see Susan D Franck, 'The Legitimacy Crisis in Investment Treaty Arbitration: Privatizing Public International Law through Inconsistent Decisions' (2005) 73 Fordham Law Review 1521.

[7] On this, see Michael Waibel and others (eds), *The Backlash against Investment Arbitration* (Kluwer Law International 2010).

[8] UNCITRAL, 'Possible Future Work in the Field of Dispute Settlement: Reforms of Investor-State Dispute Settlement (ISDS)' (20 April 2017) UN Doc A/CN.9/917, para 2.

[9] UNCITRAL (n 5) para 72.

[10] Franck and others (n 2) 466.

[11] Michael Goldhaber, 'Madame La Presidente: A Woman Who Sits as President of a Major Arbitral Tribunal Is a Rare Creature. Why?' (2004) 3 Transnational Dispute Management 1, 1.

While its importance has been brought under the spotlight over the years, it appears that diversity of arbitrators is still an unresolved concern. Certainly, diversity in investment arbitration may be linked to the aspiration of an equal opportunity for qualified persons from all groups and minorities to serve as arbitrators.[12] While equality is a laudable objective to pursue and this alone would justify fostering more diversity in arbitration, diversity may also have structural consequences on the dispute settlement mechanism as such. Particularly, one may argue that diversity can reflect on the legitimacy and quality of investment awards.

On the one hand, diversity of arbitrators appears essential for the legitimacy of investment arbitration.[13] From a logical perspective, 'it is difficult to reconcile [the] homogeneity among arbitrators with the mosaic of diverse backgrounds of the arbitration practitioners and disputing parties in international arbitration'.[14] Furthermore, from a practical point of view, the complexity of international businesses and investment activities might require further diversity among arbitrators. It is thus necessary that the pool of arbitrators expands not only with a view to ensuring an expedient procedure but also in order to encourage the transfer of knowledge from the most experienced arbitrators to the new generation of arbitrators.[15] As such, diversity in all its forms seeks to break the entry barriers for new arbitrators, who aim at positioning themselves by meritocracy.[16]

On the other hand, diversity is considered to improve the quality of the award.[17] Supporters of diversity posit that diverse groups of arbitrators produce better decisions.[18] For instance, based on social science, it is argued that diversity in decision-makers reduces the risk of groupthink.[19] Essentially, the concept of groupthink describes a scenario where a group of homogeneous people would make a poor decision given a strong conformity pressure.[20] Additionally, some studies show that arbitrators tend to have certain predisposition towards states from the same legal tradition, for instance, by rejecting jurisdiction or dismissing the claims on the merits over those states.[21] This is not at all surprising as it is inherently human to show some inclination to understand and better appreciate familiarity.[22] At the same time, and as held by Won

[12] UNCITRAL, 'Report of Working Group III (Investor-State Dispute Settlement Reform) on the Work of Its Thirty-Sixth Session' UN Doc A/CN.9/964 (6 November 2018) para 92.

[13] Andrea K Bjorklund and others, 'The Diversity Deficit in International Investment Arbitration' (2020) 21 Journal of World Investment and Trade 410, 440.

[14] Fahira Brodlija, 'Innovative Solutions for an Age-Old Issue: How Transparency and Data Analytic Tools Can Improve Diversity in International Arbitration' (2021) 5(1–2) Journal of Strategic Contracting and Negotiation 24, 25.

[15] Franck (n 2) 505.

[16] Paula Hodges, May Tai, and Elizabeth Kantor, 'Diversity: What Has Been Done So Far and Can the Arbitration Community Do More?' (22 February 2022) <www.herbertsmithfreehills.com/insight/inside-arbitration-diversity-what-has-been-done-so-far-and-can-the-arbitration-community-do>.

[17] Brodlija (n 14) 31.

[18] Lucy Greenwood, 'Tipping the Balance: Diversity and Inclusion in International Arbitration' (2017) 33(1) Arbitration International 99, 100.

[19] Bjorklund and others (n 13) 412.

[20] Hodges, Tai, and Kantor (n 16).

[21] Michael Waibel and Yanhui Wu, 'Are Arbitrators Political?' (2012) Research Paper 1, 22–23 <https://papers.ssrn.com/sol3/papers.cfm?abstract_id=2101186>.

[22] Won L Kidane, *The Culture of International Arbitration* (OUP 2017) 146.

Kidane, 'cultural familiarity is essential for the understanding of facts and interpretation and application of law'.[23] All in all, for the better appreciation of facts, and for a rigorous discourse among the arbitrators when deciding a case, diversity appears as a crucial factor for the quality of an award.

C. The Evolution of Gender Diversity in International Arbitration

1. Preliminary Assessments and International Commitments to Gender Diversity

The lack of gender diversity in investment arbitration is often attributed to, on the one hand, the so-called pipeline leak, and on the other hand, an unconscious bias in party appointments in conjunction with the circularity of appointments. The pipeline leak describes the misconceived perception that there are not enough qualified women who could serve as arbitrators in investor-state disputes.[24] The crux of the matter here is to define the pool of qualified women. Usually, it is considered that an arbitrator in investment disputes must be at the top of the legal profession, such as partners at law firms, university law professors, or judges of international courts.[25] Yet, it does not seem enough to be at such position of the legal profession to be chosen as an arbitrator.[26] There is a large pool of qualified women in international economic law, including trade and investment as well as in international arbitration but the appointment of women arbitrators in investment arbitration remains limited.[27] It is thus considered that for a woman to be appointed as an arbitrator in investment disputes, it is indispensable to have previous experience as an arbitrator.[28] Accordingly, one may challenge the traditional appraisal of a pipeline leak or lack of qualified women as a reason for a gender disparity in arbitration since experience seems to be the determinative factor more than any other qualification.

This leads to the second point often attributed to the lack of gender diversity in investment arbitration namely unconscious bias in party appointments and circularity of appointments. One of the characteristics of arbitration, and perhaps one of its most attractive features, is the appointment of arbitrators by the parties.[29] This derives from the principle of party autonomy, which not only reinforces the status quo but also 'justifies the continuation of a system where experience almost always trumps other considerations, including diversity'.[30] Yet, the system of party-appointed arbitrators is charged with an unconscious bias which directly impinges on the appointment of women as

[23] ibid 286.

[24] Lucy Greenwood and C Mark Baker, 'Is the Balance Getting Better? An Update on the Issue of Gender Diversity in International Arbitration' (2015) 31 Arbitration International 413, 418; St John and others (n 4) 3.

[25] Dos Santos (n 1) 3.

[26] St John and others (n 4) 6–7.

[27] Daniel Behn and others, 'Evidence-Guided Reform: Surveying the Empirical Research on Arbitrator Bias and Diversity in Investor-State Arbitration' in Manfred Elsig, Rodrigo Polanco, and Peter van den Bossche (eds), *International Economic Dispute Settlement: Demise or Transformation?* (OUP 2021) 284.

[28] Bjorklund and others (n 13) 429.

[29] See Richard Happ and Sebastian Wuschka, 'From the Jay Treaty Commissions towards a Multilateral Investment Court: Addressing the Enforcement Dilemma' (2017) VI(1) Indian Journal of Arbitration Law 113, 125.

[30] Bjorklund and others (n 13) 426.

arbitrators irrespective of their qualifications.[31] In a nutshell, an unconscious bias draws disputing parties and counsel to select an arbitrator that resembles the archetype of an old, western European male even though their interests might be better served with a different individual.[32] This is so, because they believe such an archetype would be able to persuade the other two alike arbitrators towards the position of the appointing party they represent.[33]

Furthermore, even beyond the archetype of arbitrator, disputing parties, and counsel may be influenced in the selection of arbitrators by the visibility and experience of the prospective candidate. From a survey of 3159 appointments of arbitrators in investment disputes, 377 arbitrators received their first appointment as arbitrators, which accounts for approx. 10 per cent of the sample, whereas fifty of the most often appointed arbitrators received 1770 of the appointments, which accounts for almost 50 per cent of the sample.[34] Accordingly, some posit that the first diversity challenge women face for becoming arbitrators is obtaining their first appointment.[35]

This creates a vicious circle where fewer women are appointed as arbitrators as the appointments are concentrated on those persons with prior experience.[36] As such, the system of party appointment builds barriers of entry for new arbitrators, and particularly for women.[37] Interestingly, two women lead the list of most often appointed arbitrators in investment disputes: Brigitte Stern and Gabrielle Kaufmann-Kohler.[38] They are however the exception in a list dominated by men.[39]

This is contrasted with the high number of women appointed by arbitral institutions. One may suggest that institutions are less susceptible to unconscious bias when appointing arbitrators since those institutions have different incentives and screening mechanisms than the disputing parties.[40] The problem is, arbitral institutions are only marginally responsible for the majority of arbitrator appointments.[41] One could suggest that arbitral institutions or even counsel should provide the parties with possible candidates as arbitrators but without revealing their gender to overcome the unconscious bias against women.[42] Another option would be to set up quotas to improve diversity in investment arbitration.[43] However, it is difficult to envisage how such proposals would work in practice. Particularly, it is unlikely that disputing parties are willing to relinquish control in the appointment process no matter how laudable the ultimate goal is.

[31] Greenwood and Baker (n 24) 419.
[32] St John and others (n 4) 9.
[33] Goldhaber (n 11) 1.
[34] Bjorklund and others (n 13) 418.
[35] Franck and others (n 2) 488.
[36] Dos Santos (n 1) 5.
[37] St John and others (n 4) 17.
[38] Malcom Langford, Daniel Behn, and Runar Hilleren Lie, 'The Revolving Door in International Investment Arbitration' (2017) 20(2) Journal of International Economic Law 301, 310.
[39] Sergio Puig, 'Social Capital in the Arbitration Market' (2014) 25(2) European Journal of International Law 387, 419.
[40] St John and others (n 4) 11–12.
[41] Greenwood (n 18) 104.
[42] See, for instance, Greenwood and Baker (n 24) 420; Dos Santos (n 1) 7.
[43] Bjorklund and others (n 13) n 9.

Thus, party appointment remains the major obstacle to more gender diversity in arbitral panels in investment arbitration.

This is unfortunately exacerbated by the asymmetry of information about the possible candidates to serve as arbitrators.[44] When faced with different candidates to appoint, a risk-averse counsel would default on the well-known and reputable arbitrator,[45] even if there might be some dissatisfaction with the awards rendered by the same arbitrator in the past.[46] The availability of information about potential candidate arbitrators is thus crucial. Accordingly, initiatives such as GAR ART[47] or Arbitrator Intelligence[48] are well received as they promote the sharing of information about possible arbitrator candidates, thereby increasing the possibilities for gender diversity. Yet, these initiatives might fall short on promoting new entrants, particularly new women arbitrators because the information is mostly based on previous cases where the individual has already served as an arbitrator.

Conversely, organizations promoting women and granting visibility to young qualified but unexperienced arbitration practitioners might be more effective in knocking off first entry barriers and thereby fostering gender diversity in arbitration. For instance, ArbitralWomen is an international non-governmental organization which has existed informally since 1993, actively since 2000, and officially as a non-profit organization since 2005. ArbitralWomen promotes women in dispute resolution through events, social gatherings, mentoring, and by sponsoring female law students in moot court competitions.

Moreover, in 2015, the Equal Representation in Arbitration (ERA) Pledge was created, whose goal is to enhance the visibility of women in international arbitration and increasing the number of women appointed to arbitral tribunals. The ERA Pledge asks counsel to attempt to send more diverse lists of potential arbitrators. It seeks to foster a broader sense of responsibility in relation to the legitimacy of ISDS, to which gender diversity contributes. Some of the steps suggested by the ERA Pledge are: first, that institutional committees, governing bodies, and conference panels include 'a fair representation of women'; second, that lists of potential arbitrators or tribunal chairs provided to parties include female names; third, that lists of potential arbitrators recommended by states for institutional panels include female names; fourth, that statistics be made available by institutions; and, fifth, that senior practitioners support and encourage women to pursue arbitrator appointments. A spin-off pledge was adopted in 2021, the Equal Representation for Expert Witnesses, which is also gaining traction.[49]

[44] Greenwood (n 18) 105–06.

[45] Brodlija (n 14) 32.

[46] Greenwood (n 18) 106.

[47] GAR's Arbitrator Research Tool (ART) is a platform that maps information about arbitrators based on their specialist knowledge, experience, and work relationships.

[48] Arbitrator Intelligence collects data through an anonymous online survey, completed by the parties and counsel following the completion of proceedings. The information is then analysed and transformed into reports on particular arbitrators.

[49] See <https://globalarbitrationreview.com/article/gender-diversity-pledge-experts-gains-traction>.

These initiatives seek to provide visibility to qualified women in international arbitration and thereby to overcome the obstacles posed by information asymmetry. It is for this reason that the visibility of qualified women and the availability of information showing their work and experience might change the level playing field of selection of arbitrators.[50] Additionally, it is suggested that visibility of qualified women should be complemented by a supportive culture in the work environment but also fostering formal or informal networking of women, which will facilitate greater visibility in the long run.[51] In this sense, these initiatives have the potential to modify the pattern of party appointments, which may ultimately result in an increased number of women appointed as arbitrators in investment disputes. All in all, this requires more transparency,[52] but also that those commitments towards diversity are seriously taken. Otherwise, there is the risk of falling into a 'diversity paradox',[53] whereby the same practitioners who support diversity initiatives fail to appoint diverse arbitrators.

2. Gender Diversity in the Last Years

The appointment of female arbitrators has certainly increased over the years. As has been reported, 'while early years of investor-state arbitration were almost completely devoid of any female arbitrators, there has been a slow increase over time'.[54] Lucy Greenwood, for instance, surmised that by 2012, approximately 5 per cent women were appointed as arbitrators, which increased to approximately 10 per cent in 2015.[55] In 2017, the number of female arbitrators was calculated at approximately 15 per cent.[56] While the number of female arbitrators seems to improve over the years, one must consider that this is highly influenced by arbitral institutions diversifying their lists of arbitrators and selecting such arbitrators when acting as appointing authorities.[57]

Some more recent statistics may be illustrative of the developments on the appointment of women arbitrators. The International Council for Commercial Arbitration (ICCA) reported in 2021 an overall average of 26.1 per cent of women appointed as arbitrators (from 5049 recorded appointments, 1317 were women).[58] This reflects a trend since the 1990s onwards where women are more and more appointed as arbitrators.[59] Historically, these numbers reveal a constant increase of women serving as arbitrators

[50] Greenwood (n 18) 107; Brodlija (n 14) 34.

[51] Katia Fach Gómez, 'Diversidad y género en el arbitraje internacional: entre los hechos y los anhelos' in Katia Fach Gómez (ed), *La política de la Unión Europea en materia de derecho de las inversiones internacionales* (JM Bosch 2017) 15–16 <https://papers.ssrn.com/sol3/papers.cfm?abstract_id=2982604>.

[52] Ruth Hosking, 'Who Is My Arbitrator? The Need for Greater Transparency in Arbitration' (*Practical Law: Arbitration Blog*, 13 September 2018) <http://arbitrationblog.practicallaw.com/who-is-my-arbitrator-the-need-for-greater-transparency-in-arbitration>.

[53] Catherine A Rogers, 'The Key to Unlocking the Arbitrator Paradox? Arbitrator Intelligence' (*Kluwer Arbitration Blog*, 27 December 2017) <http://arbitrationblog.kluwerarbitration.com/2017/12/27/on-arbitrators/?doing_wp_cron=1596049980.9639880657196044921875>.

[54] St John and others (n 4) 24.

[55] However, a disclaimer is included, as the authors are not certain whether the changing number responded to a real increase or to the paucity of information (Greenwood and Baker (n 24) 418).

[56] Greenwood (n 18) 102.

[57] Brodlija (n 14) 25.

[58] ICCA, *Report of the Cross-Institutional Task Force on Gender Diversity in Arbitral Appointments and Proceedings—2022 Update* (ICCA Reports No 8, 2022) 24.

[59] ibid 27.

since 2015 onwards both from appointments made by institutions, and appointments made by co-arbitrators. For instance, in 2021, from 1489 appointments by arbitral institutions, 545 (reflecting 37.9 per cent) were women, whereas from 638 appointments by co-arbitrators in 2021, 173 (reflecting 27.1 per cent) were women.[60] While there has been some steady progress in appointments of women by disputing parties (from an average of 7.9 per cent in 2015 to 19.4 per cent in 2020), there was a slight decrease to 17.9 per cent, this is 392 women out of 2195 of party appointments, in 2021.[61] These numbers include both commercial and investment arbitration, which does not necessarily correspond to the overall trend in investment arbitration.

In 2007, a study showed that from a pool of 145 investment treaty arbitrators, only approximately 3.5 per cent were women.[62] This low percentage of women arbitrators in investment treaty disputes was confirmed in a subsequent study in 2012, which reported that from a pool of 247 arbitrators involved in investment treaty arbitration, only 3.6 per cent were women.[63] According to the 2022 ICSID Annual report, women accounted for 24 per cent of all appointments in ICSID cases, which does not show a clear tendency considering that in 2021 women accounted for 31 per cent of all appointments, whereas in 2020 women accounted for only 14 per cent.[64] In absolute terms for 2022, of the total women serving as arbitrators, ICSID appointed 55 per cent, respondent states appointed 14 per cent, and claimants appointed 9 per cent. Furthermore, 16 per cent of female appointments were made jointly by the parties and the remaining 6 per cent were made by co-arbitrators.[65]

These statistics prove that institutions have played an essential role in the increase of women serving as arbitrators. However, this is not sufficient. Party appointments remain the core of arbitrator appointments and particularly in investment arbitration, the number of women appointed as arbitrators by the disputing parties is anything but encouraging. Moreover, those numbers may be significantly distorted by repeated appointments of individuals such as Gabrielle Kaufmann-Kohler and Brigitte Stern. While statistically women have received more appointments as arbitrators over the last years, the goal of gender diversity is far from being fully achieved.

III. Gender Diversity and Its Effects on Investment Awards

Gender diversity in investment arbitration appears desirable and the above statistics show some progress on the participation of women as arbitrators over the last years.

[60] ibid 31ff.
[61] ibid 35.
[62] Susan D Franck, 'Empirically Evaluating Claims about Investment Treaty Arbitration' (2007) 86 North Carolina Law Review 1, 81.
[63] Susan D Franck and others, 'International Arbitration: Demographics, Precision and Justice' in Anne van Aaken (ed), *ICCA Congress Series* (vol 18 ICCA Congress Series, 2015) 40.
[64] ICSID Annual Report 2022, 32 <https://icsid.worldbank.org/sites/default/files/publications/ICSID_AR.EN.pdf>.
[65] ibid.

Most importantly, while society may call for more diverse arbitrators, it is apposite to wonder whether the participation of women as arbitrators in investment disputes influences the final outcome. Accordingly, this section poses two questions for analysis: whether gender diversity improves the legitimacy of investment awards (A); whether gender diversity improves the quality of investment awards (B).

D. Legitimacy of the Investment Award

By means of investment treaty arbitration, a foreign investor claims damages caused by state actions, which bears a resemblance to administrative or constitutional procedures under domestic law.[66] As such, investment arbitration reflects a mechanism of global governance[67] that allows the adjudication of the state's exercise of public authority.[68] Precisely because of the submission of the state to such a system of adjudication, which is accountable to its people, investment treaty arbitration demands a perceived legitimacy of the arbitrators and their decision-making process.[69]

The legitimacy of an adjudicative system may be assessed from different aspects or criteria: first, it may reflect on the perception of unbiased and fair adjudicators; second, all stakeholders must be committed to the underlying normative system; and, third, some democratic institutional norms such as transparency must be followed.[70] The lack of gender diversity usually reflects some shortcomings in each of these criteria.[71]

In this context, gender diversity of arbitrators is generally considered a precondition for a greater acceptance of the arbitration process and voluntary compliance with the decisions rendered.[72] This has been stressed as one issue of concern in the process of ISDS reform at UNCITRAL. Here, different delegations have warned that the 'lack of diversity was said to be exemplified by a concentration of arbitrators from a certain region, a limited age group, *one* gender and limited ethnicity'.[73] Accordingly, it seems to be undisputed that 'the current lack of diversity in decision makers in the field of ISDS contributed to undermine the legitimacy of the ISDS regime. Relevant statistics provided by the Secretariat and presented during the session illustrated that there was indeed *lack of diversity particularly in terms of gender* and geographical representation.'[74]

[66] Gus Van Harten, *Investment Treaty Arbitration and Public Law* (OUP 2007) 68–71; Stephan W Schill, 'Enhancing International Investment Law's Legitimacy: Conceptual and Methodological Foundations of New Public Law Approach' (2011) 52 Virginia Journal of International Law 57, 78.

[67] Stephan W Schill, 'International Investment Law and Comparative Public Law—An Introduction' in Stephan W Schill (ed), *International Investment Law and Comparative Public Law* (OUP 2010) 18–19.

[68] ibid 17–18.

[69] Van Harten (n 64) 159. Similarly, Eric Stein, 'International Integration and Democracy: No Love at First Sight' (2001) 95(3) American Journal of International Law 489, 493.

[70] Nienke Grossman, 'Legitimacy and International Adjudicative Bodies' (2009) 41 George Washington International Law Review 107, 115.

[71] For a detailed account of each of the criteria of legitimacy of international adjudicative systems, see Bjorklund and others (n 13) 420ff.

[72] Dos Santos (n 1) 9; Bjorklund and others (n 13) 413; Brodlija (n 14) 31.

[73] UNCITRAL (n 5) para 70 (emphasis added).

[74] UNCITRAL (n 12) para 92 (emphasis added).

Accordingly, gender diversity constitutes a factor for the legitimacy of investment arbitration. This has a direct impact on the investment award rendered in such a dispute settlement mechanism. If the legitimacy of investment arbitration as such is in question by the lack of gender-diverse tribunals, the investment awards rendered by such tribunals would necessarily face the same legitimacy concerns. This reflects the close relationship between gender diversity in investment arbitration and the investment award. It is thus of the utmost importance to address these gender diversity gaps, otherwise the legitimacy of the entire system of ISDS and the investment awards produced thereunder cannot be defended.

Furthermore, one could even consider that an award rendered by a gender-diverse tribunal is more likely to be accepted and complied with as it would embody desired public demands for a system of investment dispute settlement that more accurately reflects its users. Indeed, it may be argued that the deliberations of a diverse tribunal have the potential of covering more comprehensively all aspects of an investment dispute, which in turn will lead to a better acceptance of the award by the disputing parties, other parties involved, and society at large.[75]

Importantly, seeking diversity for the sake of diversity should be avoided. An increase in diversity should not be merely symbolic but it must bear on the decision-making of arbitrators and the power balance within the tribunal.[76] This means that women arbitrators should not be cast aside, excluded, or simply ignored by their fellow male co-arbitrators in the decision-making process. Otherwise, gender diversity risks becoming a meaningless gesture, which would not enhance the legitimacy of the award. As long as these considerations are kept in mind, gender diversity serves as a legitimizing factor in investment arbitration and thereby in investment awards, which all stakeholders should support.

E. Quality of the Investment Award

The lack of diversity is often considered to affect the correctness of decisions by arbitral tribunals.[77] Yet, the issue of 'quality' in investment arbitration may be sometimes deceiving. For instance, the main criteria by which to judge an arbitrator's professionalism and experience are their international exposure and visibility.[78] But this is not decisive for the quality of the decisions they may render. While repeated appointments evince procedural experience, this alone does not guarantee that a particular arbitrator is the best expert for a specific issue in dispute.[79] Furthermore, even if two arbitrators are experts in a specific issue, they may reach different conclusions without this making

[75] Fach Gómez (n 51) 28.
[76] Brodlija (n 14) 31.
[77] UNCITRAL (n 5) para 70.
[78] Dos Santos (n 1) 5.
[79] ibid 5–6.

one decision wrong per se. Thus, there is no objective standard to consider whether an arbitrator has rendered a correct decision.

In this context, it is difficult to measure the quality of investment awards. Nevertheless, it is argued that gender diversity may improve the quality of an arbitral decision from a sociological point of view. As with diversity in the broader sense, a different background may provide another assessment of facts or law, prompting a deeper discussion among the arbitrators and rigor on the decisions rendered.[80] This entails that the risks of groupthink discussed above[81] are considerably reduced. In other words:

> diverse arbitrators with different ethnic and cultural backgrounds, as well as legal training, are likely to raise issues and nuances which may otherwise be overlooked by the 'ingroup'. Even if their interventions do not ultimately change the reasoning of the majority, the award will reflect a comprehensive deliberation process which should contribute to the quality of the award.[82]

While this is tenable for contrasting legal and cultural backgrounds, one may wonder how the same rationale may apply to increased gender diversity. Nevertheless, it is noted that female arbitrators still defy the archetype of an arbitrator as they are not cohesive members of the group of 'traditional' arbitrators.[83] A gender-diverse panel is thus more likely to avoid groupthink and dwell attentively on the issues before them. Yet, similarly as with the legitimacy of the investment award discussed above,[84] women arbitrators ought to have an active participation in the deliberations, assessment of facts, and law. This gives the arbitrators the opportunity to comprehensively assess the case, to consider nuances that otherwise would be ignored, and to better appreciate the divergent positions of the disputing parties. In this sense, gender diversity may effectively and positively influence the investment award.

IV. Conclusion

Gender diversity 'has emerged as a point of entry toward broader conversations about representation in investor-state arbitration',[85] but further commitment from all stakeholders is required. By no means should diversity be promoted at the expense of competence and quality,[86] which requires that those persons depicted as the archetype of arbitrator should not be alienated but rather included in the movement towards achieving gender diversity.[87] Unfortunately, gender diversity in investment arbitration

[80] Waibel and Wu (n 21) 39; Bjorklund and others (n 13) 412.
[81] See section II.B.
[82] Brodlija (n 14) 31.
[83] Dos Santos (n 1) 13.
[84] See section III.A.
[85] St John and others (n 4) 31.
[86] UNCITRAL (n 12) para 96.
[87] Hodges, Tai, and Kantor (n 16).

remains an issue of concern and its discussion at the UNCITRAL Working Group III has lagged behind. Certainly, progress has been achieved. But statistics in investment arbitration show that women appointed by the disputing parties as arbitrators remain rather the exception. While the lack of diversity undisputedly bears on the legitimacy of investment arbitration as a whole, this chapter further delves into the effects of such lack of gender diversity on the investment awards. Here, there are two points of discussion namely whether gender diversity improves the legitimacy of investment awards and whether gender diversity improves the quality of investment awards.

Gender diversity of arbitrators improves the legitimacy of the investment award as an award rendered by a gender-diverse tribunal is more likely to be accepted and complied with. Similarly, it is argued that gender diversity of arbitrators also improves the quality of the award from a sociological point of view given that a gender-diverse panel is more likely to avoid groupthink and dwell attentively on the issues before them. Yet, women arbitrators ought to have an active participation in the deliberations and should not be cast aside, excluded, or simply ignored by their fellow male co-arbitrators in the decision-making process. Otherwise, gender diversity risks becoming a meaningless gesture, which would not enhance the legitimacy or quality of the investment award.

31

The Visible and Invisible Footprint of New Technologies in Investment Awards

*Katia Fach Gómez**

I. Introduction

'Analogue awards' no longer exist today. Whether we are aware of it or not and whether we like it or not, technology is a completely ubiquitous and transversal ingredient of contemporary arbitration. As a creature of its time, the current investment award is thus a 'technological award'. That is, investment awards not only include many technological references in their drafting but have also been elaborated using different types of technology.

This chapter discusses the increasing use of new technologies in investment arbitration, focusing specifically on technology's role in investment awards. It shows how current awards bear witness to the daily use of what is known as utilitarian technology in arbitration proceedings. This is reflected in multiple references in the awards themselves, which cover matters as varied as: filing the request for arbitration electronically, the widespread use of communication technology among arbitration actors, non-presential case management conferences, the electronic submission of documents, remote hearings, remote deliberations, electronic signatures, and electronic transmission of awards (section II). The question as to whether any of the technological elements referred to in arbitration awards themselves might currently be considered a minimum form requirement for investment arbitration awards is also raised section III). Arbitrators and arbitral secretaries' use of technology—whether utilitarian or disruptive—when creating the content of investment awards is likewise analysed in this chapter. AI-led tools may not be expressly mentioned in award texts, but their use certainly has a practical impact on the awards' final configuration, which is why this chapter reflects on the appropriateness of resorting to measures, to prohibit artificial intelligence (AI) or imposing on arbitrators a duty to disclose AI usage when they draft awards (section IV).

* Katia Fach Gómez is a member of the Instituto Universitario de Derecho Europeo e Integración Regional (IDEIR), the Regional Government of Aragon Reference Research Group on Legal Management of Innovative Business, Instruments and Organisations—LegMiBIO (S12_23R), and the Spanish Research Project PID2022-137502NB-I0.

Katia Fach Gómez, *The Visible and Invisible Footprint of New Technologies in Investment Awards* In: *The Award in International Investment Arbitration*. Edited by: Katia Fach Gómez and Catharine Titi, Oxford University Press.
DOI: 10.1093/9780191975936.003.0031

II. Current Investment Awards Unanimously Attest to the Widespread Use of Utilitarian Technology during Arbitral Proceedings

In a not-too-distant past, technology was a secondary tool in investment arbitration proceedings. Some of the lawyers and arbitrators who devote themselves to investment arbitration today were already working in this field in the days when huge mountains of papers known as arbitration bundles used to arrive at their offices via expensive courier companies, and when the fastest and most technological way to keep in contact with the counterparty and arbitral panel was by setting up international conference calls. As will be made clear, the reality is completely different today, and investment awards are manifest evidence of this.[1]

Technology is often said to be one of the most reliable resources for achieving rapid and cost-effective investment conflict resolution via international arbitration.[2] The term 'technology' is extremely broad, and its content is mutable according to scientific and social progress. For the purposes of this chapter, a rough distinction is drawn between utilitarian technology and disruptive technology.[3] In simple terms, utilitarian technology is frequently used and is valued by arbitration actors, who point out its many and convincing benefits, among which are: enhancing legal productivity and efficiency; limiting expenses;[4] fairer legal services provision; protecting legal actors'

[1] With the aim of providing recent examples in this section, awards issued by different administering institutions between the years 2021 and 2023 have been consulted. Earlier awards have also been consulted on various occasions when the topic required. The awards are accessible at <www.italaw.com> and have been selected on the basis of keyword searches (electronic, videoconference, remote hearing, virtual hearing, online, technology, COVID, etc).

[2] The latest statistics from the arbitration community show that the collective relies heavily on technology to increase efficiency and that this is 'the factor most expected to influence the future evolution of international arbitration'. Queen Mary University of London and White & Case 'International Arbitration Survey: Adapting Arbitration to a Changing World' (2021) <https://arbitration.qmul.ac.uk/research/2021-international-arbitration-survey/> 20. In other contexts such as the EU judicial cooperation in civil matters, the 'digital by default' principle is clearly underlined. Fernando Gascón Inchausti, 'The New Regulation on the Digitalisation of Judicial Cooperation in the European Union: Something Old, Something New, Something Borrowed and Something Blue' *ERA Forum* (Springer 2024).

[3] It is also possible to establish a distinction between data collection and data interpretation with regard to arbitrators' decision-making process. The use of technology in arbitration is generally accepted and valued positively with respect to data collection; however, using technology in data interpretation generates more reluctance. Myriam Gicquello, 'Artificial Intelligence in International Arbitration' in Thomas Schultz and Federico Ortino (eds), *The Oxford Handbook of International Arbitration* (OUP 2020) 591, 615. Another distinction that may be relevant in this context refers to the effects of technology in the legal context, distinguishing between sustaining applications, which enable work process optimization via automation, and disruptive applications, which innovate by departing from normal processes and adopting new methods. Law Society of New South Wales Commission of Inquiry 'The Future of Law and Innovation in the Profession, FLIP report' (2017) <www.lawsociety.com.au/sites/default/files/2018-03/1272952.pdf>. More generally, distinguishing between digitization and automation: Monika Zalnieriute and Felicity Bell 'Technology and the Judicial Role' in Gabrielle Appleby and Andrew Lynch (eds), *The Judge, the Judiciary and the Court: Individual, Collegial and Institutional Judicial Dynamics in Australia* (CUP 2022) 1. In other words, when technology assists arbitrators, this is viewed as beneficial; while when technology replaces arbitrators, this is generally viewed as dangerous and even harmful. To use the terminology coined by two pioneering legaltech scholars: utilitarian technology is usually less controversial than truly transformative technology. Sophie Nappert and Paul Cohen, 'Case Study. The Practitioner´s Perspective' in Maud Piers and Christian Aschauer (eds), *Arbitration in the Digital Age: The Brave New World of Arbitration* (CUP 2018).

[4] See Hobér's commentary in this book: 'The widespread adoption of virtual conferencing has reduced concerns of time and costs associated with in-person meetings.' Kaj Hobér, 'Compensation' in Katia Fach Gómez and Catharine Titi (eds), *The Award in International Investment Arbitration* (OUP 2024).

reputations; overcoming adjudicator isolation culture; increasing diversity; and protecting the environment.[5] In contrast, what may be termed disruptive or transformative technology, such as AI-based predictive legal tools or robot arbitrators, is far more controversial, as noted in section IV.

Investment arbitration awards are characterized by their length and their provision of highly detailed information, both about the complex cases that gave rise to the claims and the legal proceedings leading to the issuance of the awards themselves. It is therefore very common for awards to refer to the use of technology throughout the arbitration proceedings in various parts (introduction and parties, arbitral tribunal, procedural history, factual background to the dispute, claims/requests for relief, objections to jurisdiction, etc).

This part of the chapter sets out several examples of ways in which the content of investment arbitration awards include express reference to the use of utilitarian technologies at different phases of arbitration proceedings.[6] As will be pointed out through this non-exhaustive sample, the successful use of non-disruptive technology in investment arbitration is directly proportional to a series of factors: the number of arbitral actors involved in the objective, their willingness to cooperate,[7] and their level of technological competence.[8] That is, implementing an investment arbitration that is well-managed at the technological level requires the participation not only of technology-savvy party representatives, but also of the arbitral institution, the arbitrators, their legal assistants, and various non-legal actors (IT experts, technology secretaries, outside IT consultants, etc).[9]

[5] Developing these arguments in detail, see Katia Fach Gómez, *The Technological Competence of Arbitrators: A Comparative and International Legal Study* (Springer 2023) ch 3.

[6] Owing to space restrictions it is not possible to cover additional topics such as cybersecurity, data protection measures, or electronic evidence here. On these issues, see Fach Gómez (n 5) ch 6, Daniel Brantes Ferreira and Elizabeta A Gromova, 'Digital Evidence: The Admissibility of Leaked and Hacked Evidence in Arbitration Proceedings' (2023) 36 International Journal for the Semiotics of Law 1.

[7] The following explanation offered by a sole arbitrator in an award is a remarkable example of the technological challenges that all arbitration actors currently have to face, as well as the realization that it is often necessary to address them collaboratively:

> On 22 May 2020, the parties provided me with a revised index to the documents in the Arbitration and with organised electronic files of the various materials, including the bundles that had been used at the hearing. I had some difficulty downloading the documents from the link provided, and there were issues with the embedded hyperlinks. On 28 May 2020, I had a short telephone meeting with Ms [X] and with Ms [Y] of [the claimant's] counsel in relation to those technical issues. The [defendant] was not able to attend that meeting, but its counsel had indicated in advance that he did not object to its taking place. On 29 May 2020, TCT sent a further link to the documents. I was able to download the documents successfully, and the issues with the hyperlinks had been resolved.

Transcanada Turbines Limited v Ministry of Electricity, Iraq, General Directorate of Electricity Al-Furat Middle Region, ICC Case No 21199/ZF/AYZ, Award (5 March 2021) [131]–[132].

[8] In more detail, see Fach Gómez (n 5) ch 4.

[9] Arbitrators are increasingly aware of the relevant role played by participants' technological competence in contemporary arbitrations. By way of an example, one tribunal: 'Directed the Parties to (i) take all necessary steps to retain an experienced remote hearing manager, at least on a contingency basis, and to start investigating the necessary preparatory steps necessary for a potential remote hearing.' *Bedri Selmani v Kosovo*, ICC Case No 24443/MHM/HBH, Award (1 August 2022) [33].

A. Electronic Filing, E-Communications, and Remote Case Management Conferences

The institutions that manage investment arbitrations currently allow non-in-person proceedings to be initiated via remote requests for arbitration.[10] Some institutions,[11] such as the Vienna International Arbitral Centre (VIAC), retain the dual option of filing the statement of the claim that begins the arbitration either in hard copy form or in electronic form.[12] Others, like the International Centre for Settlement of Investment Disputes (ICSID), have chosen to prioritize electronic filing: 'A complete request with all supporting documents should be uploaded onto ICSID's document sharing platform ('Box') and sent to the ICSID Secretariat by email. No hard copies should be sent to ICSID.'[13] This means that many investment award texts contain a record of the claimant's electronic filing, with wording such as the following: 'The Centre received an electronic copy of the Request for Arbitration (the 'ROA') submitted by the Claimant against'.[14]

Using the same pro-utilitarian-technology logic, investment awards also frequently refer to the fact that the participants have communicated with each other using electronic means during the proceedings. With respect to communication between arbitral institutions and parties, an example from a recent award reads as follows: 'By email dated ... the LCIA informed the Parties that, in accordance with Article 5 of the Arbitration Rules, the LCIA Court appointed ... to form the Arbitral Tribunal in this arbitration.'[15] With regard to communication between arbitral panels and parties, standard wording in awards is as follows: 'Notifications and communications in these arbitration proceedings are made to the representatives of the Parties indicated in the previous paragraph, to the email addresses indicated in the same section.'[16]

This is the logical consequence of investment arbitration rules' broad express recognition of email and other digital technology as valid communication mechanisms.[17] For instance, Article 14(3) of the LCIA specifies that 'the parties and the Arbitral

[10] The information on the CIETAC website seems to indicate that filing must be in hard copy form: 'Please also be reminded that all documents should be in a clean and tidy form, paged and bound together. How to Start Arbitration at CIETAC' <www.cietac.org/index.php?m=Article&a=show&id=2355&l=en>.

[11] The following arbitration institutions are studied in this chapter: ICSID, SCC, PCA, SIAC, VIAC, CIETAC, BAC–BIAC, LCIA, ICC, and the UNCITRAL Rules. Some institutions, such as ICSID, are devoted exclusively to investment arbitration. Others originally operated in commercial arbitration but now have their own investment arbitration texts (eg VIAC, CIETAC)—although these have not yet been applied to many investment cases. A third group has a single set of international arbitration rules, which is sometimes applied to investment cases (eg ICC, SCC).

[12] Vienna Investment Arbitration Rules (2021) art 7.

[13] ICSID 'How to File a Request for Arbitration—ICSID Convention Arbitration (2022 Rules)' <https://icsid.worldbank.org/procedures/arbitration/convention/how-to-file-a-request/2022>.

[14] *BSG Resources Limited, BSG Resources (Guinea) Limited and BSG Resources (Guinea) SÀRL v Guinea*, ICSID Case No ARB/14/22, Award (18 May 2022) [12].

[15] *Dunor Energia v Federal Electricity Commission (CFE) (Mexico)*, LCIA Case No 204865, Award (26 September 2022) [26].

[16] ibid [9].

[17] References of this kind also appear in commercial arbitration rules applicable to investment cases, such as the LCIA and SCC rules.

Tribunal shall make contact (whether by a hearing in person or virtually by conference call, videoconference or using other communications technology or exchange of correspondence) as soon as practicable',[18] and Article 5(2) of the 2023 Stockholm Chamber of Commerce (SCC) Arbitration Rules stipulates that 'any notice or other communication shall be delivered by courier or registered mail, email or any other means that records the sending of the communication'.[19] Article 49 of the 2019 Beijing Arbitration Commission (BAC) and Beijing International Arbitration Center (BIAC) Rules for International Investment Arbitration is more detailed and selective in this matter, establishing distinctions according to the type of document, as follows: 'Service and Time Limit: the Notice of Arbitration and the Response to the Notice of Arbitration shall be served by non-electronic means unless otherwise agreed by the Parties', whereas the remaining arbitration documents 'shall be delivered by electronic means ... unless the Parties agree or the Arbitral Tribunal orders otherwise'.[20]

It is important to take into account that this promoting of communication technologies in investment arbitration—and its expression in the wording of arbitral awards—is in fact a reflection of arbitral institutions' ultimate goals (eg efficiency, economy, celerity), which the arbitrators themselves also reflect when carrying out institutional or ad hoc arbitrations. The paradigms shaping the current arbitration world explain the inclusion in arbitration rules of provisions such as Article 14(6) of the 2020 LCIA Arbitration Rules:

The Arbitral Tribunal's power under Article 14(5) [make any procedural order it considers appropriate with regard to the fair, efficient and expeditious conduct of the arbitration] includes the making of any procedural order with a view to expediting the procedure to be adopted in the arbitration by: (iii) employing technology to enhance the efficiency and expeditious conduct of the arbitration (including any hearing).[21]

Moving forward in the arbitral proceedings, the initial meeting between the arbitrator or arbitrators and party representatives[22] is not always carried out in person. Institutions such as BAC/BIAC expressly provide for this in the investment arbitration

[18] LCIA Arbitration Rules (2020) art 14(3).

[19] Stockholm Chamber of Commerce (SCC) Arbitration Institute Arbitration Rules (2023) art 5(2). Nowadays emails are unanimously accepted as 'a means of communication that provides a record of sending'. This requirement continues to be formally included in the Arbitration Rules of various arbitration institutions. See, for instance, Article 12(3) of the Vienna Investment Arbitration Rules (2021): 'Written communications shall be sent in hard copy form by registered mail, letter with confirmation of receipt, courier service, or in electronic form, or by any other means of communication that provides a record of sending'; Article 2(1) of the Permanent Court of Arbitration (PCA) Arbitration Rules (2012): 'A notice, including a notification, communication or proposal, may be transmitted by any means of communication that provides or allows for a record of its transmission'; and Article 5(3) of the China International Economic and Trade Arbitration Commission (CIETAC) International Investment Arbitration Rules (2017): 'Any arbitration correspondence shall be deemed to have been properly served if delivered to the addressee or sent to the addressee's place of business, place of registration, domicile, habitual residence or mailing address, or ... or by any other means that can provide a record of the delivery, including but not limited to service by public notary, entrustment or retention'.

[20] Beijing Arbitration Commission (BAC) and Beijing International Arbitration Center (BIAC) Rules for International Investment Arbitration (2019) art 49.

[21] LCIA Arbitration Rules (2020) art 14.

[22] This initial meeting has a variety of names depending on the administering institution (case management conference, preliminary meeting, procedural conference, first session, preliminary conference, etc). The term 'case management conference' is used in this chapter.

context: 'The first case management conference may be conducted through a meeting in person, or by video conference, telephone conference or other means of electronic communication.'[23] Recent arbitration awards show that in practice this meeting is indeed held by videoconference ('the Tribunal held a first session with the Parties by videoconference'),[24] telephone ('the Tribunal and the Parties held a preliminary procedural consultation via telephone conference'),[25] or even email ('complying with the provisions of Article 24 of the International Chamber of Commerce (ICC) Rules, the Parties and the Tribunal carried out, through emails, the case management conference and procedural timetable').[26]

Regardless of how this initial procedural conference is held, the terms of reference—or another similarly named document—generated there are frequently shared with the parties by email. This is normally specified in the award itself, with wording such as: 'The Arbitral Tribunal circulated a signed electronic copy of the Terms of Reference [agreed during the Case Management Conference], together with Procedural Order No. 1 dated ....'[27] Furthermore, recent arbitration awards also note that arbitrators and parties sometimes sign the Terms of Reference electronically: 'The Parties and the members of the Tribunal signed the Terms of Reference (TofR) electronically, which was transmitted to the Court at its session on ... in accordance with Art 23(2) of the ICC Rules.'[28]

The investment awards discussed in this chapter include frequent references to the use of different types of technology during the usually very lengthy course of the arbitration. The following are some examples of this well-established practice: 'Claimant electronically filed its Memorial along with the following documents: ....',[29] 'the PCA received a complete electronic copy [of the Statement of Claim and the witness statement] together with exhibits ... and legal authorities ...',[30] 'the Respondent submitted the aforementioned revised materials to the record through the electronic file sharing

[23] Beijing Arbitration Commission (BAC) and Beijing International Arbitration Center (BIAC) Rules for International Investment Arbitration (2019) art 19(1). Article 3 of the Rules of Expedited Procedures for International Investment Arbitration establishes the same.

[24] *Bridgestone Licensing Services, Inc and Bridgestone Americas, Inc v Panama*, ICSID Case No ARB/16/34, Award (14 August 2020) [13].

[25] *Westmoreland Mining Holdings, LLC v Canada*, ICSID Case No UNCT/20/3, Award (31 January 2022) [20].

[26] Author translation of the original text in Spanish ('dando cumplimiento a lo establecido en el Artículo 24 de Reglamento CCI, las Partes y el Tribunal llevaron a cabo, por medio de correos electrónicos, la conferencia sobre la conducción del procedimiento y calendario procesal') *Dominicana Renovables v Dominican Republic*, ICC Case No 23364/JPA, Award (20 January 2021) [24].

[27] *Vamed Management & Services GmbH v Gabon*, ICC Case No 23975/FS (c. 23976/FS & 23977/FS), Award (21 March 2022) [30].

[28] *Reficar Columbia v CB&I Co*, ICC Case No 21747/RD, Award (2 June 2023) [42]. The use of electronic signatures (see definition of this term in section III) on diverse investment arbitration documents is not new, as this 2012 award demonstrates: 'At the initial hearing, the Terms of Appointment were agreed upon and signed by the Parties and the Tribunal, Professor [X] having authorized the use of its electronic signature. The Presiding Arbitrator signed the Procedural Rules on behalf of the Tribunal. Signed originals of each document were handed out to each Party and member of the Tribunal.' *Ulysseas, Inc v The Republic of Ecuador*, UNCITRAL, Final Award (12 June 2012) [15].

[29] *Kornikom EOOD v Serbia*, ARB/19/12, Award (20 September 2023) [48].

[30] *Fynerdale Holdings BV v Czech Republic*, PCA Case No 2018-18 (29 April 2021) [20]. Likewise: 'The Tribunal instructed the Parties to submit a timetable for the ... submission of skeleton arguments and of a joint electronic hearing bundle, and the pre-hearing conference call.' *Casinos Austria International GmbH and Casinos Austria Aktiengesellschaft v Argentina*, ICSID Case No ARB/14/32, Award (5 November 2021) [31].

platform',[31] 'the Parties informed that they couriered to the Secretary of the Tribunal five USB drives with a joint electronic bundle containing a full hyperlinked copy of the case file',[32] and so forth.

The use of technology may sometimes be a source of controversy between the parties, occasionally requiring arbitral tribunals to take positions on technological matters, as follows: 'The Parties exchanged communications regarding their disagreement with respect to the preparation of the Electronic Bundle for the Hearing ... the Tribunal provided additional instructions regarding the preparation of such Bundle',[33] and 'claimant objected to Respondent's letter, requesting that the Tribunal leave to dispense with the hard copy filing contemplated by clause 3.10 of PO 2. Claimant agreed to provide an index for its electronic submission in the form provided by clause 3.10.2 of PO 2 if leave were granted. ... Respondent reiterated its request dated 18 May 2020, arguing that clause 3(2) of PO 2 was a 'clear indication' of the supporting evidence in each submission, including with hyperlinks in the footnotes of the submission, is required'.[34] In such situations, it seems clear that the arbitrators' technological competence is a highly valued quality.[35]

These technological activities in the course of investment arbitrations show that the participants (fundamentally, party representatives and arbitrators) in administered arbitrations rely on a technology environment that supports their interventions. Digital case management platforms such as ICC Connect and the SCC Platform are proof that administering institutions have made and continue to make great pro-technology efforts. These institutions are aware of the growing number of arbitration institutions and their competitiveness when it comes to attracting clients, and also know that their technological capabilities may be a decisive element in the success or failure of their businesses. Anxious to avoid competitive disadvantage, the institutions are currently immersed in a global technological race to the top that undoubtedly benefits both arbitration users and arbitrators. That is why many arbitration awards record the arbitral actors' day-to-day activities involving technology, including those of arbitration institutions.

B. Remote Hearings

In any discussion of the ways in which contemporary investment awards reflect the use of technology at different stages of any arbitration, the hearing merits special attention. The hard and soft rules applicable to investment arbitration hearings reflect the radical changes in arbitration hearings over recent years, especially as a result of the COVID

[31] *Infinito Gold Ltd v Costa Rica*, ICSID Case No ARB/14/5, Award (3 June 2021) [24].

[32] *BayWa re Renewable Energy GmbH and BayWa re Asset Holding GmbH v Spain*, ICSID Case No ARB/15/16 (25 January 2021) [38].

[33] *Michael Anthony Lee-Chin v Dominican Republic*, ICSID Case No UNCT/18/3 (6 October 2023) [61].

[34] *JSC DTEK Krymenergo v Russia*, PCA Case No 2018-41 (1 November 2023) [60]–[61].

[35] Reflecting in detail on this question and making a distinction between 'basic' and 'premium' technological competence of arbitrators, see Fach Gómez (n 5) ch 2.

pandemic. The default rule in investment arbitration prior to lockdown was physical hearings,[36] in spite of the fact that technological elements such as the remote examination of witnesses were sometimes included in in-person hearings.[37] These technological interventions found support in provisions such as Article 28(4) of the 2012 PAC Rules of Arbitration: 'The arbitral tribunal may direct that witnesses, including expert witnesses, be examined through means of telecommunication that do not require their physical presence at the hearing (such as videoconference)',[38] text that reproduces Article 28(4) of the 2010 revised version of the UNCITRAL Arbitration Rules.[39]

As a consequence of the 2020 pandemic, there has been a striking change in the way in which arbitration hearings are conducted. In ongoing arbitrations in which the in-person hearings had not yet been held when the COVID restrictions were implemented, arbitral tribunals assumed a directive role,[40] proposing changes in the way in

[36] In other contexts, such as expedited or emergency arbitration, more frequent recourse to remote hearings was justified even before the COVID crisis. See, for example, Article 3(3) of the 2021 UNCITRAL Expedited Arbitration Rules: 'The arbitral tribunal may, after inviting the parties to express their views and taking into account the circumstances of the case, utilize any technological means as it considers appropriate to conduct the proceedings, including to communicate with the parties and to hold consultations and hearings remotely.' It is also interesting to look at the arguments surrounding the use of technology in the Explanatory Note to the UNCITRAL Expedited Arbitration Rules:

> A number of issues could be discussed during consultations so as to create a basis for a common understanding of the proceedings, for example: ... (iii) whether and how to conduct further consultations as well as hearings, including whether they would be in person or using technological means, including remotely ... Direct exchange between the parties and the arbitral tribunal at a hearing (whether in person or remotely) may facilitate a better understanding of the case and make the proceedings more efficient ... the arbitral tribunal may utilize any technological means to hold hearings without the physical presence of the parties or witnesses, including remotely.

paras 62, 72, and 76

[37] See, for instance: 'by letter transmitted by the Secretary of the Tribunal. The Tribunal wrote to the Parties concerning the examination of the witnesses and confirming that the hearing would take place on ... By this letter, the Tribunal confirmed its consent to the remote cross-examination of [X], one of the Respondent´s witnesses, at the hearing.' *Thomas Gosling and others v Mauritius*, ICSID Case No ARB/16/32, Award (18 February 2020) [30]. This was sometimes justified on medical grounds: 'The Claimant informed the Tribunal that the Parties had agreed that Mr. [X] would testify at the Hearing on the Merits through videoconference due to medical constraints.' *Infinito Gold Ltd v Costa Rica* (n 31) [52]. On other occasions, it might be due to logistical or scheduling issues: 'Claimant responded to the Tribunal's invitation regarding the examination of Mr [X] and Mr [X] by videoconference and a possibility of amending the timetable for the [in-person] hearing.' *Lion Mexico Consolidated LP v United Mexican States*, ICSID Case No ARB(AF)/15/2 (20 September 2021) [38].

[38] Permanent Court of Arbitration (PAC) Arbitration Rules (2012).

[39] UNCITRAL Arbitration Rules (2010).

[40] The importance of the principle of party autonomy in this context has also led to cases in which, in opposition to the court's proposal to hold a remote hearing, the arbitration parties' request to postpone the hearing has prevailed. For example:

> The PCA wrote to the Parties on behalf of the President of the Tribunal to inform them that, due to the propagation of COVID-19 in Europe and considering the restrictions on travel and gatherings in the Netherlands, it was unlikely that an in-person hearing could be held in late April [2020]. As such, the Tribunal invited the Parties to consider whether the Hearing could be held by video-conference, and any amendments of draft Procedural Order No 5 that may be required ... the Parties indicated that they considered that it would not be feasible to hold the Hearing by video-conference, in particular given that witnesses and experts would be cross-examined during the course of the Hearing. Both Parties thus requested the Tribunal to postpone the hearing until the fall of 2020.

Fynerdale Holdings BV v Czech Republic (n 30) [38]–[39]

On some occasions, if only one of the parties opposed the remote hearing, other types of strategies were employed to avoid it: 'The Respondent, however, resisted the Tribunal's directions to hold a remote hearing due to the C0VID-19 pandemic and then prevented the scheduled hearing from taking place by filing an unsuccessful request for the disqualification of the President.' *Triodos v Spain*, SCC Case No 2017/194, Final Award (24 October 2022) [822].

which the hearings were carried out; changes that may in turn have been adapted as the COVID crisis unfolded. For example, in the *Crescent v National Iranian Oil Company* case, the partial award contains a written record of the arbitral tribunal's lengthy reflections on the need to organize a hearing using technological tools. The PCA tribunal thus ruled out an in-person hearing, stating that:

> [i]n light of the worldwide spread of the COVID-19 coronavirus infection and resulting travel restrictions and constraints, the Tribunal had decided that it would be appropriate for the hearing to be held in London and attended in person only by a limited group, comprised of the members of the Tribunal, counsel making oral arguments, the Administrative Secretary, a staff member of the PCA, and the court reporter, providing none of these individuals presented any symptoms or had travelled from high risk areas in the preceding 14 days. All other participation would be by technical means, including access to a remote live transcript, video-conference or one-way remote live video feed.

That option seemed preferable to the arbitral tribunal than others such as 'a hearing via video only'. However, the court did not completely rule out the possibility that 'should the evolving situation render it impracticable to hold the hearing in the format described, the Tribunal would postpone the hearing'.[41]

In practice, as of 2020 many hearings on the merits are conducted partially or fully remotely.[42] Some of the references to these remote hearings[43] in the awards are worded as follows: 'The Parties confirmed their availability for a remote hearing ... a hearing on jurisdiction and the merits was held by video conference';[44] 'following exchanges between the Parties concerning the format of the hearing, the Tribunal Secretary communicated the Tribunal's decision to conduct the hearing remotely, in view of the pandemic and the consequent travel restrictions. In the same letter, the Tribunal provided logistic and administrative directions to assist with the organization of the remote

[41] *Crescent v National Iranian Oil Company*, PCA Case No 2009-20, Partial Award on Merits (27 September 2021) [223]–[224]. In this case the hearing was postponed, and 'from 3 August 2020 to 7 August 2020, a final hearing ("Final Hearing") was held, with some participants attending in-person at the IDRC in London, and others attending via the videoconferencing platform Zoom or receiving a livestream video feed.' ibid [251].

[42] The extent to which these hearings are in-person varies greatly and the peculiarities of such proceedings are taken into account when adopting a case-by-case decision. An example is provided by this court's definition of the notion of hybrid hearings:

> The Tribunal also proposed the following (the 'hybrid hearing modality'): (i) the Members of the Tribunal will use their best efforts to sit together in London, United Kingdom; (ii) as such, each Party will need to consent to hold the hearing in London in lieu of Paris pursuant to Article 63 of the ICSID Convention; (iii) core members of each Party's legal team are invited to appear in-person before the Tribunal to make oral submissions and conduct direct- and cross-examinations; and (iv) in the interest of fairness, witnesses should appear remotely.

Bay View Group LLC and The Spalena Company LLC v Rwanda, ICSID Case No ARB/18/21, Award (30 March 2022) [57]

[43] Remote hearings are hearings that are conducted in several places using communication technology such as videoconferencing. Maxi Scherer, 'Remote Hearings in International Arbitration: An Analytical Framework' (2020) 37(4) Journal of International Arbitration 407. On the basis of this author's reflections, the potentially misleading notions of virtual hearings and online hearings are therefore not used in this section unless these terms appear in a specific award or provision.

[44] *Rasia FZE and Joseph K Borkowski v Armenia*, ICSID Case No ARB/18/28, Award (20 January 2023) [48]–[73].

hearing',[45] and 'the Parties notified the Tribunal of their agreement, in light of the on-going public health circumstances, to proceed by way of a video-conference hearing ... The Parties noted that they were conferring on a remote hearing protocol'.[46]

The growing importance of remote hearings in commercial and investment arbitration as a result of the COVID crisis has been also assessed from a quantitative perspective. The 2021 Queen Mary University of London and White & Case International Arbitration Survey reported that 72 per cent of those surveyed 'sometimes, frequently or always use virtual hearing rooms.' (In the 2018 survey, 64 per cent of respondents stated that they had never used virtual hearing rooms.)[47] Likewise, an empirical study carried out by prestigious arbitrators and practitioners shows an unquestionable shift in the trend: 'The prevalence of fully remote hearings in the second quarter of 2020 was over ten times greater than at any time previously.'[48]

Administering institution rules that were drawn up or updated after the COVID pandemic bear witness to this reality, confirming that arbitral hearings can now be carried out partially or totally remotely. It is interesting to compare, for example, the 2023 version of Article 32(2) of the SCC Arbitration Rules: 'After consulting with the parties and having regard to the circumstances, the Arbitral Tribunal shall decide ... whether any hearing shall be conducted (a) in person, at a specified location, or (b) remotely, in whole or in part, by videoconference or other appropriate means of communication',[49] with the shorter 2017 version of the same provision: 'The Arbitral Tribunal shall, in consultation with the parties, determine the date, time and location of any hearing and shall provide the parties with reasonable notice thereof.'[50]

Along with these provisions, administering institutions and law firms have created a wide range of documents (ie guidelines, protocols, checklists, notes, toolkits) that address multiple practical details surrounding both the preparations for and conducting of remote hearings. After milestones such as the April 2020 Joint Declaration supporting the continuation of arbitration during the COVID crisis, signed by over a dozen prestigious arbitration institutions,[51] it seemed clear that these institutions were determined to deal with the COVID crisis by promoting the use of technology. This also meant that the particularities of non-in-person hearings had to be managed quickly and skilfully. In the investment arbitration context, organizations like ICSID made notable commitments to significant financial outlay and providing technological

[45] *Alverley Investments Limited and Germen Properties Ltd v Romania*, ICSID Case No ARB/18/30, Award (16 March 2022) [71].
[46] *Alcor Holdings Ltd v Czech Republic*, PCA Case No 2018-45, Award (2 March 2022) [47].
[47] Queen Mary University of London and White & Case (n 2).
[48] Gary Born, Anneliese Day, and Hafez Virjee, 'Remote Hearings (2020 Survey): A Spectrum of Preferences' (2021) 38(3) Journal of International Arbitration 291.
[49] SCC Arbitration Rules (2023) art 32(2).
[50] ibid.
[51] These institutions stated their ambition 'to support international arbitration's ability to contribute to stability and foreseeability in a highly unstable environment, including by ensuring that pending cases may continue and that parties may have their cases heard without undue delay.' Arbitral Institutions COVID-19 Joint Statement (2020) <https://iccwbo.org/news-publications/arbitration-adr-rules-and-tools/arbitral-institutions-joint-statement-in-the-wake-of-the-covid-19-outbreak/>.

training.[52] In the commercial arbitration field, various ICC documents on technology (especially the 'Commission Report on Leveraging Technology for Fair, Effective and Efficient International Arbitration Proceedings') are highly remarkable for their quality and modernity.[53]

This hard and soft law support for the technologization of investment arbitration hearings has been suitably reflected in the investment arbitration awards issued in recent years. When referring to the pre-hearing procedures phase, these awards give detailed accounts of the technological aspects of non-in-person hearings. The preparations for remote hearings, which require close collaboration between multiple actors, are made clear, for example, in the resulting investment award: 'the members of the Tribunal, the Tribunal Secretary, the Parties' counsel and representatives, the witness [X], Arbitration Place staff, and the court reporter held a trial videoconference to verify the proper functioning of the Zoom platform.'[54] Likewise, arbitral tribunals frequently issue very detailed procedural orders on the organizing of remote hearings,[55] documents which are also referred to in the final awards, with wording such as the following: 'The Tribunal ... proposed to conduct the hearing via the Zoom platform, and invited the Parties' comments on draft Procedural Order No 8 in respect of arrangements for a videoconference hearing ... having considered the Parties' comments, the Tribunal issued Procedural Order No 8, inter alia setting out the hearing schedule and the videoconference etiquette.'[56]

[52] International Centre for the Settlement of Investment Disputes (ICSID) 'Virtual Hearings' (2023) <https://icsid.worldbank.org/services/hearing-facilities/virtual-hearings>; ICC, 'In Focus: In-Person, Remote and Hybrid Hearings' (2023) <https://icsid.worldbank.org/resources/content/in-focus/hearing-facilities>; ICC, 'China Arbitration Summit 2020: Practical Tips for Holding Effective Remote Hearings' (2023) <https://icsid.worldbank.org/resources/multimedia/china-arbitration-summit-2020-practical-tips-holding-effective-remote-hearings>.

[53] International Chamber of Commerce (ICC) 'Guidance Note on Possible Measures Aimed at Mitigating the Effects of the COVID 19 Pandemic' (2020) <https://iccwbo.org/news-publications/arbitration-adr-rules-and-tools/icc-guidance-note-on-possible-measures-aimed-at-mitigating-the-effects-of-the-covid-19-pandemic/?dm=bypass>; ICC, 'Note to Parties and Arbitral Tribunals on the Conduct of the Arbitration' (2021) <https://iccwbo.org/news-publications/arbitration-adr-rules-and-tools/note-parties-arbitral-tribunals-conduct-arbitration/>; ICC, 'Commission Report. Leveraging Technology for Fair, Effective and Efficient International Arbitration Proceedings' (2022) <https://cdn.iccwbo.org/content/uploads/sites/3/2022/02/icc-arbitration-and-adr-commission-report-on-leveraging-technology-for-fair-effective-and-efficient-international-arbitration-proceedings.pdf>.

[54] *Lao Holdings & Sanum v Laos & al*, SIAC Case No ARB 414/17/QW, Award (11 August 2011) [47].

[55] For instance, in the case of *Gran Colombia Gold Corp v Colombia*, Procedural Order No 7 is devoted to the Organization of the [Virtual] Hearing. This 18-page document brings together the agreements reached by the parties on various issues as well as the tribunal's decisions on the remaining issues. The part referring to the organization of the hearing contains multiple sections and subsections, some devoted to the specificities of remote hearings: date and format; order of proceedings and schedule; time allocation; documents for use at the hearing (electronic hearing bundle; demonstrative exhibits and electronic presentation of evidence); audio/video recording; transcription; interpretation; post-hearing submissions and statements of costs; open hearing; and virtual hearing (testing, participants, connectivity, equipment and set-up, break-out rooms). There are also three annexes, the third of which covers the protection of confidential information, in which the virtual nature of the hearing is also taken into account. *Aris Mining Corporation (formerly known as GCM Mining Corp and Gran Colombia Gold Corp v Colombia*, Procedural Order 7 (21 September 2020).

[56] *Bank Melli Iran and Bank Saderat Iran v Bahrain*, PCA Case No 2017-25, Award (9 November 2021) [124]–[126]. In the same vein: 'The Court issued Procedural Order No. 13 with the Virtual Hearing Protocol' ('Tribunal emitió la Orden Procesal No 13 con el Protocolo de Audiencia Virtual'). *Dominicana Renovables v Dominican Republic* (n 26) [73].

Once the pre-hearing preparations have been completed, the use of technology in remote or partially remote hearings, fuelled by recent arbitral institutions' rules and documents, as noted above, has also been reflected in the wording of investment awards. Awards issued from 2020 onwards contain many examples that refer to different aspects of remote hearings in which technology plays a crucial role (opening presentations on Zoom,[57] remote witness examination, electronic transcripts and recording,[58] costs or remote hearings,[59] etc). To cite just a couple of thought-provoking examples, see, for instance, the explanation for the president of the tribunal's participation by videoconference, which would have been considered a highly odd situation not long ago:

> ICSID confirmed to the Parties that the President of the Tribunal would participate in the ... Merits Hearing by video conference. ICSID confirmed that the participants in the Hearing room in Montreal would be able to see and hear the President, and that the President would hear and see the Hearing room, including documents and presentations shown by the Parties. The Parties were invited to provide the President with an electronic copy of their presentations and any demonstrative exhibits that they intended to display at the Hearing, at least 30 minutes in advance of their presentations.[60]

It is also interesting to consider how transparency in the investment hearing context requires the use of technology:

> the Tribunal confirmed that the hearing would be 'open to the public' as required by the BIT. The President proposed to the Parties that, in light of the virtual modality of the hearing, the hearing would be made public by posting recordings, with confidential information redacted, of the hearing on the ICSID website. The Parties agreed on the record with the Tribunal's proposal. Video recordings with the Parties' agreed redactions were subsequently posted on the ICSID website.[61]

[57] See for instance: 'Claimant informed the Parties and the Tribunal that Claimant's counsel Andrea Menaker had tested positive for Covid and would, therefore, give her opening presentation and attend via Zoom.' *Kornikom EOOD v Serbia* (n 29) [fn 4].

[58] For example: 'An electronic transcript of the hearing was delivered to the Parties at the end of each hearing day.' *NJSC Naftogaz of Ukraine, PJSC State Joint Stock Company Chornomornaftogaz, PJSC Ukrtransgaz, Subsidiary Company Likvo, PJSC Ukrgasvydobuvannya, PJSC Ukrtransnafta, and Subsidiary Company Gaz Ukraiiny v The Russian Federation*, PCA Case No 2017-16, Award (12 April 2023) [50]. Likewise: 'The Tribunal invited the Parties to i) agree on a schedule for the next procedural steps; ii) submit electronic copies of the exhibits they agreed to introduce during the hearing ... Mexico confirmed that the electronic versions of the exhibits submitted during the Hearing had been uploaded to the Box folder created for this case'. *Lion Mexico Consolidated LP v Mexico* (n 37) [42].

[59] For instance: 'The Claimants insist that if the Respondents were to prevail on the merits, the Tribunal should "(a) order Respondents to pay all of the SIAC arbitration and virtual hearing costs; (b) deny Respondents any recovery of the SIAC arbitration or virtual hearing costs"', *Lao Holdings & Sanum v Laos and others* (n 54) [327].

[60] *Lone Pine Resources Inc. v The Government of Canada*, ICSID Case No UNCT/15/2, Award (21 November 2022) [98].

[61] *Bay View Group LLC and The Spalena Company LLC v Rwanda* (n 42) [69].

C. Remote Deliberations and Electronic Transmission of Awards

The use of technology does not decrease as arbitration proceedings unfold. There are, for instance, e-exchanges of post-hearing briefs, non-in-person deliberations using means such as videoconferences, email exchanges, conference calls, and the electronic transmission of awards.

One phase of proceedings in which technology may intervene is during the arbitrators' deliberations. It is interesting to look at what the rules applicable to investment cases stipulate regarding these deliberations. Some refer only to the physical place for holding them. In this vein, Article 18(2) of the UNCITRAL Arbitration Rules states: 'the arbitral tribunal may meet at any location it considers appropriate for deliberations'.[62] Other arbitration institutions have also adopted this flexible approach to the geographical location of the deliberations, with provisions such as Article 25(2) of the VIAC investment arbitration rules indicating that the location chosen for the deliberations does not affect the place of the arbitration.[63]

As well as referring to the place where the deliberations are held, other rules also clarify the way in which they are carried out, reflecting an equally accommodating approach to the latter. Thus, Article 20(3) of the BAC–BIAC Arbitration Rules stipulates that 'the Arbitral Tribunal may hold deliberations at any place or in any manner that it considers appropriate',[64] and this is also understood to cover non-face-to-face deliberations. The same interpretation ensues from the wording of ICSID Arbitration Rule 34(2): 'the Tribunal may deliberate at any place and by any means it considers appropriate'. Should any doubts remain, the ICSID website explains that 'the deliberations of the Tribunal take place in private and can be held by any means that the Tribunal considers appropriate, including in person, by telephone, videoconference or correspondence'.[65]

Even before the COVID crisis,[66] arbitration award texts included references to the different methods of holding non-in-person deliberations to be found in arbitration practice. To cite a few examples: 'The Arbitral Tribunal held deliberations in writing and through conference calls, in order to reach an agreement on the decisions taken in this Award',[67] 'the tribunal held deliberations in The Hague ... and further exchanged views through other means of communication'.[68] '[T]he Tribunal held deliberations

[62] The same wording appears in the PCA Arbitration Rules (2012) art 18(2).

[63] SCC Arbitration Rules (2023) art 25(2).

[64] Likewise, CIETAC International Investment Arbitration Rules (2017) art 20(4).

[65] ICSID (2023) 'Deliberations—ICSID Convention Arbitration (2022 Rules)' <https://icsid.worldbank.org/procedures/arbitration/convention/deliberations/2022>.

[66] This topic has been addressed for more than two decades in the judicial and academic context. See for example: 'A sentence of the Swiss Supreme Court shows that the arbitrators need not meet in person and are free to conduct deliberations by electronic means, including E-Mail, provided that suitable precautions are taken.' Richard Hill, 'On-line Arbitration: Issues and Solutions' (1999) 15(2) Arbitration International 199. Likewise, the Austrian Oberster Gerichtshof held that there is no non-recognition of an award on the grounds that the arbitrators did not meet in person to deliberate, but that the tribunal may deliberate by other means of communication. Judgment of 26 April 2006, XXXII YBCA 2007, 259.

[67] *Vito G Gallo v Canada*, Award (15 September 2011) [118].

[68] *Transban Investments Corp v Venezuela*, ICSID Case No ARB/12/24, Award (22 November 2017) [32].

immediately following the hearing, then by correspondence and at a meeting convened in London'.[69]

Scholars have recently highlighted the different ways in which new technologies can help arbitrators at the deliberation stage. A highly illustrative chapter of this book is entirely devoted to tribunal dynamics and arbitral deliberations, identifying the criteria that arbitrators should take into account when deciding how to hold their deliberations:

> The deliberation *stricto sensu* may be held in person, by video conference or by telephone, although the progress of videoconferencing has made that last solution obsolete. In the absence of previous deliberations of the arbitral tribunal, in particular post-hearing deliberation, an in-person meeting is highly recommended. When the arbitrators are already aware of their respective positions and have had the opportunity to discuss them, a videoconference is suggested to avoid unnecessary costs.[70]

Technology can also be beneficial in face-to-face deliberations, in the following sense:

> In case of a recording of the remote hearing, the tribunal is not only able to see and hear the witness at the time of the testimony, but also later, for instance during deliberations. Being able to view again a specific moment of a recorded testimony might be more helpful than just re-reading a certain passage in a transcript.[71]

Once the deliberations are concluded and the award has been drafted, it has to be communicated to the parties. The arbitration rules sometimes stipulate that this is the responsibility of the arbitration tribunal,[72] but on most occasions it is left to the arbitral institution, once it has received the award from the arbitrators.[73]

Arbitration rules specify how this communication—also known as service—should take place. Some, like VIAC, seem cautious about transmitting the award electronically:

> The Secretary General shall transmit the award to the parties in hardcopy form. If it is not possible or feasible to send the award in hardcopy form within a reasonable time,

[69] *Occidental Exploration and Production Company v Ecuador*, Final Award (1 July 2004) [24].

[70] Yves Derains, 'Tribunal Dynamics and Arbitral Deliberations' in Fach Gómez and Titi (n 4) 330. A recent ICC survey in this field notes that: 'Aspects that over 25% agreed to be less effective by video were ... tribunal deliberations and interaction (37%)'. ICC (n 53) (2022) 34.

[71] Scherer (n 43) s 5.2[b][ii].

[72] UNCITRAL Arbitration Rules (2021) art 36(2): 'Copies of the award signed by the arbitrators shall be communicated to the parties by the arbitral tribunal'. Similarly worded: 'The Arbitral Tribunal shall deliver a copy of the award to each of the parties and to the SCC without delay.' SCC Arbitration Rules (2023) art 42(4). This provision is explained in more detail in the SCC Guidelines for Arbitrators ((2023) 18):

> The tribunal should upload the award to the SCC Platform, as a signed and scanned PDF attachment, on the day that the award is rendered. The same day, the tribunal should send a signed hard-copy original of the award to the parties by courier or registered mail. Proof of dispatch of the award to the parties should be sent to the SCC together with an original hard-copy of the award.

[73] BAC–BIAC Rules for International Investment Arbitration (2019) art 42(7) and ICSID Arbitration Rules (2022) r 48(1).

> or if the parties so agree, the Secretariat may send a copy of the award in electronic form. In this case a copy of the award in hardcopy form may be sent at a later stage ... The Secretariat shall retain an original copy of the award and the documentation of proof of sending.[74]

In contrast, other arbitral institutions attach more importance to the softcopy than they would if it were merely a courtesy copy. For instance, the ICC issued in 2020 a 'Guidance Note on possible measures aimed at mitigating the effects of the Covid-19 pandemic', where it declared that 'parties are encouraged to agree, whenever possible, to the electronic notification of the award.[75] ICSID, whose rules do not refer to the electronic transmission of awards, nevertheless use this method frequently, as its website specifies that 'the Award is rendered when ICSID dispatches certified copies of the Award to the parties. This is typically done by electronic means. Certified hard copies of the Award may be requested by the parties.'[76] Going a step further, the LCIA does not only expressly authorize the electronic transmission of awards, but also establishes this as the priority form of communication: 'Such transmission may be made by any electronic means, and (if so requested by any party or if transmission by electronic means to a party is not possible) in paper form. In the event of any disparity between electronic and paper forms, the electronic form shall prevail.'[77] With reference to this LCIA policy, well-known authors consider that it does not mean that hard copy awards are simply sent electronically, but that 'fully electronic awards (i.e., for which no original exists on paper) are now possible.'[78]

Various recent investment award texts have addressed the electronic transmission of awards. Examples, which also reflect the importance of party autonomy in this issue, are as follows:[79]

> The Parties also agreed as follows in the ToR, with respect to the mechanics of executing and transmitting the eventual award in this case ... a single electronic file and

[74] VIAC Rules of Investment Arbitration and Mediation (2021) art 36(5).

[75] ICC (n 53) (2020) para 15. This phrase, however, no longer appears in 2021 ICC Note, issued when the lockdown had already ended. ICC (n 53) (2021).

[76] ICSID 'Award—ICSID Convention Arbitration (2022 Rules)' (2023) <https://icsid.worldbank.org/procedures/arbitration/convention/award/2022>.

[77] LCIA Arbitration Rules (2020) art 26.7. This wording also appears in commercial arbitration texts such as the 2021 ACICA Arbitration Rules and Expedited Arbitration Rules.

[78] Ongenae and Piers make a distinction between 'mere electronic notification [of the award]' and 'fully electronic award'. Kevin Ongenae and Maud Piers, 'Procedural Formalities in Arbitration: Towards a Technologically Neutral Legal Framework' (2021) 38(1) Journal of International Arbitration 27, 50, and 52.

[79] Party autonomy in this context may also mean that:

> the Parties have reached a mutual agreement that the award shall be executed by the members of the Arbitral Tribunal through wet-signed hardcopies. These wet-signed hard copies of the award will be promptly dispatched to the Parties at the addresses of their respective legal representatives, as identified in section I.1 supra. As a gesture of courtesy, the Parties will also receive an electronic copy of the present award via email.

WCV World Capital Ventures Cyprus Ltd & Channel Crossings Ltd v Czech Republic, PCA Case No 2016-12 (26 July 2023) [103].

notified to the parties by the Secretariat by email or any other means of telecommunication that provides a record of the sending thereof.[80]

And: 'the Parties confirmed, upon invitation of the Tribunal, that they agreed to receive a signed electronic version of the Award on Jurisdiction with the image of the signatures of each of the arbitrators.'[81]

Finally, it should also be noted that transparency, as a transversal value of investment arbitration, means in this context that many arbitration awards are nowadays published in PDF on arbitration institution websites and in legal repositories.[82]

III. Technological Requirements Forming Part of the Compulsory Content of an Investment Award: Reality or Science Fiction?

The previous section addressed the question of references in the investment awards' wording to the electronic communication of an award to the arbitration parties. This section focuses on the closely connected issue of the electronic signature of awards, taking this as a starting point from which to ponder the broader issue of whether there are any technological requirements that have to be complied with nowadays in order to fulfil the minimum content requirements of investment awards.

An examination of the provisions on awards in the investment arbitration rules covered in this chapter shows that they all require awards to be signed by the arbitral tribunal members.[83] The list of minimum contents for awards in Rule 59(2) of the ICSID Arbitration Rules includes the requisite that 'the Award shall be signed by the members of the Tribunal who voted for it'.[84] The provision also adds that the award 'may be signed by electronic means'. ICSID Additional Facility Arbitration Rule 70(2) likewise notes that 'it may be signed by electronic means'[85] and Article 26(2) LCA also includes a technological reference when dealing with the signing method: 'Any award may be signed electronically and/or in counterparts and assembled into a single instrument.'[86] In line with these provisions for electronic signatures, some recent investment awards

[80] *Bedri Selmani v Kosovo* (n 9) [17]. Signing an award in counterparts means that various copies of the award are printed so that there is a separate copy for each arbitrator to sign and, as this award specifies, all the signed copies are subsequently assembled into a single final document.

[81] *Beijing Everyway Traffic and Lighting Company Limited v Ghana*, PCA 2021-15, Award (30 January 2023) [81]; *Inter Rao v CELEC (Ecuador)*, CAM Caso No. 3568-18, Award (29 May 2023) [46].

[82] ICSID and the PCA are two institutions whose rules refer to the online publication of awards: 'If the parties agree, ICSID will publish the full text or a redacted version of the Award' ICSID Arbitration Rules (2022) r 62(2), and 'an award may be made public with the consent of all parties or where and to the extent disclosure is required of a party by legal duty, to protect or pursue a legal right or in relation to legal proceedings before a court or other competent authority' PCA Arbitration Rules (2012) art 34(5).

[83] See Article 34(4) of the UNCITRAL Arbitration Rules, 42(3) SCC, 42(6) BAC–BIAC, 47(3) CIETAC, 34(6) PCA, and 36(3) VIAC.

[84] ICSID Arbitration Rules (2022) r 59(2).

[85] ICSID Additional Facility Arbitration Rules (2022) r 70(2).

[86] LCIA Arbitration Rules (2020) art 26(2). Similar wording is also found in the commercial arbitration context. For instance: 'Unless the parties agree otherwise, or the Arbitral Tribunal or ACICA directs otherwise, any award may be signed electronically and/or in counterparts and assembled into a single instrument'. ACICA Arbitration Rules and Expedited Arbitration Rules (2021) art 42(4).

refer to signing the documents electronically, for example: 'The Tribunal invited the Parties to indicate whether they agreed to the Final Award being (i) signed electronically by the members of the Tribunal and/or (ii) notified to the Parties electronically by the ICC Court, in order to avoid important delays due to the Covid-19 pandemic.'[87] There are also investment arbitration procedural orders that contain provisions such as: 'Orders, decisions and the Award may be signed electronically.'[88]

The first issue to address here is one of terminology. These texts make only brief references to electronic signatures and provide no explanatory definitions of the term.[89] This may create doubts over interpretation, since there are currently multiple mechanisms for signing documents, which, in contrast to wet-ink signatures,[90] could be broadly labelled electronic signatures.[91] Among them are signing by typing a name or initials; drawing a signature with a finger on a touchscreen device; signing with a digital pen; scanning handwritten signatures to paste onto a document; clickwrap signatures; online signature generator platforms; password-based signatures, biometric signatures—verification via fingerprint, voice or face ID—and digital certificates issued by certificate authorities.

Scholars agree that the terms 'electronic signature' and 'digital signature' are not synonyms, and that the latter should be exclusively reserved for a qualified type of electronic signature that offers certain security levels (in terms of data integrity, guarantees of authenticity, non-repudiation, etc).[92] The same underlying idea—that not every electronic signature qualifies as a digital signature—emerges from the EU eIDAS Regulation, which distinguishes between simple, advanced and qualified electronic signatures.[93] In line with this, arbitration scholars argue that there is a technological

[87] *GBC Oil Company Ltd v Albania, Albpetrol*, ICC Case No 22676/GR, Award (6 July 2020) [259].

[88] *Suffolk (Mauritius) Limited, Mansfield (Mauritius) Limited and Silver Point Mauritius v Portuguese Republic*, ICSID Case No ARB/22/28, Procedural Order 1 (13 July 2023) [5.3]. With the same wording, see *Ruby River Capital LLC v Canada*, ICSID Case No ARB/23/5, Procedural Order 1 (23 August 2023) [5.3], and *Tayeb Benabderrahmane v State of Qatar*, ICSID Case No ARB/22/23, Procedural Order 2 (11 April 2023) [5.3].

[89] The American Arbitration Association (AAA) 2022 commercial arbitration rules do distinguish between electronic and digital signatures: 'R-48. Form of Award (a) Any award shall be in writing and signed by a majority of the arbitrators. Signatures may be executed in electronic or digital form. The award shall be executed in the form and manner required by law.'

[90] A traditional wet-ink signature is written by the person her/himself in ink.

[91] In the same vein, notions such as electronic award (e-award), digital award, which are dealt with in the previous section, can also cause disputes over interpretation.

[92] Following Gartner's 'Information Technology Glossary', a digital signature is a:

> specific type of electronic signature (e-signature) that relies on public-key cryptography to support identity authentication and provide data and transaction integrity. It is used as a means to reach a goal of providing irrefutable evidence that a specific digital object originated from a specific individual and has not been altered. The authentication mechanism supports the business need of capturing the signer's intent to sign. Digital signatures are used to support several security functions. However, the focus of this technology profile is on digital signatures used to protect the integrity and authenticity of documents, such as forms, agreements or contracts, and to demonstrate intent to sign.
> <www.gartner.com/en/information-technology/glossary/digital-signature>

Referring to digital signatures in the arbitration context, see Erik Schäfer, 'Chapter 8: E-Signature of Arbitral Awards' in Maxi Scherer and others (eds), *International Arbitration and the COVID-19 Revolution* (Kluwer Law International 2020) 154–56; Ilias Bantekas, 'Form and Contents of Award' in Ilias Bantekas and others (eds), *UNCITRAL Model Law on International Commercial Arbitration: A Commentary* (CUP 2020) 814.

[93] Regulation (EU) No 910/2014 of the European Parliament and of the Council of 23 July 2014 on electronic identification and trust services for electronic transactions in the internal market and repealing Directive 1999/93/EC. OJ L 257, 28.8.2014, 73–114.

and legal gap between an award 'issued in PDF format with bitmap copies of the original signatures on the physically existing award'[94] and an award 'that only exists in electronic format, i.e., for which no "original" counterpart exists on paper [and] it is signed with a digital signature'.[95]

With the aim of determining the characteristics of the latest practice regarding electronic signatures in investment awards, the author checked the arbitrators' signatures in the twenty-nine investment awards issued in 2023, all of which are available in PDF on italaw.[96] The most common way in which arbitrators added their signatures to these awards was by signing the signature page by hand, which is in fact what happened in thirteen cases of three-member arbitral tribunals and one case involving a sole arbitrator. These handwritten signatures can be incorporated into hard copy awards by various means: the arbitrators send the finalized hard copy award—usually, various copies—from one to another by post to obtain all their handwritten signatures; the first arbitrator signs the hard copy award by hand, scans it and sends it to another arbitrator, who prints the scanned version before signing it, and so on;[97] at their last face-to-face meeting, all the arbitrators sign on one page, which is incorporated into the paper award when it is drafted, or a meeting is held in order to for the arbitrators to physically sign the original award.[98]

Five more 2023 awards were also signed by hand, but on separate pages.[99] Each arbitrator has received her/his respective signature page and, after being signed manually, they have been incorporated into the award document.[100] There are also six cases in which the president of the tribunal has signed and sometimes dated the award by hand, but the other two arbitrators' signatures have not yet been incorporated into the document that appears on italaw. Finally, there are four awards (three from a three-member panel and one from a sole arbitrator) on which there are no handwritten signatures, but the legend '[signed]' has been typed.

In short, signatures of these types do not seem to fit the strict definition for digital signatures referred to above. There is only one 2023 award that seems to contain a digital signature, but this belongs not to an arbitrator, but to a member of the administering institution (Santiago Arbitration and Mediation Centre-CAM Santiago), who

94 Schäfer (n 92) 163.

95 Kevin Ongenae, 'Electronic Arbitral Awards: Yea or Nay? A Glimpse Inside the Minds of Arbitral Institutions' (2023) 40(3) Journal of International Arbitration 263.

96 That is the number of awards available on italaw at the time of writing (November 2023).

97 This option is undoubtedly faster than the first one and may justify the fact that signatures are sometimes in different colours. However, the first option provides three authentic handwritten signatures that have not initially been scanned. There is also the possibility that at first an electronic text is generated with the scanned signatures of the arbitrators, but that the original signature of all the arbitrators is later brought together in a single document.

98 Ongenae and Piers (n 78) 49.

99 Referring to signing awards in counterparts, ICC (n 53) (2020) para 15.

100 Therefore, arbitrators do not generally seem to incorporate a scanned handwritten signature into a soft copy version of the award. For instance, in the case of *Antonio del Valle Ruiz et al v Kingdom of Spain*, PCA Case No 2019-17, in which there is both a Spanish and an English version of the 13 March award, the three arbitrators' signatures are not identical. Likewise, differences are also visible in the signatures of the four awards signed by the arbitrator Mr. Fernández Armesto in 2023 and available on italaw. This does not completely rule out that some arbitrators do use, for instance, a sort of handwritten signature generator.

used Adobe Acrobat Sign to add her signature to the three pages containing the arbitrators' handwritten signatures.[101]

To take a step forward here, it is important to reflect on the role that electronic signatures—a not uncontroversial notion, as we have seen—play in investment awards today. The arbitration rules above that refer to the electronic signing of awards use verbs such as 'may' or 'agree', which show that signing investment awards electronically cannot be considered compulsory. That is, even though the signing of awards is one of the formal requirements of what currently constitutes the minimum content of an investment award in such important contexts such as ICSID,[102] technology has not yet permeated these requirements to the point of imposing electronic—or even digital—signatures as necessities. In fact, there is currently a series of not insignificant legal and voluntary constraints to arbitrators' use of electronic signatures in investment awards.

The legal restrictions may become especially relevant in the post-award challenge phase (award annulment or award recognition and enforcement). Rule 70(2) of the ICSID Additional Facility Arbitration Rules requires caution with regard to compliance with the law of the arbitration seat:[103] '[i]t may be signed by electronic means ... if allowed by the law of the seat of arbitration'.[104] The 2020 ICC Guidance Note declares that 'subject to any requirements of mandatory law that may be applicable, the parties may agree that ... any award be signed by the members of the tribunal in counterparts'.[105] There is also a generic reference to this restriction in the wording of investment awards themselves: 'The Parties also agreed as follows in the ToR, with respect to the mechanics of executing and transmitting the eventual award in this case: "The Parties likewise agree, again subject to any mandatory rules of law, (1) that any award may be signed by the members of the Tribunal in counterparts"'.[106]

Legislative harmonization of the requirements, characteristics, and effects of electronic signatures is still a long way off (some countries have not yet fully addressed the issue and those that have use dissimilar parameters).[107] These differences in national

[101] *Inter Rao v CELEC* (n 81). From the ICC perspective, this application provides 'signature capability, document routing, signer authentication, and security features to lock the signed document'. ICC (n 53) (2022) 25.

[102] Catharine Titi, 'What Is an Award? Concept, Content, Drafting, Effects' in Fach Gómez and Titi (n 4).

[103] The non-admissibility of electronic signatures by the law of the arbitration seat is a reality that is provided for in commercial arbitration rules such as Article 32(4) of the International Centre for Dispute Resolution (ICDR), International Dispute Resolution Procedures (2021): 'Awards, Orders, Decisions and Rulings: An order or award may be signed electronically, unless (a) the applicable law requires a physical signature, (b) the parties agree otherwise, or (c) the arbitral tribunal or Administrator determines otherwise' <www.icdr.org/rules_forms_fees>. Likewise, in the context of commercial arbitration, scholars question whether the applicable law can accept e-awards with electronic signature, since there are interpretative doubts about the stipulation that 'the award shall be made in writing', in Article 31(1) of the UNCITRAL Model Law and reproduced by many national legislatures.

[104] ICSID Additional Facility Arbitration Rules (2022) r 70(2).

[105] ICC (n 53) (2020).

[106] This generic reference to 'signed in counterparts' appears in this award as follows: pages 180, 181 and 182 have the same structure: reference to the place and date of the arbitration and name and space for the three arbitrators' signatures. Each arbitrator included her/his handwritten signature on one of the three pages—each with a different pen and in a different colour, leaving the spaces for the other two signatures blank. A single document was created from these three pages—and all the preceding ones—which was scanned and is now publicly available. *Bedri Selmani v* Kosovo (n 9) [17].

[107] See, for example, the wide range of responses from 36 ICC National Committees regarding their national law's acceptance of the practice of manually signing awards in counterparts, scanning the counterparts, and assembling them into one electronic file. ICC (n 53) (2022) 26.

legislation and standards fuel the importance of a private international law approach when referring to the legal notion of electronic signatures. The content of the applicable law is crucial in this matter, as both scholars[108] and administering institutions have pointed out:

> The powers of the tribunal are also subject to any relevant laws applicable to the arbitration ... These laws might place constraints on the use of technologies, whether such use is agreed by the parties or directed by the tribunal. Arbitrators might need to obtain advice on the applicable laws to identify those constraints and the cost of obtaining such advice should be counted as part of the costs of the arbitration. For example, arbitrators may need to establish whether it is legitimate at the seat of the arbitration to issue an electronic (i.e. e-signed) award.[109]

In this sense, a Swedish Court of Appeal recently held that the Swedish Arbitration Act (*lex arbitri*) required the—commercial in this case—award to be physically signed, and therefore rejected the arbitration tribunal's modus operandi (the arbitrators had pasted their scanned signatures onto a Word version of the award, which was subsequently converted to PDF and sent to the parties by email).[110]

Another legal circumstance, which is solely applicable to investment awards in need of enforcement in a national jurisdiction, must also be taken into account: some courts may not accept an award containing electronic signatures as a 'duly authenticated original award or a duly certified copy thereof' in the meaning of Article IV(1)(a) of the New York Convention,[111] and Article V's grounds for denying recognition and enforcement may become relevant.[112] Here again, the applicable law—in this case, that of the place of enforcement—plays an essential role, and, according to institutions such as the ICC's, brings with it a call for prudence:

[108] Beata Gessel-Kalinowska Vel Kalisz 'Admissibility of Electronic Awards in the UNCITRAL Model Law Jurisdiction: Polish Law Example' (2021) 38(2) Journal of International Arbitration 147. Reflecting on the legal concerns raised by the electronic signing of awards within the Italian legal framework: Federica Bocci 'The ICC Guidance Note on Possible Measures Aimed at Mitigating the Effects of the COVID-19 Pandemic' (2020) <www.dlapiper.com/en/insights/publications/2020/05/newsletter-dell-arbitration-team/the-icc-guidance-note-on-possible-measures-aimed-at-mitigating-the-effects-of-the-covid-19-pandemic>.

[109] Chartered Institute of Arbitrators (CIArb) 'Framework Guideline on the Use of Technology in International Arbitration' (2021) <www.ciarb.org/media/17507/ciarb-framework-guideline-on-the-use-of-technology-in-international-arbitration.pdf> 3.3.

[110] Knud Jacob Knudsen, 'Can Arbitration Awards Be Signed Electronically?' (referring to case T3385-22: *Friendly v Elsa*) (2023) <www.linkedin.com/posts/kkn_can-arbitration-awards-be-signed-electronically-activity-7060973289959022592-SCb5/>.

[111] Article 35(2) of the UNCITRAL Model Law on International Commercial Arbitration states: 'The party relying on an award or applying for its enforcement shall supply the original award or a copy thereof.'

[112] Schäfer points out that an electronically signed award under a non-EU public key infrastructure (PKI) may raise recognition and enforcement difficulties. Schäfer (n 92) 161. See also Reinmar Wolff, 'The UN Convention on the Use of Electronic Communications in International Contracts: An Overlooked Remedy for Outdated Form Provisions under the New York Convention?' in Katia Fach Gómez and Ana Mercedes López Rodríguez (eds), *60 Years of the New York Convention: Key Issues and Future Challenges* (Kluwer Law International 2019) 101; Felipe Volio Soley, 'Signing the Arbitral Award in Wet Ink: Resistance to Technological Change or A Reasonable Precaution?' (2020) <https://arbitrationblog.kluwerarbitration.com/2020/11/06/signing-the-arbitral-award-in-wet-ink-resistance-to-technological-change-or-a-reasonable-precaution/>; Omar Husain Qouteshat 'Challenges of Authentication and Certification of E-Awards in Dubai and before the Dubai International Financial Centre Courts: The Electronic Signature' (2016) 23 Digital Evidence and Electronic Signature Law Review 97.

> Given that the mutual recognition of (qualified) electronic signatures in one legal system by other legal systems is unclear (to the extent that it exists at all), coupled with uncertainties as to the technical abilities of national courts and enforcement authorities, parties may find it prudent not to rely on electronically signed award ... One cautious approach would be to produce and retain at least one hand-signed physical original of an award, of which certified true copies can be made through hand-signed notarisations.[113]

Voluntary restrictions on the use of electronic signatures in investment awards are not entirely uncoupled from legal ones, as will be pointed out below. Various provisions referring to the use of electronic signatures in these awards contain express references to party autonomy's crucial role. Thus, Rule 59(2) of the ICSID Arbitration Rules specifies that awards will only be signed electronically 'if the parties agree'.[114] The 2021 ICC Note likewise indicates that 'the parties may agree that ... any award may be signed by the members of the arbitral tribunal in counterparts'.[115] Article 26(2) of the LCIA Arbitration Rules also provides for the possibility that other key actors in arbitration investment such as the tribunal or the administering institution may not agree to the use of electronic signatures: 'Unless the parties agree otherwise, or the Arbitral Tribunal or LCIA Court directs otherwise, any award may be signed electronically and/or in counterparts and assembled into a single instrument.'[116]

Recent investment arbitration awards also reflect the practical effects of either the existence or lack of quorum among the arbitration's participants regarding the use of electronic signatures. If consensus exists: 'This document is the original of the Final Award rendered in conformity with the Rules of Arbitration of the International Chamber of Commerce and issued as an electronic document pursuant to the parties' agreement.'[117] If it does not:

> After Claimant's counsel expressed the wish that only receipt of the signed originals of the Final Award would trigger any time limits ... the Secretariat informed the Parties that it would follow its usual practice and notify the signed originals of the Final Award upon receipt from the Tribunal, and send a courtesy copy of the Final Award by email.[118]

Scholars point out that this reluctance on the part of arbitrators and parties—in their respective roles as creators and recipients of non-handwritten signatures—may arise

[113] ICC (n 53) (2022) 28–29.

[114] ICSID Arbitration Rules (2022) r 59(2).

[115] ICC (n 53) (2021) para 199.

[116] LCIA Arbitration Rules (2020) art 26.2. Similar wording is also found in the commercial arbitration context. For instance: 'Unless the parties agree otherwise, or the Arbitral Tribunal or ACICA directs otherwise, any award may be signed electronically and/or in counterparts and assembled into a single instrument.' ACICA Arbitration Rules and Expedited Arbitration Rules (2021) art 42(4).

[117] The document contains three handwritten signatures on the last page, which is part of the scanned version of the award. *Ghella v Venezuela and Metro de Valencia*, ICC Case No 24776/JPA, Award (16 March 2022) cover page.

[118] *GBC Oil Company Ltd v Albania* (n 87) [260].

from a range of circumstances: lack of personal technological competence, the effects of the digital divide and the fear that national courts may later question a signature's validity, among others.[119] Some arbitration actors even ask what is wrong with the not-so-liable electronic signatures if all those involved agree and these signatures do not seem to pose much of problem in the judicial sphere.

With regard to administering institutions in their roles as communicators of awards containing electronic signatures, a recent empirical study in which leading commercial arbitration administering institutions participated concludes that these institutions 'rarely make use of electronic awards'.[120] To the extent that this conclusion might be extrapolated to the investment arbitration context, it is also useful for explaining the institutional reluctance towards using a technological tool that is deeply interconnected with e-awards: electronic/digital signatures, the use of which would undoubtedly save arbitration participants time and money. Simply put, the study's conclusions indicate that, from the arbitration institution perspective, non-electronic awards are still considered preferable for various reasons (solemnity, integrity of the award, lower risk of interceptability, etc). These institutions believe that the time is not yet right for the widespread use of electronic awards, since 'the risk of exclusively issuing electronic awards is still too high under the current legal framework ... express provisions will be needed to provide sufficient legal certainty'.[121] These conclusions do not seem to differ much from this conservative statement, issued by the ICC in 2017: 'For the time being, original awards probably should continue to be made and signed on paper and physically served on the parties. This does not mean that electronic copies of an award or originals signed with qualified electronic signatures in accordance with the laws of the relevant country or countries could not also be communicated and used for other purposes.'[122]

In essence, everything covered so far tends to confirm that using electronic signatures is not one of the formal requirements of what currently constitutes the minimum content of investment awards. On the contrary, electronic signatures are still rare in cross-border awards, and the same can be said of fully electronic awards (that is, those for which there is no paper original).

However, this snapshot of a not-so-technological reality in late 2023 will not remain unchanged. Just as the LCIA has recently chosen electronic award transmission as its starting point for dealing with arbitration services, other arbitration institutions will also make progress in areas such as the use of electronic/digital signatures and the issuance of electronic awards. It does not seem realistic to argue that technology will go into reverse. There is even some speculation among scholars that arbitration institutions would jointly create and staff: 'A body that has the sole purpose of conceiving and implementing a virtual facility that allows secure use of electronic means for secure and reliable electronic signatures (and much more) in international arbitration.'[123]

[119] Schäfer (n 92) 162.
[120] Ongenae (n 95) 263.
[121] ibid para 102.
[122] ICC (n 53) (2017) 14.
[123] Schäfer (n 92) 164–65.

Until advances of this kind are implemented and the applicable laws and institutional rules move forward in their treatment of electronic/digital signatures,[124] party autonomy would seem to be an effective channel for achieving increased use of non-handwritten signatures in investment awards, should the will exist among the participants. One example of a useful document in this area is the ICC Appendix B 'Sample Procedural Language Relating to Technology Tools and Solutions', which asks the parties to consider technological issues such as those referring to the signing of awards before case management conferences are held.[125] Taking into account the fact that there are frequently interpretative uncertainties regarding the—usually brief—wording of hard and soft law on this matter, it would be desirable for the parties and the arbitral tribunal to provide as much detail as possible in writing with respect to their agreement on the requirements for signing awards. Including an express reference to these circumstances in the texts of final awards themselves would also be highly recommended.

IV. Technology's Invisible Footprint in Investment Awards: A Dormant Threat?

It is impossible for arbitrators to draw up investment awards nowadays without using technology. As explained in section II, the texts of the awards themselves refer to the many technological interventions throughout the arbitration proceedings, which the arbitrators endorse by signing the award. If we take a step ahead, technology is also used on many other occasions in the course of preparing investment awards, but no references subsequently appear in the text. This section brings together a series of key ideas surrounding technology's invisible footprint in investment awards, although for reasons of space a more thorough analysis of the ethical aspects of this flourishing phenomenon is undertaken in a further publication.[126]

The first aspect to note in the area, one that cannot be ignored, is the fact that professionals other than arbitrators also intervene in determining the form and content of investment awards. As has been explained in detail elsewhere,[127] arbitrators' legal assistants may assume various responsibilities related to the drafting of the award itself, and they may employ technological tools to perform these. Along the same lines, even arbitration institutions themselves sometimes scrutinize the form and content of awards, where appropriate, making suggestions that are reflected by means of technology.[128]

[124] It has also been proposed that technology such as blockchain be used to promote the use of truly digital signatures in arbitration. Pietro Ortolani, 'Recognition and Enforcement of the Outcome of Blockchain-Based Dispute Resolution' in Andrea Bonomi, Matthias Lehmann, and Shaheeza Lalani (eds), *Blockchain and Private International Law* (Brill Nijhoff 2023) 642; AJ Santos, 'Recognition of Blockchain-based Multisignature E-Awards' arXiv preprint arXiv:1911.12968 (2019).

[125] ICC (n 53) (2022) 46.

[126] Katia Fach Gómez, 'Resorting to Artificial Intelligence in Investor State Dispute Settlement: A New World of Ethical Challenges for Legal Stakeholders' in Chiara Giorgetti and Catharine Titi (eds), *Ethics and Investor-State Dispute Settlement* (Brill forthcoming).

[127] Fach Gómez (n 5) ch 4.

[128] See for instance Article 49 CIETAC: 'The arbitral tribunal shall submit its draft award to CIETAC for scrutiny before signing the award. CIETAC may bring to the attention of the arbitral tribunal issues addressed in the

Therefore, although this section refers to arbitrators in general, in reality technology's invisible footprint in investment awards is frequently due not only to arbitrators.

Arbitrators interact constantly with technological tools and many of these interactions directly affect the form and final content of awards. It is obvious, for instance, that awards are not written by hand on sheets of paper these days. Likewise, arbitrators regularly read digital versions of other awards that may be relevant to their cases, access the administering institution's digital case management platform to download documents that they may wish to cite in their award texts, review the recordings of examinations held during remote hearings and solve grammatical issues with online dictionaries if they are not writing in their native language. These types of everyday technological actions 'vont de soi' and, in principle, may be considered examples of the utilitarian technology that facilitates arbitrators' work. In that sense, the fact that arbitrators do not mention them in their arbitration award texts is so far viewed as normal and therefore acceptable.

However, the author believes that arbitrators will increasingly need to consider whether to report their use of certain technologies and the fact that they are somehow invisibly reflected in the arbitral award. There are many possible examples to illustrate this notion, and one that is addressed in another chapter is especially useful here: decision trees.[129] The chapter dealing with tribunal dynamics and arbitrator deliberations defines a decision tree as a 'decision support tool that identifies in logical sequence the decisions to be taken depending on the evidence produced with a list of the possible consequences and the resulting sub-decisions to be made'.[130] The usefulness of decision trees is highlighted in the context of arbitrators' deliberations, as they can be used to prepare preliminary reports and during post-hearing deliberations, in which case the arbitral tribunal president should 'conduct the discussion with a decision tree, ideally one of those used in previous deliberations, adapted according to the evolution of the case'.[131] Recent investment awards and procedural orders do refer to arbitration trees at different times during the proceedings, but they are meant to be used by arbitration participants other than the arbitrators: 'At the request of the Tribunal at the close of

award on the condition that the arbitral tribunal's independence in rendering the award is not affected.' CIETAC International Investment Arbitration Rules (2017); and Article 42(5) BAC–BIAC: 'The Arbitral Tribunal shall submit the draft of the award to the BAC before signing it. The BAC may make suggestions on the form of the award, and may draw the Arbitral Tribunal's attention to other matters in the award, without affecting the Arbitral Tribunal's liberty of decision.' BAC–BIAC Rules for International Investment Arbitration (2019).

[129] Decision trees are used more and more frequently in the litigation and ADR contexts. Stephen R McNeill 'Applying Decision Tree Analysis to Expedite Preference Settlements' (2015) American Bankruptcy Institute (ABI) Journal 32; Rick Weiler 'Again, with Decision Trees' (Kluwer Mediation Blog, 2020) <https://mediationblog.kluwerarbitration.com/2020/02/06/again-with-decision-trees/>. See also the very recent ICC, which approaches decision trees as an effective early risk assessment mechanism 'which can be used to assist a party in: (i) identifying the most likely outcomes of the dispute if it is fought out; (ii) attributing probabilities and financial values to each outcome; and (iii) using decision analysis techniques such as probability weighted averaging and sensitivity testing. The outputs of such analysis can help the company identify its settlement range by providing a better understanding of its risk if the dispute is litigated or arbitrated.' ICC 'Effective Conflict Management' (2023) <https://iccwbo.org/news-publications/arbitration-adr-rules-and-tools/new-report-and-guide-to-drive-thought-leadership-in-dispute-prevention-and-resolution/> para 31.

[130] Derain (n 70).

[131] ibid.

the oral proceedings, [the parties] submitted a proposed 'decision tree' to guide the Tribunal's analysis',[132] and 'the Tribunal may convene case management conferences with the parties in accordance with ICSID Arbitration Rule 31 in order to ... clarify and narrow the issues in dispute (e.g. address tribunal questions, decision tree, road map, and/or skeleton arguments)'.[133] Likewise, recent expert reports submitted in investment arbitration cases also contain graphics showing decision trees.[134]

The chapter dealing with investment arbitrator deliberations notes that a decision tree 'is a very elementary one, with no use of algorithms, usually prepared by the president, on the basis of his or her present views on what he or she considers as the more important issues to be resolved in order to reach a decision'.[135] Indeed, there is nothing to stop presiding arbitrators from preparing extremely useful decision trees using the stylus pens on their tablet computers, for instance. In the binary classification of utilitarian/disruptive technology, this type of decision tree would fall into the former category. Nevertheless, there is an unavoidable reality: more and more software is available to create decision trees[136] and, to go one step further, decision trees are one of the many instruments provided by a range of AI-powered tools for assessing, valuing and resolving complex legal disputes.[137] As this kind of AI-led technology is increasingly accessible to investment arbitration participants, arbitrators' use of it while drafting the award cannot be completely ruled out.

In fact, if we return to previous examples, which were initially classified as the utilitarian technology commonly used by arbitrators to draft arbitral awards (looking up arbitral cases on a website or solving grammar problems by using online dictionaries, etc), it turns out that these types of tasks can also be carried out by using much more disruptive technology. The constantly evolving notion of AI, in its multiple manifestations, comes into play here and is incorporated into investment awards. Nowadays, AI can assist arbitrators in legal research, automated document review and evidence analysis; facilitate document transcription, drafting, and translating; predict the outcome of legal disputes; and even act as an arbitrator in dispute resolution via decision-making tools.

This overwhelming new AI driven era seems to have caught some stakeholders off guard. If they do react, it is often when adjudicators have already been facing technological challenges in their work on a daily basis for some time. Their reactions, furthermore, are varied. On some occasions, they focus on trying to prevent the use of AI in the legal field. For instance, Article 33 of the 2019 French Law on the Programming

[132] *Itisaluna Iraq LLC and others v Iraq*, ICSID Case No ARB/17/10 (3 April 2020) [142]. In these awards, the arbitral tribunal itself did not make the decision tree, but 'the Tribunal requested the Parties to attempt to update and agree on the Decision Tree'. *Raymond Charles Eyre and Montrose Developments (Private) Limited v Democratic Socialist Sri Lanka*, ICSID Case No ARB/16/25, Award (5 March 2000) [36]–[40].

[133] *Suffolk (Mauritius) Limited, Mansfield (Mauritius) Limited and Silver Point Mauritius v Portuguese Republic* (n 88) [19.1].

[134] *Lupaka Gold Corp v Peru*, ICSID Case No ARB/20/46, Expert Report of Ms Isabel Santos and Mr Alexander Lee of AlixPartners (24 March 2022) fig 17.

[135] Derain (n 70).

[136] For instance, see Silverdecisions, EdrawMax, Creately, SmartDraw, and Visual Paradigm.

[137] The range of legal analytics and decision analysis tools currently available in the private sector is very broad: Dispute Resolution Data, Arbilex, Premonition, Blue J Legal, Solomonic, Eperoto, Lex Machina, etc.

and Reform of the Justice System prohibited analytics of judges' decisions.[138] More frequently, however, initiatives have focused on developing appropriate hard and soft law 'conciliatory measures' in support of the coexistence of AI and legal stakeholders. For instance, Canadian courts recently declared that using AI to draft court submissions is not prohibited in principle, but since it raises 'legitimate concerns about the reliability and accuracy', 'if any counsel or party relies on artificial intelligence (such as ChatGPT or any other artificial intelligence platform) ... they must advise the Court of the tool used and for what purpose'.[139]

When reflecting on how to assess technology's invisible footprint in investment awards—and whether it actually constitutes a dormant threat, initiatives from the judicial context such as that mentioned above could contribute useful guidelines in the arbitration context. The most recent survey on the question ('Artificial Intelligence in International Arbitration—AI in IA') discussed inter alia whether there should be a ban on arbitrators using AI when drafting awards. It shows that 74 per cent of respondents—a remarkably high percentage—agreed or strongly agreed that arbitrators should not use AI tools to formulate or draft adjudicatory elements of awards.[140] Another approach would be to assume that arbitrators and AI do interact. Conciliatory measures on the interconnection between AI and investment awards revolve around either party approval or arbitrator disclosure. The results of the AI in IA survey are highly significant in this sense: 59 per cent of respondents agreed or strongly agreed that arbitrators should only use AI tools with prior party approval, and 71 per cent thought arbitrators should be required to disclose the use of AI tools for any purpose in an arbitration.[141] It seems reasonable for arbitration parties to want to know if, to what extent and for what purposes investment arbitrators—or their legal assistants—have used AI to draft an investment award. This author considers that the enhanced institutional transparency recently achieved with respect to arbitrators' legal assistants[142] should also be extended to the 'true fourth arbitrator'; that is, to AI-driven technology.

[138] For instance, see Malcolm Langford and Mikael Rask Madsen 'France Criminalises Research on Judges' (2019) <https://verfassungsblog.de/france-criminalises-research-on-judges/>; Artificial Lawyer 'France Bans Judge Analytics, 5 Years in Prison for Rule Breakers' (2019) <www.artificiallawyer.com/2019/06/04/france-bans-judge-analytics-5-years-in-prison-for-rule-breakers/>.

[139] The Court of King's Bench of Manitoba stated that: 'There are legitimate concerns about the reliability and accuracy of the information generated from the use of artificial intelligence. To address these concerns, when artificial intelligence has been used in the preparation of materials filed with the court, the materials must indicate how artificial intelligence was used.' Court of King's Bench of Manitoba 'Practice Direction. Use of Artificial Intelligence in Court Submissions' (2023) <www.manitobacourts.mb.ca/court-of-queens-bench/procedure-rules-and-forms/notices-and-practice-directions/practice-directions/>. In similar terms, the Supreme Court of Yukon declared: 'If any counsel or party relies on artificial intelligence (such as ChatGPT or any other artificial intelligence platform) for their legal research or submissions in any matter and in any form before the Court, they must advise the Court of the tool used and for what purpose.' Supreme Court of Yukon, 'Practice Direction: Use of Artificial Intelligence Tools' (2023) <www.yukoncourts.ca/sites/default/files/2023-06/GENERAL-29%20Use%20of%20AI.pdf>.

[140] Bryan, Cave, Leighton, Paisner 'Annual Arbitration Survey 2023. AI in IA. The Rise of Machine Learning' (2023) <www.bclplaw.com/a/web/tUW2SW6fjHrpXVrA7AfWkS/102932-arbitration-survey-2023-report_v10.pdf> 22.

[141] ibid 23.

[142] Fach Gómez (n 5) 46–47.

In sum, arbitration stakeholders are demanding more transparency from arbitrators regarding their use of AI tools[143] because they fear that cases of improper delegation may be occurring[144] in crucial aspects such as award drafting. The use of AI to draft investment awards, apart from clouding the transparency of the decision-making process, may also bring with it other drawbacks like lack of accountability or threats to confidentiality. Furthermore, perils arising from the use of AI at key points in investment arbitration, such as the drafting of the award, may likewise have consequences in terms of the breaching of arbitrators' duties.[145] As if that were not enough, arbitrators' lack of technological competence may lead to substandard use of AI. Data provided by the survey referred to above is truly worrying in this sense: 73 per cent of arbitrator respondents rated their confidence in their own technical capability at 5 or below.[146] If these data are confirmed, it is more than justified to argue that arbitrators 'require more advanced training and assistance with respect to AI technology and its implications for the conduct of arbitration'.[147]

Well-aware of this issue's crucial importance and the urgency of ringfencing the use of AI in the arbitration world, many stakeholders are contributing enthusiastically to the current debate. They all envisage an ecosystem for the development of AI in arbitration that should be presided over by values such as transparency, explainability, robustness, human oversight, accountability, responsibility, fairness, non-discrimination, security, safety, and privacy.[148] While this ecosystem is still a work in progress at legislative and institutional levels, it is, however, important to remember that the principle of party autonomy is fully operational for arbitration participants. This is, it is highly advisable that, from the start of an arbitration, the parties and arbitrators agree[149] in as

143 It was found that 76 per cent of respondents believe there is a need for greater transparency over the use of AI tools by arbitrators. Bryan, Cave, Leighton, Paisner (n 140) 23.

144 It was found that 81 per cent of surveyors consider that a risk involved in using AI tools is improper delegation (the risk of technology being used to perform tasks that are personal in nature and fall within the mandate of legal counsel, expert, or arbitrator). ibid 15.

145 Katia Fach Gómez, *Key Duties of International Investment Arbitrators: A Transnational Study of Legal and Ethical Dilemmas* (Springer 2019).

146 It was found that 79 per cent of respondents also rated their confidence in arbitrators' technical capability to give instructions concerning the use of AI tools in arbitration at 5 or below. Bryan, Cave, Leighton, Paisner (n 140) 23.

147 Claire Morel de Westgaver in Paisner, Bryan, Cave, Leighton (n 140) 22.

148 Some key texts on this matter are: Maxi Scherer, 'International Arbitration 3.0-How Artificial Intelligence Will Change Dispute Resolution' (2019) Austrian Yearbook on International Arbitration 503; Kathleen Paisley and Edna Sussman 'Artificial Intelligence Challenges and Opportunities for International Arbitration' (2018) 11(1) New York Dispute Resolution Lawyer 35; Sophie Nappert and Paul Cohen 'Captain Kirk or Mr Spock? The Impact of IT of Arbitration Practice and Decision Making' (2016) <www.researchgate.net/publication/309120891_Captain_Kirk_or_Mr_Spock_The_Impact_of_IT_of_Arbitration_Practice_and_Decision_Making>; Sophie Nappert 'The Challenge of AI in Arbitral Decision-Making' (2018) Practical Law UK; Silicon Valley Arbitration and Mediation Center (SVAMC), 'Draft Guidelines on the Use of Artificial Intelligence in Arbitration' (2023) <https://svamc.org/svamc-draft-guidelines-released-for-public-consultation/>.

149 In this sense:

> As the use of AI tools becomes more ubiquitous in arbitration, we are likely to see a greater dialogue between the parties and the tribunal over AI usage. In many cases parties will reach a consensus on AI usage but, in cases where they can't, arbitrators will need to decide whether the tool should be used and give appropriate directions for its use. In some cases, that may result in a tribunal refusing to allow the use of a specific AI tool if it considers it would unreasonably increase time and/or costs or compromise the integrity of the proceedings.

Siobhan Abraham in Bryan, Cave, Leighton, Paisner (n 140) 21.

much detail as possible on the role that AI will be granted (a role that will be expressly recorded in the text of the award and which in turn will also possibly shape its content).

V. Conclusion

This chapter has aimed to raise awareness about the pivotal importance of technology in contemporary investment awards. It has presented multiple examples of technology's visible footprint in investment arbitration, which is reflected in the award texts themselves. The chapter has also analysed technology's growing invisible footprint in awards and reflected on how the arbitration community should respond to the use of AI-powered tools when drafting these awards.